Reading Literature

Purple Level
Yellow Level
BLUE LEVEL
Orange Level
Green Level
Red Level

Reading Literature

The McDougal, Littell English Program

McDougal, Littell & Company
Evanston, Illinois
New York   Dallas   Sacramento

Authors

Staff of McDougal, Littell & Company
Marilyn Sherman

Consultants

Stan Bidlack, Teacher, Huron Senior High School, Ann Arbor, Michigan
Patricia Ely, Teacher, Reading Senior High School, Reading, Pennsylvania
Kay Folsom, Teacher, Boulder High School, Boulder, Colorado
Hilda Guldseth, Teacher, Sammamish Senior High School, Bellevue, Washington
Deborah Heidemann, Teacher, Cicero-North Syracuse High School, Cicero, New York
Kathy Henderson, Teacher, San Gabriel High School, San Gabriel, California
Ed Johnson, Teacher, Sheldon High School, Eugene, Oregon
Linda Meixner, Teacher, Parma High School, Parma, Ohio
Paula Milano, Teacher, Central High School, Providence, Rhode Island

Frontispiece: *Little Girl of the Southwest*, 1917, ROBERT HENRI.
Delaware Art Museum, Wilmington.

Acknowledgments

Harry N. Abrams, Inc.: For "Wilma Rudolph" by Marc Pachter, from *Champions of American Sport*; published by Harry N. Abrams, Inc.; copyright © 1981. Mrs. T. D. Allen: For "Tears" by Alonzo Lopez, from *The Whispering Wind*; used by permission of the author. Agberg, Ltd. and Robert Silverberg: For "Pompeii" by Robert Silverberg,
(continued on page 684)

ISBN: 0-86609-2331

Copyright © 1985 by McDougal, Littell & Company
Box 1667, Evanston, Illinois 60204

Contents

Speaker and Tone

CHAPTER 5 *Nonfiction*   303

Handbook for Reading and Writing   *611*

Dear Educator,

Reading Literature brings to your students the greatest literature of all time. In this age of computers and VCR's, precious little of the world's great literary heritage filters through to our new generation. I don't believe you want your students to go through life without being acquainted with the short stories of Mark Twain, O. Henry, and Anton Chekhov. I don't believe you want your students to be unacquainted with the poems of Emily Dickinson, Robert Frost, and Langston Hughes. This kind of reading can provide your students with a quickened sense of life's drama and a new sense of life's possibilities. The time is now. The opportunity is here.

Your students will be reading stories, poems, nonfiction, and plays in their original form. Selections are not adapted. We have searched through the world's great literature to find selections that will stretch the students' minds, sharpen their senses, and enrich their lives.

Throughout, *Reading Literature* integrates reading and writing. Writing is presented as a process. A thorough foundation for writing is presented in a complete chapter, "How Writers Write" (see Chapter 1). The universal themes and ideas revealed by great literature make easy the task of teacher and text in guiding students to discover topics for their own writing.

I hope you will be as proud to offer *Reading Literature* to your students as we are to present it to you. I hope, too, that *Reading Literature* will assist you in helping the students to read happily, to think critically, and, above all, to meet the wondrous challenge that is life. Great writers of our time, and of earlier times, can help students in this process of growth. No other writers can do it as well.

Joseph F. Littell
Editor-in-Chief
McDougal, Littell & Company

CHAPTER 1

How Writers Write

Scissors Grinder, 1912, KASIMIR S. MALEVICH.
Yale University Art Gallery, Société Anonyme Collection,
New Haven, Connecticut.

Understanding the Process of Writing

Have you ever seen a magic act? The magician seems to do fantastic tricks without any effort. He makes magic look so easy that you might feel as if anyone could do it.

If you did try to learn magic, however, you would probably change your opinion. After working to master even a simple trick, you would understand how skilled a magician must be.

Reading is like watching a skilled magician at work. When you know what the magician is doing, you appreciate seeing it done right. When you know what goes into good writing, you get more pleasure out of reading it. In this chapter, you will learn about the steps writers follow when they write. In Chapter 3, you will study some of the techniques they use.

Most writers have discovered that their work follows a pattern. They do the same things in the same order each time they write. Together, these steps are called the **process of writing**. The three main stages of the process of writing are the following:

pre-writing—the planning stage
writing
revising—the rewriting and reworking stage

Emblems, 1913, ROGER de la FRESNAYE. The Phillips Collection, Washington, D.C.

Pre-Writing

Pre-writing is the first stage in the process of writing. It is a time to think, study, and plan. Before you even begin to write, you should follow these pre-writing steps:

1. Choose and limit a topic. Are you interested in any particular topic? Would you like to learn more about it? Do you already know a great deal about a topic? Would you like to share that information?

Make a list of possible topics. Read over the list carefully. Then make your final choice.

Once you know what you want to write about, limit your topic. Make sure it is narrow enough to be covered in the form you have chosen, such as a short story or a poem.

Professional writers agree that you should write about things that have some special importance to you. Fantasy writer C. S. Lewis advises writers: "Write about what really interests you, whether it is real things or imaginary things, and nothing else."

In order to find these interesting, important ideas, writers are always observing the world around them. Author Anne Petry says, "I get my ideas from newspapers, magazines, conversations with friends, personal experiences."

Poet Gwendolyn Brooks also gets her ideas in a variety of ways:

> I see something happening out in the street, or somebody tells me something. Or I go into my interior and pull out something and try to put it down on paper.

Try some of these pre-writing techniques in your own writing. Then develop some of your own.

2. Decide on your purpose. Your purpose is your reason for writing. Do you want to entertain your readers? Do you want to teach them about your topic? Are you trying to persuade them to agree with you? Do you want to share an experience or a feeling? To accomplish each of these purposes, you must write a little differently. You might change the level of language you use. You might also choose different details. Short story writer Flannery O'Connor noted: "Detail has to be controlled by some overall purpose, and every detail has to be put to work."

3. Decide on your audience. Think about the people who will read your writing. How should you write to be sure they understand? What ideas and details will they enjoy reading?

Poet Robert Graves thinks that it is important to keep the audience in mind:

> When anyone sits down to write, he should imagine a crowd of readers looking over his shoulder. They will be asking such questions as "What does this sentence mean? Haven't you got your ideas muddled here?"

When you have decided who will probably read your writing, think about how to reach them. Choose a topic and a style of writing that will appeal to them. Remember, both how you write and what you write change, depending on who will read your work.

4. Gather supporting information. List everything you know about your topic. Then think about questions you would want answered if you were a reader. Write down the questions. Then try to find the answers.

Suppose you are writing about a personal experience or feeling. You should list details that will make that experience or feeling seem real to your reader. To learn about other subjects, you will need to visit the library or talk to experts. Author Frank Bonham researches his subjects thoroughly. He gives this reminder to young writers:

> You can only write well about something you know about. For a book I wrote called *Durango Street*, I did "field research" at various times for a year and a half.

Take notes on your research. Without clear notes, you will not remember what you have learned.

5. Organize your ideas. Read your list of details again. Some details may not be related to what you want to say. Cross them out. You might have found a new topic that interests you more than your original topic. If you want to change, now is the time. You may find that you need to do more research. In that case, begin your research again.

Soon you will have completed a list of details. Now you must arrange those ideas in an order the reader will understand.

Events in stories are usually arranged in the order they happened. Descriptions of people and places make the most sense if details are arranged in the order you would notice them. In opinions and arguments, the reasons are arranged according to their importance.

After organizing your ideas, you can go on to the next stage in the process of writing.

> Once the material is organized, and we are satisfied that we have a sound story thread, the writing can begin.
>
> —H. A. and Margaret Rey

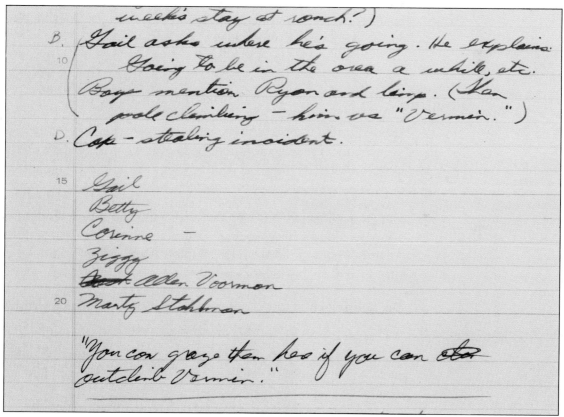

Author Frank Bonham's pre-writing notes for his novel *Devilhorn*.

Writing

Your research is done and you are ready to write. Write quickly. Keep your notes available. Follow your outline as much as possible. But if new ideas occur to you, do not be afraid to include them. Matt Christopher, writer of sports fiction, believes his outline is "not a firm, absolute path I must follow. It is there as a guiding light."

The important thing to remember when writing your first draft is to keep the words coming. This is not the time to worry about punctuation and grammar.

Read how this writer approaches the writing stage:

I do not worry or even think about spelling or grammar, paragraphing or punctuation (except periods), at this point. I will need these important mechanics of my language later. They will be priceless to me in presenting my idea formally to others. But, in the early throes of an idea there is for me only grammar of the mind, which is a flow of thought, as natural and precise as a flow of river to the sea.

—Mary O'Neill

Revising

After your first draft is written, you revise. Revising, or rewriting, is the stage when you slowly and carefully go over what you have written. You look for ways to improve your writing. Most writers agree that revision is absolutely necessary.

Rewriting, in a sense, is an author's second—and sometimes third—chance to add enriching details, to clothe the original idea, and to make the story more real. I rather like rewriting. It's a challenge.

—Ruby Zagoren

Ask yourself these questions as you read what you have written:

1. Will readers find my writing interesting? Will they want to read it?
2. Did I stay on my topic with every paragraph and sentence? Did I avoid any unnecessary details or unrelated ideas? Should I add any details?
3. Do my ideas make sense? Are they arranged logically? Are the connections between ideas clear and easy to follow?

4. Is every sentence a complete sentence? In every case, did I use the word that will best express my meaning?

Some writers feel that the opinions of others are valuable at this stage. Pura Belpre often asks for reactions to her writing.

It gives me the opportunity to see things as others see them. Living too close to the story during the writing process, I tend to lose objectivity.

Writers have many different methods of revising. Some read their writing aloud, listening for mistakes. Others, such as author Ester Weir, find it useful to set their writing aside for a while and reread it later.

When I reread a manuscript that has been allowed to "cool off" for a time, all sorts of possibilities for betterment spring to mind. Seeing the story with new eyes, I find this rewriting is automatic, so much so that I

Part of a revised draft of *Devilhorn* by Frank Bonham. Notice how the draft relates to the notes on page 5.

```
          "Well, what do you say?" Tom asked her.   "Maybe I
could pay you a little after I start selling my milk."
                     gambling man?"
          "Are you a gambling man" asked Ziggy.
                   "Depends."
     Tom shrugged.  Maybe. He could see them working up
to a joke of some kind. But I don't have much money. I'm
     "I handle Miss Farmer's business affairs," Ziggy said. And
and I'll make you a deal. You can graze your
                car
     "That's my Packard over yonder. I'll make you a deal, Fox.;
You can graze your goats around here for two weeks if you can
beat me pole-climbing."
          Tom looked the pole up and down.
          "Okay with me," Tom said, "if it's okay with Gail."
               "You're so funny, Ziggy," she laughed.
     Gail laughed.  "You guys are crazy," she said.
"But I don't care. Go ahead."

     "According to the rules," said the blond boy, "you
have to go up and ask Percy Ryan, if you lose.  Deal?"
     "Deal!2"
```

am certain a twentieth—or a hundredth—rereading would still produce something to change, to improve.

Proofreading.   When you proofread, you look for errors in grammar, punctuation, capitalization, and spelling. Your goal is to make your writing easy to understand. The readers should not be distracted by mistakes. You want them to remember your words and ideas, not your errors. Mark any corrections that are needed.

Jean George likes this late stage of revision. She says it is like "putting the trimmings on the Christmas tree, and as everyone knows, that is fun."

Preparing the Final Copy.   The final copy is what your readers will see. Try to make it as neat and attractive as possible. Copy your marked-up draft. Make all the necessary corrections and changes. Then proofread your writing one last time.

Practicing the Process of Writing

Use the ideas in this chapter every time you write. You may also refer to the Process of Writing guidelines in the Handbook for Reading and Writing at the back of this text. They can help you at every stage in the process from pre-writing to proofreading.

When you practice the writer's craft, you become a writer yourself. As a writer, you will share in the satisfaction that good writing brings.

There is nothing that can match the pleasure of creation—of creating some form of art. Not for power, not for money, but simply to say "I was here for a little while; I left this mark."
—William Faulkner

CHAPTER **1** **R**eview

Understanding the Process of Writing

Below are statements by six writers about their writing habits. About which stage in the process of writing—pre-writing, writing, or revising—is each one speaking?

1. I write swiftly without paying attention to spelling, sentence structure, details, or style. It is badly done but it's down on paper.
   —Jean Craighead George

2. I feel that a good writer can use almost any experience to good advantage by being perceptive, not only of life around him, but of the people he meets.   —Yoshiko Uchida

3. I look for hanging clauses (a great weakness of mine), extra adjectives, repetition of words or phrases. I try to use only the simplest words, whether writing for adults or for children. My object is to have my style as much like glass as possible, so that the reader may look directly at the subject, without thinking of the style.
   —Elizabeth Coatsworth

4. I go through several drafts, as many as four or five before I finish a work. I am sure that any playwright would give you practically the same description.   —Tennessee Williams

5. Take notes—take notes on anything you might possibly need later. Never trust your memory. Try to get things down exactly as you see them. . . . with your individual and special vision.
   —Frank Bonham

6. I can attack some material with a firm plan in mind, but, generally speaking, after five or six minutes of playing it lays down its own form.
   —Arthur Miller

CHAPTER 2

Short Stories

Tahitian Woman and Boy, 1899, PAUL GAUGUIN.
Norton Simon Art Foundation, Pasadena, California.

Reading Literature: Short Stories

What Is a Short Story?

A **short story** is a story short enough to be read in one sitting. Since the story is so short, the author usually concentrates on only a few characters and a single important event. Every detail must be carefully chosen to add something to the story.

All short stories share these characteristics. However, one story may be very different from another. A short story may tell about a particularly interesting event. On the other hand, it may be concerned more with exploring a character or creating a feeling. A short story may be realistic or wildly imaginative.

The History of the Short Story

People have told stories for thousands of years. Fables, myths, and legends are all stories. So are the songs and ballads once sung by minstrels. These stories were told and retold to each new generation and became part of an **oral tradition**. Such stories were actually a product of many storytellers. Each time the story was told, details might be changed or added.

The short story is different from stories of the oral tradition. A short story is written by only one person. The author chooses his or her words with great care. Once written, these words remain unchanged.

Some of the earliest short stories can be found in the Bible. They are called **parables**. Hundreds of years after those stories were written, in the late 1300's, English writer Geoffrey Chaucer wrote a book of short stories in verse. These were called *The Canterbury Tales*.

During the 1800's, many writers began writing short stories. These stories were just the right length to be printed in magazines, which were then becoming popular. In America, one of the first and finest short story writers was Edgar Allan Poe. Poe decided that each word in the story should help create a "certain unique or single effect" for the reader. The "rule" has influenced many short story writers.

The Elements of the Short Story

Elements are the basic parts that work together to make a final product. When we speak of the elements of a type of literature, we talk about its most important parts.

Character. The **characters** are the people who take part in the action of the story. A reader learns about these characters through their actions, thoughts, or words. The most important characters are called **major characters**. The story centers around their experiences. Other characters in the story are called **minor characters**.

Setting. The **setting** tells when and where the story takes place. The action or events in many short stories occur in one place during a short period of time. Sometimes the setting is very important to a story. At other times, the setting is no more than background.

Plot. The events that occur in the story make up its **plot**. The plot, or plan, of a short story often follows this pattern:

Introduction: The characters and setting are presented.
Rising Action: A conflict, or struggle, develops. The characters are faced with difficulties.
Climax: The excitement reaches a turning point.
Falling Action: The action of the story winds down as the story draws to a close.
Resolution: The action is completed. Any remaining questions are usually answered.

How To Read a Short Story

1. Allow yourself enough time to read the story carefully.
2. Decide who is telling the story. Are the events happening to the narrator or is he or she standing outside the story seeing everything that happens?
3. Pay close attention to details. In a short story only the most necessary details of setting and character are included.

Comprehension Skills: Relationships and Inferences

Understanding Relationships Among Ideas

Stories are not just events thrown together without a plan. Each event is connected in some way to the events that come before and after it. To be a thoughtful reader, you must be aware of these relationships.

The Order of Ideas

Events in a short story may be connected in a number of ways.

Chronological Order.   Sometimes events are presented in **chronological order**, or time order. One event simply follows the other.

He lifted the knocker, and it creaked up stiffly, as if it had never before been used. He let it fall, and it startled him with its booming loudness. The door remained closed. Again Rainsford lifted the heavy knocker. . . .

The order of events in this passage is clear. At other times, the writer may use such words as *first*, *next*, *then*, and *often* to signal chronological order.

Cause and Effect.   Sometimes an event depends on something that happened before. The first event that happens is the cause. The event that follows is the effect. Read the following sentence.

This river is cold because it is fed by icy mountain streams.

The cause and effect relationship in this example is signaled by the word *because*. It explains why the river is cold.

Predicting Outcomes

After you understand how events are related, you can often predict outcomes. Predicting an outcome means making an intelligent guess about what will happen next. To accurately predict an outcome, think back to what has happened so far in the story. If the story has been written in chronological order, can you determine what the next event will be? Have the characters done anything that would logically cause a certain effect, or result?

Making Inferences

As you continue to read, you will become more and more sensitive to the relationships between ideas. Understanding these relationships will allow you to make inferences about what happens in a story. An **inference** is a conclusion based on specific facts.

Read the following passage. Use the information that is provided to guess, or infer, the relationship between the writer and the boy.

I suggested that the best time for us to visit was just before supper, when I left off my writing. After that, he waited always until my typewriter had been sometime quiet. One day I worked until nearly dark. I went outside the cabin, having forgotten him. I saw him going up over the hill in twilight toward the orphanage. When I sat down on my stoop, a place was warm from his body where he had been sitting.

Exercises: Understanding Relationships and Inferences

A. Carefully read the following examples. In which example are events related in chronological order? In which are the events related by cause and effect?

1. He went on staring out to sea, watching the gulls and the incoming tide. Presently he ambled off his side of the lake, heading for the missus and home and maybe supper.

2. He knew his pursuer was coming. He heard the padding sound of feet on the soft earth, and the night breeze brought him the perfume of the general's cigarette.

B. Make a logical guess about what has happened in the excerpt below.

The sacred ground of the forum was safe no longer. It began to rock, then to pitch, then to split. As [Bimbo and Tito] stumbled out of the square, the earth wriggled like a caught snake, and all the columns of the Temple of Jupiter came down.

Vocabulary Skills: Context Clues

Using Context Clues

When you read, you often come across words you do not know. If you are to get the most out of what you read, you must develop your ability to figure out the meanings of unfamiliar words. There are several different methods you could use to do this. One of these ways is by using context clues.

Context refers to the words, sentences, and paragraphs that surround a word. Clues to the meaning of an unfamiliar word can often be found in the material around it. There are several different kinds of context clues.

Definition Clues and Restatement Clues. Sometimes a writer realizes that a certain word or term may be unfamiliar to the readers. To make the meaning clear, the writer gives the meaning, or definition of the word.

The small girl created a *diversion* by reciting a poem. In other words, she tried to entertain herself.

Certain key words often tell that the writer has included a definition clue. The key words are shown below:

is   who is   which is   that is   in other words   or

Another way writers help with an unfamiliar word is by restating the word. This means that the writer says it again in a different way.

The children moved *listlessly*, without energy or enthusiasm.

Look for these key words and key punctuation which signal restatement clues: the word *or*, dashes, commas, and parentheses.

Comparison Clues. Writers often compare things to show how they are alike. Sometimes a comparison can help you understand an unfamiliar word.

The man pointed the revolver as *rigidly* as if he were a statue.

Key words that signal comparison clues include the following:

like	similar to	than	moreover	both	all
as	and also	other	besides	the same	

Contrast Clues. Contrast clues show that the unfamiliar word is the opposite of a word or idea you already understand.

He found that he was no longer on the road, but had gone *astray*.

Inferring the Meaning of a Word

Writers don't always use key words or specific context clues to help their readers with an unfamiliar word. Many times they expect you to determine the meaning of new words from your understanding of an entire passage.

Read the following paragraph. Try to figure out the meaning of the word *slew*.

He fought the steering wheel to hold the car on a straight line. . . . He held it, then the wheel struck a rock buried in the soft dirt, and the left front tire blew out. The car *slewed*, and it was then that his mother began to scream.

Exercise: Using Context Clues

Read these sentences. Use context clues to guess the meaning of each underlined word.

1. The <u>forum</u> was the center of town, the place of shops and businesses to which everybody came at least once a day.

2. Laura looked <u>bewildered</u>, or puzzled, by the harsh laughter of her class-mates.

3. If you <u>elude</u> me for three days, you win. On the other hand, if I find you, you lose.

4. I felt as <u>elated</u> as a cab driver who has been given a gold coin by mistake.

5. He heard, far off in the jungle, the faint <u>report</u> of a pistol.

etting

You never know where a short story might take you. The stories in this section carry you to three different places and times. The setting of the first story is a space station in the future. The second story takes place on a farm in Eastern Europe. In the third story, you will visit ancient Pompeii in A.D. 79. Through short stories, you can explore any place in the world, at any time in the past or future.

Vesuvius in Eruption, 1817, JOSEPH MALLORD WILLIAM TURNER.
Yale Center for British Art, Paul Mellon Collection, New Haven, Connecticut.

Feathered Friend

ARTHUR C. CLARKE

This story couldn't happen anywhere on earth. As you read, pay attention to what makes one bird truly a "feathered friend."

To the best of my knowledge, there's never been a regulation that forbids one to keep pets in a space station. No one ever thought it was necessary—and even had such a rule existed, I am quite certain that Sven Olsen would have ignored it.

With a name like that, you will picture Sven at once as a six-foot-six Nordic giant, built like a bull and with a voice to match. Had this been so, his chances of getting a job in space would have been very slim. Actually he was a wiry little fellow, like most of the early spacers, and managed to qualify easily for the 150-pound bonus that kept so many of us on a reducing diet.

Sven was one of our best construction men. He excelled at the tricky and specialized work of collecting assorted girders as they floated around in free fall, making them do the slow-motion, three-dimensional ballet that would get them into their right positions, fusing the pieces together when they were precisely dovetailed into the intended pattern. I never tired of watching him and his gang as the station grew under their hands like a giant jigsaw puzzle.

It was a skilled and difficult job, for a space suit is not the most convenient of garbs in which to work. However, Sven's team had one great advantage over the construction gangs you see putting up skyscrapers down on Earth. They could step back and admire their handiwork without being abruptly parted from it by gravity. . . .

Don't ask me why Sven wanted a pet, or why he chose the one he did. I'm not a psychologist, but I must admit that his selection was very sensible. Claribel weighed practically nothing; her food requirements were infinitesimal—and she was not worried, as most animals would have been, by the absence of gravity.

I first became aware that Claribel was aboard when I was sitting in the little cubbyhole, laughingly called my office, checking through my lists of technical stores to decide what items we'd be running out of next. When I heard the musical whistle beside my ear, I assumed that it had come over the station intercom, and I waited for an announcement to follow. It didn't. Instead, there was a long and involved pattern of melody that made me look up with such a start that I forgot all about the beam just behind my head. When the stars had ceased to explode before my eyes, I had my first view of Claribel.

She was a small yellow canary, hanging in the air as motionless as a hummingbird— and with much less effort, for her wings were quietly folded along her sides. We stared at each other for a minute. Then, before I had quite recovered my wits, she did a curious kind of backward loop I'm sure no earthbound canary had ever managed, and departed with a few leisurely flicks. It was quite obvious that she'd already learned how to operate in the absence of gravity, and did not believe in doing unnecessary work.

Sven didn't confess to her ownership for several days, and by that time it no longer mattered, because Claribel was a general pet. He had smuggled her up on the last ferry from Earth, when he came back from leave—partly, he claimed, out of sheer scientific curiosity. He wanted to see just how a bird would operate when it had no weight but could still use its wings.

Claribel thrived and grew fat. On the whole, we had little trouble concealing our unauthorized guest when VIPs from Earth came visiting. A space station has more hiding places than you can count. The only problem was that Claribel got rather noisy when she was upset, and we sometimes had to think fast to explain the curious peeps and whistles that came from ventilating shafts and storage bulkheads. There were a

couple of narrow escapes—but then who would dream of looking for a canary in a space station?

We were now on twelve-hour watches, which was not as bad as it sounds, since you need little sleep in space. Though of course there is no "day" or "night" when you are floating in permanent sunlight, it was still convenient to stick to the terms. Certainly when I woke up that "morning" it felt like 6:00 A.M. on Earth. I had a nagging headache, and vague memories of fitful, disturbed dreams. It took me ages to undo my bunk straps, and I was still only half awake when I joined the remainder of the duty crew in the mess. Breakfast was unusually quiet, and there was one seat vacant.

"Where's Sven?" I asked, not very much caring.

"He's looking for Claribel," someone answered. "Says he can't find her anywhere. She usually wakes him up."

Before I could retort that she usually woke me up, too, Sven came in through the doorway, and we could see at once that something was wrong. He slowly opened his hand, and there lay a tiny bundle of yellow feathers, with two clenched claws sticking pathetically up into the air.

"What happened?" we asked, all equally distressed.

"I don't know," said Sven mournfully. "I just found her like this."

"Let's have a look at her," said Jock Duncan, our cook-doctor-dietician. We all waited in hushed silence while he gently held Claribel against his ear.

A designer's concept of a space station under construction, 1975–76. Rockwell International, Downey, California.

Presently he shook his head. "I can't hear anything, but that doesn't prove she's dead. I've never listened to a canary's heart," he added rather apologetically.

"Give her a shot of oxygen," suggested somebody, pointing to the green-banded emergency cylinder in its recess beside the door. Everyone agreed that this was an excellent idea. Soon Claribel was tucked snugly into a face mask that was large enough to serve as a complete oxygen tent for her.

To our delighted surprise, she revived at once. Beaming broadly, Sven removed the mask, and she hopped onto his finger. She gave her series of "Come to the cookhouse, boys" trills—then promptly keeled over again.

"I don't get it," lamented Sven. "What's wrong with her? She's never done this before."

For the last few minutes, something had been tugging at my memory. My mind seemed to be very sluggish that morning, as if I was still unable to cast off the burden of sleep. I felt that I could do with some of that oxygen—but before I could reach the mask, understanding exploded in my brain. I whirled on the duty engineer and said urgently:

"Jim! There's something wrong with the air! That's why Claribel's passed out. I've just remembered that miners used to carry canaries down to warn them of gas."

"Nonsense!" said Jim. "The alarms would have gone off. We've got duplicate circuits, operating independently."

"Er—the second alarm circuit isn't connected up yet," his assistant reminded him. That shook Jim. He left without a word, while we stood arguing and passing the oxygen bottle around like a pipe of peace.

He came back ten minutes later with a sheepish expression. It was one of those accidents that couldn't possibly happen. We'd had one of our rare eclipses by Earth's shadow that night; part of the air purifier had frozen up, and the single alarm in the circuit had failed to go off. Half a million dollars' worth of chemical and electronic engineering had let us down completely. Without Claribel, we should soon have been slightly dead.

So now, if you visit any space station, don't be surprised if you hear an inexplicable snatch of bird song. There's no need to be alarmed. On the contrary, in fact, it will mean that you're being doubly safeguarded, at practically no extra expense.

Developing Comprehension Skills

1. Sven worked on a space station. What made him well suited for his job?

2. What was the crew's attitude toward Claribel? What problems might a pet have caused aboard a space station?

3. Besides being an enjoyable pet, Claribel proved valuable in another way. Why was Sven's choice of pets especially lucky?

4. In addition to Claribel's reaction, what may have made the narrator realize that the air was bad?

5. A good short story title captures the reader's attention and suggests an important idea found in the story. What idea is suggested in the title, "Feathered Friend"? Do you think this title is a good one? Why or why not?

Reading Literature: Short Stories

1. **Recognizing Fiction.** Writing that is based on the writer's imagination is **fiction**. How do you know that "Feathered Friend" is fiction, rather than a true story?

2. **Understanding Science Fiction.** One special kind of fiction is science fiction. **Science fiction** uses a base of known scientific knowledge in an imaginative way. It often takes readers into the future. How are scientific

facts about gravity and oxygen used in the story "Feathered Friend"?

3. **Identifying Setting.** The **setting** of a short story is the place and time where it occurs. Where and when do the events in this story take place? Could these events happen in a different place and time?

4. **Identifying the Narrator.** The **narrator** in a short story is the person who tells the story. Sometimes, as in "Feathered Friend," the narrator is a character in the story.

    What do you know about the narrator of this story? Can you determine if the narrator is a man or a woman? Are there clues in the story to help you reach such a conclusion? If you had known more about the narrator, would you have enjoyed the story more?

5. **Understanding Point of View.** Some stories are written as if a person in the story is telling the story. Such a story is written from the **first-person point of view**. By using the pronoun *I,* this character tells what he or she sees, hears, and thinks. This character cannot, however, tell what anyone else in the story is thinking.

    In "Feathered Friend," the person telling the story is an unidentified crew member on a space station. What effect does this point of view have on the story? Does it help you feel as though you understand the events better? How would the story have been different if it were told by a narrator who was outside of the action?

6. **Recognizing Irony.** **Irony** is the contrast between what is thought to be true and what actually happens. The plot of this story has ironic twists. While expecting Claribel to be trouble, the crew ends up owing their lives to the bird. What is ironic about the expensive alarm devices on the space station? In your opinion, is there a message about advanced scientific knowledge in this story?

Developing Vocabulary Skills

Using Definition and Restatement Clues. You have learned that you can discover the meaning of a word by using context clues. One type of clue is **definition or restatement**. This kind of context clue tells you the meaning of an unfamiliar word by defining it or by stating it in a slightly different way.

There are several key words that tell you that a definition or restatement clue may be present. Some of these key words are, *is, which is, who is, that is, in other words,* and *or.* Consider this example:

> Claribel's food requirements were *infinitesimal,* that is, too small to be measured.

The clue words "that is" tell you that the definition of "infinitesimal" follows.

The underlined words in the following sentences can all be found in "Feathered Friend." Try to determine the meaning of each word by using context clues. Write the meaning, and then write the words that provided the clue to the underlined word.

1. The girders were <u>dovetailed</u>, or fitted together by means of special connectors.

2. His attitude was <u>unfathomable</u>. In other words, none of us could figure him out.

3. The narrator joined the crew in the <u>mess</u>— the dining area of the space station.

4. I had a nagging headache, and vague memories of <u>fitful</u> broken dreams.

5. One crew member felt <u>sluggish</u>; that is, he felt tired and dull.

6. We'd had one of our rare <u>eclipses</u>. An eclipse occurs when the light of the sun is blocked by the moon.

Developing Writing Skills

1. **Analyzing Character.** A **character trait** is a quality that a character shows by actions, statements, or thoughts. One of Sven's character traits is curiosity. For example, Sven wanted to see how a bird would operate in the zero gravity of outer space. In a paragraph, describe another of Sven's traits.

   Pre-Writing. Make a list of details about Sven from the story. Look for details that suggest something about his personality. List these details and the traits they represent. Then choose one trait as the subject of your paragraph.

   Writing. Use your pre-writing notes to write a rough draft of your paragraph. Begin your paragraph with a strong topic sentence. A **topic sentence** tells the main idea of a paragraph. In this paragraph, your topic sentence should tell the trait you are describing. Follow your topic sentence with at least two details that prove Sven has the trait.

   Revising. Read your rough draft. Did you limit your paragraph to one character trait? Does the topic sentence tell the reader what the paragraph is about? Did you provide details from the story that prove Sven has the trait you chose? Are there any unrelated details that should be removed? Make any changes that will improve your paragraph. Give your writing a thorough proofreading. Then make a clean, final copy.

2. **Describing a Setting.** The setting of a story is its place and time. "Feathered Friend" takes place sometime in the future. The action occurs on a space station far above the Earth. It is a place of construction girders, ventilating shafts, storage bulkheads, and cramped quarters for the crew members.

   Create another imaginary setting in the future. In one paragraph, describe a school, home, or other place of the 21st century. Choose specific words and details to make your description come alive.

Developing Skills in Study and Research

Understanding the Arrangement of Fiction. Books that tell of imaginary events are **fiction**. **Non-fiction** books are about real happenings. Fiction books are arranged on library shelves alphabetically by the author's last name. Find the fiction section of your library. Ask the librarian if science fiction books are in a special section. Then locate the books by Arthur C. Clarke. List the titles of his books.

Developing Skills in Critical Thinking

Identifying Cause and Effect Relationships. In a story, a writer tries to make events happen as they might in real life. Sometimes things happen as a result of events that occurred earlier. For example, an automobile skids off an icy road shortly after a snowstorm. The snowstorm is a cause. The auto accident is an effect.

In "Feathered Friend," why does the alarm system fail to operate? Does that seem to be something that could really happen? What is the cause and effect relationship in this situation? Explain your answer.

Zlateh the Goat

ISAAC BASHEVIS SINGER

A fierce blizzard leaves a boy and his friend stranded and lost. What is the most important thing the boy learns during the struggle for survival?

At Hanukkah time in early December, the road from the village to the town is usually covered with snow, but this year the winter had been a mild one. Hanukkah had almost come, yet little snow had fallen. The sun shone most of the time. The peasants complained that because of the dry weather there would be a poor harvest of winter grain. New grass sprouted, and the peasants sent their cattle out to pasture.

For Reuven, the furrier, it was a bad year, and after long hesitation he decided to sell Zlateh the goat. She was old and gave little milk. Feyvel, the town butcher, had offered eight gulden for her. Such a sum would buy Hanukkah candles, potatoes and oil for pancakes, gifts for the children, and other holiday necessaries for the house. Reuven told his oldest boy Aaron to take the goat to town.

Aaron understood what taking the goat to Feyvel meant, but he had to obey his father. Leah, his mother, wiped the tears from her eyes when she heard the news. Aaron's younger sisters, Anna and Miriam, cried loudly. Aaron put on his quilted jacket and a cap with earmuffs, bound a rope around Zlateh's neck, and took along two slices of bread with some cheese to eat on the road. Aaron was supposed to deliver the goat by evening, spend the night at the butcher's, and return the next day with the money.

While the family said goodbye to the goat, and Aaron placed the rope around her neck, Zlateh stood as patiently and good-naturedly as ever. She licked Reuven's hand. She shook her small white beard. Zlateh trusted human beings. She knew that they always fed her and never did her any harm.

When Aaron brought her out on the road to town, she seemed somewhat astonished. She'd never been led in that direction before. She looked back at him questioningly, as if to say, "Where are you taking me?" But after awhile she seemed to come to the conclusion that a goat shouldn't ask questions. Still, the road was different. They passed new fields, pastures, and huts with thatched roofs. Here and there a dog barked and came running after them, but Aaron chased it away with his stick.

The sun was shining when Aaron left the village. Suddenly the weather changed. A large black cloud with a bluish center appeared in the east and spread itself rapidly over the sky. A cold wind blew in with it. The crows flew low, croaking. At first it looked as if it would rain, but instead it began to hail as in summer. It was early in the day, but it became dark as dusk. After a while, the hail turned to snow.

In his twelve years, Aaron had seen all kinds of weather, but he had never experienced a snow like this one. It was so dense it shut out the light of the day. In a short time their path was completely covered. The wind became as cold as ice. The road to town was narrow and winding. Aaron no

I and the Village, 1911, MARC CHAGALL. Oil on canvas, 6' 3⅝" × 59⅝". The Museum of Modern Art. Mrs. Simon Guggenheim Fund, New York.

longer knew where he was. He could not see through the snow. The cold soon penetrated his quilted jacket.

At first Zlateh didn't seem to mind the change in weather. She too was twelve years old and knew what winter meant. When her legs sank deeper and deeper into the snow, she began to turn her head and look at Aaron in wonderment. Her eyes seemed to ask, "Why are we out in such a storm?" Aaron hoped that a peasant would come along in a cart, but no one passed by.

The snow grew thicker, falling to the ground in large, whirling flakes. Beneath it Aaron's boots touched the softness of a plowed field. He realized that he was no longer on the road. He had gone astray. He could no longer figure out which was east or west, which way was the village, the town. The wind whistled, howled, whirled the snow about in eddies. It looked as if white imps were playing tag on the fields. A white dust rose above the ground. Zlateh stopped. She could walk no longer. Stubbornly she anchored her cleft hooves in the earth and bleated as if pleading to be taken home. Icicles hung from her white beard, and her horns were glazed with frost.

Aaron did not want to admit the danger, but he knew just the same that if they did not find shelter, they would freeze to death. This was no ordinary storm. It was a mighty blizzard. The snowfall had reached his knees. His hands were numb, and he could no longer feel his toes. He choked when he breathed. His nose felt like wood, and he rubbed it with snow. Zlateh's bleating began to sound like crying. Those humans in whom she had so much confidence had dragged her into a trap. Aaron began to pray to God for himself and for the innocent animal.

Suddenly he made out the shape of a hill. He wondered what it could be. Who had piled snow into such a huge heap? He moved toward it, dragging Zlateh after him. When he came near it, he realized that it was a large haystack which the snow had blanketed.

Aaron realized immediately that they were saved. With great effort he dug his way through the snow. He was a village boy and knew what to do. When he reached the hay, he hollowed out a nest for himself and the goat. No matter how cold it may be outside, in the hay it is always warm, and hay was food for Zlateh. The moment she smelled it, she became contented and began to eat. Outside the snow continued to fall. It quickly covered the passageway Aaron had dug. A boy and an animal need to breathe, and there was hardly any air in their hideout. Aaron bored a kind of a window through the hay and snow and carefully kept the passage clear.

Through the window Aaron could catch a glimpse of the chaos outside. The wind carried before it whole drifts of snow. It was completely dark, and he did not know whether night had already come or whether it was the darkness of the storm. Thank God that in the hay it was not cold. The dried hay, grass, and field flowers exuded the warmth of the summer sun. Zlateh ate frequently. She nibbled from above, below, from the left and right. Her body gave forth an animal warmth, and Aaron cuddled up to her. He had always loved Zlateh, but now she was like a sister. He was alone, cut off from his family, and wanted to talk. He began to talk to Zlateh.

."Zlateh, what do you think about what has happened to us?" he asked.

"Maaaa," Zlateh answered.

"If we hadn't found this stack of hay, we would both be frozen stiff by now," Aaron said.

"Maaaa," was the goat's reply.

"If the snow keeps falling like this, we may have to stay here for days," Aaron explained.

"Maaaa," Zlateh bleated.

"What does 'Maaaa' mean?" Aaron asked. "You'd better speak up clearly."

"Maaaa. Maaaa," Zlateh tried.

"Well, let it be 'Maaaa' then," Aaron said patiently. "You can't speak, but I know you understand. I need you and you need me. Isn't that right?"

"Maaaa."

Aaron became sleepy. He made a pillow out of some hay, leaned his head on it, and dozed off. Zlateh too fell asleep.

When Aaron opened his eyes, he didn't know whether it was morning or night. The snow had blocked up his window. He tried to clear it, but when he had bored through to the length of his arm, he still hadn't reached the outside. Luckily he had his stick with him and was able to break through to the open air. It was still dark outside. The snow continued to fall and the wind wailed, first with one voice and then with many. Sometimes it had the sound of devilish laughter. Zlateh too awoke, and when Aaron greeted her, she answered, "Maaaa." Yes, Zlateh's language consisted of only one word, but it meant many things. Now she was saying, "We must accept all that God gives us—heat, cold, hunger, satisfaction, light, and darkness."

Aaron had awakened hungry. He had eaten up his food, but Zlateh had plenty of milk.

For three days Aaron and Zlateh stayed in the haystack. Aaron had always loved Zlateh, but in these three days he loved her more and more. She fed him with her milk and helped him keep warm. She comforted him with her patience. He told her many stories, and she always cocked her ears and listened. When he patted her, she licked his hand and his face. Then she said, "Maaaa," and he knew it meant, I love you too.

The snow fell for three days, though after the first day it was not as thick, and the wind quieted down. Sometimes Aaron felt that there could never have been a summer, that the snow had always fallen, ever since he could remember. He, Aaron, never had a father or mother or sisters. He was a snow child, born of the snow, and so was Zlateh. It was so quiet in the hay that his ears rang in the stillness. Aaron and Zlateh slept all night and a good part of the day. As for Aaron's dreams, they were all about warm weather. He dreamed of green fields, trees covered with blossoms, clear brooks, and

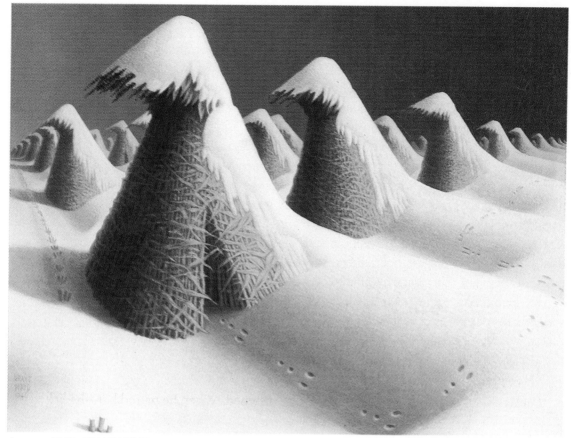

January, 1940, GRANT WOOD. Courtesy of the King W. Vidor Collection.

singing birds. By the third night the snow had stopped, but Aaron did not dare to find his way home in the darkness. The sky became clear, and the moon shone, casting silvery nets on the snow. Aaron dug his way out and looked at the world. It was all white, quiet, dreaming dreams of heavenly splendor. The stars were large and close. The moon swam in the sky as in a sea.

On the morning of the fourth day Aaron heard the ringing of sleigh bells. The hay-stack was not far from the road. The peasant who drove the sleigh pointed out the way to him—not to the town and Feyvel, the butcher, but home to the village. Aaron had decided in the haystack that he would never part with Zlateh.

Aaron's family and their neighbors had searched for the boy and the goat but had found no trace of them during the storm. They feared they were lost. Aaron's mother and sisters cried for him. His father remained silent and gloomy. Suddenly one of the neighbors came running to their house with the news that Aaron and Zlateh were coming up the road.

There was great joy in the family. Aaron told them how he had found the stack of hay and how Zlateh had fed him with her milk. Aaron's sisters kissed and hugged Zlateh and gave her a special treat of chopped carrots and potato peels, which Zlateh gobbled up hungrily.

Nobody ever again thought of selling Zlateh, and now that the cold weather had finally set in, the villagers needed the services of Reuven, the furrier, once more. When Hanukkah came, Aaron's mother was able to fry pancakes every evening, and Zlateh got her portion too. Even though Zlateh had her own pen, she often came to the kitchen, knocking on the door with her horns to indicate that she was ready to visit, and she was always admitted. In the evening Aaron, Miriam, and Anna played dreidel.[1] Zlateh sat near the stove watching the children and the flickering of the Hanukkah candles.

Once in a while Aaron would ask her, "Zlateh, do you remember the three days we spent together?"

Then Zlateh would scratch her neck with a horn, shake her white bearded head, and come out with the single sound that expressed all her thoughts, and all her love.

---

1. **dreidel**, a game of chance played at Hanukkah with a small wooden top called a dreidel.

Developing Comprehension Skills

1. At the beginning of the story, where was Aaron taking Zlateh the goat? Why?

2. Do you think Aaron's affection for Zlateh grew during their ordeal? How was her faithfulness rewarded?

3. By the end of the story, had the family changed its attitude about Zlateh? How do you know?

4. Do you think luck or intelligence played the most important role in the survival of Aaron and Zlateh? Explain your answer.

5. A sympathetic character is one you care for, feel sorry for, or understand. Which character in this story do you find most sympathetic? Explain your answer.

Reading Literature: Short Stories

1. **Identifying Setting.** Details help the reader form a mental picture of the two settings in this story. One setting is Aaron's village. Find details describing the village. What do these details tell you about the people living there? Do you think this story took place during the last twenty years? What details helped you reach this conclusion?

   What is the second setting in this story? What did Aaron learn in the second setting?

Could he have learned the same thing in the village? Explain your answer.

2. **Recognizing External Conflict.** "Zlateh the Goat" contains several conflicts. A **conflict** is any struggle within a story. An **external conflict** is a struggle between a character and another person or force. In this story, Aaron is in a struggle with a dangerous blizzard. How does he deal with this external conflict?

3. **Comparing External and Internal Conflict.** In an **internal conflict**, a character faces a decision. He or she must choose between different desires or courses of action. What internal conflict does Aaron experience following the blizzard? What decision does he make?

4. **Explaining Irony.** One method used by the writer to make this story interesting is irony. You remember that with irony, what appears to be true is eventually shown to be the opposite of the truth. Explain the irony in the statement below. It describes the situation as Zlateh is about to be led to the butcher:

Zlateh trusted human beings. She knew they always fed her and never did her any harm.

See if you can find other examples of irony in this story.

5. **Recognizing Personification.** When a writer uses **personification**, animals, objects, or ideas are given human qualities. In this story, Zlateh is given human qualities, as in the following examples:

   a. When Aaron led Zlateh toward the town, she seemed astonished.

   b. She looked at Aaron questioningly as if to say, "Where are you taking me?"

What human qualities, or traits, does Zlateh exhibit in these passages? Find at least two other passages in which Zlateh is given human qualities. Describe these qualities.

Developing Vocabulary Skills

Discovering Word Meaning with Synonyms. You may discover the meaning of an unfamiliar word by looking for a synonym. A **synonym** is a word that has almost the same meaning as another word. A writer may place synonyms in the same sentence as an unfamiliar word, or in a nearby sentence. Consider this example:

She is an *extraordinary* person. It is rare to find someone with her qualities.

You may not know the meaning of the word *extraordinary*. But the word *rare* in the next sentence is a synonym. It helps you determine the meaning of *extraordinary*.

In each of the following groups of sentences, the underlined word is drawn from the story "Zlateh the Goat." Read each group of sentences carefully. Search for a synonym for each underlined word. On your paper, write the meaning of the underlined word. Then write its synonym.

1. The peasants sent their cattle out to <u>pasture</u>. The animals fed all day on the new grass that sprouted in the fields.

2. For Reuven, the <u>furrier</u>, it was a bad year. After long hesitation, the fur seller decided to sell Zlateh the goat.

3. Zlateh looked at Aaron in <u>wonderment</u>. Her mild eyes seemed to ask in amazement, "Why are we out in such a storm?"

4. The wind whistled, howled, whirled the snow about in <u>eddies</u>. They could no longer see the road in these little whirlwinds.

5. Through the window Aaron could catch a glimpse of the <u>chaos</u> caused by the storm. In the confusion, he could not tell whether it was day or night.

Developing Writing Skills

1. **Understanding a Character's Actions.** The narrator states, "Aaron had decided in the haystack that he would never part with Zlateh." In one paragraph, explain the reasons for Aaron's new attitude. What does this new attitude tell you about Aaron? In your opinion, does this change indicate a more mature, or adult, way of thinking? Use specific details from the story to support your opinion.

2. **Narrating a Personal Experience.** In this story, Aaron develops a close bond and trusting relationship with Zlateh. In two paragraphs, describe an incident that may have helped you develop a close friendship with another person (or animal).

   Pre-Writing. Think of experiences that helped you develop closer friendships with others. Choose one experience in which you helped a friend in trouble, or in which a friend helped you. List each thing that happened in the order in which it happened. This type of organization is called **chronological, or time, order**.

   Writing. In the first paragraph, explain the troublesome situation. Why were you and your friend in this situation? Who else was involved? When and where did the incident take place? Use transitional words and phrases such as *first, next,* and *then* to make the order of events clear.

   In the second paragraph, explain how the problem was solved. How did you or your friend help? Did the situation have a happy ending? Explain how the experience strengthened your relationship.

   Revising. Ask a classmate to read your two paragraphs carefully. First ask the reader to summarize the problem you faced. Then ask the reader to explain how the problem was solved. If your reader could not answer these two questions, you may not have provided enough details. Rewrite your paragraphs, adding more details.

Developing Skills in Study and Research

Using the Card Catalog. In the library, the **card catalog** is a cabinet of small drawers. These drawers hold cards on which information about each book in the library is printed. The information in the card catalog will direct you to the location of the book on the library shelves. If the book is not listed in the card catalog, the library does not own the book.

To locate a book in the card catalog, you must know at least one thing about the book. You must know the title of the book, the name of the author, or the subject of the book. Each of these is used as a heading for a different type of catalog card.

Look in the card catalog in your library for books written by the author of "Zlateh the Goat." List the titles of at least two books written by this author.

The Dog of Pompeii

LOUIS UNTERMEYER

In the first two stories, animals acted as you might expect animals to act. Does the dog in this story show any unexpected abilities?

Tito and his dog Bimbo lived under the city wall where it joined the inner gate. They really didn't live there; they just slept there. They lived anywhere. Pompeii was one of the most festive of the old Roman towns, but although Tito was never an unhappy boy, he was not exactly a merry one. The streets were always lively with shining chariots and bright red trappings. The open-air theaters rocked with laughing crowds. Sham battles and athletic sports were free for the asking in the great stadium. Once a year the emperor visited the pleasure city, and the fireworks and other forms of entertainment lasted for days.

However, Tito saw none of these things, for he had been blind from birth. He was known to everyone in the poorer quarters. No one could say how old he was; no one remembered his parents. No one could tell where he came from. Bimbo was another mystery. As long as people could remember seeing Tito—several years at least—they had seen Bimbo. The dog never left his side. He was not only a watchdog, but mother and father to Tito.

Did I say Bimbo never left his master? (Perhaps I had better say "comrade," for if anyone was the master, it was Bimbo.) I was wrong. Bimbo did trust Tito alone exactly three times a day. It was a custom understood between boy and dog since the beginning of their friendship, and the way it worked was this.

Early in the morning, shortly after dawn, while Tito was still dreaming, Bimbo would disappear. When Tito awoke, Bimbo would be sitting quietly at his side, his ears cocked, his stump of a tail tapping the ground, and a fresh-baked loaf of bread—more like a large round roll—at his feet. Tito would stretch himself, Bimbo would yawn, and they would breakfast.

At noon, no matter where they happened to be, Bimbo would put his paw on Tito's knee, and the two of them would return to the inner gate. Tito would curl up in the corner (almost like a dog) and go to sleep, while Bimbo, looking quite important (almost like a boy), would disappear again. In a half-hour he would be back with their lunch. Sometimes it would be a piece of

Scene of Thermopolium and hanging balcony from Fausto Niccolini's *LeCase ed i Monumenti de Pompei.* . . . 1854—96.

fruit or a scrap of meat. Often it was nothing but a dry crust. Sometimes there would be one of those flat, rich cakes, sprinkled with raisins and sugar, that Tito liked so much.

At suppertime the same thing happened, although there was a little less of everything, for things were hard to snatch in the evening with the streets full of people.

Whether there was much or little, hot or cold, fresh or dry, food was always there. Tito never asked where it came from, and

Bimbo never told him. There was plenty of rain water in the hollows of soft stones; the old egg-woman at the corner sometimes gave him a cupful of strong goat's milk; in the grape season the fat wine-maker let him have drippings of the mild juice. There was no danger of going hungry or thirsty. There was plenty of everything in Pompeii if you knew where to find it—and if you had a dog like Bimbo.

As I said before, Tito was not the merriest boy in Pompeii. He could not romp with the other youngsters or play hare-and-hounds and I-spy and follow-your-master and ball-against-the-building and jackstone and kings-and-robbers with them. But that did not make him sorry for himself. If he could not see the sights that delighted the lads of Pompeii, he could hear and smell things they never noticed. When he and Bimbo went out walking, he knew just where they were going and exactly what was happening.

As they passed a handsome villa, he'd sniff and say, "Ah, Glaucus Pansa is giving a grand dinner here tonight. They're going to have three kinds of bread and roast pig and stuffed goose and a great stew—I think bear stew—and a fig pie." Bimbo would note that this would be a good place to visit tomorrow.

Or "H'm," Tito would murmur, half through his lips, half through his nostrils. "The wife of Marcus Lucretius is expecting her mother. She's airing all the linens. She's going to use the best clothes, the ones she's been keeping in pine needles and camphor, and she's got an extra servant cleaning the kitchen. Come, Bimbo, let's get out of the dust!"

Or, as they neared the forum, "Mm'm! What good things they have in the market place today! Dates from Africa and salt oysters from sea caves and cuttlefish and new honey and sweet onions and—ugh!—water-buffalo steaks. Come let's see what's what in the forum." And Bimbo, just as curious as his comrade, hurried on. Being a dog, he, too, trusted his ears and nose more than his eyes, and so the two of them entered the center of Pompeii.

The forum was the part of town to which everybody came at least once during each day. Everything happened there. There were no private houses; all was public—the chief temples, the gold and red bazaars, the silk shops, the town hall, the booths belonging to the weavers and the jewel merchants, the wealthy woolen market. Everything gleamed brightly here; the buildings looked new. The earthquake of twelve years ago had brought down all the old structures, and since the citizens of Pompeii were ambitious to rival Naples and even Rome, they had seized the opportunity to rebuild the whole town. Hence there was scarcely a building that was older than Tito.

Tito had heard a great deal about the earthquake, although, since he was only about a year old at the time, he could hardly remember it. This particular quake had been a light one, as earthquakes go. The crude houses had been shaken down, and parts of the outworn wall had been wrecked, but there had been very little loss of life.

No one knew what caused these earthquakes. Records showed they had happened in the neighborhood since the beginning of time. Sailors said that it was to teach the lazy cityfolk a lesson and make them appreciate those who risked the dangers of the sea to bring them luxuries and to protect their town from invaders. The priests said that the gods took this way of showing their anger to those who refused to worship properly or failed to bring enough sacrifices to the altars. The tradesmen said that the foreign merchants had corrupted the ground and it was no longer safe to traffic in imported goods that came from strange places and carried a curse upon them. Everyone had a different explanation, and everyone's explanation was louder and sillier than his neighbor's.

People were talking about it this afternoon as Tito and Bimbo came out of the side street into the public square. The forum was crowded. Tito's ears, as well as his nose, guided them to the place where the talk was loudest.

"I tell you," rumbled a voice which Tito recognized as that of bathmaster Rufus, "there won't be another earthquake in my lifetime or yours. There may be a tremble or two, but earthquakes, like lightning, never strike twice in the same place."

"Don't they?" asked a thin voice Tito had never heard before. It had a high, sharp ring to it, and Tito knew it as the accent of a stranger. "How about the two towns in Sicily that have been ruined three times within fifteen years by the eruptions of Mount Etna? And were they not warned? Does that column of smoke above Vesuvius mean nothing?"

"That?" Tito could hear the grunt with which one question answered another. "That's always there. We use it for our weather guide. When the smoke stands up straight, we know we'll have fair weather. When it flattens out, it's sure to be foggy. When it drifts to the east—"

"Very well, my confident friend," cut in the thin voice, which now sounded curiously flat. "We have a proverb. 'Those who will not listen to man must be taught by the gods.' I say no more. But I leave a last warning. Remember the holy ones. Look to your temples. And when the smoke tree above Vesuvius grows to the shape of an umbrella pine, look to your lives!"

Tito could hear the air whistle as the speaker drew his toga about him, and the quick shuffle of feet told him that the stranger had gone.

"Now what," said Attilio, the stone-cutter, "did he mean by that?"

"I wonder," grunted Rufus. "I wonder."

Tito wondered, too. And Bimbo, his head at a thoughtful angle, also looked as if he were doing a heavy bit of pondering. By nightfall the argument had been forgotten. If the smoke had increased, no one saw it in the dark. Besides, it was Caesar's birthday, and the town was in a holiday mood. Tito and Bimbo were among the merrymakers, dodging the charioteers, who shouted at them. Yet Tito never missed his footing. He was thankful for his keen ears and quick instinct—most thankful of all for Bimbo.

They visited the open-air theater, and then the city walls, where the people of Pompeii gathered. The crowd watched a sham naval battle in which the city, attacked from the sea, was saved after thousands of flaming arrows had been burned. Though the thrill of flaring ships and lighted skies was lost to Tito, the shouts and cheers excited him as much as anyone.

The next morning there were two of the beloved raisin cakes for his breakfast. Bimbo was unusually active and thumped his bit of a tail until Tito was afraid he would wear it out. Tito couldn't imagine whether Bimbo was urging him to some sort of game or was trying to tell him something. After a while he ceased to notice Bimbo. He felt drowsy. Last night's late hours had tired him. Besides, there was a heavy mist in the air—no, a thick fog rather than a mist—a fog that got into his throat and made him cough. He walked as far as the marine gate to get a breath of the sea, but even the salt air seemed smoky.

Tito went to bed before dusk, but he did not sleep well. He awoke early. Or rather, he was pulled awake, Bimbo doing the pulling. The dog had dragged Tito to his feet and was urging the boy along. Where, Tito did not know. His feet stumbled uncertainly; he was still half asleep. For a while he noticed nothing except the fact that it was hard to breathe. The air was hot and heavy, so heavy that he could taste it. The air, it seemed, had turned to powder, a warm powder that stung his nostrils and burned his sightless eyes.

Then he began to hear peculiar sounds. Like animals under the earth. Hissings and groanings and muffled cries. There was no doubt of it now. The noises came from underneath. He not only heard them—he could feel them. The earth twitched, the twitching changed to an uneven shrugging of the soil. Then, as Bimbo half pulled, half coaxed him along, the ground jerked away from his feet and he was thrown against a stone fountain.

The water—hot water!—splashing in his face revived him. He got to his feet, Bimbo steadying him, helping him on again. The noises grew louder, and came closer. The cries were even more animal-like than before, but now they came from human throats. A few people began to rush by; a family or two, then a group. Then, it seemed, the whole city of people. Tito, bewildered though he was, could recognize Rufus' voice as he bellowed like a water buffalo gone mad.

It was then the crashing began. First a sharp crackling, like a monstrous snapping of twigs. Then an explosion that tore earth and sky. The heavens, though Tito could not see them, were shot through with continual flickerings of fire. Lightnings above were answered by thunders beneath. A house fell. Then another. By a miracle the two companions had escaped the dangerous side streets and were in a more open space. It was the forum. They rested here awhile; how long the boy did not know.

Tito had no idea of the time of day. He could *feel* it was black—an unnatural blackness. Something inside, perhaps the lack of breakfast and lunch, told him it was past noon, but it didn't matter. Nothing seemed to matter. He was getting drowsy, too drowsy to walk, but walk he must. He knew it, Bimbo knew it; the sharp tugs told him so. Nor was it a moment too soon. The sacred ground of the forum was safe no longer. It began to rock, then to pitch, then to split. As they stumbled out of the square, the earth wriggled like a caught snake, and all the columns of the Temple of Jupiter came down. It was the end of the world, or so it seemed.

To walk was not enough now. They must run. Tito, too frightened to know what to do or where to go, had lost all sense of direction. He started to go back to the inner gate; but Bimbo, straining his back to the last inch, almost pulled his clothes from him. What did the dog want? Had he gone completely mad?

Then suddenly he understood. Bimbo was telling him the way out. The sea gate, of course. The sea gate — and then the sea, far from falling buildings, heaving ground. He turned, Bimbo guiding him across open pits and dangerous pools of bubbling mud, away from buildings that had caught fire and were dropping their burning beams.

New dangers threatened. All Pompeii seemed to be thronging toward the marine gate, and there was the chance of being trampled to death, but the chance had to be taken. It was growing harder and harder to breathe. What air there was choked him. It was all dust now, dust and pebbles as large as beans. They fell on his head, his hands — pumice stones from the black heart of Vesuvius! The mountain was turning itself inside out. Tito remembered what the stranger had said in the forum two days ago, "Those who will not listen to men must be taught by the gods." The people had refused to heed the warnings. They were being taught now, if it was not too late.

Suddenly it seemed too late for Tito. The red-hot ashes blistered his skin. The stinging vapors tore his throat. He could not go on. He staggered toward a small tree at the side of the road and fell. In a moment Bimbo was beside him. He coaxed, but there was no answer. He licked Tito's hands, his feet, his face. The boy did not stir. Then Bimbo did the thing he least wanted to do. He bit his comrade, bit him deep in the arm. With a cry of pain, Tito jumped to his feet, Bimbo after him. Tito was in despair, but Bimbo was determined. He drove the boy on, snapping at his heels, worrying his way through the crowd, barking, baring his teeth, heedless of kicks or falling stones.

Sick with hunger, half dead with fear and sulphur fumes, Tito plodded on, pursued by Bimbo. How long he never knew. At last he staggered through the marine gate and felt soft sand under him. Then Tito fainted.

Someone was dashing sea water over him. Someone else was carrying him toward a boat.

"Bimbo!" he called. And then louder, "Bimbo!" But Bimbo had disappeared.

Voices jarred against each other. "Hurry! Hurry!" "To the boats!" "Can't you see the child's frightened and starving?" "He keeps calling for someone!" "Poor child, he's out of his mind." "Here, boy, take this!"

They tucked him in among them. The oarlocks creaked; the oars splashed; the boat rode over the toppling waves. Tito was

View of a villa, Pompeii (detail). First century fresco. National Museum of Naples. Courtesy of Scala/Art Resource, New York.

safe. But he wept continually. "Bimbo!" he wailed. "Bimbo! Bimbo!"

He could not be comforted.

Eighteen hundred years passed. Scientists were restoring the ancient city. Excavators were working their way through the stones and trash that had buried the entire town. Much had already been brought to light—statues, bronze instruments, bright mosaics, household articles. Even delicate paintings that had been preserved by the ashes that had taken over two thousand lives. Columns were dug up, and the forum was beginning to emerge.

It was at a place where the ruins lay deepest that the director paused.

"Come here," he called to his assistant. "I think we've discovered the remains of a building in good shape. Here are four huge millstones that were most likely turned by slaves or mules, and here is a whole wall standing, with shelves inside it. Why, it must have been a bakery! And here is a curious thing—the skeleton of a dog!"

"Amazing!" gasped his assistant. "You'd think a dog would have had sense enough to run away at that time. What is that flat thing he's holding between his teeth? It can't be a stone."

"No. It must have come from this bakery. Do you know, it looks to me like some sort of cake, hardened with the years. And bless me, if those little black pebbles aren't raisins! A raisin cake almost two thousand years old! I wonder what made him want it at such a moment?"

"I wonder," murmured his assistant.

Developing Comprehension Skills

1. Find at least two examples of how Bimbo regularly helped Tito.

2. What unusual qualities set Bimbo apart from most other dogs? What events or details in the story show these qualities?

3. What obstacles threatened Tito's escape from the city? How did Bimbo manage to get Tito to safety?

4. Why did Bimbo leave Tito and return to the city? How did you learn Bimbo's reason for leaving Tito?

5. Were you surprised by Bimbo's reason for leaving Tito? Why or why not?

6. Do you believe that the characters in this story acted as real people and animals would? Explain your feelings.

Reading Literature: Short Stories

1. **Recognizing Setting.** The first part of "The Dog of Pompeii" re-creates the ancient city of Pompeii. The author includes many details of life in Pompeii to establish the setting. These details describe the following aspects of life in Pompeii:

houses	food
stores	transportation
clothes	entertainment

Choose three of these subjects. For each, list two specific details found in the story.

2. **Believing a Fictional Story.** Although dealing with imaginary events, a fictional story must be believable. The characters must act and speak as real people would. The events in a story must seem logical.

   In order to make "The Dog of Pompeii" seem real, the author mixed facts and fiction. For example, some of the signs on the buildings were actually found in the ruins of Pompeii. The character of Tito, however, was made up.

   Make two columns on a piece of paper. Label one *Fact* and the other *Fiction*. In each column, list at least five details from "The Dog of Pompeii" that you think fit in that category.

3. **Recognizing Foreshadowing.** A clue, or hint of some future event in a story is called **foreshadowing**. A writer uses foreshadowing to prepare the reader for an important event

in the story. In "The Dog of Pompeii," for example, the stranger in the square warns citizens to "look to your lives." What other examples of foreshadowing can you find?

4. **Appreciating Style of Writing.** A writer's **style** of writing is his or her special way of expressing ideas. The length and order of sentences is one important part of a writer's style.

In "The Dog of Pompeii," different sentence lengths help the reader appreciate the events in the story. Read this passage, which occurs early in the story.

> Early in the morning, shortly after dawn, while Tito was still dreaming, Bimbo would disappear. When Tito awoke, Bimbo would be sitting quietly at his side, his ears cocked, his stump of a tail tapping the ground, and a fresh-baked loaf of bread—more like a large round roll—at his feet.

The sentences in this passage are fairly long. They suggest a relaxed, peaceful feeling. Now read this next passage:

> Tito had no idea of the time of day. But it didn't matter. Nothing seemed to matter. He was getting drowsy, too drowsy to walk, but walk he must. He knew it, Bimbo knew it; the sharp tugs told him so. Nor was it a moment too soon. The sacred ground of the forum was safe no longer. It began to rock, then to pitch, then to split. As they stumbled out of the square, the earth wriggled like a caught snake. . . .

The sentences in this passage are shorter. Explain how these sentences suggest a feel-ing of growing tension. How does the writer's style help you appreciate the events in this story?

Developing Vocabulary Skills

Finding Word Meaning with Context Clues. Read the following sentences about "The Dog of Pompeii." Using **definition clues**, **restatement clues**, or **synonyms**, determine the meaning of each underlined word from context. On your paper, write the clue you used and the meaning of the underlined word.

1. Sham battles were presented to the citizens. A sham battle is a fake battle.
2. Tito and Bimbo searched for food near handsome villas, luxurious homes of wealthy citizens.
3. Each day, they visited the market place in the forum, or public square.
4. Bimbo and his comrade hurried on. However, his friend was growing tired.
5. The citizens of Pompeii were ambitious to rival, that is, compete with, Naples and Rome.

Developing Writing Skills

1. **Using Contrast.** The three stories in this section, "Feathered Friend," "Zlateh the Goat," and "The Dog of Pompeii," all concern the relationship between a person and an animal. Yet, this relationship differs in each situation. In each story, the human has a different attitude toward the animal. Write a paragraph contrasting these stories. Point out the differences among the relationships of the humans and animals.

Pre-Writing. Consider the human and animal relationships in the three stories. List details and quotations from the story that point out the human's attitude toward the animal. Try to group similar ideas from the three stories together.

Writing. When writing about literature, always mention the title of the selection in your opening sentence. If you are contrasting selections, the next sentence will state your purpose. For example, you might begin your paragraph with sentences similar to these.

> "Feathered Friend," "Zlateh the Goat," and "The Dog of Pompeii" are stories about a relationship between a human and an animal. The relationship is different in each story.

The rest of the paragraph should explain the differing relationships in detail. Refer to the list you prepared in pre-writing. You should include those details that best point out the differences.

Revising. Exchange your paragraph with a classmate. Read each other's writing to find the contrasting points. Is each point well supported by examples? Add any necessary details. When you are satisfied with the content of your paragraph, proofread for errors in grammar, usage, and mechanics. Then make a clean, final copy.

2. **Understanding the Importance of Setting.** In each of the stories in this section, the setting plays an important part. It affects the events and outcome of the story. Choose one story. In a paragraph, explain why the setting is so important to the story. Could the events in this story have happened in a different place or time?

Developing Skills in Speaking and Listening

Reporting a News Story. Imagine that you are a radio reporter assigned to cover the disaster at Pompeii. A good reporter describes the event so that the listener can feel as though he or she is actually there.

As you plan your report, decide what incidents you will describe. List these incidents in the order in which they occurred. This is called **chronological, or time, order**. Plan to use specific words that will help your listeners see, hear, and smell the events described in the story. Practice giving your talk before presenting it to your classmates.

Characterization

Short stories often introduce you to interesting or unusual people. From these characters, you can learn a great deal about human nature. As you meet the people in these short stories, look for the things that make them special.

Ives Field, 1964, ALEX KATZ. Weatherspoon Art Gallery, University of North Carolina at Greensboro. Gift of Burlington Industries.

The Fan Club

RONA MAYNARD

People in a select group can be cruel to others they see as different. Does Laura really understand how cruel such an attitude is?

It was Monday again. It was Monday and the day was damp and cold. Rain splattered the cover of *Algebra I* as Laura heaved her books higher on her arm and sighed. School was such a bore.

School. It loomed before her now, massive and dark against the sky. In a few minutes, she would have to face them again—Diane Goddard with her sleek blond hair and Terri Pierce in her candy-pink sweater. And Carol and Steve and Bill and Nancy. . . . There were so many of them, so exclusive as they stood in their tight little groups laughing and joking.

Why were they so cold and unkind? Was it because her long stringy hair hung in her eyes instead of dipping in graceful curls? Was it because she wrote poetry in algebra class and got A's in Latin without really trying? Shivering, Laura remembered how they would sit at the back of English class, passing notes and whispering. She thought of their identical brown loafers, their plastic purses, their hostile stares as they passed her in the corridors. She didn't care. They were clods, the whole lot of them.

She shoved her way through the door and there they were. They thronged the hall, streamed in and out of doors, clustered under red and yellow posters advertising the latest dance. Mohair sweaters, madras shirts, pea-green raincoats. They were all alike, all the same. And in the center of the group, as usual, Diane Goddard was saying, "It'll be a riot! I just can't wait to see her face when she finds out."

Laura flushed painfully. Were they talking about her?

"What a scream! Can't wait to hear what she says!"

Silently she hurried past and submerged herself in the stream of students heading for the lockers. It was then that she saw Rachel Horton—alone as always, her too-long skirt billowing over the white, heavy columns of her legs, her freckled face ringed with shapeless black curls. She called herself Horton, but everyone knew her father was Jacob Hortensky, the tailor. He ran that greasy little shop where you could always smell the cooked cabbage from the back rooms where the family lived.

"Oh, Laura!" Rachel was calling her. Laura turned, startled.

"Hi, Rachel."

"Laura, did you watch *World of Nature* last night? On Channel 11?"

"No—no, I didn't." Laura hesitated. "I almost never watch that kind of program."

"Well, gee, you missed something—last night, I mean. It was a real good show. Laura, it showed this fly being born!" Rachel was smiling now; she waved her hands as she talked.

"First the feelers and then the wings. And they're sort of wet at first, the wings are. Gosh, it was a good show."

"I bet it was." Laura tried to sound interested. She turned to go, but Rachel still stood there, her mouth half open, her pale, moon-like face strangely urgent. It was as if an invisible hand tugged at Laura's sleeve.

"And Laura," Rachel continued, "that was an awful good poem you read yesterday in English."

Laura remembered how Terri and Diane had laughed and whispered. "You really think so? Well, thanks, Rachel. I mean, not too many people care about poetry."

"Yours was real nice though. I wish I could write like you. I always like those things you write."

Laura blushed. "I'm glad you do."

"Laura, can you come over sometime after school? Tomorrow maybe? It's not very far and you can stay for dinner. I told my parents all about you!"

Laura thought of the narrow, dirty street and the tattered awning in front of the tailor shop. An awful district, the kids said. But she couldn't let that matter. "Okay," she said. And then, faking enthusiasm, "I'd be glad to come."

She turned into the algebra room, sniffing at the smell of chalk and dusty erasers. In the back row, she saw the "in" group, laughing and joking and whispering.

"What a panic!"

"Here, you make the first one."

Diane and Terri had their heads together over a lot of little cards. You could see they were cooking up something.

Fumbling through the pages of her book, she tried to memorize the theorems she hadn't looked at the night before. The laughter at the back of the room rang in her ears. Also those smiles—those heartless smiles . . . .

A bell buzzed in the corridors; students scrambled to their places. "We will now have the national anthem," said the voice on the loudspeaker. Laura shifted her weight from one foot to the other. It was so false, so pointless. How could they sing of the land of the free, when there was still discrimination. Smothered laughter behind her. Were they all looking at her?

And then it was over. Slumping in her seat, she shuffled through last week's half-finished homework papers and scribbled flowers in the margins.

"Now this one is just a direct application of the equation." The voice was hollow, distant, an echo beyond the sound of rustling papers and hushed whispers. Laura sketched a guitar on the cover of her notebook. Someday she would live in the Village[1] and there would be no more algebra classes and people would accept her.

She turned towards the back row. Diane was passing around one of her cards. Terri leaned over, smiling. "Hey, can I do the next one?"

". . . by using the distributive law." Would the class never end? Math was so dull, so painfully dull. They made you multiply and cancel and factor, multiply, cancel, and factor. Just like a machine. The steel sound of the bell shattered the silence. Scraping chairs, cries of "Hey, wait!" The crowd moved into the hallway now, a thronging, jostling mass.

Alone in the tide of faces, Laura felt someone nudge her. It was Ellen. "Hey, how's that for a smart outfit?" She pointed to the other side of the hall.

The gaudy flowers of Rachel Horton's blouse stood out among the fluffy sweaters and pleated skirts. What a lumpish, awkward creature Rachel was. Did she have to dress like that? Her socks had fallen untidily around her heavy ankles, and her slip showed a raggedy edge of lace. As she moved into the English room, shoelaces trailing, her books tumbled to the floor.

"Isn't that something?" Terri said. Little waves of mocking laughter swept through the crowd.

The bell rang; the laughter died away. As they hurried to their seats, Diane and Terri exchanged last-minute whispers. "Make one for Steve. He wants one too!"

Then Miss Merrill pushed aside the book she was holding, folded her hands, and beamed. "All right, people, that will be enough. Now, today we have our speeches. Laura, would you begin please?"

So it was her turn. Her throat tightened as she thought of Diane and Carol and Steve grinning and waiting for her to stumble. Perhaps if she was careful they'd never know she hadn't thought out everything beforehand. Careful, careful, she thought. Look confident.

"Let's try to be prompt." Miss Merrill tapped the cover of her book with her fountain pen.

Laura pushed her way to the front of the class. Before her, the room was large and still. Twenty-five round, blurred faces stared blankly. Was that Diane's laughter? She folded her hands and looked at the wall, strangely distant now, its brown paint cracked and peeling. A dusty portrait of Robert Frost, a card with the seven rules for better paragraphs, last year's calendar, and the steady, hollow ticking of the clock.

Laura cleared her throat. "Well," she began, "my speech is on civil rights." A chorus of snickers rose from the back of the room.

"Most people," Laura continued, "most people don't care enough about others. Here in New England, they think they're pretty far removed from discrimination and violence. Lots of people sit back and fold their hands and wait for somebody else to

---

1. **Village**, Greenwich Village, a section of New York City where different lifestyles are accepted.

do the work. But I think we're all responsible for people that haven't had some of the advantages. . . ."

Diane was giggling and gesturing at Steve Becker. All she ever thought about was parties and dates—and such dates! Always the president of the student council or the captain of the football team.

"A lot of people think that race prejudice is limited to the South. But most of us are prejudiced—whether we know it or not. It's not just that we don't give other people a chance; we don't give ourselves a chance either. We form narrow opinions and then we don't see the truth. We keep right on believing that we're open-minded liberals when all we're doing is deceiving ourselves."

How many of them cared about truth? Laura looked past the rows of blank, empty faces, past the bored stares and cynical grins.

"But I think we should try to forget our prejudices. We must realize now that we've done too little for too long. We must accept the fact that one person's misfortune is everyone's responsibility. We must defend the natural dignity of people—a dignity that thousands are denied."

None of them knew what it was like to be unwanted, unaccepted. Did Steve know? Did Diane?

"Most of us are proud to say that we live in a free country. But is this really true? Can we call the United States a free country when millions of people face prejudice and discrimination? As long as one person is

Figures and Screen (detail), about 1952, RAPHAEL SOYER. Collection of Arnold Lieber and Mary Soyer Lieber, New York.

forbidden to share the basic rights we take for granted, as long as we are still the victims of irrational hatreds, there can be no freedom. Only when every American learns to respect the dignity of every other American can we truly call our country free."

The class was silent. "Very nice, Laura." Things remained quiet as other students droned through their speeches. Then Miss Merrill looked briskly around the room. "Now, Rachel, I believe you're next."

There was a ripple of dry, humorless laughter—almost, Laura thought, like the sound of a rattlesnake. Rachel stood before the class now, her face red, her heavy arms piled with boxes.

Diane Goddard tossed back her head and winked at Steve.

"Well, well, don't we have lots of things to show," said Miss Merrill. "But aren't you going to put those boxes down, Rachel? No, no, not there!"

"Man, that kid's dumb," Steve muttered, and his voice could be clearly heard all through the room.

With a brisk rattle, Miss Merrill's pen tapped the desk for silence.

Rachel's slow smile twitched at the corners. She looked frightened. There was a crash and a clatter as the tower of boxes slid to the floor. Now everyone was giggling.

"Hurry and pick them up," said Miss Merrill sharply.

Rachel crouched on her knees and began very clumsily to gather her scattered treasures. Papers and boxes lay all about, and some of the boxes had broken open, spilling their contents in wild confusion. No one went to help. At last she scrambled to her feet and began fumbling with her notes.

"My—my speech is on shells."

A cold and stony silence had settled upon the room.

"Lots of people collect shells, because they're kind of pretty—sort of, and you just find them on the beach."

"Well, whaddaya know!" It was Steve's voice, softer this time, but all mock amazement. Laura jabbed her notebook with her pencil. Why were they so cruel, so thoughtless? Why did they have to laugh?

"This one," Rachel was saying as she opened one of the boxes, "it's one of the best." Off came the layers of paper and there, at last, smooth and pearly and shimmering, was the shell. Rachel turned it over lovingly in her hands. White, fluted sides, like the close-curled petals of a flower; a scrolled coral back. Laura held her breath. It was beautiful. At the back of the room snickers had begun again.

"Bet she got it at Woolworth's," somebody whispered.

"Or in a trash dump." That was Diane.

Rachel pretended not to hear, but her face was getting very red and Laura could see she was flustered.

"Here's another that's kind of pretty. I found it last summer at Ogunquit." In her outstretched hand there was a small, drab, brownish object. A common snail shell. "It's called a . . . It's called. . . ."

Rachel rustled through her notes. "I—I can't find it. But it was here. It was in here somewhere. I know it was." Her broad face had turned bright pink again. "Just can't find it. . . ." Miss Merrill stood up and strode toward her. "Rachel," she said sharply, "we are supposed to be prepared when we make a speech. Now, I'm sure you remember those rules on page twenty-one. I expect you to know these things. Next time you must have your material organized."

The bell sounded, ending the period. Miss Merrill collected her books.

Then, suddenly, chairs were shoved aside at the back of the room and there was the sound of many voices whispering. They were standing now, whole rows of them, their faces grinning with delight. Choked giggles, shuffling feet—and then applause—wild, sarcastic, malicious applause. That was when Laura saw that they were all wearing little white cards with a fat, frizzy-haired figure drawn on the front.

What did it mean? She looked more closely. "HORTENSKY FAN CLUB," said the bright-red letters.

So that was what the whispering had been about all morning. She'd been wrong. They weren't out to get her after all. It was only Rachel.

Diane was nudging her and holding out a card. "Hey, Laura, here's one for you to wear."

For a moment Laura stared at the card. She looked from Rachel's red, frightened face to Diane's mocking smile, and she heard the pulsing, frenzied rhythm of the claps and the stamping, faster and faster. Her hands trembled as she picked up the card and pinned it to her sweater. And as she turned, she saw Rachel's stricken look.

"She's a creep, isn't she?" Diane's voice was soft and intimate.

And Laura began to clap.

Developing Comprehension Skills

1. Why was Laura uncomfortable around Diane and her friends?

2. Did Laura admit to herself her real feelings about Rachel? How could you tell what her real feelings were?

3. What point was Laura making in her speech? At the end of the story, did Laura act as if she really believed in the subject of the speech? Explain your answer.

4. Why do you think Laura joined the fan club? Were you surprised at her actions? Why or why not?

5. In your opinion, which character, Laura or Diane, hurt Rachel more? Give reasons for your answer.

Reading Literature: Short Stories

1. **Understanding Characterization.** The term **characterization** refers to the methods the

writer uses to make the characters in a story come alive.

In "The Fan Club," the reader learns about Laura in a number of ways. Her thoughts and feelings present one side of Laura, but her actions present another side. What do Laura's thoughts tell you about her? What do her actions reveal?

2. **Recognizing Irony.** You may recall that in irony, the author leads the reader to believe that one thing is true or will happen. In reality, however, the opposite occurs. What, in your opinion, is ironic about the title, "The Fan Club"? What is ironic about Laura joining the fan club?

3. **Inferring Setting.** The setting of a short story refers to the time as well as the place in which the events occur. The writer of "The Fan Club" gives clues to the time period by describing the clothes and speech of the characters. List these clues. Using these clues, can you infer when the story occurs?

4. **Understanding Theme.** Writers try to discuss an important idea about life or human nature in every literary work. This idea is called the **theme**. Reread Laura's speech. It stresses the ideas of tolerance and acceptance of others. Notice how it contrasts with Laura's actions at the end of the story. What idea about human nature do you think the writer is suggesting in this story?

5. **Understanding Point of View.** The events of "The Fan Club" are told in the **third-person point of view**. This means that the narrator is outside the story. In "The Dog of Pompeii," the third-person narrator knew everything that each character was thinking. This type of third-person narrator is called **omniscient**.

In "The Fan Club," however, the narrator provides the reader with only Laura's thoughts and feelings. This kind of narrator has a **limited third-person point of view**.

What effect does the limited third-person point of view have on the story? How would the story have changed if it were told from Diane's or Rachel's point of view?

Developing Vocabulary Skills

Inferring the Meaning of a Word. You may not always find obvious clues to the meaning of an unfamiliar word. You may have to **infer**, or figure out, the meaning. To do this, you must try to understand the idea of the sentence or paragraph in which the unfamiliar word appears. For example, read the following passage:

Students *thronged* the halls. Hundreds quickly passed from classroom to classroom.

There are no specific context clues to help you figure out the meaning of "thronged." From the entire passage, however, you can infer that "thronged" means "crowded."

Read these sentences, which include words drawn from "The Fan Club." Use the entire passage to help you determine the meaning of the underlined word. Write the meaning.

1. Only the best dressed and most popular students could join their exclusive club.

2. Laura spoke against discrimination, yet when she had a chance to join the club she treated Rachel as cruelly as everyone else.

3. She was shoved from side to side and pushed against the wall by the jostling students.

4. "But most of us are prejudiced—whether we know it or not. We form narrow opinions and then we don't see the truth."

Developing Writing Skills

1. **Comparing and Contrasting Characters.** The similarities and differences between two characters provide much of the interest in "The Fan Club." Diane and Laura have different physical features and character traits. They think, act, and speak differently. However, they also share some qualities. Write a paragraph comparing and contrasting these characters. Use a list of features, traits, and details as you write.

2. **Writing a Character Sketch.** Imagine that you are preparing to write a story. Before writing your story, you must carefully plan the main character. One way to plan is by writing a **character sketch**, or short description, of your character.

   Pre-Writing. Write the names of two or three interesting people you have known. For each person, list physical features, character traits, and details of thought, action, and speech. Now choose the person you think would be most interesting to others.

   Writing. Write the first draft of the character sketch. Describe the physical features and other obvious character traits first. Finish your sketch with a description of the person's thoughts, actions, and speech. Do not limit yourself to those items on your pre-writing list. If you think of more descriptive details, use them.

   Revising. After completing the first draft of your character sketch, use the following questions to guide your revision:

   > Did I choose details that revealed important things about the person?
   > Is the sketch interesting? Will others want to read it?
   > What can I change or add to make it more interesting?
   > Did I discuss the person's physical features and character traits first?
   > Did I finish with less obvious details about the person?

Developing Skills in Critical Thinking

Understanding the Error of Bandwagon. Sometimes people decide to take a certain action simply because other people are doing so. This error in reasoning is known as **bandwagon**. One specific type of **bandwagon** error is called **snob appeal**. In this case, a person takes an action because all the "select" or "popular" people do so.

Which characters in "The Fan Club" are guilty of these errors in reasoning? Explain your answer. Can you think of any real-life examples where people simply "jump on the bandwagon"?

Developing Skills in Speaking and Listening

Participating in an Informal Discussion. The purpose of an **informal discussion** is to exchange ideas. A discussion is not an argument. Each participant should be allowed to state an opinion about the question under discussion. As a participant, you have a responsibility to listen carefully to each person's viewpoint. If you have questions or comments, wait until the person is finished speaking before you seek an answer.

Take part in an informal discussion about the following statement:

> People cannot always be judged by what they say or how they look.

A Mother in Mannville

It is sometimes difficult to reveal personal feelings to others. What is Jerry's secret? Why does he hide the truth from one he cares for?

MARJORIE KINNAN RAWLINGS

The orphanage is high in the Carolina mountains. Sometimes in winter the snowdrifts are so deep that the institution is cut off from the village below, from all the world. Fog hides the mountain peaks, the snow swirls down the valleys, and a wind blows so bitterly that the orphanage boys who take the milk twice daily to the baby cottage reach the door with fingers stiff in an agony of numbness.

"Or when we carry trays from the cookhouse for the ones that are sick," Jerry said, "we get our faces frostbit, because we can't put our hands over them. I have gloves," he added. "Some of the boys don't have any."

He liked the late spring, he said. The rhododendron was in bloom, a carpet of color, across the mountainsides, soft as the May winds that stirred the hemlocks. He called it laurel.

"It's pretty when the laurel blooms," he said. "Some's pink and some's white."

I was there in the autumn. I wanted quiet, isolation, to do some troublesome writing. I wanted mountain air to blow out the malaria from too long a time in the subtropics. I was homesick, too, for the flaming of maples in October, and for corn shocks[1] and pumpkins and black-walnut trees and the lift of hills. I found them all, living in a cabin that belonged to the orphanage, half a mile beyond the orphanage farm. When I took the cabin, I asked for a boy or man to come and chop wood for the fireplace. The first few days were warm, I found what wood I needed about the cabin, no one came, and I forgot the order.

I looked up from my typewriter one late afternoon, a little startled. A boy stood at the door, and my pointer dog, my companion, was at his side and had not barked to warn me. The boy was probably twelve years old, but undersized. He wore overalls and a torn shirt, and was barefooted.

He said, "I can chop some wood today."

I said, "But I have a boy coming from the orphanage."

---

1. **corn shocks**, stalks of corn heaped together in small piles in the field, for drying.

Gathering Autumn Leaves, 1873, WINSLOW HOMER.
Cooper-Hewitt Museum, the Smithsonian Institution's National Museum of Design, Washington, D.C. Gift of Charles Savage Homer.

"I'm the boy."

"You? But you're small."

"Size don't matter, chopping wood," he said. "Some of the big boys don't chop good. I've been chopping wood at the orphanage a long time."

I visualized mangled and inadequate branches for my fires. I was well into my work and not inclined to conversation. I was a little blunt.

"Very well. There's the ax. Go ahead and see what you can do."

I went back to work, closing the door. At first the sound of the boy dragging brush annoyed me. Then he began to chop. The blows were rhythmic and steady, and shortly I had forgotten him. The sound was no more of an interruption than a steady rain. I suppose an hour and a half passed, for when I stopped and stretched, and heard the boy's steps on the cabin stoop, the sun was dropping behind the farthest mountain, and the valleys were purple with something deeper than the asters.

The boy said, "I have to go to supper now. I can come again tomorrow evening."

I said, "I'll pay you now for what you've done," thinking I should probably have to insist on an older boy. "Ten cents an hour?"

"Anything is all right."

We went together back of the cabin. An astonishing amount of solid wood had been cut. There were cherry logs and heavy roots of rhododendron, and blocks from the waste pine and oak left from the building of the cabin.

"But you've done as much as a man." I said. "This is a splendid pile."

I looked at him, actually, for the first time. His hair was the color of the corn shocks. His eyes, very direct, were like the mountain sky when rain is pending—gray, with a shadowing of that miraculous blue.

As I spoke, a light came over him, as though the setting sun had touched him with the same suffused glory with which it touched the mountains. I gave him a quarter.

"You may come tomorrow," I said, "and thank you very much."

He looked at me, and at the coin, and seemed to want to speak, but could not, and turned away.

"I'll split kindling tomorrow," he said over his thin ragged shoulder. "You'll need kindling and medium wood and logs and backlogs."

At daylight I was half wakened by the sound of chopping. Again it was so even in texture that I went back to sleep. When I left my bed in the cool morning, the boy had come and gone, and a stack of kindling was neat against the cabin wall. He came again after school in the afternoon and worked until time to return to the orphanage. His name was Jerry. He was twelve years old, and he had been at the orphanage since he was four. I could picture him at four, with the same grave gray-blue eyes and the same—independence? No, the word that comes to me is "integrity."

The word means something very special to me, and the quality for which I use it is a rare one. My father had it. But almost no man of my acquaintance possesses it with the clarity, the purity, and the simplicity of a mountain stream. But the boy Jerry had it. It is bedded on courage, but it is more than brave. It is honest, but it is more than honesty. The ax handle broke one day. Jerry said the woodshop at the orphanage would repair it. I brought money to pay for the job and he refused it.

"I'll pay for it," he said. "I broke it. I brought the ax down careless."

"But no one hits accurately every time," I told him. "The fault was in the wood of the handle. I'll see the man from whom I bought it."

It was only then that he would take the money. He was standing back of his own carelessness. He was a free-will agent and he chose to do careful work. If he failed, he took the responsibility without subterfuge.

He did for me the unnecessary thing, the gracious thing, that we find done only by the great of heart. Things no training can teach, for they are done on the instant, with no experience. He found a cubbyhole beside the fireplace that I had not noticed. There, of his own accord, he put kindling and "medium" wood, so that I might always have dry fire material ready in case of sudden wet weather. A stone was loose in the rough walk to the cabin. He dug a deeper hole and steadied it. I found that when I tried to return his thoughtfulness with such things as candy and apples, he was wordless. "Thank you" was, perhaps, an expression for which he had had no use, for his courtesy was instinctive. He only looked at the gift and at me, and a curtain lifted, so that I saw deep into the clear well of his eyes, and gratitude was there, and affection, soft over the firm granite of his character.

He made simple excuses to come and sit with me. I could no more have turned him away than if he had been physically hungry. I suggested once that the best time for us to visit was just before supper, when I left off my writing. After that, he waited always until my typewriter had been quiet some time. One day I worked until nearly dark. I went outside the cabin, having forgotten him. I saw him going up over the hill in the twilight toward the orphanage. When I sat down on my stoop, a place was warm from his body where he had been sitting.

He became friendly, of course, with my pointer, Pat. There is a strange communion between a boy and a dog. Perhaps they possess the same singleness of spirit, the same kind of wisdom. It is difficult to explain, but it exists. When I went across the state for a weekend, I left the dog in Jerry's charge. I gave him the dog whistle and the key to the cabin, and left food. He was to come two or three times a day and let out the dog, and feed and exercise him. I should return Sunday night, and Jerry would take out the dog for the last time Sunday afternoon and then leave the key under an agreed hiding place.

My return was belated and fog filled the mountain passes so treacherously that I dared not drive at night. The fog held the next morning, and it was Monday noon before I reached the cabin. The dog had been fed and cared for that morning. Jerry came early in the afternoon, anxious.

"The superintendent said nobody would drive in the fog," he said. "I came just before bedtime last night and you hadn't come. So I brought Pat some of my breakfast this morning. I wouldn't have let anything happen to him."

"I was sure of that. I didn't worry."

"When I heard about the fog, I thought you'd know."

He was needed for work at the orphanage and he had to return at once. I gave him a dollar in payment, and he looked at it and went away. But that night he came in the darkness and knocked at the door.

"Come in, Jerry," I said, "if you're allowed to be away this late."

"I told maybe a story," he said. "I told them I thought you would want to see me."

"That's true," I assured him, and I saw his relief. "I want to hear about how you managed with the dog."

He sat by the fire with me, with no other light, and told me of their two days together. The dog lay close to him, and found a comfort there that I did not have for him. It seemed to me that being with my dog, and caring for him, had brought the boy and me, too, together, so that he felt that he belonged to me as well as to the animal.

"He stayed right with me," he told me, "except when he ran in the laurel. He likes the laurel. I took him up over the hill and we both ran fast. There was a place where the grass was high and I lay down in it and hid. I could hear Pat hunting for me. He found my trail and he barked. When he found me, he acted crazy, and he ran around and around me, in circles."

We watched the flames.

"That's an apple log," he said. "It burns the prettiest of any wood."

We were very close.

He was suddenly impelled to speak of things he had not spoken of before, nor had I cared to ask him.

"You look a little bit like my mother," he said, "especially in the dark, by the fire."

"But you were only four, Jerry, when you came here. You have remembered how she looked, all these years?"

"My mother lives in Mannville," he said.

For a moment, finding that he had a mother shocked me as greatly as anything in my life has ever done. I did not know why it disturbed me. Then I understood my distress. I was filled with a passionate resentment that any woman should go away and leave her son. A fresh anger added itself— to leave a son like this one! The orphanage was a wholesome place, the executives were kind, good people. The food was more than adequate. The boys were healthy. A ragged shirt was no hardship, nor was the doing of clean labor. Granted, perhaps, that the boy felt no lack, what blood fed a woman who did not yearn over this child that had come out of her own body? At four he would have looked the same as now. Nothing, I thought, nothing in life could change those eyes. His quality must be apparent to an idiot, a fool. I burned with questions I could not ask. In any, I was afraid, there would be pain.

"Have you seen her, Jerry—lately?"

"I see her every summer. She sends for me to come."

I wanted to cry out, "Why are you not with her? How can she let you go away?"

He said, "She comes up here from Mannville whenever she can. She doesn't have a job now."

His face shone in the firelight.

"She wanted to give me a puppy, but they can't let any one boy keep a puppy. You remember the suit I had on last Sunday?" He was plainly proud. "She sent me that for Christmas. The Christmas before that"—he drew a long breath, savoring the memory—"she sent me a pair of skates."

"Roller skates?"

My mind was busy, making pictures of her, trying to understand her. She had not, then, entirely deserted or forgotten him. But why, then—I thought, "I must not condemn her without knowing."

"Roller skates. I let the other boys use them. They're always borrowing them. But they're careful of them."

What circumstance other than poverty—

"I'm going to take the dollar you gave me for taking care of Pat," he said, "and buy her a pair of gloves."

I could only say, "That will be nice. Do you know her size?"

"I think it's 8½," he said.

He looked at my hands.

"Do you wear 8½?" he asked.

"No, I wear a smaller size, a 6."

"Oh! Then I guess her hands are bigger than yours."

I hated her. Poverty or no, there was other food than bread, and the soul could starve as quickly as the body. He was taking his dollar to buy gloves for her big stupid hands, and she lived away from him, in

Mannville, and contented herself with sending him skates.

"She likes white gloves," he said. "Do you think I can get them for a dollar?"

"I think so," I said.

I decided that I should not leave the mountains without seeing her and knowing for myself why she had done this thing.

The human mind scatters its interests as though made of thistledown, and every wind stirs and moves it. I finished my work. It did not please me, and I gave my thoughts to another field. I should need some Mexican material.

I made arrangements to close my Florida place and travel to Mexico immediately. I would do the writing there, if conditions were favorable. Then—Alaska with my brother. After that, heaven knew what or where.

I did not take time to go to Mannville to see Jerry's mother, nor even to talk with the orphanage about her. I was a trifle distracted because of my work and plans. After my first fury at her—we did not speak of her again—his having a mother, any sort at all, not far away, in Mannville, relieved me of the ache I had had about him. He did not question the strange relationship. He was not lonely. It was not my concern.

He came every day and cut my wood and did small helpful favors and stayed to talk. The days had become cold, and often I let him come inside the cabin. He would lie on the floor in front of the fire, with one arm across the dog, and they would both doze and wait quietly for me. Other days they ran

Pattern of Leaves, 1924, GEORGIA O'KEEFFE.
The Phillips Collection, Washington, D.C.

with a common ecstasy through the laurel, and since the asters were now gone, he brought me back crimson maple leaves, and chestnut boughs dripping with imperial yellow. I was ready to go.

I said to him, "You have been my good friend, Jerry. I shall often think of you and miss you. Pat will miss you too. I am leaving tomorrow."

He did not answer. When he went away, I remember that a new moon hung over the mountains, and I watched him go in silence up the hill. I expected him the next day, but he did not come. The details of packing my personal belongings, loading my car, arranging the bed over the seat, where the dog would ride, occupied me until late in the day. I closed the cabin and started the car, noticing that the sun was in the west and I should do well to be out of the mountains by nightfall. I stopped by the orphanage and left the cabin key and money for my light bill with Miss Clark.

"And will you call Jerry for me to say good-by to him?"

"I don't know where he is," she said. "I'm afraid he's not well. He didn't eat his dinner this noon. One of the other boys saw him going over the hill into the laurel. He was supposed to fire the boiler this afternoon. It's not like him; he's always been unusually reliable."

I was almost relieved, for I knew I should never see him again, and it would be easier not to say good-by to him.

I said, "I wanted to talk with you about his mother—why he's here—but I'm in more of a hurry than I expected to be. It's out of the question for me to see her now, too. But here's some money I'd like to leave with you to buy things for him at Christmas and on his birthday. It will be better than for me to try to send him things. I could so easily duplicate—skates, for instance."

She blinked her honest eyes.

"There's not much use for skates here," she said.

Her stupidity annoyed me.

"What I mean," I said, "is that I don't want to duplicate things his mother sends him. I might have chosen skates if I didn't know she had already given them to him."

She stared at me.

"I don't understand," she said. "He has no mother. He has no skates."

Developing Comprehension Skills

1. How did the narrator first meet Jerry? Was he what she expected?

2. Why was the relationship with the narrator important to Jerry?

3. When she was told that Jerry had no mother, how do you think she felt?

4. Can you understand why Jerry lied about his mother? Explain your reasoning.

5. Do you think the narrator really understood Jerry? What makes you think so? Do you think she loved Jerry? Find evidence from the story to support your opinion.

Reading Literature: Short Stories

1. **Analyzing the Narrator.** "A Mother in Mannville" is written from the first-person point of view. The narrator is a character in the story. She uses the pronoun *I* in relating the events of the story. The reader can know only what the narrator sees and what she experiences.

What does the narrator in "A Mother in Mannville" tell about herself? Why has she come to the mountain? What do you learn about the narrator from the way she reacts to Jerry?

2. **Inferring Character Traits.** The narrator describes Jerry as a person of integrity, courage, and graciousness. Do you agree with that description? Find details in the story that support your answer.

What other character traits, or qualities, can you infer about Jerry from these words and actions:

a. his caring for and feeding the narrator's dog

b. his avoidance of the narrator on the last days of her stay

c. his comment, "You look a bit like my mother"

3. **Identifying Conflicts.** In this story, most of the conflicts, or struggles, take place within each character. As you recall, these are internal conflicts. For instance, Jerry struggles with opposing feelings about his relationship with the narrator. At times he seems to want to keep his distance from her. At other times he appears to care for her very much. Can you explain Jerry's difficulty in placing his trust and love in another person?

4. **Understanding Metaphor.** A comparison between two unlike things is a **metaphor**. In referring to Jerry, for example, the narrator uses the metaphor "the firm granite of his character." What things are being compared in this metaphor? What does this metaphor tell you about Jerry's character and values? Do you think this is a good comparison? Why or why not?

Developing Vocabulary Skills

Using Antonyms as Context Clues. Words that are nearly opposite in meaning are called **antonyms**. An antonym can sometimes be used as a context clue. It helps you understand a new word by telling you what it is not. An antonym can appear in the same sentence as the unfamiliar word, or in a nearby sentence. It is often signaled by a key word such as *not*, *but*, or *however*. Consider this example:

She did not *prosper*. She failed.

You may not be familiar with the verb *prosper*. However, the word *not* signals a context clue that can help determine meaning. The verb *fail* in the next sentence is an antonym of *prosper*. Therefore, you can figure out that *prosper* means "to succeed" or "to do well."

Read the statements below. Each sentence or group of sentences contains an underlined word taken from "A Mother in Mannville." Write the word on your paper. Then, write its antonym. The antonym will be found in either the same sentence or a nearby sentence. Finally, determine the meaning of the underlined word by using its antonym.

1. I visualized a pile of mangled and inadequate branches for my fires, but the ones I found were quite suitable.

2. If the boy failed, he took the responsibility without subterfuge. He accepted it with total honesty.

3. The boy's courtesy was instinctive; it was not artificial or forced.

4. I knew I must not condemn Jerry's mother, but forgive her for whatever reason.

5. Her voice was soft and intimate, not distant as always before.

Developing Writing Skills

1. **Understanding the Impact of an Experience.** The narrator's experience with Jerry was a powerful, emotional one. Do you think the experience changed her at all? Write a paragraph in which you tell what you think the narrator learned about herself and others.

2. **Writing a Description.** Descriptive paragraphs are often used in stories. They help to create the setting for the story. They can also help set the mood. Marjorie Kinnan Rawlings uses descriptions throughout "A Mother in Mannville" for both these purposes.

   Write a description. Try to create not only a physical description, but also a mood.

   Pre-Writing. Decide on a subject for your description. Try to choose a place that had a strong emotional effect on you. It might be a carnival, the seashore, the woods, or a bustling city street. Write down as many details as you can about this place. Then list sensory details that will help you describe the details well. Try to choose adjectives and adverbs that will create the mood you want your reader to feel.

   Writing. Using your list of details, make a rough draft of your description. Present your details in **spatial order**. That is, describe the scene from front to back, near to far, side to side, or in some other order that makes sense. Use transitional words and phrases such as *in front of*, *next to*, and *behind* to create a clear image in your reader's mind.

   Revising. Ask a classmate to read your description. Ask that person what feeling your description creates. Are there any words or phrases that misled your reader?

Replace them. Also add any details that you think would make your description clearer. Finally, check the order of your details. Did you present them in an order that makes sense? Did you use good transitional words and phrases? When you are satisfied with your description, make a clean, final copy.

Developing Skills in Critical Thinking

Defining a Term. As you think about ideas and speak with others, you will often find it necessary to define a word. A good definition involves three parts. First, the definition gives the subject, or word to be defined. Then, the definition places the subject in a general class. Finally, it shows how the subject differs from all other members of its class. It does this by giving specific characteristics of the subject. Look at the following examples:

   A *mandolin* is a musical instrument with four or five pairs of strings and a deep, rounded sound box.

   Pride is the feeling you get when you are pleased with something you've done.

In a paragraph, define one of these personal qualities: *courage, heroism,* or *friendship.* Look at the author's definition of *integrity* in "A Mother in Mannville" for ideas. Make sure your definition does the following:

1. puts the subject in its general class

2. gives specific characteristics of the subject

3. uses specific examples to develop a general definition

You may find it easier to decide on your personal definition if you first think of a person who has the quality.

The Storyteller

SAKI

Is a happy ending the key to a good story? Or is there a more important ingredient? Read to discover the secret of the storyteller.

It was a hot afternoon, and the railway carriage was correspondingly sultry. The next stop was at Templecombe, nearly an hour ahead. The occupants of the carriage were a small girl, and a smaller girl, and a small boy. An aunt belonging to the children occupied one corner seat, and the further corner seat on the opposite side was occupied by a bachelor who was a stranger to their party, but the small girls and the small boy emphatically occupied the compartment. Both the aunt and the children were conversational in a limited, persistent way, reminding one of the attentions of a housefly that refused to be discouraged. Most of the aunt's remarks seemed to begin with "Don't," and nearly all of the children's remarks began with "Why?" The bachelor said nothing out loud.

"Don't, Cyril, don't," exclaimed the aunt, as the small boy began smacking the cushions of the seat, producing a cloud of dust at each blow.

"Come and look out of the window," she added.

The child moved reluctantly to the window. "Why are those sheep being driven out of that field?" he asked.

"I expect they are being driven to another field where there is more grass," said the aunt weakly.

"But there is lots of grass in that field," protested the boy; "there's nothing else but grass there. Aunt, there's lots of grass in that field."

"Perhaps the grass in the other field is better," suggested the aunt foolishly.

"Why is it better?" came the swift, inevitable question.

"Oh, look at those wonderful cows!" exclaimed the aunt. Nearly every field along the line had contained cows or bulls, but she spoke as though she were drawing attention to a rarity.

"Why is the grass in the other field better?" persisted Cyril.

The frown on the bachelor's face was deepening to a scowl. He was a hard, unsympathetic man, the aunt decided in her mind. She was utterly unable to come to any satisfactory decision about the grass in the other field.

The smaller girl created a diversion by beginning to recite "On the Road to Mandalay." She only knew the first line, but she put her limited knowledge to the fullest possible use. She repeated the line over and over again in a dreamy but resolute and very audible voice. It seemed to the bachelor as though someone had had a bet with her that she could not repeat the line aloud two thousand times without stopping. Whoever it was who had made the wager was likely to lose his bet.

"Come over here and listen to a story," said the aunt, when the bachelor had looked twice at her and once at the communication cord.

The children moved listlessly towards the aunt's end of the carriage. Evidently her reputation as a storyteller did not rank high in their estimation.

In a low, confidential voice, interrupted at frequent intervals by loud, impatient questions from her listeners, she began a deplorably uninteresting story about a little girl who was good. She made friends with every one on account of her goodness, and was finally saved from a mad bull by a number of rescuers who admired her moral character.

"Wouldn't they have saved her if she hadn't been good?" demanded the bigger of the small girls. It was exactly the question that the bachelor had wanted to ask.

"Well, yes," admitted the aunt lamely, "but I don't think they would have run quite so fast to help her if they had not liked her so much."

"It's the stupidest story I've ever heard," said the bigger of the small girls, with immense conviction.

"I didn't listen after the first bit, it was so stupid," said Cyril.

The smaller girl made no actual comment on the story, but she had long ago recommenced a murmured repetition of her favorite line.

"You don't seem to be a success as a storyteller," said the bachelor suddenly from his corner.

The aunt bristled in instant defense at this unexpected attack.

"It's a very difficult thing to tell stories that children can both understand and appreciate," she said stiffly.

"I don't agree with you," said the bachelor calmly.

"Perhaps you would like to tell them a story," was the aunt's retort.

"Tell us a story," demanded the bigger of the small girls.

"Once upon a time," began the bachelor, "there was a little girl called Bertha, who was extraordinarily good."

The children's momentarily-aroused interest began at once to flicker. All stories seemed dreadfully alike, no matter who told them.

"She did all that she was told. She was always truthful. She kept her clothes clean, ate milk puddings as though they were jam tarts, learned her lessons perfectly, and was polite in her manners."

"Was she pretty?" asked the bigger of the small girls.

"Not as pretty as any of you," said the bachelor, "but she was horribly good."

There was a wave of reaction in favor of the story. The word horrible in connection with goodness was a novelty that commended itself. It seemed to introduce a ring of truth that was absent from the aunt's tales of infant life.

"She was so good," continued the bachelor, "that she won several medals for goodness, which she always wore, pinned on to her dress. There was a medal for obedience, another medal for punctuality, and a third for good behavior. They were large medals and they clinked against one another as she walked. No other child in the town where she lived had as many as three medals, so everybody knew that she must be an extra good child."

"Horribly good," quoted Cyril.

"Everybody talked about her goodness. The Prince of the country got to hear about it, and he said that as she was so very good she might be allowed once a week to walk in his park, which was just outside the town. It was a beautiful park, and no children were ever allowed in it, so it was a great honor for Bertha to be allowed to go there."

"Were there any sheep in the park?" demanded Cyril.

"No," said the bachelor, "there were no sheep."

"Why weren't there any sheep?" came the inevitable question arising out of that answer.

The aunt permitted herself a smile, which might almost have been described as a grin.

"There were no sheep in the park," said the bachelor. "because the Prince's mother had once had a dream that her son would be killed either by a sheep or else by a clock falling on him. For that reason the Prince never kept a sheep in his park or a clock in his palace."

The aunt suppressed a gasp of admiration.

"Was the Prince killed by a sheep or by a clock?" asked Cyril.

"He is still alive, so we can't tell whether the dream will come true," said the bachelor; "anyway, there were no sheep in the park, but there were lots of little pigs running all over the place."

"What color were they?"

"Black with white faces, white with black spots, black all over, grey with white patches, and some were white all over."

The storyteller paused to let a full idea of the parks' treasures sink into the children's imaginations. Then he resumed:

"Bertha was rather sorry to find that there were no flowers in the park. She had promised her aunts, with tears in her eyes, that she would not pick any of the kind Prince's flowers. And she had meant to keep her promise, so of course it made her feel silly to find that there were no flowers to pick."

"Why weren't there any flowers?"

"Because the pigs had eaten them all." said the bachelor promptly. "The gardeners had told the Prince that you couldn't have

Pig and the Train, 1978, JAMIE WYETH. Copyright © 1978 Jamie Wyeth.

pigs and flowers, so he decided to have pigs and no flowers."

There was a murmur of approval at the excellence of the Prince's decision, so many people would have decided the other way.

"There were lots of other delightful things in the park. There were ponds with gold and blue and green fish in them, and trees with beautiful parrots that said clever things at a moment's notice, and humming birds that hummed all the popular tunes of the day. Bertha walked up and down and enjoyed herself immensely, and thought to herself: 'If I were not so extraordinarily good I should not have been allowed to come into this beautiful park and enjoy all that there is to be seen in it.' Her three medals clinked against one another as she walked and helped to remind her how very good she really was. Just then an enormous wolf came prowling into the park to see if it could catch a fat little pig for its supper."

"What color was it?" asked the children, amid an immediate quickening of interest.

"Mud-color all over, with a black tongue and pale grey eyes that gleamed with unspeakable ferocity. The first thing that it saw in the park was Bertha. Her pinafore was so spotlessly white and clean that it could be seen from a great distance. Bertha saw the wolf and saw that it was sneaking towards her. She began to wish that she had never been allowed to come into the park. She ran as hard as she could, and the wolf came after her with huge leaps and bounds. She managed to reach a shrubbery of myrtle bushes and she hid herself in one of the thickest of the bushes. The wolf came sniffing among the branches, its black tongue lolling out of its mouth and its pale grey eyes glaring with rage.

"Bertha was terribly frightened, and thought to herself: 'If I had not been so extraordinarily good I should have been safe in the town at this moment.' However, the scent of the myrtle was so strong that the wolf could not sniff out where Bertha was hiding, and the bushes were so thick that he might have hunted about in them for a long time without catching sight of her, so he thought he might as well go off and catch a little pig instead. Bertha was trembling very much at having the wolf prowling and sniffing so near her. As she trembled the medal for obedience clinked against the medals for good conduct and punctuality. The wolf was just moving away when he heard the sound of the medals clinking and stopped to listen. They clinked again in a bush quite near him. He dashed into the bush, his pale grey eyes gleaming with ferocity and triumph, and he dragged Bertha out and devoured her to the last morsel. All that was left of her were her shoes, bits of clothing, and the three medals for goodness."

"Were any of the little pigs killed?"

"No, they all escaped."

"The story began badly," said the smaller of the small girls, "but it had a beautiful ending."

"It is the most beautiful story that I ever heard," said the bigger of the small girls, with immense decision.

"It is the only beautiful story I have ever heard." said Cyril.

A different opinion came from the aunt.

"A most improper story to tell to young children! You have undermined the effect of years of careful teaching."

"At any rate," said the bachelor, collecting his belongings preparatory to leaving the carriage, "I kept them quiet for ten minutes, which was more than you were able to do."

"Unhappy woman!" he observed to himself as he walked down the platform of Templecombe station: "for the next six months or so those children will assail her in public with demands for an improper story!"

Developing Comprehension Skills

1. What annoyed the children about their aunt?

2. Why did the children find the bachelor's story more interesting than their aunt's story?

3. What was the bachelor's purpose in telling the story? Did he tell it to entertain? Was he trying to prove something to the aunt? Explain your answer.

4. If the aunt had told the bachelor's story, how would she have ended it?

5. The aunt says the bachelor's story is "most inappropriate." Do you agree? What is your definition of "appropriate"?

Reading Literature: Short Stories

1. **Identifying Contrasts in Characters.** What a character says often reveals what the character is like. In this selection, the story told by each adult says something about the character of each. What do you learn about the bachelor and the aunt from their stories? In what ways are the characters different?

2. **Explaining Conflict.** The main conflict, or struggle, in this story is external. It is between the bachelor and the children. He is trying to capture their interest. In what ways do the children try to block the bachelor's efforts? How does he meet these challenges? Find specific passages that highlight this conflict. How does this conflict make the story interesting?

3. **Appreciating Language.** In a well-told story, words do more than simply relate the events. The writer chooses words carefully for the effect they will have on the reader. For example, at one point in the bachelor's story, the little girl is described as "horribly good." This unexpected combination of words catches the children's interest in a way the aunt's stories could not.

Why do you think the writer chose the underlined word or phrase in each of the following sentences? Explain its effect on the meaning of the sentence.

a. An aunt belonging to the children occupied one corner seat.

b. The small girls and the small boy emphatically occupied the compartment.

c. She began a deplorably uninteresting story about a little girl who was good.

d. "It is the most beautiful story that I ever heard," said the bigger of the small girls, with immense decision.

4. **Recognizing Parody.** Sometimes a writer makes fun of another kind of literature by imitating it in an exaggerated or humorous way. This is called **parody**. A parody often points out the humor in something that is usually taken seriously. The bachelor's story is a parody of a fairy tale. Explain how it parodies, or makes fun of, these common elements of fairy tales:

a. an innocent heroine

b. a curse on a prince or other member of royalty

c. goodness being rewarded

d. an ending in which everyone lives happily ever after

Developing Vocabulary Skills

Recognizing Context Clues. Each of the underlined words in the following sentences was drawn from "The Storyteller." You can determine the meaning of each by using the following context clues:

a. a **definition or restatement clue**, which either directly states the meaning of a word or restates the meaning in a slightly different way

b. **synonyms**, or words that have nearly the same meaning as unfamiliar words

c. **antonyms**, which provide the opposite meaning of the unfamiliar word

d. **inference clues**, which enable you to figure out the meaning of an unfamiliar word by determining the main idea of a sentence or paragraph

For each of the following sentences, determine the context clue to be used in finding the meaning of the underlined word. Write the clue you use to unlock the meaning of the word. Then, write the meaning of the word.

1. The children persisted in asking questions. They would not be discouraged by silence or angry looks.

2. The little girl stated emphatically that she did not care about the story. On that one point she was quite firm.

3. Whoever it was who had made the wager was likely to lose the bet.

4. The children sat listlessly in their seats. They were clearly bored and seemed to have no hope that the situation would improve in the near future.

5. The storyteller recommenced his tale after the long interruption.

6. The bachelor's story was a novelty, not at all the same as all the other stories that had been inflicted on them.

Developing Writing Skills

1. **Creating the Mood.** In "The Storyteller," the writer describes the uncomfortable situation in a railway car. He uses strong adjectives and specific details to create a tense, uncomfortable atmosphere. For example, the railway carriage is described as being sultry as the hot afternoon. When the small boy begins smacking the seat cushions, clouds of dust fill the car. The annoying activities of the children and their aunt heighten the feeling of discomfort.

   In one paragraph, write a description of a place familiar to you. Decide on the impression you want to create. Will it be pleasant, frightening, depressing, or thrilling? Choose words and details that will help to create this mood.

2. **Writing a Children's Story.** The bachelor in "The Story teller" entertains the two children with an imaginary tale. This tale is a parody of a typical children's story. In these stories, humans, or animals with human traits, are often placed in threatening situations. After much difficulty, these characters usually manage to overcome their problems. They generally do so with great courage and wisdom and are often aided by magic or other special powers.

   Write your own children's story. If you liked the bachelor's story, you may choose to write a parody instead.

   Pre-Writing. Plan your story or parody carefully. First, list a number of incidents that could be the subject of the story or parody. Here are some possibilities:

   a. a child of poor parents saves the life of the king's only child

b. a brother and sister are separated from their parents at an early age
c. a youngster discovers that he or she has an invisible friend

List the characters that will be involved in your story. Decide from which point of view your story will be told. Next, list the events that will occur in chronological, or time, order.

Writing. Refer to your pre-writing notes as you write your story. However, don't limit yourself to the items on your list. Add new ideas as they occur. Include enough specific details in telling your story to make the characters and situations vivid for your reader.

Revising. Revise your story with the following questions in mind:

Is my story lively and interesting?
Did I include enough specific details to tell the story well?

Did I use clear chronological, or time, order in presenting the incidents?
Did I use the same point of view throughout the story?

Developing Skills in Critical Thinking

Understanding Classification. When you **classify**, you place people, things, or ideas into groups. Each member of the group has at least one similar quality, or one thing in common. For example, each story in this chapter is classified as a short story.

The stories can be classified in smaller groups, also. For example, you could separate those with first-person point of view from those with third-person point of view. Think of two other ways of classifying the six stories you have read. On your paper, list your categories and the stories in each group.

*lot*

Plot is the series of related events in a story. A good plot holds your attention. It makes you wonder, "What will happen next? How will this story work itself out?" The following short stories will keep you in suspense up to the final paragraph.

Death on the Ridge Road, 1934, GRANT WOOD. Williams College Museum of Art, Gift of Cole Porter, Williamstown, Massachusetts.

Reading Literature: More About Short Stories

Other Elements of the Short Story

You understand the importance of characters, setting, and plot to a short story. However, there are other elements that are equally important. These elements of a short story are point of view, mood, and theme.

Point of View

Point of view refers to the person who is telling the story. A story may be written from the first-person or the third-person point of view.

In a story told from the **first-person point of view**, the narrator, or person who tells the story, is a character in the story. This narrator uses the pronouns *I* and *we* in relating events. The character is also part of the action. The reader can see and understand only what the character sees and understands. An example of a story written in the first-person point of view is "Feathered Friend."

Other writers decide that their stories should be told from the **third-person point of view**. The narrator is then someone outside the story. Third-person point of view can be either omniscient or limited.

In a story written from the third-person omniscient point of view, the narrator knows everything that happens. The narrator knows what everyone is thinking and feeling as well. "Zlateh the Goat" is written from the third-person omniscient point of view. The reader knows the thoughts of the boy in the story, and even those of the goat.

The narrator of a story written from the third-person limited point of view tells only what one character can see. The reader must recognize that the story is being colored by that character's feelings and beliefs. "The Fan Club" is an example of a story written from the third-person limited point of view. The reader learns about the characters in the story through the eyes of one girl who feels that she is an outcast.

Mood

The **mood** of the story is the feeling you get as you read. Some stories make you feel anxious or uneasy. Others make you feel relaxed or happy.

The writer carefully controls your feelings in a number of ways. The choice of setting may influence your feelings. For example, a story set in a lonely mountain cabin may make you feel lonely too. Another way the writer can control your emotions is by his or her choice of words. A mountain cabin that seemed lonely in the writer's story could seem safe and snug in a different story.

Look again at "Feathered Friend," one of the stories you read in the first part of this chapter. The situation faced by the characters aboard the space station was dangerous. But the mood of the story was rather calm. The writer controlled your feelings through his choice of words. He carefully avoided such words as *panic*, or *fear*, and instead used such words as *delighted* and *laughingly*.

Theme

Short story writers often see their stories as a way to share some of their ideas and concerns about life with the reader. The idea that is expressed is called the **theme** of the story.

The theme of the story is usually not stated directly. A thoughtful reader can figure out the theme of the story by thinking about what happened in it. For example, in this chapter, the theme of "Feathered Friend" may be that people cannot always depend on machines. The theme of "The Fan Club" may be how easy it is for people to be cruel to others, especially when they feel frightened. You may see other themes in these stories. That is not surprising. A good story may have several themes.

To discover the theme of a story, think about your feelings as you read it and after you read it. Who were your favorite characters? What did you admire about them? Did the events in the story remind you of things that happen in your life? As you think about the answers to these questions, you may understand what the writer was saying about not only the characters, but about each one of us, as well.

The Test

THEODORE L. THOMAS

A responsible young man faces a crisis on the highway. As you read, try to predict the outcome of the young man's terrifying drive.

Robert Proctor was a good driver for so young a man. The turnpike curved gently ahead of him, lightly travelled on this cool morning in May. He felt relaxed and alert. Two hours of driving had not yet produced the twinges of fatigue that appeared first in the muscles in the base of the neck. The sun was bright, but not glaring, and the air smelled fresh and clean. He breathed it in deeply, and blew it out noisily. It was a good day for driving.

He glanced quickly at the slim, grey-haired woman sitting in the front seat with him. Her mouth was curved in a quiet smile. She watched the trees and the fields slip by on her side of the pike. Robert Proctor immediately looked back at the road. He said, "Enjoying it, Mom?"

"Yes, Robert." Her voice was as cool as the morning. "It is very pleasant to sit here. I was thinking of the driving I did for you when you were little. I wonder if you enjoyed it as much as I enjoy this."

He smiled, embarrassed. "Sure I did."

She reached over, patted him on the arm, and then turned back to the scenery.

He listened to the smooth purr of the engine. Up ahead he saw a great truck, spouting a geyser of smoke as it sped along the turnpike. Behind it, not passing it, was a long blue convertible, content to drive in the wake of the truck. Robert Proctor noted the arrangement and filed it in the back of his mind. He was slowly overtaking them, but he would not reach them for another minute or two.

He listened to the purr of the engine, and he was pleased with the sound. He had tuned that engine himself over the objections of the mechanic. The engine idled rough now, but it ran smoothly at high speed. You needed a special feel to do good work on engines, and Robert Proctor knew he had it. No one in the world had a feel like his for the tune of an engine.

It was a good morning for driving, and his mind was filled with good thoughts. He pulled nearly abreast of the blue convertible and began to pass it. His speed was a few miles per hour above the turnpike limit, but his car was under perfect control. The blue convertible suddenly swung out from behind the truck. It swung out, without warning and struck his car near the right front fender, knocking his car to the shoulder on the left side of the turnpike lane.

Robert Proctor was a good driver, too wise to slam on the brakes. He fought the steering wheel to hold the car on a straight path. The left wheels sank into the soft left shoulder, and the car tugged to pull to the left and cross the island and enter the lanes carrying the cars heading in the opposite direction. He held it, then the wheel struck a rock buried in the soft dirt, and the left front tire blew out. The car slewed, and it was then that his mother began to scream.

The car turned sideways and skidded part of the way out into the other lanes. Robert Proctor fought against the steering wheel to straighten out the car, but the drag of the blown tire was too much. The scream rang steadily in his ears, and even as he strained at the wheel one part of his mind wondered coolly how a scream could so long be sustained without a breath. An oncoming car struck his radiator from the side and spun him viciously, full into the left-hand lanes.

He was flung into his mother's lap, and she was thrown against the right door. It held. With his left hand he reached for the steering wheel and pulled himself erect against the force of the spin. He turned the wheel to the left, and tried to stop the spin and careen out of the lanes of oncoming traffic. His mother was unable to right herself. She lay against the door, her cry rising and falling with the spin of the car.

The car lost some of its momentum. During one of the spins he twisted the wheel straight, and the car wobblingly stopped spinning and headed down the lane. Before Robert Proctor could turn it off the pike to safety a car loomed ahead of him, bearing down on him. There was a man at the wheel of that other car, sitting rigid, unable to move, eyes wide and staring and filled with fright. Alongside the man was a girl, her head against the back of the seat, soft curls framing a lovely face, her eyes closed in easy sleep. It was not the fear in the man that reached into Robert Proctor. It was the trusting helplessness in the face of the sleeping girl. The two cars sped closer to each other, and Robert Proctor could not change the direction of his car. The driver of the other car remained frozen at the wheel. At the last moment Robert Proctor sat motionless staring into the face of the onrushing, sleeping girl, his mother's cry still sounding in his ears. He heard no crash when the two cars collided head-on at a high rate of speed. He felt something push into his stomach, and the world began to go grey. Just before he lost consciousness he heard the scream stop, and he knew then that he had been hearing a single, short-lived scream that had only seemed to drag on and on. There came a painless wrench, and then darkness.

Robert Proctor seemed to be at the bottom of a deep black well. There was a spot of faint light in the far distance, and he could hear the rumble of a distant voice. He tried to pull himself toward the light and

Demolished Vehicle, 1970, JOHN SALT. Housatonic Museum of Art, Bridgeport, Connecticut.

the sound, but the effort was too great. He lay still and gathered himself and tried again. The light grew brighter and the voice louder. He tried harder, again, and he drew closer. Then he opened his eyes full and looked at the man sitting in front of him.

"You all right, Son?" asked the man. He wore a blue uniform, and his round, beefy face was familiar.

Robert Proctor tentatively moved his head, and discovered he was sitting in a reclining chair, unharmed, and able to move his arms and legs with no trouble. He looked around the room, and he remembered.

The man in the uniform saw the growing intelligence in his eyes and he said, "No harm done, Son. You just took the last part of your driver's test."

Robert Proctor focused his eyes on the man. Though he saw the man clearly, he seemed to see the faint face of the sleeping girl in front of him.

The uniformed man continued to speak. "We put you through an accident under hypnosis—do it to everybody these days before they can get their driver's licenses. Makes better drivers of them, more careful drivers the rest of their lives. Remember it now? Coming in here and all?"

Robert Proctor nodded, thinking of the sleeping girl. She never would have awakened. She would have passed right from a sweet, temporary sleep into the dark heavy sleep of death, nothing in between. His mother would have been bad enough; after all, she was pretty old. The sleeping girl was downright waste.

The uniformed man was still speaking. "So you're all set now. You pay me the ten dollar fee, and sign this application, and we'll have your license in the mail in a day or two." He did not look up.

Robert Proctor placed a ten dollar bill on the table in front of him, glanced over the application and signed it. He looked up to find two white-uniformed men, standing one on each side of him, and he frowned. He started to speak, but the uniformed man spoke first. "Sorry, Son. You failed. You're sick. You need treatment."

The two men lifted Robert Proctor to his feet, and he said, "Take your hands off me. What is this?"

The uniformed man said, "Nobody should want to drive a car after going through what you just went through. It should take months before you can even think of driving again, but you're ready right now. Killing people doesn't bother you. We don't let your kind run around loose in society any more. But don't you worry now, Son. They'll take good care of you, and they'll fix you up." He nodded to the two men, and they began to march Robert Proctor out.

At the door he spoke, and his voice was so urgent the two men paused. Robert Proctor said, "You can't really mean this. I'm still dreaming, aren't I? This is still part of the test, isn't it?"

The uniformed man said, "How do any of us know?" And they dragged Robert Proctor out the door, knees stiff, feet dragging, his rubber heels sliding along the two grooves worn into the floor.

Silverheels, 1963, JOHN CHAMBERLAIN. Courtesy of Leo Castelli Gallery, New York.

Developing Comprehension Skills

1. Why did Robert feel confident as he drove with his mother?

2. What was the uniformed man's reaction when Robert signed the application for the license? Why did he have this reaction?

3. What did the authorities consider the most important quality of a good driver? Do you think the authorities were right to make this the most important factor in the test? Explain your answer.

4. At the end of the story, what do the "two grooves worn into the floor" tell you about others taking the driving test?

5. In your opinion, was the driving test fair? Why or why not? Find details in the story to support your opinion.

Reading Literature: Short Stories

1. **Determining the Setting.** At the beginning of "The Test," the reader is led to believe that the setting of the story is the inside of a car. At a certain point in the story, however, it becomes clear that the car is not the real setting. When do you discover the real setting? Is there evidence to suggest that this story takes place some time other than today or somewhere other than our country? Explain your answer.

2. **Identifying Conflict.** Robert Proctor faces a number of conflicts in this story. One conflict involves the events that occurred while Robert was under hypnosis. Another conflict involves Robert and the uniformed man. Describe these conflicts in detail. How is each resolved? Can you identify any other conflicts in the story?

3. **Plotting a Short Story.** The plot is the series of events that take place in the story. The plot of a story usually includes these parts:

> **Introduction:** The main character and setting are introduced.
> **Rising Action:** The main character struggles with a conflict.
> **Climax:** This is the most exciting part of the story. The main character makes a discovery or decision, or takes some action that affects the outcome of the story.
> **Falling Action:** The story draws to a close.
> **Resolution:** In most stories, any remaining questions are answered.

The parts of a plot can be shown in a plot diagram. The diagram on the following page,

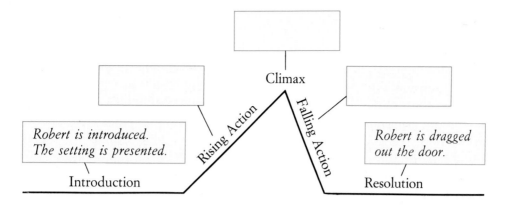

Climax

Rising Action

Falling Action

Robert is introduced.
The setting is presented.

Robert is dragged
out the door.

Introduction

Resolution

for "The Test," is partly filled in. Tell what events belong in the rising action, climax, and falling action.

Compare your answers with those of your classmates. Did each of you view the story in the same way? Remember there is often room for discussion and disagreement about literature.

Developing Vocabulary Skills

Using Comparison and Contrast Clues. Two other types of context clues can help you determine the meaning of a new word. These are comparison and contrast clues. When a **comparison** word is used, a writer relates an unfamiliar word to a similar, but familiar, idea. Consider this example.

The *ramshackle* old house looked like little more than a neglected shack.

From this clue you can infer that *ramshackle* means "likely to fall to pieces." The key word is *like*. Other key words and phrases indicating comparison clues are *as, in the same way, just as,* and *similar to.*

When a **contrast** clue is used, a writer compares an unfamiliar word with an idea that is different or opposite. Look at this passage.

Shirley easily became *exasperated.* Her sister, on the other hand, was always quite patient.

From this example, you can guess that *exasperated* means "irritated or annoyed." The key phrase is *on the other hand.* Other key words and phrases are *although, but, however, unlike, on the contrary, different from,* and *in contrast.*

The underlined words in each of the following sentences were drawn from the stories in this chapter. Write whether the sentence contains a comparison clue or a contrast clue. Also write the key word that signals the clue. Finally, write the meaning of the underlined word.

1. To Jeanie's surprise, the teacher did not disparage her writing. On the contrary, she praised it.

2. Jerry felt an ecstasy when running with the dog that was similar to the joy he felt when we walked through the fields.

3. The railway car was as sultry as a hot, humid summer day.

4. The car slewed on the icy road; however, the driver managed to straighten it out again.

5. In contrast to Robert's tentative actions, the man in the uniform knew exactly what he should do.

Developing Writing Skills

1. **Developing an Argument.** In your opinion, did Robert deserve to pass the test, or was the examiner correct in denying Robert his license? Write a paragraph in which you state and support your opinion.

   Pre-Writing. If you feel that Robert should have received his license, list evidence of Robert's driving skill in your pre-writing notes. If you agree with the examiner, list evidence of Robert's shortcomings.

   Writing. Begin the paragraph with a topic sentence that immediately gives your opinion. For example, your first sentence might say, "Robert Proctor deserved to pass his driver's test." Following the topic sentence, attempt to persuade your reader that your opinion is correct. To do this successfully, you must support your opinion with evidence from the story. You may wish to list evidence in the order of its importance. Start with the least important reason, and end with the most important. Use transitional phrases such as *first of all* and *most important* to move from one idea to the next.

   Revising. Check your paragraph by answering the following questions:

   Does my topic sentence present a clear opinion?
   Have I supported my opinion with evidence from the story?
   Is my paragraph convincing?
   Can I think of other convincing evidence?

   When you are finished with the content of your paragraph, proofread it carefully for mistakes in grammar, usage, and mechanics. Then make a final copy.

2. **Writing a Definition.** What is your definition of a "good driver"? Write one paragraph explaining the skills and personality traits needed to be a good driver. Skills are physical abilities, such as quick reflexes. Personality traits are qualities such as patience and good judgment. Provide reasons why you chose each skill and personality trait.

Developing Skills in Critical Thinking

Recognizing Generalizations. After reading "The Test," some readers might make statements similar to these:

The men who gave the test had no compassion for those who failed the test.

The government that made people take the test was unjust and cruel.

These are examples of generalizations. A **generalization** is a broad statement based on several specific facts. If there are not enough supporting facts, the statement is unfair.

Read the following specific facts based on "The Test":

Robert takes a test under hypnosis.
During the test, Robert "experiences" an accident.
Robert still wants his license after the test.
Robert is denied his license.
People who fail the test are taken away for treatment.

Are these facts enough to support the broad statements about the examiners and the government given above? If not, choose one of the generalizations. List other additional questions you would need to have answered before such a statement could be considered a fair generalization. Does the story give any of the answers?

The Beau Catcher

FREDERICK LAING

At some time, almost everyone feels lonely and shy. Read to discover what one girl learns about the "secret" of popularity.

What had really brought her into Waller's department store was something definitely not romantic. She had promised her mother to get herself a pair of boots. As she wandered through she was looking wistfully at the things she couldn't afford or wouldn't be allowed to wear. That two-piece bathing suit, for instance. Renee Weston had one like it. . . .

Renee Weston, yes . . . whom Bert Howland was taking to the benefit dance this Saturday, this very night. And as for herself, who had asked her to go to the dance at the country club? Why, nobody. For who was going to ask bashful Genevieve Smith?

She was walking along the aisles with her head down and her heart, to judge from the way she felt, dragging on the floor behind her. It was the sign in front of these hair ribbons that stopped her cold.

BEAU CATCHERS, it said.

And around the sign was a selection of those bow ribbons for your hair. Every color of the rainbow, it said—pick a color to suit your personality.

She stood there a moment with her head down. No, her mother wouldn't let her wear a bow that big and showy, even if she had the nerve, which she hadn't. These beau catchers, they were the kind . . .

The kind Renee Weston would wear, she had started to think, when the saleslady broke into her train of thought: "This would be a nice one for you, dear."

"Oh, no, I'm afraid I couldn't wear anything like that," she answered. But at the same time she was reaching wistfully for the green ribbon.

The saleslady looked surprised. "With that lovely copper-colored hair and those pretty eyes? Why, child, you could wear anything."

Maybe it was only a sales talk, but the ribbon was attached to a comb, and because she didn't need much urging, she fastened it into her hair.

"No, a little farther front," the saleslady said. "One thing you have to remember, honey, if you're going to wear anything a little out of the ordinary, wear it like nobody had a better right than you. In this world, you gotta hold your head up." She looked at the position of the ribbon critically. "That's better. Why, you look positively . . . exciting."

She looked in the mirror and, sure enough, the green color of the ribbon and the hint of red in her hair with the green of her eyes . . .

"I'll take it," she said, a little surprised at the note of decision in her voice.

"Now if you wanted to get another for formal wear," the saleslady said, "one like this, for instance, if you were going to a party or a dance . . . ."

It was the last thing she wanted to talk about. She paid for the ribbon and started to get out of there so fast that she bumped smack into a big woman with a lot of packages, and almost got knocked silly.

As she neared the door, a funny old man was staring at her. A man with black eyes and a droopy gray mustache under a green hat. You could tell from his eyes that he was smiling under the gray mustache. Smiling and looking at the beau catcher.

It was a conquest, even if it wasn't much. She gave him a glance. Just the merest passing look, but . . .

The next moment a shiver of fright went through her, for the silly old thing was actually following her. That beau catcher couldn't . . . but this was really dreadful. She started to look around and then she heard him say, "Hey, keedo!" She ran like a rabbit and didn't stop running until she was a block down the street.

Then suddenly she found herself in front of Carson's drugstore and she knew for sure it was where she'd been intending to go from the start. Because practically any girl in town knew this was the drugstore where Bert Howland hung around Saturday afternoons, talking with his friends or playing the pinball machine.

She hesitated just a moment before she entered the drugstore. Then she took a deep breath.

He was there all right. He was sitting at the soda counter, and the minute she saw him—the way he was hunched over a cup of coffee, not drinking it, just looking ahead—she thought, Renee turned him down. She's going to the dance with somebody else.

She sat down at the other corner of the counter facing his profile, and Harry, the soda jerk, came over to take her order.

"Bring me a black and white soda," she said to him.

And as he went to get her the soda, she saw, out of the side of her eyelashes, that Bert Howland had turned and was staring at her.

She sat up straight, holding her head high, conscious, very conscious of that green beau catcher.

After a while he said, "Hi, Genevieve."

She turned, and did a neat little job there of looking surprised. "Why, Bert Howland," she said, "how long have you been sitting here?"

"All my life," he said. "Just waiting here for you."

Snack Bar, about 1954, ISABEL BISHOP. Oil on masonite, 13½" × 11⅛". Columbus Museum of Art, Museum Purchase: Howald Fund 54.47. Columbus, Ohio.

It was only a line, but ordinarily it would have left her stuttering. She wanted to reach up and make a few touches at her hair, just to feel the beau catcher to give her confidence, but she restrained herself.

"Flatterer," she said.

A moment later, he was sitting on the stool beside her, looking at her in that same way, as though he'd just noticed that she was alive.

"Wearing your hair a different way or something, aren't you?" he asked.

She reached for her soda and took a gulp. "Do you usually notice things like that?" she asked.

"No," he said. "I guess it's just the way you're holding your head up. Like you thought I ought to notice something."

She felt a slight flush at her cheeks and the tips of her ears. "Is that a crack?"

"Maybe," he said, grinning, "and maybe not. Maybe I sort of like to see you hold your head like that."

It was about ten minutes afterward that the unbelievable happened. He said, "You know, they're having a dance at the country club tonight."

And when he actually came across with it, the invitation and everything, it was all she could do to keep from throwing her arms around him.

They left the drugstore a little later, and he offered to walk home with her. Suddenly she remembered that formal beau catcher, the one you wore to a party or a dance. She couldn't wear the one she had on. She would have to have one to match her evening dress. And so, though only this morning she would have practically wept for joy at the chance to have Bert Howland walk home with her, she told him now that she simply had to get to Waller's before it closed.

She got there just as the doors were being shut. A man tried to keep her out, but she brushed past him and dashed to the ribbon counter.

She looked for the blue-and-gold one. Gone! If they didn't have another . . . .

The saleslady smiled when she saw who it was. "I knew you'd be back."

"H . . . how?" she asked, out of breath.

The saleslady reached under the counter. "I've been saving it for you." But the beau catcher she brought out was not the blue-and-gold one. It wasn't even formal at all. In fact, it was . . . .

"That's like the one I just bought," she said, puzzled.

And then she was standing with her mouth opened in amazement. Why, when the big woman had bumped into her it must have been knocked off. . . .

"It is the same one," the saleslady explained.

And with that knowledge a lot of things began to flash through Genevieve's mind. But suddenly she began to smile and then somehow she couldn't stop smiling. She let her head lift easily while half of her listened to the saleslady's story—a story about a man who had found his way to the ribbon counter with her beau catcher, a jolly old man in a green hat.

Developing Comprehension Skills

1. Why did Genevieve buy a beau catcher?

2. How did the advice the saleslady gave her affect Genevieve's actions?

3. The bow seemed to change Genevieve's mood and her entire personality. How could a simple a piece of ribbon have this kind of effect? Explain your answer.

4. For what two reasons was the old man in the store important to the story?

5. What connection did this story make between self-confidence and popularity? In your opinion, is self-confidence the most important key to popularity? Explain.

Reading Literature: Short Stories

1. **Understanding Conflict.** The conflict in this story is internal. Genevieve must decide between two different outlooks, or attitudes. What are these outlooks? How does she eventually decide to act? How does the beau catcher affect her decision?

2. **Making Inferences About Character.** A reader can often make an inference about a character's personality from details given in the story. These details may concern thoughts, actions, or physical characteristics. For example, Genevieve thought of herself as "bashful Genevieve Smith." What can you infer about her self-confidence from this self-image? Can you find other details that help you make an inference about her?

3. **Recognizing the Falling Action.** In the **falling action** of a plot, the story draws to a close. This happens as a result of the main character's discovery, decision, or action at or directly after the climax.

In "The Beau Catcher," the climax occurs when Bert Howland asks Genevieve to the country club dance. What happens in the falling action of the story?

Developing Vocabulary Skills

Using Example Clues. A writer may give a clue to the meaning of an unfamiliar word by providing an **example**. If the example is a familiar word or term, you can then guess the meaning of the unknown word. For instance:

> *Marsupials* like the kangaroo and the opossum carry their young in a pouch.

Sometimes the unfamiliar word itself is given as an example of something the writer has described. Consider this sentence.

> Diving birds, such as the *loon*, have sharp bills and webbed feet.

Like other context clues, an example may be signaled by key words. These key words and phrases include *for example, one kind, for instance, like, especially, and other*, and *such as*.

Read the following sentences. Each contains a word drawn from stories in this chapter. A comparison, contrast, or example clue will help you determine the meaning of each underlined word. Look for key words and phrases that signal the clue in each sentence. For each sentence, write the type of clue you used and the meaning of the underlined word.

1. The wife of Marcus Lucretius protects her best clothes from moths with repellents such as pine needles and camphor.

2. They fell on his head, his hands—pumice and other volcanic stones from the black heart of Vesuvius!

3. Jerry looked as <u>wistful</u> as a child outside a pet store.

4. Even though the saleslady was <u>critical</u> about the placement of the ribbon, she praised Genevieve for her choice of color.

5. For the dance, she needed <u>formal</u> wear such as a long gown, white gloves, and high heels.

6. The <u>vermilion</u> leaves fluttered like thousands of tiny red flags.

Developing Writing Skills

1. **Stating an Opinion.** An **adage** is a traditional saying that is thought by some to express a basic truth or useful thought. One adage states, "You can't tell a book by its cover." Write a paragraph about this adage. First explain what it means to you. Then say whether you agree or disagree with it.

2. **Planning the Introduction of a Story.** In the introduction of a story, the writer establishes the setting and introduces the main character. The introduction also introduces the problem the main character will face in the story. Develop your own idea for a short story. Then write an introduction that introduces the important elements.

    Pre-Writing. Use several sources to find story ideas. Skim newspapers, magazines, and books. When you have decided on an idea, list the information you will include in the introduction. Decide on a setting, including a description of the time and place of the story. Create a main character. List details in a physical description of that character. Also list personality traits of the main character. Finally, note a problem that will confront the main character.

    Writing. Write an introduction to your story. Try to introduce your elements indirectly. Don't simply tell your reader everything. Show them, through the speech and actions of your characters.

    Revising. Reread the first draft of your introduction. Refer to the following questions to guide your revision:

    Does my introduction describe the time and place of the story?
    Did I use specific words to describe the setting?
    Are the physical characteristics and personality traits of the main character described in my second paragraph?
    Is the problem confronting my main character introduced?

Developing Skills in Speaking and Listening

Telling an Anecdote. An anecdote is a short, interesting story about a personal experience. A speaker may tell an anecdote to explain or support an opinion or statement. Consider these statements or opinions:

1. Self-confidence is as important as talent or good looks.

2. Sometimes the price of popularity can be too high.

3. People are not always what you expect them to be.

Choose one of these statements or one of your own. Make a list of details about an anecdote relating to the statement. Using this list, practice telling the anecdote. When you feel comfortable with your anecdote, tell it to classmates in a small group.

The Most Dangerous Game

RICHARD CONNELL

A famous hunter is trapped on a mysterious island. How does he react when he discovers the identity of the most dangerous game?

"Off there to the right—somewhere—is a large island," said Whitney. "It's rather a mystery—"

"What island is it?" Rainsford asked.

"The old charts call it 'Ship-Trap Island,'" Whitney replied. "A suggestive name, isn't it? Sailors have a curious dread of the place. I don't know why. Some superstition—"

"Can't see it," remarked Rainsford, trying to peer through the dank tropical night that pressed its thick warm blackness in upon the yacht.

"You've good eyes," said Whitney, with a laugh, "and I've seen you pick off a moose moving in the brown fall bush at four hundred yards, but even you can't see four miles or so through a moonless Caribbean night."

"Nor four yards," admitted Rainsford. "Ugh! It's like moist velvet."

"It will be light enough in Rio," promised Whitney. "We should make it in a few days. I hope the jaguar guns have come from Purdey's. We should have some good hunting farther up the Amazon. Great sport, hunting."

"The best sport in the world," agreed Rainsford.

"For the hunter," amended Whitney. "Not for the jaguar."

"Don't talk rot, Whitney," said Rainsford. "You're a big-game hunter, not a philosopher. Who cares how a jaguar feels?"

"Perhaps the jaguar does," observed Whitney.

"Bah! They've no understanding."

"Even so, I rather think they understand one thing at least—fear. The fear of pain and the fear of death."

"Nonsense," and Rainsford laughed. "This hot weather is making you soft, Whitney. Be a realist. The world is made up of two classes—the hunters and the hunted. Luckily, you and I are hunters. Do you think we've passed that island yet?"

"I can't tell in the dark. I hope so."

"Why?" asked Rainsford.

"The place has quite a reputation—a bad one."

"Cannibals?" suggested Rainsford.

"Hardly. Even cannibals wouldn't live in such a God-forsaken place. But it's got into sailor lore, somehow. Didn't you notice that the crew's nerves seem a bit jumpy today?"

"They were a bit strange, now you mention it. Even Captain Nielsen—"

"Yes, even that tough-minded old sailor, who'd go up to the devil himself and ask him for a light. Those fishy blue eyes held a look I never saw there before. All I could get out of him was, 'This place has an evil name among seafaring men, sir.' Then he said to me very gravely, 'Don't you feel anything?'—as if the air about us was actually poisonous. Now, you mustn't laugh when I tell you this. I did feel something like a sudden chill.

"There was no breeze. The sea was as flat as a plate-glass window. We were drawing near the island then. What I felt was a—a mental chill—a sort of sudden dread."

"Pure imagination," said Rainsford. "One superstitious sailor can taint the whole ship's company with his fear."

"Maybe. But sometimes I think sailors have an extra sense that tells them when they are in danger. Sometimes I think evil is a tangible thing—with wave lengths, just as sound and light have. An evil place can, so to speak, broadcast vibrations of evil. Anyhow, I'm glad we're getting out of this zone. Well, I think I'll turn in now, Rainsford."

"I'm not sleepy," said Rainsford. "I'm going on deck to smoke another pipe."

"Good night, then, Rainsford. See you at breakfast."

"Right. Good night, Whitney."

There was no sound in the night as Rainsford sat there but for the muffled throb of the engine that drove the yacht swiftly through the darkness, and the swish and ripple of the wash of the propeller.

Rainsford, reclining in a steamer chair, lazily puffed on his favorite pipe. The sensuous drowsiness of the night was on him. "It's so dark," he thought, "that I could sleep without closing my eyes; the night would be my eyelids—"

An abrupt sound startled him. Off to the right he heard it, and his ears, expert in such matters, could not be mistaken. Again he heard the sound, and again. Somewhere, off in the blackness, someone had fired a gun three times.

Rainsford sprang up and moved quickly to the rail, mystified. He strained his eyes in the direction from which the reports had come, but it was like trying to see through a blanket. He leaped upon the rail and balanced himself there, to get greater elevation. His pipe, striking a rope, was knocked from his mouth. He lunged for it. A short, hoarse cry came from his lips as he realized he had reached too far and had lost his balance. The cry was pinched off short as the blood-warm waters of the Caribbean Sea closed over his head.

He struggled up to the surface and tried to cry out, but the wash from the speeding yacht slapped him in the face and the salt water in his open mouth made him gag and strangle. Desperately he struck out with strong strokes after the receding lights of the yacht. But he stopped before he had swum fifty feet. A certain cool-headedness had come to him. It was not the first time he had been in a tight place. There was a chance that his cries could be heard by someone aboard the yacht, but that chance was slender, and grew more slender as the yacht raced on. He wrestled himself out of his clothes, and shouted with all his power. The lights of the yacht became faint as ever-vanishing fireflies. Then they were blotted out entirely by the night.

Rainsford remembered the shots. They had come from the right, and doggedly he swam in that direction, swimming with slow, deliberate strokes, conserving his strength. For a seemingly endless time he fought the sea. He began to count his strokes desperately. He could do possibly a hundred more and then—

Rainsford heard a sound. It came out of the darkness, a high, screaming sound, the sound of an animal in anguish and terror.

He did not recognize the animal that made the sound. He did not try to. With fresh vitality he swam toward the sound. He heard it again. Then it was cut short by another noise, crisp, staccato.

"Pistol shot," muttered Rainsford, swimming on.

Ten minutes of determined effort brought another sound to his ears—the most welcome he had ever heard—the muttering and growling of the sea breaking on a rocky shore. He was almost on the rocks before he saw them. On a night less calm he would have been shattered against them. With his remaining strength he dragged himself from the swirling waters. Jagged crags appeared to jut up into the darkness. He forced himself upward, hand over hand. Gasping, his hands raw, he reached a flat place at the top. Dense jungle came down to the very edge of the cliffs. What perils that tangle of trees and under-brush might hold for him did not concern Rainsford just then. All he knew was that he was safe from his enemy, the sea, and that utter weariness was on him. He flung him-self down at the jungle edge and slept.

When he opened his eyes he knew from the position of the sun that it was late in the afternoon. Sleep had given him new vigor; a sharp hunger was picking at him. He looked about him, almost cheerfully.

"Where there are pistol shots, there are men. Where there are men, there is food," he thought. But what kind of men, he wondered, in so forbidding a place? An unbroken front of snarled and jagged jungle fringed the shore.

He saw no sign of a trail through the closely knit web of weeds and trees. It was easier to go along the shore, and Rainsford floundered along by the water. Not far from where he had landed, he stopped.

Some wounded thing, by the evidence a large animal, had thrashed about in the underbrush. The jungle weeds were crushed down and the moss was lacerated. One patch of weeds was stained crimson. A small, glittering object not far away caught Rainsford's eye and he picked it up. It was an empty cartridge.

"A twenty-two," he remarked. "That's odd. It must have been a fairly large animal, too. The hunter had his nerve to tackle it with a light gun. It's clear that the brute put up a fight. I suppose the first three shots I heard was when the hunter flushed his quarry and wounded it. The last shot was when he trailed it here and finished it."

He examined the ground closely and found what he had hoped to find—the

The Equatorial Jungle, 1909, HENRI ROUSSEAU. National Gallery of Art, Chester Dale Collection, 1962, Washington, D.C.

print of hunting boots. They pointed along the cliff in the direction he had been going. Eagerly he hurried along, now slipping on a rotten log or a loose stone, but making headway. Night was beginning to settle down on the island.

Bleak darkness was blacking out the sea and jungle when Rainsford sighted the lights. He came upon them as he turned a crook in the coastline. His first thought was that he had come upon a village, for there were many lights. But as he forged along he saw to his great astonishment that all the lights were in one enormous building—a lofty structure with pointed towers plunging upward into the gloom. His eyes made out the shadowy outlines of a palatial chateau. It was set on a high bluff, and on three sides of it cliffs dived down to where the sea licked greedy lips in the shadows.

"Mirage," thought Rainsford. It was no mirage, he found, when he opened the tall spiked iron gate. The stone steps were real enough. The massive door with a leering carved monster for a knocker was definitely real enough. Yet about it all hung an air of unreality.

He lifted the knocker, and it creaked up stiffly, as if it had never before been used. He let it fall, and it startled him with its booming loudness. He thought he heard footsteps within. The door remained closed. Again Rainsford lifted the heavy knocker, and let it fall. The door opened then, opened as suddenly as if it were on a spring. Rainsford stood blinking in the river of glaring gold light that poured out. The

first thing Rainsford's eyes discerned was the largest man Rainsford had ever seen—a gigantic creature, solidly made and black-bearded to the waist. In his hand the man held a long-barrel revolver, and he was pointing it straight at Rainsford's heart.

Out of the snarl of beard two small eyes regarded Rainsford.

"Don't be alarmed," said Rainsford, with a smile which he hoped was disarming. "I'm no robber. I fell off a yacht. My name is Sanger Rainsford of New York City."

The menacing look in the eyes did not change. The revolver pointed as rigidly as if the giant were a statue. He gave no sign that he understood Rainsford's words, or that he had even heard them. He was dressed in uniform, a black uniform trimmed with gray fur.

"I'm Sanger Rainsford of New York," Rainsford began again. "I fell off a yacht. I am hungry."

The man's only answer was to raise with his thumb the hammer of his revolver. Then Rainsford saw the man's free hand go to his forehead in a military salute, and he saw him click his heels together and stand at attention. Another man was coming down the broad marble steps, an erect, slender man in evening clothes. He advanced to Rainsford and held out his hand.

In a cultivated voice marked by a slight accent that gave it added precision and deliberateness, he said, "It is a very great pleasure and honor to welcome Mr. Sanger Rainsford, the celebrated hunter, to my home."

Automatically, Rainsford shook the man's hand.

"I've read your book about hunting snow leopards in Tibet, you see," explained the man. "I am General Zaroff."

Rainsford's first impression was that the man was unusually handsome. His second was that there was an original, almost bizarre quality about the general's face. He was a tall man past middle age, for his hair was a vivid white. But his thick eyebrows and pointed military mustache were as black as the night from which Rainsford had come. His eyes, too, were black and very bright. He had high cheekbones, a sharp-cut nose, a spare, dark face, the face of a man used to giving orders. Turning to the giant, the general made a sign. The giant put away his pistol, saluted, withdrew.

"Ivan is an incredibly strong fellow," remarked the general, "but he has the misfortune to be deaf and dumb. A simple fellow, but I'm afraid, like all his race, a bit of a savage."

"Is he Russian?"

"He is a Cossack,"[1] said the general, and his smile showed red lips and pointed teeth. "So am I.

"Come," he said, "we shouldn't be chatting here. We can talk later. Now you want clothes, food, rest. You shall have them. This is a most restful spot."

Ivan had reappeared, and the general spoke to him with lips that moved but gave forth no sound.

---

1. **Cossack,** a military horseman from South Russia.

"Follow Ivan, if you please, Mr. Rainsford," said the general. "I was about to have my dinner when you came. I'll wait for you. You'll find that my clothes will fit you, I think."

It was to a huge, beam-ceilinged bedroom with a canopied bed that Rainsford followed the silent giant. Ivan laid out an evening suit. Rainsford, as he put it on, noticed that it came from a London tailor who ordinarily cut and sewed for none below the rank of duke.

The dining room to which Ivan conducted him was in many ways remarkable. There was a medieval magnificence about it. About the hall were the mounted heads of many animals—lions, tigers, elephants, moose, bears. Larger or more perfect specimens Rainsford had never seen. At the great table the general was sitting, alone.

"You'll have a cocktail, Mr. Rainsford," he suggested. The cocktail was surpassingly good. And, Rainsford noted, that the table appointments were of the finest, the linen, the crystal, the silver, the china.

They were eating *borsch*, the rich, red beet soup with sour cream so dear to Russian tastes. Half apologetically General Zaroff said, "We do our best to preserve civilization here. Please forgive any lapses. We are well off the beaten track, you know. Do you think the champagne has suffered from its long ocean trip?"

"Not in the least," declared Rainsford. He was finding the general a most thoughtful and friendly host, a true gentleman. However, there was one small trait of the general's that made Rainsford uncomfortable. Whenever he looked up from his plate he found that the general was studying him, carefully.

"Perhaps," said General Zaroff, "you were surprised that I recognized your name. You see, I read all books on hunting published in English, French, and Russian. I have but one passion in my life, Mr. Rainsford, and it is the hunt."

"You have some wonderful heads here," said Rainsford as he ate a particularly well cooked filet mignon. "That Cape buffalo is the largest I ever saw."

"Oh, that fellow. Yes, he was a real monster."

"Did he charge you?"

"Hurled me against a tree," said the general. "Fractured my skull. But I got the brute."

"I've always thought," said Rainsford, "that the Cape buffalo is the most dangerous of all big game."

For a moment the general did not reply. He was smiling his curious red-lipped smile. Then he said slowly, "No. You are wrong, sir. The Cape buffalo is not the most dangerous big game." He sipped his wine. "Here in my preserve on this island," he said in the same slow tone, "I hunt more dangerous game."

Rainsford expressed his surprise. "Is there big game on this island?"

The general nodded. "The biggest."

"Really?"

"Oh, it isn't here naturally, of course. I have to stock the island."

"What have you imported, General?" Rainsford asked. "Tigers?"

The general smiled. "No," he said. "Hunting tigers ceased to interest me some years ago. I exhausted their possibilities, you see. No thrill left in tigers, no real danger. I live for danger, Mr. Rainsford."

The general took from his pocket a gold cigarette case and offered his guest a long black cigarette with a silver tip. It was perfumed and gave off a smell like incense.

"We will have some capital hunting, you and I," said the general. "I shall be most glad to have your society."

"But what game—" began Rainsford.

"I'll tell you," said the general. "You will be amused, I know. I think I may say, in all modesty, that I have done a rare thing. I have invented a new sensation. May I pour you another glass of port, Mr. Rainsford?"

"Thank you, General."

The general filled both glasses and said, "God makes some men poets. Some He makes kings, some beggars. Me He made a hunter. My hand was made for the trigger, my father said. He was a very rich man with a quarter of a million acres in the Crimea, and he was a serious sportsman. When I was only five years old he gave me a little gun, specially made in Moscow for me, to shoot sparrows with. When I shot some of his prize turkeys with it, he did not punish me. He complimented me on my marksmanship. I killed my first bear when I was ten. My whole life has been one prolonged hunt. I went into the army and for a time commanded a division of Cossack cavalry, but my real interest was always the hunt. I have hunted every kind of game in every land. It would be impossible for me to tell you how many animals I have killed."

The general puffed at his cigarette.

"After the revolution in Russia I left the country, for it was imprudent for an officer of the Czar to stay there. Many noble Russians lost everything. I, luckily, had invested heavily in American securities, so I shall never have to open a tearoom in Monte Carlo or drive a taxi in Paris. Naturally, I continued to hunt—grizzlies in your Rockies, crocodiles in the Ganges, rhinoceroses in East Africa. It was in Africa that the Cape buffalo hit me and laid me up for six months. As soon as I recovered I started for the Amazon to hunt jaguars, for I had heard they were unusually cunning. They weren't." The Cossack sighed. "They were no match at all for a hunter with his wits about him and a high-powered rifle. I was bitterly disappointed. I was lying in my tent with a splitting headache one night when a terrible thought pushed its way into my mind. Hunting was beginning to bore me! And hunting, remember, had been my life. I have heard that in America businessmen often go to pieces when they give up the business that has been their life."

"Yes, that's so," said Rainsford.

The general smiled. "I had no wish to go to pieces," he said. "I must do something. Now, mine is an analytical mind, Mr. Rainsford. Doubtless that is why I enjoy the problems of the chase."

"No doubt, General Zaroff."

"So," continued the general, "I asked myself why the hunt no longer fascinated me. You are much younger than I am, Mr. Rainsford, and have not hunted as much, but you perhaps can guess the answer."

"What was it?"

"Simply this: hunting had ceased to be what you call 'a sporting proposition.' It had become too easy. I always got my quarry. Always. There is no greater bore than perfection."

The general lit a fresh cigarette.

"No animal had a chance with me any more. That is no boast; it is a mathematical certainty. The animal had nothing but his legs and his instinct. Instinct is no match for reason. When I thought of this it was a tragic moment for me, I can tell you."

Rainsford leaned across the table, absorbed in what his host was saying.

"It came to me as an inspiration what I must do," the general went on.

"And that was?"

The general smiled the quiet smile of one who has faced an obstacle and surmounted it with success. "I had to invent a new animal to hunt," he said.

"A new animal? You are joking."

"Not at all," said the general. "I never joke about hunting. I needed a new animal. I found one. So I bought this island, built this house, and here I do my hunting. The island is perfect for my purposes—there are jungles with a maze of trails in them, hills, swamps—"

"But the animal, General Zaroff?"

"Oh," said the general, "it supplies me with the most exciting hunting in the world. No other hunting compares with it for an instant. Every day I hunt, and I never grow bored now, for I have a quarry with which I can match my wits."

Rainsford's bewilderment showed in the expression on his face.

"I wanted the ideal animal to hunt," explained the general. "So I said, 'What are the attributes of an ideal quarry?' And the answer was, of course, 'It must have courage, cunning, and, above all, it must be able to reason.'"

"But no animal can reason," objected Rainsford.

"My dear fellow," said the general, "there is one that can."

"But you can't mean—" gasped Rainsford.

"And why not?"

"I can't believe you are serious, General Zaroff. This is a grisly joke."

"Why should I not be serious? I am speaking of hunting."

"Hunting? Good God, Zaroff, what you speak of is murder."

The general laughed with entire good nature. He regarded Rainsford quizzically. "I refuse to believe that so modern and civilized a young man as you seem to be harbors romantic ideas about the value of human life. Surely your experiences in the war—" He stopped.

"Did not make me condone cold-blooded murder," finished Rainsford stiffly.

Laughter shook the general. "How extraordinarily amusing you are!" he said. "One does not expect nowadays to find a young man of the educated class, even in America, with such a naïve point of view. I'll wager you'll forget your notions when you go hunting with me. You've a genuine new thrill in store for you, Mr. Rainsford."

"Thank you, but I'm a hunter, not a murderer."

"Dear me," said the general, quite unruffled, "again that unpleasant word. But I think I can show you that your doubts are quite ill founded."

"Yes?"

"Life is for the strong, to be lived by the strong, and, if needs be, taken by the strong. The weak of the world were put here to give the strong pleasure. I am strong. Why should I not use my gift? If I wish to hunt, why should I not? I hunt the scum of the earth—sailors from tramp ships—a thoroughbred horse or hound is worth more than a score of them."

"But they are men," said Rainsford hotly.

"Precisely," said the general. "That is why I use them. It gives me pleasure. They can reason, after a fashion. So they are dangerous."

"But where do you get them?"

The general's left eyelid fluttered down in a wink. "This island is called Ship-Trap," he answered. "Sometimes an angry god of the high seas sends them to me. Sometimes, when Providence is not so kind, I help Providence a bit. Come to the window."

Rainsford went to the window and looked out toward the sea.

"Watch! Out there!" exclaimed the general, pointing into the night. Rainsford's eyes saw only blackness, and then, as the general pressed a button, far out to sea Rainsford saw the flash of lights.

The general chuckled. "They indicate a channel," he said, "where there is none. Giant rocks with razor edges crouch like a sea monster with wide-open jaws. They can crush a ship as easily as I crush this nut." He dropped a walnut on the hardwood floor and brought his heel grinding down on it. "Oh, yes," he said casually, as if in answer to a question, "I have electricity. We try to be civilized here."

"Civilized? And you shoot down men?"

A trace of anger was in the general's black eyes. But it was there for but a second, and he said, in his most pleasant manner: "Dear me, what a righteous young man you are! I assure you I do not do the thing you suggest. That would be barbarous. I treat these visitors with every consideration. They get plenty of good food and exercise. They get into splendid physical condition. You shall see for yourself tomorrow."

"What do you mean?"

"We'll visit my training school." The general smiled. "It's in the cellar. I have about a dozen pupils down there now. They're from the Spanish vessel *San Lucar* that had the bad luck to go on the rocks out there. A very inferior lot, I regret to say. Poor specimens, and more accustomed to the deck than to the jungle."

He raised his hand, and Ivan, who served as waiter, brought thick Turkish coffee. Rainsford, with an effort, held his tongue in check.

"It's a game, you see," pursued the general blandly. "I suggest to one of them that we go hunting. I give him a supply of food and an excellent hunting knife. I give him three hours' start. I am to follow, armed only with a pistol of the smallest caliber and range. If my quarry eludes me for three whole days, he wins the game. If I find him—" the general smiled—"he loses."

"Suppose he refuses to be hunted?"

"Oh," said the general, "I give him his option, of course. He need not play that game if he doesn't wish to. If he does not wish to hunt, I turn him over to Ivan. Ivan once had the honor of serving as official flogger to the Great White Czar, and he has his own ideas of sport. Invariably, Mr. Rainsford, invariably they choose the hunt."

"And if they win?"

The smile on the general's face widened. "To date I have not lost," he said.

Then he added, hastily, "I don't wish you to think me a braggart, Mr. Rainsford. Many of them afford only the most elementary sort of problem. Occasionally I get more than I bargained for. One almost did win. I eventually had to use the dogs."

"The dogs?"

"This way, please. I'll show you."

The general steered Rainsford to a window. The lights from the windows sent a flickering illumination that made grotesque patterns on the courtyard below, and Rainsford could see moving about there a dozen or so huge black shapes; as they turned toward him, their eyes glittered greenly.

"A rather good lot, I think," observed the general. "They are let out at seven every night. If anyone should try to get into my house—or out of it—something extremely regrettable would occur to him."

"And now," said the general, "I want to show you my new collection of heads. Will you come with me to the library?"

"I hope," said Rainsford, "that you will excuse me tonight, General Zaroff. I'm really not feeling at all well."

"Ah, indeed?" the general inquired solicitously. "Well, I suppose that's only natural, after your long swim. You need a good, restful night's sleep. Tomorrow you'll feel like a new man, I'll wager. Then we'll hunt, eh? I've one rather promising prospect—"

Rainsford was hurrying from the room.

"Sorry you can't go with me tonight," called the general. "I expect rather fair sport—a big, strong sailor. He looks resourceful—Well, good night Mr. Rainsford; I hope that you have a good night's rest."

The bed was good and the pajamas of the softest silk. He was tired in every fiber of his being, but nevertheless Rainsford could not quiet his brain with sleep. He lay, eyes wide open. Once he thought he heard stealthy steps in the corridor outside his room. He sought to throw open the door. It would not open. He went to the window and looked out. His room was high up in one of the towers. The lights of the château were out now, and it was dark and silent. But there was a fragment of moon, and by its light he could see, dimly, the courtyard. There weaving in and out in the pattern of shadow, were black, noiseless forms. The hounds heard him at the window and looked up, expectantly, with their green eyes. Rainsford went back to the bed and lay down. By many methods he tried to put himself to sleep. He had achieved a doze when, just as morning began to come, he heard, far off in the jungle, the faint report of a pistol.

General Zaroff did not appear until luncheon. He was dressed faultlessly in the tweeds of a country gentleman. He asked about the state of Rainsford's health.

"As for me," sighed the general, "I do not feel so well. I am worried, Mr. Rainsford. Last night I detected traces of my old illness."

To Rainsford's questioning glance the general said, "Boredom."

Then, taking a second helping of crepes suzette, the general explained, "The hunting was not good last night. The fellow lost his head. He made a straight trail that offered no problems at all. That's the trouble with these sailors. They have dull brains to begin with, and they do not know how to get about in the woods. They do excessively stupid and obvious things. It's becoming most annoying. Will you have more, Mr. Rainsford?"

"General," said Rainsford firmly, "I wish to leave this island at once."

The general raised his thickets of eyebrows. He seemed hurt. "But, my dear fellow," the general protested, "you've only just come. You've had no hunting—"

"I wish to go today," said Rainsford. He saw the dead black eyes of the general on him, studying him. General Zaroff's face suddenly brightened.

He filled Rainsford's glass from a dusty bottle.

"Tonight," said the general, "we will hunt—you and I."

Rainsford shook his head. "No, General," he said, "I will not hunt."

The general shrugged his shoulders and delicately ate a hothouse grape. "As you wish, my friend," he said. "The choice rests entirely with you. But may I not venture to suggest that you will find my idea of sport more interesting than Ivan's?"

He nodded toward the corner to where the giant stood, scowling, his thick arms crossed on his huge chest.

"You don't mean—" cried Rainsford.

"My dear fellow," said the general, "have I not told you I always mean what I say about hunting? This is really an inspiration. I drink to a foe worthy of me at last."

The general raised his glass, but Rainsford sat staring at him.

"You'll find this game worth playing," the general said enthusiastically. "Your brain against mine. Your woodcraft against mine. Your strength and stamina against mine. Outdoor chess! And the stake is not without value, eh?"

 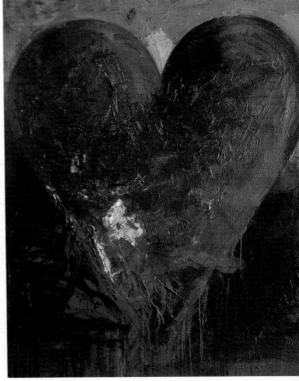

"And if I should win—" began Rainsford huskily.

"I'll cheerfully acknowledge myself defeated if I do not find you by midnight of the third day," said Zaroff. "My ship will place you on the mainland near a town."

The general read what Rainsford was thinking.

"Oh, you can trust me," said the Cossack. "I will give you my word as a gentleman and a sportsman. Of course you, in turn, must agree to say nothing of your visit here."

"I'll agree to nothing of the kind," said Rainsford.

"Oh," said the general, "in that case— But why discuss it now? Three days hence we can discuss it, unless—"

The general sipped his wine.

Then a businesslike air animated him. "Ivan," he said to Rainsford, "will supply you with hunting clothes, food, a knife. I suggest you wear moccasins. They leave a poorer trail. I suggest too that you avoid the big swamp in the southeast corner of the island. We call it Death Swamp. There's quicksand there. One foolish fellow tried it. The deplorable part of it was that Lazarus followed him. You can imagine my feelings, Mr. Rainsford. I loved Lazarus. He was the finest hound in my pack. Well, I must beg you to excuse me now. I always take a siesta after lunch. You'll hardly have time for a nap, I fear. You'll want to start, no doubt. I shall not follow till dusk. Hunting at night is so much more exciting than by day, don't you think? *Au revoir*, Mr. Rainsford, until we meet again."

General Zaroff, with a deep, courtly bow, strolled from the room.

From another door came Ivan. Under one arm he carried khaki hunting clothes, a haversack of food, and a leather sheath containing a long-bladed hunting knife. His right hand rested on a cocked revolver thrust in the crimson sash about his waist. . . .

Rainsford had fought his way through the bush for two hours. "I must keep my nerve. I must keep my nerve," he said through tight teeth.

He had not been entirely clear-headed when the château gates snapped shut be-

Painting (Cruising) LaChase (detail), 1981, JIM DINE.
Courtesy of Pace Gallery, New York.

hind him. His whole idea at first was to put distance between himself and General Zaroff, and, to this end, he had plunged along, spurred on by the sharp stabs of something very like panic. Now he had got a grip on himself, he had stopped, and was taking stock of himself and the situation.

He saw that straight flight was futile. Inevitably it would bring him face to face with the sea. He was in a picture with a frame of water, and his operations, clearly, must take place within that frame.

"I'll give him a trail to follow," muttered Rainsford, and he struck off from the path he had been following into the trackless wilderness. He executed a series of intricate loops. He doubled on his trail again and again, recalling all the lore of the fox hunt, and all the dodges of the fox. Night found him leg-weary, with hands and face lashed by the branches, on a thickly wooded ridge. He knew it would be insane to blunder on through the dark, even if he had the strength. His need for rest was imperative and he thought, "I have played the fox, now I must play the cat of the fable." A big tree with a thick trunk and outspread branches was nearby, and, taking care to leave not the slightest mark, he climbed up, stretched out on one of the broad limbs, and rested after a fashion. Rest brought him new confidence and almost a feeling of security. Even such a hunter as General Zaroff could not trace him there, he told himself. Only the devil himself could follow that complicated trail through the jungle after dark. But, perhaps, the general was a devil—

An apprehensive night crawled slowly by like a wounded snake. Sleep did not visit Rainsford, although the silence of a dead world was on the jungle. Toward morning when a dingy gray was painting the sky, the cry of some startled bird focused Rainsford's attention in that direction. Something was coming through the bush, coming slowly, carefully, coming by the same winding way Rainsford had come. He flattened himself down on the limb, and through a screen of leaves almost as thick as carpet, he watched. The thing that was approaching him was a man.

It was General Zaroff. He made his way along with his eyes fixed in careful concentration on the ground before him. He paused, almost beneath the tree, dropped to his knees and studied the ground. Rainsford's impulse was to hurl himself down like a panther, but he saw that the general's right hand held something small and metallic—an automatic pistol.

The hunter shook his head several times, as if he were puzzled. Then he straightened up and took from his case one of his black cigarettes. Its pungent incense-like smoke floated up to Rainsford's nostrils. Rainsford held his breath. The general's eyes had left the ground and were traveling inch by inch up the tree. Rainsford froze there, every muscle tensed for a spring. But the sharp eyes of the hunter stopped before they reached the limb where Rainsford lay. A smile spread over his brown face. Very deliberately he blew a smoke ring into the air. Then he turned his back on the tree and walked carelessly away, back along the trail he had come. The swish of the underbrush against his hunting boots grew fainter and fainter.

The pent-up air burst hotly from Rainsford's lungs. His first thought made him feel sick and numb. The general could follow a trail through the woods at night. He could follow an extremely difficult trail. He must have uncanny powers. Only by the merest chance had the Cossack failed to see his quarry.

Rainsford's second thought was even more terrible. It sent a shudder of cold horror through his whole being. Why had the general smiled? Why had he turned back?

Rainsford did not want to believe what his reason told him was true, but the truth was as evident as the sun that had by now pushed through the morning mist. The general was playing with him! The general was saving him for another day's sport! The Cossack was the cat. He was the mouse. Then it was that Rainsford knew the full meaning of terror.

"I will not lose my nerve. I will not."

He slid down from the tree, and struck off again into the woods. His face was set and he forced the machinery of his mind to function. Three hundred yards from his hiding place he stopped where a huge dead tree leaned on a smaller, living one. Throwing off his sack of food, Rainsford took his knife from its sheath and began to work with all his energy.

The job was finished at last, and he threw himself down behind a fallen log a hundred feet away. He did not have to wait long. The cat was coming again to play with the mouse.

Following the trail with the sureness of a bloodhound came General Zaroff. Nothing escaped those searching black eyes, no crushed blade of grass, no bent twig, no mark, no matter how faint, in the moss. So intent was the Cossack on his stalking that he was upon the thing Rainsford had made before he saw it. His foot touched the protruding bough that was the trigger. Even as he touched it, the general sensed his danger and leaped back with the agility of an ape. But he was not quite quick enough. The dead tree, delicately adjusted to rest on the cut living one, crashed down and struck the general a glancing blow on the shoulder as it fell. But for his alertness, he would have been smashed beneath it. He staggered but he did not fall. Nor did he drop his revolver. He stood there, rubbing his injured shoulder, and Rainsford, with fear again gripping his heart, heard the general's mocking laugh ring through the jungle.

"Rainsford," called the general, "if you are within sound of my voice, as I suppose you are, let me congratulate you. Not many men know how to make a Malay mancatcher. Luckily for me, I too have hunted in Malaya. You are proving interesting, Mr. Rainsford. I am going now to have my wound dressed. It's only a slight one. Then I shall be back. I shall be back."

When the general, nursing his bruised shoulder, had gone, Rainsford took up his flight again. It was flight now, a desperate, hopeless flight that carried him on for some hours. Dusk came, then darkness, and still he pressed on. The ground grew softer under his moccasins. The vegetation grew ranker, denser. Insects bit him savagely. Then, as he stepped forward, his foot sank into the ooze. He tried to wrench it back, but the muck sucked viciously at his foot as if it were a giant leech. With a violent effort, he tore his foot loose. He knew where he was now. Death Swamp and its quicksand.

His hands were closed tight as if his nerve were something that someone in the darkness was trying to tear from his grip. The softness of the earth had given him an idea. He stepped back from the quicksand a dozen feet or so and, like some huge prehistoric beaver, he began to dig.

Rainsford had dug himself in during the war, when a second's delay meant death. That had been a peaceful pastime compared to his digging now. The pit grew deeper. When it was above his shoulders, he climbed out and from some hard saplings, cut stakes and sharpened them to a fine point. These stakes he planted in the bottom of the pit with the points sticking up. With flying fingers he wove a rough carpet of weeds and branches and with it he covered the mouth of the pit. Then, wet with sweat and aching with tiredness, he crouched behind the stump of a fallen tree.

He knew his pursuer was coming. He heard the padding sound of feet on the soft earth, and the night breeze brought him the perfume of the general's cigarette. It seemed to Rainsford that the general was coming with unusual swiftness. He was not feeling his way along, foot by foot. Rainsford, crouching there, could not see the general, nor could he see the pit. He lived a year in a minute. Then he felt an impulse to cry aloud with joy, for he heard the sharp crackle of the breaking branches as the cover of the pit gave way. He heard the sharp scream of pain as the pointed stakes found their mark. He leaped up from his place of hiding. Then he cowered back. Three feet from the pit a man was standing, with an electric torch in his hand.

"You've done well, Rainsford," the voice of the general called. "Your Burmese tiger pit has claimed one of my best dogs. Again you score. I think, Mr. Rainsford, I'll see what you can do against my whole pack. I'm going home for a rest now. Thank you for a most amusing evening."

At daybreak Rainsford, lying near the swamp, was awakened by a sound that made him know that he had new things to learn about fear. It was a distant sound, faint and wavering, but he knew it. It was the baying of a pack of hounds.

Rainsford knew he could do one of two things. He could stay where he was and wait. That was suicide. He could flee. That was postponing the inevitable. For a moment he stood there, thinking. An idea that held a wild chance came to him, and, tightening his belt, he headed away from the swamp.

The baying of the hounds drew nearer, then still nearer, nearer, ever nearer. On a ridge Rainsford climbed a tree. Not a quarter of a mile away, he could see the bush moving. Straining his eyes, he saw the lean figure of General Zaroff. Just ahead of him Rainsford made out another figure whose wide shoulders surged through the tall jungle weeds. It was the giant Ivan, and he seemed pulled forward by some unseen force. Rainsford knew that Ivan must be holding the pack in leash.

They would be on him any minute now. His mind worked frantically. He thought of a native trick he had learned in Uganda. He slid down the tree. He caught hold of a springy young sapling and to it he fastened his hunting knife, with the blade pointing down the trail. With a bit of wild grapevine he tied back the sapling. Then he ran for his life. The hounds raised their voices as they hit the fresh scent. Rainsford knew now how a hunted animal feels.

He had to stop to get his breath. The baying of the hounds stopped abruptly, and Rainsford's heart stopped too. They must have reached the knife.

He shinnied excitedly up a tree and looked back. His pursuers had stopped, but the hope that was in Rainsford's brain when he climbed died. For he saw in the shallow valley that General Zaroff was still on his feet—but Ivan was not. The knife, driven by the recoil of the spring tree, had not wholly failed.

Rainsford had hardly tumbled to the ground when the pack took up the cry again.

"Nerve, nerve, nerve!" he panted, as he dashed along. A blue gap showed between the trees dead ahead. Ever nearer drew the hounds. Rainsford forced himself on toward the gap. He reached it. It was the shore of the sea. Across a cove he could see the gloomy gray stone of the château. Twenty feet below him the sea rumbled and hissed. Rainsford hesitated. He heard the hounds. Then he leaped into the sea. . . .

When the general and his pack reached the place by the sea, the Cossack stopped. For some minutes he stood regarding the blue-green expanse of water. He shrugged his shoulders. Then he sat down, took a drink of brandy from a silver flask, lit a perfumed cigarette, and hummed a tune.

General Zaroff had an exceedingly good dinner in his great paneled dining hall that evening. Two slight annoyances kept him from perfect enjoyment. One was the thought that it would be difficult to replace Ivan. The other was that his quarry had escaped him. Of course, the American hadn't played the game—so thought the general as he tasted his after-dinner liqueur. In his library he read, to soothe himself. At ten he went up to his bedroom. He was deliciously tired, he said to himself, as he locked himself in. There was a little moonlight, so, before turning on his light, he went to the window and looked down at the courtyard. He could see the great hounds, and he called, "Better luck another time," to them. Then he switched on the light.

A man, who had been hiding in the curtains of the bed, was standing there.

"Rainsford!" screamed the general. "How in God's name did you get here?"

"Swam," said Rainsford. "I found it quicker than walking through the jungle."

The general sucked in his breath and smiled. "I congratulate you," he said. "You have won the game."

Rainsford did not smile. "I am still a hunted beast," he said, in a low, hoarse voice. "Get ready, General Zaroff."

The general made one of his deepest bows. "I see," he said. "Splendid! One of us is to furnish a meal for the hounds. The other will sleep in this very excellent bed. On guard, Rainsford. . . ."

He had never slept in a better bed, Rainsford decided.

Developing Comprehension Skills

1. How did Rainsford learn the reputation of Ship-Trap Island?

2. Why had General Zaroff lost interest in the sport of hunting? How did he regain his interest?

3. Rainsford managed to escape Zaroff during the hunt. Was this due to luck or skill? Find examples to support your answer.

4. When Rainsford escaped, General Zaroff thought, "Of course, the American hadn't played the game." Do you think that it was possible to play General Zaroff's game by a "fair" set of rules? Why or why not?

5. General Zaroff appears to be a refined gentleman. What details indicate that he is a man of culture? Do his actions and beliefs match his appearance? Explain your answer.

6. The title, "The Most Dangerous Game" has more than one meaning. What might those meanings be?

Reading Literature: Short Stories

1. **Inferring Character Traits.** Rainsford, like Zaroff, is an enthusiastic hunter. Review his conversation with Whitney at the beginning of the story. What can you determine about Rainsford from this conversation? What clues are present to support your inference? By the end of the story, do you think Rainsford has changed in any way? Find evidence in the story to support your answer.

2. **Identifying Foreshadowing.** A writer will sometimes create **tension** through the use of foreshadowing. **Foreshadowing** is the use of clues or hints to indicate events that will occur later in the story. In "The Most Dangerous Game," several examples of foreshadowing occur near the beginning of the story. For example, Whitney tells Rainsford of his first experience with Ship-Trap Island. He says, "We were drawing near the island then. What I felt was a—a mental chill—a sort of sudden dread." He also says, "An evil place can, so to speak, broadcast vibrations of evil." How are these comments examples of foreshadowing? Can you locate other examples of foreshadowing in the story? Explain the event your clue foreshadows.

3. **Understanding Rising Action.** In the rising action of the story, the main character is

involved in conflict. This conflict develops and the action builds to the climax of the story. Rainsford struggles with several conflicts in "The Most Dangerous Game." He struggles against the General, nature, and himself. Discuss one of these conflicts in more detail. How does the conflict develop during the rising action of this story? What is the climax to which it leads?

4. **Building Suspense.** Suspense can build during the rising action of a story. **Suspense** occurs when the main character struggles with a conflict and a number of outcomes become possible.

How does the writer of "The Most Dangerous Game" create suspense? Which situations in the story have several possible outcomes? At what point in the story does the suspense finally end?

5. **Appreciating the Mood of a Story.** The **mood** of a story is the feeling the story creates in the reader. Writers choose their words carefully to create a mood. The writer of "The Most Dangerous Game" creates a mysterious and evil mood. Zaroff is described as having 'thick eyebrows, black eyes and pointed teeth.' Zaroff's castle has a spiked iron gate and a 'massive door with a leering carved monster for a knocker.' The island itself is described as dense jungle meeting jagged cliffs. What mood do these descriptions create? Find other specific descriptive words and phrases that help to create this mood.

6. **Understanding How Setting Reflects Character.** The writer of "The Most Dangerous Game" draws strong comparison between Zaroff and his island. Both have touches of civilization, but both are also quite wild and savage. Find at least two physical similarities between General Zaroff and his island. In your opinion, why does the writer make these comparisons between the setting and a major character in the story?

Developing Vocabulary Skills

Inferring Word Meaning from Context. You can figure out, or infer, the meaning of a word even though no specific context clue is present. For example, read this passage.

"I suppose the first three shots I heard was when the hunter flushed his *quarry* and wounded it. The last shot was when he trailed it here and finished it."

From this sentence, you can infer that "quarry" is the object of a hunt. Read the following passages which use words from "The Most Dangerous Game." Use the meaning of the sentence or paragraph as a whole to help you determine the meaning of each underlined word. Then use the dictionary to check your definition.

1. Darkness had just overcome the island when Rainsford saw the lighted towers of a huge chateau.

2. Everything about the building seemed so unreal he thought it was a mirage.

3. "Don't be alarmed," said Rainsford, with a smile which he hoped was disarming. "I'm no robber."

4. The general explained that it was imprudent for any governmental officials to stay in Russia after the people revolted.

5. Rainsford valued human life and so did not condone the general's idea of hunting.

6. The general explained that he gave his "guests" an <u>option</u>. Each man could choose between playing the game or being turned over to Ivan.

7. Rainsford felt <u>apprehensive</u> as he watched Ivan head toward the trap.

8. Rainsford knew he could not run much longer. His need for rest was <u>imperative</u>.

Developing Writing Skills

1. **Making Comparisons and Contrasts.** When you make a comparison, you are looking for similarities between things. When you contrast things or ideas, you are looking for differences. Write two paragraphs comparing and contrasting the characters of General Zaroff and Rainsford.

   Pre-Writing. Think carefully about Zaroff and Rainsford. Refer to the story several times if necessary. Write the words *Similarities* and *Differences* at the top of a piece of paper. List as many details as you can under each column.

   Writing. Use your pre-writing notes to compose a first draft. Plan a topic sentence for each paragraph. In the first paragraph, discuss the similarities between the two characters. In the second paragraph, discuss the differences between Zaroff and Rainsford. Use transitional words and phrases to signal comparisons and contrasts. Such words include *similarly, also, on the other hand, however,* and *unlike.*

   Revising. Read your two paragraphs carefully. Is there a topic sentence for each paragraph? Have you chosen the best evidence from the story to point out the similarities and differences between the two characters? Could one or both paragraphs be improved with additional information? After you are satisfied with the content, proofread your paper and make a final, neat copy.

2. **Preparing an Interview.** In an interview, one person questions another to obtain information. The questions are prepared in advance after the interviewer has carefully considered exactly what information he or she wants to know. The questions should be worded so that the person interviewed gives in-depth answers. Simple *yes* or *no* answers provide little information.

   Imagine that you have the opportunity to interview Rainsford at the end of the story. Decide what you would really like to know about him and his experience. Then, write six questions you would ask him.

Developing Skills in Critical Thinking

Drawing Conclusions from Specific Facts. One type of reasoning involves reaching a conclusion based on specific information. In "The Most Dangerous Game," Rainsford finds himself exhausted and hungry on the rocky shore of a mysterious island. He cheers up when he recalls hearing gunshots on the island. He reasons, "Where there are pistol shots there are men. Where there are men, there is food." He concludes that there is food on the island.

Another example of this type of reasoning follows shortly after the first on page 88. Locate this passage. Explain the reasoning process that Rainsford used.

 *heme*

Every short story has at least one theme. A theme is an idea that the writer wants to share with you. That is one reason why literature is so exciting. Themes can make you aware of some truths in life. They can teach you about others. They can even help you learn more about yourself. In the following stories, look for the main idea the writer wishes to share. How is this idea important in your own life?

Door Street, about 1953, COLLEEN BROWNING. Milwaukee Art Museum Collection. Gift of Mrs. Harry Lynde Bradley.

Humans Are Different

ALAN BLOCH

How might an alien scientist feel about humans? Read to discover what this unusual scientist understands about humans. . . and what it doesn't understand.

I'm an archaeologist, and Humans are my business. Just the same I wonder if we'll ever find out what made Humans different from us Robots—by digging around on the dead planets. You see, I lived with a Human once, and I know it isn't as simple as they told us back in school.

We have a few records, of course, and Robots like me are filling in some of the gaps, but I think now that we aren't really getting anywhere. We know, or at least the historians say we know, that Humans came from a planet called Earth. We know, too, that they rode out bravely from star to star and wherever they stopped, they left colonies—Humans, Robots, and sometimes both—against their return. But they never came back.

Those were the shining days of the world. But are we so old now? Humans had a bright flame—the old word is "divine," I think—that flung them far across the night skies, and we have lost the strands of the web they wove.

Microscopic view of a computer chip. Photograph by Mortimer Abramowitz, Olympus Corporation, New York.

Our scientists tell us that Humans were very much like us. The skeleton of a Human is, to be sure, almost the same as the skeleton of a Robot, except that it's made of some calcium compound instead of titanium. They speak learnedly of "population pressure" as a "driving force toward the stars." Just the same, though, there are other differences.

It was on my last field trip, to one of the inner planets, that I met the Human. It must have been the Last Human in this sytem and it had forgotten how to talk—it had been alone so long. Once it learned our language we got along fine together, and I planned to bring it back with me. Something happened to it, though.

One day, for no reason at all, it complained of the heat. I checked its temperature and decided that its thermostat circuits were shot. I had a kit of field spares with me, and it was obviously out of order, so I went to work. I turned it off without any trouble. I pushed the needle into its neck to operate the cutoff switch, and it stopped moving. Just like a Robot! But when I opened it up it wasn't the same inside. And when I put it back together, I couldn't get it running again. Then it sort of weathered away—and by the time I was ready to come home, about a year later, there was nothing left of it but bones. Yes, Humans are indeed different.

Developing Comprehension Skills

1. Describe the experience that the Robot had with a Human. What eventually happened to the Human?

2. What is the setting for "Humans Are Different"? Is the place as important as the time? Explain your answer.

3. What is the Robot's attitude toward the Humans?

4. Why was the Robot unable to get the Human running again?

5. At the end of the story, the Robot concludes that "Humans are different." How would the Robot explain the differences? How would you explain the differences?

6. The narrator in this story seems to feel that Robots and Humans are each superior in certain ways. In what ways would the narrator say that Robots are superior to Humans?

In what ways are Humans superior to Robots? Would you agree with the narrator's conclusions? Explain your answer.

Reading Literature: Short Stories

1. **Identifying the Introduction.** The introduction of a story presents the setting and introduces the main character or characters. In "Humans Are Different," the introduction is the first two paragraphs of the story. What do you learn about the main character in the introduction? Describe the setting of the story from the information provided in the introduction. Are you able to determine the time and place of the setting? What clues did you use?

2. **Identifying Point of View.** The narrator in "Humans Are Different" tells the story using the first-person point of view. A story is told

from the first-person point of view when the narrator's thoughts or reactions to a situation are important. The narrator in this story is not Human. It is a Robot. In what ways is this narrator similar to a Human? How is it different? How do these differences make the Robot an interesting narrator? Explain your answer.

3. **Recognizing Irony.** This story's interest comes from its ironies. The Robot speaks of a time long ago when Humans left Earth to colonize the stars. It says that they left colonies of Humans and Robots wherever they went. Why do you think Humans originally brought the Robots with them? Do you think the Robot understands that its ancestors were created by Humans? Find evidence in the story to support your answer. What is ironic about the fact that the Robots, not the Humans, survived?

4. **Identifying Theme.** The **theme** of a story is the main idea a writer wants the reader to understand. What point do you think the author of "Humans Are Different" is trying to make about humans? What is he saying about their developing technology, and their future?

Developing Vocabulary Skills

Finding the Meaning of Words. There will be times when you cannot figure out the meaning of an unfamiliar word by using context clues. Instead, you will have to refer to a dictionary or a glossary to determine the meaning. The **glossary** lists words used in a book that may be new to the reader. The glossary for this text can be found at the back of the book. Look at the following sentence:

"Perhaps the grass in the other field is better," suggested the aunt *fatuously*.

There are no context clues in this sentence to suggest that "fatuously" means "in a silly or foolish manner." You would have to consult a glossary or dictionary to find the meaning. Look at each of the following sentences. If context clues are present, write down the words that help you determine the meaning of the underlined words. Then write the meaning of the word. If no context clues are present, write *Use Dictionary*. Then look up the word and write its meaning.

1. I am an <u>archaeologist</u>, a scientist who tries to learn about ancient cultures by studying their remains.

2. Humans had a <u>divine</u> spark, an almost god-like quality.

3. The perfectly preserved <u>artifacts</u> gave the scientists some idea of what life was like in the twentieth century.

4. We based our conclusions on the <u>premise</u> that the humans had left their home because of population pressures.

5. I checked its temperature and decided that its <u>thermostat</u> must have broken.

6. The Human slowly <u>weathered</u> away until only its bones were left.

Developing Writing Skills

1. **Imagining the Background of a Story.** In "Humans Are Different," it appears that one of humankind's machines has outlived the human race. The Robot-narrator does not explain why the human race died while Robots survived. Can you imagine why that

might have happened? Write two paragraphs explaining what may have happened. Give reasons why the Robots were able to survive while Humans could not.

Pre-Writing. This is an assignment calling for critical thinking skills and imagination. How might the human race have ended? Disaster? Illness? Warfare? List all the possibilities you can imagine. Choose the explanations that could best explain why Robots survived despite these problems. Then, list the differences between Robots and Humans that might account for the Robot's survival.

Writing. Use your pre-writing notes to write a rough draft of your explanation. In your first paragraph, explain possible reasons why Humans did not survive. In the second paragraph, explain the differences between Robots and Humans that might account for the Robots' survival. You may want to discuss the differences in the order of importance. In this case, you would start with the strongest or most obvious reason. You could then present other reasons that also make sense.

Use transitional words and phrases to help you express your ideas logically. These transitions include such words as *first, the first reason, more important*, and *finally*.

Revising. In small groups of four or five, discuss your explanations. Which explanation seemed most interesting? Which seemed most likely? A good explanation will give specific reasons for the Robots' survival. Revise your paragraph according to your classmates' suggestions. Then proofread your writing for errors in grammar, usage, and mechanics and make a clean, final copy.

2. **Using Point of View.** Imagine that you are an alien scientist studying twentieth-century America. You might be especially interested in rock music, shopping malls, cars, and computers. Write a paragraph in which you describe what you observe. Use the first-person point of view and the pronoun "I" to record what you see. Remember, you are seeing these things for the first time. Also remember that, because you are an alien, some of your conclusions may be wrong. Describe the appearance of the subject. Then, try to describe the actions and purpose.

Developing Skills in Study and Research

Using the Encyclopedia. As you know, the encyclopedia is a reference book found in most libraries. **Encyclopedias** provide factual information on a wide range of topics. Subjects are entered alphabetically. An index in the last volume can refer you to entries.

Look up *Robot* in an encyclopedia in your library. Read the entry carefully. Now read the entry for *Robot* in a different set of encyclopedias. Compare the two entries by answering these questions:

1. Which entry gives more complete or varied information about robots?

2. Does either entry have helpful illustrations or photographs? How do these help you to increase your understanding of robots? Which entry has the most helpful illustrations and photographs?

3. Does either entry guide you to other entries or other books about robots?

What does this comparison tell you about the value of using more than one encyclopedia?

Beauty Is Truth

ANNA GUEST

Jeanie discovers the meaning of beauty and truth in her life. Read to see if others can understand how she feels.

At 125th Street, they all got off, Jeanie and her friend, Barbara, and a crowd of other boys and girls who went to the same downtown high school. Through the train window, Jeanie thought she saw the remaining passengers look at them with relief and disdain. Around her the boys and girls pressed forward with noisy gaiety. They were all friends now. They were home again in Harlem.

They passed the big ice-cream parlor window, cluttered with candy boxes and ornate with curly lettering. They could see the jukebox near the door and some boys and girls sitting down at a table. It looked warm and friendly.

"I think I'll stop in. I'm awful thirsty," said Barbara.

Jeanie shrugged.

"So long then."

"So long."

She walked along the busy street, aimlessly looking in the store windows, turned the corner, and walked the few blocks to her house. Though it was chilly, each brownstone or gray stoop had its cluster of people clinging to the iron railings.

Her little brother Billy was playing in front of the stoop with three or four other kids. They were bending over something on the sidewalk, in a closed circle. Pitching pennies again, she thought with distaste. She was going to pass them and started up the three stone steps to the doorway. A window on the ground floor opened, and Fat Mary leaned out.

"Now you're going to catch it, Billy Boy. Your sister's going to tell your mamma you been pitching pennies again."

Jeanie did not pause.

Billy sprang up. "Hi, Jeanie. Jeanie, gimme a nickel. I need a nickel. A nickel, a nickel. I gotta have a nickel."

The other little boys quickly took up the chant. "A nickel, a nickel. Billy needs a nickel."

She threw them a furious glance and went in. The kitchen smelled dank and unused, and the opening of the door dislodged a flake of green plaster. A black dress someone had given her mother lay over the chair before the sewing machine.

She sat down on the bed and opened her loose-leaf notebook at random. A page fell out. Today's English. Some poem about a vase, and youths and maidens. Why did everybody get so excited about the Greeks? It was so long ago. "Wonderful! Wonderful!" Miss Lowy had exclaimed. How could anybody get so stirred up over a poem? She meant it, too. You could tell from her expression.

"Beauty is truth, truth beauty,"—that is all Ye know on earth, and all ye need to know.

There it was, copied into her notebook. Caught by something in the lines, she tried to find the poem in her tattered anthology, not bothering about the index, but riffling the pages to and fro. John Keats, at last— "On First Looking into Chapman's Homer." More Greeks. Here it was— "Ode on a Grecian Urn." The poem, all squeezed together in the middle of the page, looked dry and dusty, withered and far away, at the bottom of a dry well. Recognizing the last lines, she heard them again, falling so roundly, so perfectly, from the lips of Miss Lowy.

"Write about beauty and truth. Write about life," Miss Lowy had said.

She tore a page out of her notebook and opened her pen. Pulling over a chair, she rested her book on the sooty window sill. She stared out at the dusk falling sadly, sadly, thickening into darkness over the coal yards.

A crash of the kitchen door caused a reverberation in the window sill. The notebook slipped out of her hands.

"Where'd you get that bottle of pop?" She heard her mother's voice, hard and sounding more Southern than usual.

"I asked you. Where'd you get that pop? You better tell me."

"A lady gave me a nickel. A lady came down the street and ask me—"

"You lying. I know where you got that money for that pop. Gambling, that's what you was doing."

"I was only pitching pennies, Ma. It's only a game, Ma."

"Gambling and stealing and associating with bad friends. I told you to stay away from them boys. Didn't I? Didn't I?" Her mother's voice rose. "I'm going to give you a beating you ain't going to forget for a good long time."

Billy wailed on a long descending note.

Jeanie could hear each impact of the strap and her mother's heavy breathing.

"I want you to grow up good, not lying and gambling and stealing," her mother gasped, "and I'm going to make you good. You ain't never going to forget this." When it had been going on forever, it stopped. A final slap of the strap. "And you ain't going to get any supper either. You can go now. You can go to bed and reflect on what I told you." He stumbled past her, whimpering; fists grinding into eyes, and into the dark little alcove which was his room.

Her mother appeared in the doorway. She wore her hat and coat.

"Come help me get supper, Jeanie. You should have got things started." Her voice was tired and trembling and held no blame.

"I don't want any supper, Ma."

Her mother came in and sat down heavily on the bed, taking off her hat, and letting her coat fall open.

"I had a hard day. I worked hard every minute," she said. "I brought you something extra nice for dessert. I stood in line to get some of them tarts from Sutter's."

Jeanie rose and silently put her mother's hat on the shelf. She held out her hand for her mother's coat and hung it up.

Together they opened the paper bags on the kitchen table. She set the water to boil.

As they ate in silence, the three tarts shone like jewels on a plate at one end of the chipped porcelain table. Her mother looked tired and stern.

"You better fix your brother up a plate," she said, still stern. "Put it on a tray. Here, take this." She put on the tray the most luscious, the most perfect of the tarts. "Wait." She went heavily over to her swollen black handbag, took out a small clasp purse, opened it, and carefully, seriously, deliberately, picked out a coin, rejected it, and took out another. "Give him this." It was a quarter.

After the dishes were washed, Jeanie brought her books into the kitchen and spread them out under the glaring overhead light. Billy had been asleep, huddled in his clothes. Tears had left dusty streaks on his face.

Her mother sat in the armchair, ripping out the sides of the black dress. Her spectacles made her look strange. "Beauty is truth," Jeanie read in her notebook. Hastily, carelessly, defiantly disregarding margins and doubtful spellings, letting her pen dig into the paper, she began to write: "Last night my brother Billy got a terrible beating. . . ."

Get to English early. Slip her composition in under the others, sit in the last seat. Don't bother me. I am in a bad mood. Rows and rows of seats. Rows and rows of windows opposite. A poem about a skylark. From where she sat, she could see about a square foot of sky drained of all color by the looming school walls. Miss Lowy read clearly, standing all alone at the front of the room in her clean white blouse and with her smooth blond hair.

Miss Lowy, maybe you see skylarks. Me, I'd be glad to see some sky, she thought and nearly uttered it. It had been a mistake to write as she had done about her brother's beating. They would laugh if they knew. No danger, though, that her story would be read. Only the best manuscripts were read. She remembered keenly the blotched appearance of the paper, the lines crossed out, and the words whose spelling she could never be sure of. Oh, well, she didn't care. One more period and then the weekend.

The bell rang, and the pens dropped. The books were closed with a clatter. She slipped out ahead of the pushing, jostling boys and girls.

Monday, Miss Lowy had on still another perfect white blouse. She stood facing the class, holding a sheaf of papers in her hand.

"I spent a very enjoyable time this weekend, reading your work," said Miss Lowy, waiting for the class to smile.

"Seriously, though, many of your pieces were most interesting, even though they were unconventional about spelling and punctuation." A smile was obviously indicated here too, and the class obeyed. She paused. "Sometimes, however, a piece of writing is so honest and human that you have to forgive the technical weaknesses. Not that they aren't important," she said hastily, "but what the writer has to say is more significant."

The three best students in the class looked confused. It was their pride not to have technical errors.

"When you hear this," Miss Lowy continued, "I think you'll agree with me. I know it brought tears to my eyes."

The class looked incredulous.

"It's called 'Evening Comes to 128th Street.' " Her face took on that rapt look.

Jeanie's heart beat painfully. She picked up a pencil but dropped it, so unsteady were her fingers. Everyone was listening. Even the classes in the other wing of the building across the courtyard, seemed fixed, row on row, in an attitude of listening. Miss Lowy read on. It was all there, the coal yards and Fat Mary, the stoop and the tarts from Sutter's, Billy asleep with the tears dried on his face, the clasp purse and the quarter.

" 'The funny part of it was, when I woke him, Billy wasn't mad. He was glad about the quarter, and ate his supper, dessert and all, but Mama never did eat her tart, so I put it away.' "

The pain of remembrance swept over Jeanie, then shame and regret. It was no business of theirs, these strange people.

No one spoke. The silence was unbearable. Finally Marion, the incomparable Marion, raised her hand.

"It was so real," she said, "you felt you were right there in that kitchen."

"You didn't know who to feel sorry for," said another student. "You wanted to cry with the mother and you wanted to cry with Billy."

"With the girl too," said another.

Several heads nodded.

"You see," said Miss Lowy. "It's literature. It's life. It's pain and truth and beauty."

Jeanie's heart beat so, it made a mist come before her eyes. Through the blue she heard Miss Lowy say it was good enough to be sent to a magazine. It showed talent, it showed promise. She heard her name called and shrank from the eyes turned upon her.

After school she hurried out and caught the first train. She did not want to meet anyone, not even Barbara.

Was that Billy among the kids on the stoop?

"Billy," she called. "Billy."

What would she say to him? Beauty is truth, truth beauty?

"Billy," she called again urgently.

Billy lifted his head, and seeing who it was, tore himself reluctantly away from his friends and took a step toward her.

Developing Comprehension Skills

1. What sort of neighborhood did Jeanie live in? What proof can be found in the first paragraph that Jeanie went to school in a different neighborhood?

2. Jeanie thought, "Miss Lowy, maybe you see skylarks. Me, I'd be glad to see some sky." What does this thought reveal about Jeanie's feelings and her life?

3. Explain why Jeanie's mother beat Billy, then treated him to a tart. What did this say about her feelings for her son?

4. After Jeanie's story was read aloud in class, the narrator states:

> A pain of remembrance swept over Jeanie, then shame and regret. It was no business of theirs.

In your opinion, why was Jeanie ashamed of opening herself up to strangers? What sorts of comments did she expect from the other students?

5. When Jeanie hurried home and called out for Billy, do you think she was feeling proud or ashamed that she had written truthfully

about her life? What do you think she wanted to tell him?

6. After her writing was praised, Jeanie avoided the other students and hurried home. What do you think she was feeling? Do you think most people would react this way?

Reading Literature: Short Stories

1. **Understanding Theme.** You have learned that **theme** refers to a concern, or idea, that a writer wishes to communicate to the reader. The title "Beauty Is Truth" states an important theme in this story. Read the complete quotation from the Keats poem. The word "beauty" does not refer to physical beauty in this case. It refers to a quality pleasing or satisfying to the mind. In this story, Jeanie's writing about her life is beautiful. What do Jeanie's teacher and her classmates find beautiful in her writing?

2. **Making Inferences About Character.** We learn about the problems that Jeanie's mother is experiencing through specific details in the story. From these details, we are able to infer, or figure out, the kind of person her mother is. Explain what the following details reveal about the mother's character:

   a. her beating Billy for pitching pennies
   b. her grammar, as in, "You ain't never going to forget this."
   c. the fact that she doesn't eat the tart

3. **Appreciating Character Development.** A character in a short story will sometimes change during the course of a story. Such a character is called a **dynamic** character. This change may occur as a result of the conflict experienced by the character.

Jeanie experiences conflict both at school and at home. What disturbs Jeanie about her situation? Find details in the story that support your answer.

What about Jeanie has changed by the end of the story when she calls out to her brother? What is responsible for this change?

Developing Vocabulary Skills

Inferring Meanings from Familiar Word Parts. You have learned that you should use the dictionary if context clues do not help you figure out the meaning of an unfamiliar word. Before you turn to the dictionary, however, look carefully at the word. Perhaps you are familiar with part of the word. This word part may help you unlock the meaning of the entire word.

For example, if you know that the meaning of *apology* is "a request for pardon," then you can guess the meaning of the italicized word in the following sentence:

"I suppose I never really considered your feelings," he said *apologetically*.

Study the meaning of each word in the following list. Check the dictionary if you are not sure of a meaning. Then read the sentences below using words drawn from stories in this chapter. Each underlined word is based on one of the words in the list. Determine the meaning of each word from what you know about the word in the list. Write the meaning of each underlined word as it is used in the sentence.

1. vary   3. defy   5. explain
2. tremble   4. compare   6. diet

   a. To have money of her own, she was clerking after school in a small <u>variety</u> store.

b. Her voice was tired and <u>tremulous</u>.

c. She <u>defiantly</u> disregarded margins and spellings.

d. Just as Jeanie had feared, Marion, the <u>incomparable</u> Marion, raised her hand to speak.

e. Jack Duncan, our cook-doctor-<u>dietician</u>, did everything he could for the bird.

f. When visiting a space station, don't be surprised if you hear the <u>inexplicable</u> melody of a bird song.

Developing Writing Skills

1. **Explaining an Opinion.** Choose one of the following statements. Write one paragraph telling whether you agree or disagree with the statement. Support your opinion with evidence from the story or from your own experiences.

   a. Jeanie was wrong to tell about what happened in her family.

   b. The truth is not always beautiful.

   c. Jeanie was wrong when she said that the experiences she had written about were "no business of theirs."

2. **Comparing Stories.** "The Fan Club" and "Beauty Is Truth" both deal with school situations. The main character in each story is a high school girl. Write four paragraphs in which you compare the stories. This means that you will look for similarities. Do not contrast, or look for differences. Compare the two stories by examining any or all of these major elements:

   a. main character

   b. setting

   c. conflict

   d. theme

Pre-Writing. Prepare a list of similarities for each of the four categories. Find specific details from each story to support statements about similarities. Then, choose the elements about which you can say the most.

Writing. Begin your comparison with a paragraph that explains what you are doing. Let your reader know which stories you are comparing and which topics you are writing about. However, avoid such weak and uninteresting beginnings as "I am going to write about . . ." or "The purpose of this paper is. . . ."

Begin each body paragraph with a topic sentence. Each topic sentence should tell the reader what the paragraph will be about. For example, the topic in one of your paragraphs might be similar to this:

> The main characters in each story have much in common.

As you write, refer to your list for similarities, but do not limit your paragraph to items on that list. You may think of additional similarities as you are writing. Remember, you are not looking for contrasts in this writing assignment.

Revising. Consider the following questions as you revise your comparison:

> Did my introductory paragraph give the purpose of the writing assignment?
>
> Did I discuss each element in a separate paragraph?
>
> Did I include enough details to make each comparison clear?
>
> Did I limit this assignment to comparisons not contrasts?
>
> Was it clear at all times which story I was discussing?

Developing Skills in Study and Research

Locating Literary References. A writer will often refer to another literary work in order to highlight or illustrate an idea. It may be necessary for the reader to be familiar with that work to fully appreciate the story. In "Beauty Is Truth," there is reference to a poem by John Keats. If you wished to learn the title of this poem, you could refer to *Bartlett's Familiar Quotations*. This book contains thousands of well known quotations and lists the source of each one. It is found in the reference section of many libraries.

There are other reference books about literature in the library. Some of them contain information on the history of literature. Some contain analyses of stories, poems, and plays.

Others list quotations and proverbs. In still others, you can find information about writers themselves. Check to see which of the following literary references can be found in your library:

Book Review Digest
Contemporary Poets
Encyclopedia of World Drama
A Literary History of England
A Literary History of the United States
The Oxford Companion to American Literature

List those references you found in your library. Note the location on the reference shelf. Then choose one and write a paragraph explaining the types of information found in it.

The Force of Luck

As you read this folk tale, try to decide whether luck, money, or something else helps a poor but honest miller fulfill his dreams.

LATIN AMERICAN FOLK LEGEND
Retold by Rudolfo A. Anaya

Once two wealthy friends got into a heated argument. One said that it was money that made a man prosperous, and the other maintained that it wasn't money, but luck, which made the man. They argued for some time and finally decided that, if only they could find an honorable man, then perhaps they could prove their respective points of view.

One day while they were passing through a small village they came upon a miller who was grinding corn and wheat. They paused to ask the man how he ran his business. The miller replied that he worked for a master and that he earned only four bits a day. With that he had to support a family of five.

The friends were surprised. "Do you mean to tell us you can maintain a family of five on only fifteen dollars a month?" one asked.

"I live modestly to make ends meet," the humble miller replied.

The two friends privately agreed that, if they put this man to a test, perhaps they could resolve their argument.

"I am going to make you an offer," one of them said to the miller. "I will give you two hundred dollars and you may do whatever you want with the money."

"But why would you give me this money when you've just met me?" the miller asked.

"Well, my good man, my friend and I have a long standing argument. He contends that it is luck that elevates a man to high position, and I say it is money. By giving you this money perhaps we can settle our argument. Here, take it, and do with it what you want!"

The poor miller took the money and spent the rest of the day thinking about the strange meeting, which had presented him with more money than he had ever seen. What could he possibly do with all this money? Be that as it may, he had the money in his pocket and he could do with it whatever he wanted.

When the day's work was done, the miller decided the first thing he would do would be to buy food for his family. He took out ten dollars and wrapped the rest of the money in a cloth and put the bundle in his bag. Then he went to the market and bought supplies and a good piece of meat to take home.

On the way home he was attacked by a hawk that had smelled the meat that the miller carried. The miller fought off the bird but in the struggle he lost the bundle of money. Before the miller knew what was happening the hawk grabbed the bag and flew away with it. When he realized what had happened he fell into deep thought.

"Ah," he moaned, "wouldn't it have been better to let that hungry bird have the meat! I could have bought a lot more meat with the money he took. Alas, now I'm in the same poverty as before! And worse, because now those two men will say I am a thief! I should have thought carefully and bought nothing. Yes, I should have gone straight home and this wouldn't have happened!"

So he gathered what was left of his provisions and continued home and, when he arrived, he told his family the entire story.

When he was finished telling his story, his wife said, "It has been our lot to be poor, but have faith in God and maybe someday our luck will change."

The next day the miller got up and went to work as usual. He wondered what the two men would say about his story. Since he had never been a man of money, however, he soon forgot the entire matter.

Three months after he had lost the money to the hawk, it happened that the two wealthy men returned to the village. As soon as they saw the miller they approached him to ask if his luck had changed. When the miller saw them, he felt ashamed and afraid that they would think that he had squandered the money on worthless things. Yet he decided to tell them the truth and, as soon as they had greeted each other, he told his story. The men believed him. In fact, the one who insisted that it was money and not luck that made a man prosper took out another two hundred dollars and gave it to the miller.

"Let's try again," he said, "and let's see what happens this time."

The miller didn't know what to think. "Kind sir, maybe it would be better if you put this money in the hands of another man," he said.

"No," the man insisted, "I want to give it to you because you are an honest man, and if we are going to settle our argument you have to take the money!"

The miller thanked them and promised to do his best. Then as soon as the two men left he began to think what to do with the money so that it wouldn't disappear as it had the first time. The thing to do was to take the money straight home. He took out ten dollars, wrapped the rest in a cloth, and headed home.

When he arrived his wife wasn't at home. At first he didn't know what to do with the money. He went to the pantry where he had stored a large earthenware jar filled with bran. That was as safe a place as any to hide the money, he thought, so he emptied out the grain and put the bundle of money at the bottom of the jar, then covered it up with the grain. Satisfied that the money was safe he returned to work.

That afternoon when he arrived home from work he was greeted by his wife.

"Look, my husband, today I bought some good clay with which to whitewash the entire house."

"And how did you buy the clay if we don't have any money?" he asked.

"Well, the man who was selling the clay was willing to trade for jewelry, money, or anything of value," she said. "The only thing we had of value was the jar full of bran, so I traded it for the clay. Isn't it wonderful, I think we have enough clay to whitewash these two rooms!"

The man groaned and pulled his hair.

"Oh, you crazy woman! What have you done? We're ruined again!"

"But why?" she asked, unable to understand his anguish.

"Today I met the same two friends who gave me the two hundred dollars three months ago," he explained. "And after I told them how I lost the money, they gave me another two hundred. And I, to make sure the money was safe, came home and hid it inside the jar of bran—the same jar you have traded for dirt! Now we're as poor as we were before! And what am I going to tell the two men? They'll think I'm a liar and a thief for sure!"

"Let them think what they want," his wife said calmly. "We will only have in our lives what the good Lord wants us to have.

It is our lot to be poor until God wills it otherwise."

So the miller was consoled and the next day he went to work as usual. Time came and went, and one day the two wealthy friends returned to ask the miller how he had done with the second two hundred dollars. When the poor miller saw them he was afraid they would accuse him of being a liar and a spendthrift. Still he decided to be truthful and, as soon as they had greeted each other, he told them what had happened to the money.

"That is why poor men remain honest," the man who had given him the money said. "Because they don't have money they can't get into trouble. But I find your stories hard to believe. I think you gambled and lost the money. That's why you're telling us these wild stories.

"Either way," he continued, "I still believe that it is money and not luck that makes a man prosper."

"Well, you certainly didn't prove your point by giving the money to this poor miller," his friend reminded him. "Good evening, you luckless man," he said to the miller.

"Thank you, friends," the miller said.

"Oh, by the way, here is a worthless piece of lead I've been carrying around. Maybe you can use it for something," said the man who believed in luck. Then the men left, still debating their points of view on life.

Since the lead was practically worthless, the miller thought nothing of it and put it in his jacket pocket. He forgot all about it

The Farmhouse, Mont-roig, 1921–22, JOAN MIRÓ. Collection of Mrs. Ernest Hemingway, New York.
Copyright © 1985 A.D.A.G.P., Paris/V.A.G.A., New York.

until he arrived home. When he threw his jacket on a chair he heard a thump and he remembered the piece of lead. He took it out of the pocket and threw it under the table. Later that night after the family had eaten and gone to bed, they heard a knock at the door.

"Who is it? What do you want?" the miller asked.

"It's me, your neighbor," a voice answered. The miller recognized the fisherman's wife. "My husband sent me to ask you if you have any lead you can spare. He is going fishing tomorrow and he needs the lead to weight down the nets."

The miller remembered the lead he had thrown under the table. He got up, found it, and gave it to the woman.

"Thank you very much, neighbor," the woman said. "I promise you the first fish my husband catches will be yours."

"Think nothing of it," the miller said and returned to bed. The next day he got up and went to work without thinking any more of the incident. However, in the afternoon when he returned home he found his wife cooking a big fish for dinner.

"Since when are we so well off we can afford fish for supper?" he asked his wife.

"Don't you remember that our neighbor promised us the first fish her husband caught?" his wife reminded him. "Well this was the fish he caught the first time he threw his net. So it's ours, and it's a beauty. But you should have been here when I gutted him! I found a large piece of glass in his stomach!"

"And what did you do with it?"

"Oh, I gave it to the children to play with," she shrugged.

When the miller saw the piece of glass, he noticed it shone so brightly it appeared to illuminate the room, but because he knew nothing about jewels he didn't realize its value and left it to the children. The bright glass was such a novelty that the children were soon fighting over it.

Now it so happened that the miller and his wife had other neighbors who were jewelers. The following morning when the miller had gone to work the jeweler's wife visited the miller's wife to complain about all the noise her children had made.

"We couldn't get any sleep last night," she moaned.

"I know, and I'm sorry, but you know how it is with a large family," the miller's wife explained. "Yesterday we found a beautiful piece of glass and I gave it to my youngest one to play with and when the others tried to take it from him he raised a storm."

The jeweler's wife took interest. "Won't you show me that piece of glass?" she asked.

"But of course. Here it is."

"Ah, yes, it's a pretty piece of glass. Where did you find it?"

"Our neighbor gave us a fish yesterday and, when I was cleaning it, I found the glass in its stomach."

"Why don't you let me take it home for just a moment. You see, I have one just like it, and I want to compare them."

"Yes, why not? Take it," answered the miller's wife.

So the jeweler's wife ran off with the glass to show it to her husband. When the jeweler saw the glass he knew it was one of the finest diamonds he had ever seen.

"It's a diamond!" he exclaimed.

"I thought so," his wife nodded eagerly. "What shall we do?"

"Go tell the neighbor we'll give her fifty dollars for it, but don't tell her it's a diamond!"

"No, no," his wife chuckled, "of course not." She ran to her neighbor's house. "Ah yes, we have one exactly like this," she told the miller's wife. "My husband is willing to buy it for fifty dollars—only so we can have a pair, you understand."

"I can't sell it," the miller's wife answered. "You will have to wait until my husband returns from work."

That evening when the miller came home from work his wife told him about the offer the jeweler had made for the piece of glass.

"But why would they offer fifty dollars for a worthless piece of glass?" the miller wondered aloud. Before his wife could answer they were interrupted by the jeweler's wife.

"What do you say, will you take fifty dollars for the glass?" she asked.

"No, that's not enough," the miller said cautiously. "Offer more."

"I'll give you fifty thousand!" the jeweler's wife blurted out.

"A little bit more," the miller replied.

"Impossible!" the jeweler's wife cried, "I can't offer any more without consulting my husband." She ran off to tell her husband how the bargaining was going, and he told her he was prepared to pay a hundred thousand dollars to acquire the diamond.

He handed her seventy-five thousand dollars and said, "Take this and tell him that tomorrow, as soon as I open my shop, he'll have the rest."

When the miller heard the offer and saw the money he couldn't believe his eyes. He imagined the jeweler's wife was jesting with him, but it was a true offer and he received the hundred thousand dollars for the diamond. The miller had never seen so much money, but he still didn't quite trust the jeweler.

"I don't know about this money," he confided to his wife. "Maybe the jeweler plans to accuse us of robbing him and thus get it back."

"Oh no," his wife assured him, "the money is ours. We sold the diamond fair and square—we didn't rob anyone."

"I think I'll still go to work tomorrow," the miller said. "Who knows, something might happen and the money will disappear, then we would be without money and work. Then how would we live?"

So he went to work the next day, and all day he thought about how he could use the money. When he returned home that afternoon his wife asked him what he had decided to do with their new fortune.

"I think I will start my own mill," he answered, "like the one I operate for my master. Once I set up my business, we'll see how our luck changes."

The next day he set about buying everything he needed to establish his mill and to build a new home. Soon he had everything going.

Six months had passed, more or less, since he had seen the two men who had given him the four hundred dollars and the piece of lead. He was eager to see them again and to tell them how the piece of lead had changed his luck and made him wealthy.

Time passed and the miller prospered. His business grew and he even built a summer cottage where he could take his family on vacation. He had many employees who worked for him. One day while he was at his store he saw his two benefactors riding by. He rushed out into the street to greet them and ask them to come in. He was overjoyed to see them, and he was happy to see that they admired his store.

"Tell us the truth," the man who had given him the four hundred dollars said. "You used that money I gave you to set up this business."

The miller swore he hadn't, and he told them how he had given the piece of lead to his neighbor and how the fisherman had, in return, given him a fish with a very large diamond in its stomach. He then told them how he had sold the diamond to the jeweler and his wife.

"And that's how I acquired this business and many other things I want to show you," he said. "But it's time to eat. Let's eat first then I'll show you everything I have now."

The men agreed, but one of them still doubted the miller's story. So they ate and then the miller had three horses saddled and they rode out to see his summer home. The cabin was on the other side of the river where the mountains were cool and beautiful. When they arrived the men admired the place very much. It was such a peaceful place that they rode all afternoon through the forest. During their ride they came upon a tall pine tree.

"What is that on top of the tree?" one of them asked.

"That's the nest of a hawk," the miller replied.

"I have never seen one; I would like to take a closer look at it!"

"Of course," the miller said, and he ordered a servant to climb the tree and bring down the nest so his friend could see how it was built. When the hawk's nest was on the ground, they examined it carefully. They noticed that there was a cloth bag at the bottom of the nest. When the miller saw the bag, he immediately knew that it was the very same bag he had lost to the hawk which fought him for the piece of meat years ago.

"You won't believe me, friends, but this is the very same bag in which I put the first two hundred dollars you gave me," he told them.

"If it's the same bag," the man who had doubted him said, "then the money you said the hawk took should be there."

"No doubt about that," the miller said. "Let's see what we find."

The three of them examined the old, weatherbeaten bag. Although it was full of holes and crumbling, when they tore it apart they found the money intact. The two men remembered what the miller had told them, and they agreed he was an honest and honorable man. Still, the man who had given him the money wasn't completely satisfied. He wondered what had really happened to the second two hundred he had given the miller.

They spent the rest of the day riding in the mountains and returned very late to the house.

As he unsaddled their horses, the servant in charge of grooming and feeding the horses suddenly realized that he had no grain for them. He ran to the barn and checked, but there was no grain for the hungry horses. So he ran to the neighbor's granary and there he was able to buy a large clay jar of bran. He carried the jar home and emptied the bran into a bucket to wet it before he fed it to the horses. When he got to the bottom of the jar he noticed a large lump which turned out to be a rag covered package. He examined it and felt something inside. He immediately went to give it to his master who had been eating dinner.

"Master," he said, "look at this package which I found in an earthenware jar of grain which I just bought from our neighbor!"

The three men carefully unraveled the cloth and found the other one hundred and ninety dollars which the miller had told them he had lost. That is how the miller proved to his friends that he was truly an honest man.

Then they had to decide for themselves whether it had been luck or money that had made the miller a wealthy man!

Developing Comprehension Skills

1. Why did the two wealthy friends decide to give a poor man money?

2. Did the miller lose the four hundred dollars through bad luck or carelessness? Explain your answer.

3. Why was the miller afraid to tell the truth about what happened to the money? Why do you think he told anyway?

4. How does the miller's wife explain the miller's misfortune?

5. In your opinion, did the story prove that luck or money is the key to success? Or, did it suggest that something else brings success? Explain your answer.

Reading Literature: Short Stories

1. **Appreciating Folk Tales.** "The Force of Luck" is an old folk tale from Latin America. A **folk tale** is a story that is passed on in spoken form from generation to generation. Therefore, its author is usually unknown. Why do you think most people would find this story an appealing one to tell again and again?

2. **Identifying Elements of Folk Tales.** Folk tales often have a number of things in common. The main character is often a poor but honest person struggling to survive. Another common element in folk tales is a wealthy or powerful stranger who changes the main character's life. Something quite unexpected, or miraculous, nearly always occurs in a folk tale. This unexpected event usually brings joy to a long suffering main character. Finally, there is often a lesson to be learned from a folk tale. What details and events in "The Force of Luck" fit these characteristics of a folk tale?

3. **Evaluating a Character.** Characters in folk tales usually have only one or two character

traits. The reader quickly associates the character with the most obvious trait. In "The Force of Luck," the miller is honest. What trait do you associate with the miller's wife? What traits do you associate with the jeweler and his wife? Why do you think characters in folk tales have only one or two character traits?

4. **Identifying Theme.** What point do you think this story makes about what is necessary for success? Do you agree?

Developing Vocabulary Skills

Using Synonyms and Antonyms. It is often possible to determine the meaning of an unknown word by finding synonyms or antonyms. As you know, **synonyms** are words that are very close in meaning. **Antonyms** are words that are nearly opposite in meaning.

Read these passages, which use words drawn from stories in this chapter. Find the synonym or antonym to determine the meaning of the underlined word. On your paper, write the synonym or antonym and the meaning of the underlined word.

1. Jeanie searched in her anthology for the title. In the story collection, she found the poem Miss Lowy had read.

2. Billy reluctantly left his friends, but he was soon willingly following his older sister.

3. The two men hoped to turn the miller into a prosperous man, one who was successful and wealthy.

4. The humble miller lived modestly. He did not dress well nor live extravagantly.

5. The miller had never squandered his money. In fact, he had never wasted anything.

6. He thought the neighbor was jesting, but her proposal was quite serious.

Developing Writing Skills

1. **Writing an Explanation.** The characters in this folktale are not given names. Why do you think the storyteller chose not to name the characters? Write one paragraph explaining your opinion.

2. **Writing a Definition.** Nearly everyone wants to be successful in life. Yet, each person defines success in a very personal way. Some may link success with money. Others may link success with happiness. Still others might link success with the achievement of personal goals. Write one paragraph in which you explain what it will take for you to achieve success in life.

Pre-Writing. List those things that would make you feel successful. You may wish to include personal accomplishments, activities, family situations, and relationships. Indicate the order of their importance to you by placing a number beside each one.

Writing. Begin your paragraph with a topic sentence giving your general definition of success. Then, discuss the things that you feel are part of your personal idea of success. You may wish to present your ideas in the order of their importance to you. This is one effective way of organizing. For example, your ideas might begin with the most important element and then tell what other elements are also important to you.

Revising. Did you begin your paragraph with a topic sentence stating your general definition of success? Did you discuss the items necessary for your success in order of their importance to you? Does your definition include all things necessary to your personal success? When you are satisfied with the content, proofread for mistakes in grammar, capitalization, punctuation, and spelling. Then make a clean, final copy.

Developing Skills in Speaking and Listening

Telling a Tale. Prepare a folk tale to present before a group.

First, locate a book of folk tales in your library. You can find such a collection by looking up *Folk tales* in the subject cards of the card catalog. Select a tale that interests you.

Become familiar with the folk tale by reading the story several times. Take a few notes on the main events in the story. Then practice telling the story in your own words. Refer to your notes if you wish as you practice telling the story.

Try to be relaxed as you speak. Tell your story just as you would tell a joke or a personal experience to a friend. Plan where to pause. Decide where a change in the pitch or volume of your voice might be interesting.

When you feel you are ready, tell your story to a group of classmates. Remember to use the gestures you planned. Also, try to look into the eyes of your listeners as you tell the story. Above all, let your listeners know that you are enjoying the story.

When you are listening to others deliver their folk tales, consider these questions:

Is the storyteller familiar with the story he or she is telling?

Does this storyteller hold the audience's attention?

Does the storyteller use gestures and changes in voice to add meaning and emphasis to the story?

The Confession

ANTON CHEKHOV

This story is the public confession of a young man arrested for thievery. As you read, see if you think Gregory Kuzmich is to blame for his situation.

It was a cold clear day. I felt as elated as a cab driver who has been given a gold coin by mistake. I wanted to laugh, to cry, to pray. I was in seventh heaven: I had just been made a cashier! But I was rejoicing not because I now could get my hands on something—I was not a thief, and would have destroyed anyone who had told me that in time I should be one—I was rejoicing over the promotion and the slight increase in salary, nothing more.

Also I was happy for another reason: on becoming a cashier I suddenly felt as if I were wearing rose-colored glasses. All at once people appeared to have changed. My word of honor! Everyone seemed to have improved! The ugly became beautiful, the wicked, good; the proud became humble, the miserly, generous. It was as if my eyes had been opened, and I beheld all man's wonderful, until now unsuspected qualities. "Strange," I said to myself, "either something has happened to them, or I have been stupid not to have noticed these qualities before. How charming everyone is!"

On the day of my promotion, even Z. N. Kazusov changed. He was a member of the board of directors, a haughty, proud man who always ignored the small fry. He approached me and—what had happened to him?—smiling affectionately, he clapped me on the back.

"You're too young to be so proud, my boy. It's unforgivable!" he said. "Why don't you ever drop in on us? It's shameful of you not to visit. The young people generally gather at our house, and it's always festive there. My daughters are forever asking me: 'Why don't you invite Gregory Kuzmich, Papa? He's so nice!' But is it possible to get him to come? Well, in any case, I'll try, I told them. I'll ask him. Now, don't give yourself airs, my boy, do come."

Amazing! What had happened to Mr. Kazusov? Had he gone out of his mind? He had always been a regular ogre, and now look at him!

On returning home that same day I was astounded: Mama served not the usual two courses at dinner, but four! For tea in the evening there was jam and white bread. The following day, again four courses, again jam; and when guests dropped in, we drank chocolate. The third day it was the same.

Self-Portrait, 1913, OSKAR KOKOSCHKA. Oil on canvas, 32⅛″ × 19½″. The Museum of Modern Art, New York. Purchase.

"Mama," I said, "what's the matter with you? Why this burst of generosity? You know, my salary wasn't doubled. The increase was trifling."

Mama looked at me in surprise. "Humph! What do you expect to do with money—save it?"

God only knows what got into them. Papa ordered a fur coat, bought a new cap, took a relaxing vacation, and began to eat grapes—in winter!

Within a few days I received a letter from my brother. This brother could not endure me. We had parted over a difference of opinion: he considered me a selfish parasite, incapable of self-sacrifice, and for this he despised me. In his letter he now wrote: "Dear brother, I love you, and you cannot imagine what hellish torture our quarrel has caused me. Let us make it up. Let us each extend a hand to the other, and may peace triumph! I beg you! Awaiting your reply, I embrace you and remain your most loving and affectionate brother, Yevlampy." Oh, my dear brother! I answered him saying that I embraced him and rejoiced. Within a week I received a telegram: "Thanks. Happy. Send hundred rubles. Most urgent. Embrace you. Yevlampy." I sent the hundred rubles.

Even she changed. She did not love me. Once when I had made so bold as to hint that I admired her, she laughed in my face. On meeting me a week after my promotion, however, she dimpled, smiled, and looked flustered. "What's happened to you?" she asked, gazing at me. "You've grown so handsome. When did you manage to do that?" And then, "Let's dance. . . ."

Sweetheart! Within a month she had given me a mother-in-law. I had become that handsome! When money was needed for the wedding I took three hundred rubles out of the cash box. Why not take it, when you know you are going to put it back as soon as you receive your raise? At the same time I took out a hundred rubles for Kazusov. He had asked for a loan and it was impossible to refuse him; he was a big wheel in the office and could have anyone fired at a moment's notice.

A week before the arrest it was suggested that I give a party. What the devil, let them guzzle and gorge, if that's what they want! I did not count the guests that evening, but I recall that all eight of my rooms were swarming with people, young and old. There were those before whom even Kazusov had to show humility.

His daughters—the oldest being my treasure—were in dazzling attire. The flowers alone with which they covered themselves cost me over a thousand rubles. It was very festive, with glittering chandeliers, deafening music, and plenty of champagne. There were long speeches and short toasts; one journalist presented me with a poem, another with a song. "We in Russia do not know how to appreciate such men as Gregory Kuzmich," cried Kazusov. "It's a shame! Russia is to be pitied!"

All those who were shouting, applauding and kissing me, were whispering behind my back, thumbing their noses at me. I saw their smiles and heard their sighs. "He stole it, the crook!" they whispered, with evil grins. But their sighing and smirking did not prevent them from eating, drinking, and enjoying themselves. Wolves never ate as they did.

My wife, flashing gold and diamonds, came up to me and whispered: "They are saying that you stole the money. If it's true, I warn you, I cannot go on living with a thief. I'll leave!" And she smoothed down her five-thousand ruble gown. The devil take them all! That very evening Kazusov had five thousand from me. Yevlampy took an equal amount. "If what they are whispering about you is true," said my ethical brother, as he pocketed the money, "watch out! I will not be brother to a thief!"

After the party I drove them all to the country in a sleigh. We finished up at six in the morning. Exhausted, they lay back in the sleigh, and, as they started off for home, cried out in farewell: "Inspection tomorrow! Thanks."

My dear ladies and gentlemen, I got caught; or, to state it more fully: yesterday I was respected and honored on all sides. Today I am a scoundrel and a thief. . . . Cry out, now, accuse me, spread the news, judge and wonder. Banish me, write editorials and throw stones, only, please—not everyone, not everyone!

Developing Comprehension Skills

1. After his promotion to cashier, Gregory Kuzmich was treated differently by other people. List three or more of these people and describe how each of them changed his or her attitude toward him.

2. Gregory's troubles began when he tried to please others. Why do you think he was so willing to take risks for them?

3. How was Gregory able to convince himself that taking money from the cash box was justified?

4. Gregory said, "Yesterday I was respected and honored. Today I am a scoundrel." Do you think he was ever really respected and honored? Explain your answer.

5. In your opinion, was Gregory the only guilty person in this story? Were any others even more guilty than he was? Support your answer with "evidence" from the story.

6. Do you feel sorry for Gregory, or do you think he was foolish? Why?

Reading Literature: Short Stories

1. **Understanding Theme.** The writer of "The Confession" appears to be concerned about certain characteristics of human nature. What point do you think he is trying to make about the affection and loyalty of certain people? In your opinion, what is the theme of this story?

2. **Appreciating Form.** "The Confession" has an unusual form for a short story. The story begins with an admission by Gregory that he was guilty of theft. In most short stories, such information would be found in the resolution, the end of the story. Why did the writer choose to place this key information at the beginning of the story? How did this knowledge affect your expectations of what you were about to read? Did it also affect your opinion of Gregory as you read the story? Explain your answers.

3. **Analyzing Point of View.** The main character, Gregory Kuzmich, is the narrator of this story. We see the events of the story through his eyes. We know about the other characters only what Gregory tells us about them. How does the first-person point of view affect the reader's opinions of Gregory and the other characters? Would other characters tell the same story about specific incidents? For example, would Gregory's sweetheart have described their courtship in the same way he did? How might her explanation have differed?

4. **Recognizing Irony.** Irony is contrast between what is thought to be true and what is actually true. This situation can surprise the reader and heighten interest. In "The Confession," the narrator tells how wonderful the people were when he gave them money and gifts. The narrator seems convinced of their sincerity. What is ironic about this situation? What can the reader see that the narrator cannot?

Developing Vocabulary Skills

Recognizing Cause and Effect Clues. Events are often related by cause and effect. In other words, the first event causes the second event. You can often infer the meaning of an unfamiliar word if you understand that it refers to either the cause or the result of another situation. Read the sentence on the following page.

Because he had studied so hard, Josh was *optimistic* that he would pass the test.

From this sentence, you can infer that Josh's studying caused him to feel hopeful that he would do well. Therefore, *optimistic* must mean "hopeful," or "expecting the best outcome." The key word that tells you that there is a cause and effect clue is *because*. Other key words and phrases are *since, therefore, in order that, so that, for this reason, that is why, as a result,* and *consequently*.

The following sentences or groups of sentences use words drawn from the stories in this chapter. Identify the cause and effect relationship in each example. From that relationship, try to infer the meaning of each underlined word. Write the word and its meaning on your paper.

1. The little girl was very bored with the story. Consequently, she looked for a <u>diversion</u>.

2. The museum curators stored the ancient relics and paintings very carefully so that their beauty would be <u>preserved</u>.

3. In order to maintain the car's <u>momentum</u>, the driver had to keep a steady foot on the accelerator.

4. Because the jungle underbrush was so thick, the hunter found it <u>futile</u> to make any kind of trail.

5. Gregory had just been made a cashier and received a raise. As a result, he was <u>elated</u>.

6. The miller's wife did her best to soothe the anguished miller, and soon he felt <u>consoled</u>.

Developing Writing Skills

1. **Comparing and Contrasting Theme.** In three of the four stories in this section, "Beauty Is Truth," "The Force of Luck," and "The Confession," the main character learns something about the value of honesty. Compare and contrast what these characters learned. Which character do you think benefited most from the lesson?

2. **Building to the Climax of a Story.** During the rising action of a story, excitement builds as the main character struggles with a problem. The climax, or turning point, of a short story occurs when the main character takes an action that ends the conflict. It may also be marked by discovery or a decision the character makes about the problem. This is usually the most exciting part of the story.

Read the following introduction to a short story. Using your imagination, continue this story to the climax, or turning point.

Larry winced as the stinging November wind slapped at his face. He barely noticed the first snowflakes of the season being driven to the ground as he made his way up the fourteen steps to the front entrance of the high school.

Only one thought occupied Larry's mind this morning. Unless he passed the math test today, there would be no basketball game for him this weekend. This test was going to be the toughest one yet in a class that had been difficult all year. Sure, he had studied. He studied more for this class than any other. Yet, he was barely maintaining a passing grade. If he didn't pass this test, his math grade might make him ineligible for the most important game of the season.

Pre-Writing. You have just read the introduction to a short story. The setting and main character have been introduced. You have also been given an idea of the problem confronting the main character. Think about the many ways this story could develop from this point. What sort of conflict might Larry deal with? Could he be faced with a decision of whether to remain honest or to find another way to pass the test?

List the events that will occur in the rising action of the story. Remember, suspense makes a story interesting. Decide upon the turning point, or climax of your story. Save your work for later use in this chapter.

Writing. Continue this story through the climax. Make sure that the action Larry takes is in keeping with what you know about him from the introduction. As you write, try to use dialogue to advance the action of the story.

Revising. Read your story. Did you keep the same point of view throughout? Are your characters and dialogue realistic? Check to see that the incidents you create in the rising action are consistent with what you learned in the introduction. Does the action taken by the main character at the climax of the story seem natural for that character?

After completing this assignment, save it for use in a later lesson.

Developing Skills in Critical Thinking

Distinguishing Between Objective and Subjective Language. Gregory Kuzmich's confession is a story of his misfortune. He does not tell the story simply to record the events. He tells it to get the reader's sympathy. In doing so Gregory uses words and phrases that show his feelings about other people. For example, Gregory describes Kazusov as "a haughty, proud man who always ignored the small fry." The words *haughty*, *proud*, and *small fry* are examples of subjective language. **Subjective language** gives a personal opinion. **Objective language** is fair and impersonal. It simply conveys information without stating personal opinion.

Can you find other examples of Gregory's use of subjective language? Explain why Gregory uses specific subjective words. Did Gregory's use of subjective language make you sympathetic to his situation? Why or why not?

Mood

What feeling do you get when you read a story? The emotion you experience is called the *mood*. The moods in the following stories range from humorous to dreamlike. See how the writers created the moods with their careful choice of words.

Foghorns, 1929, ARTHUR DOVE. Colorado Springs Fine Arts Center Collection. Anonymous Gift.

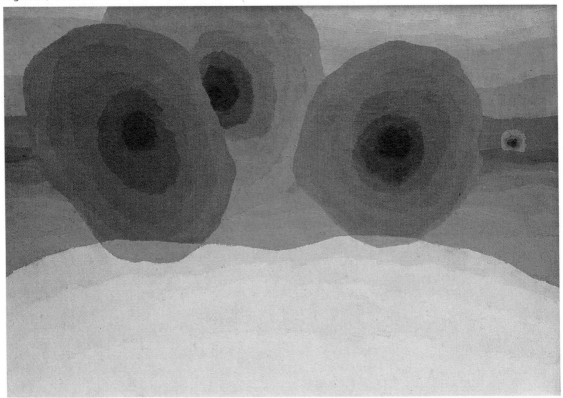

The Ransom of Red Chief

O. HENRY

The kidnappers in this story aren't quite what you might expect them to be. What surprise awaits them and the reader as they carry out their plan?

It looked like a good thing: but wait till I tell you. We were down South, in Alabama—Bill Driscoll and myself—when this kidnapping idea struck us. It was, as Bill afterward expressed it, "during a moment of temporary mental apparition." But we didn't find that out till later.

There was a town down there, as flat as a flannel-cake, and called Summit, of course. It contained inhabitants of as self-satisfied a class of peasantry as ever clustered around a Maypole.

Bill and me had a joint capital of about six hundred dollars, and we needed just two thousand dollars more to pull off a fraudulent town-lot scheme in Western Illinois with. We talked it over on the front steps of the Hotel. Philoprogenitiveness, says we, is strong in semi-rural communities. Therefore, and for other reasons, a kidnapping project ought to do better there than in the radius of newspapers that send reporters out in plain clothes to stir up talk about such things. We knew that Summit couldn't get after us with anything stronger than constables, some lackadaisical blood-hounds, and a diatribe or two in the *Weekly Farmers' Budget*. So, it looked good.

We selected for our victim the only child of a prominent citizen named Ebenezer Dorset. The father was respectable and tight, a mortgage fancier and a stern, upright collection-plate passer and forecloser. The kid was a boy of ten, with bas-relief freckles, and hair the color of the cover of the magazine you buy at the newsstand when you want to catch a train. Bill and me figured that Ebenezer would melt down for a ransom of two thousand dollars to a cent. But wait till I tell you.

About two miles from Summit was a little mountain, covered with a dense cedar brake. On the rear elevation of this mountain was a cave. There we stored provisions.

One evening after sundown, we drove in a buggy past old Dorset's house. The kid was in the street, throwing rocks at a kitten on the opposite fence.

"Hey, little boy!" says Bill, "Would you like to have a bag of candy and a nice ride?"

The boy catches Bill neatly in the eye with a piece of brick.

"That will cost the old man an extra five hundred dollars," says Bill, climbing over the wheel.

That boy put up a fight like a welterweight cinnamon bear. At last, we got him down in the bottom of the buggy and drove away. We took him up to the cave, and I hitched the horse in the cedar brake. After dark I drove the buggy to the little village three miles away, where we had hired it, and walked back to the mountain.

Bill was pasting court-plaster over the scratches and bruises on his features. There was a fire burning behind the big rock at the entrance of the cave, and the boy was watching a pot of boiling coffee, with two buzzard tail-feathers stuck in his red hair. He points a stick at me when I come up, and says: "Ha! Cursed paleface, do you dare to enter the camp of Red Chief, the terror of the plains?"

"He's all right now," says Bill, rolling up his trousers and examining some bruises on his shins. "We're playing Indian. We're making Buffalo Bill's show look like magic-lantern views of Palestine in the town hall. I'm Old Hank, the Trapper, Red Chief's captive, and I'm to be scalped at daybreak. By Geronimo! that kid can kick hard."

Yes, sir, that boy seemed to be having the time of his life. The fun of camping out in a cave had made him forget that he was a captive himself. He immediately christened me Snake-eye, the Spy, and announced that, when his mighty band of braves returned from the warpath, I was to be broiled at the stake at sunrise.

Then we had supper. He filled his mouth full of bacon and bread and gravy and began to talk. He made a during-dinner speech something like this: "I like this fine. I never camped out before; but I had a pet 'possum once, and I was nine last birthday. I hate to go to school. Rats ate up sixteen of Jimmy Talbot's aunt's speckled hen's eggs. Are there any real Indians in these woods? I want some more gravy. Does the trees moving make the wind blow? We had five puppies. What makes your nose so red, Hank? My father has lots of money. Are the stars hot? I whipped Ed Walker twice, Saturday. I don't like girls. You dassent catch toads unless with a string. Do oxen make any noise? Why are oranges round? Have you got beds to sleep on in this cave? Amos Murray has got six toes. A parrot can talk, but a monkey or a fish can't. How many does it take to make twelve?"

Every few minutes he would remember that he was a pesky redskin, and pick up his stick rifle and tiptoe to the mouth of the cave to look for the scouts of the hated paleface. Now and then he would let out a war-whoop that made Old Hank the Trapper shiver. That boy had Bill terrorized from the start.

"Red Chief," says I to the kid, "would you like to go home?"

"Aw, what for?" says he. "I don't have any fun at home. I hate to go to school. I like to camp out. You won't take me back home again, Snake-eye, will you?"

"Not right away," says I. "We'll stay here in the cave awhile."

"All right!" says he. "That'll be fine. I never had such fun in all my life."

We went to bed about eleven o'clock. We spread down some wide blankets and quilts and put Red Chief between us. We weren't afraid he'd run away. He kept us awake for three hours, jumping up and reaching for his rifle and screeching: "Hist! pard," in mine and Bill's ears, as the fancied crackle of a twig or the rustle of a leaf revealed to his young imagination the stealthy approach of the outlaw band. At last, I fell into a troubled sleep, and dreamed that I had been kidnapped and chained to a tree by a ferocious pirate with red hair.

Just at daybreak, I was awakened by a series of awful screams from Bill. They weren't yells, or howls, or shouts, or whoops, or yawps, such as you'd expect from a manly set of vocal organs. They were simply indecent, terrifying, humiliating screams, such as women emit when they see ghosts or caterpillars. It's an awful thing to hear a strong, desperate, fat man scream uncontrollably in a cave at daybreak.

I jumped up to see what the matter was. Red Chief was sitting on Bill's chest, with one hand twined in Bill's hair. In the other he had the sharp case-knife we used for slicing bacon. He was industriously and realistically trying to take Bill's scalp, according to the sentence that had been pronounced upon him the evening before.

I got the knife away from the kid and made him lie down again. But, from that moment, Bill's spirit was broken. He laid down on his side of the bed, but he never closed an eye again in sleep as long as that boy was with us. I dozed off for a while, but along toward sun-up I remembered that Red Chief had said I was to be burned at the stake at the rising of the sun. I wasn't nervous or afraid; but I sat up and lit my pipe and leaned against a rock.

"What you getting up so soon for, Sam?" asked Bill.

"Me?" says I. "Oh, I got a kind of pain in my shoulder. I thought sitting up would rest it."

"You're a liar!" says Bill. "You're afraid. You was to be burned at sunrise, and you was afraid he'd do it. And he would, too, if he could find a match. Ain't it awful, Sam? Do you think anybody will pay out money to get a little imp like that back home?"

"Sure," said I. "A rowdy kid like that is just the kind that parents dote on. Now, you and the Chief get up and cook breakfast, while I go up on the top of this mountain and reconnoitre."

I went up on the peak of the little mountain and ran my eye over the vicinity. Over towards Summit I expected to see the sturdy folks of the village armed with scythes and pitchforks beating the countryside for the dastardly kidnappers. What I actually saw was a peaceful landscape dotted with one man ploughing with a mule. Nobody was dragging the creek. No couriers dashed hither and yon, bringing tidings of no news to the distracted parents. There was a sylvan attitude of somnolent sleepiness pervading that section of the external outward surface of Alabama that lay exposed to my view. "Perhaps," says I to myself, "it has not yet been discovered that the wolves have borne away the tender lambkin from the fold. Heaven help the wolves!" says I, and I went down the mountain to breakfast.

When I got to the cave I found Bill backed up against the side of it, breathing hard, and the boy threatening to smash him with a rock half as big as a coconut.

"He put a red-hot boiled potato down my back," explained Bill, "and then mashed it with his foot; and I boxed his ears. Have you got a gun about you, Sam?"

I took the rock away from the boy and kind of patched up the argument. "I'll fix you," says the kid to Bill. "No man ever yet struck the Red Chief but he got paid for it. You better beware!"

After breakfast the kid takes a piece of leather with strings wrapped around it out of his pocket and goes outside the cave unwinding it.

"What's he up to now?" says Bill, anxiously. "You don't think he'll run away, do you, Sam?"

"No fear of it," says I. "He don't seem to be much of a home body. But we've got to fix up some plan about the ransom. There don't seem to be much excitement around Summit on account of his disappearance. Maybe they haven't realized yet that he's gone. His folks may think he's spending the night with Aunt Jane or one of the neighbors. Anyhow, he'll be missed today. Tonight we must get a message to his father demanding the two thousand dollars for his return."

Just then we heard a kind of war-whoop, such as David might have emitted when he knocked out the champion Goliath. It was a sling that Red Chief had pulled out of his pocket, and he was whirling it around his head.

I dodged, and heard a heavy thud and a kind of sigh from Bill, like a horse gives out when you take his saddle off. A rock the size of an egg had caught Bill just behind his left ear. He loosened himself all over and fell in the fire across the frying pan of hot water for washing the dishes. I dragged him out and poured cold water on his head for half an hour.

By and by, Bill sits up and feels behind his ear and says: "Sam, do you know who my favorite Biblical character is?"

"Take it easy," says I. "You'll come to your senses presently."

"King Herod," says he. "You won't go away and leave me alone, will you, Sam?"

I went out and caught that boy and shook him until his freckles rattled.

"If you don't behave," says I, "I'll take you straight home. Now, are you going to be good, or not?"

"I was only funning," says he, sullenly. "I didn't mean to hurt Old Hank. But what did he hit me for? I'll behave, Snake-eye, if you won't send me home, and if you'll let me play the Black Scout today."

"I don't know the game," says I. "That's for you and Mr. Bill to decide. He's your

playmate for the day. I'm going away for a while, on business. Now, you come in and make friends with him and say you are sorry for hurting him, or home you go, at once."

I made him and Bill shake hands, and then I took Bill aside and told him I was going to Poplar Grove, a little village three miles from the cave, and find out what I could about how the kidnapping had been regarded in Summit. Also, I thought it best to send a letter to old man Dorset that day, demanding the ransom and dictating how it should be paid.

"You know, Sam," says Bill, "I've stood by you without batting an eye in earthquakes, fire, and flood—in poker games, dynamite outrages, police raids, train robberies, and cyclones. I never lost my nerve yet till we kidnapped that two-legged sky-rocket of a kid. He's got me going. You won't leave me alone long with him, will you, Sam?"

"I'll be back some time this afternoon," says I. "You must keep the boy amused and quiet till I return. And now we'll write the letter to old Dorset."

Bill and I got paper and pencil and worked on the letter while Red Chief, with a blanket wrapped around him, strutted up and down, guarding the mouth of the cave. Bill begged me tearfully to make the ransom fifteen hundred dollars instead of two thousand. "I ain't attempting," says he, "to decry the celebrated moral aspect of parental affection, but we're dealing with humans, and it ain't human for anybody to give up two thousand dollars for that forty-pound chunk of freckled wildcat. I'm willing to take a chance at fifteen hundred dollars. You can charge the difference up to me."

So, to relieve Bill, I agreed, and we cooperated a letter that ran this way:

Ebenezer Dorset, Esq.:

We have your boy concealed in a place far from Summit. It is useless for you or the most skillful detectives to attempt to find him. Absolutely, the only terms on which you can have him restored to you are these: We demand fifteen hundred dollars in large bills for his return; the money to be left at midnight tonight at the same spot and in the same box as your reply—as hereinafter described. If you agree to these terms, send your answer in writing by a solitary messenger tonight at half-past eight o'clock. After crossing Owl Creek on the road to Poplar Grove, there are three large trees about a hundred yards apart, close to the fence of the wheat field on the right-hand side. At the bottom of the fence-post, opposite the third tree, will be found a small pasteboard box.

The messenger will place the answer in this box and return immediately to Summit.

If you attempt any treachery or fail to comply with our demand as stated, you will never see your boy again.

If you pay the money as demanded, he will be returned to you safe and well within three hours. These terms are final, and if you do not agree to them no further communication will be attempted.

TWO DESPERATE MEN

I addressed this letter to Dorset, and put it in my pocket. As I was about to start, the kid comes up to me and says:

"Aw, Snake-eye, you said I could play the Black Scout while you was gone."

"Play it, of course," says I. "Mr Bill will play with you. What kind of a game is it?"

"I'm the Black Scout," says Red Chief, "and I have to ride to the stockade to warn the settlers that the Indians are coming. I'm tired of playing Indian myself. I want to be the Black Scout."

"All right," says I. "It sounds harmless to me. I guess Mr. Bill will help you foil the pesky savages."

"What am I to do?" asks Bill, looking at the kid suspiciously.

"You are the hoss," says Black Scout. "Get down on your hands and knees. How can I ride to the stockade without a hoss?"

"You'd better keep him interested," said I, "till we get the scheme going. Just loosen up a little."

Bill gets down on his all fours, and a look comes in his eye like a rabbit's when you catch it in a trap.

"How far is it to the stockade, kid?" he asks, in a husky manner of voice.

"Ninety miles," says the Black Scout. "And you have to hurry yourself to get there on time. Whoa, now!"

The Black Scout jumps on Bill's back and digs his heels in his side.

"For Heaven's sake," says Bill, "hurry back, Sam, as soon as you can. I wish we hadn't made the ransom more than a thousand. Say, you quit kicking me or I'll get up and warm you good."

I walked over to Poplar Grove and sat around the post office and store, talking with the chaw-bacons that came in to trade. One whiskerando says that he hears Summit is all upset on account of Elder Ebenezer Dorset's boy having been lost or stolen. That was all I wanted to know. I bought some smoking tobacco, referred casually to the price of black-eyed peas, posted my letter, and came away. The postmaster said the mail-carrier would come by in an hour to take the mail to Summit.

When I got back to the cave, Bill and the boy were not to be found. I explored the vicinity of the cave, and risked a yodel or two, but there was no response.

So I lighted my pipe and sat down on a mossy bank to await developments.

In about half an hour I heard the bushes rustle, and Bill wobbled out into the little glade in front of the cave. Behind him was the kid, stepping softly like a scout, with a broad grin on his face. Bill stopped, took off his hat, and wiped his face with a red handkerchief. The kid stopped about eight feet behind him.

"Sam," says Bill, "I suppose you'll think I'm a renegade, but I couldn't help it. I'm a grown person with masculine habits of self-defense. There is a time when all systems of egotism and predominance fail. The boy is gone. I sent him home. All is off. There was martyrs in old times," goes on Bill, "that suffered death rather than give up the particular graft they enjoyed. None of 'em ever was put through such supernatural tortures as I have been. I tried to be faithful to our plan, but there came a limit."

"What's the trouble, Bill?" I asks him.

"I was rode," says Bill, "the ninety miles to the stockade, not barring an inch. Then, when the settlers were rescued, I was given oats. Sand ain't a palatable substitute. And then, for an hour I had to try to explain to him why there was nothin' in holes, how a road can run both ways, and what makes the grass green. I tell you, Sam, a human can only stand so much. I takes him by the neck of his clothes and drags him down the mountain. On the way he kicks my legs black and blue from the knees down; and I've got to have two or three bites on my thumb and hand cauterized.

"But he's gone"—continues Bill—"gone home. I showed him the road to Summit and kicked him about eight feet nearer there at one kick. I'm sorry we lose the ransom, but it was either that or Bill Driscoll to the madhouse."

Bill is puffing and blowing, but there is a look of peace and growing content on his rose-pink features.

"Bill," says I, "there isn't any heart disease in your family, is there?"

"No," says Bill, "nothing chronic except malaria and accidents. Why?"

"Then you might turn around," says I, "and have a look behind you."

Bill turns and sees the boy, and loses his complexion and sits down plump on the ground and begins to pluck aimlessly at grass and little sticks. For an hour I was afraid for his mind. Then I told him that my scheme was to put the whole job through immediately and that we would get the ransom and be off with it by midnight if old Dorset fell in with our proposition. So Bill braced up enough to give the kid a weak sort of a smile and a promise to play the Russian in a Japanese war with him as soon as he felt a little better.

I had a scheme for collecting that ransom without danger of being caught by counterplots that ought to commend itself to professional kidnappers. The tree under which the answer was to be left—and the money later on—was close to the road fence with big, bare fields on all sides. If a gang of constables should be watching for anyone to come for the note, they could see him a long way off crossing the fields or in the road. But no, sirree! At half-past eight I was up in that tree as well hidden as a tree toad, waiting for the messenger to arrive.

Exactly on time, a half-grown boy rides up the road on a bicycle, locates the pasteboard box at the foot of the fencepost, slips a folded piece of paper into it, and pedals away again back toward Summit.

I waited an hour and then concluded the thing was square. I slid down the tree, got the note, slipped along the fence till I struck the woods, and was back at the cave in another half an hour. I opened the note, got near the lantern, and read it to Bill. It was written with a pen in a crabbed hand, and the sum and substance of it was this:

TWO DESPERATE MEN

Gentlemen:

I received your letter today by post, in regard to the ransom you ask for the return of my son. I think you are a little high in your demands, and I hereby make you a counter-proposition, which I am inclined to believe you will accept. You bring Johnny home and pay me two hundred and fifty dollars in cash, and I agree to take him off your hands. You had better come at night, for the neighbors believe he is lost, and I couldn't be responsible for what they would do to anybody they saw bringing him back.

Very respectfully,
Ebenezer Dorset

"Great Pirates of Penzance," says I; "of all the impudent—"

But I glanced at Bill, and hesitated. He had the most appealing look in his eyes I ever saw on the face of a dumb or talking brute.

"Sam," says he, "what's two hundred and fifty dollars, after all? We've got the money. One more night of this kid will send me to an asylum. Besides being a thorough gentleman, I think Mr. Dorset is a spendthrift for making us such a liberal offer. You ain't going to let the chance go, are you?"

"Tell you the truth, Bill," says I, "this little lamb has somewhat got on my nerves too. We'll take him home, pay the ransom, and make our getaway."

We took him home that night. We got him to go by telling him that his father had bought a silver-mounted rifle and a pair of moccasins for him, and we were to hunt bears the next day.

It was just twelve o'clock when we knocked at Ebenezer's front door. Just at the moment when I should have been abstracting the fifteen hundred dollars from the box under the tree, according to the original proposition, Bill was counting out two hundred and fifty dollars into Dorset's hand.

When the kid found out we were going to leave him at home he started up a howl like a calliope and fastened himself as tight as a leech to Bill's leg. His father peeled him away gradually, like a porous plaster.

"How long can you hold him?" asks Bill.

"I'm not as strong as I used to be," says old Dorset. "But I think I can promise you ten minutes."

"Enough," says Bill. "In ten minutes I shall cross the Central, Southern, and Middle Western States, and be legging it trippingly for the Canadian border."

And, as dark as it was, and as fat as Bill was, and as good a runner as I am, he was a good mile and a half out of Summit before I could catch up with him.

Developing Comprehension Skills

1. Why did Bill and Sam decide to kidnap Ebenezer Dorset's son?

2. Why were Bill and Sam shocked by Ebenezer Dorset's response to the ransom demand?

3. What did Dorset's letter tell you about his relationship with his son?

4. In your opinion, which parts of the story are most humorous? Explain why you chose those parts.

5. Do you think events like those described in this story could happen today? Explain why or why not.

Reading Literature: Short Stories

1. **Identifying Mood.** The feeling a story creates within a reader is called the **mood**. The mood may be serious, light, humorous, or sorrowful, for example. What is the mood of "The Ransom of Red Chief"?

2. **Appreciating Surprise Endings.** O. Henry was known for his use of the unexpected surprise ending. A **surprise ending** is an unexpected turn at the end of a story. The surprise ending in "The Ransom of Red Chief" adds to the enjoyment of the story. How would you expect a kidnap story to end? How does this story end? Does the surprise

ending add humor to this story? Explain your answer.

3. **Understanding Indirect Description.** A writer often describes a character directly. The writer does this by telling the reader how a character looks, acts, and feels. A reader can also learn much about a character through indirect description. For example, much is revealed about a character through his or her speech. In this story, Sam's style of speaking is marked by at least two distinct characteristics:

    a. exaggeration

    b. the use and misuse of big words.

Find examples of each of these characteristics of Sam's speech. What other things do you notice about the way Sam talks? What do each of these tell you about Sam?

4. **Recognizing Allusions.** A writer's reference to a well-known work of literature, a famous person, or a historical event is an **allusion**. Allusions often help to emphasize ideas, events, or characters. The narrator of this story alludes to the Biblical story of David and Goliath when Red Chief uses his slingshot. According to the Bible, David used his slingshot to conquer the giant Goliath. How does this allusion add to the humor of the situation?

Bill makes another allusion when he says that his favorite Biblical character is King Herod. Herod was a brutal king known for killing children. What does this allusion tell you about Bill's attitude toward Red Chief?

5. **Analyzing Conflict and Climax.** The plot of this story involves kidnappers who take a small boy but soon wish to be rid of him.

There is more than one conflict in this story. The most obvious conflict is between the kidnappers and Red Chief. Another conflict exists between the kidnappers and Dorset. Before a story ends, conflicts usually reach a high point, or climax, and are then resolved. What is the high point or climax of each of these conflicts? How are the conflicts resolved in the story?

Developing Vocabulary Skills

Using the Dictionary for the Exact Meaning. Read the following sentences. Each contains a word drawn from one of the stories in this chapter. Use context clues to define each underlined word. Look for help from *definition and restatement clues, synonym or antonym clues, example clues, comparison and contrast clues,* or *cause and effect clues.* Then check the exact meaning in the dictionary.

1. Rainsford took a moment to <u>reconnoitre</u>. He knew he must examine the situation carefully if he were to make useful plans.

2. Sam <u>cauterized</u> the bites on his thumb. He burned them with a hot needle to prevent the spread of infection.

3. The kidnappers knew that only the <u>constables</u> would chase them. These local police would never be able to find them.

4. Sam thought the town would be in an uproar. Instead, it was drowsy and <u>somnolent</u>.

5. Billy's room was little more than an <u>alcove</u>. On the other hand, his friend's room was large and comfortable.

6. The events on the island were a part of sailor <u>lore</u>, as essential as knowing how to read the stars or raise a sail.

7. Jeanie's writing was quite <u>subtle</u>. It was not forced and obvious.

8. Rainsford's favorite <u>brier</u> was similar to a pipe belonging to the captain of the ship.

Developing Writing Skills

1. **Creating Humor with Contrast.** The writer of "The Ransom of Red Chief" does not portray the two kidnappers as heartless, hardened criminals. This is one reason that the story is so humorous. In two paragraphs, explain how the characters of Bill and Sam contrast with the usual image of criminals. When you look for contrasts, you are looking for differences.

Pre-Writing. What sort of character traits would you normally expect in criminals? How would you expect them to act and talk? In your pre-writing notes, list specific words and phrases that would describe criminal qualities. For example, the words "cruel" and "crafty" could describe frightening and very intelligent criminals. How many more descriptive words or phrases can you think of? Now, find passages from the story that contrast with the words you have just listed.

Writing. Use your pre-writing notes to begin your rough draft. In your first paragraph, you will write about the usual image of criminals. In your second paragraph, you will discuss how Bill and Sam do not fit this usual image. Begin each paragraph with a topic sentence that states the main idea of the paragraph. In the remainder of the paragraph, support the topic sentence with details listed in your pre-writing notes.

Revising. Review your paragraphs. Did you include enough convincing evidence to show that Bill and Sam are not the usual sort of criminals? Is each point in the first paragraph matched with one in the second? If you feel more explanation is needed to point out the contrast, add it now.

2. **Using Specific Language To Create a Mood.** Think about a memorable personal experience. It may have been frightening or exciting. It may have been funny or sad. Perhaps it was unexpectedly dangerous. Relate the experience in one paragraph.

As you write, use words that help the reader feel what you felt at the time. If you were frightened, for example, you would use words such as *terrifying, horrible, dark, ghastly, screams*, and *deserted*. These words can help form a picture of fear in the reader's mind.

Developing Skills in Study and Research

Finding the Story Collection. Libraries often shelve their books of short stories in a special section. This section is called the Story Collection, and books in this section are marked SC. They are arranged alphabetically on the shelves by the author's last name.

See if your library has a special section for short story books. If the short stories are not located in a special section, they may be in the 800's with other literature books or on the fiction shelves, organized by the author's last name.

Use the card catalog to find out if your library has any books of short stories by O. Henry. Locate author cards in the card catalog by looking up O. Henry's name. Then write down the book titles and locate at least one.

The Old Man

DAPHNE du MAURIER

The old man demands strict obedience from his family. Read to discover the penalty a son must pay for disobeying his father.

Did I hear you asking about the Old Man? I thought so. You're a newcomer to the district, here on holiday. We get plenty these days, during the summer months. Somehow they always find their way eventually over the cliffs down to the beach, and then they pause and look from the sea back to the lake. Just as you did.

It's a lovely spot, isn't it? Quiet and remote. You can't wonder at the old man choosing to live here.

I don't remember when he first came. Nobody can. Many years ago, it must have been. He was here when I arrived, long before the war. Perhaps he came to escape from civilization, much as I did myself. Or maybe, where he lived before, the folks around made things too hot for him. It's hard to say. I had the feeling, from the very first, that he had done something, or something had been done to him, that gave him a grudge against the world. I remember the first time I set eyes on him I said to myself, "I bet that old fellow is quite a character."

Yes, he was living here beside the lake, with his missus. Funny sort of shack they had, exposed to all the weather, but they didn't seem to mind.

I had been warned about him by one of the fellows from the farm, who advised me, with a grin, to give the old man who lived down by the lake a wide berth. He didn't care for strangers. So I went carefully, and I didn't stay to pass the time of day. Nor would it have been any use if I had, not knowing a word of his lingo. The first time I saw him he was standing by the edge of the lake looking out to sea. I avoided the piece of planking over the stream, which meant passing close to him, and crossed to the other side of the lake by the beach instead. Then, with an awkward feeling that I was trespassing and had no business to be there, I bobbed down behind a clump of bristle, took out my spyglass, and had a peep.

He was a big fellow, broad and strong. He's aged, of course, lately. I'm speaking of several years back—but even now you can see what he must have been once. Such power and drive behind him, and that fine head, which he carried like a king. There's an idea in that, too. No, I'm not joking.

Who knows what royal blood he carries inside him, harking back to some remote ancestor? Also now and again, surging in him—not through his own fault—it gets the better of him and drives him fighting mad. I didn't think about that at the time. I just looked at him and ducked behind the shrubbery when I saw him turn. I wondered to myself what went on in his mind, whether he knew I was there, watching him.

If he should decide to come up the lake after me I should look pretty foolish. He must have thought better of it, though, or perhaps he did not care. He went on staring out to sea, watching the gulls and the incoming tide, and presently he ambled off his side of the lake, heading for the missus and home and maybe supper.

I didn't catch a glimpse of her that first day. She just wasn't around. Living as they do, close in by the left bank of the lake, with no proper track to the place, I hardly had the nerve to venture close and come upon her face to face. When I did see her, though, I was disappointed. She wasn't much to look at after all. What I mean is, she hadn't got anything like his character. A calm, mild-tempered creature, I judged her.

They had both come back from fishing when I saw them, and were making their way up from the beach to the lake. He was in front, of course. She tagged along behind. Neither of them took the slightest notice of me, and I was glad. The old man might have paused, and waited, and told her to get on back home, and then come down towards the rocks where I was sitting

but he didn't. You ask what I would have said, had he done so? I'm hanged if I know. Maybe I would have got up, whistling and seeming unconcerned, and then, with a nod and a smile, said good day and pottered off. I don't think he would have done anything. He'd just have stared after me, with those strange narrow eyes of his, and let me go.

After that, winter and summer, I was always down on the beach or the rocks. They went on living their curious, remote existence, sometimes fishing in the lake, sometimes at sea. Occasionally, I'd come across them in the harbor on the inlet, taking a look at the yachts anchored there, and the shipping. I used to wonder which of them made the suggestion. Perhaps suddenly he would be lured by the thought of the bustle and life of the harbor, and all the things he had either wantonly given up or never known, and he would say to her, "Today we are going into town." And she, happy to do whatever pleased him best, followed along.

You see, one thing that stood out—and you couldn't help noticing it—was that the pair of them were devoted to one another. I've seen her greet him when he came back from a day's fishing and had left her back home. Towards evening she'd come down the lake and onto the beach and down to the sea to wait for him. She'd see him coming from a long way off, and I would see him too, rounding the corner of the bay. He'd come straight in to the beach, and she would go to meet him, and they would embrace each other, not caring who saw

The Old Man 147

them. It was touching, if you know what I mean. You felt there was something lovable about the old man, if that's how things were between them. He might be a devil to outsiders, but he was all the world to her. It gave me a warm feeling for him, when I saw them together like that.

You asked if they had any family. I was coming to that. It's about the family I really wanted to tell you. Because there was a tragedy, you see. And nobody knows anything about it except me. I suppose I could have told someone, but if I had, I don't know. . . . They might have taken the old man away, and she'd have broken her heart without him. And anyway, when all's said and done, it wasn't my business. I know the evidence against the old man was strong, but I hadn't positive proof, it might have been some sort of accident, and anyway, nobody made any inquiries at the time the boy disappeared, so who was I to turn busybody and informer?

I'll try and explain what happened. But you must understand that all this took place over quite a time, and sometimes I was away from home or busy, and didn't go near the lake. Nobody seemed to take any interest in the couple living there but myself. It was only what I observed with my own eyes that makes this story, nothing that I heard from anybody else, no scraps of gossip, or tales told about them behind their backs.

Yes, they weren't always alone, as they are now. They had four kids. Three girls and a boy. They brought up the four of them in that ramshackle old place by the lake. It was always a wonder to me how they did it. I've known days when the rain lashed the lake into little waves that burst and broke on the muddy shore near their place, and turned the marsh into a swamp, with the wind driving straight in. You'd have thought anyone with a grain of sense would have taken his missus and his kids out of it and gone off somewhere where they could get some creature comforts at least. Not the old man. If he could stick it, I guess he decided she could too, and the kids as well. Maybe he wanted to bring them up the hard way.

Mark you, they were attractive youngsters. Especially the youngest girl. I never knew her name, but I called her Tiny. She had so much to her. Chip off the old block, in spite of her size.

I can see her now, as a little thing, the first to venture in the lake, on a fine morning, way ahead of her sisters and brother.

The brother I nicknamed Boy. He was the eldest and, between you and me, a bit of a fool. He hadn't the looks of his sisters and was a clumsy sort of fellow. The girls would play around on their own and go fishing. He'd hang about in the background, not knowing what to do with himself. If he possibly could, he'd stay around home, near his mother. A mama's boy. That's why I gave him the name. Not that she seemed to fuss over him any more than she did the others. She treated the four alike, as far as I could tell. Her thoughts were always for the old man rather than for them. But Boy was just a big baby. I have an idea he was simple.

Like their parents, the youngsters kept to themselves. Been drummed into them, I dare say, by the old man. They never came down to the beach on their own and played. It must have been a temptation, I thought, in full summer, when people came walking over the cliffs down to the beach to bathe and picnic. I suppose, for those strange reasons best known to himself, the old man had warned them to have nothing to do with strangers.

They were used to me puttering, day in, day out, fetching driftwood and such. And often I would pause and watch the kids playing by the lake. I didn't talk to them, though. They might have gone back and told the old man. They used to look up when I passed by, then glance away again, sort of shy. All but Tiny. Tiny would give a toss of her head and do a somersault, just to show off.

I sometimes watched them go off, the six of them—the old man, the missus, Boy, and the three girls, for a day's fishing out to sea. The old man, of course, in charge; Tiny eager to help, close to her dad; the missus looking about her to see if the weather was going to keep fine; the two other girls alongside; and Boy, poor simple Boy, always the last to leave home. I never knew what sport they had. They used to stay out late, and I'd have left the beach by the time they came back again. But I guess they did well. They must have lived almost entirely on what they caught. Well, fish is said to be full of vitamins, isn't it? Perhaps the old man was a food faddist in his way.

Time passed, and the youngsters began to grow up. Tiny lost something of her individuality then, it seemed to me. She grew more like her sisters. They were a nice-looking trio, all the same. Quiet, you know, well-behaved.

As for Boy, he was enormous. Almost as big as the old man, but with what a difference! He had none of his father's looks, or strength, or personality. He was nothing but a great clumsy lout. And the trouble was, I believe the old man was ashamed of him. He didn't pull his weight in the home, I'm certain of that. And out fishing he was perfectly useless. The girls would work away like beetles, with Boy, always in the background, making a mess of things. If his mother was there he stayed by her side.

I could see it rattled the old man to have such an oaf of a son. Irritated him, too, because Boy was so big. It probably didn't make sense to his intolerant mind. Strength and stupidity didn't go together. In any normal family, of course, Boy would have left home by now and gone out to work. I used to wonder if they argued about it back in the evenings, the missus and the old man, or if it was something never admitted between them but silently understood—Boy was just no good.

Well, they did leave home at last. At least, the girls did.

I'll tell you how it happened.

It was a day in late autumn, and I happened to be over doing some shopping in the little town overlooking the harbor, three miles from this place. And suddenly I saw the old man, the missus, the three girls and Boy all making their way up to Pont— that's at the head of a creek going eastward from the harbor. There are a few cottages at Pont, and a farm and a church behind. The family looked washed and spruced up, and so did the old man and the missus, and I wondered if they were going visiting. If they were, it was an unusual thing for them to do. But it's possible they had friends or acquaintances up there, of whom I knew nothing. Anyway, that was the last I saw of them, on the fine Saturday afternoon, making for Pont.

It blew hard over the weekend, a proper easterly gale. I kept indoors and didn't go out at all. I knew the seas would be breaking good and hard on the beach. I wondered if the old man and the family had been able to get back. They would have been wise to stay with their friends up at Pont, if they had friends there.

It was Tuesday before the wind dropped and I went down to the beach again. Seaweed, driftwood, tar and oil all over the place. It's always the same after an easterly blow. I looked up the lake, towards the old man's shack, and I saw him there, with the missus, just by the edge of the lake. But there was no sign of the youngsters.

I thought it a bit funny, and waited around in case they should appear. They never did. I walked right round the lake, and from the opposite bank I had a good view of their place, and even took out my old spyglass to have a closer look. They just weren't there. The old man was puttering about as he often did when he wasn't fishing, and the missus had settled herself down to bask in the sun. There was only one explanation. They had left the family with friends in Pont. They had sent the family for a holiday.

I can't help admitting I was relieved, because for one frightful moment I thought maybe they had started off back home on the Saturday night and got struck by the gale; and, well—that the old man and his missus had got back safely, but not the kids. It couldn't be that, though. I should have heard. Someone would have said something. The old man wouldn't be puttering there in his usual unconcerned fashion and the missus basking in the sun. No, that must have been it. They had left the family with friends. Or maybe the girls and Boy had gone up country to find jobs at last.

Somehow it left a gap. I felt sad. So long now I had been used to seeing them all around, Tiny and the others. I had a strange sort of feeling that they had gone for good. Silly, wasn't it? To mind, I mean. There was the old man, and his missus, and the four youngsters, and I'd more or less watched them grow up, and now for no reason they had gone.

I wished then I knew even a word or two of his language, so that I could have called out to him, neighbor-like, and said, "I see you and the missus are on your own. Nothing wrong, I hope?"

But it wasn't any use. He'd have looked at me with his strange eyes and told me to go away.

I never saw the girls again. No, never. They just didn't come back. Once I thought I saw Tiny, somewhere up the inlet, with a group of friends, but I couldn't be sure. If it was, she'd grown. She looked different. I tell you what I think. I think the old man and the missus took them with a definite end in view, that last weekend, and either settled them with friends they knew or told them to shift for themselves.

I know it sounds hard, not what you'd do for your own son and daughters. But you have to remember the old man was a tough customer, a law unto himself. No doubt he thought it would be for the best, and so it probably was. If only I could know for certain what happened to the girls, especially Tiny, I wouldn't worry.

But I do worry sometimes, because of what happened to Boy.

You see, Boy was fool enough to come back. He came back about three weeks after that final weekend. I had walked down through the woods—not my usual way, but down to the lake by the stream that feeds it from a higher level. I rounded the lake by the marshes to the north, some distance from the old man's place, and the first thing I saw was Boy.

He wasn't doing anything. He was just standing by the marsh. He looked dazed. He was too far off for me to hail him; besides, I didn't have the nerve. But I watched him, as he stood there in his clumsy loutish way, and I saw him staring at the far end of the lake. He was staring in the direction of the old man.

The old man, and the missus with him, took not the slightest notice of Boy. They were close to the beach, and were either just going out to fish or coming back. And here was Boy, with his dazed stupid face, but not only stupid—frightened.

I wanted to say, "Is anything the matter?" but I didn't know how to say it. I stood there, like Boy, staring at the old man.

Then what we both must have feared would happen, happened.

The old man lifted his head and saw Boy.

He must have said a word to his missus, because she didn't move, she stayed where she was, by the bridge. But the old man turned like a flash of lightning and came down the other side of the lake towards the marshes, towards Boy. He looked terrible. I shall never forget his appearance. That magnificent head I had always admired now angry, evil; and he was cursing Boy as he came. I tell you, I heard him.

Boy, bewildered, scared, looked hopelessly about him for cover. There was none. Only the thin reeds that grew beside the marsh. But the poor fellow was so dumb he went in there, and crouched, and believed himself safe—it was a horrible sight.

I was just getting my own courage up to interfere when the old man stopped suddenly in his tracks, pulled up short as it were, and then, still cursing, muttering, turned back again and returned to the bridge. Boy watched him from his cover of reeds, then, poor clot that he was, came out onto the marsh again, with some idea, I suppose, of striking for home.

I looked about me. There was no one to call. No one to give any help. And if I went and tried to get someone from the farm they would tell me not to interfere, that the old man was best left alone when he got in one of his rages. And anyway that Boy was old enough to take care of himself. He could give as good as he got. I knew different. Boy was no fighter. He didn't know how.

I waited quite a time beside the lake but nothing happened. It began to grow dark. It was no use my waiting there. The old man and the missus left the bridge and went on home. Boy was still standing there on the marsh, by the lake's edge.

I called to him, softly. "It's no use. He won't let you in. Go back to Pont, or wherever it is you've been. Go to some place, anywhere, but get out of here."

He looked up, that same strange dazed expression on his face. I could tell he hadn't understood a word I said.

I felt powerless to do any more. I went home. But I thought about Boy all evening, and in the morning I went down to the lake again, and I took a great stick with me to give me courage. Not that it would have been much good. Not against the old man.

Well . . . I suppose they had come to some sort of agreement, during the night. There was Boy, by his mother's side, and the old man was puttering on his own.

I must say, it was a great relief. Because after all, what could I have said or done? If the old man didn't want Boy home, it was really his affair. And if Boy was too stupid to go, that was Boy's affair.

But I blamed the mother a good deal. After all, it was up to her to tell Boy he was in the way, and the old man was in one of his moods, and Boy had best get out while the going was good. But I never did think she had great intelligence. She did not seem to show much spirit at any time.

However, what arrangement they had come to worked for a time. Boy stuck close to his mother—I suppose he helped her at home, I don't really know—and the old man left them alone and was more and more by himself.

He took to sitting down by the bridge, humped, staring out to sea, with an odd brooding look on him. He seemed strange, and lonely. I didn't like it. I don't know what his thoughts were, but I'm sure they were evil. It suddenly seemed a very long time since he and the missus and the whole family had gone fishing, a happy, contented party. Now everything had changed for him. He was thrust out in the cold, and the missus and Boy stayed together.

I felt sorry for him, but I felt frightened, too. Because I felt it could not go on like this indefinitely. Something would happen.

One day I went down to the beach for driftwood and when I glanced towards the lake I saw that Boy wasn't with his mother. He was back where I had seen him that first day, on the edge of the marsh. He was as big as his father. If he'd known how to use his strength he'd have been a match for him any day, but he hadn't the brains. There he was, back on the marsh, a great big frightened foolish fellow. And there was the old

The Sea—Evening, 1907, DWIGHT WILLIAM TRYON. Freer Gallery of Art, Smithsonian Institution, Washington, D.C.

man, outside his home, staring down towards his son with murder in his eyes.

I said to myself, "He's going to kill him." But I didn't know how or when or where. Whether by night, when they were sleeping, or by day, when they were fishing. The mother was useless. She would not prevent it. It was no use appealing to her. If only Boy would use a grain of sense, and go. . . .

I watched and waited until nightfall. Nothing happened.

It rained in the night. It was grey, and cold, and dim. December was everywhere,

trees all bare and bleak. I couldn't get down to the lake until late afternoon. Then the skies had cleared and the sun was shining in that watery way it does in winter, a burst of it, just before setting below the sea.

I saw the old man, and the missus, too. They were close together, by the old shack, and they saw me coming for they looked towards me. Boy wasn't there. He wasn't on the marsh, nor by the side of the lake.

I crossed the bridge and went along the right bank of the lake, and I had my spyglass with me, but I couldn't see Boy. Yet all the time I was aware of the old man watching me.

Then I saw him. I scrambled down the bank, and crossed the marsh, and went to the thing I saw lying behind the reeds.

He was dead. There was a great gash on his body. Dried blood on his back. But he had lain there all night. His body was soaked with the rain.

Maybe you'll think I'm a fool, but I began to cry, like an idiot, and I shouted across to the old man, "You murderer, you bloody murderer." He did not answer. He did not move. He stood there, outside his shack with the missus, watching me.

You'll want to know what I did. I went back and got a spade, and I dug a grave for Boy, in the reeds behind the marsh. I said one of my prayers for him, being uncertain of his religion. When I had finished I looked across the lake to the old man.

And do you know what I saw?

I saw him lower his great head, and bend towards her and embrace her. And she lifted her head to him and embraced him, too. It was both a requiem and a benediction. An atonement, and a giving of praise. In their strange way they knew they had done evil, but now it was over, because I had buried Boy and he was gone. They were free to be together again, and there was no longer a third to divide them.

They came out into the middle of the lake, and suddenly I saw the old man stretch his neck and beat his wings, and he took off from the water, full of power, and she followed him. I watched the two swans fly out to sea right into the face of the setting sun, and I tell you it was one of the most beautiful sights I ever saw in my life: the two swans flying, there, alone, in winter.

Developing Comprehension Skills

1. What was the old man's attitude toward the folks living in the area?

2. Who tells the story of the old man? What do you know about the narrator?

3. In what ways did Boy displease or disappoint his father?

4. Shortly after Boy returned from Pont, the narrator became concerned that the old man was going to harm his son. What details or events led the narrator to this conclusion?

5. What unexpected information do you get in the last paragraph of the story? How does this information affect your feelings about the old man? Explain your answer.

Reading Literature: Short Stories

1. **Recognizing Shifts in Mood.** You remember that mood is the feeling that a story creates in the reader. The mood changes several times during "The Old Man." At times, the mood is relaxed and warm. At other times,

the mood is sinister, even terrifying. Describe the points in the story where you feel that there is a change in mood. How does the author achieve these changes?

2. **Making Inferences About Character.** The narrator of this story deliberately leads the reader to believe that the old man and his family are humans. For example, she gives the family nicknames that imply that they are people. She describes their home by the lake as though it were a shack instead of a shelter made of reeds. Can you find other instances in which the narrator speaks of the family in human terms? Why do you think the narrator described the old man and his family in this manner?

3. **Recognizing Foreshadowing.** You remember that foreshadowing is a technique in which the author or narrator hints about events to come. Foreshadowing helps to create the sinister feeling that gradually becomes the mood of "The Old Man." The following statement, for instance, is one example of foreshadowing.

It's about the family I really wanted to tell you. There was a tragedy, you see.

How does this statement prepare the reader for what is to come? Find other comments that foreshadow the tragedy in the story.

4. **Analyzing Suspense. Suspense** is the feeling created when the reader becomes unsure of the outcome of events. In this story the reader develops a concern for Boy. As the events unfold, it becomes apparent that Boy is in danger. The reader becomes concerned about what will happen to him. Find specific details in this story that build suspense.

5. **Understanding the Surprise Ending.** Both "The Test" and "The Old Man" end in unexpected ways. In the first story, the reader discovers that the setting is not what it appears to be. In "The Old Man," it is the characters who are not what they seem.

There are several hints in "The Old Man" that might prepare the reader for the surprise ending. For example, it is unusual that during the entire time the narrator watches the "children" grow up, he never once speaks to them or learns their names. Look for at least four other details that may have seemed strange to you the first time you read the story.

Developing Vocabulary Skills

Referring to the Dictionary or Glossary. Each of the following sentences contains words drawn from "The Old Man." See if you can determine the meaning of the underlined word by using context clues. If you can, write the clue and the meaning of the word. If there are no context clues, write *Use Dictionary*. Then look up the word and write its meaning.

1. Tiny was always the first to venture into the lake, her explorations soon imitated by her sisters and brother.

2. Perhaps the old man thought of things he had wantonly given up when younger.

3. The old man was intolerant of Boy's weaknesses, but his missus seemed more forgiving of her awkward son.

4. A gale blew in from the ocean like a miniature hurricane.

5. Once I saw Tiny and her friends, somewhere up the inlet.

6. The situation could not go on <u>indefinitely</u>. Something would have to happen soon.

Developing Writing Skills

1. **Understanding the Conclusion.** "The Old Man" seems at first to be a story of suspense about the murder of a boy by his own father. Only at the end does the reader realize that the story is about a very common event in nature. How does the ending affect the mood of the entire story?

2. **Using Personification.** When writers use personification, they give human qualities to nonhuman creatures or things. The author of "The Old Man" used this technique to create a tale of suspense out of an ordinary event. Try this technique. Choose an animal and an activity in which the animal might be involved. Describe both in human terms.

   Pre-Writing. Choose an animal and an incident that you feel you could describe well. For example, you might choose a bird building a nest or a dog hunting a rabbit. In your pre-writing notes, list each step of the incident in **chronological, or time, order**. This means that you will list the steps in the order in which they occurred.

   Writing. Work on a rough draft of your story. Try to choose words that do not show that you are writing about an animal. For example, a bird's nest could simply be called its home. A hunting dog could be referred to only as "the hunter." Close your story with a sentence that reveals what the central character actually is.

   Revising. Read over your rough draft. Check your language carefully. Could you add words to make the incident more vivid? Should you replace any words that might give away the surprise? Make sure your sentences flow smoothly. If necessary, add transitional words such as *then*, *next*, and *soon* to connect ideas.

Developing Skills in Critical Thinking

Recognizing Rationalization. Sometimes a person gives believable reasons for an action, but the reasons are not the true ones. The person may do this because he or she feels that the real reasons might not be acceptable to others. Giving false reasons in this way is called **rationalizing**.

In "The Old Man," the narrator gives reasons for not interfering in the activities of the family. Find at least three of those reasons. Do you think they are the real reasons, or do you think the narrator is rationalizing? Explain your answer.

The Richer, the Poorer

DOROTHY WEST

One sister cherishes her money. The other thinks money is the least important thing life has to offer. See if this story convinces you that one woman is wiser than the other.

Over the years Lottie had urged her sister Bess to prepare for her old age. Over the years Bess had lived each day as if there were no other. Now they were both past sixty, the time for summing up. Lottie had a bank account that had never grown lean. Bess had the clothes on her back, and the rest of her worldly possessions in a battered suitcase.

Lottie had hated being a child, hearing her parents' skimping and scraping. Bess had never seemed to notice. All she ever wanted was to go outside and play. She learned to skate on borrowed skates. She rode a borrowed bicycle. Lottie couldn't wait to grow up and buy herself the best of everything.

As soon as anyone would hire her, Lottie put herself to work. She minded babies, she ran errands for the old.

She never touched a penny of her money, though her child's mouth watered for ice cream and candy. But she could not bear to share with Bess, who never had anything to share with her. When the dimes began to add up to dollars, she lost her taste for sweets.

By the time she was twelve, she was clerking after school in a small variety store. Saturdays she worked as long as she was wanted. She decided to keep her money for clothes. When she entered high school, she would wear a wardrobe that neither she nor anyone else would be able to match.

But her freshman year found her unable to indulge so frivolous a whim, particularly when her admiring instructors advised her to think seriously of college. No one in her family had ever gone to college, and certainly Bess would never get there. She would show them all what she could do, if she put her mind to it.

She began to bank her money, and her bank account became her most private and precious possession.

In her third year of high school she found a job in a small but expanding restaurant, where she cashiered from the busy hour until closing. In her last year, the business increased so rapidly that Lottie was faced with the choice of staying in school or working fulltime.

She made her choice easily. A job in hand was worth two in the future.

Bess had a boyfriend in the school band, who had no other ambition except to play a horn. Lottie expected to be settled with a home and family while Bess was still waiting for Harry to earn enough to buy a marriage license.

That Bess married Harry straight out of high school was not surprising. That Lottie never married at all was not really surprising either. Two or three times she was halfway persuaded, but to give up a job that paid well for a homemaking job that paid nothing was a risk she was unable to take.

Bess's married life was nothing for Lottie to envy. She and Harry lived like gypsies, Harry playing in second-rate bands all over the country, even getting himself and Bess stranded in Europe. They were often in rags and never in riches.

Bess grieved because she had no child, not having sense enough to know she was better off without one. Lottie was certainly better off without nieces and nephews to feel sorry for. Very likely Bess would have dumped them on her doorstep.

That Lottie had a doorstep they might have been left on was only because her boss, having bought a second house, offered Lottie his first house at a price so low and terms so reasonable that it would have been like losing money to refuse.

Victorian Survival, 1931, GRANT WOOD. Private Collection.

She shut off the rooms she didn't use, letting them go to ruin. Since she ate her meals out, she had no food at home, and did not encourage callers, who always expected a cup of tea.

Her way of life was mean and miserly, but she did not know it. She thought she lived frugally in her middle years so that she could live in comfort and ease when she most needed peace of mind.

The years, after forty, began to race. Suddenly Lottie was sixty and retired from her job by her boss's son, who had no sentimental feeling about keeping her on until she was ready to quit.

She made several attempts to find other employment, but her dowdy appearance made her look old and inefficient. For the first time in her life Lottie would gladly have worked for nothing, to have some place to go, something to do with her day.

Harry died abroad, in a third-rate hotel, with Bess weeping as much as if he had left her a fortune. He had left her nothing but his horn. There wasn't even money for her passage home.

Lottie, trapped by the blood tie, knew she would not only have to send for her sister, but take her in when she returned. It didn't seem fair that Bess should reap the harvest of Lottie's lifetime of self-denial.

It took Lottie a week to get a bedroom ready, a week of hard work and hard cash. There was everything to do, everything to replace or paint. When she was through, the room looked so fresh and new that Lottie felt she deserved it more than Bess.

She would let Bess have her room, but the mattress was so lumpy, the carpet so worn, the curtains so threadbare that Lottie's conscience bothered her. She supposed she would have to redo that room, too, and went about doing it with an eagerness that she mistook for haste.

When she was through upstairs, she was shocked to see how dismal the downstairs looked by comparison. She tried to ignore it, but, with nowhere to go to escape it, the contrast grew more intolerable.

She worked her way from kitchen to parlor, persuading herself she was only putting the rooms right to give herself something to do. At night she slept like a child after a long and happy day of playing house. She was having more fun than she had ever had in her life. She was living each precious hour for itself.

There was only a day now before Bess would arrive. Passing her gleaming mirrors, at first with vague awareness, then with painful clarity, Lottie saw herself as others saw her, and could not stand the sight.

She went on a spending spree from specialty shops to beauty salon, emerging transformed into a woman who believed in miracles.

She was in the kitchen basting a turkey when Bess rang the bell. Her heart raced, and she wondered if the heat from the oven was responsible.

She went to the door, and Bess stood before her. Stiffly she suffered Bess's embrace, her heart racing harder, her eyes suddenly smarting from the onrush of cold air.

"Oh, Lottie, it's good to see you," Bess said, but saying nothing about Lottie's splendid appearance. Upstairs Bess, putting down her shabby suitcase, said, "I'll sleep like a rock tonight," without a word of praise for her lovely room. At the lavish table, top-heavy with turkey, Bess said, "I'll take light and dark both," with no marveling at the size of the bird, or that there was turkey for two elderly women, one of them too poor to buy her own bread.

With the glow of good food in her stomach, Bess began to spin stories. They were rich with places and people, most of them lowly, all of them magnificent. Her face reflected her telling, the joys and sorrows of her remembering, and above all, the love

Victorian Interior, 1946, HORACE PIPPIN. The Metropolitan Museum of Art, Arthur H. Hearn Fund, 1958, (58-26)

she lived by that enhanced the poorest place, the humblest person.

Then it was that Lottie knew why Bess had made no mention of her finery, or the shining room, or the twelve-pound turkey. She had not even seen them. Tomorrow she would see the room as it really looked, and Lottie as she really looked, and the warmed-over turkey in its second-day glory. Tonight she saw only what she had come seeking, a place in her sister's home and heart.

She said, "That's enough about me. How have the years used you?"

"It was me who didn't use them," said Lottie wistfully, "I saved for them. I forgot the best of them would go without my ever spending a day or a dollar enjoying them. That's my life story in those few words, a life never lived.

"Now it's too near the end to try."

Bess said, "To know how much there is to know is the beginning of learning to live. Don't count the years that are left us. At our time of life it's the days that count. You've too much catching up to do to waste a minute of a waking hour feeling sorry for yourself."

Lottie grinned, a real wide open grin, "Well, to tell the truth I felt sorry for you. Maybe if I had any sense I'd feel sorry for myself, after all. I know I'm too old to kick up my heels, but I'm going to let you try to show me how. If I land on my head, I guess it won't matter much. I feel giddy already, and I like it."

Developing Comprehension Skills

1. List at least three ways in which Lottie and Bess were different as children. Did these differences remain as they grew older?

2. Before Bess arrived, why did Lottie suddenly become aware of her house and personal appearance?

3. During dinner with Bess, Lottie discovered something about herself. What was that discovery? What led Lottie to this new understanding?

4. What things did each sister sacrifice for her beliefs? Who do you think sacrificed more? Explain your answer.

5. The story suggests that Bess was wiser in her outlook on life than was Lottie. Do you agree? Why or why not?

Reading Literature: Short Stories

1. **Understanding Static and Dynamic Characters.** Some characters in short stories stay the same throughout the stories. They are called **static**, or unchanging, characters. Other characters change over the course of the story. They are called **dynamic** characters. Which sister in the story is a dynamic character? What is this character's **motive**, or reason, for wanting to change?

2. **Identifying the Theme.** The title of this story, "The Richer, the Poorer," reflects its theme, or main idea. What does this story have to say about different kinds of wealth? Now think about how the title applies to the two sisters. Which sister is richer, and which is poorer? Explain your answer.

3. **Recognizing Tone.** The **tone** of a story is the author's attitude toward the subject. The tone may be amused, critical, detached, or horrified, for example. Sometimes the author's attitude is very similar to those of the characters in the story. At other times, it is quite different.

In "The Richer, the Poorer," information is sometimes presented as though Lottie herself were telling the story:

Bess grieved because she had no child, not having sense enough to know she was better off without one.

At other times, the information is presented as though a second narrator were taking a critical look at Lottie herself:

Her way of life was miserly, but she did not know it.

Find other sentences in the story that sound as though Lottie were presenting the information. Then locate sentences in which the narrator seems slightly critical of Lottie. Which sentences do you think represent the attitude, or tone, of the author? How do you think the author viewed both Lottie's life and Bess's life?

Developing Vocabulary Skills

Inferring Meaning with Analogies. An **analogy** contains two pairs of words. Each pair is related in the same way. Look at this example.

hammer is to *carpenter* as *brush* is to _____.

a. canvas   c. painter
b. picture   d. bristle

The first two words, *hammer* and *carpenter*, have a certain relationship to each other. This relationship can be expressed in a sentence: A hammer is a tool used by a carpenter. To complete the analogy, you must choose a word that has the same relationship to the word *brush* as *carpenter* has to *hammer*. You can check your choice by substituting the new pair of words in the same sentence you used before: A *brush* is a tool used by a _____. The correct answer is c: painter.

Complete the following analogies. You may find it necessary to refer to a dictionary.

1. Create is to produce, as verify is to _____.
   a. relate   c. prove
   b. judge   d. report

2. Fawn is to deer, as gosling is to _____.
   a. monkey   c. goat
   b. goose   d. fish

3. Moss is to trees, as algae is to _____.
   a. water   c. shrubs
   b. underground   d. green

4. Flood is to water, as avalanche is to _____.
   a. ice   c. cold
   b. snow   d. white

5. Fad is to clothes, as slang is to _____.
   a. language   c. education
   b. food   d. cool

Developing Writing Skills

1. **Analyzing Irony.** Lottie dedicated herself to saving money so that she could have a much better life than the one she had as a child. What is ironic about the results of her choices? In a paragraph explain your answer.

2. **Using Indirect Description.** In "The Richer, the Poorer," the writer implies things about the character by describing the way she lives, dresses, speaks, and thinks. This is called **indirect description**.

   Try writing an indirect description yourself. Choose an interesting person to write about. Describe that person so that your reader infers the character's personality from the details you provide.

Pre-Writing. Decide on a subject for your description. Then, ask yourself questions such as the following:

What sort of clothes would such a person wear? How would he or she stand or speak? What would the interests of this person be? Would there be any family or friends?

Writing. Write a rough draft of your paragraph. As you write, try to reveal things about the character's personality through the way he or she speaks, dresses, acts, or thinks.

Revising. Have a friend read through your draft. Then ask your reader to describe your character to you. Did you create the impression you wanted to, or did your reader see your character in a way you didn't intend? Change any misleading details and substitute new ones.

Developing Skills in Critical Thinking

1. **Recognizing Slanted Language.** Sometimes a speaker or writer tries to influence an audience in indirect ways. This is often accomplished through the use of slanted language. **Slanted language** is words or phrases that have a strong emotional effect.

   Read the following passage from "The Richer, the Poorer":

   > Bess's married life was nothing for Lottie to envy. She and Harry *lived like gypsies*, Harry playing in *second-rate* bands all over the country, even getting himself and Bess *stranded* in Europe. They were often in *rags*, and never in riches.

   What effect do the italicized words have on the reader? Can you rewrite the passage

so that Bess's married life *does* sound like something to envy? You may wish to use slanted language that has a positive emotional effect.

2. **Understanding Analogies.** Look again at the analogies under Developing Vocabulary Skills. Explain the relationship that exists between each pair of words.

Developing Skills in Speaking and Listening

Taking Part in a Discussion. Sometimes, it is necessary for a group to reach an agreement, or **consensus**, on the idea being discussed. This means that the group must reach a conclusion about the discussion topic.

Organize a discussion with four or five of your classmates. Try to find an answer to the following question: "What are the three most important requirements for a happy life?" Follow these steps:

1. Think about the question carefully. Write on a piece of paper the three requirements you would choose.

2. Compare your list with those of the rest of the group. Be sure to give reasons for your choices. Determine which requirements appear on members' lists most often. Also decide which requirements were supported by the best reasons. Write these requirements on a group list.

3. Now discuss the requirements on the group list. Let each member express an opinion on which requirements should be on the final list of three. After the discussion, see if the group can reach a decision, or **consensus**, on the three most important requirements.

The Foghorn

RAY BRADBURY

Two men confront terror on a gloomy November night. What do they learn in spite of their fear?

Out there in the cold water, far from land, we waited every night for the coming of the fog, and it came, and we oiled the brass machinery and lit the fog light up in the stone tower. Feeling like two birds in the grey sky, McDunn and I sent the light touching out, red, then white, then red again, to eye the lonely ships. If they did not see our light, then there was always our Voice, the great deep cry of our Fog Horn. It shuddered through the rags of mist to startle the gulls away like decks of scattered cards and make the waves turn high and foam.

"It's a lonely life, but you're used to it now, aren't you?" asked McDunn.

"Yes," I said. "You're a good talker, thank the Lord."

"Well, it's your turn on land tomorrow," he said, smiling, "to dance with the ladies and drink gin."

"What do you think, McDunn, when I leave you out here alone?"

"On the mysteries of the sea." McDunn lit his pipe. It was a quarter past seven on a cold November evening, the heat on, the light switching its tail in two hundred directions, the Fog Horn bumbling in the high throat of the tower. There wasn't a town for a hundred miles down the coast, just a road, which came lonely through dead country to the sea, with few cars on it. Two miles of cold water separated our rock, and rare few ships passed.

"The mysteries of the sea," said McDunn thoughtfully. "You know, the ocean's the biggest snowflake ever? It rolls and swells a thousand shapes and colors, no two alike. Strange. One night, years ago, I was here alone, when all of the fish of the sea surfaced out there. Something made them swim in and lie in the bay, sort of trembling. They stared up at the tower light going red, white, red, white across them so I could see their funny eyes. I turned cold. They were like a big peacock's tail, moving out there until midnight. Then, without so much as a sound, they slipped away. The million of them was gone. I kind of think maybe, in some sort of way, they came all those miles to worship. Strange. But think how the tower must look to them, standing seventy feet above the water, the God-light flashing out from it, and the tower declaring itself with a monster voice. They never came back, those fish, but don't you think for a little while they thought they were in God's presence?"

I shivered. I looked out at the long grey lawn of the sea stretching away into nothing and nowhere.

"Oh, the sea's full." McDunn puffed his pipe nervously, blinking. He had been nervous all day and hadn't said why. "For all our engines and so-called submarines, it'll be ten thousand centuries before we set foot on the real bottom of the sunken lands, in the fairy kingdoms there, and know real terror. Think of it. It's still the year 300,000 Before Christ down under there. While we've paraded around with trumpets, lopping off each other's countries and heads, they have been living beneath the sea twelve miles deep and cold in a time as old as the beard of a comet."

"Yes, it's an old world."

"Come on. I got something special I been saving up to tell you."

We ascended the eighty steps, talking and taking our time. At the top, McDunn switched off the room lights so there'd be no reflection in the plate glass. The great eye of the light was humming, turning easily in its oiled socket. The Fog Horn was blowing steadily, once every fifteen seconds.

"Sounds like an animal, don't it?" McDunn nodded to himself. "A big lonely animal crying in the night. Sitting here on the edge of ten billion years calling out to the Deeps, 'I'm here, I'm here, I'm here.' And the Deeps do answer, yes, they do. You been here now for three months, Johnny, so I better prepare you. About this time of year," he said, studying the murk and fog, "something comes to visit the lighthouse."

"The swarms of fish like you said?"

"No, this is something else. I've put off telling you because you might think I'm daft. But tonight's the latest I can put it off, for if my calendar's marked right from last year, tonight's the night it comes. I won't go into detail; you'll have to see it yourself. Just sit down there. If you want, tomorrow you can pack your duffel and take the motorboat into land and get your car parked there at the dinghy pier on the cape. You can drive on back to some little inland town and keep your lights burning nights. I won't question or blame you. It's happened three years now, and this is the only time anyone's been here with me to verify it. You wait and watch."

Half an hour passed with only a few whispers between us. When we grew tired waiting, McDunn began describing some of his ideas to me. He had some theories about the Fog Horn itself.

"One day many years ago a man walked along and stood in the sound of the ocean on a cold sunless shore and said, 'We need a voice to call across the water, to warn ships; I'll make one. I'll make a voice like all of time and all of the fog that ever was. I'll make a voice that is like an empty bed beside you all night long, and like an empty house when you open the door, and like trees in autumn with no leaves. A sound like the birds flying south, crying, and a sound like November wind and the sea on the hard, cold shore. I'll make a sound that's so alone that no one can miss it, that whoever hears it will weep in their souls. Hearths will seem warmer, and being inside will seem better to all who hear it in the distant towns. I'll make me a sound and an apparatus and they'll call it a Fog Horn. Whoever hears it will know the sadness of eternity and the briefness of life.' "

The Fog Horn blew.

"I made up that story," said McDunn quietly, "to try to explain why this thing keeps coming back to the lighthouse every year. The Fog Horn calls it, I think, and it comes. . . ."

"But—" I said.

"Sssst!" said McDunn. "There!" He nodded out to the Deeps.

Something was swimming toward the lighthouse tower.

It was a cold night, as I have said. The high tower was cold. The light was coming and going, and the Fog Horn, calling and calling through the raveling mist. You couldn't see far and you couldn't see plain, but there was the deep sea moving on its way about the night earth, flat and quiet, the color of grey mud. Here were the two of us alone in the high tower. There, far out at first, was a ripple, followed by a wave, a rising, a bubble, a bit of froth. And then, from the surface of the cold sea came a head, a large head, dark-colored, with im-

mense eyes, and then a neck. And then—not a body—but more neck and more! The head rose a full forty feet above the water on a slender and beautiful dark neck. Only then did the body, like a slender little island of black coral and shells and crayfish, drip up from the subterranean. There was a flicker of tail. In all, from head to tip of tail, I estimated the monster at ninety or a hundred feet.

I don't know what I said. It seems I said something.

"Steady, boy," whispered McDunn.

"It's impossible!" I said.

"No, Johnny, we're impossible. It's like it always was ten million years ago. It hasn't changed. It's us and the land that've changed, become impossible. Us!"

It swam slowly and with a great dark majesty out of the icy waters, far away. The fog came and went about it, momentarily erasing its shape. One of the monster eyes caught and held and flashed back our immense light, red, white, red, white, like a disc held high and sending a message in primeval code. It was as silent as the fog through which it swam.

"It's a dinosaur of some sort!" I crouched down, holding to the stair rail.

"Yes, one of the tribe."

"But they died out!"

"No, only hid away in the Deeps. Deep, deep down in the deepest Deeps. Isn't that a word now, Johnny, a real word, it says so much: the Deeps. There's all the coldness and darkness and deepness in the world in a word like that."

"What'll we do?"

"Do? We got our job, we can't leave. Besides, we're safer here than in any boat trying to get to land. That thing's as big as a destroyer and almost as swift."

"But here, why does it come here?"

The next moment I had my answer.

The Fog Horn blew.

And the monster answered.

A cry came across a million years of water and mist. A cry so anguished and alone that it shuddered in my head and my body. The monster cried out at the tower. The Fog Horn blew. The monster roared again. The Fog Horn blew. The monster opened its great toothed mouth and the sound that came from it was the sound of the Fog Horn itself. Lonely and vast and far away. The sound of isolation, a viewless sea, a cold night, apartness. That was the sound.

"Now," whispered McDunn, "do you know why it comes here?"

I nodded.

"All year long, Johnny, that poor monster there lying far out, a thousand miles at sea, and twenty miles deep maybe, biding its time. Perhaps it's a million years old, this one creature. Think of it, waiting a million years. Could you wait that long? Maybe it's the last of its kind. I sort of think that's true. Anyway, here come men on land and build this lighthouse, five years ago. And set up their Fog Horn and sound it and sound it out toward the place where you bury yourself in sleep and sea memories of a world where there were thousands like yourself. But now you're alone, all alone in a world not made for you, a world where you have to hide.

"But the sound of the Fog Horn comes and goes, comes and goes, and you stir from the muddy bottom of the Deeps. And your eyes open like the lenses of two-foot cameras and you move, slow, slow, for you have the ocean sea on your shoulders, heavy. But that Fog Horn comes through a thousand miles of water, faint and familiar. The furnace in your belly stokes up, and you begin to rise, slow, slow. You feed yourself on great slakes of cod and minnow, on rivers of jellyfish, and you rise slow through the autumn months, through September when the fogs started, through October with more fog and the horn still calling you on. And then, late in November, after pressurizing yourself day by day, a few feet higher every hour, you are near the surface and still alive. You've got to go slow. If you surfaced all at once you'd explode. So it takes you all of three months to surface, and then a number of days to swim through the cold waters to the lighthouse. And there you are, out there, in the night, Johnny, the biggest monster in creation. And here's the lighthouse calling to you, with a long neck like your neck sticking way up out of the water, and a body like your body, and, most important of all, a voice like your voice. Do you understand now, Johnny, do you understand?"

The Fog Horn blew.

The monster answered.

I saw it all, I knew it all—the million years of waiting alone, for someone to come

back who never came back. The million
years of isolation at the bottom of the sea,
the insanity of time there, while the skies
cleared of reptile-birds. The swamps dried
on the lands. The sloths and sabre-tooths
had their day and sank in tar pits, and men
ran like white ants upon the hills.

The Fog Horn blew.

"Last year," said McDunn, "that creature swam round and round, round and
round, all night. Not coming too near, puzzled, I say. Afraid, maybe. And a bit angry
after coming all this way. But the next day,
unexpectedly, the fog lifted, the sun came
out fresh, the sky was as blue as a painting.
And the monster swam off away from the
heat and the silence and didn't come back. I
suppose it's been brooding for a year now,
thinking it over from every which way."

The monster was only a hundred yards
off now, it and the Fog Horn crying at each
other. As the lights hit them, the monster's
eyes were fire and ice, fire and ice.

"That's life for you," said McDunn.
"Someone always waiting for someone who
never comes home. Always someone loving
some thing more than that thing loves them.
And after a while you want to destroy whatever that thing is, so it can't hurt you no
more."

The monster was rushing at the lighthouse.

The Fog Horn blew.

"Let's see what happens," said McDunn.

He switched the Fog Horn off.

The ensuing minute of silence was so
intense that we could hear our hearts

pounding in the glassed area of the tower,
could hear the slow greased turn of the
light.

The monster stopped and froze. Its great
lantern eyes blinked. Its mouth gaped. It
gave a sort of rumble, like a volcano. It
twitched its head this way and that, as if to
seek the sounds now dwindled off into the
fog. It peered at the lighthouse. It rumbled
again. Then its eyes caught fire. It reared
up, threshed the water, and rushed at the
tower, its eyes filled with angry torment.

What Are the Wild Waves Saying?, 1859, JAMES HAMILTON. The Chrysler Museum. Gift of Walter P. Chrysler, Jr., Norfolk, Virginia.

"McDunn!" I cried. "Switch on the horn!"

McDunn fumbled with the switch. But even as he flicked it on, the monster was rearing up. I had a glimpse of its gigantic paws, fishskin glittering in webs between the finger-like projections, clawing at the tower. The huge eye on the right side of its anguished head glittered before me like a cauldron into which I might drop, screaming. The tower shook. The Fog Horn cried, the monster cried. It seized the tower and gnashed at the glass, which shattered in upon us.

McDunn seized my arm. "Downstairs!"

The tower rocked, trembled, and started to give. The Fog Horn and the monster roared. We stumbled and half fell down the stairs. "Quick!"

We reached the bottom as the tower buckled down toward us. We ducked under the stairs into the small stone cellar. There were a thousand concussions as the rocks rained down. The Fog Horn stopped abruptly. The monster crashed upon the tower. The tower fell. We knelt together, McDunn and I, holding tight, while our world exploded.

Then it was over, and there was nothing but darkness and the wash of the sea on the raw stones.

That and the other sound.

"Listen," said McDunn. "Listen."

We waited a moment. And then I began to hear it. First a great vacuumed sucking of air, and then the lament, the bewilderment, the loneliness of the great monster, folded over and over upon us, above us. The sickening reek of its body filled the air, a stone's thickness away from our cellar. The monster gasped and cried. The tower was gone. The light was gone. The thing that had called to it across a million years was gone. And the monster was opening its mouth and sending out great sounds. The sounds of a Fog Horn, again and again. And ships far at sea, not finding the light, not seeing anything, but passing and hearing late that night, must've thought: There it is, the lonely sound, the Lonesome Bay horn. All's well. We've rounded the cape.

And so it went for the rest of that night.

The sun was hot and yellow the next afternoon when the rescuers came out to dig us from our stoned-under cellar.

"It fell apart, is all," said Mr. McDunn gravely. "We had a few bad knocks from the waves and it just crumbled." He pinched my arm.

There was nothing to see. The ocean was calm, the sky blue. The only thing was a great algaic stink from the green matter that covered the fallen tower stones and the shore rocks. Flies buzzed about. The ocean washed empty on the shore.

The next year they built a new lighthouse, but by that time I had a job in the little town and a wife. I had a good small warm house that glowed yellow on autumn nights, the doors locked, the chimney puffed smoke. As for McDunn, he was master of the new lighthouse, built to his own specifications, out of steel-reinforced concrete. "Just in case," he said.

The new lighthouse was ready in November. I drove down alone one evening late and parked my car. I looked across the grey waters and listened to the new horn sounding, once, twice, three, four times a minute far out there, by itself.

The monster?

It never came back.

"It's gone away," said McDunn. "It's gone back to the Deeps. It's learned you can't love anything too much in this world. It's gone into the deepest Deeps to wait another million years. Ah, the poor thing! Waiting out there, and waiting out there, while man comes and goes on this pitiful little planet. Waiting and waiting."

I sat in my car, listening. I couldn't see the lighthouse or the light standing out in Lonesome Bay. I could only hear the Horn, the Horn, the Horn. It sounded like the monster calling.

I sat there wishing there was something I could say.

Developing Comprehension Skills

1. What is the purpose of the Fog Horn?

2. What did McDunn think drew the monster to the lighthouse each year?

3. Johnny stated that the monster was impossible. McDunn replied, "It's us and the land that've changed, become impossible. *Us!*" What do you think he meant by this?

4. Why do you think the monster did not return?

5. McDunn didn't tell the rescuers about the monster. Was he right to think that no one would believe him? Do you think there might sometimes be cases when people should give such unbelievable stories the benefit of the doubt? Explain.

Reading Literature: Short Stories

1. **Understanding Mood.** A writer can create mood through the careful choice of setting, details, and language. The use of techniques such as foreshadowing can also strengthen a mood.

   In "The Fog Horn," the mood is very powerful. What feelings do you get when you read this story? Explain what you think the mood is. Then find details or passages from the story that help to create this mood.

2. **Understanding Theme.** A **universal theme** is one that is concerned with feelings and ideas all people share. Explain this statement by McDunn, which he uses to help Johnny understand the monster's pain: "That's life for you. Someone always waiting for someone who never comes home. Always someone loving some thing more than that thing loves them. And after a while you want to destroy whatever that thing is, so it can't hurt you no more." In your opinion, what does this statement suggest about loneliness and being human? What explanation does it give for people who destroy the very thing they love the most?

3. **Recognizing Symbols.** A **symbol** is an object or idea that has its own meaning but is used to represent something else. For example, a dove is a bird, but it is also used to represent peace. Black is a color, but it can also represent mourning.

   In this story, the Fog Horn is an instrument for warning ships at sea. However, it takes on an additional meaning for the keepers of the Fog Horn and for the monster who comes to find it. What emotion does the Fog Horn represent to these three characters? What details about the Fog Horn make it an appropriate symbol for this feeling?

Developing Vocabulary Skills

Using Context Clues. Read the following sentences, which use words drawn from the stories in this chapter. Find a context clue to help you determine the meaning of each underlined word. Write the word or phrase you used as a context clue. If you inferred the meaning from the entire passage, write *Inference*. Then write the meaning of the underlined word.

1. The authorities put each applicant through an accident under hypnosis—a sleeplike condition in which a person is conscious and responds.

2. He always takes a siesta after lunch. He usually naps for at least an hour or two.

3. Because of the family's strange and unpredictable ways, he walked <u>warily</u> toward the house.

4. The ugly became beautiful, the wicked, good; the proud became humble, the <u>miserly</u>, generous.

5. It happened millions of years ago when the sloths, the sabre-tooths, and other <u>extinct</u> animals sank into the tar pits.

6. Although the monster really existed, McDunn was afraid that people would think he was <u>daft</u>.

Developing Writing Skills

1. **Comparing Short Stories.** When you compare two items, you are looking for similarities. Write a paragraph on one of the following topics:

   a. Compare the narrator in "The Old Man" to the narrator in "The Fog Horn."

   b. Compare the Human in "Humans Are Different" to the monster in "The Fog Horn."

   c. Compare the theme of loneliness in "The Fog Horn" with the loneliness of "A Mother in Mannville."

2. **Creating a Mood.** The introduction of a story sets the time and place of the events. A description of the physical setting of a story is an obvious place to help create a mood. Think of an interesting place you know. It can be mysterious, frightening, cheerful, or simply unusual. Write one paragraph describing the place as if it were the setting for a short story. Try to choose precise words and phrases that would create an emotional reaction in the reader.

Pre-Writing. Think of the place you will describe. List the details of its physical appearance. Then determine the overall feeling this place gives you. List specific descriptive words and phrases that would help create that feeling. For example, you might describe a door in an old house as a rotting piece of wood, while one in a mansion would be an ornate entranceway. Organize your details in a natural order. For a description, you would probably use **spatial order**. This is the order in which details are related in space. Spatial orders include front to back, side to side, top to bottom (or the reverse), and near to far.

Writing. Write the rough draft of your paragraph as though you were beginning a short story. Set the scene for the story with your description. Refer to your list of descriptive words and phrases as you describe the setting. In writing your description in this manner, try to create a strong mood.

Revising. Read your paragraph. Do the words and descriptive phrases you used create the kind of mood you intended? Are there any additional descriptive words you might use? Are your details presented in spatial order? When you have finished revising the content of your paper, proofread it and make a final copy.

3. **Planning a Short Story.** You know that the plot of a short story can be divided into five parts: introduction, rising action, climax or turning point, falling action, and resolution. Look at the plot diagram at the top of the next page. It diagrams the story you began on page 132 in the writing exercise of "The Confession."

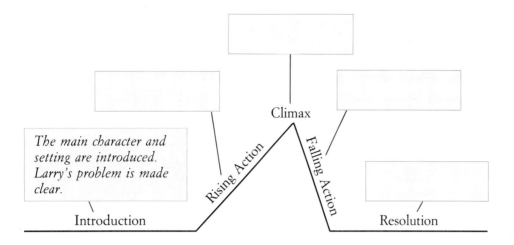

The main character and setting are introduced. Larry's problem is made clear.

Climax

Rising Action

Falling Action

Introduction

Resolution

Because the story was started for you, the introduction of the plot diagram is already filled in. Sketch the diagram on your own paper. If you completed this writing exercise earlier, you will be able to fill in the *rising action* and the *climax* by recalling how you continued the story. Now, plan how the story will end. Fill in the falling action and the resolution in the plot diagram. Then write the rest of your story.

Developing Skills in Study and Research

Locating Biographical References. An encyclopedia can provide information about the life of a well-known person. In addition, most libraries have additional specialized reference books. Some of these contain biographical information.

Locate the reference section in your library. Then, see if you can locate one of the following biographical references:

> *Twentieth Century Authors*
> *Current Biography*
> *Dictionary of National Biography*
> *Dictionary of American Biography*
> *Who's Who*

Find an entry about one of the authors in this unit. Write down the title of the reference book in which you found it. Then write down the page number, and the number of pages in the entry. Read the information about the author. List three facts about the author's life that you find interesting.

CHAPTER 2 **R**eview

Using Your Skills in Reading Short Stories

The following paragraph introduces the short story "The Confidence Game" by Pat Carr. Read the passage and answer the questions that follow.

My confidence started draining out my toes the day Angela Brady showed up at the pool for workout. I even started to chew the inside of my cheek, a nervous habit I usually reserve for fighting the fear that clutches at me just before a race. In a way, I guess I knew it *was* a race between Angela and me for the backstroke position on our team relay for National Championship.

I hadn't even seen her swim yet, but the whole team knew she had been swimming for a famous club in California. We were just a small city team, only two years old. But we had a coach whose middle name was motivation. He'd motivated me into swimming a grueling three miles a day, and now I was actually in the running to compete at the Nationals. Or I was until Angela showed up.

1. What can you determine about the setting of the story?
2. What do you learn about the person telling the story?
3. From what point of view is the short story told?
4. What conflict do you suppose may develop?

Using Your Comprehension Skills

Read the following poem from Chapter 4, "Lodged," by Robert Frost. What is the cause and effect relationship that is expressed? Now look at the speaker's reaction to the event. What can you infer about his feelings?

The rain to the wind said,
"You push and I'll pelt."
They so smote the garden bed
That the flowers actually knelt,
And lay lodged—though not dead.
I know how the flowers felt.

Using Your Vocabulary Skills

Read the following passages from poems you will read in Chapter 4. Use context clues to determine the meaning of each underlined word.

1. For one white singing hour of peace
   Count many a year of strife well lost

2. For something is amiss or out of place
   When mice with wings can wear a human face.

3. Bewildered stands the fox, too many streets lead off too many ways,

4. riding over / heaving surges / of the open sea

5. We are spendthrifts with words,
   We squander them, / Toss them like pennies in the air—

Using Your Writing Skills

Choose one of the writing assignments below.

1. A hero or heroine is a character noted for strength, bravery, or nobility. Of all the characters in the short stories in this chapter, which one did you find most heroic? Write a composition explaining why you think that character is heroic. In the introduction to your composition, be sure to present your definition of *heroic*. In three separate paragraphs, identify three traits that make the character heroic. Give specific examples, incidents, and quotations to develop each paragraph.

2. Imagine that you are going to write a short story. Describe a setting that creates a mood of loneliness. Use specific sensory details that will allow your reader to feel this mood.

Using Your Skills in Critical Thinking

1. You have learned that a generalization is a general statement based on specific facts. The stories "Zlateh the Goat," "The Dog of Pompeii," and "The Fan Club" are all concerned with the idea of loyalty. What generalizations can you make about loyalty, based on these three stories?

2. The ability to classify things, or group them according to certain similarities, is a very useful skill. Which stories in this chapter would you classify as science fiction? as folktales? as humor? Explain why you classified each story as you did.

Techniques Writers Use

The Vegetable Man, 16th Century, ARCIMBOLDO.
(Turn book for hidden image.) Cremona Municipal Museum, Italy.
Courtesy of Scala/Art Resource, New York.

Using the Sounds of Language

Writers consider both the sound and the meaning of each word they use. The sound of a well chosen word can help create feeling and reinforce meaning. It can also give a musical quality to a work. In this chapter, you will learn about the following ways that writers use the sounds of language:

alliteration   assonance   rhyme   rhythm   onomatopoeia

Brookside Music, (*Pussywillow, Song, Sparrow, Sunlit Stream*), 1950, CHARLES BURCHFIELD.
Dr. and Mrs. Jerome Rapháel Collection. Courtesy of Kennedy Galleries, New York.

Alliteration

> **Alliteration** is the repetition of a consonant sound at the beginning of words.
>
> Examples: tried and true   live and let live
>   sink or swim   jump for joy

Alliteration in Prose.   Alliteration is used frequently in prose. You probably use it now without realizing it. Phrases such as "safe and sound," "bread and butter," and "rock and roll" contain alliteration. The repetition of sounds makes these phrases fun to say and hear. It also makes them easy to remember.

Writers use alliteration to emphasize certain words. Words that begin with the same consonant sound stand out from the rest of the sentence. Notice how alliteration emphasizes words in the following examples:

> The mass of men lead lives of quiet desperation.
> —Henry David Thoreau, *Walden*

> The animal was depressed by the tremendous cold. It knew that it was no time for traveling. Its instinct told it a truer tale than was told to the man by the man's judgment.
> —Jack London, "To Build a Fire"

Alliteration in Poetry.   Alliteration draws attention to particular words in poetry too. Words that begin with the same sound stand out from other words. In addition, a poet may use alliteration to create a rhythm, or a musical effect. Here are a few examples:

> Deep into the darkness peering,
>   long I stood there, wondering, fearing,
> Doubting, dreaming dreams no mortal
>   ever dared to dream before;
>
>   —Edgar Allan Poe, "The Raven"

Up among the branches a summer bee still sings,
But winter is a whisper in its wings.

> —Patricia Hubbell, "Autumn"

Alliteration can also reinforce the meaning or mood of a poem. Mood is the feeling a writer creates for the reader. Notice how the *w* sound is repeated in the following example. The sound is soft and helps to create a peaceful mood.

We shall walk in velvet shoes:
    Wherever we go
Silence will fall like dews
    On white silence below.
    We shall walk in the snow.

> —Elinor Wylie, "Velvet Shoes"

Exercises: Using Alliteration

A. Identify the consonant sounds that are repeated in the following examples. How do they help to emphasize ideas, create rhythm, and add to the mood?

1. I know my friends from the feel of their faces. But I cannot really picture their personalities by touch.
    > —Helen Keller, "The Seeing See Little"

2. Nature's first green is gold,
   Her hardest hue to hold.
    > —Robert Frost, "Nothing Gold Can Stay"

3. Zinnias, stout and stiff,
   Stand no nonsense: their colors
   Stare   —Valerie Worth, "Zinnias"

4. The locusts were started, and the fire flies were out, and a few frogs were flopping in the dewy grass.
    > —James Agee, *A Death in the Family*

B. Write a three or four sentence description of a sports event. Use alliteration at least twice.

Assonance

> **Assonance** is the repetition of a vowel sound within words.
>
> Examples: rise and shine   down and out

Assonance in Prose. Writers use repeated vowel sounds to stress particular words. Like alliteration, this technique draws attention to the words in which it is used.

Assonance also helps to create different moods. In the following example, a short *a* sound is repeated. The short *a* sound is like a cry—a cry for help. The mood, then, could be one of despair.

> My soul is more than matched; she's over-manned; and by a madman!
> —Herman Melville, *Moby Dick*

Notice that alliteration is also used in the above example. This is not unusual. Used together, assonance and alliteration can create a more effective mood.

Can you find both the assonance and alliteration in the following example? What mood do you think the writer is creating with his words?

> Under the cool double moons of Mars the midnight cities were bone and dust.   —Ray Bradbury, "The Blue Bottle"

Assonance in Poetry. Assonance can stress a word or an idea in poetry, too. The repetition of a vowel sound can also be used to create a rhythm. This adds a musical quality to the poem. Finally, assonance can also create a certain mood, depending on which vowel sound is repeated.

What vowel sounds are repeated in the following examples? What mood do they help create?

> Look out how you use proud words.
> When you let proud words go, it is not easy to call them back.
> —Carl Sandburg, "Primer Lesson"

The grey winds, the cold winds are blowing.
  Where I go.
I hear the noise of many waters
  Far below.
All day, all night, I hear them flowing
  To and fro.

—James Joyce, "The Noise of Waters"

Exercises: **Using Assonance**

A. Find the examples of assonance in the following selections.

1. While in the wild wood I did lie,
   A child—with a most knowing eye.
   —Edgar Allan Poe, "Romance"

2. Roll on, thou deep and dark blue Ocean—roll!
   Ten thousand fleets sweep over thee in vain;
   —George Gordon, Lord Byron, "Childe Harold's
   Pilgrimage"

3. O world, I cannot hold thee close enough!
   Thy winds, thy wide gray skies!
   Thy mists that roll and rise!
   —Edna St. Vincent Millay, "God's World"

4. The crows flew low, croaking.
   —Isaac Bashevis Singer, "Zlateh the Goat"

5. A bright fire glowed in the stove and the cat lay stretched before it, watching the table with a drowsy eye.
   —Edith Wharton, *Ethan Frome*

B. Write three sentences using assonance. Repeat the vowel sound at least twice in each sentence. Make sure the vowel sounds you choose match the meaning of your sentences.

Rhyme

> **Rhyme** is the repetition of sounds at the ends of words. Rhyme may involve one or more syllables.
>
> Example: Thirty days has September,
>   April, June, and November.

Rhyme in Prose.   Rhyme is rare in prose. It is usually reserved for poetry. However, rhyme can occasionally be found in sayings and proverbs. In such cases, the use of rhyme makes a saying easy to remember, and enjoyable to listen to.

Red sky in the morning, sailors take warning.

Besides being pleasing to the ear, rhyme can stress an idea in a piece of prose. For example, in the following selection the sounds of battle are reinforced by the rhyming of *flash* and *crash.*

Other shells homed in, each arriving with a whistle and a hiss, a flash and a crash.   —Frank Bonham, *The Ghost Front*

Rhyme in Poetry.   Poets use rhyme to create a musical quality in their work. Usually the rhyme is found at the end of lines. This end rhyme can follow different patterns. The pattern of rhyme in a poem is called its **rhyme scheme.**

A special code is used to represent the rhyme scheme of a poem. A letter of the alphabet is assigned to each rhyme sound. When lines end with the same sound, they are assigned the same letter.

In the following poem, all the lines in the stanza rhyme. Therefore they are assigned the same letter.

He clasps the crag with crooked hands;   a
Close to the sun in lonely lands,   a
Ring'd with the azure world, he stands.   a

—Alfred, Lord Tennyson, "The Eagle"

In the poem below, each stanza has four lines. The first two lines rhyme and the second two lines rhyme. Notice the letter assigned to each line.

I must go down to the seas again, to the lonely sea and the sky,	a
And all I ask is a tall ship and a star to steer her by;	a
And the wheel's kick and the wind's song and the white sail's shaking,	b
And the gray mist on the sea's face, and a gray dawn breaking.	b

—John Masefield, "Sea-Fever"

End rhyme is the most common type of rhyme. However, rhyme does not always occur at the end of lines. It may occur within a line. This is known as **internal rhyme.** In the following line, for example, the word *fast* within the line rhymes with the last word, *blast.*

The ship drove fast, loud roared the blast.
—Samuel Taylor Coleridge, "The Rime of the Ancient Mariner"

Exercises: Using Rhyme

A. Identify the rhyme scheme for each of the following poems.

1. I have been one acquainted with the night.
   I have walked out in rain—and back in rain.
   I have outwalked the furthest city light.

   I have looked down the saddest city lane.
   I have passed by the watchman on his beat
   And dropped my eyes, unwilling to explain.
   —Robert Frost, "Acquainted with the Night"

2. I have fallen in love with American names,
   The sharp names that never get fat,
   The snakeskin-titles of mining-claims,
   The plumed war-bonnet of Medicine Hat,
   Tucson and Deadwood and lost Mule Flat.
   —Stephen Vincent Benét, "American Names"

B. Write a four-line poem using the **a a b b** rhyme scheme.

Rhythm

Rhythm is the pattern of stressed (/) and unstressed (◡) syllables in a sentence or a line of poetry. The pattern is shown by marking each syllable with these symbols:

Example: ◡ / ◡ / ◡ / ◡ / On this green bank, by this soft stream
◡ / ◡ / ◡ / ◡ / We set today a votive stone.

—Ralph Waldo Emerson, "Concord Hymn"

Rhythm in Prose.   Prose makes use of the natural rhythm of language. To express different moods, people naturally speak in different rhythms. Writers, like speakers, match the rhythm of their words with their mood. This is done by using words of different lengths. In addition, stressed syllables, punctuation, and pauses affect rhythm.

In the following example, the rhythm creates excitement.

> He woke with the jerk of his right fist coming up against his face and the line burning out through his right hand. He had no feeling of his left hand but he braked all he could with his right and the line rushed out. Finally his left hand found the line and he leaned back against the line and now it burned his back and his left hand, and his left hand was taking all the strain and cutting badly. Just then the fish jumped making a great bursting of the ocean and then a heavy fall.
>
> —Ernest Hemingway, *The Old Man and the Sea*

Rhythm in Poetry.   Rhythm in poetry emphasizes and adds meaning to words. In the following example, short, quick syllables create rhythm. The result is a rhythm that almost sounds like a lively march.

> We're going West tomorrow, where the promises can't fail.
> O'er the hills in legions, boys, and crowd the dusty trail!
> We shall starve and freeze and suffer. We shall die, and tame
>   the lands.
> But we're going West tomorrow, with our fortune in our hands.
>
> —Stephen Vincent Benét, "Western Wagons"

Compare that lively rhythm with the rhythm of the next poem. The long, drawn out syllables create a slow pace, or rhythm.

The long canoe
Toward the shadowy shore,
One . . . two . . .
Three . . . four . . .
The paddle dips,
Turns in the wake,
Pauses, then
Forward again.

—Robert Hillyer, "Lullaby"

Exercises: Using Rhythm

A. How would you describe the rhythm of the following poem? How does the rhythm match the subject of the poem?

Across the dim frozen fields of night
Where is it going? Where is it going?
No throb of wheels, no rush of light.
Only a whistle blowing, blowing.
Only a whistle blowing.

—Robert Francis, "Night Train"

B. The following selection has a tense, suspenseful mood. How did the writer use the rhythm of language to create the mood?

At first Donald lay still. Scarcely a muscle moved. Excitement held him motionless. His hands gripped the short grass and his toes dug into the dry earth. Cautiously he raised himself on his elbows and gazed at the scene below him.

—Gladys Frances Lewis, "The Black Stallion and the Red Mare"

Onomatopoeia

> **Onomatopoeia** is the use of words that imitate sounds.
>
> Examples: whirr, creak, clunk, quack

Onomatopoeia in Prose. Sometimes when writers are describing sounds, they use a word that reminds the reader of that sound. *Squeak* and *hiss* are examples of words that suggest sounds. At other times, writers may simply invent a new word to re-create a sound.

Find the onomatopoeia in the following example:

> A buzz arose in the court as if a cloud of great blue-flies were swarming about the prisoner.
>
> —Charles Dickens, *A Tale of Two Cities*

Onomatopoeia in Poetry. The following poem allows the reader to "hear" the noise of a wrecking ball tearing down a building.

> Crash goes a chimney,
> Pow goes a hall,
> Zowie goes a doorway,
> Zam goes a wall.　　—Eve Merriam, "Bam, Bam, Bam"

Exercises: **Using Onomatopoeia**

A. Find the onomatopoeia in the following sentences and lines.

1. Go wind, blow
   Push wind, swoosh.　—Lilian Moore, "Go Wind"

2. When I lay me down to sleep
   My waterbed says, "Gurgle-gleep,"
   　　　　　—John Updike, "Insomnia the Gem of
   　　　　　　　the Ocean"

B. Use onomatopoeia in three sentences to imitate three sounds. You may use real words that suggest sounds or you may use words you have invented.

Using Figures of Speech

Writers often have special ways of looking at the world. These writers help readers see ordinary things in a different way. The language they use to do this is known as figurative language. You will learn about the following figures of speech in this chapter:

simile   personification
metaphor   hyperbole

Dynamism of a Soccer Player, 1913, UMBERTO BOCCIONI. Oil on canvas, 6' 4⅛" × 6' 7⅛".
The Museum of Modern Art. Gift of the Sidney and Harriet Janis Collection, New York.

Simile

A **simile** is a comparison that uses *like* or *as*. It shows how two unlike things are alike in some way.

Examples: The still lake reflects the mountains like a mirror.

The old basement was as damp as an underground cave.

Similes in Prose.   Similes help you see similarities between things that are not really alike. For example, you may not consider a person or a mule to be alike. However, when the simile "stubborn as a mule" is used, you can see a similarity. Both a person and a mule can be stubborn. Good similes surprise you. They can show you a new way of looking at familiar things.

What two things are compared in each of the following similes? How are the two things alike?

The sunlight poured over them like a warm bath.

—James Ramsey Ullman, "A Boy and a Man"

This man was hunting about the hotel lobby like a starved dog that has forgotten where he has buried a bone.

—O. Henry, "A Municipal Report"

Similes in Poetry.   Similes help to create images in poetry. Writers can give a new or surprising meaning to an object when they compare it to something familiar. Notice how the following simile uses a familiar sight in its description.

At the corner
of the lake and the river.
Houses on stilts
climbing the hill like goats.

—José Coronel Urtecho, "San Carlos"

Similes also add to the mood of a poem. A good simile creates an image for the reader. The image, in turn, may cause the reader to feel joy, sorrow, fear, or some other emotion. This feeling is the mood.

The moods of the following two poems are different. The first has a discouraging, even depressing mood. The second example has a cheerful, active mood. How do the similes in each poem affect the mood of the poem?

Our dried voices, when
We whisper together
Are quiet and meaningless
As wind in dry grass
Or rats' feet over broken glass
In our dry cellar
—T.S. Eliot, "The Hollow Men"

My hair flopped to the side
like the mane of a horse in the wind.
—May Swenson, "The Centaur"

Exercises: Using Similes

A. Identify the two things that are compared in each of the following similes. Whenever possible, tell how the simile affects the mood of the selection.

1. Friends are like melons. Shall I tell you why? To find one good, you must a hundred try. —Claude Mermet, "Epigram on Friends"

2. At the end of the pasture, the pond gleamed brightly, like an open eye.
   —Jean Lively, "The Flight of the Snowbird"

3. And trains pass with windows shining
   Like a smile full of teeth
   —Richard Garcia, "The City Is So Big"

B. Write three original similes. Try to surprise your readers with an unusual, but true, comparison. You may want to describe one of the following things:

an animal	a washing machine
a bus	an alarm clock

Metaphor

> A **metaphor** is a comparison that states, or suggests, that two unlike things are the same or have something in common. Unlike similes, metaphors do not contain the words *like* or *as.* They make the comparison directly.
>
> Examples: A book is a ship that takes you to distant lands.
>
> The branches of the trees are sweeping the sky.

Metaphors in Prose.   Metaphors present images that help readers picture things and people clearly. Picture the river shore in the following example.

> The shore, muffled in thick scarves of drifting mist, looked scarcely different from the miles of unbroken forest they had seen for the past week.   —Elizabeth George Speare, *The Witch of Blackbird Pond*

The metaphor in the above sentence compares mist to thick scarves. What two things are being compared in each of the following examples?

> Some books are to be tasted, others to be swallowed, and some few to be chewed and digested.
>
> —Francis Bacon, "Of Studies"

> Only his daughter had the power of charming this black brooding from his mind. She was the golden thread that united him to a Past beyond his misery.   —Charles Dickens, *A Tale of Two Cities*

Metaphors in Poetry.   Metaphors are used in poetry just as they are used in prose. The poem on the following page creates a clear image. What two things are being compared?

A ghostly snow
floats
out of the sky
tonight,
and snow moths
dance
in the pale street light.

—Lilian Moore, "Night Snow"

When a writer compares two things in a number of different ways, he or she is using an **extended metaphor**. Notice how the writer of the next example compares good conversation to serving food to guests:

Conversation is but carving!
Give no more to every guest
Than he's able to digest.
Give him always of the prime
And but little at a time
Carve to all but just enough
Let them neither starve nor stuff.

—Jonathan Swift, "Conversation"

Exercises: Using Metaphors

A. What two things are compared in each of the following metaphors? How does the metaphor affect the mood of the piece?

1. Iced, red laughter
   of summer,
   a slice
   of watermelon!   —José Juan Tablada, "Haikus"

2. Listen a while, the moon is a lovely woman, a lonely woman,
   lost in a silver dress, lost in a circus-rider's silver dress.
                    —Carl Sandburg, "Night Stuff"

B. Write three sentences containing original metaphors. To begin, think of questions such as these: To what can you compare rain? To what can you compare your mind? your eyes? your hands?

Personification

Personification is another type of comparison. It gives human qualities to an object, an animal, or an idea.

Examples: The wind whispered.

The city shivered during the snowstorm.

Personification in Prose.   Personification can be used to set the mood of a piece of writing quickly and vividly. How would you describe the mood of the following example?

The battle flag in the distance jerked about madly. It seemed to be struggling to free itself from an agony.

—Stephen Crane, *The Red Badge of Courage*

When ideas are personified, a picture is placed in the reader's mind. As a result, the reader understands the ideas more easily. In the following example, the reader can "see" hunger.

Hunger had always been more or less at my elbow when I played, but now I began to wake up at night to find hunger standing at my bedside, staring at me gauntly.

—Richard Wright, "The Street"

Personification in Poetry.   In this poem, ideas you cannot see, hear, or feel have human qualities. Which two ideas are personified?

Because I could not stop for Death—
He kindly stopped for me—
The Carriage held but just Ourselves—
And Immortality.

—Emily Dickinson, "Because I Could Not Stop for Death"

In the poem on the following page, the poet shows his special vision of one of the simple things in life—a vegetable.

The soft-hearted
artichoke
put on armor,
stood at attention, raised
a small turret
and kept itself
watertight
under
its scales.

— Pablo Neruda, "Ode to an Artichoke"

Exercises: Using Personification

A. What is personified in each of the following examples? Describe the mood that is created.

1. The little boat at anchor
   in the black water sat murmuring
   to the tall black sky.

   — Carl Sandburg, "Fourth of July Night"

2. Night comes close to the window,
   breathing against the pane,

   — Elizabeth Coatsworth, "Song to Night"

3. Spring skips lightly on a thin crust of snow,
   Pokes her fragrant fingers in the ground far below,
   Searches for the sleeping seeds hiding in cracked earth,
   Sticks a straw of sunshine down and whispers words to grow.

   — Myra Cohn Livingston, *A Circle of Seasons*

B. Write three original sentences using personification. You may want to choose an animal or an object that *does* something. Then you will find it easier to relate its actions to human actions. Here are some possible subjects:

| a toaster | the rain | a rocket |
| a moving van | the wind | |

Hyperbole

> **Hyperbole** is exaggeration. It puts an unusual or especially vivid image into the reader's mind.
>
> Examples: The whistle blast made me jump ten feet in the air.
>
> This suit is older than the hills.

Hyperbole in Prose.   Hyperbole is often used in humorous writing. The images it creates are sometimes ridiculous. Look at the following example from an American tall tale:

> The cold was mighty intense. It went down to 70 degrees below zero. The men couldn't blow out the candles at night, because the flames were frozen, so they had to crack the flames off and toss them outdoors. (When the warm weather came, the flames melted and started quite a forest fire.)   —Maurice Dolbier, "Paul Bunyan's Been There"

Ridiculous exaggeration is not limited to tall tales. This example is from a twentieth-century play.

> It's simply freezing; the dogs are sticking to the sidewalks; can anybody explain that?   —Thornton Wilder, *The Skin of Our Teeth*

What is being exaggerated in the following example?

> One day Davy had a raccoon up a tree. It looked so solemn that Davy couldn't keep from laughing. He just stood there on the ground and grinned. And the first thing he knew, he'd grinned that raccoon right out of the tree. He had done it without firing a shot.
> —Michael Gorham, "Davy Crockett"

Hyperbole in Poetry.   Humorous poetry also uses hyperbole. Notice how the exaggeration in the poem on the following page is similar to the hyperbole used in the tall tale.

The ostrich is a silly bird,
   With scarcely any mind.
He often runs so very fast,
   He leaves himself behind.
                           —Mary E. Wilkins Freeman, "The Ostrich Is A
                               Silly Bird"

Hyperbole is not always humorous. It can also describe strong or·
unusual sensations. Read this description of the intense heat of a summer afternoon.

I am becoming sunlight.
My hair is on fire. My boots run like tar.
I am hung-up by the bright air.
                           —Ralph Pomeroy, "Corner"

In the following poem, hyperbole is used to emphasize an important idea.

Here once the embattled farmer stood
   And fired the shot heard round the world.
                           —Ralph Waldo Emerson, "Concord Hymn"

Exercises: Using Hyperbole

A. Read the following examples of hyperbole. For each one, decide what is
being exaggerated.

1. A sudden sneeze by the kid in the middle of any of these configurations
   could trigger a chain reaction that sent kids flying in all directions.
                           —Sam Levenson, "Sleeping Arrangements"

2. There were fogs so thick that you could cut houses out of them, the way
   they do with snow and ice in the far north.
                           —Maurice Dolbier, "Paul Bunyan's Been There"

B. Write an original hyperbole. You may want to imitate one of the examples
in this section. You can write a humorous hyperbole or one that describes a
sensation or an emotion.

CHAPTER **3** **R***eview*

Understanding the Sounds of Language

Read each of the following selections carefully. Look for examples of alliteration, assonance, rhyme, rhythm, and onomatopoeia. Then explain how each technique helps the reader understand or appreciate the selection.

1. The lake roared in. A vast steam leaped up, white in the sudden dark under the moon. There was a hiss, a gushing whirl, and then silence.
   —J.R.R. Tolkien, *The Hobbit*

2. My first glimpse of the flat black stretches of Chicago depressed and dismayed me, mocked all my fantasies.
   —Richard Wright, *American Hunger*

3. His arms were thick as hickory logs
       Whittled to little wrists;
   Strong as the teeth of terrier dogs
       Were the fingers of his fists.
   —Elinor Wylie, "The Puritan's Ballad"

Understanding Figures of Speech

In the following selections, find at least one example of each of the following figures of speech: simile, metaphor, personification, hyperbole. Identify each figure of speech that you find. If you find a comparison, tell what two things are being compared and how they are alike.

1. Let the rain kiss you.
   Let the rain beat upon your head with silver liquid drops.
   —Langston Hughes, "April Rain Song"

2. Some people brag that they sleep like a rock. I slept *on* one. Mama's pillows were about the size of a home movie screen and were as hard as bags of cement.   —Sam Levenson, "Sleeping Arrangements"

3. Hope is the thing with feathers
   That perches in the soul
   —Emily Dickinson, "Hope Is the Thing with Feathers"

CHAPTER 4

Waves at Matsushima, 17th Century, SOTATSU.
The Freer Gallery of Art, Smithsonian Institution, Washington, D.C.

Reading Literature: Poetry

What Is Poetry?

Poetry is a special, exciting way of using language. Poets present ideas and feelings in a few exact words. They use sound and rhythm to emphasize these ideas. A poet also tries to appeal to the reader's emotions. That is why poetry is more than just the reading of words. It is an experience to be enjoyed and remembered.

The History of Poetry

Poetry is an ancient form of literature. Thousands of years ago, people began using the musiclike rhythm and rhyme of poetry to pass on stories they did not want to be forgotten. They used poetry in their chants, their songs, and their prayers.

In ancient Greece and Rome, poetry continued to be the favorite way to tell stories. Most plays were written in poetry. So were the long stories, called **epics**, that told of brave heroes and fantastic adventures. This tradition continued in other times and other cultures. Storytellers the world over passed on legends through poetry and song. In the 1500's, playwright William Shakespeare reminded audiences of the beauty and power of poetry by using it in his plays.

Today, poetry is seldom used in plays. Storytellers do not travel around the country telling epics. Instead, modern poets write to share their feelings. They write to help readers see their world in a deeper, more personal way.

The Elements of Poetry

Form. Poems are easy to recognize because they usually look different from other types of writing. They are written in lines instead of sentences. The lines are grouped together in stanzas instead of paragraphs. Sometimes the poet uses line lengths and placement to create an actual shape on the page. The shape can add meaning.

Sound. Poetry depends on the sound as well as the meaning of its words. You learned about many of the techniques that poets use in Chapter 3. As you read poems, look for examples of **alliteration**, **assonance**, and **onomatopoeia**.

Rhyme. Words that rhyme end with the same syllable sound. Poets usually rhyme words at the end of lines. This kind of rhyme is called **end rhyme**. The pattern in which a poem rhymes is called its **rhyme scheme**. You can determine the rhyme scheme of a poem by assigning a letter of the alphabet to each rhyming sound at the end of a line. Lines that end with the same sound are assigned the same letter. Refer to Chapter 3 for an example of how to determine a rhyme scheme.

Rhythm. Rhythm is the pattern of stressed and unstressed syllables in a poem. Some poems have a steady, regular rhythm or beat. In others, the rhythm resembles normal speech. This type of rhythm is called **free verse**.

How To Read a Poem

1. Read each poem aloud. Listen carefully to the sounds as you say them. Remember that the sounds of a poem work together with the meanings of the words. You need to hear the sounds to completely understand and appreciate a poem.

2. Read the poem several times, slowly. Think about the meaning of the words as you read. Also think about the feelings the words create in you.

3. Look at the way the poem appears on the page. Does it seem to have a special shape? Are capitalization, punctuation, and spelling used in special ways? What additional meaning might these details add?

4. Try to find the purpose, or message, of each poem that you read. Some poets write simply to entertain. Others write to share some valuable thoughts or feelings about life. Give each poet a chance to speak to you.

Comprehension Skills: Structure and Meaning

Understanding Unusual Word Order

In prose, the subject of a sentence usually comes first. It is followed by the verb. The verb tells *what is* or *what is happening*.

I loved my friend.

   subject   verb

This order is often reversed in poetry.

Bewildered stands the fox.

     verb   subject

It is not difficult to understand sentences with unusual word order. First, find the verb. Then find the word the verb tells about. Finally, put the sentence in the usual order: *The fox stands bewildered.*

Understanding Long Sentences

Many poems are made up of one or more long sentences. To understand what the poet is saying, you must break the sentence down.

She stands
In the quiet darkness,
This troubled woman
Bowed by
Weariness and pain
Like an
Autumn flower
In the frozen rain . . .

This sentence combines several different ideas. First, decide who or what the sentence is about: the troubled woman. Then, look for words and phrases that describe the subject. In this sentence, there are a number of phrases that describe the woman. From these descriptive phrases, can you tell what the speaker's feelings are about her?

Using Punctuation Clues

Poems are usually written in lines. When you read a poem, it is natural to expect to pause at the end of each line. However, the end of a line of poetry does not always signal the end of a complete thought. If you pause at the end of every line, the poem may not make sense. Look for periods, question marks, and exclamation marks to tell you that you have come to the end of a complete idea. Use commas to help you separate the parts of a complete idea. Read these lines from a poem. Notice how the idea extends over two lines.

> The bicycles lie
> In the woods, in the dew.

It would not make sense to stop at the end of the first line. The idea, or thought, would not be complete. Some poems, such as the following poem, use almost no punctuation. They require special attention.

> ever been kidnapped
> by a poet
> if i were a poet
> i'd kidnap you

You may have to read poems like this one several times. As you read slowly and thoughtfully, try to identify the poet's complete thoughts.

Exercises: Understanding Structure and Meaning

A. Rearrange the words in this part of a poem. Put the subject first, followed by the verb.

> Couched in his kennel, like a log,
> With paws of silver sleeps the dog;

B. Break down this sentence into smaller parts. Decide what the sentence is about. Then find words or phrases that describe the subject.

> The fox at midnight in the city square
> knows there's a way, but knows not which it is,
> a path that leads to fields and woods and lair,
> leaves underfoot, earth and the stirring air.

$\mathcal{V}$ocabulary Skills: The Dictionary

Using the Dictionary

When context clues cannot help you figure out the meaning of an unfamiliar word, use a dictionary. The dictionary lists words in alphabetical order. It provides useful information about these words.

entry word   pronunciation   part of speech   origin   meaning

cre·vasse (kri vas′) *n.* [Fr. < OFr. *crevace,* CREVICE] **1.** a deep crack or fissure, esp. in a glacier ☆**2.** a break in a levee, as of a river

Each word listed on a dictionary page is called an **entry word**. The dictionary provides the following information for each entry word:

1. **How to divide words into syllables.** Entry words are printed in heavy black type. Spaces or dots between letters show where the syllables are divided: **cre·vasse**.

2. **The pronunciation of a word.** The pronunciation tells you how to pronounce the entry word correctly. It is usually found in parentheses following the word: (kri vas′) Symbols show you each sound in the word. The symbols are explained in the pronunciation key at the bottom of the dictionary page. Accent marks (′) tell you which syllables are stressed when pronouncing the word.

3. **The origin of the word.** Words have entered our language in a variety of ways. The dictionary briefly lists where each entry word came from. Its origin, or source, is in brackets. Abbreviations are used to show the language a word originally came from. Common abbreviations are L. (Latin), Fr. (French), and Ger. (German).

4. **The part of speech of the word.** In each dictionary entry, you will find the part of speech of the word abbreviated as follows:

n. —noun	*pro.* —pronoun	*prep.* —preposition
v. —verb	*adv.* —adverb	*conj.* —conjunction
	adj. —adjective	*interj.* —interjection

5. **The definition of the word.** Many words have more than one definition. Each definition in an entry is assigned a number.

   Some words are used as more than one part of speech. If so, all the meanings for that part of speech appear together.

Exercises: **Using the Dictionary**

A. Use this entry to answer the following questions.

> **op·ti·mism** (äp′tə miz′m) *n.* [< Fr. < L. *optimus,* best (see OPTIMUM)] **1.** the belief that the existing world is the best possible **2.** the tendency to take the most hopeful or cheerful view of matters. —**op′ti·mist** (-mist) *n.* —**op′ti·mis′tic** (-mis′tik), —**op′ti·mis′ti·cal** *adj.* —**op′ti·mis′ti·cal·ly** *adv.*

1. How many syllables are there in the word *optimism*?
2. On which syllable is the accent placed?
3. What part of speech is *optimism*?
4. What languages does *optimism* come from?
5. What does the word *optimism* mean?

B. Study the following dictionary entry. Then answer the questions that follow the entry.

> **coun·te·nance** (koun′tə nəns) *n.* [< OFr. < L. *continentia,* bearing < *continere,* CONTAIN] **1.** the look on a person's face that shows his nature or feelings [a friendly *countenance*] **2.** the face; facial features [a smile spread over his *countenance*] **3.** *a)* a look of approval *b)* approval; support [to give *countenance* to a plan] **4.** calm control; composure —*v.* **-nanced, -nanc·ing** to give support to; approve [I will not *countenance* such rudeness]

1. How many syllables are there in *countenance*? Which syllable is stressed?
2. Can *countenance* be used as more than one part of speech? List these parts of speech. Then, write two sentences. Each should use *countenance* as a different part of speech.
3. Which languages did the word *countenance* originally come from?

Sound

Poetry allows writers to use language in beautiful and unusual ways. Poets choose words for their sound as well as their meaning. Think of how a songwriter carefully arranges each note to achieve a special sound and effect. In the same way, the poet also selects words to achieve a special sound and effect. As you read these poems, listen carefully to the song the poet creates.

Flood, 1967, HELEN FRANKENTHALER. The Whitney Museum of American Art.
Gift of the Friends of the Whitney Museum of American Art, New York.

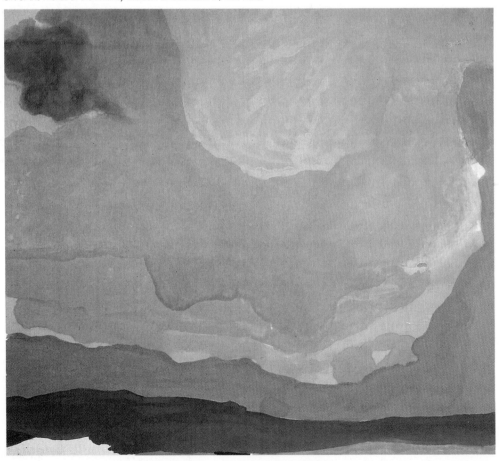

The Optileast and the Pessimost

EVE MERRIAM

Do you ever feel that you are really two different people? Read this poem to find out about the little creatures who cause this feeling.

The Optileast
Is a cheerful beast;
The least little thing
Makes his joy-bells ring.

The Pessimost
Is given to boast
That there's always room
For more and more gloom.

Now these two creatures, queer to relate,
Whom nature would scarcely be able to mate;
Who neither the other could ever abide,
Who surely could never live side by side—
Queer as can be, although they're not kin,
They dwell within the very same skin.

Times when my Optileast is here,
My Pessimost does not appear,
And yet he's somewhere down below
Even though he does not show;
So do not be alarmed or shout
If he should suddenly break out.

Then when my Pessimost is seen
And acting bigly mean as mean;
Without any warning in advance,
My Optileast begins to dance:
The smallest flower, or nothing at all,
Can make him leap up laughing tall.

Strange Optileast and Pessimost,
Neither is guest, neither is host;
They couldn't be brothers, they couldn't be wed,
Yet they'll live together until they're dead.
For however peculiar it may be,
They're both alive, alive in me.

Two Heads, 1932, PAUL KLÉE.
Norton Simon Museum of Art. The Blue Four
Galka Scheyer Collection, Pasadena, California.

Developing Comprehension Skills

1. This poem changes the word *optimist* and *pessimist* to *Optileast* and *Pessimost.* How does the speaker explain these new names? Look in the first two stanzas for clues.

2. What types of creatures are the Optileast and the Pessimost?

3. What kinds of things make the Optileast appear?

4. What does it mean when the speaker says that the Optileast and the Pessimost "dwell within the very same skin"?

5. What does "acting bigly mean as mean" mean?

6. What is the poet saying about people's personalities? Do you agree with her idea?

Reading Literature: Poetry

1. **Identifying the Speaker.** A poet is the writer of a poem. A **speaker** is the voice that "speaks" the poem. The speaker in a poem is much like the narrator in a short story.

   Sometimes the poet and the speaker share the same feelings and ideas. Sometimes the two are quite different. In this poem, how would you describe the tone, or attitude, of the speaker? Do you think the poet shares this feeling?

2. **Identifying Form.** Poems are organized in lines rather than sentences. These lines are grouped in stanzas, which are similar to paragraphs. Each stanza usually deals with one main idea.

   How many stanzas are in this poem? How many lines are in each stanza? Why do you think the poet made the first two stanzas different lengths than the others?

3. **Recognizing Rhyme Scheme.** The pattern of rhyme in a poem is called a **rhyme scheme**. A rhyme scheme is shown by using letters of the alphabet. Lines that rhyme are labeled with the same letter. Look at the rhyme scheme for the first stanza of "The Optileast and the Pessimost":

The Optileast	a
Is a cheerful beast;	a
The least little thing	b
Makes his joy-bells ring.	b

   Chart the rhyme scheme for the rest of this poem. Use a new letter for each new rhyme.

4. **Understanding Mood.** Mood is the feeling the reader gets from a poem. You might describe the mood of a poem as serious, cheerful, depressing, or a combination of these or any other feelings. What is the mood of this poem? How is it created?

Rain

RICHARD ARMOUR

Do you ever have mixed feelings about a person or thing? As you read this poem, try to decide how you feel about rain.

Rain that fosters growing plants
Takes the creases out of pants.

Rain that settles summer dust
Causes mildew, causes rust.

Rain that, with its cleansing fall,
Washes autos, makes them stall.

Rain that fills the dried-up creek
Causes people's roofs to leak.

Rain that cools you when it's hot
Makes you shiver when it's not.

Rain's a mixed-up sort of weather,
Pro and con all rolled together.

Rain is nasty, rain is nifty,
In proportion, fifty-fifty.

Children Singing in the Rain, 1951, BARBARA MORGAN. From *Summer's Children* by Barbara Morgan, copyright © 1951 Barbara Morgan, published by Morgan & Morgan, Inc., Dobbs Ferry, New York. Photo copyright © 1980 Barbara Morgan.

Developing Comprehension Skills

1. Name one good thing that rain does. Then name the corresponding, annoying thing that happens when it rains.

2. How does the speaker feel about rain? How can you tell?

3. Line 13 says "Rain is nasty, rain is nifty." In your opinion, can the same thing really be described by such opposite words?

4. If you had written a poem about rain, would you have come to the same conclusion as the speaker? Explain your reasons.

Reading Literature: Poetry

1. **Identifying Rhythm.** The rhythm, or beat, of a poem is measured in accented syllables (/) and unaccented syllables (◡). When the pattern of syllables repeats itself without any changes, the rhythm is said to be regular. If there are differences in the pattern, the rhythm is irregular.

    The rhythm of the first stanza of "Rain" would be shown like this.

    / ◡ / ◡ / ◡ /
    Rain that fosters growing plants
    / ◡ / ◡ / ◡ /
    Takes the creases out of pants.

    Copy the rest of the poem. Mark the accented and unaccented syllables. Is the rhythm of the poem regular or irregular? How does the rhythm affect what is being said in the poem?

2. **Understanding Form.** This poem is divided into seven stanzas of two lines each. In addition to the lines, what else has the poet organized in pairs?

3. **Understanding Rhyme.** What is the rhyme scheme of this poem? How does the rhyme scheme fit the ideas and form of the poem?

Developing Vocabulary Skills

Using Guide Words. The words in bold type at the top of a dictionary page are called **guide words**. The left guide word tells you the first word on that page. The right guide word tells you the last word.

The following list of words is from the poems you have read. In parentheses after each word are two possible guide words for a dictionary page. Decide whether each of the words would come *before*, *on*, or *after* that dictionary page.

    a. abide (abacus-abridge)
    b. foster (fortress-fossil)
    c. proportion (propaganda-proponent)
    d. mildew (migrate, militia)

Developing Writing Skills

1. **Expressing Your Opinion.** Choose one of the poems you have studied so far. State the reasons why you did or did not like the poem.

    Pre-Writing. Reread your poem carefully. Then list the reasons for your opinion. Consider subject matter, tone, rhyme, rhythm, vocabulary or any other element that would support your opinion.

    Writing. Write a topic sentence that states your opinion. Write several sentences explaining your opinion. Do not cover more than one reason in a sentence. Be sure that you support each reason with specific examples from the poem. Arrange your reasons from least important to most important.

    Revising. Make sure the paragraph clearly explains your opinion. Be sure each reason makes sense. Check to see that each reason supports your topic sentence. After you revise your paragraph, let someone else read it. Ask that person to tell you the main idea and to list the reasons you gave.

2. **Presenting Different Views.** Write a paragraph or poem of your own in which you present two very different views of the same thing. Possible subjects might be a pet, a sport, a holiday, or a place.

Developing Skills in Study and Research

Using the Parts of a Book. Most nonfiction books have a table of contents and an index. The table of contents is at the front of the book. It lists the major topics you can find in the book in the order in which they appear. The index is at the back of the book. It is an alphabetical listing of all the topics covered. This list shows the pages on which you will find the topic discussed. Both sections can help you become familiar with a book. They can also help you locate specific items within a book.

Find the table of contents and index in this book. Answer these questions:

1. Does the book have any poems by Langston Hughes? How many?

2. Can you find the poem "Barter" by Sara Teasdale in the book?

3. Does the table of contents list all the titles of the poems in the book? Does it group any of the poems together? If so, what are two of the titles for the groupings?

Developing Skills in Speaking and Listening

Interpreting a Poem Orally. Some of the activities in this chapter will ask you to present a poem orally to the class. The following suggestions will help you prepare, read, and listen to poems.

1. **Preparing the Poem.** Choose a poem whose sound and meaning you enjoy. Read your poem to yourself at least twice. Think about the meaning of the words as you read. Now read the poem aloud. Stress the important words. Lower or raise your voice to create a mood. Pause where a pause makes sense. Pay attention to commas, periods, or other breaks in the thought.

   Ask a friend to listen to you read the poem. Are you pronouncing every word correctly? Does your voice help create a mood? Are you reading at a good speed?

2. **Presenting the Poem.** Read loud enough for everyone to hear you. Remember all the things you practiced. Try to appear relaxed. Show your audience that you are enjoying yourself.

3. **Listening to a Poem.** When someone else presents a poem, concentrate on what he or she is saying. Can you understand all the words? Was the reader's voice the right volume and speed? Did the reader capture the mood of the poem and use effective emphasis so that you enjoyed the poem more?

The Sloth

THEODORE ROETHKE

The sloth lives in trees in the jungles of Central and South America. What makes the sloth an interesting and amusing creature?

In moving-slow he has no Peer.
You ask him something in his ear;
He thinks about it for a Year;

And then, before he says a Word
There, upside down (unlike a Bird)
He will assume that you have Heard—

A most Ex-as-per-at-ing Lug.
But should you call his manner Smug,
He'll sigh and give his Branch a Hug;

Then off again to Sleep he goes,
Still swaying gently by his Toes,
And you must know he knows he knows.

Developing Comprehension Skills

1. How does the sloth cling to the branches of trees?

2. What is the sloth's most obvious characteristic? What does the phrase "In moving-slow he has no Peer" mean?

3. Is the sloth interested in showing off his knowledge? What phrases support your answer?

4. Do you think that the poet successfully shows the reader the personality of the sloth? Give examples to support your opinion.

Reading Literature: Poetry

1. **Understanding Personification.** Personification occurs when a writer gives human qualities to an animal, an object, or an idea. The poet personifies the sloth in this poem. What words in the poem show that the sloth has human qualities?

2. **Recognizing Rhyme.** Chart the rhyme scheme of this poem. Use the same letter to label lines that end with rhyming sounds. How does the rhyme scheme add to what the poem says about the sloth being a slow-moving animal?

3. **Understanding Punctuation.** In the third stanza of the poem, the word *Ex-as-per-at-ing* is interrupted by several dashes. Does this speed up or slow down your reading? Why do you think the poet used this punctuation?

4. **Understanding Repetition.** Writers use repetition to create a particular effect or emphasis. Look at the last stanza of "The Sloth." Why do you think the poet chose to repeat "he knows" in the final line of the poem? What effect does this repetition have?

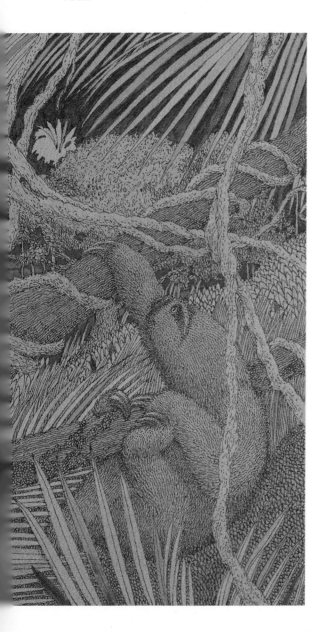

The Bat

The bat seems harmless enough during the day. But what happens at night? Read to find out.

THEODORE ROETHKE

By day the bat is cousin to the mouse.
He likes the attic of an aging house.

His fingers make a hat about his head.
His pulse beat is so slow we think him dead.

He loops in crazy figures half the night
Among the trees that face the corner light.

But when he brushes up against a screen,
We are afraid of what our eyes have seen:

For something is amiss or out of place
When mice with wings can wear a human face.

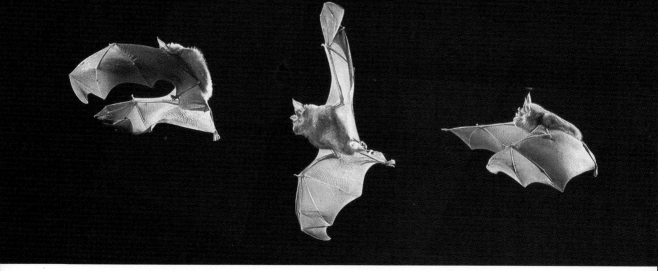

Greater horseshoe bat in flight. Animals, Animals/Oxford Scientific Films, New York. Photograph by Dalton.

Developing Comprehension Skills

1. To what other animal is the bat compared? In what ways are they similar?

2. How do the bat's actions change from night to day? How is this different from the actions of most other animals?

3. What about the bat most frightens people?

4. What feeling do you think the poet was trying to create about the bat?

Reading Literature: Poetry

1. **Understanding Figurative Language.** Language that describes things in a fresh new way is called **figurative language**. By using figurative language, the poet helps the reader see more vividly what is being described. For example, the line "His fingers make a hat about his head" adds interest and meaning to a common action of the bat. Find one other example of figurative language in this poem.

2. **Identifying Rhythm.** The basic unit of rhythm in poetry is called a **foot**. A foot is a combination of stressed and unstressed syllables. One type of two-syllable foot has this pattern: ⌣╱ as in ă mó̇ng. This foot is called the **iamb**.

   Look at the lines below from "The Bat." The stressed and unstressed syllables are marked. How many feet does each line have? Do the other lines of this poem follow a similar pattern?

   > He loops in crazy figures half the night
   > Among the trees that face the corner
   > light

3. **Identifying Couplets.** A couplet is a pair of lines in a poem that rhyme. Chart the rhyme scheme of "The Bat." Is it written in couplets? What other poem that you have read so far is also written in couplets?

Life

PAUL LAURENCE DUNBAR

A crust of bread and a corner to sleep in,
A minute to smile and an hour to weep in,
A pint of joy to a peck of trouble,
And never a laugh but the moans come double:
  And that is life!

A crust and a corner that love makes precious,
With the smile to warm and the tears to refresh us;
And joy seems sweeter when cares come after,
And a moan is the finest of foils for laughter:
  And that is life!

Developing Comprehension Skills

1. According to the first stanza, does life contain more joy or more sorrow?

2. What is meant by the line "And never a laugh but the moans come double"?

3. What message is presented in the first stanza of this poem? How does the second stanza soften this message?

4. Do you agree that the unhappy things in life are necessary to make us appreciate the good things?

Reading Literature: Poetry

1. **Recognizing Form.** This poem is built on contrasts, or differences. For example, compare the first lines in each stanza. Both talk about a crust and a corner. However, each line shows a very different feeling about life.

Compare and contrast the second, third, and fourth lines in the same way. First tell how the first stanza describes life. Then explain how the second stanza gives a different view.

The Banjo Lesson, 1893, HENRY OSSAWA TANNER. Hampton University Museum, Hampton, Virginia.

2. **Recognizing Alliteration.** The repetition of a consonant sound at the beginnings of words is called **alliteration**. In the first line, *crust* and *corner* both begin with *c*. Find three other lines that use alliteration.

3. **Appreciating Rhyme.** Chart the rhyme scheme for this poem. Explain how the rhyme scheme helps to emphasize what is being said in the poem.

4. **Understanding Repetition.** When a word, phrase, or line is repeated, the poet is using **repetition**. A poet may use repetition for emphasis or to create a certain effect. Why do you think the poet repeats the line "And that is life!" at the end of each stanza?

Developing Vocabulary Skills

Understanding Alphabetical Order of Special Entries. In most dictionaries, each entry is alphabetized as if it were a single word. Main entries include abbreviations, suffixes, prefixes, phrases, and hyphenated words. Study the list of entry words on the next page.

R.D.   reach
re-   rect.
REA

The word at the top of each of the three lists below is from a poem you have read. Alphabetize each of the lists.

rain	advance	beast
railroad	-acious	beanbag
R. and D.	ad lib	beast of burden
rain forest	adverb	B-cell

Developing Writing Skills

1. **Comparing and Contrasting Poems.** Write a paragraph comparing and contrasting any two poems you have studied so far. When you compare, you describe the ways in which the poems are alike. When you contrast, you tell how they are different.

   Pre-Writing. Reread all the poems. Choose two poems that are either very similar or very different. You might consider comparing "The Sloth" and "The Bat," or "Rain" and "Life." Make a chart like the sample below:

	Poem I	Poem II
Mood	cheerful	mysterious
Rhyme	a a b b	a b a b
Rhythm	regular	regular

   You may also want to compare such things as subject, form, and your reaction to the poem. Note the ways in which the poems are alike. Then note the ways they differ. Choose three of the elements to compare or contrast in your paragraph.

   Writing. Write a topic sentence that names the poems you are comparing and tells a general idea about them. Write at least two sentences about each element you are comparing. The first sentence should tell how the first poem uses that element. The second sentence should tell how the second poem uses it. To connect the two sentences, use words and phrases that signal comparisons and contrasts, such as *like, same, however,* and *unlike.*

   Revising. Look over your writing carefully. Did you connect your ideas smoothly? Are the similarities and differences between the poems clear? Check your capitalization, punctuation, and spelling.

2. **Writing a Poem.** Write a poem similar to the poems of Theodore Roethke in this chapter. Choose any animal for the subject. Use the same rhyme scheme as "The Sloth" or "The Bat." The poem should have at least six lines. Use the iambic rhythm pattern ($\smile$/). Try to use alliteration at least once. Use humor if possible.

Developing Skills in Speaking and Listening

Interpreting the Mood of a Poem. Choose one of the poems from this section to read orally. First decide what the mood of the poem is. Let your voice reflect that feeling. If the poem changes mood, as the poem "Life" does, be sure to make the mood change clear.

hape

When artists put paint on canvas, they carefully arrange the shapes and colors to achieve a certain effect. A poet can arrange words on a piece of paper in much the same way. A poem may resemble something as simple as a crow or as awesome as the universe. A poem may even look like a football field. Poets have fun with their poems, and you can, too. As you read the poems in this section, see how the shape of the poem adds to your enjoyment.

The Second Orange Clamp (detail), 1983, JIM DINE. Courtesy of the Pace Gallery, New York.

Reading Literature: More About Poetry

Other Elements of Poetry

Speaker. The speaker is the person, or voice, through which the poet speaks to the reader. The speaker is not necessarily the poet. It is important to know who the speaker is in order to understand a poem. The speaker in the poem below is a young person. What proves this?

> Grandma sleeps with
> my sick
> > grand-
> pa so she
> can get him
> during the night
> medicine
> to stop
> > the pain.

Imagery. Poets try to make readers experience ideas and events of a poem with their senses. Poets choose words that help readers *see, hear, feel, taste,* and *smell* the things being described. In the following poem, the poet uses sight images to help the reader "see" the birds.

> Between the under and the upper blue
> All day the seagulls climb and swerve and soar,

Sometimes words appeal to more than one sense.

> black on white
> crow in snow
> > hunched
> > wet lump
> on brittle branch
> remembering warmth
> remembering corn

Which words help you be part of the crow and her world?

Figurative Language. Poets often use figurative language to create their word pictures. Figurative language can create a new, fascinating way of looking at common, as well as unusual subjects.

A **simile** compares two unlike things using the words *like* or *as*. Such a comparison can help the reader gain a better understanding of the poet's intended meaning. For example,

> We are spendthrifts with words,
> We squander them,
> Toss them like pennies in the air—

By comparing words to nearly worthless pennies tossed aside, the poet tells the reader just how careless we are with the words we use.

A **metaphor** is a direct comparison of unlike things. The words *like* or *as* are not used. In this poem bicycles are compared to monsters.

> And you can't
> Wake them up!
> > Petrified monsters,
> > Their chains entwined.

The technique in which the poet gives human qualities to an animal, object, or idea is called **personification**. Personification in poetry helps the poet create an image, mood, or feeling about the poem. In this poem, the personification of "the blues" brings to mind the people who are feeling down.

> Blues
> Never climb a hill
> Or sit on a roof
> In starlight.

Tone. The attitude the writer has toward the subject is the tone. It may be serious, lighthearted, or humorous, depending on the words the writer uses. Can you guess the writer's attitude in this poem?

> I'm nobody! Who are you?
> Are you nobody, too?
> Then there's a pair of us—don't tell!
> They'd banish us, you know.

Football

WALT MASON

Football can be a hard-hitting, dangerous game. What position would you like to play on this team?

The Game was ended, and the noise at last had died away, and now they gathered up the boys where they in pieces lay. And one was hammered in the ground by many a jolt and jar; some fragments never have been found, they flew away so far. They found a stack of tawny hair, some fourteen cubits high; it was the halfback, lying there, where he had crawled to die. They placed the pieces on a door, and from the crimson field, that hero then they gently bore, like soldier on his shield. The surgeon toiled the livelong night above the gory wreck; he got the ribs adjusted right, the wishbone and the neck. He soldered on the ears and toes, and got the spine in place, and fixed a gutta-percha nose upon the mangled face. And then he washed his hands and said: "I'm glad that task is done!" The halfback raised his fractured head and cried: "I call this fun!"

Developing Comprehension Skills

1. What happens to the halfback in this poem?

2. What does the surgeon do for the half-back?

3. Is the poet describing a real event? How can you tell? Why do you think he chose to write about football in this way?

4. Who or what is "the gory wreck"?

5. What is surprising about the last line of the poem?

6. What does the poet's opinion of football and football players seem to be? Do you agree with this opinion?

Reading Literature: Poetry

1. **Understanding Hyperbole.** You recall that hyperbole is a type of figurative language. It exaggerates an idea in order to create a vivid picture. Hyperbole is often used to create a humorous or shocking effect. Find two examples of hyperbole in "Football." How does hyperbole affect the mood of the poem?

2. **Understanding Concrete Poetry.** This poem does not look like most of the other poems you have read. This is because it is a concrete poem. A **concrete poem** is one in which the shape of the poem suggests something important about the meaning. For example, a poem about flowers might resemble the shape of a flower.

Look at the form of "Football" once again. What does the form remind you of? Why might the poet have chosen this form?

3. **Recognizing Figures of Speech.** In addition to hyperbole, this poem also contains two other types of figures of speech: simile and metaphor. A **simile** is a comparison between two unlike things that uses the words *like* or *as*. A **metaphor** is a comparison between two unlike things that does not use the words *like* or *as*. Find one example of each figure of speech in this poem. What image is created by each one?

4. **Identifying Rhyme Scheme.** At first it may be hard to recognize the rhyme scheme in this poem. This is because the rhymes do not appear at the ends of the lines. Read "Football" aloud. Listen for the rhyming words. Then chart the rhyme scheme.

5. **Recognizing Alliteration.** You know that alliteration is the repetition of consonant sounds at the beginnings of words. Find the alliteration in this part of the poem:

> And one was hammered in the ground by
> many a jolt and jar; some fragments never
> have been found, they flew away so far.

What effect does the alliteration have? What ideas or feelings are emphasized?

Arithmetic

Compare this definition of arithmetic to the one you find in the dictionary. Which do you think is more accurate?

CARL SANDBURG

Arithmetic is where numbers fly like pigeons in and out of your
    head.
Arithmetic tells you how many you lose or win if you know how
    many you had before you lost or won.
Arithmetic is seven eleven all good children go to heaven—or five
    six bundle of sticks.
Arithmetic is numbers you squeeze from your head to your hand to
    your pencil to your paper till you get the answer.
Arithmetic is where the answer is right and everything is nice and
    you can look out of the window and see the blue sky—or the
    answer is wrong and you have to start all over and try again and
    see how it comes out this time.
If you take a number and double it and double it again and then
    double it a few more times, the number gets bigger and bigger
    and goes higher and higher and only arithmetic can tell you
    what the number is when you decide to quit doubling.
Arithmetic is where you have to multiply—and you carry the
    multiplication table in your head and hope you won't lose it.
If you have two animal crackers, one good and one bad, and you eat
    one and a striped zebra with streaks all over him eats the other,
    how many animal crackers will you have if somebody offers you
    five six seven and you say No no no and you say Nay nay nay
    and you say Nix nix nix?
If you ask your mother for one fried egg for breakfast and she gives
    you two fried eggs and you eat both of them, who is better in
    arithmetic, you or your mother?

Numbers in Color (detail), 1959, JASPER JOHNS. Encaustic and newspaper on canvas, 66½" × 49½". Albright-Knox Art Gallery. Gift of Seymour H. Knox, 1959, Buffalo, New York.

Developing Comprehension Skills

1. In the first sentence, what are numbers compared to?

2. Does this poet seem to be interested more in facts or in feelings? Explain your answer.

3. Do you think this poem is directed at children, adults, or both? Use passages from the poem to support your opinion.

4. Are these definitions of arithmetic good ones? Why or why not?

Reading Literature: Poetry

1. **Appreciating Form.** "Arithmetic" is nine sentences long. The first word or first two words of each sentence extend out to the left of the rest of the sentence. Why do you think the poet arranged the poem this way?

2. **Understanding Language.** Sandburg creates a very childlike feeling in this poem. Study the poem. How does Sandburg use words and sentence structure to make the poem sound as though it were written by a child?

3. **Recognizing Humor.** Sandburg uses a great deal of humor in this poem. He creates humor by first remembering how we felt about arithmetic as children. Then he puts that feeling into words so that we can see it, recognize it, and laugh at it.

Look at the eighth line, which deals with animal crackers. What is Sandburg remembering and making fun of?

Medicine

ALICE WALKER

Some people say that laughter is the best medicine. What else can be used to fight illness?

Grandma sleeps with
my sick
            grand-
pa so she
can get him
during the night
medicine
to stop
   the pain

      In
   the morning
      clumsily
         I
      wake
         them

Her eyes
look at me
from under-
               neath
his withered
arm

      The
   medicine
      is all
         in
   her long
         un-
               braided
                     hair.

Developing Comprehension Skills

1. Who is the speaker in this poem?

2. Why does the grandmother sleep with her sick husband?

3. What does "The medicine is all in her long unbraided hair" mean?

4. How do you think the speaker feels about her grandparents? How do you know?

5. What do you think is the best treatment for an illness—love or medicine? Explain your answer.

Reading Literature: Poetry

1. **Understanding Shape.** The shape of this poem catches your attention immediately. There are never more than three words in a line. What picture is created by this unusual shape? Look for a hint in the poem itself.

2. **Understanding Mood.** How would you describe the mood of this poem? How is the mood created? Study the vocabulary, the shape of the poem, and the description of the characters.

3. **Recognizing Unusual Word Order.** Look at the first and second "sentences" of the poem. Which words seem out of order? Why do you think the poet placed these words where she did?

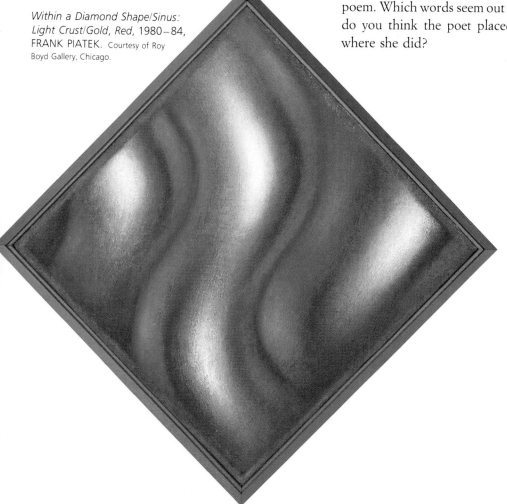

Within a Diamond Shape/Sinus: Light Crust/Gold, Red, 1980–84, FRANK PIATEK. Courtesy of Roy Boyd Gallery, Chicago.

How does a poet behave? Would you recognize one if you saw one?

Voice in the Crowd

TED JOANS

If you should see/a man/walking
    down a crowded street/talking aloud/to himself
        don't run/in the opposite direction
            but run toward him/for he is a *poet!*

        You have nothing to fear/from the poet
        but the truth

Developing Comprehension Skills

1. How does the poet act as he walks down the street? Why might this behavior make someone run away?

2. Why should a person run toward this odd individual?

3. To whom is the speaker addressing this advice?

4. The poem says "You have nothing to fear / from the poet / but the truth." Why might people fear the truth? Give examples to support your answer.

Reading Literature: Poetry

1. **Understanding Punctuation in Poetry.** Why is the poem punctuated in such an unusual way? How do the slashes (/) between the words affect the rate at which you read? Do the slashes have any other effect? Why do you think there is no other punctuation in the poem?

2. **Inferring a Poet's Character Traits.** What attitude does the writer of this poem seem to have toward poets? Remember, the writer is a poet himself. What does this tell you about how he sees himself?

Developing Vocabulary Skills

Understanding Multiple Meanings. The same word may have several different meanings. It may also be used as different parts of speech. These multiple meanings and uses are listed in the dictionary entry for that word.

Look at each underlined word in the sentences below. Then look the word up in the dictionary and read the possible meanings. Try to decide how the word is being used. Write the part of speech of the word and the correct definition. Then write a sentence that uses the word with a different meaning or as a different part of speech.

1. Without any warning in <u>advance</u>,
   My Optileast begins to dance:

2. Rain that fosters growing <u>plants</u>
   Takes the creases out of pants.

3. He'll sigh and give his <u>Branch</u> a Hug;

4. But when he <u>brushes</u> up against a screen,
   We are afraid of what our eyes have seen:

5. And joy seems sweeter when <u>cares</u> come after,

Developing Writing Skills

1. **Analyzing Mood.** Write a paragraph that examines how a poet creates the mood of a poem. Choose either "Football" or "Medicine." In your topic sentence, mention both the poem and the mood it creates. Then discuss how factors such as topic, shape, vocabulary, theme, and sound help create mood.

2. **Using the First-Person Point of View.** Reread the poem "Football." Then write a paragraph or poem that describes the game from the halfback's point of view.

Pre-Writing. Imagine the sights, sounds, smells, and emotions the halfback might experience. List them. Use words that show the player's attitude toward the game.

Writing. Keeping your notes in mind, write your poem or paragraph. Try to describe the game vividly. Use precise words and figurative language to create strong images. Put the details in an order that imitates the way the halfback would be aware of them. If you write a poem, you may use rhyme. You may also choose to write a concrete poem so that the shape of the poem adds to the meaning.

Revising. Reread your poem or paragraph. Make sure that all your details fit the halfback's point of view. Also check your word choice. Replace dull words with vivid words. Replace weak verbs with strong ones. If you wrote a concrete poem, ask several people if the shape of your poem reminds them of anything related to football.

3. **Using Poetry To Define.** Choose a term or an idea to define. Then write a poem like Sandburg's "Arithmetic" that explains the word in an unusual way. Try to create a definite tone and mood.

Developing Skills in Speaking and Listening

Listening to a Poet. Many libraries have a catalog that lists the titles of all records, tapes, films, and filmstrips the library has. Use the audio-visual catalog to locate a record of Carl Sandburg reading his own poems. Listen to how he uses pitch and volume to make his meaning clear. If possible, refer to a copy of one of his poems as he recites it.

Tears

ALONZO LOPEZ

Do tears always mean sorrow? As you read this poem, try to feel the different moods that are described.

Tears of loneliness
    rinse my memory;
Tears of memory
    cleanse my heart;
Tears of sadness
    bathe my eyes;
Tears of hate
    build up
    to drown me.

Developing Comprehension Skills

1. What are the different types of tears? How does each type affect the speaker?

2. The speaker of the poem implies that some types of crying are comforting. Do you agree? Give examples to support your answer.

3. Which kind of tears is destructive? Why do you suppose this is so?

Reading Literature: Poetry

1. **Recognizing Parallelism.** Poets often emphasize an idea by repeating the same type of word, phrase, or sentence several times. What word is repeated in this poem? What sentence structure is repeated? Where does the poet depart from this pattern? What effect does this change have?

2. **Appreciating Imagery.** Alonzo Lopez uses imagery to express the ideas in this poem. These images are meant to be taken figuratively. In other words, the reader is supposed to look beyond the everyday, ordinary meanings of the words to the special meaning beneath them.

   For example, does the poet mean that tears actually *rinse* the memory and *cleanse* the heart? What is the meaning he hopes his readers will get from these images?

3. **Symbol.** The poet has endless ways to describe the woman in the poem, but he chooses only memory, heart, and eyes. These might be considered symbols, things that represent something else. If memory represents the past, what might the heart and eyes of the woman stand for?

4. **Alliteration.** One sound is repeated in 7 of the 9 lines in this poem. What is this sound? What does the repetition of this sound add to the overall effect of the poem?

who knows if the moon's

e. e. cummings

Where does your imagination take you when you want to escape? Read about one place where you might like to go.

who knows if the moon's
a balloon, coming out of a keen city
in the sky—filled with pretty people?
(and if you and i should

get into it, if they
should take me and take you into their balloon,
why then
we'd go up higher with all the pretty people

than houses and steeples and clouds:
go sailing
away and away sailing into a keen
city which nobody's ever visited, where

always
        it's
            Spring) and everyone's
in love and flowers pick themselves

Developing Comprehension Skills

1. To what is the moon compared in this poem?

2. What might the moon / balloon come from?

3. What is meant by the phrase "and flowers pick themselves"? How does this phrase add to the mood of the poem?

4. Describe the place where the balloon is going. Is it a place where you would like to go? Explain why or why not.

5. What do you learn about the speaker from this poem? What kind of personality does the speaker seem to have?

Reading Literature: Poetry

1. **Understanding Punctuation and Capitalization.** e.e. cummings has his own system of capitalization and punctuation. For example, the only word that is capitalized in this poem is *Spring*. There are no periods, although there is other punctuation. How does this affect the poem? Why are the parentheses placed where they are? Does the unusual style make the poem easier or harder to understand? How does it emphasize certain words?

2. **Appreciating Form.** The form of this poem is very loose and unstructured. Why do you suppose cummings set up the poem in this way?

3. **Noticing Repetition.** Sometimes writers repeat words, phrases, or ideas. They do this to provide emphasis or to create a certain effect in their writing.

   Look at the part of the poem inside the parentheses. What ideas are repeated from somewhere else in the poem? How does the wording change when each idea is repeated? What effect do you think the writer was trying to create?

4. **Identifying Alliteration and Assonance.** You know that alliteration is the repetition of consonant sounds at the beginnings of words. Look for a phrase in this poem in which the *p* sound is repeated. Are any other sounds repeated?

   Assonance is the repetition of vowel sounds within words. What vowel sounds are repeated in the following phrases?
   a. who knows if the moon's a balloon,
   b. than houses and steeples and clouds:
   c. go sailing away and away sailing into a keen city

The Red Balloon, 1922, PAUL KLÉE.
Solomon R. Guggenheim Museum, New York.
Photograph by David Heald.

Absolutes

GUSTAVE KEYSER
From an ink painting by Seiho

An ink painting inspired this
poem. Notice how the poet
imitates the mood of this bleak
black and white drawing.

black on white
crow in snow
      hunched
       wet lump
on brittle branch
remembering warmth
remembering corn
miserable
as life
is
black on white

Crows in the Night Snow,
1775, DAGYOKU SANJIN.
The Shin'enkan Collection.

Developing Comprehension Skills

1. This poem describes a scene. What is the black object in the scene? Why is the background white?

2. What is the crow thinking about? What is his mood?

3. What is the mood of the poem as a whole? How do the adjectives help create the mood?

4. Look at the title and the last four lines of the poem. What is the theme, or main idea, that the poet is trying to express? Do you agree with this idea?

5. Notice the position of the word *miserable* in the poem. Do you think this word refers to the crow or to life in general? Explain your answer.

Reading Literature: Poetry

1. **Understanding Concrete Poems.** You know that the shape of a concrete poem tells something about the subject of the poem. What does the shape of this poem remind you of?

2. **Identifying the Sounds of Language.** Find an example of alliteration in this poem. Why do you think the poet repeated this particular sound? Now find three examples of assonance in the poem. How does each vowel sound add to the total effect of the poem?

3. **Feeling the Rhythm of a Poem.** "Absolutes" is made up of short words and short lines. How does this affect the way you read the poem? In what way does this rhythm reinforce the meaning of the poem?

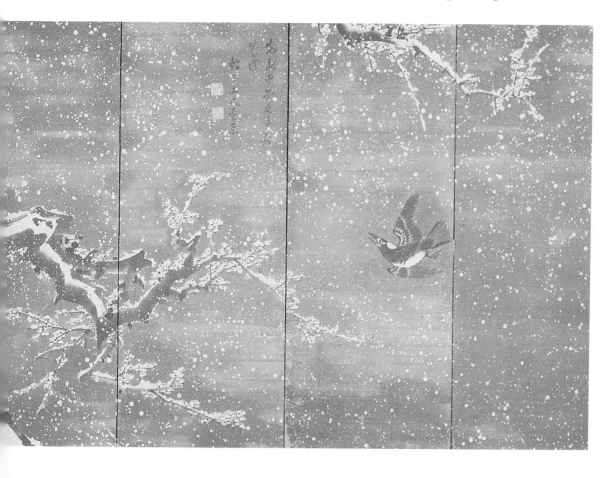

The Universe

How did the universe begin?
How far does it reach? And why
do we ask ourselves impossible
questions like this?

MAY SWENSON

What
is it about,
the universe,
the universe about us stretching out?
We, within our brains,
within it,
think

we must unspin
the laws that spin it.
We think *why*
because we think
because.
Because we think,
we think
the universe about us.

But does it think,
the universe?
Then what about?
About us?
If not,
must there be cause
in the universe?
Must it have laws?
And what
if the universe
is not about us?
Then what?
What
is it about?
And what
about *us?*

Developing Comprehension Skills

1. Why do we want answers about how the universe works?

2. What is meant by "we, within our brains, within it"?

3. You are probably familiar with the phrase "we think the world of her." What does the poet mean by "Because we think we think the universe about us."

4. If the universe does not think about us, what might no longer be true?

5. Who or what does the speaker imply we must worry about if the universe is not aware of us?

6. The speaker may be hinting that we are not as important as we think we are. How important do you think humankind is in the universe?

Reading Literature: Poetry

Understanding Form Look at the paragraph below. It is "The Universe" written in prose form. Read the paragraph to yourself several times. How did the form of the poem affect your understanding of it? Did it make it more confusing? Does the form add meaning to the words? What does the shape of the poem remind you of? Why is this shape appropriate?

What is it about, the universe about us stretching out? We within our brains within it think we must unspin the laws that spin it. We think *why* because we think because, Because we think we think the universe about us. But does it think, the universe? Then what about? About us? If not, must there be cause in the universe? Must it have laws? And what if the universe is *not about* us? Then what? What is it about and what about *us*?

Developing Vocabulary Skills

Identifying Homographs. Sometimes you will find that a word is listed as an entry word in a dictionary more than once. These words are called homographs. **Homographs** are words that have the same spelling but different, unrelated meanings. Most homographs have the same pronunciation, but some do not. Read these entries for *row*.

row[1] (rō) *n.* a number of people in a straight line.
row[2] (rō) *v.* to move a boat on water by using oars.
row[3] (rou) *n.* a noisy quarrel.

Find the following words in the poems you have read. Reread the parts of the poems that contain these words. Then, using a dictionary, write the word and its homograph number, the respelling of the word, and the correct meaning of the word as it is used in the poem.

1. *mate*, "The Optileast and the Pessimost," line 10

2. *host*, "The Optileast and the Pessimost," line 28

3. *stall*, "Rain," line 6

4. *minute*, "Life," line 1

5. *peck*, "Life," line 3

6. *foils*, "Life," line 9

7. *bore*, "Football," line 12

8. *toiled*, "Football," line 13

Developing Writing Skills

1. **Comparing Images.** Both "who knows if the moon's" and "Absolutes" present clear images. Compare these images in two paragraphs. First, describe the pictures both poems paint. Compare differences and similarities. Be sure to think about the mood each image creates. Then tell which of the images you like best and why.

2. **Writing a Poem from a Picture.** Choose a picture from this book. Write a short poem inspired by the picture.

   Pre-Writing. Page through the book. Choose five pictures that appeal to you. Write down their page numbers. Go back and study each one carefully. Then choose one picture to write about. List details about the picture. Think about the subject, the colors, and the shapes. Also, think about the feelings that the picture gives you.

   Writing. Use your notes to write a short poem. Try to give your reader some idea of what the picture looks like. Also try to express a feeling or attitude about this picture just as the writer of "Absolutes" did. If possible, use a rhythm that adds to the meaning of the poem.

   Revising. Work in small groups of three or four people. Have the group listen as each member reads his or her poem. Then look at the picture on which the poem is based. Decide which words or lines are most effective in describing the picture. As you read your poem aloud, you may hear words you want to change. If so, mark the changes after you finish reading.

Developing Skills in Study and Research

Sometimes you want to present the main ideas of a piece of writing in a report, speech, or discussion. You can do this by preparing a paraphrase of the material. When you write a paraphrase, you simplify material and put it in your own words.

Reread "The Universe," by May Swenson. Look at one idea at a time. Try to restate each idea in your own words. When you are done, look at these notes carefully. Then write a paragraph that presents all of the ideas in a clear, organized manner.

Developing Skills in Speaking and Listening

Using Music To Interpret a Poem. Choose one of the poems from this section. Find some music that has the same mood as the poem. Play the music on a record player or tape recorder as you read the poem aloud. The music should help set the mood for your reading.

If you choose to read "who knows if the moon's" or "The Universe," first read your poem to someone who has never heard it before. See if that person can understand the poem from the way you are reading it.

Speaker and Tone

The speaker is the person, or voice, speaking the words of the poem. Often, the poet is the speaker. Sometimes however, the poet imagines the words that another person might say.

To really understand a poem, first decide who the speaker is. Then ask yourself these questions. How does the speaker feel about the subject? Is the attitude respectful and serious? Is it sarcastic or amused? Is it optimistic or pessimistic? This attitude is often the tone of the poem. The better you understand the tone, the more you will enjoy the poem.

Portrait of Scott, 1968, ROBERT VICKREY. Collection of Remson Scott Vickrey.

The Way It Is

GLORIA ODEN

Parents play a central role in every person's life. How important are they in shaping their children's character?

Forever Free, 1933, SARGENT JOHNSON.
Wood with lacquer on cloth, 36" × 11½" × 9½"
(91.5 × 29.2 × 24.2 cm.). San Francisco Museum of Art.
Gift of Mrs. E.D. Lederman. Photograph by Phillip Galgiani.

I have always known
that had I been blonde
blue-eyed
with skin fabled white as the unicorn's
with cheeks tinted and pearled
as May morning on the lips of a rose
such commercial virtues
could never have led me to assume myself
anywhere near as beautiful as
my mother
whose willow fall of black hair
—now pirate silver—
I brushed as a child
(earning five cents)
when shaken free from the bun
as wrapped round and pinned
it billowed in a fine mist
from her proud shoulders
to her waist.

Brown as I am, she is browner.
Walnut
like the satin leaves of the oak
that fallen overwinter in woods
where night comes quickly
and whose wind-peaked piles
deepen the shadows of
such seizure.

Moreover, she is tall.
At her side standing
I feel I am still
the scarecrow child of
yesteryear:

owl-eyed
toothed, boned, and angled
opposite to her
soft southern presence—
an inaudible allegiance
but sweetening her attendance
upon strangers and friends.

Dark hair, dark skin
these are the dominant measures of
my sense of beauty
which explains possibly
why being a black girl
in a country of white strangers
I am so pleased with myself.

Developing Comprehension Skills

1. As described in the poem, what is society's version of "perfect" beauty? Is this the speaker's view, too?

2. Do you think the mother and daughter have a loving relationship? Why or why not?

3. How does her mother's beauty make the speaker feel? Does this feeling bother her?

4. What does the speaker mean by "a country of white strangers"?

5. What is the speaker grateful to her mother for? In your opinion, what are the most important things a parent can give a child?

Reading Literature: Poetry

1. **Inferring Character.** Most of this poem deals with outward, or physical, description. Little is said directly about the personality of the speaker or her mother. However, the reader can infer a great deal from the tone and words of the speaker.

   What kind of person do you think the mother is? How does she view herself? Because of the mother, how does the speaker feel about herself?

2. **Recognizing Metaphors.** Find the two metaphors that describe the mother's hair. Why do you think the poet used these metaphors?

3. **Understanding Rhythm.** The rhythm of this poem is not regular. There is no set pattern of accented and unaccented syllables. Yet the poem still has rhythm. It is the natural rhythm of every day speech. This rhythm is called **free verse.** Why do you think the poet chose to write this poem in free verse?

Youth to Age

PAULI MURRAY

How we see life often depends on our age. According to this poem, what do the young and old have in common?

Aged one and wise,
Were you twenty-two again
Would you risk all for fame?
Conform?
Or go your way alone?

But how can you reply, being seventy-two?
Your path is fogged with memories
As mine with fears.

Developing Comprehension Skills

1. How old is the "aged one" in the poem? How old is the speaker? How do you know?

2. What are the decisions that the speaker is trying to make? What are the possible choices?

3. Does the speaker think the older person will be able to provide answers to any of the questions? Why can't the speaker find the answers without help?

4. In your own words, tell what these lines mean: "Your path is fogged with memories As mine with fears."

5. This poem suggests that life is like a path. Do you think this is a good metaphor for life? Why or why not? What other metaphors might be used to describe life?

Reading Literature: Poetry

1. **Analyzing the Speaker.** The age of the speaker is clear from the poem. What else can you tell about this person from the questions he or she asks? What additional insights might you get from the second stanza? Finally, what is the tone, or attitude, of the speaker?

2. **Understanding the Stanza.** You know that lines of poetry are grouped together in stanzas. The break between stanzas often signals that the poet is changing ideas, mood, or tone. Studying stanza breaks can help you understand a poem. Explain the difference between the first and the second stanzas in "Youth to Age."

A Pair of Boots, 1887, VINCENT van GOGH. The Baltimore Museum of Art. The Cone Collection, formed by Dr. Claribel Cone and Miss Etta Cone of Baltimore, Maryland. (BMA 1950.302)

Kidnap Poem

NIKKI GIOVANNI

Can you find the words in this poem that refer to poetry? As you read, watch for surprising uses of familiar words.

ever been kidnapped
by a poet
if i were a poet
i'd kidnap you
put you in my phrases and meter
you to jones beach
or maybe coney island
or maybe just to my house

lyric you in lilacs
dash you in the rain
blend into the beach
to complement my sea
play the lyre for you
ode you with my love song
anything to win you
wrap you in the red Black green
show you off to mama
yeah if i were a poet i'd kid
nap you

Towards Disappearance, II, 1958, SAM FRANCIS. Oil on canvas, 9' ½" × 10' 5⅞". Museum of Modern Art, New York. Blanchette Rockefeller Fund.

Developing Comprehension Skills

1. What are some of the things the speaker would do if she were a poet?

2. What do you think the poet means by "lyric you in lilacs / dash you in the rain"?

3. What is the speaker's relationship with the person she is talking to? How do you know?

4. Does the speaker mean she would actually kidnap the person she is speaking to? If not, what does she mean? Why do you think she chose the idea of kidnapping to express her thoughts?

5. This poem seems to have been meant as a love poem. If you received it, would you be touched? Why or why not?

1. **Identifying Tone.** A kidnapping should be a frightening, serious matter. Is this the tone of "Kidnap Poem"? If not, what would you say the tone is?

2. **Appreciating Style.** Nikki Giovanni wrote this poem without any capitalization or punctuation. What effect does this have on the poem? To answer, ask yourself how the lack of these familiar "signposts" affects the way you read the poem. Also consider what the poet might have been feeling that would make these details unimportant.

3. **Recognizing Alliteration.** There is a great deal of musical feeling to this poem. One technique the writer uses to accomplish this is alliteration. **Alliteration**, you recall, is the repetition of a consonant sound at the beginnings of words. Find two examples of alliteration in the second stanza of the poem. What does this add to the poem?

4. **Noticing Unusual Uses of Language.** Language can be used in unusual ways to create humor or interest for the reader. What is unusual about Giovanni's use of the poetic term "meter" in this poem? What other words does she use in surprising ways? Finally, how do these unexpected uses of language affect the tone of the poem as a whole?

I'm Nobody!
Who Are You?

EMILY DICKINSON

Would you like to be famous, or would you be happier with a quiet life? What does the speaker in this poem prefer?

I'm nobody! Who are you?
Are you nobody, too?
Then there's a pair of us—don't tell!
They'd banish us, you know.

How dreary to be somebody!
How public, like a frog
To tell your name the livelong day
To an admiring bog!

Seated Girl with Dog, 1944, MILTON AVERY.
Collection of Roy R. Neuberger, New York. Photograph
copyright © M. Varon.

Developing Comprehension Skills

1. What happens to "nobodies," according to the speaker?

2. What are "nobodies"? What are "somebodies"?

3. Does the speaker in the poem want to be a "somebody"? How can you tell?

4. Do you agree with the speaker's opinions about privacy and fame? Explain why or why not.

Reading Literature: Poetry

1. **Understanding Similes.** What is the simile in this poem? How are the two things being compared alike? Do you think this comparison is effective?

2. **Recognizing Tone.** The poem seems to have a tone of humor and lightheartedness. However, there may be another feeling in the poem. For example, who or what is the "admiring bog"? What does the use of the word *bog* tell you about the speaker's attitude?

3. **Identifying Theme.** Theme is the main idea about life that the poet wants to share with the reader. What is the theme of this poem?

Developing Vocabulary Skills

Using Synonyms and Antonyms. Many words in our language have similar meanings. These words are called **synonyms**. When writers compose they try to select just the right synonym with just the right shade of meaning.

Dictionaries can help with this process. Many entries contain **synonymies** at the end of certain entries. These synonymies contain all of the synonyms for the entry word. Some synonymies also contain **antonyms**, or words with the opposite meaning.

Look at the synonyms for the word *proud*, which was used in "The Way It Is." Do you think the writer chose the best synonym? What word could have been used to show the opposite of proud? Write a sentence for each synonym. Make sure that each sentence fits the precise shade of meaning of the word.

> *SYN.*—**proud** having proper self-respect or pride (a *proud* expression); **arrogant** implies the forceful presenting of oneself as having superior importance (the *arrogant* colonel); **haughty** implies great awareness of one's high position, rank, etc., that shows itself in scorn for those one considers beneath one (a *haughty* princess); **overbearing** implies extreme haughtiness made clear in insulting behavior (an *overbearing* supervisor); **disdainful** implies very strong and obvious scorn for that which is beneath one—*ANT.* humble

Developing Writing Skills

1. **Understanding Themes in Poetry.** The poems "The Way It Is" and "Youth to Age" discuss some things we can and cannot learn from older people. In a few paragraphs, discuss what these things are.

   Pre-Writing. Reread the two poems. Take notes on what each speaker was or was not able to learn from the older person. Then think about why there are some things we must learn on our own. You may wish to discuss this with others. As you think and talk, jot down interesting ideas. Finally, put your ideas in logical groups. You may want to put the things we can learn in one group, and the things we can't learn in a second group, and your explanations or conclusions in a third group.

Writing. Using your notes, write a rough draft of your paragraphs. Try to express your ideas simply and clearly. Use examples from the poem or from your own experiences to support each idea.

Revising. Read your paragraphs to another person. Are your ideas clear and easy to understand? Do the ideas seem to flow smoothly as you read them? Make any corrections that are necessary, and rewrite your paragraphs neatly.

2. **Describing a Person.** Describe a person you knew when you were very young. Think about the qualities you remember best. List details about how the person looked and sounded. Then write a poem or a paragraph describing the person as you remember him or her. Try to create a definite tone and mood as you write.

3. **Using Words in Unusual Ways.** Make up a list of terms from specialized areas. You might choose music, sports, or computers, for example. Write a poem or paragraph in which these terms are used in unexpected ways. Reread the "Kidnap Poem" for ideas.

Developing Skills in Study and Research

Developing Skimming and Scanning Techniques. Skimming and scanning are two types of fast reading that will help you read and study effectively. **Skimming** is used to get a general idea of the content of a selection. When you skim, you move your eyes quickly over the material. You look at titles, headings, and illustrations. You also read the first and last sentence of each paragraph.

Scanning is used to find the answer to a specific question. Again, you do not read every word. You look for key words that are related to the information you need. Once you find the information, you read more carefully to get the correct answer.

Find an encyclopedia article about the poet, Emily Dickinson. Skim the article. What information do you find as you skim?

Now scan the encyclopedia article about Emily Dickinson and answer these questions.

1. Was Emily Dickinson an American?

2. When did she live?

3. Was she famous as a poet during her lifetime?

Developing Skills in Critical Thinking

Defining Terms. Words, or terms, can mean different things to different people. It is important to define terms clearly when you are speaking or writing. The writer of "The Way It Is" has a personal definition of beauty. Your definition of beauty may be quite different.

Work with a partner. Discuss what beauty means. It may help to consult a dictionary at first. Think about what makes a person beautiful. Think about people you consider beautiful. Write a definition that satisfies both of you. Then, with your partner, define the following terms:

youth	love	privacy
old age	fame	

Two Friends

DAVID IGNATOW

Are you able to talk to your friends? And do they really listen? Read this poem to find out what kind of relationship these two friends have.

I have something to tell you.
I'm listening.
I'm dying.
I'm sorry to hear.
I'm growing old.
It's terrible.
It is, I thought you should know.
Of course and I'm sorry. Keep in touch.
I will and you too.
And let me know what's new.
Certainly, though it can't be much.
And stay well.
And you too.
And go slow.
And you too.

Old Friends, 1983, SANDRA RICE. Baked clay and acrylic. Collection of Dr. Howard and Muriel Pottak. Courtesy of Jay Johnson Gallery, New York.

Developing Comprehension Skills

1. What is wrong with the first speaker?

2. How does one friend react to the news that the other is dying? Are you surprised by this response? Why or why not?

3. How can you tell that the second speaker is not really listening to what the first speaker is saying?

4. What is the theme of this poem?

5. Considering your own relationships with friends, do you think this poem gives a realistic view of most friendships? Do you feel it is too negative? Explain your answer.

Reading Literature: Poetry

1. **Understanding More Than One Speaker.** Two people are involved in conversation in this poem. How can you tell which friend is speaking? Look at the statements of first one friend, and then the other. How would you describe each person?

2. **Appreciating Irony.** You remember that the contrast between what is expected or thought to be true and what is actually true is called irony. What is ironic about the title of this poem? What is ironic about the lines "And let me know what's new"?

Poem

Love for a friend may run very deep. But what happens when the friend goes away?

LANGSTON HUGHES

I loved my friend.
He went away from me.
There's nothing more to say.
The poem ends,
Soft as it began—
I loved my friend.

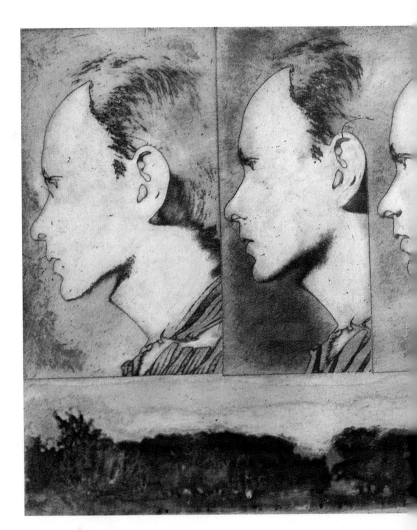

Developing Comprehension Skills

1. How does the speaker feel about his friend?

2. What happened to the friend?

3. Why does the speaker say, "There's nothing more to say"? Why do you think the speaker chooses not to explain any details?

4. Look at the lines "The poem ends/Soft as it began—" What else is ending besides the poem? Why does the poet use the word *soft* to describe the ending?

5. Compare this poem to "Two Friends." Which do you think is the more realistic version of most friendships?

6. Do you think this poem reflects the way most people feel when a friendship ends? Why?

Reading Literature: Poetry

1. **Relating Poetry to Personal Experience.** Have you ever experienced the loss of someone you loved? Did this poem remind you of the feelings you had then? How?

2. **Identifying Mood.** What is the mood of this poem? What techniques does the poet use to create this mood?

3. **Understanding Repetition.** The first line of the poem is repeated as the last line. How does this repetition add to the mood and the ideas in the poem? What does it show is most important to the speaker? How does the reader's understanding of the line change by the second reading?

Figure in Landscape, 1966, KEITH A. SMITH.
Photo-etching 9 × 12". Museum of Modern Art, New York. Purchase.

Where the Rainbow Ends

RICHARD RIVE

A legend says that you can find a pot of gold at the end of a rainbow. Read the poem to discover what kind of treasure the speaker in this poem hopes to find.

Where the rainbow ends
There's going to be a place, brother,
Where the world can sing all sorts of songs,
And we're going to sing together, brother,
You and I, though you're white and I'm not.
It's going to be a sad song, brother,
Because we don't know the tune,
And it's a difficult tune to learn.
But we can learn, brother, you and I.
There's no such tune as a black tune.
There's no such tune as a white tune.
There's only music, brother,
And it's music we're going to sing
Where the rainbow ends.

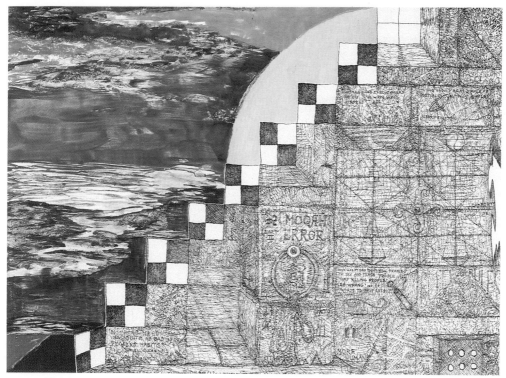

No Room for Error, 1983, WILLIAM T. WILEY. Frumkin and Struve Gallery, Chicago.

Developing Comprehension Skills

1. Is the speaker of this poem white or black?

2. What is the song the speaker mentions? Why will it be sad? What does the speaker mean by "there's no such tune as a black tune" or a white tune?

3. Do you think that the speaker is optimistic or pessimistic about reaching the rainbow's end? What is your own opinion? Give reasons for your answer.

Reading Literature: Poetry

1. **Understanding Mood.** This poem can make you feel hopeful, almost joyful. Yet, at the same time, you may feel other emotions. What are these feelings? Find the phrases in the poem that made you feel each way.

2. **Understanding a Symbol.** A symbol is a person, place, object, or idea that stands for something other than itself. For example, a flag might stand for patriotism. Blue skies could symbolize happiness. By using symbols, a writer tells you more about his ideas than is apparent on the surface.

   In this poem, both music and the rainbow stand for something other than themselves. What are some of the qualities of music? Why would the poet want you to think about these qualities when you read the poem? Now think about all the ideas and feelings that a rainbow brings to mind. Why are these important to the poem?

Friendship

What do you look for in a friend? Read to see whether the qualities mentioned in this poem are important to you.

OGLALA SIOUX

Friend, whatever hardships threaten
If thou call me,
I'll befriend thee;
All-enduring, fearlessly,
I'll befriend thee.

Osage Friendship Blanket, 1900. Cranbrook Institute of Science, Bloomfield Hills, Michigan.

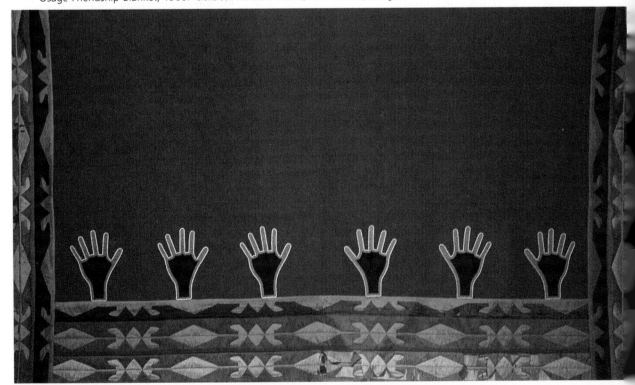

Developing Comprehension Skills

1. To whom is the poem addressed?

2. What does the speaker believe a good friend should be willing to do?

3. Instead of saying, "I will help you" the speaker says "I'll befriend thee." Why do you think the second phrase was used instead of the first?

4. Based on the poems you have read so far in this section of the chapter, how would you define a friend?

Reading Literature: Poetry

1. **Understanding Repetition.** In this short poem, the poet has chosen to repeat this line: "I'll befriend thee." Why did the poet write this line twice?

2. **Understanding Mood.** What is the mood of this poem? How does the language and word choice help create this mood?

Developing Vocabulary Skills

Identifying Inflected Forms. Many words are formed by adding endings to other words. For example, -s or -es is added to most nouns to form plurals. The suffixes -ed and -ing are used to change the tense of verbs. The suffixes -er and -est are used to form comparisons of adjectives and adverbs. These plurals, comparative forms, and different tenses are called the **inflected forms** of a word. Most dictionaries show the inflected forms if there are any unusual changes made to the base word when the endings are added. The inflected forms are shown in boldface type following the part of speech label. Sometimes only the part of the word that changes is shown.

The following words are main entries in a dictionary. Write one inflected form that is shown for each word.

kneel	crazy	fish	memory
leap	mice	repairman	mighty
assume	wrap	least	child

Developing Writing Skills

1. **Writing About Friendship.** Each of the poems in this section is about friendship. Write a composition about the kinds of friendship described in these poems. Include a paragraph telling which qualities you yourself think a friend should have.

Pre-Writing. Reread all four poems. As you finish each one, jot down a few ideas about the kind of friendship presented in the poem. Also write down any qualities of a friend that are mentioned in the poem. When you are done reading, organize your ideas logically. For example, you may want to organize the paragraph by listing the qualities you would select in the order of their importance to you.

Writing. Your first paragraph should tell which poems you will discuss and the idea you will be exploring. For the body paragraphs, use your notes to write one or two paragraphs about the types of friendship covered in the poems. Then write a paragraph that lists the qualities you feel are important. Write a final paragraph that states your conclusions about friendship.

Revising. Reread your rough draft carefully. Does every paragraph have a topic sentence? Do all details relate to the topic? Are all your details accurate? Did you make a statement connecting all three poems in the introduction?

2. **Writing a Poem.** The poet who wrote "Where the Rainbow Ends" describes a place where black people and white people will live together peacefully. What other treasures can you find at the rainbow's end? Write a poem describing your hopes and dreams for the future. You might begin it with the same words as "Where the Rainbow Ends":

> Where the rainbow ends
> There's going to be a place . . .

Developing Skills in Study and Research

Using the Vertical File. Many libraries have a vertical file. A vertical file is a cabinet that contains brochures, pamphlets, catalogs, and other information on a variety of subjects. The subjects are listed in alphabetical order. You might consult the vertical file if you need up-to-date information or pictures for a report.

Locate the vertical file in your library. Look up the topic "American Indian" or "Native Americans." Make a list of all the materials the file contains on this subject. See if the file has any information about the Oglala Sioux, the tribe from which the poem "Friendship" comes.

Developing Skills in Speaking and Listening

Interpretation of Poems on a Theme. Prepare an oral reading of three of the poems on the subject of friendship. Work in a group of four. Two group members will work together on an oral interpretation of "Two Friends," each taking the part of one of the speakers. Each of the other two members of the group will choose either "Poem" or "Friendship." Practice your poems individually and then as a group. Make sure the audience will be able to hear the differences in each poem's mood and view of friendship.

Imagery and Mood

In some ways, a poem is like a photograph. It is a reflection of real life. Poet Nikki Giovanni explains what poetry means to her:

A poem is a way of capturing a moment. I want my camera and film to record what my eye and my heart saw.

As you read poems, try to see the picture that the poet has created.

Apparition, 1947, HANS HOFMANN. Krannert Art Museum, University of Illinois, Urbana-Champaign, Illinois. Festival of Arts Purchase Fund.

Troubled Woman

LANGSTON HUGHES

Sometimes pain can be reflected in a person's appearance. As you read this poem, try to imagine the events that have hurt the woman so deeply.

She stands
In the quiet darkness,
This troubled woman
Bowed by
Weariness and pain
Like an
Autumn flower
In the frozen rain,
Like a
Wind-blown autumn flower
That never lifts its head
Again.

Developing Comprehension Skills

1. How does the woman in this poem look?

2. What types of experiences has her life been filled with? How do you know?

3. How is the woman like the flower? Do you think that the comparison is a good one? Why or why not?

4. Does the speaker think the woman will ever be happy again? Find evidence in the poem to support your answer.

5. How does the speaker feel about this woman? How do you know?

Reading Literature: Poetry

1. **Appreciating Imagery.** This poem is built on one strong sight image. What simile is used to create this image? What picture forms in your mind as you read the poem? Do you see the woman, the flower, or both? What meaning does the flower comparison add to the poem?

2. **Understanding How Description Adds to a Mood.** In this poem the poet uses adjective/noun combinations that help strengthen the main image and mood. One example is "quiet darkness." This adjective/noun combination tells the reader that it is dark, probably lonely, where the woman is. It is quiet and still, with no noise to disturb the mood.

   Find four more adjective/noun combinations in this poem. Tell how they contribute to the overall image and mood of the poem.

3. **Recognizing Free Verse.** This poem is written in free verse. It does not have a rhyme scheme, and it has no set rhythm. There are, however, three words in the poem that rhyme. What are those three words? Why do you think the poet chose these words to rhyme? Read the poem aloud. What does the insertion of these rhyming words add to the overall impact of the poem?

Dead Sunflower, 1917, CHARLES BURCHFIELD.
Munson-Williams-Proctor Institute, Utica, New York.
Edward W. Root bequest.

Driving to Town Late To Mail a Letter

ROBERT BLY

Do you like cold, snowy evenings? Read the poem to find what one person enjoys about such nights.

It is a cold and snowy night. The main street is deserted.
The only things moving are swirls of snow.
As I lift the mailbox door, I feel its cold iron.
There is a privacy I love in this snowy night.
Driving around, I will waste more time.

Developing Comprehension Skills

1. Why is the speaker out on the cold and snowy night?

2. What do the streets and town look like?

3. What does the speaker mean by "There is a privacy I love in this snowy night"?

4. In the last line, the speaker says that he or she will drive around and "waste more time." Why do you think the speaker wishes to do this?

5. A cold winter night usually keeps people inside. What does this poem tell you about the importance of a person's attitude or point of view?

Reading Literature: Poetry

1. **Recognizing Mood.** How would you describe the mood of this poem? Find specific words that help to create the mood.

2. **Recognizing Imagery.** This poem creates a clear picture of a snowy night. It appeals strongly to the senses. Which images are strongest? How does the writer help readers to see, hear, and feel the night?

3. **Identifying Assonance.** You will recall that assonance is the repetition of vowel sounds within words. Read the poem aloud. What vowel sound is repeated two or three times in every line? What effect does the use of assonance have on the sound and meaning of the poem?

4. **Identifying the Speaker of a Poem.** Describe the speaker in the poem. What kind of person do you think he or she is? Can you infer anything about the speaker's attitude toward life? Explain your answer by telling what words or phrases in the poem helped form your opinion.

Bicycles

ANDREI VOZNESENSKY
Translated by Anselm Hollo

As you read this poem, look for the image that the riderless bicycles are being compared to.

The bicycles lie
In the woods, in the dew.
    Between the birch trees
    The highroad gleams.

They fell, fell down
Mudguard to mudguard,
    Handlebar to handlebar
    Pedal to pedal.

And you can't
Wake them up!
    Petrified monsters,
    Their chains entwined.

Huge and surprised
They stare at the sky.
    Above them, green dusk
    Resin, and bumblebees.

In the luxurious
Rustling of camomile, peppermint
    Leaves they lie, Forgotten,
    Asleep. Asleep.

Developing Comprehension Skills

1. Where do the bicycles lie?

2. How do you suppose the bicycles got where they are? Who may have left them there? Explain your answer.

3. To what are the bicycles compared? How are the two things similar? What unusual qualities does this comparison give to the bicycles?

4. Describe how the bicycles are contrasted with their surroundings. How does this contrast add to the mood?

5. The poet seems to feel sorry for the bicycles. People often develop feelings for non-living objects. Can you think of some examples?

Reading Literature: Poetry

1. **Recognizing Imagery.** Describe the image, or mental picture, that you liked best as you read the poem. How did the poet create the image?

2. **Identifying Mood.** What is the mood or feeling of this poem? Point out specific words and lines to support your answer.

3. **Understanding Repetition.** What words are repeated in the second and last stanzas? What effect does the repetition have on the meaning and the mood?

4. **Understanding Theme.** Sometimes a poem may not contain a definite theme or message for the reader. In your opinion, does "Bicycles" have a specific theme? What do you think the poet wanted to communicate by writing this poem?

5. **Appreciating Form.** In each stanza, two lines are indented. Do you see any similarities in these indented lines? in the unindented lines? What purpose might the poet have had for arranging the lines this way?

6. **Identifying Figures of Speech.** Review the figures of speech described on page 223. Which ones can be found in this poem?

Concrete Trap

ELIZABETH COATSWORTH

An unfamiliar place can be bewildering and frightening. What is the one hope for the fox in this poem?

The fox at midnight in the city square
knows there's a way, but knows not which it is,
a path that leads to fields and woods and lair,
leaves underfoot, earth and the stirring air.
Bewildered stands the fox, too many streets
lead off too many ways, yet there is one
leads to the woods and to tomorrow's sun.
Under street lamps, between the straight house walls,
hard, geometric, baffling nose and eyes,
escape is there for him to recognize.
Bewildered stands the fox, questing the way,
and in the yards the dogs begin to bay.

Developing Comprehension Skills

1. Describe where the fox is and where it would like to be.

2. How does the fox feel? Why does it feel this way? Give evidence from the poem to support your answer.

3. What phrase does the poet repeat in the poem? Why do you suppose she does this?

4. What threat may soon face the fox?

5. What does the title of the poem mean?

6. How successful do you think the poet was in making the reader understand the feelings of the fox?

Reading Literature: Poetry

1. **Understanding Contrast.** The poet uses contrast between the natural world and the "civilized" world to emphasize the problem the fox is faced with. Make two lists. Write *Civilization* at the top of one list. Write *Nature* at the top of the second. List words

A La Pintura #12, 1975, ROBERT MOTHERWELL. Collection of the Artist.
Courtesy of M. Knoedler and Co. Gallery, New York.

and images from the poem that fall into each of the two categories. Do you think that the use of contrast is effective? Why or why not? Give reasons for your answer.

2. **Understanding Symbolism.** You know that a symbol is a person, place, thing, or idea that represents something other than itself. Do you think that the fox seeking a way out of the city is meant to symbolize something else? What might this be? Support your answer. Do you think the symbol is effective?

3. **Using Capitalization and Punctuation To Aid Understanding.** The word order in this poem is often unusual. Therefore, the ideas are sometimes difficult to follow. How does the capitalization show where new ideas begin in this poem? How do the periods help the reader? What are the commas used for? Choose a sentence from the poem and explain how the punctuation helps the reader understand ideas. Why do you think the poem was punctuated in this way?

time and space

NAOSHI KORIYAMA

Do you ever think about the endless nature of time and space? As you read this poem, notice how one image flows into the next one.

the ocean liner
keeps on sailing
gallantly
riding over
heaving surges
of the open sea
as time flows on
ceaselessly
through
the heartbeat
of the passenger
who is leaning
against the railing
of the topmost deck
looking up
into the sky
where
millions of stars
too
are sailing
through
time
and
space
silently

Nocturne in Black and Gold, the Falling Rocket, about 1874,
JAMES ABBOTT McNEILL WHISTLER. Oil on panel. The Detroit Institute of Arts.
Gift of Dexter M. Ferry, Jr.

Developing Comprehension Skills

1. Describe the setting of this poem.

2. What three things in this poem are moving through time and space?

3. How does the poet change the reader's focus from the ship to the passenger to the stars?

4. Why do you think that the poet chose the image of an ocean liner sailing on the night sea for this poem? Do you think the choice is a good one?

Reading Literature: Poetry

1. **Understanding How Word Choice Creates Mood.** Study the verbs and the adverbs in this poem. Think about their sounds and how they describe what is happening in the poem. Then think about the meaning and mood of the poem. How do the verbs and adverbs add to what is being said?

2. **Recognizing the Theme of a Poem.** Think about the different images in this poem. What ideas are similar to all of them? What message is the poet trying to get across? In your own words, state the theme of this poem.

3. **Noticing Punctuation and Capitalization in Poetry.** Why do you think the poet chose not to use any punctuation or capitalization in this poem? How does the choice contribute to the theme of the poem?

Developing Vocabulary Skills

Using the Best Method To Determine Meaning. Read the following groups of lines. Each is from a poem you have read. If the meaning of

the underlined word can be figured out from the context of the sentence, write *Context Clues*. If you need to use the dictionary to find the meaning, write *Dictionary*. Then write the meaning of each word.

1. And you can't / Wake them up!
   <u>Petrified</u> monsters / Their chains <u>entwined</u>.

2. Above them, green dusk
   <u>Resin</u>, and bumblebees

3. In the luxurious
   Rustling of <u>camomile</u>, peppermint
   Leaves they lie, Forgotten,

4. The main street is <u>deserted</u>.
   The only things moving are <u>swirls</u> of snow.

5. . . . between the straight house walls,
   hard, <u>geometric</u>, baffling nose and eyes

6. Bewildered stands the fox,
   <u>questing</u> the way

7. the ocean liner / keeps on sailing / gallantly / riding over / heaving <u>surges</u>

Developing Writing Skills

1. **Evaluating Imagery.** Choose the image you like best from each of the five poems in this section. The image can be in the form of a simile or a metaphor. It may also be simply a strong description that appeals to the senses. In a paragraph, explain why this image was your favorite.

   Pre-Writing. List the sensory details or images that made an impression on you. Choose the one you like best from each poem. Decide why you chose that image. Did it surprise you with its comparison? Did it appeal strongly to one of your senses?

   Writing. Write a clear topic sentence that introduces the poem and the purpose of the paragraph. Describe the image that appealed to you. Then tell why you think that image is the best. Be specific. Tell how the image affected you. Point out specific words that made the image so vivid.

Revising. Work with a partner. Read each other's compositions. Can each reader picture the image from its description in the paragraph? Are the writer's reasons for choosing that image clear? If your partner cannot understand any of these points, rewrite the paragraph more clearly until he or she does understand.

2. **Writing a Descriptive Poem.** Write a poem that describes a scene. First, think of a place that has a certain atmosphere. It can suggest any mood from sunny and cheerful to dark and eerie. Next list details about the place. What do you see or hear? How would you feel if you were there?

Now write a poem describing the scene. Use images, figures of speech, and sound devices to make the scene come alive.

Developing Skills in Critical Thinking

Classifying Poems. The poems you have read so far have been presented in groups. The poems in each group share certain qualities or characteristics in common with the other poems in the group. For example, the first group of poems used sound in special ways. The second group of poems had interesting shapes.

There are many other ways that these poems can be grouped, or *classified*. For example, poems that are humorous may be grouped together. You could group poems that use rhyme together. Decide on different ways to classify the poems you have read so far in this chapter. Write a title for each group that tells what element the poems have in common.

Figurative Language

Poets know something that the rest of us too often forget. Language is meant to be enjoyable and exciting as well as informative! Poets try to share the joy of words with the reader by using figurative language. They describe things in unusual ways. They exaggerate, sometimes with humorous results. In short, poets use the language to help the reader look at something in an entirely new way. As you read the next few poems, see how language can be much more than words on paper.

River Pond, 1967–75, WAYNE THIEBAUD. University of Rochester Memorial Art Gallery. Joseph C. Wilson Memorial Fund, Rochester, New York.

What are the beautiful things in life worth? Read to see the value one person places on loveliness.

Barter

SARA TEASDALE

Life has loveliness to sell,
　　All beautiful and splendid things,
Blue waves whitened on a cliff,
　　Soaring fire that sways and sings,
And children's faces looking up
Holding wonder like a cup.

Life has loveliness to sell,
　　Music like a curve of gold,
Scent of pine trees in the rain,
　　Eyes that love you, arms that hold,
And for your spirit's still delight,
Holy thoughts that star the night.

Spend all you have for loveliness,
　　Buy it and never count the cost;
For one white singing hour of peace
　　Count many a year of strife well lost,
And for a breath of ecstasy
Give all you have been, or could be.

Carnation, Lily, Lily, Rose, 1886, JOHN SINGER SARGENT. The Tate Gallery, London.

Developing Comprehension Skills

1. What are some of the lovely things in life, according to this poem?

2. What advice does the speaker in this poem give?

3. How can a person "buy" loveliness? What does the speaker mean by "Give all you have been, or could be"?

4. What must a person sometimes trade for an hour of peace?

5. The word *barter* means "to trade or exchange." Why was this used as the title of the poem? Is this choice of a title surprising?

6. Would the speaker in this poem agree or disagree with this statement: "The best things in life are free"? Explain your answer.

Reading Literature: Poetry

1. **Appreciating Imagery.** You know that images are pictures that a writer paints with words. Identify the images in this poem. Tell what senses they appeal to. Then answer the following questions.

   a. How can blue waves be "whitened on a cliff"?

   b. How can fire sing?

   c. Why would music be compared to a curve of gold?

   d. Why would the poet use the words *white* and *singing* to describe an hour of peace?

2. **Understanding Main Ideas.** State the main idea of each stanza. How does the third stanza differ from the first two. Why did the poet change ideas there?

3. **Identifying Figures of Speech.** Read the following lines from the poem. Identify the simile, the metaphor, and the example of personification.

   a. Soaring fire that sways and sings,

   b. And children's faces looking up
   Holding wonder like a cup.

   c. Holy thoughts that star the night.

   Find one other example of each type of figure of speech. Why is each one an effective comparison?

4. **Identifying Rhyme Patterns.** Chart the rhyme scheme for this poem. Is the pattern for each stanza the same? Notice that not every line has a line that rhymes with it. Does the regular rhyme pattern suit the subject? Would free verse be just as effective?

5. **Identifying Alliteration.** In addition to the imagery and figurative language, there are also many examples of alliteration in this poem. One can be found in the first line. Find at least three other examples.

The Distant Drum

CALVIN C. HERNTON

As you read this poem, think about the speaker and the tone of voice. What does the speaker want to tell you?

I am not a metaphor or symbol.
This you hear is not the wind in the trees,
Nor a cat being maimed in the street.
I am being maimed in the street.
It is I who weep, laugh, feel pain or joy,
Speak this because I exist.
This is my voice.
These words are my words,
My mouth speaks them,
My hand writes them—
I am a poet
It is my fist you hear
Beating against your ear.

Developing Comprehension Skills

1. What does the speaker say he is *not*?

2. Explain the first five lines in the poem. What does the poet want his readers to realize about metaphors, symbols, and writers?

3. What do the last two lines of the poem tell you about the message the poet is sending?

4. Why is this poem called "The Distant Drum"? What feelings or ideas does the word "drum" bring to your mind?

5. What experiences do you think may have caused the writer to write this poem?

Reading Literature: Poetry

1. **Understanding Figurative Language.** The writer uses a strong metaphor to conclude his poem. What is the meaning of the lines "It is my fist you hear / Beating against your ear"? How is the figurative language that the poet uses more powerful than a simple statement of the same idea?

2. **Identifying Tone.** How does the poet feel about his subject and about the reader? How would you describe the tone of his voice that comes to you through the poem?

Get Up, Blues

JAMES A. EMANUEL

*Everybody "sings the blues"
sometimes. But what happens
when the song goes on too long?*

Blues
Never climb a hill
Or sit on a roof
In starlight.

Blues
Just bend low
And moan in the street
And shake a borrowed cup.

Blues
Just sit around
Sipping.
Hatching yesterdays.

Get up, Blues.
Fly.
Learn what it means
To be up high.

Argosy, 1958, ADOLPH GOTTLIEB. Oil on Canvas 92 × 72".
Copyright © 1980 Adolph and Esther Gottlieb Foundation, New York.

Developing Comprehension Skills

1. What does the speaker say Blues can and cannot do?

2. In which direction do Blues never go or look?

3. People who feel low often sit around remembering things that happened to them and chances they missed. Which stanza describes people like this? What phrase in particular presents this idea?

4. What does the speaker mean when he tells Blues: "Fly. Learn what it means to be up high"?

5. Consider this poem and "Barter." They both deal with people's attitude toward life. Think of a general statement about life that both poems would agree with.

Reading Literature: Poetry

1. **Identifying Tone.** What is the speaker's attitude toward life? How do you think he feels about people who let themselves feel depressed all of the time? Is he angry? impatient? pitying? caring? Which words tell you this?

2. **Recognizing Theme.** The theme of this poem may lie in the last stanza. Study it and explain what you think the theme is.

3. **Identifying Personification.** What kind of person does Blues become in the second stanza? in the third? Do you think the use of personification makes this a better poem than it might have been otherwise? Explain your answer.

4. **Hearing Assonance.** Assonance sometimes reflects, or imitates, what it is describing. Look at the second stanza. What sound is repeated? What word in the stanza does this sound bring to mind?

5. **Recognizing Repetition.** What is the pattern of repetition in this poem? How does it add to the overall effect?

You know that a pun is a play on words. As you read this poem, watch for the pun it contains.

A Penguin

OLIVER HERFORD

The Pen-guin sits up-on the shore
And loves the lit-tle fish to bore;
He has one en-er-vat-ing joke
That would a very Saint pro-voke:
"The *Pen*-guin's might-i-er than the *Sword*-fish";
He tells this dai-ly to the bored fish,
Un-til they are so weak, they float
With-out re-sis-tance down his throat.

Antarctic emperor penguins.
Animals Animals, New York. Photograph by G. L. Kooyman.

Developing Comprehension Skills

1. Where is the penguin sitting and what is he doing?

2. How do the fish respond to the penguin's joke? What comment might the poet be making about people who tell this type of joke?

3. What is the penguin's purpose in boring the fish?

4. Do you think this poem is humorous? Why or why not?

Reading Literature: Poetry

1. **Recognizing Puns.** The penguin's pun was: "The *Pen*guin's mightier than the *Sword*-fish." This is a pun based on a saying you may have heard: "The pen is mightier than the sword." What does the saying "The pen is mightier than the sword" mean? Why is the penguin's version so ridiculous?

2. **Recognizing Special Techniques.** Usually, it is better not to read poems in a sing-song way, overstressing the accented syllables. In this poem, however, the poet wants you to read this poem that way. What special technique does the poet use that forces you to read this poem like a jump-rope rhyme? Why do you think he wants the poem read this way?

3. **Identifying Rhythm.** This poem has a regular rhythm pattern. How many times is the iambic ($\cup$/) pattern repeated in each line?

4. **Identifying Rhyme.** Chart the rhyme scheme of this poem. Does it follow a regular pattern? How does the rhyme scheme contribute to the overall feeling of the poem?

Words

PAULI MURRAY

A spendthrift is a person who wastes money. What else do we waste just as foolishly?

We are spendthrifts with words,
We squander them,
Toss them like pennies in the air—
Arrogant words,
Angry words,
Cruel words,
Comradely words,
Shy words tiptoeing from mouth to ear.

But the slowly wrought words of love
And the thunderous words of heartbreak—
These we hoard.

Developing Comprehension Skills

1. What does the speaker say we do with words?

2. What kinds of words do we use all the time, sometimes carelessly?

3. Why do people find the words of love and the words of heartbreak hardest to say?

4. Do you think the poet is asking us to do or change something? What might this be?

Reading Literature: Poetry

1. **Understanding Similes.** Reread this simile about words: "We toss them like pennies in the air." Do you think this is a good image for the way we use words? Why or why not?

2. **Appreciating Language.** Pauli Murray uses unusual adjectives to describe the last two types of words. What does "slowly wrought" imply about the words of love? What does "thunderous" say about the words of heartbreak?

3. **Recognizing Personification.** In addition to comparing words to coins, the poet gives them human qualities. Find several examples of this. What additional meaning do these figures of speech add to the poem?

Developing Vocabulary Skills

Recognizing Idioms. Idioms are colorful phrases used in everyday conversation. They have a meaning that cannot be figured out from the individual words in the phrase. An example is the phrase *to keep one's head*. This phrase means "to remain in control of oneself." It has nothing to do with keeping your head attached to your body.

Sometimes you will have to look up an unusual idiom in order to understand its meaning. Idioms can be found in the entry of the most important word in the phrase. For example, you would look up *to keep one's head* under the word *head*.

Each of the following sentences contains an idiom. The main word in each idiom can be found in one of the poems in this chapter. Write the phrase and its meaning. Use a dictionary if necessary.

    a. The guest <u>praised</u> the guest of honor <u>to the skies</u>.
    b. During the squabble, someone shouted, "Hey! <u>Break it up</u>!"
    c. The chosen players were eager <u>to get the show on the road</u>.
    d. Pam was afraid the team captain would <u>light into</u> her when she was late for practice.
    e. Tanya's younger brother always <u>takes</u> her teasing <u>to heart</u>.

Developing Writing Skills

1. **Analyzing a Poem.** Choose one poem from this section. In a few paragraphs, tell how the poet uses figurative language to add to the ideas and feelings of the poem.

    Pre-Writing. Reread the poems and choose one that you feel uses figurative language in an especially interesting way. Answer the following questions and make notes on your answers.

    What does each figurative phrase mean?
    What images does the phrase create in your mind?
    What is the effect of figurative language on the poem? How does it affect the mood? What meaning does it add?

Writing. Write an introduction that states the title of your poem and introduces the topic of figurative language. Then write one or two paragraphs in which you describe and analyze the figurative language in the poem. Be sure that the ideas follow a logical organization. Be sure to restate each image before you explain what it means. Make the connections between your ideas clear and smooth.

Revising. Read over your draft. Check to see that every sentence is a complete thought. Are all the ideas stated clearly? Do the sentences flow smoothly from one to the other?

2. **Writing About Poets.** You have read two poems about poets, "Voice in the Crowd" and "The Distant Drum." Think about the ideas in those poems and in the other poems you have studied. Write a paragraph or poem explaining what a poet is and what a poet tries to accomplish.

   Include some of your own feelings about poets and your opinions about why they write poetry.

Developing Skills in Critical Thinking

Understanding Generalizations. Generalizations are broad statements based on specific facts. For example, imagine that you noticed that when the wind came from the east, it rained. You could keep records for a while to see if it rained every time the wind was from the east. If so, you could make the following generalization: When the wind comes from the east, there will be rain.

If, however, it did not rain under those conditions on even one occasion, your generalization would be faulty. You would then have to make a change in your generalization. You could make it valid by limiting it in this way: It *often* rains when the wind comes from the east.

The poem "Words" contains some generalizations about how people use words and express emotions. Find the generalizations. Can you think of exceptions to any of these statements? If the generalizations are too broad, how could they be changed or limited to make them valid?

heme

The theme of a literary selection is an idea about life that the writer wishes to share with the reader. Poets try to speak about life truthfully, hoping to share some feelings with the reader. They may share knowledge or they may question. They may share fears or offer hope. You may not agree with every poet's ideas or conclusions. That is to be expected. The poet would probably say that it's enough that you think about the ideas.

Dicomano V, 1982, SUSAN SENSEMANN. Courtesy of Roy Boyd Gallery, Chicago and Los Angeles.

Lodged

ROBERT FROST

Do you ever see your own moods reflected in your surroundings? As you read this poem, think about why the speaker sees the way he does.

The rain to the wind said,
"You push and I'll pelt."
They so smote the garden bed
That the flowers actually knelt,
And lay lodged—though not dead.
I know how the flowers felt.

Developing Comprehension Skills

1. What did the rain and the wind do to the garden?

2. How does the speaker in this poem feel? What type of situation may have caused this?

3. What might be important about the fact that the flowers, although beaten, are not dead?

4. Do you agree that our mood can affect the way we see things? Give several examples.

Reading Literature: Poetry

1. **Understanding Theme.** Consider what the poet is saying about himself, and about how people can face hardship. In your own words, state the theme of the poem. Then explain how you can relate the theme to your own life.

2. **Identifying Figures of Speech.** How does the poet use personification in this poem? How does this technique affect the reader's picture of the garden? How does it affect the meaning of the poem?

3. **Identifying Alliteration.** Find three examples of alliteration in the poem. How do the repeated sounds echo what is being said in the poem?

4. **Identifying Rhyme Scheme.** Chart the rhyme scheme of this poem. How many different rhymes are there? Is there a recognizable pattern to the scheme?

Seagulls

ROBERT FRANCIS

What qualities in nature are beautiful to you? As you read this description of seagulls, try to decide why the speaker is fascinated by them.

White Bird, 1957, WILLIAM BAZIOTES. Oil on canvas, 60″ × 48″. Albright-Knox Art Gallery. Gift of Seymour H. Knox, 1957, Buffalo, New York.

Between the under and the upper blue
All day the seagulls climb and swerve and soar,
Arc intersecting arc, curve over curve.

And you may watch them weaving a long time
And never see their pattern twice the same
And never see their pattern once imperfect.

Take any moment they are in the air—
If you could change them, if you had the power
How would you place them other than they are?

What we have labored all our lives to have
And failed, these birds effortlessly achieve:
Freedom that flows in form and still is free.

Developing Comprehension Skills

1. What are the seagulls doing? Why is the speaker attracted to them?

2. What are the "under" and the "upper blue"?

3. In the third stanza, the speaker asks what you would change about the seagulls if you could. Does he expect that you would have a suggestion?

4. Explain the last three lines of the poem. Do you think the goal mentioned here is worth working "all our lives" for? Explain.

Reading Literature: Poetry

1. **Identifying the Speaker.** What do you learn about the speaker from reading the poem? How is he feeling as he watches the graceful birds? In a few sentences, describe your mental picture of the speaker.

2. **Stating the Theme.** Look again at the third stanza of the poem. What do you think the theme of this poem is? Is the theme uplifting, saddening, or something else?

3. **Recognizing Imagery.** The sight images in this poem are clear and easy to imagine. Which words and phrases do you find most striking?

4. **Appreciating Technique.** Find an example of alliteration in each stanza. Also look for the repetition of words, phrases, and ideas. How do these techniques add to the meaning and imagery of the poem?

Ride a Wild Horse

HANNAH KAHN

Is there anything that you would like to do but have only dreamed about doing? As you read this poem, see what this speaker suggests.

Ride a wild horse
with purple wings
striped yellow and black
except his head
which must be red.

Ride a wild horse
against the sky—
hold tight to his wings

before you die
whatever else you leave undone—
once ride a wild horse
into the sun.

Apollo, 1905–1910, ODILON REDON. Yale University Art Gallery.
Philip L. Goodwin Collection, New Haven, Connecticut.

Developing Comprehension Skills

1. What does the wild horse in this poem look like?

2. The poet does not really mean for anyone to ride a multi-colored wild horse into the sun. What is she asking us to do?

3. Do you think that the advice given in this poem is worth listening to? Explain.

Reading Literature: Poetry

1. **Understanding Theme.** What idea about living is the poet trying to share? Do you think we need to be reminded of this idea?

2. **Appreciating Imagery.** The poet creates a wild, fantastic creature to be the central image of this poem. Why do you think she chose this type of image? What does it suggest about the things we should do before we die?

3. **Recognizing Tone.** How would you describe the tone of this poem? Is this tone a good one to use with the ideas the writer presents?

4. **Understanding Structure.** Study the structure of this poem. Notice the number of lines in each stanza, the length of the lines, and which lines rhyme. Why do you think the poet structured her words in this way? How does the structure add to the meaning of the poem?

Television-Movie

KIRBY CONGDON

We enjoy watching monster movies and horror shows that show people in terrifying situations. Is real life, however, even more frightening?

The monster is loose.
This is an emergency area.
Leave your homes.
There is no time
to gather your belongings.
The highways are jammed,
the trains, derailed.
The planes have crashed
and the bridges are collapsing.
There is no escape.

Aunt Harriet has fallen down,
trying to escape.
The baby is hysterical.
The radio's broken.
The neighbors are gone.
Susie forgot her doll.
I can't find the insurance papers.
The monster has knocked over
the Tower of London.
The Empire State Building
is breaking in half.
Everyone is drowning
in Times Square.

In Tokyo
all the poor people
have fallen into a crevasse
which is now closing up,
even on United States citizens.
The ship's piano is rolling
across the ballroom floor.
The cargo is crushing the coolies.
The Army is out of ammunition.
The President has declared
a national state of affairs.
The almanacs were wrong.
The computers were in error.
Where will it all end?

The baby has stopped crying.
You hold her now; I'm tired.
Aunt Harriet wants to stay
one more week.
I can't say no. You tell her.
The radio repairman will come for sure
—if he can make it.
The neighbors said it's too loud.
Fix Susie's doll; the squeak's gone.

The insurance papers
are in the bottom left-hand drawer
right where you put them.
If they're not there,
keep looking.
Will you get paid tomorrow?
Did you mail my letter?
Did you set the alarm?

The monster is dead.
He is never coming back.
And if he does come,
someone will kill it.
And we will all go on
just like always.
There is no escape.

Developing Comprehension Skills

1. What types of movies are described in this poem?

2. Which stanzas seem to be about movies? Which stanzas seem to be about real life?

3. Which people, things, and incidents are mentioned in both the movie section and the real-life section of this poem? What differences do you see the second time?

4. According to the poet, which are more horrible: the movie situations or those in real life? Why is this so? Do you agree?

Reading Literature: Poetry

1. **Identifying Mood.** The mood in this poem changes about two-thirds of the way through. What is the mood of the first section? What is the mood of the second section? What idea do you think the poet was trying to get across by making this shift?

2. **Understanding a Theme.** Look at the last line of the poem. What is there no escape from? Based on this and other ideas in the poem, what do you think the theme is? Do you think there is any truth to what the poet says?

Developing Vocabulary Skills

Reviewing Context Clues. You now are familiar with different ways the dictionary can be used to unlock word meaning. However, you should always try first to find the meaning by using context clues.

The following sentences are from the poems in this unit. First, try to unlock the meanings of the underlined words with context clues. If this is not possible, use the dictionary. Next to each definition, write the method you used:

definition/restatement   example clues
synonym/antonym   inference
comparison/contrast   dictionary

1. The rain to the wind said,
   "You push and I'll pelt."
   And so smote the garden bed . . .

2. All day the seagulls climb and swerve and soar,
   Arc intersecting arc, curve, over curve.

3. In Tokyo / all the poor people
   have fallen into a crevasse
   which is now closing up,

4. What we have labored all our lives to have
   And failed, these birds effortlessly achieve:

5. Aunt Harriet has fallen down,
   trying to escape.
   The baby is hysterical.
   The radio's broken.

6. The almanacs were wrong.
   The computers were in error.

Developing Writing Skills

1. **Making Comparisons.** In two poems you have read, "Troubled Woman" and "Lodged," people have been compared to flowers. Write two paragraphs. In the first one, tell how "Troubled Woman" used the comparison and what effect it had. In the second paragraph, tell how the comparison was presented in "Lodged." In both paragraphs, explain your personal reaction to the images.

2. **Writing a Poem.** "Television-Movie" and "Ride a Wild Horse" show two different ways of looking at the future. Write a poem that expresses your own ideas about what the future holds.

   Pre-Writing. When you think about your future, what do you see? What will you be doing in two years? five years? ten years? How will you reach those goals? Make a list of the emotions you feel and the thoughts that go through your mind. Then try to express your attitude in one or two sentences.

   Writing. Write a poem expressing your view of the future. Every line should help create a mood. Include details to make your image vivid. Try to express your theme or attitude clearly. Emphasize ideas with figurative language and sound devices.

   Revising. Reread your poem. Did you accomplish your purpose? That is, did you convey your theme and mood? Will other people understand your writing? Did you use strong, active verbs and precise adjectives?

Developing Skills in Speaking and Listening

Presenting a Choral Interpretation. Prepare an oral interpretation of "Television-Movie." Work with a group. First, discuss the poem so that the group is in general agreement on what it is about. Then decide who should say which lines. Finally, discuss the way the poem should be read. Should certain lines be said fast or slow, loudly or softly? Do you want to say any words or lines in groups? Practice your parts individually. Then practice together.

Richard Cory

EDWIN ARLINGTON ROBINSON

Richard Cory was one of the town's leading citizens. All the towns-people envied him. But did they really know him?

Whenever Richard Cory went down town,
We people on the pavement looked at him:
He was a gentleman from sole to crown,
Clean favored, and imperially slim.

And he was always quietly arrayed,
And he was always human when he talked;
But still he fluttered pulses when he said,
"Good-morning," and he glittered when he walked.

And he was rich—yes, richer than a king—
And admirably schooled in every grace:
In fine, we thought that he was everything
To make us wish that we were in his place.

So on we worked, and waited for the light,
And went without the meat, and cursed the bread;
And Richard Cory, one calm summer night,
Went home and put a bullet through his head.

Bathing in Levantine Afternoons, 1979,
JIM DINE. Collection of Stefan T. Edlis.

Developing Comprehension Skills

1. Describe Richard Cory's appearance.

2. Who are the "people on the pavement"? How do they differ from Richard Cory?

3. What did Richard Cory do one night? Why is the last line of the poem so unexpected?

4. What sorts of things might have led Cory to kill himself?

5. What does the poet want to say about the importance of looking beyond the outward appearances of people? What can we learn from this poem that could help us be more sensitive to other people?

Reading Literature: Poetry

1. **Recognizing Irony.** How does the poet use the technique of irony in this poem?

2. **Understanding Imagery.** Richard Cory is described almost as though he were royalty. What words and phrases does the poet use to give us this image of Richard Cory?

3. **Analyzing Rhyme and Form.** Chart the rhyme scheme of this poem. Then look at the form. How many lines are in each stanza? How many iambic feet ($\cup$/) are in each line? Why might the poet have chosen such a regular rhyme scheme and form?

Earth

How might we appear to beings from another planet? As you read this poem, decide what the observer has really seen.

JOHN HALL WHEELOCK

"A planet doesn't explode of itself," said drily
The Martian astronomer, gazing off into the air—
"That they were able to do it is proof that highly
Intelligent beings must have been living there."

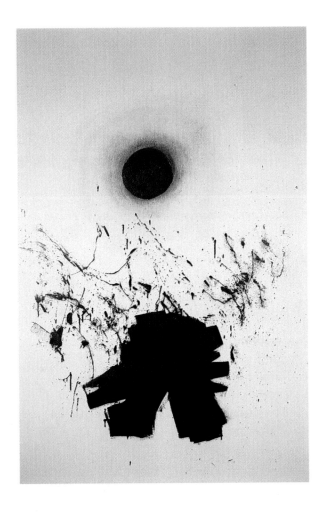

Burst II, 1972, ADOLPH GOTTLIEB. Oil and acrylic on canvas, 90 × 60". Copyright © 1980 Adolph and Esther Gottlieb Foundation, New York.

Developing Comprehension Skills

1. What has happened to the earth? Who or what was responsible?

2. How does this observer seem to feel about the event? How do you know?

3. The Martian astronomer observes that "highly intelligent beings" must have lived on Earth. Do you agree that the destruction of the earth was proof of intelligence?

Reading Literature: Poetry

1. **Understanding Satire and Irony.** Writing that is critical and humorous at the same time is called **satire**. **Irony** is the contrast between what is thought to be true and what is actually true. How does the poet use both satire and irony in this poem?

2. **Understanding and Stating a Theme.** State the theme of this poem in your own words.

Saying Yes

DIANA CHANG

Most people are aware of their cultural heritage. They know who their ancestors were and where they came from. As you read this poem, note how the speaker feels about her two cultures.

"Are you Chinese?"
"Yes."

"American?"
"Yes."

"*Really* Chinese?"
"No . . . not quite."

"*Really* American?"
"Well, actually, you see . . ."

But I would rather say
yes

Not neither-nor,
not maybe,
but both, and not only

The homes I've had,
the ways I am

I'd rather say it
twice,
yes

Developing Comprehension Skills

1. Who are the speakers in this poem?

2. Why does the main speaker hesitate when she is asked whether she is "Really Chinese" or American?

3. How does the main speaker feel about being both Chinese and American? Why does she want to say "yes" twice?

4. In what way might the speaker represent all of us?

5. Do you think it is possible to hold onto your own cultural heritage and still be an American? Explain.

Reading Literature: Poetry

1. **Identifying the Speaker.** Describe the main speaker of the poem. Tell not only what her heritage is, but also some of her feelings about her background.

2. **Recognizing Dialogue.** This poem uses the technique of dialogue to present ideas. You know that a dialogue is a conversation. Why is dialogue effective for this particular poem? What does it tell you about the problems or questions the speaker faces each day?

3. **Understanding Theme.** What is the theme of this poem? In what ways is this theme appropriate for every reader?

Developing Vocabulary Skills

Understanding Usage Labels. When you write or speak, you must use language that is suitable for your purpose and audience. For example, in casual writing or conversation, you could use slang or other popular phrases. In a formal paper, however, you would not write a sentence such as "The soldiers *zapped* the enemy troops."

A dictionary has usage labels to tell you the particular level of usage for a word. Here are some of these usage labels:

Colloquial—informal language that is acceptable in casual communication

Slang—used only in very informal speaking

Dialect—used only in certain regions of the country

Usage labels are usually enclosed in brackets or italicized. Some may be abbreviated.

The following words are from poems in this chapter. Find them in a dictionary. Find a special usage label in the entry for that word. Read the definition that follows. Then write a more formal word that could be used in the same situation.

break	con	keen	blue
nifty	peck	yeah	square

1. **Expressing an Opinion.** The poems in this last section all have strong themes. From among "Earth," "Saying Yes," and "Richard Cory," choose the poem you like best. Explain why you chose that poem. Consider the theme of the poem and any of these other factors:

topic	mood	figurative language
rhythm	rhyme	word choice

Pre-Writing. After you have chosen the poem, make notes on any of the points listed above. Use these notes to try to understand which parts of the poem appealed to you the most. List lines and phrases from the poem that could be used as examples. Choose three or four points to discuss.

Writing. Begin with a topic sentence telling which poem you have chosen, and your reaction to it. Arrange the reasons for your choice in the order of their importance to you, or in the order of their impact on the poem. Use lines and phrases from the poem to support your opinion.

Revising. Have a partner read your writing. Ask him or her to write down your main idea and to list the reasons you gave. If the reader cannot list all the reasons, rewrite any parts that were unclear.

2. **Using Dialogue.** "Saying Yes" and "Two Friends" both use conversations between two people. In "Saying Yes," one person asks questions and the other answers. In "Two Friends," the two people take turns speaking.

Write a poem that uses dialogue. Try to make it illustrate some theme or idea.

3. **Imagining Your Reaction.** The townspeople envied Richard Cory for his wealth and position. How do you think they felt after he killed himself? Did they understand why he did it? Were they shocked? Did they feel guilty? Did it make them look at their own lives in a new way? How would you have reacted to the news of Richard Cory's death? Write about the experience. Tell about the emotions and thoughts you would have. You may choose to write your thoughts in the form of a dialogue with another person who represents another way of thinking.

Developing Skills in Study and Research

Writing a Paraphrase. You are often asked to write reports that require research. In your research, you may find paragraphs like the following from *Living Authors: A Book of Biographies*. This passage is about Edwin Arlington Robinson, who wrote the poem "Richard Cory."

Edwin Arlington Robinson was one of the foremost poets in the United States during the first half of the twentieth century. He was awarded the Pulitzer Prize for poetry three times. His poetry reflected a somber, almost hopeless, view of life. Many of Robinson's poems focus on sad or confused people. He said, "The failures are so much more interesting. There is a world of tragedy in the individual's futile struggles against a fate too powerful for him."

If you were writing a report on Edwin Arlington Robinson, you might find this paragraph useful. However, you could not just repeat the paragraph, word for word. You would have to paraphrase what the author has written. When you **paraphrase**, you identify the main ideas of a selection. Then you put these ideas into your own words. The first sentence of the passage about Robinson could be paraphrased like this: *Edwin Arlington Robinson was a respected twentieth-century American poet.*

Paraphrase the rest of the paragraph. Choose the most important ideas and put them in your own words.

Using Your Skills in Reading Poetry

Read the following stanza from the poem "The Last Mystery" by Jon Stallworthy. Then follow these directions:

1. Find two examples of alliteration.

2. Find one simile. How does this comparison add to the idea being expressed?

3. Listen for the rhythm of this poem. Is it regular or irregular? Why do you think the poet chose this kind of rhythm?

> He knew that coastline—no man better—
> Knew all its rocks and currents, like the veins
> And knuckles on the brown back of his hand;
> The leap-frog rollers and tall tons that batter
> Boat-rib and man-rib into grains
> Of indistinguishable sand:
> He had known them all since he could stand.

Using Your Comprehension Skills

The following sentences are from nonfiction selections that you will read in Chapter 5. Find the *subject* and *verb* in these long sentences with unusual word order. Then rephrase the sentences so that the verb comes after the subject. Explain, too, how punctuation helps you to understand each sentence.

1. In the year 1904, there appeared in Berlin a Russian horse known as Clever Hans.

2. At the north end, on the fourth side, stood the temple of Jupiter, Juno, and Minerva, raised on a podium ten feet high.

3. Overlooked in the confusion was Vesonius' black watchdog, chained in the courtyard.

4. On the walls of the buildings are election slogans and the scrawlings of unruly boys.

Using Your Vocabulary Skills

The following sentences are from nonfiction selections that you will read in Chapter 5. Look up each underlined word in a dictionary. For each word, identify the following:

    a. the number of syllables in the word
    b. the accented syllable
    c. the part of speech for the word as it is used in the sentence
    d. the definition that best fits the sentence

1. We gingerly tested each toehold and fingerhold for loose rock before putting our weight on it.

2. I found my way into the dingy labyrinth which housed the Wildlife Service.

3. At the moving passages, be moved—but only according to the degree of your intimacy with the parties giving the entertainment.

4. As salesman for a soft-drink bottler in Newark, he had an income of thirty dollars a week . . . and took in threadbare relatives.

5. I am persuaded that the average ant is a sham.

6. Wisps of evening fog below grew luminous in the approaching dark.

Using Your Writing Skills

Choose one of the following writing assignments.

1. Compare and contrast these three poems about poets: "The Distant Drum," "Voice in the Crowd," and "Kidnap Poem." Explain how they are alike and how they are different. Consider at least three of these aspects: theme, mood, tone, figurative language, imagery, sound, and form.

2. Write a poem about a powerful experience or important idea you have had. Use at least one of these figures of speech to describe your feelings: simile, metaphor, personification, or hyperbole. Use alliteration, assonance, rhyme, rhythm, or onomatopoeia to create a special effect. Choose specific, descriptive words to suit the mood and tone of your poem.

Using Your Skills in Study and Research

Visit a library. Ask the librarian to direct you to the poetry section. Look through the poetry anthologies and other collections. Find one other poem that could fit in each of the classifications used in this chapter.

Nonfiction

Rocky Mountains in the Selkirk Range near the Canadian Border,
1889, ALBERT BIERSTADT. New Bedford Free Public Library, Massachusetts.

Reading Literature: Nonfiction

What Is Nonfiction?

Nonfiction is writing that is based on facts. Nonfiction tells about real people, places, and events. Nonfiction can be the most interesting kind of literature. The selections in this chapter offer proof that truth is often more exciting than fiction.

Nonfiction and History

Since nonfiction is about real people, it has existed as long as people have. There are many different types of nonfiction. Each has its own purpose and style.

Journals. Journals, the oldest kind of nonfiction, are records of people's activities, thoughts, and feelings. Because the entries are written by the people involved in the events, journals have the freshness of an eye-witness account. Travelers often use journals to record the events of their journeys. A journal written by William Bradford in 1620 tells of the founding of Plymouth Colony by the Pilgrims. Journals can bring history to life in an exciting way.

True Adventure Stories. These stories often begin as journals. They are exciting records of memorable events. World travelers, adventurers, and common people caught up in unusual, exciting events have told of their experiences for thousands of years. For example, as early as 50 B.C., Julius Caesar, the emperor of Rome, wrote of his military experiences. His journals bring the battles to life.

Biographies. Throughout the centuries, writers have examined the lives of others, hoping to understand those people better. Their studies resulted in biographies. Biographies from 5,000 years ago can be found in the ancient tombs of the rulers of Egypt. More recent biographies have studied both the lives of well known people and those who lived quiet, but interesting lives.

Autobiographies. Sometimes a person will write an autobiography—a book about his or her own life. Autobiographies may tell of exciting adventures or thoughtful moments. They help a reader to understand the writer's failures and achievements, fears and dreams.

Essays. This form of nonfiction appeared in the 1500's. Essays express a writer's personal feelings on a subject. Some essays are informative. They teach about a subject the writer knows well. Other essays are simply expressions of the writer's personal opinion. Essays can be serious or humorous.

Articles. Newspapers and magazines often contain short, nonfiction selections called articles. They point out the interesting, unusual, thoughtful, and exciting aspects of everyday life.

The Elements of Nonfiction

Nonfiction, like fiction, has characters, setting, and plot. Conflict may also be present. In nonfiction, however, these elements are real. Refer to pages 13 and 70–71 for a review of these elements.

Another important element of nonfiction is the writer's purpose. Nonfiction writers try to inform, teach, persuade, or entertain. Sometimes they try to achieve more than one of these purposes. When you read nonfiction, try to tell what the writer was trying to accomplish.

How To Read Nonfiction

1. As you read a nonfiction selection, pay attention to the key elements in the selection. Ask yourself these questions:

   Who are the major characters?
   What is the setting?
   How do the events in the plot relate to each other?
   Is conflict present? If so, what kind of conflict is it?

2. Think about the writer's purpose. Is the writer trying to explain, persuade, or simply entertain?
3. Look for the organization of the ideas in the selection.

Comprehension Skills: Evaluating Nonfiction

Being an Active Reader

While good nonfiction is entertaining, it can also teach or persuade. Therefore, it is not enough to simply read nonfiction. To get the most from a selection, the reader must evaluate it. In other words, the reader must examine the selection carefully and judge the ideas it contains.

Determining the Author's Purpose.   The author's purpose is the reason why he or she wrote the selection. Authors write for many reasons. They may wish to entertain, inform, or persuade. Writers may also wish to express emotions or to tell personal experiences. Knowing the purpose will help the reader judge the writer and the selection fairly. Has the writer included details that help achieve the purpose? Were these details presented well?

Distinguishing Between Fact and Opinion.   A **fact** is a statement that can be proved true. It can be proved by personal observation or by checking a reliable source. An **opinion** is a statement that cannot be proved true. It is simply someone's personal view. Opinions may or may not be based on facts.

A nonfiction article may contain both facts and opinions. The reader must determine which is which. If a statement is an opinion, the reader should try to determine if the opinion is supported with facts. Then the reader can decide whether to agree with the opinion.

Recognizing Errors in Reasoning.   Writers are sometimes guilty of errors in reasoning. One example of such weak reasoning is a **faulty cause and effect relationship**. For example, when one event follows another, some people might think that the first event caused the second. However, the first event may have had nothing to do with the second. A person who walks under a ladder may later have an accident. But the accident did not happen because he or she walked under the ladder.

Another type of faulty thinking is called **circular reasoning**. Writers may try to prove a statement by repeating it in different words. For example, a writer could say, "Babe Didrikson Zaharias was an excellent athlete." To prove the statement, the writer might say, "She was good at sports." This writer is simply saying the same thing twice, using different words. The second statement gives no evidence to prove the first statement.

A third type of faulty thinking is **overgeneralization**. A generalization is a broad statement based on specific facts. Consider this statement: "Many Americans watch five hours of television every day." This statement is based on facts that can be proved. However, the statement, "Americans watch too much television," is an overgeneralization. Not all Americans watch television, and not all who do watch too much.

Slanted Writing. Writers often try to persuade readers to agree with their opinions. To do so, they sometimes use words with strong connotations. **Connotations** are the ideas and feelings a word brings to mind. Connotations can be positive or negative. The following sentences both describe the same person. Notice how the strong connotations of the words influence your opinions of the person.

Scott is an intelligent member of the student council.
Scott is a pushy know-it-all.

Exercise: Recognizing Errors in Reasoning

Read the following situations carefully. There is an error in reasoning in each passage. Decide whether the error is one of *faulty cause and effect, circular reasoning, overgeneralization,* or *slanted writing.*

1. A political candidate says that she is the best person for the office. As proof of this, she says that she is "better qualified" than her opponents.

2. A commercial uses the following slogan: Nature Flakes—the all natural cereal with a golden drop of honey in every delicious bite.

3. A television commentator tells his audience, "People just don't care about each other any more. Everyone just looks out for himself."

4. A student goes to the movies the night before an exam. He gets an "A" on the exam. The student decides to go to the movies before each exam from now on.

Vocabulary Skills: Using Word Parts

Word Parts

There are three kinds of word parts. The **base word** is the main word to which parts are added. It contains the basic meaning. A **prefix** is a word part added to the beginning of a base word. A **suffix** is a word part added to the end of a base word.

Prefix + Base Word = New Word
un- + popular = unpopular

Base Word + Suffix = New Word
hair + -less = hairless

When you look at each part of an unfamiliar word separately, you can often guess at its meaning. Refer to the following information when you need to find out the meaning of a word made from word parts. Note that the spelling of a part may change when it is combined with another part.

Commonly Used Prefixes

Prefix	Meaning	Example
anti-	against	antislavery
extra-	beyond, outside	extrasensory
pre-	before	prejudge
post-	after	postwar
sub-	under, beneath	substandard
super-	over, above	supernatural

Prefix	Meaning	Example
in-, ir-, im-, il- dis-, un-, non-	"not" or "the opposite of"	in + active = inactive (not active)

Commonly Used Suffixes

Suffix	Meaning	Example
-er, -or, -ist, -ian	"one who does something"	act + or = actor (one who acts)
-ous, -ful	"full of"	glory + ous = glorious (full of glory)
-able (-ible), -less, -like, -most	These suffixes mean what they say.	read + able = readable (able to be read)

Greek and Latin Roots

Some words are built around Latin or Greek roots. A root is a word part that contains the word's basic meaning. A root cannot stand alone. Many English words are based on Greek and Latin roots. If you know the meaning of these roots, you can often figure out the meanings of a number of unfamiliar words.

The following chart lists some commonly used roots.

Greek Roots	Meaning	Latin Roots	Meaning
auto	self, alone	cred	believe
bio	life	dic, dict	speak, tell
graph	write	mit, mis	send
logy	study of	spect	look at
		vid, vis	see

Exercise: Using Word Parts To Determine Meaning

Identify base words, prefixes, suffixes, and roots in the words below.

1. magician
2. graphology
3. careless
4. missile
5. postdate
6. dictionary
7. superhero
8. biography
9. automobile
10. predawn

True Adventure Stories

Nonfiction can be exciting literature. True adventure stories can be the most exciting of all. The stories you are about to read are personal accounts of actual events. Through them, you will meet two boys who scaled sheer rock cliffs. You will be part of a dangerous escape attempt during wartime. You will come face to face with dangerous, wild animals. You will share the fears and achievements of the characters as you read these true stories.

The Trapper, 1921, ROCKWELL KENT. The Whitney Museum of American Art, New York

From

Of Men and Mountains

WILLIAM O. DOUGLAS

Two teenaged boys face death on a treacherous mountain. Read this true story to discover what they learn about courage—and about themselves.

Kloochman Rock stands on the southern side of the Tieton Basin in the Cascades Mountains in the state of Washington. It is an oval-shaped lava rock, running lengthwise northwest by southeast, a half-mile or more. It rises 2,000 feet above the basin. The first third of its elevation is gained through gentle slopes of pine and fir. Next are a few hundred yards of tumbled rock. Then there is the cliff rising to the sky, 1,200 feet or more—straight as the Washington Monument and over twice as high.

It was in 1913, when Doug Corpron was nineteen and I was not quite fifteen, that the two of us made this climb of Kloochman. Doug and I were camped in the Tieton Basin at a spring. We were traveling light, one blanket each. The night, I recall, was so bitter cold that we took turns refueling the campfire so that we could keep our backs warm enough to sleep. We rose at the first show of dawn and cooked frying-pan bread and trout for breakfast. We had not planned to climb Kloochman, but the challenge came as the sun struck her crest.

Southeast Face of Kloochman

After breakfast we started circling the rock. There are fairly easy routes up Kloochman, but we shunned them. When we came to the southeast face[1] (the one that never has been conquered, I believe), we chose it. The July day was warm and cloudless. Doug led. The beginning was easy. For 100 feet or so, we found ledges six to twelve inches wide that we could follow to the left or right. Some ledges ran up the rock ten feet or more at a gentle grade. Others were merely steps to a higher ledge. Thus, by hugging the wall, we could either ease upward or hoist ourselves from one ledge to another.

When we were about 100 feet up the wall, the ledges became narrower and footwork more risky. Doug suggested that we take off our shoes. This we did, tying them behind us on our belts. In stocking feet we wormed up the wall, clinging like flies to the rock. We gingerly tested each toehold

---

1. **face**, in mountaineering, the side of a mountain.

and fingerhold for loose rock before putting our weight on it. At times we had to inch along sidewise, our stomachs pressing tightly against the rock, in order to gain a point where we could reach the ledge above. If we got on a ledge that turned out to be a cul-de-sac, the much more dangerous task of going down the rock wall would confront us. Hence, we picked our route with care and weighed the advantages of several choices that frequently were given us. At times we could not climb easily from one ledge to another. The one above might be a foot or so high. Then we would have to reach it with one knee, slowly bringing the other knee up. Then, delicately balancing on both knees on the upper ledge, we would come slowly to our feet by pressing close to the wall and getting such a handhold with our fingers as the lava rock permitted us.

In that tortuous way, we made perhaps 600 feet in two hours. It was late forenoon when we stopped to appraise our situation. We were in serious trouble. We had reached the feared cul-de-sac. The two- or three-inch ledge on which we stood ended. There seemed none above us within Doug's reach. I was longer-legged than Doug, so perhaps I could have reached some ledge with my fingers if I were ahead. However, it was impossible for us to change positions on the wall.

Doug's Jump

Feeling along the wall, Doug discovered a tiny groove into which he could press the tips of the fingers of his left hand. It might help him maintain balance as his weight began to shift from the lower ledge to the upper one. Still, there was not even a lip of rock for his right hand within reach. Just out of reach, however, was a substantial crevice, one that would hold several men. How could Doug reach it? I could not boost him, for my own balance was insecure. Clearly, Doug would have to jump to reach it—and he would have but one jump. Since he was standing on a ledge only a few inches wide, he could not expect to jump for his handhold, miss it, and land safely. A slip meant he would go hurtling down some 600 feet onto the rocks. After much discussion and indecision, Doug decided to take the chance.

He asked me to do him a favor. If he failed and fell, I might still make it, since I was longer-legged. Would I please give certain messages to his family in that event? I nodded.

"Then listen carefully," he told me. "Tell Mother that I love her dearly. Tell her I think she is the most wonderful person in the world. Tell her not to worry—that I did not suffer, that God willed it so. Tell my sister that I have been a mean little devil, but I had no hatred toward her. Tell her I love her, too—that some day I wanted to marry a girl as wholesome and cheery and good as she.

"Tell Dad I was brave and died unafraid. Tell him about our climb in detail. Tell Dad I have always been proud of him, that someday I had planned to be a doctor, too. Tell him I lived a clean life, that I never did anything to make him ashamed. . . . Tell Mother, Sister, and Dad I prayed for them."

Every word burned into me. My heart was sick. My lips quivered. I pressed my face against the rock. I wept.

All was silent. A pebble fell from the ledge on which I squeezed. I counted seconds before it hit 600 feet below with a faint, faraway tinkling sound. Would Doug drop through the same space? Would I follow? When you fall 600 feet, do you die before you hit the bottom? Closing my eyes, I asked God to help Doug up the wall.

In a second Doug said in a cheery voice, "Well, here goes."

A false bravado took hold of us. I said he could do it. He said he would. He wiped first one hand, then the other on his trousers. He placed both palms against the wall, bent his knees slowly, paused a split second, and jumped straight up. It was not much of a jump—only six inches or so. But that jump by one pressed against a cliff 600 feet in the air had dare-devil proportions. I held my breath; my heart pounded.

Doug made the jump, and in a second was hanging by two hands from a strong wide ledge. There was no toehold. He would have to hoist himself by his arms alone. His body went slowly up as if pulled by some unseen winch.[2] Soon he had the

weight of his body above the ledge and was resting on the palms of his hands. He then put his left knee on the ledge, rolled over on his side, and chuckled as he said, "Nothing to it."

Doug's exploration of the ledge showed he was in a final cul-de-sac. There was no way up. There was not even a higher ledge he could reach by jumping. We went down backwards, weaving a strange pattern across the face of the cliff as we moved from one side to the other. It was perhaps mid-afternoon when we finally reached the bottom.

The Northwest Face

Being young, we were determined to climb the rock. So once more we started to circle. When we came to the northwest wall, we selected it as our route. Here, too, was a cliff rising 1,000 feet like some unfinished pyramid. But close examination showed numerous toeholds and fingerholds that made the start, at least, fairly easy.

Again, it was fairly easy going for 100 feet or so. Then Doug, who was ahead, came to a ledge to which he could not step.

He hitched up his trousers and grasped a tiny groove of rock with the tips of the fingers of his left hand. He pressed his right hand flat against the smooth rock wall as if it had magical sticking power. Slowly he lifted his left knee until it was slightly over the ledge above him. To do so he had to stand tiptoe on his right foot. Pulling with his left hand, he brought his right knee up. Doug was now on both knees on the upper

---

2. **winch**, an apparatus for lifting or pulling, consisting of a handle, a drum, and a rope that is wound around the drum.

Kloochman Rock, Wenatchee National Forest. USDA Forest Service. Photograph by Larry Miller.

ledge. If he could find good holds overhead he was safe. His hands explored the wall above him. He moved them slowly over most of it without finding a hold. Then he reached straight above his head and cried out, "This is our lucky day."

He had found strong, rough edges of rock, and on this quickly pulled himself up. His hands were on a ledge a foot wide. He lay down on it and grasped my outstretched hand. The pull of his strong arm against the drop of 100 feet or more was as comforting an experience as any I can recall. In a jiffy, I was at his side. We pounded each other on the shoulders and laughed.

Bill in Trouble

My own most serious trouble was yet to come. For a while, Doug and I were separated. I worked sideways along a ledge to the south, found easier going, and in a short time was 200 feet or more up the rock wall. I was above Doug, 25 feet or so, and 50 feet to his right. We had been extremely careful to test each hold before putting our trust in it. Kloochman is full of treacherous rocks. We often discovered thin ledges that crumbled under pressure and showered handfuls of rock and dust down below. Perhaps I was careless. Whatever the cause, the thin ledge on which I was standing gave way.

As I felt it slip, I grabbed for a hold above me. The crevasse I seized was solid. There I was, hanging by my hands 200 feet in the air, my feet pawing the rock. To make matters worse, my camera had swung between me and the cliff when I slipped. Its bulk was actually pushing me from the cliff. I twisted in an attempt to get rid of it, but it was firmly lodged between me and the wall.

I yelled to Doug for help. He at once started edging toward me. It seemed hours, though it was probably not over a few minutes. He shouted, "Hang on, I'll be there!"

Hang on I did. My fingers ached beyond description. They were frozen to the rock. My exertion in pawing with my feet had added to the fatigue. The ache of my fingers extended to my wrists and then along my arms. I stopped thrashing around and hung like a sack, motionless. Every second seemed a minute, every minute an hour. I did not see how I could possibly hold.

I would slip, I thought, slip to sure death. I could not look down because of my position. In my mind's eye, though, I saw in sharp outline the jagged rocks that seemed to pull me toward them. The camera kept pushing my fingers from the ledge. I felt them move. They began to give way before the pull of a force too great for flesh to resist.

Fright grew in me. The idea of hanging helpless 200 feet above the abyss brought panic. I cried out to Doug, but the words caught in my dry throat. I was like one in a nightmare who struggles to shout—who is then seized with a fear that promises to destroy him.

Then there flashed through my mind a family scene. Mother was sitting in the living room talking to me, telling me what a wonderful man Father was. She told me of his last illness and his death. She told me of his departure from Cleveland to Portland, Oregon, for what proved to be a fatal operation. His last words to her were: "If I die, it will be glory. If I live, it will be grace."

The panic passed. The memory of my father's words restored my reason. Glory to die? I could not understand why it would be glory to die. It would be glory to live. But as Father said, it might take grace to live, grace from One more powerful than Doug or I.

Again that day I prayed. I asked God to save my life, to save me from destruction on this rock wall. I asked God to make my fingers strong, to give me strength to hang on. I asked God to give me courage, to make me unafraid. I asked God to give me guts, to give me power to do the impossible.

My fingers were as numb as flesh full of novocaine.[3] They seemed detached from me, as if they belonged to someone else. My wrists, my shoulders cried out for respite from the pain.

Hang on? You can't hang on. You are a weakling. The weaklings die in the woods.

Weakling? I'll show you. How long must I hang on? All day? OK, all day then. I'll hang on, I'll hang on. O God, dear God, help me hang on!

I felt someone pushing my left foot upwards. It was Doug. As if through a dream, his voice was saying, "Your feet are 18 inches below your toehold." Doug found those toeholds for my feet.

I felt my shoes resting in solid cracks. I pulled myself up and leaned on my elbows on the ledge to which my hands had been glued. I flexed my fingers and bent my wrists to bring life back.

It was shortly above the point where Doug saved my life that we discovered a classic path up Kloochman. It was a three-sided chimney chute, a few feet wide, that led almost to the top.

The sun was setting when we reached the top. We were happy and buoyant. We talked about the glories of the scene in front of us. We bragged a bit about our skill—how we must be part mountain goat to have reached the top. We shouted and hallooed to meadows far below us.

On Kloochman Rock that July afternoon, both Doug and I valued life more because death had passed so close. It was wonderful to be alive, breathing, shouting, seeing.

On the road leading back to camp, Doug said, "You know, Bill, there is power in prayer."

That night I prayed again. I knelt on a bed of white fir boughs beside the embers of a campfire and thanked God for saving Doug's life and mine, for giving us the strength to save each other.

---

3. **novocaine**, a drug used as a local anesthetic, often used by dentists to avoid causing pain. It paralyzes nerves for a short time without causing permanent damage.

Developing Comprehension Skills

1. Why did Doug and the narrator decide to climb the southeast face of Kloochman Rock?

2. When Doug thought he might die, he gave his friend a message for his family. Besides the traits mentioned by Doug, what did the message reveal about him?

3. When the narrator came close to death, he remembered his father's words: "If I die, it will be glory. If I live, it will be grace." How did these words help the narrator face this difficult situation?

4. How did Doug and the narrator help each other survive their climb up the mountain?

5. After each brush with death, the two boys continued the climb. Do you think they were brave or foolish? Explain your answer.

6. Following their climb, Doug and the narrator seemed to look at life differently than before. What accounted for this change?

Reading Literature: Nonfiction

1. **Recognizing Nonfiction.** "Of Men and Mountains" sounds like a short story. It has characters, conflict, and a strong story line. However, it is in the nonfiction chapter. Would you have realized that this adventure story was nonfiction even if it did not appear in this chapter? Why or why not? What clues in the selection show you that this event really happened?

2. **Analyzing Setting.** The setting for "Of Men and Mountains" is a mountain in the Cascades range of the northwestern United States. As Douglas describes Kloochman Rock, he notes the following dangers:

a. the steepness of its face
b. its height
c. the tendency of its ledges to crumble

Find passages describing each of these aspects of the mountain. Why are these details important to the story?

3. **Recognizing External Conflict.** Every true adventure story concerns an external conflict. As you remember, an **external conflict** is a struggle between the main character and another character or outside force. Explain the external conflict in "Of Men and Mountains."

4. **Recognizing Internal Conflict.** An **internal conflict**, you remember, is a struggle within a person faced with a choice. Consider the following dialogue from this story:

Hang on? You can't hang on. You are a weakling. The weaklings die in the woods.
Weakling? I'll show you. . . . I'll hang on.

Who is speaking? Explain the internal conflict.

5. **Inferring Character Traits.** Just as in fiction, the actions, words, and thoughts of nonfiction characters help to reveal their personality traits. What do the following show about the narrator?

a. his tears when Doug reveals his message for his family
b. his determination to climb Kloochman Rock following two close brushes with death
c. his efforts to continue to hang from the crevasse until Doug rescues him
d. his prayers

6. **Appreciating Point of View.** Every nonfiction selection is told from a certain point of view. The writer of this selection uses the first-person point of view. How does this point of view make the story more exciting than if it were told in third person?

7. **Recognizing Style.** An author's style is the special way that writer uses words. One characteristic of the writer's style in "Of Men and Mountains" is his use of **similes**, which are comparisons that use the words *like* or *as*. Explain the following comparisons and the pictures or feeling each one creates:

   a. In stocking feet we wormed up the wall, clinging like flies to the rock.
   b. His body went slowly up as if pulled by some unseen winch.
   c. Here, too, was a cliff rising 1,000 feet like some unfinished pyramid.
   d. I was like one in a nightmare who struggles to shout.
   e. My fingers were as numb as flesh full of novocaine.

Developing Vocabulary Skills

Identifying Word Parts. In this chapter you will learn to determine the meaning of a word by examining the parts that make up that word. Remember that there are three kinds of word parts: prefixes, suffixes, and base words.

Make four columns on your paper. Label them *Prefix, Base Word, Suffix,* and *Meaning.* Examine the following words taken from "Of Men and Mountains." Divide each word into its parts. Put each part in the proper column. Then give the meaning of the word. If a word has no prefix or suffix, put *0* in the column. You may wish to refer back to pages 308–309.

Example:

Prefix	Base Word	Suffix	Meaning
un	seen	0	not seen

cloudless   motionless   refuel
unseen   powerful   unafraid
dangerous   careless   discover
insecure

Developing Writing Skills

1. **Analyzing Motivation.** In your opinion, what causes people to seek excitement in dangerous sports such as mountain climbing and sky diving? State your opinion and support it in two or three paragraphs.

   Pre-Writing. Hold a discussion with your family or your classmates. Seek different ideas on the question of why some people seek danger. List possible reasons. Select one or two that make the most sense to you. Write down incidents or examples that support each reason. You may wish to use details from "Of Men and Mountains."

   Writing. Write an introduction that includes your opinion. Follow this introduction with paragraphs that support your opinion. Cover one strong reason in each paragraph. Give specific examples to help prove each reason.

   Revising. Exchange papers with two other students who will act as your editor and proofreader. The student acting as your editor should make suggestions about how to improve the content and organization of your composition. The student acting as your proofreader should check the spelling, punctuation, and usage in your composition. At the same time, you should edit or proofread these students' compositions.

2. **Writing a Letter.** Imagine that you are about to face a life-or-death situation. You want to convey a message either to your family or to your closest friend. Write your message. You might want to explain what you have learned about your life so far or what your family or friend has taught you about life.

3. **Using Similes.** Write a paragraph explaining an experience you had in which your courage was tested. Like the author of this selection, use comparisons, or similes, to explain some of the feelings you experienced. Refer to the last exercise under Reading Literature for examples.

Developing Skills in Study and Research

1. **Using Biographical References.** The author of this true adventure story is a well-known American. He is famous for his accomplishments in a field other than mountain climbing. In your library, look for information about William O. Douglas. Consult the following biographical sources located on the reference shelf or ask the reference librarian to recommend others.

   a. an encyclopedia
   b. a biographical encyclopedia
   c. *Dictionary of American Biography*

Take notes on the information you find in these references. Save these notes. You will use them again.

2. **Summarizing a Reading Selection.** Sometimes you will want to record or restate only the most important ideas of a selection. For example, you may wish to include only a brief version of a chapter or an article in a report. You can do this by writing a summary. A **summary** is a short version of the original material.

   To summarize a selection, first read the material carefully. Look for a key sentence that gives the writer's main point. Then, in your own words, note important ideas in the order in which they occur. Omit unnecessary details, examples, and anecdotes.

   When you write the summary, try to restate the material in your own words. Also try to keep your summary much shorter than the original. When you are finished with your draft, check your summary to see if you have included all the important ideas.

   In one paragraph, summarize the most interesting article that you found on the career of William O. Douglas. Study the notes you took in the first exercise and decide which information is the most important. Make sure that your paragraph begins with a strong topic sentence.

Not To Go with the Others

JOHN HERSEY

> *In a prison camp during World War II, Zaremski seems to face certain death. Which decisions could save his life? Which ones could condemn him to death?*

Late in the evening of Wednesday, January 17, 1945, three days before Lodz was to fall to the Russians, all the prisoners were gathered on the third and fourth floors of the main building, even those who were sick. There they all lay down on wooden bunks and floors to try to sleep. At about two in the morning, guards came and ordered them to get up for roll call.

They divided the prisoners into groups of about twenty each and lined up the groups in pairs. Zaremski was in the second group. SS[1] men led it down concrete stairs in a brick-walled stairwell at one end of the building and halted it on a landing of the stairway, near a door opening into a large loft on the second floor. The first group had apparently been led down to the ground floor.

Someone gave an order that the prisoners should run in pairs into the loft as fast as they could. When the first pair of Zaremski's group ran in, SS men with their backs

to the wall inside the room began to shoot at them from behind. Zaremski's turn came. He ran in terror. A bullet burned through his trouser leg. Another grazed his thigh. He fell down and pretended to be dead.

Others from Zaremski's and later groups ran into the hall and were shot and fell dead or wounded on top of Zaremski and those who had gone first. At one time Zaremski heard the Polish national anthem being sung somewhere.

Finally the running and shooting ended, and there ensued some shooting on the upper floors, perhaps of people who had refused to run downstairs.

SS men with flashlights waded among the bodies, shining lights in the faces of the prostrate victims. Any wounded who moaned or moved, or any whose eyes reacted when the shafts of light hit their faces, were dispatched with pistol shots. Somehow Zaremski passed the test.

As dawn began to break, Zaremski heard the iron doors of the main building being

---

1. **SS**, special military police force in Nazi Germany.

locked, and he heard some sort of grenades or bombs being thrown into the lowest hall and exploding there. They seemed to him to make only smoke, but they may have been incendiaries. Later, in any case, the ground floor began to burn. Perhaps gasoline had been poured around. Zaremski was still lying among the bodies of others.

There were several who were still alive, and they began jumping out of the burning building, some from windows on the upper stories. A few broke through a skylight to the roof, tied blankets from the prisoners' bunks into long ropes and let themselves down outside. Zaremski, now scurrying about the building, held back to see what would happen. Those who jumped or climbed down were shot at leisure in the camp enclosure by SS men in the turrets on the walls. Zaremski decided to try to stay inside.

On the fourth floor, at the top of the reinforced concrete staircase, in the bricked stairwell at the end of the building, Zaremski found the plant's water tank. For a time he and others poured water over the wounded lying on the wooden floors in the main rooms. Later Zaremski took all his clothes off, soaked them in the tank, and put them back on. He lay down and kept

Flame, 1934—1938, JACKSON POLLOCK. Oil on canvas on composition board, 20½" × 30". The Museum of Modern Art, New York. Purchase.

pouring water over himself. He put a soaked blanket around his head.

The tank was a tall one, separated from the main room by the stairwell's brick wall. When the fire began to eat through the wooden floor of the fourth story and the heat in the stairwell grew unbearable, Zaremski climbed up and got right into the water in the tank. He stayed immersed there all day long. Every few minutes he could hear shots from the wall turrets. He heard floors of the main halls fall and heard the side walls collapse. The staircase shell and the concrete stairs remained standing.

It was evening before the shooting and the fire died down. When he felt sure both had ended, Zaremski pulled himself out of the tank and lay awhile on the cement floor beside it. Then, his strength somewhat restored, he made his way down the stairs, and on the way he found six others who were wounded but could walk.

The seven went outside. Dusk. All quiet. They thought the Germans had left, and they wanted to climb the wall and escape. The first three climbed up and dropped away in apparent safety, but then the lights flashed on in the turrets and bursts of firing broke out. Three of the remaining four decided to take their chances at climbing out after total darkness. They did not know whether the first three had been killed or had escaped. Only Zaremski stayed.

The three climbed, but this time the lights came sooner and the guards killed all three while they were still scaling the wall.

Zaremski crept into the camp's storehouse in a separate building. Finding some damp blankets, he wrapped them around himself and climbed into a big box, where he stayed all night. Once during the night he heard steps outside the building and in the early morning he heard walking again. This time the footsteps approached the storeroom door. The door opened. The steps entered. Through the cracks of the box Zaremski sensed that the beam of a flashlight was probing the room. Zaremski could hear box tops opening and slamming and a foot kicking barrels. He held the lid of his box from the inside. Steps came near, a hand tried the lid, but Zaremski held tight, and the searcher must have decided the box was locked or nailed down. The footsteps went away.

Later two others came at different times and inspected the room but neither tried Zaremski's box; the third hunter locked the door from the outside.

Much later Zaremski heard a car start and drive away.

Much later still—some time on the nineteenth of January in the year of victory—Zaremski heard the Polish language being spoken, even by the voices of women and children. He jumped out of the box and broke the window of the storehouse and climbed out to his countrymen.

Developing Comprehension Skills

1. How did Zaremski survive the mass shooting by the SS men? How did Zaremski keep from being burned alive while the building was on fire?

2. Instead of climbing out of the building with the seven remaining prisoners, where did Zaremski hide from the SS men?

3. How long did Zaremski hide inside the building? How did he know when it was safe to emerge from his hiding place?

4. Did the prisoners seem to pose any threat to the SS men? What does Zaremski's treatment at Lodz reveal about the SS men?

5. Zaremski survived after all the other prisoners died. Do you think he survived because of luck or cleverness? Explain your answer.

6. There is an expression, "Truth is stranger than fiction." If you had not known that Zaremski's story was true, would you have found it believable? What do you find "strangest" about this true story?

Reading Literature: Nonfiction

1. **Understanding Purpose in Nonfiction.** Nonfiction can help readers to understand history in a way that facts and statistics cannot. "Not To Go with the Others" presents one person's experiences, but the story also reflects a portion of history. What insights into history does this story give you that a history book might not?

2. **Inferring Setting.** The setting for "Not To Go with the Others" is never explained directly. The reader must pick up clues about where and when the story takes place.

What clues can you find in this selection to tell you that the events took place during World War II? What clues tell you that Lodz is a prison camp in Poland run by Germans? That Zaremski is Polish?

3. **Recognizing Conflict.** Conflict, as you remember, is a struggle between one character and other characters or forces. Explain the conflicts facing Zaremski in "Not To Go with the Others." Which conflict did you find most interesting? Explain your answer.

4. **Identifying Suspense.** Suspense is the growing tension that a reader feels when the outcome of a story is uncertain. In true adventures, a writer builds suspense by describing threatening situations that the main character faces. In "Not To Go with the Others," the author builds suspense with a series of events. List four threatening situations that Zaremski faces. Choose one, and explain how the author builds suspense within that incident.

5. **Analyzing Tone.** Tone, as you remember, is the author's attitude toward the characters and events. An author's tone may be humorous or serious, light or thoughtful. On the other hand, the author may simply report the events of a story without showing concern for the characters and their problems. This is called an objective tone. Does this true adventure remind you of an objective newspaper report? If so, does this tone add or detract from the horror of the situation? Explain your answer.

6. **Recognizing Theme in a Title.** The title "Not To Go with the Others" emphasizes Zaremski's decisions not to follow the

crowd. It also expresses the theme of the true story. What main idea about life does Hersey convey in "Not To Go with the Others"?

Developing Vocabulary Skills

Using Prefixes. On page 308, you studied several prefixes that mean "not" or "the opposite of." The sentences below contain base words in parentheses. Add a prefix that means "not" or "the opposite of" to each base word so that the sentence is logical. Write the new words on your paper and give their meaning. If you are not sure which prefix to use, you may refer to a dictionary.

1. Zaremski lay (mobile) as the soldiers searched among the bodies for anyone who was still alive.
2. The heat became so (bearable) that Zaremski climbed into the water tank.
3. Zaremski held tightly to the lid of the box to prevent the soldier from (covering) him.
4. After hearing guns fire at the escaping men, it was (logical) to assume that one could get over the wall safely.
5. Death seemed to be (escapable), but Zaremski managed to survive.
6. Is "Not To Go with the Others" fiction or (fiction)?

Developing Writing Skills

1. **Analyzing Character Traits.** "Not To Go with the Others" tells about personal traits that are important in a crisis. Write a brief composition explaining these admirable traits, or qualities, that Zaremski possesses.

    Pre-Writing. List the admirable traits that Zaremski demonstrates. For each trait make notes on actions that reveal that quality. Organize these traits in the order of their importance.

    Writing. Write an introduction that presents the question of what traits are necessary for people to overcome difficult situations. In each body paragraph, explain one trait and show how Zaremski illustrates it. Include a good topic sentence in each paragraph. Write a conclusion that ties the composition together.

    Revising. Ask someone else to read your paragraphs. Ask the person what point each paragraph makes and how clear each paragraph is. See if the person understands your main ideas. If not, revise each paragraph beginning with a stronger topic sentence and more logically related examples.

2. **Using First-Person Point of View.** Point of view can affect a reader's reaction to a story. "Not To Go with the Others" is written from the third-person point of view. The narrator does, however, know what Zaremski is thinking and feeling. Do you think this point of view is effective in showing Zaremski's thoughts and feelings?

    Imagine yourself in Zaremski's place, trying to survive in the prison camp. Using first-person point of view, write one paragraph describing your feelings as you hide in the water tank or in the box in the storeroom. Use words and sensory details that show how you would react to the danger, the waiting, and the fear.

Developing Skills in Critical Thinking

Evaluating Facts and Opinions. A fact can be proven by observing the subject directly. It can also be proven by consulting an expert source. An opinion cannot be proven. It is one person's belief. Which of these statements are facts, and which are opinions?

1. On Wednesday, January 17, 1945, all the prisoners gathered on the third and fourth floors of the main building.

2. The prisoners who obeyed the order to run to the loft were foolish.

3. Several prisoners tried to escape by jumping out of upper-story windows and were shot.

4. The prisoners who jumped out of the windows weren't thinking clearly.

Is there enough evidence in the story to support the opinions? Explain why you think so.

Developing Skills in Speaking and Listening

Conducting an Interview. Interviews can help you find new ideas or information. Imagine that you have been assigned a report on World War II. First find and narrow a topic. Then conduct an interview with a person who was involved in World War II or who is well informed about that period. You might interview a history teacher, for example. When you conduct the interview, remember these guidelines:

1. Make an appointment for the interview, and arrive on time.

2. Do basic research on the subject so that you can ask informed questions.

3. Prepare questions in advance in order to get the information you need.

4. Avoid wording of questions that will result in simple "yes" or "no" answers.

5. Pay close attention to what the person says.

6. Take notes or ask if you may use a tape recorder during the interview.

Rattlesnake Hunt

MARJORIE KINNAN RAWLINGS

Can fear be overcome with knowledge? Read to see if the narrator of this true adventure learns enough to conquer her fear of snakes.

Ross Allen, a young Florida herpetologist, invited me to join him on a hunt in the upper Everglades, the swamps of southern Florida—for rattlesnakes to milk for snakebite serum.

The hunting ground was Big Prairie, south of Arcadia and west of the northern tip of Lake Okeechobee. Big Prairie is a desolate cattle country, half marsh, half pasture, with islands of palm trees and cypresses and oaks. At that time of year, the cattlemen and Indians were burning the country, on the theory that the young fresh wire grass that springs up from the roots after a fire is the best cattle forage. Ross planned to hunt his rattlers in the forefront of the fires. They lived in winter, he said, in gopher holes, coming out in the midday warmth to forage. They would move ahead of the flames and be easily taken. We joined forces with a big fellow named Will, his snake-hunting companion of the territory, and set out in early morning, after a long rough drive over deep-rutted roads into the open wilds.

I hope never in my life to be so frightened as I was in those first few hours. I kept on Ross's footsteps. I moved when he moved, sometimes jolting into him when I thought he might leave me behind. He does not use the forked stick of conventional snake hunting, but a steel prong, shaped like an L, at the end of a long stout stick. He hunted casually, calling my attention to the varying vegetation, to hawks overhead, to a pair of rare whooping cranes that flapped over us. In midmorning he stopped short, dropped his stick, and brought up a five-foot rattlesnake draped limply over the steel L. It seemed to me that I should drop in my tracks.

"They're not active at this season," he said quietly. "A snake takes on the temperature of its surroundings. They can't stand too much heat for that reason, and when the weather is cool, they're sluggish."

The sun was bright overhead, the sky a translucent blue, and it seemed to me that it was warm enough for any snake to do as it willed. The sweat poured down my back.

Ross dropped the rattler in a sack and Will carried it. By noon, he had caught four. I felt faint and ill. We stopped by a pond and went swimming. The region was flat, the horizon limitless, and as I came out of the cool blue water, I expected to find myself surrounded by a ring of rattlers. There were only Ross and Will, opening the lunch basket. I could not eat. Will went back and drove his truck closer, for Ross expected the hunting to be better in the afternoon. The hunting was much better. When we went back to the truck to deposit two more rattlers into the wire cage, there was a rattlesnake lying under the truck.

Ross said, "Whenever I leave my car or truck with snakes already in it, other rattlers always appear. I don't know whether this is because they scent or sense the presence of other snakes, or whether in this arid area they come to the car for shade in the heat of the day."

The problem was scientific, but I had no interest.

That night, Ross and Will and I camped out in the vast spaces of the Everglades' prairies. We got water from an abandoned well and cooked supper under buttonwood bushes by a flowing stream. The campfire blazed cheerfully under the stars and a new moon lifted in the sky. Will told tall tales of the cattlemen and the Indians and we were at peace.

Ross said, "We couldn't have a better night for catching water snakes."

After the rattlers, water snakes seemed harmless enough. We worked along the edge of the stream and here Ross did not use his L-shaped steel. He reached under rocks and along the edge of the water and brought out harmless reptiles with his hands. I had said nothing to him of my fears, but he understood them. He brought a small dark snake from underneath a willow root.

"Wouldn't you like to hold it?" he asked. "People think snakes are cold and clammy, but they aren't. Take it in your hands. You'll see that it is warm."

Because I was ashamed, I took the snake in my hands. It was not cold, it was not clammy, and it lay trustingly in my hands, a thing that lived and breathed and had mortality like the rest of us. I felt a sudden rise in my spirits.

The next day was magnificent. The air was crystal, the sky was aquamarine, and the far horizon of palms and oaks lay against the sky. I felt a new boldness and followed Ross bravely. He was making the rounds of the gopher holes. The rattlers came out in the midmorning warmth and were never far away. He could tell by their tails whether one had come out or was still in the hole. Sometimes the two men dug the snake out. At times, it was down so long and winding a tunnel that the digging was hopeless. Then they blocked the entrance and went on to other holes. In an hour or so, they made the original rounds, unblocking the holes. The rattler in every case came out hurriedly, as though anything was preferable to being shut in. All the time Ross talked to me, telling me the scientific facts

Concealing Coloration in the Animal Kingdom: Copperhead Snake on Dead Leaves, 1900–1909,
ABBOTT HANDERSON THAYER with GERALD THAYER, EMMA THAYER and ROCKWELL KENT.
National Museum of American Art, Smithsonian Institution. Gift of the heirs of Abbott H. Thayer, Washington, D.C.

he had discovered about the habits of the rattlers.

"They pay no attention to a man standing perfectly still," he said, and proved it by letting Will unblock a hole while he stood at the entrance as the snake came out. It was exciting to watch the snake crawl slowly beside and past the man's legs. When it was at a safe distance, he walked within its range of vision, which he had proved to be no higher than a man's knee. The snake whirled and drew back in an attitude of defense. The rattler strikes only for paralyzing and killing its food, and for defense.

"It is a slow and heavy snake," Ross said. "It lies in wait on a small game trail and strikes the rat or rabbit passing by. It waits a few minutes, then follows along the trail, coming to the small animal, now dead or dying. It noses it from all sides, making sure that it is its own kill, and that it is dead and ready for swallowing."

A rattler will lie quietly without revealing itself if a man passes by and it thinks it is not seen. It slips away without fighting if given the chance. Only Ross's sharp eyes sometimes picked out the gray and yellow diamond pattern, camouflaged among the grasses. In the cool of the morning, chilled by the January air, the snakes showed no fight. They could be looped up simply over the steel L and dropped in a sack or up into the wire cage on the back of Will's truck. As the sun mounted in the sky and warmed the moist Everglades' earth, the snakes were warmed, too. Ross warned that it was time to go more cautiously. Yet, having learned that it was we who were the aggressors; that immobility meant complete safety; that the snakes, for all their lightning flash in striking, were inaccurate in their aim, and had limited vision; having watched again and again the liquid grace of movement, the beauty of pattern, suddenly I understood that I was relaxed. I was drinking in freely the magnificent sweep of the horizon, with no fear of what might be at the moment under my feet. I went off hunting by myself. Though I found no snakes, I should have known what to do.

The sun was dropping low in the west. Masses of white clouds hung above the flat marshy plain and seemed to be tangled in the tops of distant palms and cypresses. The sky turned orange, then saffron. I walked leisurely back toward the truck. In the distance I could see Ross and Will making their way in, too. The season was more advanced than at the Creek, two hundred miles to the north, and I noticed that spring flowers were blooming among the lumpy hummocks. I leaned over to pick a violet. There was a rattlesnake under the violet.

If this had happened the week before, if it had happened the day before, I think I should have lain down and died on top of the rattlesnake, with no need of being struck and poisoned. The snake did not coil, but lifted its head and whirred its rattles lightly. I stepped back slowly and put the violet in a buttonhole. I reached forward and laid the steel L across the snake's neck, just back of the head. I called to Ross: "I've got one."

He strolled toward me.

"Well, pick it up," he said.

I released it and slipped the L under the middle of the thick body.

"Go put it in the box."

He went ahead of me and lifted the top of the wire cage. I made the truck with the rattler, but when I reached up the six feet to drop it in the cage, it slipped off the stick and dropped on Ross's feet. It made no effort to strike.

"Pick it up again," he said. "If you'll pin it down lightly and reach just back of its head with your hand, as you've seen me do, you can drop it in more easily."

I pinned it and leaned over.

"I'm awfully sorry," I said, "but you're pushing me a little too fast."

He grinned. I lifted it on the stick and again as I had it at head height, it slipped off, down Ross's boots and on top of his feet. He stood as still as a stump. I dropped the snake on his feet for the third time. It seemed to me that the most patient of rattlers might in time resent being hauled up and down. For all the man's quiet certainty that in standing motionless there was no danger, it would strike at whatever was nearest and that would be Ross.

I said, "I'm just not man enough to keep this up any longer," and he laughed and reached down with his smooth quickness and lifted the snake back of the head and dropped it in the cage. It slid in among its mates and settled in a corner. The hunt was over and we drove back over the uneven trail to Will's village and left him and went on to Arcadia and home. Our catch for the two days was thirty-two rattlers.

I said to Ross, "I believe that tomorrow I could have picked up that snake."

Back at the Creek, I felt a new lightness. I had done battle with a great fear, and the victory was mine.

Developing Comprehension Skills

1. Why did Ross choose to hunt snakes in warm weather?

2. What surprised the narrator upon first handling a snake? What had the narrator expected?

3. What did Ross want people to understand about snakes? Why was this important to him?

4. Based on the information in this story, do you think a fear of snakes is justified? Why or why not?

5. What advice would you give to someone who spots a snake?

Reading Literature: Nonfiction

1. **Observing Character Development.** In some stories—true or imaginary—readers can watch characters change, or develop. In "Rattlesnake Hunt" the narrator begins by being terrified of snakes. Later she becomes calmer, more informed, and less afraid. At what point does the narrator begin to change her attitude toward snakes? List the things that she learns about snakes that account for her more relaxed approach.

2. **Appreciating Description.** Marjorie Kinnan Rawlings's style involves the careful use of sensory details. These are details that appeal to the five senses. For example, her descriptions of the land, the water, the sky, the camp, and the weather appeal strongly to the sense of sight. Find two passages that help you to imagine the setting of this story. What words and phrases makes these passages so vivid?

3. **Determining the Author's Purpose.** Writers usually have a purpose for each piece of writing they create. They may wish their writing to inform, to entertain, or to persuade. What do you think the author's purpose was in writing "Rattlesnake Hunt"? Could there have been more than one purpose? Find specific evidence from this true adventure to support your opinion.

Developing Vocabulary Skills

Using Prefixes To Determine Word Meaning. Each of the following sentences contains an underlined word formed from a base word and a prefix from page 308. Write each underlined word on your paper. Give the meaning of the prefix. Then give the meaning of the entire word.

1. William Douglas and his friend did not pre-arrange their climb up Kloochman Rock.

2. The two young climbers made a superhuman effort to scale the southeast face of the mountain.

3. Zaremski stayed submerged in the water tank all day.

4. Something in Zaremski's subconscious mind kept him from trying to escape with the others.

5. Postwar investigations uncovered many prison camps such as Zaremski's.

6. Before the hunt, Marjorie Kinnan Rawlings had many preconceived ideas about snakes.

7. The author of "Rattlesnake Hunt" made an extraordinary effort to conquer her fear of snakes.

8. Ross Allen was hunting rattlesnakes to milk for antivenin serum.

Developing Writing Skills

1. **Using Comparison and Contrast.** In "Of Men and Mountains" and "Rattlesnake Hunt," a main character meets a great challenge and overcomes fear. In two paragraphs, compare and contrast the main characters in each selection. How are the characters similar? How are they different? Consider the characters' fears and goals, and what they did to achieve their goals.

2. **Writing About a Personal Experience.** Have you ever been afraid of someone or something? Perhaps you were afraid when you first rode a bike, drove a car, or tried some dangerous sport. In three paragraphs tell a true story of being afraid.

Pre-Writing. Jot down what happened when you were afraid. List the sequence of events in chronological order. Picture the events in your mind and recall your feelings as they occurred. Try to find words and phrases that will re-create those feelings.

Writing. Combine the ideas in clear sentences. Use transitional words such as *first*, *then*, *next*, *while*, *after*, and *last* to link your ideas. Convey your fear by including details that describe your feelings. Create suspense by keeping the reader uncertain of the outcome.

Revising. Ask a classmate to read your composition. Does the person get a strong sense of your fearfulness and its cause? If not, add more details that show the reason for your fear.

Developing Skills in Study and Research

Understanding Skimming and Scanning. When you study written material, you can use several types of reading. Each has a different purpose. **In-depth reading** is used when you want to get the full benefit of a piece of writing. It calls for careful, thoughtful reading and re-reading of paragraphs. Fast reading is useful for surveying or reviewing material. Two types of fast reading are skimming and scanning.

Skimming is used to get a general idea of the content of the selection. When you skim a selection, move your eyes quickly over the material. Do not read every word. Glance at titles, subtitles, headings, pictures, and graphic aids. Look at the first and final sentences in each paragraph.

Scanning is used to locate specific information. When you scan a selection, move your eyes quickly across each line or down each page. Locate words or phrases related to the information you need. When you spot the key word or phrase, stop scanning and read more slowly.

Scan "Rattlesnake Hunt" to find factual information about water snakes. List the information you find.

Developing Skills in Critical Thinking

Identifying Judgment Words. An opinion, you remember, is a statement that cannot be proved true. It is an expression of one person's feelings about a subject.

An opinion often contains one or more judgment words. **Judgment words** are words that express feelings. Judgment words, such as *disgusting* and *ineffective*, for example, show disapproval. Words such as *pleasing* and *capable* show approval. Learn to notice judgment words as you read.

Which are the judgment words in these passages? Which sentences show positive feelings? Which show negative feelings?

1. Big Prairie is a desolate cattle country, half marsh, half pasture . . .

2. We couldn't have a better night for catching snakes.

3. At times, it was down so long and winding a tunnel that digging was hopeless.

4. . . . having watched again and again the liquid grace of movement, the beauty of pattern, suddenly I understood that I was drinking in freely the magnificent sweep of the horizon . . .

From

Never Cry Wolf

FARLEY MOWAT

Why would anyone want to face dangerous wolves in the barren marshland of northern Canada? Read to discover what biologist Farley Mowat learns about wolves, and what he learns from them.

At an early age, Canadian naturalist Farley Mowat became fascinated by animals. A childhood of carefree animal observation led to formal university training as a biologist. During college, he decided that research in the field would interest him more than laboratory work. After his graduation, Mowat began his career with the government Wildlife Service.

I received a summons from the Dominion Wildlife Service informing me that I had been hired at the munificent salary of one hundred and twenty dollars a month, and that I "would" report to Ottawa at once.

I arrived in the windswept, gray-souled capital of Canada and found my way into the dingy labyrinth that housed the Wildlife Service. Early one morning I was called to the office of the senior officer who was my direct chief, for a final interview before departing "into the field."

"As you are aware, Lieutenant Mowat," my chief began, "the *canis lupus* problem has become one of national importance. Within the past year alone this Department has received no less than thirty-seven memoranda from Members of the House of Commons, all saying that we ought to do something about the wolf. Most of the complaints have come from such civic-minded and disinterested groups as various Fish and Game clubs. Members of the business community—in particular the manufacturers of some well-known brands of ammunition—have lent their weight to the support of these legitimate grievances of the voting public of this Great Dominion. Their grievance is the complaint that the wolves are killing all the deer, and more and more of our citizens are coming back from more and more hunts with less and less deer.

"The Department of Mines and Resources is determined to do everything in its power to curb this killing of the deer population by hordes of wolves. A full-scale investigation of this problem, employing the full resources of the Department, is to be launched at once.

"You, Lieutenant Mowat, have been chosen for this great task! It only remains for you to go out into the field at once and tackle this work in a manner worthy of the great traditions of this Department. The wolf, Lieutenant, is now your problem!"

Somehow I staggered to my feet, and with an involuntary motion brought my right hand up in a smart salute before fleeing from the room.

I fled from Ottawa, too . . . that same night, aboard a Canadian Air Force transport plane. My immediate destination was Churchill, on the western shore of Hudson Bay; but beyond that, somewhere in the desolate wastes of the subarctic Barren Lands, lay my ultimate objective—the wolf himself.

He Finds a Wolf

I had arrived safely at my base. As I looked about me at the stark and cloud-topped hills, the waste of pressure-rippled ice, and, beyond the valley, to the desolate and treeless roll of tundra, I had no doubt that this was excellent wolf country.

As I was a newcomer to the Barrens, it behooved me to familiarize myself with the country in a cautious manner. Hence, on my first expedition afield I contented myself with making a circular tour on a radius of about three hundred yards from the cabin.

This expedition revealed little except the presence of four or five hundred caribou skeletons; indeed, the entire area surrounding the cabin seemed to be carpeted in caribou bones. Since I knew from my researches in Churchill that trappers never shot caribou, I could only assume that these animals had been killed by wolves.

After this dismaying tour of the boneyard it was three days before I found time for another trip afield. Carrying a rifle and wearing my revolver, I went a quarter-mile on this second expedition—but saw no wolves.

Meantime spring had come to the Barrens with volcanic violence. The snows melted so fast that the frozen rivers could not carry the melted water, which flowed six feet deep on top of the ice. Finally the ice let go, with a thunderous explosion; then it promptly jammed, and in short order the river beside which I was living had entered into the cabin.

Eventually the jam broke and the waters subsided; but the cabin had lost its charm, for the debris on the floor was a foot thick. I decided to pitch my tent on a gravel ridge above the cabin. Here, I was vainly trying to go to sleep that evening when I became aware of unfamiliar sounds. Sitting bolt upright, I listened intently.

The sounds were coming from just across the river, to the north, and they were a weird mixture of whines, whimpers, and small howls. My grip on the rifle slowly relaxed. The cries were obviously those of a Husky, probably a young one that had got lost, and was now begging for someone to come and be nice to it.

Sunset on the tundra, Churchill, Manitoba. Earth Scenes. Copyright © 1984. Photograph by John Nees.

I was delighted. If that pup needed a friend, a chum, I was its man! I climbed hastily into my clothes, ran down to the riverbank, launched the canoe, and paddled lustily for the far bank.

The pup had never ceased its mournful cry and I was about to call out reassuringly when it occurred to me that an unfamiliar human voice might frighten it. I decided to stalk it instead, and to betray my presence only when I was close enough for soothing murmurs.

From the nature of the sounds, I had assumed the dog was only a few yards away from the far bank. However, as I made my way in the dim half-light, over broken boulders and across gravel ridges the sounds seemed to remain at the same volume while I appeared to be getting no closer. I assumed the pup was retreating, perhaps out of shyness. In my anxiety not to startle it away entirely, I still kept quiet, even when the whimpering wail stopped, leaving me uncertain about the right direction to pursue. I saw a steep ridge looming ahead of me, and I suspected that, once I gained its summit, I would have a clear enough view to enable me to locate the lost animal. As I neared the crest of the ridge, I got down on my stomach (practicing the fieldcraft I had learned in the Boy Scouts) and cautiously inched my way the last few feet.

My head came slowly over the crest—and there was my quarry. He was lying down, evidently resting after his mournful singsong, and his nose was about six feet from mine. We stared at one another in silence. I do not know what went on in his massive skull, but my head was full of the most disturbing thoughts. I was peering straight into the amber gaze of a fully grown arctic wolf, who probably weighed more than I did and who was certainly a lot better versed in close-combat techniques than I would ever be.

For some seconds neither of us moved but continued to stare hypnotically into one another's eyes. The wolf was the first to break the spell. With a spring that would have done justice to a Russian dancer, he leaped about a yard straight into the air and came down running. The textbooks say a wolf can run twenty-five miles an hour, but this one did not appear to be running, so much as flying low. Within seconds he had vanished from my sight.

My own reaction was not so dramatic, although I may very well have set some sort of record for a cross-country run myself. My return over the river was accomplished with such verve that I paddled the canoe almost her full length up on the beach on the other side. Then, remembering my responsibilities to my scientific supplies, I entered the cabin, barred the door, and, re-gardless of the discomfort caused by the debris on the floor, made myself as comfortable as I could on top of the table.

It had been a strenuous interlude, but I could congratulate myself that I had, at last, established contact—no matter how briefly—with the study species.

The Wolf Family

What with one thing and another, I found it difficult to get to sleep. The table was too short and too hard; the atmosphere in the cabin was far too thick; and the memory of my recent encounter with the wolf was too vivid. I tried counting sheep, but they kept turning into wolves, leaving me more wakeful than ever. Finally, when some red-backed mice who lived under the floor began to produce noises that sounded to me like the sounds a wolf might make if he were snuffling at the door, I gave up all idea of sleep, lit my oil lantern, and resigned myself to waiting for the dawn.

I allowed my thoughts to return to the events of the evening. Considering how brief the encounter with the wolf had been, I was amazed to discover the wealth of detail I could recall. In my mind's eye I could visualize the wolf as if I had known him or her for years. The image of that massive head with its broad white ruff, short pricked ears, yellow eyes, and grizzled muzzle was fixed in my memory. So, too, was the image of the wolf in flight; the lean and muscular motion and the overall impression of a beast the size of a small pony; an impression that implied killing strength.

As the light grew stronger, I even began to suspect that I had muffed an opportunity—one that might never again recur. It was borne in upon me that I should have followed the wolf and endeavored to gain his confidence, or at least to convince him that I harbored no ill will toward his kind.

The Canada jays who came each day to scavenge the debris in the dooryard were now becoming active. I lit the stove and cooked my breakfast. Then, filled with resolution, I packed some food in a haversack, saw to the supply of ammunition for my rifle and revolver, slung my binoculars around my neck, and set out to make good my failure of the previous evening. My plan was straightforward. I intended to go directly to the spot where I had seen the wolf disappear, pick up his trail, and follow until I found him.

The going was rough and rocky at first, and I took a good deal longer to cover the ground than the wolf had done. Eventually I scaled the low crest where I had last seen him or her. Ahead of me I found a vast expanse of marsh that promised well for tracks; and indeed I found a set of footprints almost immediately, leading off across a patch of chocolate-colored bog.

I should have felt overjoyed, yet somehow I did not. The truth is that my first sight of the wolf's paw-prints was a revelation for which I was quite unprepared. It is one thing to read in a textbook that the footprints of an arctic wolf measure six inches in diameter; but it is quite another thing to see them laid out before you. It has

a dampening effect on one's enthusiasm. The mammoth prints before me, combined as they were with a forty-inch stride, suggested that the beast was built on approximately the scale of a grizzly bear.

I studied those prints for quite a long time, and might perhaps have studied them for even longer had I not made the discovery that I had neglected to bring my pocket compass with me. Since it would have been foolhardy to proceed into an unmarked wilderness without it, I regretfully decided to return to the cabin.

When I got back to the cabin, the compass was not where I had left it. In fact, I couldn't remember where I had left it or even if I had seen it since leaving Ottawa. In order not to waste my time, I got down one of the standard books with which the Department had equipped me and consulted the section on wolves. I had, of course, read this section many times before, but some of the facts had evidently failed to impress themselves clearly on my mind. Now, with my capacity for mental imagery sharpened by my first look at a set of real wolf tracks, I reread the piece with new interest and appreciation.

Arctic wolves, the author informed me, were the largest of the many subspecies or races of *canis lupus*. Specimens had been examined that weighed one hundred and seventy pounds; measured eight feet seven inches from tip of nose to tip of tail; and that stood forty-two inches high at the shoulders. An adult of the arctic race could eat (and presumably did on favorable occasions) thirty pounds of raw meat at a sitting. The teeth were "massive in construction and capable of both tearing and grinding action, which enables the owner to dismember the largest mammals with ease and to crush even the strongest bones." The section closed with the following remarks: "The wolf is a savage, powerful killer. It is one of the most feared and hated animals known to man, and with excellent reason."

I was very thoughtful for the balance of the day. There were moments when I wondered if my hopes of gaining the confidence of the wolves might not be overly optimistic. As to demonstrating that I bore them no ill will—this I felt would be easy enough to do, but would be of little value unless the wolves felt like reciprocating.

The next morning I undertook to clean up the mess in the cabin, and in the process I uncovered my compass. I set it on the windowsill while I continued with my work, but the sun caught its brass surface, and it glittered at me so accusingly that I resigned myself to making another effort to restore the lost contact between me and the wolves.

My progress on this second safari was even slower, since I was carrying my rifle, shotgun, pistol and pistol belt, a small hatchet, and my hunting knife.

It was a hot day, and spring days in the subarctic can be nearly as hot as in the tropics. The first mosquitoes were already heralding the approach of the sky-filling swarms that would soon make travel a veritable trip through hell. I located the wolf tracks and set out upon the trail.

It led directly across the marsh for several miles; but although the wolf had sunk in only three or four inches, my steps sank in until I reached solid ice a foot beneath the surface. It was with great relief that I finally crossed another gravel ridge and lost all trace of the wolf tracks.

I felt lonelier than I had ever felt in all my life. No friendly sound of aircraft engines broke the silence of that empty sky. No distant rumble of traffic set the ground beneath my feet to shaking. Only the birdsong of an unseen plover gave any indication that life existed anywhere in all this lunar land where no tree grew.

I found a niche amongst some moss-covered rocks and, having firmly jammed myself into it, ate and drank my lunch. Then I picked up the binoculars and began to scan the barren landscape for some signs of life.

Directly in front of me was the ice-covered bay of a great lake, and on the far side of this bay was something which at least relieved the somber monotony of the marsh. It was a yellow sand esker, rising to a height of fifty or sixty feet and winding sinuously away like a gigantic snake.

These barren land eskers are the inverted beds of long-vanished rivers that once flowed through and over the glaciers that, ten thousand years ago, covered the Keewatin Barrens to a depth of several thousand feet. When the ice melted, sandy riverbeds were deposited on the land below. They provide almost the sole visual relief in the bleak monotony of the tundra plains.

I gazed at this one with affection, studying it closely; and, as I swept it with my glasses, I saw something move. The distance was great, but the impression I had was of someone, just the other side of the esker crest, waving his arm above his head. Much excited, I stumbled to my feet and trotted along the ridge to its termination on the shore of the bay. I was then not more than three hundred yards from the esker and when I got my breath back I took another look through the glasses.

The object I had previously glimpsed was still in view, but now it looked like a white feather boa being waved by persons or person unseen. It was a most inexplicable object, and nothing I had ever heard of in my study of natural history seemed to fit it. As I stared, the first boa was joined by a second one, also waving furiously. Both boas began to move slowly along, parallel to the crest of the esker.

I began to feel somewhat uneasy, for here was a phenomenon that did not seem to be subject to scientific explanation. In fact, I was on the point of abandoning my interest in the spectacle until some expert in psychic research happened along—when, without warning, both boas turned toward me, began rising higher and higher, and finally revealed themselves as the tails of two wolves proceeding to top the esker.

Arctic wolf, Baffin Island Tundra.

The esker overlooked my position on the bay's shore. Hunkering down to make myself as small as possible, I wormed my way into the rocks and did my best to be unobtrusive. I need not have worried. The wolves paid no attention to me, if indeed they even saw me. They were far too engrossed in their own affairs, which, as I slowly and incredulously began to realize, were at that moment centered around the playing of a game of tag.

It was difficult to believe my eyes. The wolves were romping like a pair of month-old pups! The smaller wolf took the initiative. Putting her head down on her forepaws and elevating her posterior in a most undignified manner, she suddenly pounced toward the much larger male, whom I now recognized as my acquaintance of two days earlier. He, in his attempt to evade her, tripped and went sprawling. Instantly she was upon him, nipping him smartly in the backside before leaping away to run around him in frenzied circles. The male scrambled to his feet and gave chase, but only by the most strenuous efforts was he able to close the gap until he, in his turn, was able to nip her backside. Thereupon the roles were again reversed, and the female began to pursue the male, who led her on a wild scrabble up, over, down, and back across the esker until finally both wolves lost their footing on the steep slope and went skidding down it together.

When they reached the bottom they shook the sand out of their hair, and stood panting heavily, almost nose to nose. Then the female reared up and quite literally embraced the male with both forepaws while she proceeded to smother him in kisses.

The male appeared to be enduring this overt display of affection, rather than enjoying it. He bore it patiently until the female tired. Turning from him, she climbed halfway up the esker slope and . . . disappeared.

She seemed to have vanished off the face of the earth without leaving a trace behind her. Not until I swung the glasses back toward a dark shadow in a fold of the esker near where I had last seen her did I understand. The dark shadow was the mouth of a cave, or den, and the female wolf had almost certainly gone into it.

I was so elated by the realization that I had not only located a pair of wolves, but by an incredible stroke of fortune had found their den as well, that I forgot all caution and ran to a nearby knoll in order to gain a better view of the den mouth.

The male wolf, who had been loafing about the foot of the esker after the departure of his wife, instantly saw me. In three or four bounds, he reached the ridge of the esker, where he stood facing me in an attitude of tense and threatening vigilance. He no longer seemed like a playful pup, but had become a magnificent engine of destruction.

I decided I had better not disturb the wolf family any more that day, for fear of upsetting them and perhaps forcing them to move away. So I withdrew. It was not an easy withdrawal, for one of the most difficult things I know of is to walk backward up a broken rocky slope for three quarters of a mile, carrying the tools of a scientist's trade.

When I reached the ridge from which I had first seen the wolves, I took a last quick look through the binoculars. The female was still invisible, and the male had so far relaxed his attitude of vigilance as to lie down on the crest of the esker. While I watched, he turned around two or three times, as a dog will, and then settled himself, nose under tail, with the evident intention of having a nap.

I was much relieved to see he was no longer interested in me. It would have been a tragedy if my accidental intrusion had unduly disturbed these wolves, thereby prejudicing what promised to be a unique opportunity to study the beasts I had come so far to find.

Developing Comprehension Skills

1. What was the purpose of Mowat's assignment in the Barren Lands? How did he find his first wolf?

2. Each time Mowat set out to track wolves he took more weapons. Why?

3. Mowat observed a male wolf and a female wolf. In what ways did the wolves' behavior seem human?

4. How did Mowat discover a wolf's den? What do you think he did for the next few weeks after this discovery?

5. Would you have liked living the adventures that Mowat experienced? Why or why not?

6. Mowat read that "The wolf is a savage, powerful killer. It is one of the most feared and hated animals known to man." Does anything in Mowat's account contradict this image? How do you think the wolf's savage image came to be?

Reading Literature: Nonfiction

1. **Recognizing Nonfiction.** This excerpt from the book *Never Cry Wolf* is a true story of Farley Mowat's scientific work with wolves. It is a true adventure because it tells of the challenge of facing wolves in the wilderness. How does the fact that it is true affect your reaction to the story? What incidents in Mowat's story interest you the most?

2. **Analyzing Effective Introductions.** A good introduction provides enough background information to get a reader into the selection quickly. It also sparks the reader's interest. What do you learn about Farley Mowat in this introduction? What information sug-

gests the adventures that lie ahead for Mowat? What was unusual, and therefore interesting, about this introduction?

3. **Understanding the Narrator.** Part of the charm of Mowat's story lies in the character of Mowat himself. Many of his actions and reactions are not what you would expect of a skilled scientist. For example, when Mowat first meets the wolf he has been seeking, he runs in terror.

Reread the last five paragraphs of this true story. Which of Mowat's actions are different from what you would expect of a skillful, objective scientist? How does Mowat's honesty about those things he cannot do show his sense of humor? How does it affect your response to his story? Explain your answer.

4. **Recognizing Understatement.** Mowat creates humor by using understatement. **Understatement** occurs when a speaker makes a calm, simple statement even though the situation calls for something more forceful. For example, Mowat says that seeing a wolf has "a dampening effect on one's enthusiasm." What does he really mean? Find one other example of understatement in the selection. Explain how it adds to the humor of the story.

5. **Identifying Narration, Description, and Exposition.** Nonfiction can include narration, description, and exposition. Narration tells a story. Description creates word pictures. Exposition explains how or why something is done.

Find one example each of description, narration, and exposition in this story. Explain what each kind of writing adds to the

story. Is "Never Cry Wolf" primarily narration, description, or exposition?

Developing Vocabulary Skills

Learning New Prefixes. You have already studied many prefixes. The chart below contains three more commonly used English prefixes:

Prefix	Meaning	Example
en-	to cause to be	endanger
inter-	between, among	interstate
re-	again, back	reuse

The following words are from "Never Cry Wolf." Determine their meaning by using your knowledge of prefixes and base words. Write the meaning of each word on your paper.

1. interview
2. reassure
3. enable
4. involuntary
5. subarctic
6. recall
7. discomfort
8. subspecies

Developing Writing Skills

1. **Using Comparison.** The narrators of both "Never Cry Wolf" and "Rattlesnake Hunt" encounter fear of an animal and try to overcome it. What helps to reduce the narrator's fear in each story? Write a paragraph comparing the narrators' response to fear, and the actions taken to overcome the fear.

2. **Writing for Different Purposes.** "Arctic wolves," Mowat's book tells him, "were the largest of the many subspecies or races of *Canis lupus*." Reread the dry, scientific description of wolves on pages 337–338. It contrasts with Mowat's lively, personal description on page 336, which begins "The image of that massive head with its broad

white ruff, short pricked ears, yellow eyes, and grizzled muzzle was fixed in my memory.''

Write two descriptions about an animal or object of your own choosing. You might choose an insect, a cloud, or the moon, for example. Make one description impersonal and scientific by including facts from an encyclopedia. Make the other description vivid and lively by including interesting and personal observations.

Pre-Writing. Observe your subject carefully. You might also watch a documentary or movie about it. Note your observations. Include sensory details about appearance, and any behavior or abilities. Then, consult an encyclopedia or other references for facts and statistics about your subject. Organize your ideas in some type of spatial order, or in another order that makes sense.

Writing. Using your notes, write first drafts of each description. Begin your first paragraph with a good topic sentence that presents your subject. Then describe your subject using sensory details from your observation. In the second paragraph, describe your subject using the facts and statistics.

Revising. Read your descriptions aloud. Ask your listeners to try to picture what you are describing. Ask them to think of additional details and facts that will add to each description.

Developing Skills in Study and Research

1. **Using an Atlas.** Every library has at least one atlas, which is a book of maps. An atlas is a useful reference tool for learning where the places you read about are located.

Locate an international atlas in your library. Use its index to find a map of Canada. Read the legend, which explains the various symbols used on the map, as well as the scale of distance. On the map, locate the places that Mowat mentions: the Barren Lands, Ottawa, Keewatin, Oakville, Ontario, Churchill, and Hudson Bay. Use the legend to determine the approximate distance Mowat traveled from Ottawa to the Barren Lands.

2. **Using the *Readers' Guide*.** The *Readers' Guide to Periodical Literature* is an index to magazine articles. Your library has a bound volume of past *Readers' Guides*, along with more current monthly indexes. If you are searching for current information on a topic, look up your subject in the *Readers' Guide*'s alphabetical listing.

Each entry in *Readers' Guide* lists the subject, article title, name, and date of the magazine in which the article appears. It also lists the page number of the article. Here is a sample entry:

Lish, Gordon
   A protecting father. il *N Y Times Mag* p50 Jl 15 '84
Lisp (Computer language)
   Swift mechanical logic. J. Raloff. il *Sci News* 125:346-7 Je 2 '84
Lispector, Clarice
   Pig Latin [story]; tr. by Alexis Levitin il *Ms* 13:68-9 Jl '84
Listening
   Getting kids to listen. G. N. Edelman. il *Parents* 59:52-6 Jl '84
Lite food *See* Food
Literacy education
   One-on-one against illiteracy. D. A. Williams. il *Newsweek* 104:78 Jl 30 '84

Use the *Readers' Guide* in your library to locate articles written about wolves in the past three years. Write down the title and date of the magazine, along with the title and page number of each article. Find one article, and read it carefully, taking notes on important information so that you can report to the class.

Developing Skills in Critical Thinking

1. **Distinguishing Fact from Opinion.** Reread the reference book material about wolves that appears on pages 337–338. At what point does the article switch from fact to opinion? What judgment words does the book use to create emotion in the reader?

2. **Recognizing Faulty Logic.** One type of faulty logic is called **either/or thinking**. In such a case, a person wrongly assumes that there are only two possibilities, rather than many. "If she doesn't agree with us, then she must be against us" is an example of this error in reasoning. In fact, "she" might be neutral. She might also only partly agree. Explain how Farley Mowat demonstrates this flaw in reasoning in the following paragraph:

> The entire area surrounding the cabin seemed to be carpeted in caribou bones. Since I knew from my researches in Churchill that trappers never shot caribou, I could only assume that these animals had been killed by wolves.

3. **Evaluating Stereotypes.** A **stereotype** is a distorted image that is believed to be true by a group. It represents an oversimplified opinion, and is often harmful or dangerous. What is the common stereotype of wolves? How does the government's book reinforce this stereotype? What does Mowat see that contradicts the stereotype?

*B*iographies

Biographies are the true stories of people's lives. In this section you will read about three famous women who set standards for others to follow. They were leaders admired by millions. The personal lives of these women were filled with the same mixture of happiness, tragedy, success, and failure that all people experience. But each had something extra, something within her that set her above the rest. As you read these biographies, look for these qualities.

Wilma Rudolph displaying her three gold medals from the 1960 Olympics, Rome. UPI/Bettmann, New York.

Babe Didrikson Zaharias

HARRY GERSH

Babe Didrikson was a pioneer in women's professional sports. Read her biography to see what made her excel on the playing field, and in her private life as well.

Ole Didrikson was a Norwegian seaman who sailed around Cape Horn seventeen times before settling in Port Arthur, Texas. There he got married, learned the furniture-finishing trade, and fathered seven children. Mildred, whom everyone called Babe, was one of the youngest.

Raising seven children on a furniture worker's pay in the 1920's meant scrimping and scraping, so there were no nickels or even pennies to spare for the children. Yet Ole Didrikson said, "I can build them good bodies, and that's better than nickels and dimes for candy and movies."

He built a trapeze and bars in the back yard. He put together a weight-lifting machine from old iron and rope. Then he taught his children to use them. The Didrikson kids became the best athletes in town—which isn't always good. After a bit the other children refused to play ball with them unless they split up, otherwise they always won. The Didrikson kids refused to split up though. They were a team.

When there was no work in the furniture factory, Mrs. Didrikson took in washing and Ole Didrikson had to ship out again as a sailor. With Father away at sea and Mother washing all day to earn enough to feed them, the Didrikson kids had to take care of the many chores that seem to multiply in a seven-child household. The chores took them away from their beloved sports, but Babe found a way to keep in trim.

Her chore was scrubbing the floors of the entire house. Once she got past the kitchen and where her mother couldn't see her, Babe strapped the scrubbing brushes on her feet and skated over the soapy water until the floors shone. One sportswriter later wrote, "Maybe that's where Babe developed the muscles and the balance that made her the greatest athlete of her time."

Life was hard for the Didrikson children, and the parents were strict—but lovingly strict. Disobedience earned a slap or a licking. Almost always it was followed by a kiss to take the sting away.

Once when Babe was eleven, her mother made her a new dress. New dresses were rare in the Didrikson house, and anyone

Babe Didrikson (front, center), about age 6, with father, brothers and sister. Gray Library, Lamar University, Beaumont, Texas.

getting one knew she had to treasure it. Babe forgot one day. She had worn the dress to school and was on her way home to change it—a strict rule—when she suddenly found herself playing baseball with some boys. The dress ripped during a slide to home base. But she was safe, and her team won.

Babe knew better than to try to hide the tragedy. She marched into the kitchen and showed the damage. Mrs. Didrikson was sitting shelling peas with one leg up on a chair to ease an ankle she had sprained in a fall the previous day. She became so angry at the sight of the ruined dress that she rose, grabbed a stick, and began hobbling toward Babe. Babe dodged behind the table, with her mother in full chase.

Suddenly Babe stopped running from the threatening stick. The sight of her mother hobbling on a swollen ankle touched her.

"Momma, stop running," she said, "You'll hurt your ankle worse. I'll wait for you."

By the time Mrs. Didrikson came up to her daughter, she hadn't the heart to spank or punish her. Instead they both burst out laughing.

Babe played basketball in junior high school. She never grew very tall, and at fourteen she wasn't even five feet. The girls' basketball coach looked at her, looked at the towering seniors, and told Babe that she wasn't cut out for basketball.

The next day she turned out for boys' basketball practice. "Just to watch," she told someone who asked her what she was doing there. She was there the following day, and the next, and the next. The boys' coach was surprised to see the little skinny girl turn up for practice every day, but suspected she had a crush on one of the players. When Babe began nagging him about why this was done and how that was done, he found out she was interested only in basketball, not basketball players.

When the players were resting, or after they had finished for the day, little Babe Didrikson bounced barefoot onto the court—she didn't own a pair of sneakers—in a ragged tee shirt and jeans, and took command of the ball. After she sank five baskets in a row from the center court, she didn't have to nag the coach any more. He was quite willing to show her anything she wanted to know.

A few weeks later Babe told the boys' coach, "Go tell the girls' coach that I can play basketball." He did, and Babe was on the Beaumont, Texas, High School girls' basketball team.

She was high scorer not only in the first inter-high-school game she played, but she was high scorer for the entire season. Her team didn't lose a single game all year.

Basketball was an important girls' sport in the 1930's, and many companies supported employee teams for the advertising. Even in those years of great unemployment, a good basketball player was sure of a job. Babe, not quite sixteen, was offered a job by the Employers' Casualty Insurance Company so she could play on the company's basketball team.

It was a double opportunity—she could continue to play basketball, and she could help support her family. After long discussions around the dinner table, Babe accepted the offer. She moved to Dallas and began earning seventy-five dollars a month. Forty-five dollars went home to help the Didriksons; five dollars a month went for rent; she lived on the remaining twenty-five dollars a month. She owned one pair of shoes and made skirts from clothes the other girls on the team passed on to her.

She was named All-American girls' basketball player that year—and the next year, and the year after that.

The basketball season lasted only six months, which left Babe another six months without athletic competition. Babe solved this problem by suggesting to the company that it sponsor a girls' track-and-field team. The company was willing to do anything for its All-American athlete, so a call was sent out for track-and-field candidates.

At the first meeting of candidates for the new team, the girls were asked what sports they wanted to try out for.

"I'll try discus," said one girl.

"Hurdles for me," said a second.

"I'm a javelin thrower," said a third.

"What are you going to try out for, Babe?" asked the coach.

"How many events are there?" asked Babe.

"Oh, nine or ten."

"Well," said Babe, "I guess maybe I'll try them all."

The gymnasium rocked with laughter. Babe was like that, half innocent and half boastful. They couldn't decide which half was speaking then.

When Babe Didrikson entered all ten of the events at her first track-and-field meet and won eight, they cheered.

In 1932 the national women's track championships were combined with the tryouts for the team that would represent the United States of America at the Olympic games. The Employers' Casualty Insurance Company, Babe's employer, sent a team to the meet in the Chicago area. The team consisted of two women—Babe Didrikson and a chaperone, Mrs. Wood.

Babe went to bed rather early the night before the meet, but she couldn't sleep. Her stomach felt as if she had eaten ground glass, and she was racked by spasms. Her tossing and groaning woke Mrs. Wood, who became frightened and called a doctor. She thought Babe might be having an appendicitis attack.

The doctor examined Babe and asked a great many questions. None of the answers seemed to satisfy him. Babe and Mrs. Wood got more and more frightened. Finally he asked what they were doing in Chicago.

"I'm competing in the national track championships," Babe said.

The doctor began packing his bag. "That's it, then," he said. "There's nothing wrong with you except nervousness and excitement. It ought to go away when you're on the field."

Even though they were reassured, Babe and Mrs. Wood didn't fall asleep until dawn. That's why they overslept. When they finally awoke and saw the time, they threw on their clothes, dashed out of the hotel without breakfast, and jumped into the first taxi they saw.

"Where to, ladies?" the cabbie asked.

"The stadium in Evanston," they both yelled.

"Not me. That's out of town and I don't drive outside Chicago."

So they jumped out of that cab. Another drew up in front of the hotel. But that one wouldn't leave the city limits either. They finally persuaded a third driver to make the trip.

Traffic was slow, and Mrs. Wood kept looking at her watch every two minutes.

"We'll never make it," she wailed. "You won't have time to change clothes before they call the first event."

Babe was just as worried, but she was cooler. "I'll change while we're driving," she said.

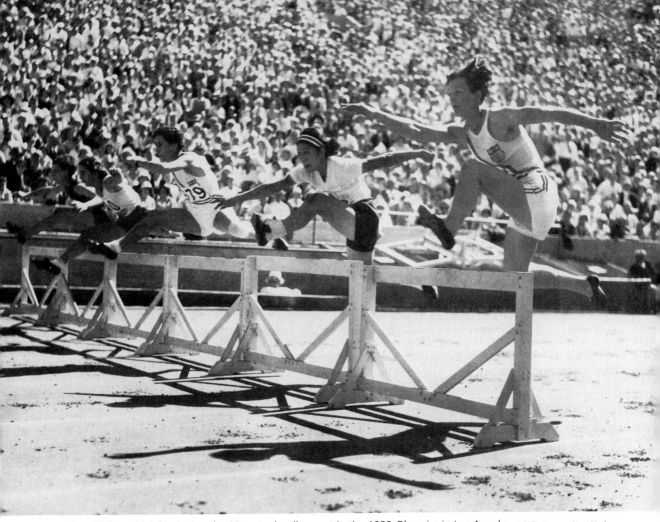

Babe Didrikson (right), winning the 80-meter hurdle event in the 1932 Olympics in Los Angeles. UPI/Bettmann, New York.

So while Mrs. Wood held a blanket around her, Babe changed into her track clothes in the taxi passing through the crowded streets in the middle of Chicago. When the cab drew up before the contestants' entrance, she jumped out in tee shirt, shorts, and spiked shoes, ready to go.

Even as they entered the stadium, the loud speakers were calling the teams for the parade onto the field. When the Illinois Women's Athletic Club was called, twenty-two athletes marched forward. A second club fielded fifteen girls, another twelve. All in all there were more than 200 female athletes on the field. When they called the team of the Employers' Casualty Insurance Company of Dallas, Texas, one lonely girl marched bravely down the field. The crowd roared.

Babe had entered eight of the individual events in the meet; she wasn't eligible for the team events like the relays. She ran a heat of the 80-meter hurdles, took a high jump, threw the javelin, then went back to run the second heat of the hurdles. When she finished that, they were waiting for her at the pit for the 8-pound shot.

The one-woman team of the Employers' Casualty Company won that track meet. Babe Didrikson won first place in five of the eight events she entered, tied for first place in the sixth event, placed in the seventh. She was out of the running in only one event. Her team—made up of Babe Didrikson and chaperone—took first place with thirty points. The twenty-two-woman team of the Illinois Athletic Club took second place with twenty-two points. While she was about it, Babe also broke the world's records for throwing the javelin, running the 80-meter hurdles, and the high jump.

That summer, Babe Didrikson was on the team that represented her country at the Olympics in Los Angeles. She was entered in only three events because Olympic games rules limited contestants to three individual events.

The Olympic games are opened with a parade of teams from all the competing nations, each team in its own costume and carrying its national flag. The girls on the American team were issued uniforms of red, white, and blue dresses, stockings, and white shoes. These were the first silk stockings Babe had ever owned. They felt fine. The shoes, however, were killing her. When the athletes of all the nations lined up in mid-field for the opening ceremonies, Babe

slipped out of her shoes. There she stood, before 80,000 people, in her stocking feet—but comfortable.

She got stubborn about the track shoes. The committee provided each contestant with the finest track shoes available, but Babe refused to use them. She insisted on running in the old, broken-down shoes that had carried her so well in Evanston.

The first event in which she was a contestant was the javelin throw. It was late in the day when that event was called. Shadows dimmed the field, and the air was cool. Babe was so entranced by the sight of the great stadium filled with so many thousands of people and by the thousands of athletes from faraway lands, she forgot to keep warm and supple. When her name was announced and she stepped up to the throwing line, her muscles were tight.

Babe picked up the long, slim spear and balanced it in her hand. She looked down the course 129 feet to where a small flag marked the current Olympic record. The record had been made by a German girl, so the flag marking it was the German flag. Her eyes on that flag, Babe reached far back with the javelin. She waited a long moment, then she brought the spear forward.

But she wasn't properly warmed up or loosened up. As she released the javelin, her hand slipped off the cord binding of the handle. Instead of arching high and away in a proper course, the javelin sped straight away, like a line drive from the bat of a great baseball slugger. It was the wrong way to throw the javelin. It couldn't possibly reach the record flag without the aid of arching flight. But it did reach the record flag—and went well beyond. Babe Didrikson's first throw in the Olympic javelin event came to rest 143 feet, 4 inches away from the starting line. It was a new Olympic record.

It wasn't until the distance had been measured and announced and the crowd had finished its thunderous applause that Babe became conscious of a sharp pain.

The finals of the 80-meter hurdles were held three days later. In her anxiety to be off and running, Babe began her sprint a split second before the starting gun went off. It was a foul and the runners were recalled. Babe was embarrassed and worried. Olympic rules say that a runner who jumps the gun twice is disqualified. So she held back in the second start until the other contestants were off. She didn't catch the field until the fifth hurdle. Then she passed them. Her time of 11.7 seconds—with a slow start—was enough to win another gold medal for the United States team, and set another Olympic record.

Babe ran into hard luck again in the third event, the high jump. She used a western roll to get over the bar—the only woman contestant to use this unorthodox jump—and the judges were unaccustomed to it. Babe and another American contestant had both cleared the bar at five feet, five and a quarter inches when the judges disqualified Babe for diving over the bar. She had to be satisfied with second place in that event.

With two firsts and one second in the three events in which she was allowed to compete, Babe Didrikson was the star of the Olympics.

The day after the high jump, Babe began to play a new game in which she was to become the world's greatest. A group of sportswriters invited her to play a round of golf with them. They accepted her protests that she had never played before and assured her that they would be both charitable and helpful.

They met at the country club and, while the men were having some coffee, Babe excused herself to borrow a set of clubs. She hurried around to the professional's shop and explained to the pro that she had never played before. She wanted him to show her in five minutes enough "so I won't look so bad out there."

The pro gave her a five-minute demonstration in how to grip the club, how to swing, and how to stand. Every time Babe exclaimed that she could never do it right without long lessons, the pro would say, "Just look at the ball real hard. Look at the ball real hard every time."

The men invited Babe to drive the first ball. She walked to the first tee, placed her ball on the grass, and stepped back a bit to get room to swing.

"Hey, Babe," yelled Grantland Rice, one of the nation's greatest sportswriters, "don't you know enough to use a tee?"

Babe looked confused, so the sportswriter came forward and placed Babe's ball on the little wooden pin that lifted it clear of the grass. She was proud ever after that the first ball she ever drove down a fairway had been teed up by Grantland Rice. It was a good luck omen.

Babe took a few practice swings and addressed the ball. "Look at the ball real hard. Look at the ball real hard," she kept repeating to herself. So she looked at the ball hard and swung with all her trained strength. The ball sailed straight and true down the fairway. It came to rest 240 yards from the tee. It was a better and longer drive than any of her partners made that day. Nor would they believe that she had never played golf before.

After the Olympics, Babe returned to her job at the insurance company. She got a lot more money, but it was still only $300 a month.

Babe entered her first golf tournament in November, 1934. She scored a 77 in her first round, but she wasn't skillful enough or well enough trained to win the tournament. She did win the Texas women's championship four months later. That year she was forced to turn professional.

It was during the Los Angeles Open Tournament in 1938 that Babe Didrikson met George Zaharias, a husky, black-haired, professional wrestler. They were accidentally paired in a mixed foursome and George asked Babe if she would have a soda after the game. He took her to dinner the second day; dancing, the third; to a party, the fourth. They saw each other every night during the two weeks of the tournament and were married shortly after.

Babe Didrikson Zaharias was the world's greatest woman golfer for more than ten years. In 1947, for example, she won fifteen championships in a row. Her greatest battle was still before her. Babe was entered in a tournament in Seattle in May 1952 and was expected to win, as usual. However, her drives were short, her approach shots didn't reach the green, and her putting was weak. She dragged around the course and finished the eighteen holes. She came in eleventh, the lowest she had ever scored in tournament play.

The next day she was operated on for a strangulated hernia as soon as the doctors could get her ready for surgery. Not too serious in itself, the hernia had been neglected for so long that it might have killed Babe soon.

In a few months, Babe Zaharias was back on the golf circuit, but she couldn't seem to come back to her former form and condition. She felt tired all the time. Still she played on and on.

In March of 1953, Babe returned to Texas to play in a great championship tournament named for her, the Babe Zaharias Open. It was her tournament, in her home town, in her home state. She wanted to win it very much. Although she knew she needed medical treatment right away and made an appointment to see her doctor, the appointment was for the day after the tournament was scheduled to end.

Babe Didrikson Zaharias was ahead on the first two rounds of the 1953 Babe Zaharias Open but winning those rounds had taken every reserve of strength. She began the third round on sheer nerve.

Babe finished the sixteenth hole with a total score of 210. She was so tired she thought she'd never raise her arms again. Going against long-established custom and superstition, she asked how the other leading contenders had finished. Louise Suggs was leading with a total for the three rounds of 218 strokes. Babe would have to do the last two holes in seven strokes or less to win her championship.

Her drive off the seventeenth tee was perfect. The ball came to rest only twelve feet from the hole—an easy two strokes for the great Babe. She was trembling with exhaustion, though, and it took three putts to sink her ball. She had only three strokes left for the last hole if she was to win the tournament—and the eighteenth was a par-four hole. A par-four hole is one that takes four strokes if played exactly right.

Babe's drive off the eighteenth tee was bad. It hooked around some trees. She went to the ball, stood over it so long the crowd got restless, and then she summoned every reserve in her fine athlete's body and every bit of courage in her great heart. She blasted that ball to within six feet of the hole, sank it with one putt—and won the Babe Zaharias Open with a 217, one stroke under Louise Suggs.

A few hours later she was lying on the doctor's examination table. He probed for a while and said with relief, "Well, everything looks all right." However, his trained hands continued their search even while he spoke. Suddenly they stopped, and searched again, and froze. The doctor's face froze too. When he became conscious that Babe was watching his face, the doctor turned away.

"It's cancer, isn't it, Doc?" she said quietly. There were no fear and no tears in her voice.

They operated on Babe a few weeks later. During the weeks of preparation for surgery, half the world seemed to be watching for news from the hospital in Texas. Messages and flowers from the great and small of the sports world and the newspaper world and the entertainment world, and from the millions who had thrilled to the greatest woman athlete of the century, filled the hospital.

When they had first wheeled her into the hospital, Babe had told George, "Get my golf clubs out of the car and put them in the corner over there where I can see them."

When she opened her eyes after the operation, she saw two things, her husband and the tools of her trade. When she was wheeled out to go home and recover, she said, "Don't forget my clubs, George. We'll be playing soon."

Three and a half months later, Babe Zaharias went to Chicago to compete in the Tam O'Shanter All American Championship, one of golfdom's greatest. She asked for only one favor: that she be paired with a golfer who knew her condition and would be able to help if she needed it.

Babe stepped to the first tee at the opening round of the tournament and smiled to the great crowd that had come to see a champion who wouldn't let illness and sur-

Babe Didrikson Zaharias playing golf in Agua, California, August, 1946. Wide World Photos, New York.

gery beat her. They knew of her operation and its results, and they waited to see if Babe Zaharias could come back from her terrible ordeal.

She sent that first ball 250 yards straight and true down the fairway. It was farther than most men could drive, but she couldn't keep it up. The first day wasn't so good. The second day was worse. Behind her always smiling face Babe began to have doubts. Not so much about winning, but about herself.

The third round started badly and soon became worse. She couldn't hit, she couldn't chip, she couldn't find the cup with her putts. At the fifth hole she missed an easy shot and took three putts to sink her ball from ten feet away. She walked to the sixth tee, sat down, put her face in her hands and cried. George came running and folded her in his great wrestler's arms.

"That's enough," he said. "Pick up your ball and leave. Everyone will understand."

Babe stopped crying immediately. She shrugged her husband's hands off her shoulders. "I don't pick up. Good or bad, I finish."

She shot the last nine holes of that round in 34, two under men's par.

In the next year, 1954, Babe Zaharias won the National Women's Open championship. It was a great year for Babe Zaharias—she finished in the top three in every tournament she entered—but it was her last great year.

Babe wrote her autobiography in 1955. The closing words were, "In the future, maybe I'll have to limit myself to just a few of the most important tournaments each year. But I expect to be shooting for championships for a good many years to come. My autobiography isn't finished yet."

She died of cancer in 1956, at the age of forty-four. But she was right. Her autobiography wasn't finished. She became a legend, and she lives on. Wherever people know the excitement of sports and the thrill of competition and wherever they respect the great heart and courage of the true champion, they remember and talk about Babe Didrikson Zaharias.

Developing Comprehension Skills

1. How did Babe's father help his children develop their athletic ability?

2. Because of her size, Babe at first was not accepted on the girls' basketball team. How did she make the team? What do her methods reveal about her character?

3. How did Babe gain national recognition as an athlete? Why was Babe considered the star of the Olympics?

4. How did Babe become a golfer?

5. Cancer threatened to defeat Babe as no athlete could. What inner resources did Babe use to fight cancer?

6. Weakened by her illness during a golf game, Babe said "Good or bad, I finish." What does this comment say about Babe?

Reading Literature: Nonfiction

1. **Understanding Biography.** A well written biography captures the most important and interesting aspects of a person and his or her life. What important information does "Babe" give you about Didrikson's career, her personal life, and her personality?

2. **Making Inferences About Character Traits.** A biography often includes statements made by the subject. These remarks help to reveal character. What conclusions can you draw about Babe's character from these remarks?

   a. When her mother tries to discipline her: "Momma, stop running. You'll hurt your ankle worse. I'll wait for you."

   b. Upon being told that there were ten events in track and field: "Well, I guess I'll try them all."

   c. After her operation: "Don't forget my clubs, George. We'll be playing soon."

3. **Evaluating Point of View.** Who do you think is better qualified to write about Babe Didrikson's life—Babe or an outside researcher? Explain your answer.

Developing Vocabulary Skills

Using Suffixes. On page 309, you studied several suffixes that mean "a person or thing that does something." Two others are:

Suffix	Example
-ant	participant
-eer	puppeteer

Complete each sentence below by writing the missing word. Use the clues given in parentheses. Each new word should include a suffix that means "a person or thing that does something."

1. William O. Douglas was an amateur _____. (one who climbs mountains)

2. The German soldiers were killing _____. (those who are confined to a prison)

3. Ross Allen was a _____. (one who is an expert in herpetology)

4. Canadian Farley Mowat was a _____. (one who studies nature)

5. Before Ole Didrikson settled down, he was a _____. (one who sails)

6. Babe Didrikson was the last _____ (one who is entered in a contest) to arrive at the national track championship of 1932.

Developing Writing Skills

1. **Analyzing Character.** Babe Didrikson had a winning attitude toward sports and life. In

three paragraphs, explain how this attitude helped Babe achieve her goals.

Pre-Writing. Reread "Babe," and jot down examples of Babe's winning attitude during her childhood, her career in sports, and her illness. You may organize the three paragraphs of your essay around these ideas.

Writing. Compose a strong topic sentence for each paragraph. Develop each main idea with plenty of examples from the biography. You may also include quotations.

Revising. Check to see if you have at least three examples or quotations to support each topic sentence. Make sure that each detail relates to the topic sentence.

2. **Contrasting Confidence and Conceit.** Babe was a confident person in sports and her personal life. Confidence is a positive trait. If a person becomes overly confident, however, he or she can become conceited. What is the difference between the two?

In one paragraph, explain your definition of confidence. Then, in the second paragraph, explain your definition of conceit. Finally, contrast the traits of confidence and conceit. Use personal examples to explain the differences between the two qualities.

Developing Skills in Study and Research

1. **Planning a Report.** A report is a special kind of composition. It is based on facts that you gather from books, magazines, interviews, and other sources. You then present this information in a clear, organized manner.

In this chapter, you are going to write a five-paragraph biographical report. The first step is to list the names of a few famous people you might be interested in reporting on. Then do some general reading about each possible subject. Skim encyclopedia articles, magazine articles, and books. Choose one person to be the subject of your report. You may then wish to narrow your subject further. Do this by focusing on one very interesting aspect of that person's life, personality, or accomplishments.

2. **Selecting Sources.** Once you have chosen a subject, you must gather your information. Use the card catalog and the *Readers' Guide to Periodical Literature* to find possible sources. Skim these sources to find out if they have useful information. For books, scanning the table of contents may help you decide.

When you decide on a source, make a bibliography card for it. A bibliography card should include the following information:

Book: author, title, publisher, date published

Magazine: author of article (if there is one), title of article, name of magazine, date published, page

Encyclopedia: author of article (if there is one), name of encyclopedia, volume and page, date published

Newspaper: author of article (if there is one), title of article, name of newspaper, date published, section, page, and column number

As you are making bibliography cards, give each card a number. These numbers will help you as you write your note cards. Save your cards and any other information in a folder titled *Report*. You will use this material later in the chapter.

Wilma Rudolph

MARC DACHTER

Wilma Rudolph could not walk until she was eight years old. How, then, did she learn to run so fast that she broke world records?

Wilma Rudolph had to relearn to walk before she could run. An early childhood bout of pneumonia and scarlet fever had left her left leg paralyzed. She went through years of confinement to bed or chair before special shoes put her back on her feet at the age of eight.

It did not take long for her body to find its natural tone. By thirteen, she had made her high-school basketball team and, at fifteen was a certified athletic marvel. She was known throughout the black community of Clarksville, Tennessee, as an all-state player who had scored 803 points in twenty-five games. Her coach, Clinton Gray, who called her "Skeeter" (mosquito) because she was "always buzzing around," took the suggestion of the great track coach Ed Temple to start her running. After one year she had already qualified, at sixteen, for a place on the 1956 Olympic team at Melbourne, where she shared in a bronze-medal win for the 400-meter relay.

That was only the beginning. Within one year she was running full time for Ed Tem-

ple at Tennessee Agricultural and Industrial State College in the best women's track program in the nation. Rudolph's genius was honed by hard competition. "Her teammates are the next three fastest girls in the country," said her coach. "Rudolph runs fast because she is pressed so hard in practice. Without it she wouldn't be nearly as good as she is." Temple's point was proven when the entire 400-meter women's relay

team for the 1960 Olympics was chosen out of his squad.

Never able to count on her health, Rudolph went through a debilitating illness that canceled her 1958 track season. She pulled a left thigh muscle in 1959 and suffered serious complications from a tonsil operation in the Olympic year of 1960. When it was time to go to Rome, though, she was ready. How ready became obvious

Wilma Rudolph (left) winning the 100-meter dash in the 1960 Rome Olympics. Wide World Photos, New York.

in her first event, the 100-meter dash, when she broke away from the competition at the halfway point and won, three yards ahead of the silver medalist in 11 seconds flat. Her second Olympic record and gold medal came in the 200-meter dash, at 24 seconds, when she again showed the stride which, one reporter wrote, "made the rest of the pack seem to be churning on a treadmill." The Rudolph trademark was composure— a quality of smooth, effortless, impassive speed. Her third gold medal came to her, as if by right, when she anchored the United States 400-meter relay team: Wilma and her Tennessee A & I classmates set both world and Olympic marks at 44.5 seconds.

On tour throughout Europe with her teammates, Rudolph was hailed as a goddess of sport. "*La Gazella Nera*" (Black Gazelle) to the Italians, "*La Perle Noire*" (Black Pearl) and "*La Chattanooga Choo Choo*" to the French, she was mobbed wherever she went. Once her shoes were pulled off her feet. A wax statue was made of her in Madame Tussaud's London Museum. Overwhelmed by the hoopla, she returned to America for a new round of celebrations, banquets, and carnivals in her honor. Winning gold medals must have seemed easier.

She had not finished yet. Runner-up in 1960 for the Amateur Athletic Union's Sullivan trophy as outstanding amateur of the year, she took it that next year, only the third woman to do so. She was the first woman in thirty years to be invited to participate in the celebrated Millrose Games at Madison Square Garden. There, she was clocked at 6.9 seconds in the 60-yard dash, tying her own world record. She trimmed it to 6.8 seconds at the New York Athletic Club games two weeks later. By the end of the year, she owned the world's records for the 70-yard dash and the 100-meter event. That was enough. She retired, at the height of her glory, to the quieter life of a schoolteacher.

Developing Comprehension Skills

1. What physical disabilities did Wilma Rudolph overcome during her lifetime? What were her most memorable accomplishments?

2. Many events were held in Wilma's honor. Referring to these, Wilma said, "Winning gold medals must have been easier." What does the statement tell you about Wilma?

3. Why do you think a physically disabled person would attempt to become a runner? Is it wise to set seemingly impossible goals?

4. Wilma was given the nicknames "Skeeter," "La Gazella Nera," "La Perle Noire," and "La Chattanooga Choo Choo." How does each name fit her?

5. Wilma retired at the peak of her fame to become a teacher. Why do you think she

made this decision? Would you have made the same choice? Explain your answer.

Reading Literature: Nonfiction

1. **Comparing Biographies.** Why is "Wilma Rudolph" classified as a biography? Compare and contrast it with the preceding biography, "Babe." Look for similarities and differences in the manner in which the two selections do the following:

   a. Present facts about the subject's childhood.

   b. Explain how the subject overcame problems to achieve success.

   c. Discuss the subject's personal as well as public life.

   d. Show the personal thoughts of the subject as well as the thoughts of others.

   Which biography do you think is more effective? Why?

2. **Identifying Sequence.** The author of Wilma Rudolph's biography presents events in chronological, or time, order. Decide the proper sequence for these events:

   a. Wilma wins an Olympic gold medal in the 200-meter dash.

   b. Wilma is the first woman in thirty years to participate in the Melrose games at Madison Square Garden.

   c. Wilma scores 803 points in twenty-five basketball games.

   d. Wilma and her Tennessee teammates set World and Olympic records as a 400-meter relay team.

   e. Wilma sets an Olympic record in the 100-meter dash.

3. **Characterizing Tone.** The **tone** of a biography is the author's attitude toward the subject. For example, the tone may be formal, casual, serious, or humorous. What is the tone of Wilma Rudolph's biography?

4. **Understanding an Adage.** An **adage** is a saying that states a commonly-believed bit of wisdom. One adage states, "You have to learn to walk before you run." What does this mean? How does it apply to Wilma? Does it apply in more than a physical way? With this adage in mind, explain the significance of the first sentence in this selection.

Developing Vocabulary Skills

Using Suffixes That Make Abstract Words. Suffixes are often used to make abstract words. Abstract words are those that refer to a quality or state of being rather than to a definite object. For example, a friend is a real person, but friend*ship* is a quality or idea. Study the following list.

Suffix	Example
-ance, -ence	experience
-ation, -ition	competition
-hood	parenthood
-ism	capitalism
-ment	contentment
-ness	kindness
-ship	friendship
-ty, -ity	creativity

Turn the following base words into abstract words by adding suffixes from the list above. Note that the spelling of the base word may change when a suffix is added.

1. professional
2. effortless
3. innocent
4. disobedient
5. sportsman
6. unemploy
7. nervous
8. individual
9. frustrate
10. mother

Developing Writing Skills

1. **Supporting an Opinion.** Do you think talent, hard work, or determination is most important for success in athletics? Write a paragraph supporting your opinion with logical reasons and specific examples.

2. **Writing a Dialogue.** Imagine that you are interviewing Olympic medal winner Wilma Rudolph. Write an imaginary dialogue focusing on how Rudolph overcame great odds to become a star athlete.

   Pre-Writing. Prepare for your imaginary interview as you would for a real interview (see page 325). Review Rudolph's biography, and list questions you would like to ask Rudolph about her accomplishments. Based on your understanding of Rudolph's attitudes, decide how Rudolph would answer each question. Make notes.

   Writing. Develop your questions and answers into a dialogue, using complete sentences. Try to make the sentences reflect both your personality and Rudolph's. As you write, use lead-in phrases such as "then I asked," or "next she said." Begin a new paragraph each time the speaker changes.

   Revising. Review the rules for punctuating dialogue. Check your punctuation of quotations. Make sure that your dialogue reveals Rudolph's attitudes toward sports and winning.

Developing Skills in Study and Research

Taking Notes. You have now chosen your topic and found some good sources for a report. The next step is to gather information. As you read from your sources, look for facts or ideas you think you might want to include in your report. Avoid opinions, unless you plan to note them as opinions. Record your information on note cards. Use the following guidelines:

1. Use a separate 3″ × 5″ note card for each fact.

2. Write the notes in your own words. Copying another writer's work word for word is called **plagiarism**. Plagiarism is dishonest and unacceptable. If you wish to quote a source directly, copy the words exactly and enclose them in quotation marks.

3. At the top of each card, write a key phrase that tells the main idea of the note.

4. Label each card with the number given to that source on its bibliography card. Also note the exact page number.

When you have completed your research, complete the critical thinking activity below.

Developing Skills in Critical Thinking

Organizing Report Information. After you have taken notes, you must organize your information. Begin by looking through your note cards. Separate them into several piles. Each pile should contain cards dealing with one main idea. For example, one pile of cards might be about your subject's childhood. Another might deal with the subject's career or life's work. Each pile of cards will provide the information for one paragraph in the body of your report.

Finally, decide the order in which you will present your ideas in your report. For a biographical report, a logical organization is chronological, or time order. Arrange the groups, and then the cards within each group, in order. Save the cards for later use.

Eleanor Roosevelt:
Citizen of the World

AYLESA FORSEE

Eleanor Roosevelt was a shy young woman from a distinguished family. She did not seek the spotlight. How, then, did she become one of the greatest stateswomen of her time?

When Eleanor Roosevelt was five years old, the family went to Europe. On a sightseeing trip to Sorrento, Italy, her father rented a donkey. Astride the small, big-eared animal, Eleanor rode off happily with a bare-footed boy as guide. Her father was surprised later to see them returning with the guide riding the mule. "What happened?" he asked.

"My guide cut his foot," explained Eleanor. "I made him ride."

In later life the same kind of concern for others, linked with a relentless energy, set her off on a campaign for social justice that made her an international celebrity. Columnist, lecturer, globe-trotter, at one time the first lady of the land, Eleanor Roosevelt was also the first woman to be the United States Representative to the General Assembly of the United Nations.

She was born October 11, 1884, in New York City. Her father, a wealthy, personable, and charming man, was the younger brother of Theodore Roosevelt. Eleanor's mother came from an equally impressive and wealthy family, noted for distinguished appearance and social grace. She was descended from Philip Livingston, a signer of the Declaration of Independence.

Childhood was a time of frustration and unhappiness for Eleanor. Although her eyes were lovely and her hair beautiful, she had protruding teeth and a plainness that made her feel like an ugly duckling compared to her beautiful mother. Her self-conscious shyness became all the more painful when her mother, with no thought of wounding her, sometimes called her Granny because she was so serious and old-fashioned. Quite often she failed to do what her mother considered "proper." Then she got the idea she would never be able to do what her mother expected.

With her father, to whom she was devoted, Eleanor could forget her shyness. However, Mr. Roosevelt had had poor health even as an adolescent. Now under the strain of business and social activities Mr. Roosevelt became ill. For long periods at a time he would be in a sanitarium where Eleanor was not permitted to visit him. To her loneliness for her father was added worry about what might be wrong with him.

Then, when Eleanor was five, there was the European trip, when she and her father set forth on delightful adventures. In Venice they boated down canals, with her father singing like a gondolier. On a visit to Mt. Vesuvius, they tossed pennies into a crater and got them back lava-coated.

While the family was in Paris, Mr. Roosevelt entered a French sanitarium. Shortly afterward, Eleanor's baby brother Hall was born, and Mrs. Roosevelt took her three small children back to America. At home, a governess was engaged to teach them. Even with a governess, Eleanor was often too timid to recite, although she might know her lesson perfectly.

Eleanor was only eight when her mother died of diphtheria. Her maternal grandmother, Mrs. Valentine G. Hall, took the three youngsters into her fashionable but somber New York City home on West Thirty-Seventh street. Mr. Roosevelt came for the funeral but left shortly afterwards. "Write to me, and study hard," he told Eleanor. "Be a good girl and grow into a woman I'll be proud of."

Eleanor tried, but her life seemed one continuous struggle for self-improvement. She had to wear braces to correct a curvature of the spine and braces to straighten her teeth. Grandmother Hall was a strict disciplinarian and was constantly nagging at Eleanor to improve her skills or manners. There were endless Bible verses to be learned in French and rules to be obeyed.

"It's lots easier for Grandmother to say no than it is for her to say yes," Eleanor told her brother, Ellie.

Lonely for her father, sensitive to criticism, ashamed of her awkwardness, Eleanor retreated more and more into herself. The death of Ellie the same winter she lost her mother increased her loneliness. On the few occasions when she was with other children, aside from her brother Hall, Eleanor found herself poorly prepared for their sports and light-hearted fun. She was tortured by the feeling that she was odd.

Despite her own unhappiness, or perhaps because of it, Eleanor was very sympathetic toward the needs of others. When her Uncle Vallie took her along to help with the Christmas tree in Hell's Kitchen in New York City, she was shocked by what she saw in this slum area. Young as she was, she felt she must do something for these people in torn and faded clothing.

She was just as touched by a visit to crippled children at Orthopedic Hospital and she tried to comfort the tiny patients by showing them the brace she wore. "See all I can do with it," she told them.

Living at Grandmother Hall's had some bright spots. Eleanor loved to read, and she was well supplied with books from her grandfather's library. She especially liked the ones that pictured life in other countries; they left her with a longing to visit these far-away places.

The best days of Eleanor's childhood came when her father visited. At the sound of his voice, she would slide down the bannisters and catapult into his arms. Always he had a delightful surprise for her—a toy, a pet, a ride in a high dog cart. These happy, carefree days ended with her father's death when Eleanor was nine. After this she took refuge in a dream world in which she pretended she and her father were doing things together.

Summers spent at Grandmother Hall's estate at Oak Terrace on the Hudson River helped Eleanor forget her grief. There she had a playhouse in the woods, a bicycle, and a pony. She loved the horses and dogs, especially a dog named Mickey that looked like a polar bear. Until they were caught she and her brother Hall found it amusing to climb out an upstairs window and walk around on the gutter to a window on the opposite side of the house.

Once a summer Eleanor visited her Uncle Teddy's great gabled house called Sagamore Hill on Long Island Sound. With her cousins, whooping with delight, she would slide, roll, tumble at a dizzy pace down Cooper's Bluff, a sandy incline sloping sharply to the beach. When the children tired of swimming, riding horseback, rowing boats, they would gather around Uncle Teddy, who told exciting stories of cowboys, cattle thieves, grizzly bears and Indians. In the telling, he hammered home the necessity for courage and moral stamina.

In Eleanor's early teens, the highlight of the year was always a Christmas party at the home of Auntie Corrine. This was partly painful because Eleanor stood in awe of her sophisticated cousin Alice. There was,

however, one great satisfaction—Cousin Franklin gave most of his attention to her.

When she was fifteen, Eleanor entered Allenswood School in England. She enjoyed her classes with Mlle. Souvestre, headmistress of the school, a vivid and entertaining person. While at the school, Eleanor, who had never excelled at sports, became a very good hockey player and for the first time in her life she had the feeling of really belonging to a group.

Eleanor Roosevelt at age 15. Franklin D. Roosevelt Library, Hyde Park, New York.

During school vacations Eleanor visited friends or relatives in England or on the continent, or traveled with Mlle. Souvestre. The wise and understanding headmistress, wanting to foster Eleanor's self-reliance, assigned her such responsibilities as ticket buying. Under her teacher's guidance, Eleanor developed a deep appreciation of na-

Eleanor Roosevelt (top row, third from right) with her class at Mlle. Souvestre's School, South Fields, England in 1900. *Franklin D. Roosevelt Library, Hyde Park, New York.*

ture and of the customs of different people. She learned to find beauty in every form — in the colored sail of a fishing boat or a cathedral spire in moonlight.

After three happy years at Allenswood, Eleanor wanted to stay on for a fourth, but her grandmother ordered her to come home. "Eighteen," she insisted, "is the age for coming out."[1]

Because of Grandmother Hall, Eleanor's name was on all the right lists. At dinners,

dances, and parties, the tall, shy girl, unaware of her sparkling blue eyes, sweet smile, interesting hands, felt herself something of a wallflower.

Rebelling at the rigidity of being with the so-called right people, attending endless parties, reading only certain prescribed books, Eleanor began taking on projects. She investigated working conditions in factories and taught calisthenics and dancing at a settlement house.

Eleanor became better acquainted with her cheerful, self-confident cousin Franklin. It was easy for her to talk to him about

---

1. **coming out**, the time upper-class girls are introduced to society.

things they were both interested in — literature, history, foreign lands. Soon they fell in love. Franklin's mother disapproved of Eleanor as a future wife for her son, however, and hustled him off on a cruise to the West Indies. She hoped he would change his mind.

During a visit with her Aunt Bye in Washington, D.C., plenty of eligible escorts surrounded Eleanor, but none interested her as much as Franklin. In her battle against sensitivity, Aunt Bye was a big help. "Just be sure you would not be ashamed to explain your actions to someone you love, and then do what seems right," she told Eleanor.

The cruise didn't change Franklin's mind. Shortly after he returned, the engagement was announced. Shortly before the wedding, the lovers saw their Uncle Teddy inaugurated as President of the United States.

Eleanor and Franklin

For the wedding on March 17, 1905, Eleanor wore a heavy satin dress with shirred tulle in the neck and long sleeves. The bride received less attention than Uncle Teddy.

Because Franklin was still in Law School at Columbia University, the honeymoon was put off until the summer after the wedding. Then the happy couple went to Europe, where they attended the theater in Paris, motored through the Alps, floated down Venetian canals, rode across the moors of Scotland.

During the early years of her married life, Eleanor had to make many difficult adjustments. Strict and methodical in her habits, she often found it hard to go along with Franklin's easy-going ways, although they were in agreement on basic values.

The birth of baby Anna on May 3, 1906, brought new responsibilities. Anna was followed by James and Elliott. Franklin Delano, Junior, born in 1909, died when only a few months old.

When Franklin was elected a state senator, Eleanor moved to Albany reluctantly, dreading public life. Yet, she had been trained to do what she ought to do, not what she wanted to do. Feeling it was her duty to be interested in her husband's work, she frequently sat in the visitors' gallery at the state legislature. Impelled to do something about problems she heard discussed, she tried to get women interested in political campaigns and elections.

In the spring of 1913, Franklin was appointed Assistant Secretary of the Navy. This meant living in Washington, where Eleanor could run her own household. Still shy, she was a little awed by the people into whose orbit Franklin's work drew her, but she was very conscientious in her duties as a government official's wife. As she gave of her energy and interest, she developed poise and new understanding of the world around her. The political scene fascinated her, but she felt her first duty was to the children. The family spent many evenings listening to music, reading aloud or just talking. Speaking of that period of her life

Eleanor said, "I wish now I could have taught them more wisdom somehow—saved them more heartaches and mistakes."

A second child named Franklin was born in 1914, John in 1916. When the United States became involved in World War I, Eleanor did Red Cross work, served as hostess at a canteen, and visited the wounded in hospitals.

In the summer of 1921, the family vacationed at their summer home on Campobello Island, New Brunswick, Canada. When a forest fire broke out, Franklin volunteered as a firefighter. After the fire was under control, he came home and took a swim. Later he complained of chills and fatigue. Before he could be gotten to a hospital, paralysis had set in.

"Infantile paralysis,"[2] the doctors told Eleanor. "He'll be in a wheelchair the rest of his life."

Franklin's mother and his friends took this to mean that his political career was at an end, but his doctor and his wife would not have it that way. To help keep Franklin's name before the public, Eleanor embarked on a series of speeches, although her shyness made public appearances an ordeal. She invited political leaders to come in for conferences with her husband, became finance chairman of the New York Democratic State Committee, and took a position teaching history and literature several days a week at the Todhunter School for Girls.

---

2. **Infantile paralysis**, the disease now called polio.

When Franklin went to Warm Springs, Georgia, for treatment, Eleanor realized that the children were going to miss his companionship. Trying to make up some of the loss, she learned to swim, so that she could supervise the children in the water. She rode horseback with the youngsters and took them on camping trips.

Shuttling back and forth between New York and Warm Springs, Eleanor encouraged Franklin to greater physical, mental, and political achievements. By 1928, he could walk with the aid of a cane. That same year he became the Governor of New York.

The Presidency

Franklin's election as President of the United States four years later left Eleanor both elated and sad. She knew how much it would change their personal lives.

On the eve of the inauguration, young Democrats were singing "Happy Days are Here Again," but the occasion was far from a light-hearted one for the Roosevelts. They were conscious of an America plunged into depression. In Washington there were breadlines, soup kitchens, and men sleeping on park benches. Soberly, the Roosevelts moved to the White House.

Eleanor found it hard to remember she was the wife of the President and often did not conform to tradition. She startled the household staff by helping to rearrange furniture and running the elevator herself. At the first few parties, she forgot that none of the guests could leave until she left. The

speak. In case of differences of opinion on issues, Franklin encouraged her to go ahead and state her own views.

When the United States entered World War II after the attack on Pearl Harbor, Eleanor expressed sympathy for the Americans of Japanese descent being herded into internment camps. Her comments brought criticism swirling about her. Undaunted, she shuttled back and forth across the country, appraising the state of the nation and promoting civil defense.

To obtain better understanding of a wartime ally, the President sent her to England. A guest of the King and Queen at Buckingham Palace, Eleanor found windowpanes broken by bombing. The palace was cold and the food plain. Visiting military bases, shipyards, factories, air raid shelters, and bombed-out areas, Eleanor marveled at the people's ability to carry on.

Back home, she watched as eagerly as any mother for letters from James, Elliott, Franklin Jr., and John, who were overseas. Although the boys made exceptional military records, there were charges that they were shown favoritism.

Her hardest assignment came when the President asked her to make a tour of the Pacific. She flew or sailed over mine-infested seas to visit hospitals, rest camps, recreation centers. Keeping up a machine-gun pace, she got up before 6 A.M. to eat with enlisted men and to watch jungle warfare. On besieged islands she spoke to huge audiences. "She did more for our morale than a dozen shows," soldiers said of her.

Thinner by thirty pounds and more tired than she had ever been in her life, Eleanor came home bringing hundreds of addresses of relatives of boys in service to call upon or to write to. About the trip she said, "I wished I could be changed in some magic way into the mother or sweetheart, wife or sister these men longed to see."

Because of duties in Washington, Mrs. Roosevelt stayed behind when the President, in April 1945, went to Warm Springs, Georgia, for a rest. There he was taken ill. A short time later a call from the White House came to Eleanor while she was attending a benefit. Her heart froze. She was almost certain what the message would be.

Even in her grief over her husband's death, Eleanor's thoughts reached out to people who, having lost their leader in the midst of a critical stage of the war, were anxious and disturbed.

She had no definite plans for the future, but it was with relief that she moved out of the White House where she had lived for twelve years under the pitiless searchlight of public opinion.

Eleanor left behind her a trail of shattered traditions. She had almost completely changed the citizen's idea of what the president's wife should be. Refusing round-the-clock secret service surveillance, she had driven her own car or traveled on buses and planes chatting with fellow passengers, workers, and housewives. The White House had become a more friendly place, where a duke and a farmer might sit down at the same table to eat corned beef.

Believing people had a right to know what was going on, Eleanor had inaugurated the custom of strictly feminine news conferences. Treating the women of the press as people whose good judgment and loyalty could be trusted, she answered questions frankly and good-humoredly.

World Citizen

As is customary for the wives of ex-presidents, Eleanor disappeared from the public scene. For a time she enjoyed a quiet existence. Then the old tempest of energy began once more to rage within her.

Vigorously she undertook a colossal daily schedule that often left her doing two things at once. With the help of a secretary, she answered the staggering piles of mail that continued to come her way. Especially interested in the queries of girls wanting to know about the world of politics, she gave detailed advice: any girl interested in politics as a career should be active in school organizations, acquire an understanding of government and laws from the local to the international level, and learn at least one foreign language. She should read newspapers and news magazines, listen to newscasts, try to understand the shades of opinion represented but form her own opinions. Ability to speak fluently and clearly is invaluable, and any girl who expects to enter politics should get all the experience possible in making public appearances. She should learn to meet people easily and to understand them. Working with the political party in her community, ringing doorbells at election time, stuffing envelopes, poll watching all give excellent experience. Politics is no place for the weak of heart, but it is a fertile field for any intelligent girl who has the courage to stand for her convictions even in the face of pressure or defeat.

When Eleanor received word that she had been appointed to serve as United States representative to the General Assembly of the United Nations, she thought she had no background for such an assignment. As the only woman on the United States delegation for the meeting of the General Assembly in London, she felt unwelcome and conducted herself with shyness.

Throwing her heart and soul into the work, she soon astonished everyone by her grasp of world affairs. Outspoken, straightforward, she gave opinions that were both fearless and wise. If she became involved in a debate in which bitter statements were made, she saw them as a difference of opinion and not a personal attack on her. Even when others around her became ruffled or angry, she remained poised and serene. With brilliance and energetic drive she concerned herself with refugees, world health, equality. A great idealist, but also a doer, she served capably as chairperson of the Human Rights Commission, cutting red tape to a minimum. Accused of being too idealistic, she answered, "Remember that every step forward is the product of someone who dreamed dreams."

On a trip to India, Eleanor maintained a pace which brought assistants practically to

Eleanor Roosevelt speaking at a United Nations conference in Rome on March 15, 1955. Wide World Photos, New York.

the verge of collapse. She spoke to the Indian parliament, visited mud huts and tenements, talked to veiled women, and taught teen-agers to dance. On a scorching hot day in Bombay, thousands of people milled about in front of the hotel where Eleanor was staying. When she came out to a waiting automobile they shouted, "Eleanor Roosevelt, zindabad!" (Long live Eleanor Roosevelt.) Before entering the car, Eleanor bowed her head and pressed her palms together in the Hindu posture of friendship. Flattered that she had taken the trou-

ble to learn a respected custom, the crowd went wild.

With the endurance of a circus trouper, Eleanor went on to Singapore and other Far Eastern cities.

In January of 1953, after seven years in the United Nations where she had become one of the most popular members, Eleanor resigned.

Back home Eleanor spent much time out-of-doors, swimming daily and taking long walks. Wearing a seersucker dress and trailed by her black Scottie, "Mr. Duffie," she looked much like a country grandmother as she gathered pansies, picked raspberries or staged picnics for guests ranging from her grandchildren to the Emperor of Ethiopia.

Her other routines were far from grandmotherly. She continued to attend meetings, lecture, appear on radio and television, write, and cope with stacks of mail. She went on working for the American Association for the United Nations. "If you abandon faith in the world, what's the use of living?" she asked those who said the United Nations was a failure.

At home and abroad, honors continued to come Eleanor's way. Many institutions of higher learning, including England's famous Oxford University, conferred degrees upon Eleanor. Her picture appeared upon the stamps of Lebanon and El Salvador. In polls, she has run far ahead of any other woman in the esteem of the public.

As basic to her success as her energy was Eleanor Roosevelt's early acceptance of the belief that life requires tremendous self-discipline. She also learned that the way to conquer the self-indulgence of shyness was to have outgoing interests. Goodness, just simple goodness, was the quality that most impressed those who knew her. A reporter who went to Hyde Park on a muggy day to cover details of one of her numerous parties for underprivileged boys found her looking hot but cheerful as she buttered dozens of hot dog rolls.

"Why butter them?" he queried. "The boys will eat them anyway."

"When the King and Queen of England had hot dogs here we buttered the rolls," she replied. "Why should I do less for these boys?"

Because of Eleanor Roosevelt's interest in people of all races, religions, and creeds, women are a little closer to equality, workers are less likely to be exploited, and blacks have won a little more recognition. Newspaper columnist Westbrook Pegler, often her severest critic, once conceded, "There is no other who works as hard or knows the low-down truth about people and the troubles in their hearts as she does."

A society girl who found social life boring, born to wealth but with a deep concern for the poor, Eleanor Roosevelt became a defender of human rights, a friend of the forgotten, and a citizen of the world. Her influence on her times has seldom been equaled by any other woman.

Developing Comprehension Skills

1. Name three tragedies that occurred during Eleanor Roosevelt's childhood. What other problems made her childhood unhappy?

2. How did Eleanor overcome her shyness?

3. How did Franklin's political career change the direction of Eleanor's life? How did his illness affect her?

4. Which groups of people did Eleanor work the hardest for? Why do you think she was so sensitive to the needs of others?

5. According to this biography, what made Eleanor one of the most popular members of the United Nations General Assembly?

6. In your opinion, what was Eleanor Roosevelt's most important achievement?

Reading Literature: Nonfiction

1. **Evaluating Biography.** A good biography focuses on a person's personality. At the same time, it gives details about the times when that person lived. As you read "Eleanor Roosevelt," how much do you learn about our country as it was during her lifetime? Does this information add to your understanding of her as a person? Explain your answer.

2. **Identifying Character Traits.** The biography of Eleanor Roosevelt contains many brief anecdotes and quotations. Each reveals something about Eleanor's personality. Explain what character trait each of the following incidents reveals:

a. While on a tour, Eleanor walks and allows her guide to ride her mule.

b. Eleanor gives ten dollars to a jobless man and believes he will use it well.

c. In India, she learns and uses the Hindu posture of friendship.

d. She butters rolls for underprivileged boys, just as she did for the King and Queen of England.

Now explain what character traits the following comments by Eleanor reveal:

a. At large gatherings, Eleanor says she notices ". . . faces. I think, 'what a pretty face. What a kind face.' "

b. "I wished I could be changed in some magic way into the mother or sweetheart, wife or sister these men longed to see."

c. "Remember that every step forward is the product of someone who dreamed dreams."

3. **Recognizing Parallelism.** The technique of **parallelism** is the use of paired words, phrases, or sentences. This technique is used to emphasize a point or simply make the writing pleasing to read or listen to.

Parallelism is one part of the writer's style in "Eleanor Roosevelt." For example, this sentence contains parallel phrases: "She had to wear *braces to correct a curvature of the spine, braces to straighten her teeth.*" Identify the use of parallelism in the final paragraph of "Eleanor Roosevelt." What effect does this parallelism have on the reader?

Developing Vocabulary Skills

Using Word Parts To Determine Meaning. The sentences below are from "Eleanor Roosevelt: Citizen of the World." Use your knowledge of prefixes and suffixes to determine the meaning of the underlined words. Write each word and its meaning on your paper.

1. . . . the same concern for others, linked with a relentless energy. . . .

2. Grandmother was a strict disciplinarian.

3. Rebelling at the rigidity of being with the so-called right people . . . Eleanor began taking on projects.

4. With the endurance of a circus trouper, Eleanor went on to Singapore . . .

5. . . . she moved out of the White House where she had lived for twelve years under the pitiless searchlight of public opinion.

6. Because of Eleanor Roosevelt's interest . . . women are a little closer to equality. . . .

Developing Writing Skills

1. **Using Comparison.** What traits do Eleanor Roosevelt, Wilma Rudolph, and Babe Didrikson have in common? Write a five-paragraph essay that discusses one important trait these three famous women share.

Pre-Writing. Think about the biographies of Roosevelt, Rudolph, and Didrikson. List the most outstanding character traits of each. Choose a trait that they have in common. Jot down evidence of the trait in each woman. Then organize your composition. A logical way might be to focus on a different woman in each of the three body paragraphs.

Writing. In the introduction, use an attention-getting opening sentence that states the purpose of your composition. Develop each paragraph with several examples. Your conclusion should summarize your main point.

Revising. Help your readers see the similarity in these women's characters by adding strong transitional words and phrases that show comparison. Use words such as *likewise*, *in comparison*, and *similarly* to stress the comparisons. Ask someone to read your composition and judge if you have used enough examples.

2. **Writing a Speech.** Imagine that Eleanor Roosevelt is visiting a small town. A major industry has closed down, leaving several hundred people out of work. These people have come to hear Mrs. Roosevelt speak. What might she say to them? Write the speech that she might have given. Make sure her concern for others and her practical wisdom are evident.

Developing Skills in Study and Research

Making an Outline for a Report. You have now completed the research for your report. You have also organized the information you gathered. You must now make an outline of your report. An outline is a more formal and detailed way of organizing your notes. You will follow the outline when writing the first draft.

Study the sample outline below. All outlines follow the same form. Roman numerals indicate main ideas. Under main ideas, capital letters indicate subtopics. Under subtopics, Arabic numerals indicate details. You must have no fewer than two main topics or subtopics.

Eleanor Roosevelt, the First
Modern Political Woman

I. Introduction
   A. Definition of a modern woman
   B. Definition of a political person

II. Childhood
   A. Family Life
      1. Troubles
      2. Advantages
   B. Education

III. Marriage to Franklin
   A. Life before the Presidency
   B. Life during the Presidency
      1. Private life
      2. Public life

IV. Life after Franklin's death
   A. Political life
      1. In the United States
      2. In other countries
   B. Final Years

V. Conclusion

Notice how indentation, capitalization, and punctuation are used.

Now make an outline for your own report. Use the information from your organized note cards. When you are finished, save this outline in your report folder.

Developing Skills in Critical Thinking

Recognizing the Error of Stacking. A good biography presents a true, accurate picture of a person. The writer, or biographer, should include both the positive and negative details of the subject. If a biographer fails to do this, he or she may be guilty of stacking. **Stacking** occurs when a speaker or writer presents only one side of a subject in order to make a point.

Find and read two encyclopedia articles on Eleanor Roosevelt. In your opinion, is there evidence of stacking in the biography you have just read? If so, what point do you think the writer was trying to make? Do you think the stacking was justified?

Autobiographies

Autobiographies are the most personal, and often the most memorable, kind of nonfiction. An autobiography is the writer's own account of his or her life.

The four autobiographies in this section are written by people of very different backgrounds and experiences. As you read each selection, look for proof that no one but the writer could have told the story quite so well.

Martial Memory, 1941, PHILIP GUSTON. The St. Louis Art Museum, Missouri.

From

Everything But Money

SAM LEVENSON

Sam Levenson's family did not have much money. In what ways, though, was his family wealthy?

As long as Papa was at the head of the table we were made aware of the unity of body and soul. There were rituals surrounding the care and feeding of both. Papa would take a small piece of bread in his hand, say the blessing, sprinkle some salt on it, then chew it slowly, thoughtfully, gratefully. He would then turn to the family and give the signal for the beginning of the meal with the words "Eat and remember." Once again we had been reminded that man is not an unthinking animal, and home is not a stable—certainly not our home.

Friday night's dinner was a testimonial banquet to Papa. For that hour, at least, he was no longer the oppressed victim of the sweatshops, the harassed, frightened, and unsuccessful breadwinner, but the master to whom all heads bowed and upon whom all honor was bestowed. He was our father, our teacher, our wise man, our elder statesman, our tribal leader.

I was aware even as a child that my parents through their traditions had the power to separate mundane time from sacred time, to declare one day out of seven above and beyond the slavish struggle for survival. What a sense of power for a man to be able to borrow a segment of time out of eternity, to ask it into his home for twenty-four hours, to feel himself transfigured by it from man into Man.

The transformation of time began when Mama would usher in the sabbath at twilight. As we stood there watching her bless the candles and murmuring prayers, we could feel the metamorphosis of a weekday into a holy day. The candles threw ghostly lights and shadows on the walls. The mystery and the magnitude of the experience affected our behavior. We stopped shouting and talked softly to each other without having to be told to do so.

For us kids, the Sabbath also had a special secular virtue; we were not spanked on that day. But after sunset you had better look out!

Mama's relationship with God was different from Papa's. He taught us to worship God formally, using prayers we had memorized. Mama's was an intimate, personal kinship. God was her Father and our

Grandfather. She appealed to God directly: "Dear God, how long will this strike go on? Have a little mercy. The children need shoes." Although she stood in awe of the holy word, she said her prayers as she felt them. When the fourth kid went down with the measles, she began to lose patience. "Enough already, dear God. How much do you think I can take?"

Mama transmitted her personal relationship with God to us. If I found a penny, it was because God wanted me to find it; if I lost a penny, I must have deserved it. I must help Mama with her bundles because God said, "Thou Shalt Honor Thy Father and Thy Mother." I mustn't fight with Henry because God said, "Love Thy Neighbor." I can't take Harold's bike because God said, "Thou Shalt Not Covet Thy Neighbor's Goods." "So why did Papa take away the dollar Aunt Bessie gave me for my birthday?" "Because Thou Shalt Honor Thy Father and Thy Mother," said Mama.

For the Passover[1] our home had to be converted into a temple in which rites of all kinds would be conducted—prayers, feasts, songs, even games, all related to one of mankind's greatest epics—the exodus from Egypt.

Our home had to be cleansed of all traces of bread. Papa turned sleuth. We followed him through every corner of the house tracking down every last crumb. It was a

sort of game we played with Papa, perhaps the only game we ever played together. We placed little pieces of bread on windowsills and in corners, then later pretended to "discover" them. The punishment was standard—death by fire. The bread-burning, too, was both a ritual and a game. Token pieces of bread were placed in a wooden spoon, wrapped in cloth, and cremated in small bonfires on the street by kids who were paid a few cents for "buying" our bread and helping us purify our homes in honor of the arrival of the Passover.

As though keeping dairy dishes at a respectable distance from meat dishes were not enough of a job, Passover required the use of all "new" dishes, which were kept in old barrels in the cellar. Operation Dishes included pans, kettles, crocks, graters, sieves, buckets, knives, forks, spoons, ladles, chopping bowls, glasses, bottles, jars, mugs, jugs, platters, dippers, cake pans, coffeepots, teapots. The year-round dishes had to be taken to the cellar or to some other neutral place. After a dozen trips to the cellar, one of the brothers always asked, "Why can't we all just move to the cellar for the holidays?"

There was great excitement in removing the faded newspaper wrappings from the holiday dishes and recognizing the familiar designs. These were more than just dishes. They had a history, and they brought with them the promise of family living on a higher plane than we lived the rest of the year. Each played a part in the folklore of the Passover season. Our mouths watered

1. **Passover**, the eight-day Jewish spring holiday that celebrates the deliverance of the ancient Hebrews from Egypt.

with anticipation as we unwrapped each dish and foretasted the thrills, both gastronomical and emotional, which would be forthcoming when these inanimate utensils would come to life again as part of the symbolism of the Seder service.

About three days before the Passover, there was a knock on the door: "Your order is here." The Israelites took less out of Egypt with them than Mama brought in for the holidays. We were prepared for forty years of desert living. For weeks we felt our way amongst crates of eggs, sacks of flour, farfel and matzohs—matzohs in closets, on mantel-pieces, under beds, under tables, under sinks, on the fire escape, on the piano: egg matzohs, plain matzohs, long matzohs, short matzohs, round matzohs, square matzohs.

My folks refused to accept the idea that good wine could be bought. Every year they brought home baskets of wine grapes which they squeezed through sieves, filtered through sacks and finally deposited in barrels next to my bed. During the night bubbles would burst and send heady little wine-breezes floating about the room. How could I ever explain to the teacher why I was late for school?

I don't remember just how long it took, but after a certain period Papa would taste the purple froth. He kept his judgment to himself until after Mama had tasted it. Then Papa would say it needed more sugar and Mama would say it was too sweet. The neighbors were called in. They, too, were divided into opposing groups of "too sweet" or "too sour." "Since when did you become a connoisseur?" "This is vinegar, not wine." "You used the wrong grapes." "For whiskey it's too weak, and for wine it's too strong." "What is it?"

The folks thanked everybody and ignored the comments. But every night Papa secretly put in more sugar and Mama secretly put in more water. We had to secretly bring up more barrels from the cellar. The wine was still not sweet enough and too watery.

One Passover Papa gave up in disgust and bought wine. With a smirk he poured a glass of the commercial stuff, tasted it, then gave some to Mama to taste. "It needs more sugar," said Papa.

The Seder[2] was conducted by King Papa with the utmost solemnity. We princelings sat around the table with Queen Mama, all of us looking cleaner and shinier and more vibrant than at any other time of the year. This was an important event, and by participation in it we became important people. We were retelling, as were our kinfolk all over the world, at this same moment, in the very same words, a chapter of man's search for freedom. The text was sacred and we repeated it with awe, reciting aloud our identification of the symbols of our history before us on the table: the bitter herbs to remind us of the bitterness of slavery; a little mound of chopped fruits and nuts signifying the mortar that went into the bricks

---

2. **Seder**, the feast and the special service held on the first and second evenings of the Passover.

Majolica Seder plate,
19th century, Padua, Italy.
Israel Museum, Jerusalem.

with which our ancestors built the pyramids when they were slaves to the Pharaohs; the roasted egg recalling the sacrifices made in the temple; the roasted lamb bone symbolizing the paschal lamb the Israelites sacri- ficed on the evening before they left Egypt; beads of blood-red wine dropped into a bowl, the curses visited upon Pharaoh; and the matzohs, the unleavened bread our ancestors took with them into the desert.

In the wine-stained Haggadah[3] before me, I could see woodcuts of the crossing of the Red Sea, Pharaoh's terrified soldiers on horseback being swallowed up by the waves, Moses pleading for freedom, and Hebrews being whipped by their oppressors. Before I could read, I had already become familiar with biblical accounts of disastrous upheavals in nature, miraculous victories, dramatic chronicles like Joseph and his Brethren and Moses on Mount Sinai.

For me, the youngest child, the Seder service held moments of great fear. I had to ask the Four Questions. The answers, which would be given in chorus by the rest of the family, explained the meaning of Passover. My brothers would become abnormally quiet to be sure to catch every crack in my voice. I could see the twinkle in their eyes as I rose to deliver the traditional paragraphs. "Wherefore is this night different from all other nights . . . .?" They were with me all the way, but they mischievously hoped for some small fluff as a subject of conversation for the rest of the year. While no applause was permissible, I could tell whether I had done well and would be held over for another year by the enthusiasm with which the chorus responded, "Slaves were we unto Pharaoh in Egypt. . . ."

As the evening went on, the mood became lighter. Between dishes made with as much love as chicken fat, and much singing, aided and abetted by the third and fourth glasses of wine, and the children's game of treasure hunting for the hidden matzoh (afikomen) for a reward, this was indeed a night to remember. How good it was to be slaves no longer, to sing our songs surrounded by our brethren, to feel rich and magnanimous enough to announce, "Let all those who are hungry come and eat with us" (even though it meant cutting down my portion), to talk of days when "all men shall be free" and "live in peace," to welcome the prophet Elijah into our homes, to drink the cup of wine that we had set aside for him, and for me to really see the wine go down in the cup as he drank. This night I belonged to history and history belonged to me.

Passover ended, and we became ordinary mortals again. The dishes were repacked and returned to the cellar, the good suit was hung up in the closet, but the matzohs died a lingering death. There were still about a dozen boxes to be finished off. We took matzoh sandwiches to school, to the movies, to the park. We left a trail of matzoh confetti behind us for weeks.

The very same foods tasted differently after the holiday was over. The spell was broken. Life was different now. Papa was not going to be king again for quite a while; Mama was also dethroned; and while we kids were not slaves unto Pharaoh any more, the landlord was still around, and we were back in the tenement, just a little bit let down, not quite sure that this was real freedom.

---

3. **Haggadah**, the story of the escape from Egypt, read by all the participants at the Seder service.

Developing Comprehension Skills

1. In the Levenson household, how was Friday turned from an ordinary day into a sacred one? What rituals brought about this change?

2. How do you think Sam Levenson felt toward his mother and father? In his eyes, how did religious rituals transform his parents?

3. What is different about his mother's relationship with God and his father's? What does Levenson seem to think of each relationship?

4. Why is the Seder meal described as a royal meal?

5. Levenson's title may be a reference to the saying "Money isn't everything." How appropriate is the title "Everything But Money" for his autobiography?

Reading Literature: Nonfiction

1. **Recognizing Autobiography.** An autobiography is written from a special viewpoint. It is written by the subject, not by an observer or a reporter. How does this different point of view affect what you learn about the subject? What information does it give you that a biography does not?

2. **Appreciating Humor.** Humor is an important element in Sam Levenson's writing. Explain the humor in these statements:

   a. For us kids the Sabbath also had another virtue; we were not spanked on that day. . . . But after sunset you had better look out!

   b. I can't take Harold's bike because God said, "Thou Shalt Not Covet Thy Neighbor's Goods." So why did Papa take away the dollar Aunt Bessie gave me for my birthday? "Because Thou Shalt Honor Thy Father and Mother," said Mama.

3. **Identifying Hyperbole.** As you know, hyperbole is exaggeration. It is often used to create humor or make a point. Explain the humor in Levenson's hyperbole:

   The Israelites took less out of Egypt with them than Mama brought in for the holidays.

4. **Understanding Symbols.** You have learned that a symbol is a person, place, or thing that stands for something other than itself. The Jewish rituals that Levenson describes contain many symbols. For example, at the Passover meal the bitter herbs symbolize the bitterness of slavery.

   Symbols can also exist in everyday life. Explain what these symbols meant to Levenson:

   a. the holiday dishes
   b. the bread hunt
   c. the Sabbath candles

Developing Vocabulary Skills

Learning About Adjective Suffixes. When some suffixes are added to a noun, they turn the noun into an adjective. On page 309, you studied the adjective suffixes -ous, and -ful, which mean "full of." The following adjective suffixes mean "relating to" or "like."

Suffix	Example
-al	musical
-ic	angelic
-ical	historical
-ative, itive	talkative
-ish	selfish

Notice that some base words change their spelling when a suffix is added.

The following adjectives are from "Eleanor Roosevelt" and "Everything But Money." Write each adjective suffix and its meaning. Then write a definition of the entire word. If you need help, refer to a dictionary.

slavish   tribal
biblical   conscientious
miraculous   sympathetic
methodical   fanatical
tactful   continuous
sensitive   ritual

Developing Writing Skills

1. **Analyzing Theme.** Based on your reading of "Everything But Money," what do you think Sam Levenson learned from his mother and father? Write a short composition discussing the lessons you think his parents taught him. Could these lessons be important to you, too? How could they affect your life?

2. **Writing an Explanation.** Think back to a holiday you celebrated as a child. How are your feelings about that holiday different now? In one paragraph, explain how your feelings and attitudes have changed.

3. **Writing the First Draft.** A report, like other kinds of writing, has three parts. The **introduction** introduces the subject to your readers. The **body** develops the subject with supporting ideas and details. The **conclusion** summarizes the important information presented in your report.

You are now ready to begin writing the first draft of your report. Make sure your introduction presents the topic of your report. You may also wish to include an anecdote or one or two interesting facts or details to capture your readers' interest.

The body of your report will develop your main ideas. Use each of your main outline headings as a guide to writing the topic sentence of each paragraph. The subtopics on the outline will provide details to develop each paragraph. Be sure to use quotation marks when you use the exact words of another writer. Give the writer credit by using a phrase such as *according to . . .* , or something similar. As you write, avoid the first person point of view. The words *I*, *me*, or *my* should not be included.

The conclusion of your report should tie ideas together naturally. When you have finished your first draft, save it in your folder.

Developing Skills in Speaking and Listening

Telling a Humorous Anecdote. The writing of Sam Levenson could be described as a series of anecdotes. An **anecdote** is a brief story. It is often used as an introduction to a piece of writing or an informal speech.

Think of an amusing situation you or a friend experienced. Practice telling your anecdote before a mirror. As you practice, use gestures to help get your ideas across to an audience. Practice your delivery until you feel confident. Then tell your anecdote to classmates.

"Not Poor, Just Broke"

DICK GREGORY

Dick Gregory tells of his own experiences of growing up poor and black. What hardships does he face? How does his mother help him?

Like a lot of black kids, we never would have made it without our Momma. When there was no fatback to go with the beans, no socks to go with the shoes, no hope to go with tomorrow, she'd smile and say: "We ain't poor, we're just broke." Poor is a state of mind you never grow out of, but being broke is just a temporary condition. She always had a big smile, even when her legs and feet swelled from high blood pressure and she collapsed across the table with sugar diabetes. You have to smile twenty-four hours a day, Momma would say. If you walk through life showing the aggravation you've gone through, people will feel sorry for you, and they'll never respect you. She taught us that man has two ways out in life—laughing or crying. There's more hope in laughing. A man can fall down the stairs and lie there in such pain and horror that his own wife will collapse and faint at the sight. But if he can just hold back his pain for a minute she might be able to collect herself and call the doctor. It might mean the difference between his living to laugh again or dying there on the spot.

So you laugh, so you smile. Once a month the big gray relief truck would pull up in front of our house and Momma would flash that big smile and stretch out her hands. "Who else you know in this neighborhood gets this kind of service?" We could all feel proud when the neighbors, folks who weren't on relief, folks who had Daddies in their houses, would come by the back porch for some of those hundred pounds of potatoes, for some sugar and flour and salty fish. We'd stand out there on the back porch and hand out the food like we were in charge of helping poor people, and then we'd take the food they brought us in return.

Momma came home one hot summer day and found we'd been evicted, thrown out into the streetcar zone with all our orange-crate chairs and secondhand lamps. She flashed that big smile and dried our tears and brought some penny Kool-Aid. We stood out there and sold drinks to thirsty people coming off the streetcar, and we thought nobody knew we were kicked out—figured they thought we wanted to be there. Momma went off to talk the landlord into letting us back in on credit.

But I wonder about my Momma sometimes, and all the other black mothers who got up at 6 A.M. to go to the white man's house with sacks over their shoes because it was so wet and cold. I wonder how they made it. They worked very hard for the man, they made his breakfast and they scrubbed his floors and they diapered his babies. They didn't have too much time left for us.

I wonder about my Momma, who walked out of a white woman's clean house at midnight and came back to her own where the lights had been out for three months, and the pipes were frozen and the wind came in through the cracks. She'd have to make deals with the rats: leave some food out for them so they wouldn't gnaw on the doors or bite the babies. The roaches, they were just like part of the family.

I wonder how she felt telling those white kids she took care of to wash their hands before they ate and to brush their teeth after they ate. She could never tell her own kids because there wasn't soap or water back home.

I wonder how Momma felt when we came home from school with a list of vitamins and pills and cod liver oils the school nurse said we had to have. Momma would cry all night, and then go out and spend most of the rent money for pills. A week later, the white man would come for his eighteen dollars rent and Momma would plead with him to wait until tomorrow. She had lost her pocketbook. The relief check was coming. The white folks had some money for her. Tomorrow. I'd be hiding in the coal closet because there was only supposed to be two kids in the flat, and I could hear the rent man curse my Momma and call her a liar. When he finally went away, Momma put the sacks on her shoes and went off to the rich folks' house to dress the rich white kids so their mother could take them to a special baby doctor.

Momma had to take us to Homer G. Phillips, the free hospital for blacks. We'd stand in line and wait for hours, smiling and Uncle Tomming every time a doctor or a nurse passed by. We'd feel good when one of them smiled back and didn't look at us as though we were dirty and had no right coming down there. All the doctors and nurses at Homer G. Phillips were black, too.

I remember one time when a doctor in white walked up and said: "What's wrong with him?" as if he didn't believe that anything was.

Momma looked at me and looked at him and shook her head. "I sure don't know, Doctor, but he cried all night long. Held his stomach."

"Bring him in and get his damned clothes off."

I was so mad at the way he was talking to my Momma that I bit down hard on the thermometer. It broke in my mouth. The doctor slapped me across the face.

"Both of you go and stand in the back of the line and wait your turn."

My Momma had to say: "I'm sorry, Doctor," and go to the back of the line. She had five other kids at home and she never knew when she'd have to bring another down to the City Hospital.

Those rich white folks Momma was so proud of. She'd sit around with the other women and they'd talk about how good their white folks were. They'd lie about how rich they were, what nice parties they gave, what good clothes they wore. And how they were going to be remembered in their white folks' wills. The next morning the white lady would say, "We're going on vacation for two months, Lucille, we won't be needing you until we get back." Two-month vacation without pay.

I wonder how my Momma stayed so good and beautiful in her soul when she worked seven days a week on swollen legs and feet, how she kept teaching us to smile and laugh when the house was dark and cold and she never knew when one of her hungry kids was going to ask about Daddy.

I wonder how she kept from teaching us hate when the social worker came around. She was a nasty woman with a pinched face who said: "We have reason to suspect you are working, Miss Gregory, and you can be sure I'm going to check on you. We don't stand for welfare cheaters."

Momma, a welfare cheater. A criminal who couldn't stand to see her kids go hungry, or grow up in slums and end up mug-ging people in dark corners. I guess the system didn't want her to get off relief, the way it kept sending social workers around to be sure Momma wasn't trying to make things better.

I remember how that social worker would poke around the house, wrinkling her nose at the coal dust on the chilly linoleum floor, shaking her head at the bugs crawling over the dirty dishes in the sink. My Momma would have to stand there and make like she was too lazy to keep her own house clean. She could never let on that she spent all day cleaning another woman's house for two dollars and carfare. She would have to follow that nasty woman around those drafty three rooms, keeping her fingers crossed that the telephone hidden in the closet wouldn't ring. Welfare cases weren't supposed to have telephones.

But Momma figured that some day the Gregory kids were going to get off North Taylor Street and into a world where they would have to compete with kids who grew up with telephones in their houses. She didn't want us to be at a disadvantage. She couldn't explain that while she was out spoon-feeding somebody else's kids, she was worrying about her own kids, that she could rest her mind by picking up the telephone and calling us—to find out if we had bread for our baloney or baloney for our bread, to see if any of us had gotten run over by the streetcar while we played in the gutter, to make sure the house hadn't burnt down from the papers and magazines we

Rag in Window, 1959,
ALICE NEEL. Collection of Arthur
M. Bullowa, New York City. Courtesy
of Robert Miller Gallery, New York.

stuffed in the stove when there was no money for coal.

But sometimes when she called there would be no answer. Home was a place to be only when all other places were closed.

I never learned hate at home, or shame. I had to go to school for that. I was about seven years old when I got my first big lesson. I was in love with a little girl named Helene Tucker, a light-complected little girl with pigtails and nice manners. She was always clean and she was smart in school. I think I went to school then mostly to look at her. I brushed my hair and even got me a little old handkerchief. It was a lady's handkerchief, but I didn't want Helene to see me wipe my nose on my hand. The pipes were frozen again, there was no water in the house, but I washed my socks and shirt every night. I'd get a pot, and go over to Mister Ben's grocery store, and stick my pot down into his soda machine. Scoop out some chopped ice. By evening the ice melted to water for washing. I got sick a lot that winter because the fire would go out at night before the clothes were dry. In the morning I'd put them on, wet or dry, because they were the only clothes I had.

Everybody's got a Helene Tucker, a symbol of everything you want. I loved her for her goodness, her cleanness, her popularity. She'd walk down my street and my brothers and sisters would yell, "Here comes Helene," and I'd rub my tennis sneakers on the back of my pants and wish my hair wasn't so nappy and the white folks' shirt fit me better. I'd run out on the street. If I knew my place and didn't come too close, she'd wink at me and say hello. That was a good feeling. Sometimes I'd follow her all the way home, and shovel the snow off her walk and try to make friends with her Momma and her aunts. I'd drop money on her stoop late at night on my way back from shining shoes at the taverns. And she had a Daddy, and he had a good job. He was a paper hanger.

I guess I would have gotten over Helene by summertime, but something happened in that classroom that made her face hang in front of me for the next twenty-two years.

When I played the drums in high school it was for Helene and when I broke track records in college it was for Helene and when I started standing behind microphones and heard applause I wished Helene could hear it, too. It wasn't until I was twenty-nine years old and married and making money that I finally got her out of my system. Helene was sitting in that classroom when I learned to be ashamed of myself.

It was on a Thursday. I was sitting in the back of the room, in a seat with a chalk circle drawn around it. The idiot's seat, the troublemaker's seat.

The teacher thought I was stupid. Couldn't spell, couldn't read, couldn't do arithmetic. Just stupid. Teachers were never interested in finding out that you couldn't concentrate because you were so hungry, because you hadn't had any breakfast. All you could think about was noontime, would it ever come? Maybe you could sneak into the cloakroom and steal a bit of some kid's lunch out of a coat pocket. A bit of something. Paste. You can't really make a meal out of the paste, or put it on bread for a sandwich, but sometimes I'd scoop a few spoonfuls out of the paste jar in the back of the room. Pregnant people get strange tastes. I was pregnant with poverty. Pregnant with dirt and pregnant with smells that made people turn away, pregnant with cold and pregnant with shoes that were never bought for me, pregnant with five other people in my bed and no Daddy in the next room, and pregnant with hunger.

Paste doesn't taste too bad when you're hungry.

The teacher thought I was a trouble-maker. All she saw from the front of the room was a little black boy who squirmed in his idiot's seat and made noises and poked the kids around him. I guess she couldn't see a kid who made noises because he wanted someone to know he was there.

It was on a Thursday, the day before the black payday. The eagle always flew on Friday. The teacher was asking each student how much his father would give to the Community Chest. On Friday night, each kid would get the money from his father, and on Monday he would bring it to the school. I decided I was going to buy me a Daddy right then. I had money in my pocket from shining shoes and selling papers, and whatever Helene Tucker pledged for her Daddy I was going to top it. And I'd hand the money right in. I wasn't going to wait until Monday to buy me a Daddy.

"Helene Tucker?"

"My Daddy said he'd give me two dollars and fifty cents."

"That's very nice, Helene. Very, very nice indeed."

That made me feel pretty good. It wouldn't take too much to top that. I had almost three dollars in dimes and quarters in my pocket. I stuck my hand in my pocket and held onto the money, waiting for her to call my name. But the teacher closed the book after she called on everybody else in the class.

I stood up and raised my hand.

"What is it now?"

"You forgot me."

She turned toward the blackboard. "I don't have time to be playing with you, Richard."

"My Daddy said he'd . . ."

"Sit down, Richard, you're disturbing the class."

"My Daddy said he'd give . . . fifteen dollars."

She turned around and looked mad. "We are collecting this money for you and your kind, Richard Gregory. If your Daddy can give fifteen dollars you have no business being on relief."

"I got it right now, I got it right now, my Daddy gave it to me to turn in today, my Daddy said . . ."

"And furthermore," she said, looking right at me, her nostrils getting big and her lips getting thin and her eyes opening wide, "we know you don't have a Daddy."

Helene Tucker turned around, her eyes full of tears. She felt sorry for me. Then I couldn't see her too well because I was crying, too.

"Sit down, Richard."

And I always thought the teacher kind of liked me. She always picked me to wash the blackboard on Friday, after school. That was a big thrill, it made me feel important. If I didn't wash it, come Monday the school might not function right.

"Where are you going, Richard?"

I walked out of school that day, and for a long time I didn't go back very often. There was shame there.

Now there was shame everywhere. It seemed like the whole world had been inside that classroom, everyone had heard what the teacher had said, everyone had turned around and felt sorry for me. There was shame in going to the Worthy Boys Annual Christmas Dinner for you and your kind, because everybody knew what a worthy boy was. Why couldn't they just call it the Boys Annual Dinner, why'd they have to give it a name? There was shame in wearing the brown and orange and white plaid mackinaw the welfare gave to 3,000 boys. Why'd it have to be the same for everybody so when you walked down the street the people could see you were on relief? It was a nice warm mackinaw and it had a hood, and my Momma beat me and called me a little rat when she found out I stuffed it in the bottom of a pail full of garbage way over on Cottage Street. There was shame in running over to Mister Ben's at the end of the day and asking for his rotten peaches, there was shame in asking Mrs. Simmons for a spoonful of sugar, there was shame in running out to meet the relief truck. I hated that truck, full of food for you and your kind. I ran into the house and hid when it came. And then I started to sneak through alleys, to take the long way home so the people going into White's Eat Shop wouldn't see me. Yeah, the whole world heard the teacher that day, we all know you don't have a Daddy.

It lasted for a while, this kind of numbness. I spent a lot of time feeling sorry for myself. And then one day I met this old derelict in a restaurant. I'd been out hustling all day, shining shoes, selling newspapers, and I had goo-gobs of money in my pocket. Bought me a bowl of chili for fiteen cents, and a cheeseburger for fifteen cents, and a Pepsi for five cents, and a piece of chocolate cake for ten cents. That was a good meal. I was eating when this old guy came in. I love derelicts because they never hurt anyone but themselves.

He sat down at the counter and ordered twenty-six cents worth of food. He ate it like he really enjoyed it. When the owner, Mister Williams, asked him to pay the check, the old guy didn't lie or go through his pocket like he suddenly found a hole.

He just said: "Don't have no money."

The owner yelled: "Why do you come in here and eat my food if you don't have no money? That food costs me money."

Mister Williams jumped over the counter and knocked the derelict off his stool and beat him over the head with a pop bottle. Then he stepped back and watched the man bleed. Then he kicked him. And he kicked him again.

I looked at the derelict with blood all over his face and I went over. "Leave him alone, Mister Williams. I'll pay the twenty-six cents."

The old man got up, slowly, pulling himself up to the stool, then up to the counter, holding on for a minute until his legs stopped shaking so bad. He looked at me with pure hate. "Keep your twenty-six cents. You don't have to pay, not now. I just finished paying for it."

He started to walk out, and as he passed me, he reached down and touched my shoulder. "Thanks, sonny, but it's too late now. Why didn't you pay it before?"

I was pretty sick about that. I waited too long to help another man.

I remember a white lady who came to our door once around Thanksgiving time. She wore a wooly, green bonnet around her head, and she smiled a lot.

"Is your mother home, little boy?"

"No, she ain't."

"May I come in?"

"What do you want, ma'am?"

She didn't stop smiling once, but she sighed a little when she bent down and lifted up a big yellow basket. The kind I saw around church that were called Baskets for the Needy.

"This is for you."

"What's in there?"

"All sorts of good things," she said, smiling. "There's candy and potatoes and cake and cranberry sauce and"—she made a funny little face at me by wrinkling up her nose—"and a great big fat turkey for Thanksgiving dinner."

"Is it cooked?"

"A big fat juicy turkey, all plucked clean for you. . . ."

"Is it cooked?"

"No, it's not. . . ."

"We ain't got nothing in the house to cook it with, lady."

I slammed the door in her face. Wouldn't that be something, to have a turkey like that in the house with no way to cook it? No gas, no electricity, no coal, just a big fat juicy raw turkey.

I remember Mister Ben, the grocery-store man, a round little white man with funny little tufts of white hair on his head and a sad look in his eyes. His face was kind of gray-colored, and the skin was loose and shook when he talked.

"Momma want a loaf of bread, Mister Ben, fresh bread."

"Right away, Richard," he'd say and get the bread he bought three days old from the bakeries downtown. It was the only kind he had for his credit-book customers. He dropped it on the counter. Clunk.

I'd hand him the credit book, that green tablet with the picture of the snuff can on it, to write down how much we owed him. He'd lick the tip of that stubby pencil he kept behind his ear. Six cents.

"How you like school, Richard?"

"I like school fine, Mister Ben."

"Good boy, you study, get smart."

I'd run home to Momma and tell her that the bread wasn't fresh bread, it was stale bread. She'd flash the big smile.

"Oh, that Mister Ben, he knew I was fixin to make toast."

The peaches were rotten and the bread wasn't fresh and sometimes the butter was green, but when it came down to the nitty-gritty you could always go to Mister Ben. Before a Jewish holiday he'd take all the food that was going to spoil while the store was shut and bring it over to our house. Before Christmas he'd send over some meat even though he knew it was going on the tablet and he might never see his money. When the push came to the shove and every hungry belly in the house was beginning to eat on itself, Momma could go to Mister Ben and always get enough for dinner.

But I can remember three days in a row I went into Mister Ben's and asked him for a penny Mr. Goodbar from the window.

Three days in a row he said: "Out, out, or I'll tell your Momma you been begging."

One night I threw a brick through his window and took it.

The next day I went into Mister Ben's to get some bread for Momma and his skin was shaking and I heard him tell a lady, "I can't understand why should anybody break my window for a penny piece of candy, a lousy piece of candy, all they got to do is ask, that's all, and I give."

Developing Comprehension Skills

1. Dick Gregory wrote, "Home was a place to be only when all other places were closed." What did he mean by this? What did Gregory lack at home?

2. Gregory's mother saw a difference between being poor and being broke. How did she explain the difference? How would you explain the difference?

3. What advice did Dick Gregory's mother give her children? Did she seem to follow this advice herself? Explain.

4. In several cases, Gregory's mother had to act in ways she despised in order to survive. Explain one situation.

5. What did Helene Tucker represent to Gregory? How does her crying affect him?

6. Explain how Gregory felt about Mr. Ben. Was he right to feel as he did?

Reading Literature: Nonfiction

1. **Understanding Purpose in Autobiography.** In writing an autobiography, an author selects events in his or her life to tell about. These events are chosen to suit a specific purpose. Review the events Gregory tells about in "Not Poor, Just Broke." What do you think that his purpose was in writing his autobiography? What effect do you think Gregory wanted it to have on readers?

2. **Making Inferences About Character.** Find the passages in "Not Poor, Just Broke" that tell about the following:
   a. his mother's job
   b. her response to the relief truck
   c. her actions when her family is evicted
   d. her reasons for having a telephone

   What does each of the above reveal about the character of Gregory's mother?

3. **Recognizing Conflict.** Conflict, as you know, is the problem facing a character. "Not Poor, Just Broke" contains several conflicts. Find at least three of these conflicts. In each, does Gregory struggle against another character, against nature, against society, or against himself? Explain your answers.

4. **Recognizing Irony.** One type of irony is the contrast between what seems to be true and what actually is true. What is ironic about the following situations?

   a. I wonder about my Momma, who walked out of a white woman's clean house at midnight and came back to her own where the lights had been out for three months, and the pipes were frozen.

   b. My Momma would have to stand there and make like she was too lazy to keep her own house clean.

   Find two other examples of irony in this autobiography. Explain the contrast in each.

5. **Identifying Tone.** You recall that tone is the author's attitude toward the characters and events in a selection. Would you describe Gregory's tone as one of anger, amusement, sorrow, or bitterness? Find at least two phrases that you believe reveal Gregory's tone. Explain how each phrase reveals his attitude toward the events he is telling about.

6. **Explaining Theme.** Like fiction, nonfiction can have a theme. Theme is the main idea that the writer wants the reader to consider in a selection.

   In your opinion, what was the cause of the many hardships Gregory suffered as a child?

What ideas do you think the author wants the reader to consider while reading this autobiography? Support your opinion with evidence from the selection.

Developing Vocabulary Skills

Using Word Parts To Determine Meaning. The column on the left below lists words from the selections you have read. These words use the adjective suffixes *-able*, *-less*, *-like*, and *-most*. Match the words with the definitions on the right by writing the correct letter on your paper next to the number of the word. Use your knowledge of word parts to help you choose the right answer.

1. available	a. having a value too great to measure
2. jobless	b. without feeling, cruel
3. invaluable	c. able to be used or gotten
4. pitiless	d. highest place
5. respectable	e. unable to relax
6. restless	f. worthy of esteem
7. uppermost	g. generous in giving aid to those in need
8. childlike	h. most distant
9. charitable	i. possessing qualities similar to those of a child
10. furthermost	j. without employment

Developing Writing Skills

1. **Comparing Themes.** Review Anna Guest's short story "Beauty Is Truth," in Chapter 2. Recall the theme of the story. Do you think Dick Gregory would agree with the theme? What were some problems both authors

were concerned with? Write a composition explaining how the two authors might agree or disagree about solutions to those problems.

2. **Revising the First Draft.** You are now ready to revise the first draft of your biographical report. Take your draft from your report folder. Try reading it aloud to yourself. It is likely that you will catch errors you missed when you wrote the first draft. As you read, ask yourself these questions.

a. Does my introduction tell the reader what the report will be about? ~~my in~~troduction capture the att reader?

b. Does the report follow m

c. Is each paragraph abou' Does each fact in that p or support that main i

d. Have I included str tween sentences and

e. Have I summarized t clusion?

f. Are all dates, fac' rate? Are all nam

g. Have I indicated quotation mark

The next step reading. Check f capitalization, You may wish to

this stage. Another person can often spot errors you have missed.

Rewrite the first draft, making any changes you think are necessary. Only one step remains in preparing your report. You will learn about it on page 403.

Developing Skills in Critical Thinking

1. **Identifying Stereotypes.** A **stereotype** is an unfair generalization about members of a specific group. It can lead to misunderstandings and feelings of prejudice.

Dick Gregory's teacher uses the phrase "you and your kind." What stereotype does ~~h~~e seem to hold? How does "Not Poor, Just ~~Br~~oke" reveal the harmful results of stereo~~ty~~ping and prejudice? Use incidents and ~~qu~~otations from the selection to support ~~y~~our opinion.

~~R~~ecognizing **Subjective Language.** The writer of an autobiography often uses subjective language in relating his or her experiences. That is, he or she allows feelings and attitudes to be reflected in the writing. Autobiography is seldom objective, or simply factual. Do you think a person could write an autobiography such as "Not Poor, Just Broke" using only objective language? Do you think it would be worth reading if it were written objectively? Why or why not?

From
Growing Up

RUSSELL BAKER

Russell Baker's mother decides that her son should learn the value of hard work. What does he learn instead from his disastrous first job?

I began working in journalism when I was eight years old. It was my mother's idea. She wanted me to "make something" of myself. After a levelheaded appraisal of my various strengths, she decided I had better start young if I was to have any chance of keeping up with the competition.

The flaw in my character which she had already spotted was lack of "gumption." My idea of a perfect afternoon was lying in front of the radio rereading my favorite Big Little Book, *Dick Tracy Meets Stooge Viller.* My mother despised inactivity. Seeing me having a good time in repose, she was powerless to hide her disgust. "You've got no more gumption than a bump on a log," she said. "Get out in the kitchen and help Doris do those dirty dishes."

My sister Doris, though two years younger than I, had enough gumption for a dozen people. She positively enjoyed washing dishes, making beds, and cleaning the house. When she was only seven she could carry a piece of short-weighted cheese back to the A&P. She would threaten the man-

ager with legal action, and come back triumphantly with the full quarter-pound we'd paid for and a few ounces extra thrown in for forgiveness. Doris could have made something of herself if she hadn't been a girl. Because of this defect, however, the best she could hope for was a career as a nurse or schoolteacher. That was the only work that capable females were considered up to in those days.

This must have saddened my mother, this twist of fate that had given all the gumption to the daughter and left her with a son who was content with Dick Tracy and Stooge Viller. If disappointed, though, she wasted no energy on self-pity. She would make me make something of myself whether I wanted to or not. "The Lord helps those who help themselves," she said. That was the way her mind worked.

She was realistic about the difficulty. Having sized up the material the Lord had given her to mold, she didn't overestimate what she could do with it. She didn't insist that I grow up to be President of the United States.

Fifty years ago parents still asked boys if they wanted to grow up to be President, and asked it not jokingly but seriously. Many parents who were hardly more than paupers still believed their sons could do it. Abraham Lincoln had done it. We were only sixty-five years from Lincoln. Many a grandfather who walked among us could remember Lincoln's time. Men of grand-fatherly age were the worst for asking if you wanted to grow up to be President. A sur-prising number of little boys said "yes" and meant it.

I was asked it many times myself. No, I would say, I didn't want to grow up to be President. My mother was present during one of these interrogations. An elderly un-cle, having posed the usual question and exposed my lack of interest in the Presi-dency, asked, "Well, what do you want to be when you grow up?"

I loved to pick through trash piles and collect empty bottles, tin cans with pretty labels, and old magazines. The most desir-able job on earth sprang instantly to mind. "I want to be a garbage man," I said.

My uncle smiled, but my mother had seen the first distressing evidence of a bump budding on a log. "Have a little gumption, Russell," she said. Her calling me Russell was a signal of unhappiness. When she ap-proved of me I was always "Buddy."

When I turned eight years old, she de-cided that the job of starting me on the road toward making something of myself could no longer be safely delayed. "Buddy," she said one day, "I want you to come home right after school this afternoon. Some-body's coming and I want you to meet him."

When I burst in that afternoon she was in conference in the parlor with an executive of the Curtis Publishing Company. She in-troduced me. He bent low from the waist and shook my hand. Was it true as my mother had told him, he asked, that I longed for the opportunity to conquer the world of business?

My mother replied that I was blessed with a rare determination to make some-thing of myself.

"That's right," I whispered.

"But have you got the grit, the character, the never-say-quit spirit it takes to succeed in business?"

My mother said I certainly did.

"That's right," I said.

He eyed me silently for a long pause, as though weighing whether I could be trusted to keep his confidence, then spoke man-to-man. Before taking a crucial step, he said, he wanted to advise me that working for the Curtis Publishing Company placed enor-mous responsibility on a young man. It was one of the great companies of America. Per-haps the greatest publishing house in the world. I had heard, no doubt, of the *Satur-day Evening Post?*

Heard of it? My mother said that every-one in our house had heard of the *Saturday Post* and that I, in fact, read it with religious devotion.

Then doubtless, he said, we were also familiar with those two monthly pillars of

Russell and Doris Baker. Collection of Russell Baker.

the magazine world, the *Ladies Home Journal* and the *Country Gentleman*.

Indeed we were familiar with them, said my mother.

Representing the *Saturday Evening Post* was one of the weightiest honors that could be bestowed in the world of business, he said. He was personally proud of being a part of that great corporation.

My mother said he had a right to be.

Again he studied me as though debating whether I was worthy of a knighthood. Finally: "Are you trustworthy?"

My mother said I was the soul of honesty.

"That's right," I said.

The caller smiled for the first time. He told me I was a lucky young man. He admired my spunk. Too many young men thought life was all play. Those young men would not go far in this world. Only a young man willing to work and save and keep his face washed and his hair neatly combed could hope to come out on top in a world such as ours. Did I truly and sincerely believe that I was such a young man?

"He certainly does," said my mother.

"That's right," I said.

He said he had been so impressed by what he had seen of me that he was going to make me a representative of the Curtis Publishing Company. On the following Tuesday, he said, thirty freshly printed copies of the *Saturday Evening Post* would be delivered at our door. I would place these magazines, still damp with the ink of the presses, in a handsome canvas bag, sling it over my shoulder, and set forth through the streets to bring the best in journalism, fiction, and cartoons to the public.

He had brought the canvas bag with him. He presented it with reverence fit for a chasuble.[1] He showed me how to drape the sling over my left shoulder and across the chest so that the pouch lay easily accessible to my right hand. It allowed the best in journalism, fiction, and cartoons to be swiftly extracted and sold to a citizenery whose happiness and security depended upon us soldiers of the free press.

---

1. **chasuble**, a garment worn by a priest saying Mass.

The following Tuesday I raced home from school and put the canvas bag over my shoulder. I dumped the magazines in, and, tilting to the left to balance their weight, embarked on the highway of journalism.

We lived in Belleville, New Jersey, a commuter town at the northern fringe of Newark. It was 1932, the bleakest year of the Depression. My father had died two years before, leaving us with a few pieces of Sears, Roebuck furniture and not much else, and my mother had taken Doris and me to live with one of her younger brothers. This was my Uncle Allen. Uncle Allen had made something of himself by 1932. As salesman for a soft-drink bottler in Newark, he had an income of $30 a week; wore pearl-gray spats, detachable collars, and a three-piece suit; was happily married; and took in threadbare relatives.

With my load of magazines I headed toward Belleville Avenue. That's where the people were. There were two filling stations at the intersection with Union Avenue, as well as an A&P, a fruit stand, a bakery, a barber shop, Zuccarelli's drugstore, and a diner shaped like a railroad car. For several hours I made myself highly visible, shifting position now and then from corner to corner, from shop window to shop window, to make sure everyone could see the heavy black lettering on the canvas bag that said THE SATURDAY EVENING POST. When the angle of the light indicated it was suppertime, I walked back to the house.

How many did you sell, Buddy?" my mother asked.

"None."

"Where did you go?"

"The corner of Belleville and Union Avenues."

"What did you do?"

"Stood on the corner waiting for somebody to buy a *Saturday Evening Post*."

"You just stood there?"

"Didn't sell a single one."

"For God's sake, Russell!"

Uncle Allen intervened. "I've been thinking about it for some time," he said, "and I've about decided to take the *Post* regularly. Put me down as a regular customer." I handed him a magazine and he paid me a nickel. It was the first nickel I earned.

Afterwards my mother instructed me in salesmanship. I would have to ring doorbells, address adults with charming self-confidence, and break down resistance with a sales talk. I should point out that no one, no matter how poor, could afford to be without the *Saturday Evening Post*.

I told my mother I'd changed my mind about wanting to succeed in the magazine business.

"If you think I'm going to raise a good-for-nothing," she replied, "you've got another think coming." She told me to hit the streets with the canvas bag and start ringing doorbells the instant school was out the next day. When I objected that I didn't feel any aptitude for salesmanship, she asked how I'd like to lend her my leather belt so she could whack some sense into me. I bowed to superior will and entered journalism with a heavy heart.

Introducing me to the *Saturday Evening Post,* she was trying to wean me as early as possible from my father's world where men left with their lunch pails at sunup, worked with their hands until the grime ate into the pores, and died with a few sticks of mail-order furniture as their legacy. In my mother's vision of the better life there were desks and white collars, well-pressed suits, evenings of reading and lively talk, and perhaps—if a man were very, very lucky and hit the jackpot, really made something important of himself—perhaps there might be a fantastic salary of $5,000 a year to support a big house and a Buick with a rumble seat and a vacation in Atlantic City.

And so I set forth with my sack of magazines. I was afraid of the dogs that snarled behind the doors of potential buyers. I was timid about ringing the doorbells of strangers, relieved when no one came to the door, and scared when someone did. Despite my mother's instructions, I could not deliver an engaging sales pitch. When a door opened I simply asked, "Want to buy a *Saturday Evening Post?*" In Belleville few persons did. It was a town of 30,000 people, and most weeks I rang a fair majority of its doorbells. But I rarely sold my thirty copies. Some weeks I canvassed the entire town for six days and still had four or five unsold magazines on Monday evening; then I dreaded the coming of Tuesday morning, when a batch of thirty fresh *Saturday Evening Post*s was due at the front door.

"Better get out there and sell those magazines tonight," my mother would say.

I usually posted myself then at a busy intersection where a traffic light controlled commuter flow from Newark. When the light turned red I stood on the curb and shouted my sales pitch at the motorists waiting in their cars.

"Want to buy a *Saturday Evening Post?*"

One rainy night when car windows were sealed against me I came back soaked and with not a single sale to report. My mother beckoned to Doris.

"Go back down there with Buddy and show him how to sell these magazines," she said.

Brimming with zest, Doris who was then seven years old, returned with me to the corner. She took a magazine from the bag, and when the light turned red she strode to the nearest car and banged her small fist against the closed window. The driver, probably startled at what he took to be a midget assaulting his car, lowered the window to stare, and Doris thrust a *Saturday Evening Post* at him.

"You need this magazine," she piped, "and it only costs a nickel."

Her salesmanship was irresistible. Before the light changed half a dozen times she disposed of the entire batch. I didn't feel humiliated. To the contrary I was so happy I decided to give her a treat. Leading her to the vegetable store on Belleville Avenue, I bought three apples, which cost a nickel, and gave her one.

"You shouldn't waste money," she said.

"Eat your apple." I bit into mine.

"You shouldn't eat before supper," she said. "It'll spoil your appetite."

Back at the house that evening, she dutifully reported me for wasting a nickel. Instead of scolding, I was rewarded with a pat on the back for having the good sense to buy fruit instead of candy. My mother reached into her bottomless supply of maxims and told Doris, "An apple a day keeps the doctor away."

By the time I was ten I had learned all my mother's maxims by heart. Asking to stay up past normal bedtime, I knew that a refusal would be explained with, "Early to bed and early to rise, makes a man healthy, wealthy, and wise." If I whimpered about having to get up early in the morning, I could depend on her to say, "The early bird gets the worm."

The one I most despised was, "If at first you don't succeed, try, try again." This was the battle cry with which she constantly sent me back into the hopeless struggle whenever I moaned that I had rung every doorbell in town and knew there wasn't a single potential buyer left in Belleville that week. After listening to my explanation, she handed me the canvas bag and said, "If at first you don't succeed . . . ."

Three years in that job, which I would gladly have quit after the first day except for her insistence, produced at least one valuable result. My mother finally concluded that I would never make something of myself by pursuing a life in business and started considering careers that demanded less competitive zeal.

One evening when I was eleven I brought home a short "composition" on my summer vacation which the teacher had graded with an A. Reading it with her own schoolteacher's eye, my mother agreed that it was top-drawer seventh grade prose and complimented me. Nothing more was said about it immediately, but a new idea had taken life in her mind. Halfway through supper she suddenly interrupted the conversation.

"Buddy," she said, "maybe you could be a writer."

I clasped the idea to my heart. I had never met a writer, had shown no previous urge to write, and hadn't a notion how to become a writer. I loved stories, however, and thought that making up stories must surely be almost as much fun as reading them. Best of all, though, and what really gladdened my heart, was the ease of the writer's life. Writers did not have to trudge through the town peddling from canvas bags, defending themselves against angry dogs, being rejected by surly strangers. Writers did not have to ring doorbells. So far as I could make out, what writers did couldn't even be classified as work.

I was enchanted. Writers didn't have to have any gumption at all. I did not dare tell anybody for fear of being laughed at in the schoolyard, but secretly I decided that what I'd like to be when I grew up was a writer.

Developing Comprehension Skills

1. Why did Russell Baker's mother conclude that he had no "gumption"? Do you think she was correct? Explain your answer.

2. How did Mrs. Baker define success? What did she expect from her son?

3. Why did Mrs. Baker force her son to sell magazines? Explain the problems that Russell had with the magazine job.

4. How well do you think Mrs. Baker understood her son?

5. How was Doris different from her brother? How did Doris's career opportunities differ from her brother's? What accounted for this difference?

6. Why did being a writer appeal to Baker? Do you think that these were his real reasons for becoming a writer? Explain your answer.

Reading Literature: Nonfiction

1. **Evaluating Autobiography.** Russell Baker tells the story of his magazine job to make a point about himself and his childhood. Why do you think he chose this incident? What does it reveal about Russell Baker's family? What does it show about his own goals and personality?

2. **Identifying Character Traits.** Russell Baker thinks he is not suited for the life of a salesperson. Do you agree? What character traits does Baker reveal as he attempts to sell magazines?

3. **Evaluating Setting.** The setting for Baker's autobiography is 1932 during the Great Depression. How do you think Mrs. Baker's attitudes about her son's career are affected by the times during which they lived? How

were Doris's opportunities limited by attitudes toward women's roles at that time?

4. **Appreciating Humor.** Humor is a trademark of Russell Baker's style. What is humorous about the interview involving Baker, his mother, and the Curtis Publishing Company executive? What is amusing about the executive's approach? What is humorous about the answers he received?

5. **Appreciating Irony.** Read this comment about Doris:

> Doris could have made something of herself if she hadn't been a girl. Because of this defect, however, the best she could hope for was a career as a nurse or school-teacher.

Does Baker really think that being a girl is a "defect," or is his use of the word ironic? Explain your answer.

Developing Vocabulary Skills

Using Prefixes and Suffixes To Make New Words. Choose five of the people you have read about in this chapter and write their names on your paper. Under each name, write three words that tell about that person. Your words must include a suffix, a prefix, or both. Draw a line under each prefix or suffix in the word. Then write the meaning of the word.

Example: Babe Didrikson
competitive—likes to compete

Developing Writing Skills

1. **Writing an Autobiographical Incident.** In three or more paragraphs, write about a humorous experience that you had while you were growing up.

Pre-Writing. Think about funny incidents that have happened in your family. You might consult with other family members for ideas. When you decide on a topic, list as many details as you can think of about the incident. Later, organize your list in chronological order.

Writing. As you write the first draft of your story, include specific details. Try to make the tone of your writing as humorous as possible.

Revising. Ask a family member to read your composition. Does this person agree with your version of the experience? See if the person can remember other details. Add these, if they improve the story. Then check your writing to make sure that you have used chronological order throughout.

2. **Analyzing Character.** The women whose biographies appeared in the "Biography" section grew up during the same era as Doris and Russell Baker. Did Eleanor Roosevelt, Babe Didrikson, and Wilma Rudolph act as stereotyped women of the times? How do you think these women were able to break away from what society expected of them? Explain your answer.

Developing Skills in Study and Research

Preparing a Bibliography. Now that you have completed your biographical report, you are ready to prepare a bibliography. A **bibliography** is a complete list of the sources you used in preparing your report. It appears on a separate page following your report.

A bibliography is arranged alphabetically by the last name of the author. Every line after the first line of an entry is indented. If no author is given, use the first main word of the title to determine the proper order. Look at the correct form for each source given below:

Newspaper
"President Johnson Sends a Message to Eleanor Roosevelt." *New York Times*, 13 April 1965, Sec. A, p. 13, col. 1.

Magazine
Huber, R. G. "William O. Douglas and the Environment." *Environmental Affairs*, Spring 1976, pp. 209–212.

Encyclopedia
"Willie Mays." *The World Book Encyclopedia*. 1984 ed.

Book
Hahn, James, and Lynn Hahn. *Zaharias: The Sports Career of Mildred Didrikson Zaharias*. Mankato, MN.: Crestwood House, 1981.

Prepare a bibliography for your report. Use your bibliography cards to provide the necessary information for each entry.

Developing Skills in Critical Thinking

Identifying Exaggeration in Autobiography. You have seen that the writer of an autobiography may slant the writing to suit his or her purposes. One of Russell Baker's main purposes is to amuse and entertain. To add to the humor, do you think he exaggerates any of these elements:

his own gumption?
his problems selling magazines?
his sister's behavior?
his mother's use of maxims?

Explain each exaggeration and its effect.

From
My Life In and Out of Baseball

WILLIE MAYS
As told to Charles Einstein

Willie Mays learned all about baseball from his father. What other important lessons did "Kitty-Kat" teach his son?

My oldest memory is of a radio and a silly cowboy song, but even before that, from the time I was less than two, my father started me with a ball. He was Kitty-Kat—that was his nickname, that's what the other players called him on the pickup semipro teams around Birmingham. They called him that for a reason. He was the most graceful fielder, they said, that anybody ever saw.

"Buck," Piper Davis[1] said to me, last time I saw him, a couple of years back, "you get the greatest instinctive jump on a ball I ever saw, except for maybe Joe D. or his brother Vince. But you've got more range than either of them, and you field ground balls better, and your arm is maybe the most dangerous since Ruth himself and more accurate than anybody except maybe Henrich's. And you don't know how to look bad under a fly ball."

Willie Mays, 1951. UPI/Bettmann, New York

"Sounds like I'm pretty good," I said.

"Only one better," he said. "Your old man. Kitty-Kat. Lot of things you can do, he couldn't do. But graceful? Man, he was a

---

1. **Piper Davis**, manager of the Birmingham Barons of the Negro National League and Willie's first professional manager.

poem. He was Shakespeare and that other cat Dante rolled into one. Know the difference, Buck? You don't pounce. You're a grabber. The old man, though—that's why we called him Kitty-Kat—now, he knew how to pounce!" He grinned. "I've seen you on the bases. Passed ball, no more than three foot away, and you explode. Explode, that's the word for it. Better than Jackie, better than anybody. But, Buck you don't pounce. You just never learned how."

And that was the game, when I was two years old. My dad would roll the ball at me, easy, and I'd stop it and then take it in my right hand and throw it back. And that was it—no matter how bad I threw it, he'd catch it. Like Piper said, Kitty-Kat would pounce. Till I wanted to pounce too, so instead of rolling it, he'd loft it a little ways in the air, and I learned to catch it.

The older I got, the more complicated the game got, but it was still the same game. When I was 10 years old, it was Kitty-Kat throwing the ball at me so it would bounce just in front of me and I'd have to "scoop" it—make the "pickup." For many big-leaguers, this is the most difficult fielding play of all. For me, simply on the basis of all that training over all those years, it actually became easier than some catches.

Little League

Us poor kids of my generation—we never had any Little League.

Don't mistake me. I believe in Little League. but I believe in it because at today's prices, for everything from tape to wind a ball, to a vacant lot to play in, a lot of places it's Little League or nothing.

But in my day we didn't have to worry about that. We found a roll of friction tape and we found a vacant lot, so what we did was play ball. I don't say there's a choice today, but I do say we had it better. We didn't have uniforms or screaming mothers or concession stands or crazy men who didn't know a thing about baseball but wound up managing because their son was playing and because nobody else wanted the job. We didn't fill out insurance forms so in case somebody got hurt, somebody else paid. Maybe that was a bad part. I'm all for insurance. The point is, if a kid didn't get hurt playing baseball, he'd get hurt doing something else. Today so many more of them spend so much time playing baseball, it's a good thing there's insurance, and it's a good thing they've got good equipment and adults around.

Main thing, what's going on today isn't like what was going on when I was a kid. More kids, higher prices, less land.

Today has its good side, and it's necessary. But my day had its good side, too. Chances were, adults would either leave you alone or, if they took an interest in you, they knew what they were talking about.

In the Bay area of San Francisco, there's a rich man I've been told about who has a back yard so big it's a Little League field all by itself. And because he wanted his own kid to play he installed a pitching machine back there and managed a team and made all the kids on the team report to his house for practice against the pitching machine. He also drives two Cadillacs.

He doesn't know very much about baseball either.

I think youngsters who have a future in baseball can survive undercoaching—things they're not taught because their Little League manager just doesn't know them to begin with—far better than they can weather overcoaching!

Knowing how to play a Little Leaguer is one thing. Knowing *when* to play him is a far greater gift, I think. If you've got a new 10-year-old who obviously isn't a match for the real good pitching in the league, don't go changing him around because he isn't hitting. And don't go letting him play every game—although I know there are some parents who think the only object of the Little League is for every boy to get into every game. For the boy's sake, whether he's a real good player or not, spot him against the "off" pitching.

I've found that the parents sometimes think the boy's happy if he gets up to bat. I think the truth is he's really happy not by getting to bat with no chance, but by getting to bat with a real chance. What doesn't occur to the parents is that he doesn't want to bat for the sake of batting. He wants to bat for the sake of getting on base.

The same parents who think it's a crime if a boy doesn't get into the game would think it was cruel of the manager who not only put him in the game but made him pitch to the big hitters on the other team. Sometimes I think we should all remember that all of us—and that includes 10-year-old boys—don't just want to do. What we want is the chance to do well.

It isn't a crime to want to win at the Little League level, either. Not because winning is so important at that level. But because if you criticize a boy after a defeat, it sounds like blame. When you spell out his mistakes after the team has won, he learns. The difference between criticism and blame is not what you did but how the team did.

If I talk about boys with talent and coaches without it, nobody should think I believe baseball is only for winners. Baseball is for anybody who wants to play it. And losing isn't the worst thing in the world (but winning isn't either). What I don't like to see is boys who are made to play because "everybody else does it." Beyond that, I think today's programs, for Little Leagues and others, are considerably more on the plus side than the minus. Like I say, 25 years ago I would have said no—but 25 years ago is a different world.

Growing Older

One of the sad things in growing older is learning what isn't glamour about what you used to think was glamorous. One time, outside of a flower store, I saw an emblem of this guy with wings that said you could send flowers by wire. And when the wind blew on the overhead utility lines and made the wires sing, I'd always think to myself that must be flowers going through the wires, somebody sending them to somebody else.

Five or six times—maybe more than that—when I was a kid, I'd get to sneak into games of the Birmingham club of the Southern Association. The thing that really thrilled me most was that they were the only team in the league that was allowed to wear white uniforms. Everybody else had to wear gray.

My daddy even pulled the old joke on me one time, when I couldn't have been much more than five or six years old, taking me to a ball game and then announcing he was a magician. When he said, "Stand up," everybody in the place would stand up, and when he said, "Sit down," everybody would sit down. I didn't learn about the seventh inning stretch[2] till long after that.

There's a story about me that the only job I ever had as a kid was washing dishes at a lunch counter, and that the job just lasted one day, and I took a look at a pile of dishes and said, "Tell the boss I said good-bye, and don't worry about one day's pay."

The story happens to be absolutely true.

It implies, though, that I never earned any money—and that part isn't true. From the time I was 13, 14 years old, my old man would take me along as an extra man whenever there was a ball game to be played. If the score was lopsided or we didn't have enough players or something, I'd get to play. And they'd pass the hat or maybe charge a small admission or something, and afterward they'd split up the money. Even though I was just a kid and an extra hand, they always made sure I got a full share just like everybody else. Some days it didn't come to more than $10 or $12, but it was money, and you'd get maybe 20 paydays a summer.

When we had these semipro and pickup games back home, if I got in at all, it was as an outfielder. I was a big kid, and I played all sports and all positions. You'd have to say basketball was my best sport. Jim McWilliams, the football coach at Fairfield Industrial High School, made me a passer because I could throw for long distance, but some of those big linemen racked me up good a couple of times, and Charley Willis, who played on the same team, got smeared so bad one game he was out for the rest of the season. So I started going more for basketball. The year I was a sophomore I was high scorer in the county.

I've never minded physical contact in the sense of being afraid of it—except maybe with a catcher named Foiles, who used to play for Pittsburgh, and man, don't go sliding into him—he was built like a brick wall. But I'm not one of those people who get some special kick out of it either. In fact, I wish once in a while some small pitcher would throw at my head. Seems like all I get is the big ones.

I did, though, have one thing, and it came out mostly in basketball. It's kind of a disease, if you want to call it that. They call it "peripheral vision." Otto Graham had it.

_____

2. **seventh inning stretch**, time when all at the baseball game stand up to stretch in the middle of the seventh inning.

I'd be coming down the basketball court with the ball and suddenly I'd throw a perfect pass to somebody else without even looking at him. The fact is, I was looking, but my eyes could see a lot farther to either side than most people's.

It's for this same reason that I've had so few collisions with other fielders going after fly balls, and so few accidents from running into the fences. Seems like I can see the ball and somebody or something else all at the same time.

This of course is a real help playing the outfield, but even though DiMaggio was my idol, I kind of accidentally fell into playing that position. My ambition was to be a pitcher, like my grandfather. My father'd gone for the outfield for himself because, he said, "Pitchers don't work every day."

In my case, though, what happened was this: One day I was pitching for a sandlot team, and I went nine innings and then hit a home run inside the park. After I finished crossing home plate I suddenly went all dizzy. My eyes were open, but I couldn't see anything. When I came to, my father was bending over me. "You were bearing down too hard out there," he said. "This is what happens."

Fifteen years later, a team of doctors would look at me solemnly and say those same words: "You were bearing down too hard out there. This is what happens."

Anyway, with one thing and another, I stopped pitching and became an outfielder.

It had been only a passing dizzy spell, anyhow. I only had one injury that meant anything while I was growing up. I guess you could call it an athletic injury. I shinnied up a tree to watch a football game, fell out, and broke my leg.

Baseball Wisdom

The one thing that never stops amazing me is the number of things I still have to learn about baseball.

At the beginning, my daddy went to Piper Davis and said, "Give him a contract. He can play."

"He thinks he's DiMaggio," Davis said.

"What's wrong with that?"

"He's a smaller man, that's what wrong. More he copies himself after Joe D., more he's got to unlearn."

"Then unlearn him," my father said. "But he can play, and you know it."

"Ain't much money," Davis said.

"How much ain't much?"

"Seventy a month?"

"You're right. That ain't."

"I'll up it five every month he's over .300," Davis said.

"With you changing him around," my father said, "he'd never collect."

"Why don't you talk to him?" Davis said.

So my dad talked to me.

"I can get you down in the mill," he said. "Only trouble is, once you get in you never get out. I think maybe you can make better money doing something else."

"Baseball?"

"Doesn't have to be baseball. You got a trade."

That "you got a trade" was kind of a fancy way of saying I'd taken a special course in cleaning and pressing at school. The idea was, I could enter into that field for a living, and baseball could always be something extra on the side.

"I think I can play for Piper Davis," I said.

"So does he," my dad said. "He's got a lot he wants to teach you. Hit a curve ball, quit crowding the plate, and so forth."

"Then what do you think?" I said.

"I think you like baseball," he said.

It was as simple as that.

No. Not quite that simple. Because the next night, for what was to be the last time, my dad and I played together on the same team. He was in center field. I was in left. He was something like 36, 37, at the time, but his condition was fine, and he could still go get them.

It was a game between a couple of factory teams, but they had some good ballplayers. In the second inning, one of the hitters, a left-handed batter, looped a long, sinking liner to left-center, the wrong field for him,

Night Game— 'Tis a Bunt, 1981. RALPH FASANELLA. Collection of the artist.

and I heard my father say, "All right, all right, let me take it!" But then I was aware that the ball was sinking and he was too far back, and I knew if I cut in front of him I could handle it, so I did, and caught it off the grass-tops.

And I knew that I'd shown him up.

And he knew it.

I've never apologized to him for making the play.

He's never apologized to me for trying to call me off.

We both wanted the same thing—to get away from the situation where I had to play side by side in the same outfield with my own father.

Because even the great Kitty-Kat was beginning to slow down, the same as his son will slow down, and the only thing worse than being shown up by youth is being shown up by your own flesh and blood.

Because then you've got to pretend that you like it.

I think he had four or five years, maybe more, of part-time ball left in his system, my old man, but he didn't play them. I went with the Barons, and "One in a family is enough!" he'd say happily to anybody who asked, but I'd gone and knocked him out of the one thing he loved and lived for. He knew it and I knew it. It's great for a man to see his son do something he always wanted to do but couldn't. It's great for a man to see his son want to follow in his father's footsteps.

But don't play in the same outfield together. It's like a father and a son chasing the same girl.

Things will never be the same between you again.

All I had to do was let him have that baseball for himself, out there that twilight in left-center field.

I could have said: "Take it—it's yours!"

But I didn't. And I can't buy it back.

Developing Comprehension Skills

1. What was Kitty-Kat's special skill? How did he teach his son about baseball?

2. What are the advantages and disadvantages of today's Little League, according to Mays? Do you agree?

3. What special talent made Willie an excellent basketball player? How did this talent help him succeed in baseball, too?

4. What role did Mays's father play during Willie's early career in baseball? Do you think the competition between them was friendly or uncomfortable?

5. In one memorable game, Willie caught a fly ball that his father had called for. What effect did this have on their relationship? Did Willie seem to regret his action?

6. How did Willie Mays's attitude toward baseball change as he grew up? Explain your answer.

Reading Literature: Nonfiction

1. **Evaluating Autobiography.** Mays's autobiography is titled "My Life In and Out of Baseball." What parts of Mays's life does this excerpt cover? Why do you think Mays felt it was important to include information about his life outside of baseball?

2. **Identifying Style.** The style of this autobiography is casual and conversational. For example, Mays writes, "Main thing, what's going on today isn't like what was going on when I was a kid." Find two other passages that show this conversational style.

   Mays also uses slang phrases, such as "racked me up" and "got smeared so bad." How does this casual language affect the selection? How does it affect the reader? Do you enjoy this style?

3. **Identifying Character Traits.** A person's thoughts and ideas often reveal his or her character. Tell what each of the following comments reveals about Willie Mays:

   a. What we want is the chance to do well.
   b. I think the truth is [a boy is] really happy not by getting to bat with no chance, but by getting to bat with a real chance.
   c. Losing isn't the worst thing in the world (but winning isn't either).
   d. The only thing worse than being shown up by youth is being shown up by your own flesh and blood.

4. **Recognizing Essays.** A short composition that expresses an opinion on a subject is called an **essay**. In this autobiography, Willie Mays sometimes strays from the story of his childhood to give his point of view on subjects he is interested in. For example, he includes a short essay about little league baseball. In your opinion, are essays appropriate in an autobiography? Why or why not?

Developing Vocabulary Skills

Joining Word Parts To Make New Words. The following base words are from "Willie Mays: My Life In and Out of Baseball." Each word can be combined with at least one of the prefixes or suffixes you have studied. Make as many new words as you can by joining word parts. Next to each new word, write its meaning. You may want to refer to the lists of prefixes and suffixes on pages 308–309, 342, 356, 361, and 383.

1. season	9. learn
2. interest	10. outfield
3. reason	11. play
4. accurate	12. paid
5. fill	13. perfect
6. cruel	14. machine
7. wire	15. memory
8. glamour	

Developing Writing Skills

1. **Using Comparison and Contrast.** Willie Mays's father not only helped him develop skill in baseball, but also inspired in him a love of the sport. In four or five paragraphs, compare and contrast Willie Mays's father with Russell Baker's mother.

   Pre-Writing. As you reread the autobiographies of Baker and Mays, jot down similarities and differences in their parents' attitudes about life and raising children. Include specific incidents to support each point.

Make an outline to organize your notes. You might use these topics: attitudes toward their children, expectations, demands, methods of teaching.

Writing. Use an attention-getting introduction. Then develop each main point with specific examples from the autobiographies. Use transitional words and phrases to signal comparisons and contrasts.

Revising. Check to see if you have followed a logical organization. Does each paragraph have a topic sentence supported with details and quotes from the selection?

2. **Explaining an Idea.** Willie Mays writes, "One of the sad things in growing older is learning what isn't glamorous about what you used to think was glamorous." In two paragraphs, explain Mays's idea by giving examples both from Mays's autobiography and from your own experience.

3. **Writing an Autobiography.** In five or more paragraphs, write a selection that might be included in your own autobiography. Select an incident that has been significant in your life, and tell about it in detail.

Developing Skills in Speaking and Listening

Delivering a Sportscast. Sportscasting is an exciting activity. It requires knowledge of a sport, good observation skills, imagination, and the ability to speak clearly and forcefully.

Attend a sports event in your school or community. Take notes for about a five minute period during the game. Include in your notes descriptions of the plays, game strategy, actions of players and coaches, and fan reaction.

After the game, write an informal script of your sportscast. Then give your sportscast to a small group. Ask the listeners to judge your performance according to this checklist:

1. Does the announcer seem to understand the rules and strategy of the game?

2. Does the announcer describe the action of the game in detail?

3. Does the announcer use specific, exciting words to describe the action?

4. Does the announcer vary the tone of voice to keep the listeners interested?

5. Does the announcer speak clearly?

*J*ournals

Journals are similar to diaries. Journals are regular records of events in a person's life. Much of our knowledge of history comes to us through the journals of people who took part in historic events. Some of our understanding of the world comes from travelers who used journals to record their thoughts and experiences. In this section, you will read entries from journals of three well known travelers. As you read, imagine yourself traveling with the writer. What would you have recorded in your journal?

Still Life with Straws, 1978, RALPH GOINGS. Collection of A. Barry Hirschfeld.

From
Travels with Charley

JOHN STEINBECK

During a visit to Yellowstone Park, John Steinbeck has an astonishing experience with his dog Charley. What changes Charley into a "new" dog?

I must confess to a laxness in the matter of National Parks. I haven't visited many of them. Perhaps this is because they enclose the unique, the spectacular, the astounding—the greatest waterfall, the deepest canyon, the highest cliff, the most stupendous works of man or nature. And I would rather see a good Brady photograph than Mount Rushmore. For it is my opinion that we enclose and celebrate the freaks of our nation and of our civilization. Yellowstone National Park is no more representative of America than is Disneyland.

This being my natural attitude, I don't know what made me turn sharply south and cross a state line to take a look at Yellowstone. Perhaps it was a fear of my neighbors. I could hear them say, "You mean you were that near to Yellowstone and didn't go? You must be crazy." Again it might have been the American tendency in travel. One goes, not so much to see but to tell afterward. Whatever my purpose in going to Yellowstone, I'm glad I went because I discovered something about Charley I might never have known.

A pleasant-looking National Park man checked me in and then he said, "How about that dog? They aren't permitted in except on leash."

"Why?" I asked.

"Because of the bears."

"Sir," I said, "this is an unique dog. He does not live by tooth or fang. He respects the right of cats to be cats although he doesn't admire them. He turns his steps rather than disturb an earnest caterpillar. His greatest fear is that someone will point out a rabbit and suggest that he chase it. This is a dog of peace and tranquillity. I suggest that the greatest danger is that your bears will be offended at being ignored."

The young man laughed. "I wasn't so much worried about the bears," he said. "But our bears have developed an intolerance for dogs. One of them might demonstrate his prejudice with a clip on the chin, and then—no dog."

"I'll lock him in the back, sir. I promise you Charley will cause no ripple in the bear world, and, as an old bear-looker, neither will I."

"I just have to warn you," he said. "I have no doubt your dog has the best of intentions. On the other hand, our bears have the worst. Don't leave food about. Not only do they steal but they are critical of anyone who tries to reform them. In a word, don't believe their sweet faces or you might get clobbered. And don't let the dog wander. Bears don't argue."

We went on our way into the wonderland of nature gone nuts, and you will have to believe what happened. The only way I can prove it would be to get a bear.

Less than a mile from the entrance I saw a bear beside the road, and it ambled out as though to flag me down. Instantly a change came over Charley. He shrieked with rage. His lips flared, showing wicked teeth that

Bear Totem, 1984, DON NICE.
Courtesy of Nancy Hoffman Gallery, New York.

have some trouble with a dog biscuit. He screeched insults at the bear, which hearing, the bear reared up and seemed to me to over top our truck. Frantically I rolled the windows shut and, swinging quickly to the left, grazed the animal, then scuttled on while Charley raved and ranted beside me, describing in detail what he would do to that bear if he could get at him. I was never so astonished in my life. To the best of my knowledge Charley had never seen a bear, and in his whole history had showed great tolerance for every living thing. Besides all this, Charley is a coward, so deep-seated a coward that he has developed a technique for concealing it. And yet he showed every evidence of wanting to get out and murder a bear that outweighed him a thousand to one. I don't understand it.

A little farther along two bears showed up, and the effect was doubled. Charley became a maniac. He leaped all over me, he cursed and growled, snarled and screamed. I didn't know he had the ability to snarl. Where did he learn it? Bears were in good supply, and the road became a nightmare. For the first time in his life Charley resisted reason, even resisted a cuff on the ear. He became a primitive killer lusting for the blood of his enemy, and up to this moment he had had no enemies. In a bearless stretch, I opened the cab, took Charley by the collar, and locked him in the house. But that did no good. When we passed other bears he leaped on the table and scratched at the windows trying to get out at them. I could hear canned goods crashing as he

struggled in his mania. Bears simply brought out the Hyde in my Jekyll-headed dog.[1] What could have caused it? Was it a pre-breed memory of a time when the wolf was in him? I know him well. Once in a while he tries a bluff, but it is an obvious lie. I swear that this was no lie. I am certain that if he were released he would have charged every bear we passed and found victory or death.

It was too nerve-wracking, a shocking spectacle, like seeing an old, calm friend go insane. No amount of natural wonders, of rigid cliffs and belching waters, of smoking springs could even engage my attention while that pandemonium went on. After about the fifth encounter I gave up, turned the truck about, and retraced my way. If I had stopped the night and bears had gathered to my cooking, I dare not think what would have happened.

At the gate the park guard checked me out. "You didn't stay long. Where's the dog?"

"Locked up back there. And I owe you an apology. That dog has the heart and soul of a bear-killer and I didn't know it. Heretofore he has been a little tender-hearted toward an underdone steak."

"Yeah!" he said. "That happens sometimes. That's why I warned you. A bear dog would know his chances, but I've seen a

---

1. **the Hyde in my Jekyll-headed dog**, a reference to *The Strange Case of Dr. Jekyll and Mr. Hyde*, a novel by Robert Louis Stevenson. In the story, the good Dr. Jekyll takes a drug that changes him into a new person, Mr. Hyde, who is ugly and evil.

Pomeranian go up like a puff of smoke. You know, a well-favored bear can bat a dog like a tennis ball."

I moved fast, back the way I had come, and I was reluctant to camp for fear there might be some unofficial non-government bears about. That night I spent in a pretty auto court. I had my dinner in a restaurant, and when I had settled in with a comfortable chair and my bathed bare feet on a carpet with red roses, I inspected Charley. He was dazed. His eyes held a faraway look and he was totally exhausted, emotionally no doubt. Mostly he reminded me of a man coming out of a long, hard drunk—worn out, collapsed. He couldn't eat his dinner, he refused the evening walk, and, once we were in he collapsed on the floor and went to sleep. In the night I heard him whining and yapping. When I turned on the light his feet were making running gestures and his body jerked and his eyes were wide open, but it was only a night bear. I awakened him and gave him some water. This time he went to sleep and didn't stir all night. In the morning he was still tired. I wonder why we think the thoughts and emotions of animals are simple.

Developing Comprehension Skills

1. According to John Steinbeck, what was Charley usually like?

2. What great change came over Charley when he saw his first bear?

3. Does Steinbeck seem shocked, upset, or amused by his dog's behavior? Find examples in the story to support your answer.

4. What possible reasons does Steinbeck give for the dog's extreme reaction to bears? Which one do you think is most logical?

5. Steinbeck writes of travel, "One goes, not so much to see, but to tell afterward." What does he mean? Do you agree with this?

Reading Literature: Nonfiction

1. **Recognizing Journals.** A **journal** is a record of events and personal feelings. It may be written in either a formal or informal manner. In other words, the writer may simply record thoughts and observations in a natural, unstructured way. Or, the writer may plan the journal entry carefully, using more formal language. Which method did Steinbeck use in "Travels with Charley"? Why do you think Steinbeck chose this method?

2. **Identifying Personification.** In this journal, Steinbeck personifies Charley. This means that he gives Charley human qualities. Explain these examples of personification:
   a. He shrieked with rage.
   b. He screeched insults at the bear.
   c. Charley raved and ranted beside me, describing in detail what he would do to that bear if he could get at him.

3. **Appreciating Humorous Language.** Steinbeck's style in "Travels with Charley" is hu-

morous. To achieve humor, he combines words that are not usually used together. He also tells about commonplace things in new, unexpected ways. Explain how Steinbeck's language adds to the humor in these statements:

a. Heretofore he had been a little tenderhearted toward an underdone steak.

b. We went our way into the wonderland of nature gone nuts . . .

c. . . . showing wicked teeth that have some trouble with a dog biscuit.

Find another passage with language that you consider humorous. Explain why you think the passage is humorous.

4. **Analyzing Dialogue.** Steinbeck's journal presents conversations between himself and the park guard. However, his dialogue does not seem to show the way people really talk. For example, according to Steinbeck, the guard says, "Our bears have developed an intolerance for dogs. One of them might demonstrate his prejudice with a clip on the chin and then—no dog." What seems unusual about this dialogue? In your opinion, would Steinbeck's journal have been more or less interesting if he had recorded "real" dialogue? Explain your answer.

5. **Recognizing Allusions.** An allusion is a reference to a well known person, place, historical event, or work of literature. Writers often use an allusion to make a point. Steinbeck makes an allusion to the well known literary characters Dr. Jekyll and Mr. Hyde. "Bears simply brought out the Hyde in my Jekyll-headed dog," Steinbeck writes. Explain how this allusion adds to your understanding of the change in Charley.

Developing Vocabulary Skills

Reviewing Context Clues. In Chapter 2, you learned that context clues can help unlock the meaning of unfamiliar words. The sentences below are from selections you have read in this chapter. Write the meaning of the underlined word in each sentence. Tell whether you used definition/restatement, example, or inference to determine the meaning.

1. Only Ross's sharp eyes sometimes picked out the gray and yellow diamond pattern, camouflaged among the grasses.

2. I found a niche amongst some moss-covered rocks and having firmly jammed myself into it, ate and drank my lunch.

3. My mother reached into her bottomless supply of maxims and told Doris, "An apple a day keeps the doctor away."

4. I was asked it many times myself. No, I would say, I didn't want to grow up to be President. My mother was present during one of these interrogations.

5. But have you got the grit, the character, the never-say-quit spirit it takes to succeed in business?

6. Some weeks I canvassed the entire town for six days and still had four or five unsold magazines. . . .

Developing Writing Skills

1. **Supporting an Opinion.** John Steinbeck is a writer who believes in the importance of typical, ordinary American experiences. He writes, "It is my opinion that we enclose and celebrate the freaks of our nation and civilization." What do you think he means by this statement? Do you agree that our country

has the wrong idea of what is important? Write one paragraph that tells whether you agree or disagree with Steinbeck. Use specific examples and personal experiences to support your opinion.

Pre-Writing. Review Steinbeck's comments about Americans' ideas of what's important. Then think about your own ideas of what is important in America. Write your opinion in sentence form. Jot down convincing reasons. Add examples to make each reason clear and convincing. Finally, decide on a logical order for presenting your reasons.

Writing. Write a topic sentence stating your opinion. Add your reasons in logical order. Include specific facts and examples to support your opinion. Use transitional words and phrases to tie your ideas together.

Revising. Work with a group of students to revise your writing. Each writer should read his or her paragraph aloud. Then, the rest of the group can give the writer suggestions for improving the writing. Keep the following points in mind as you listen:

Is the opinion clearly stated?
Are the reasons convincing and logical?
Do the ideas flow smoothly?
Could the paragraph persuade others?

After the revision session, make changes to correct weaknesses in your own paragraph.

2. **Writing a Journal Entry.** You recall that some journal entries are very informal. These entries show the natural flow of thoughts and feelings. Write a journal entry about a recent experience you had that was unusual.

Record thoughts and feelings in the order they occur to you.

Developing Skills In Critical Thinking

Analyzing Cause-Effect Relationships. An early event is sometimes the reason for a later event. The two events are said to have a **cause and effect relationship**. For example, Steinbeck said, "he was afraid his neighbors would call him crazy, so he went to look at Yellowstone Park." What does Steinbeck identify as the cause for his visit to Yellowstone?

Later, Steinbeck tries to explain the cause for Charley's violent reaction to bears. "What could have caused it?" he asks. "Was it a pre-breed memory of a time when the wolf was in him?" What cause-effect relationship does Steinbeck suggest? Do you think this is a likely explanation? What other explanations can you think of? Which one seems most likely?

Developing Skills in Speaking and Listening

Observing Good Speaking Habits. Carefully observe a comedian performing on television. Try to choose a comedian who tells stories similar to the one about Charley. Take notes on the comedian's posture, use of gestures, use of eye contact, and tone of voice. What good speaking habits does the comedian display? What speaking habits add to the comedian's humor? When you tell a story in front of a group, which techniques would you like to imitate? Practice by reading aloud passages from Steinbeck's writing as a good comedian would read them.

From
Blue Highways

WILLIAM LEAST HEAT MOON

William Least Heat Moon sets off on a journey along America's back roads, the highways colored blue on road maps. What does he discover along the forgotten roads of small town America?

Had it not been raining hard that morning I never would have learned of Nameless, Tennessee. Waiting for the rain to ease, I lay on my bunk and read the atlas to pass time rather than to see where I might go. In Kentucky were towns with fine names like Boreing, Bear Wallow, Decoy, Subtle, Mud Lick, Mummie, Neon; Belcher was just down the road from Mouthcard, and Minnie was only ten miles away from Mousie.

I looked at Tennessee. Turtletown eight miles from Ducktown. And also: Peavine, Wheel, Milky Way, Love Joy, Dull, Weakly, Fly, Spot, Miser Station, Only, McBurg, Peeled Chestnut, Clouds, Topsy, Isoline. And the best of all, Nameless. The logic! I was heading east, and Nameless lay forty-five miles west. I decided to go anyway.

The rain stopped, but things looked saturated, even bricks. In Gainesboro, a hill town with a square of businesses around the Jackson County Courthouse, I stopped for directions and breakfast. There is one almost infallible way to find honest food at just prices in blue-highway America: count the wall calendars in a cafe.

No calendar: Same as an interstate pitstop.
One calendar: Preprocessed food assembled in New Jersey.
Two calendars: Only if fish trophies present.
Three calendars: Can't miss on the farmboy breakfasts.
Four calendars: Try the ho-made pie, too.
Five calendars: Keep it under your hat, or they'll franchise.

One time I found a six-calendar cafe in the Ozarks, which served fried chicken, peach pie, and chocolate malts, that left me searching for another ever since. I've never seen a seven-calendar place. But old-time travelers—road men in a day when cars had running boards and lunchroom windows said *AIR COOLED* in blue letters with icicles dripping from the tops—those travelers have told me the golden legends of seven-calendar cafes.

To the rider of back roads, nothing shows the tone, the voice of a small town more quickly than the breakfast grill or the

*Pee Wee's Diner,
Warnerville, New York,
1977, RALPH GOINGS.*
Private collection. Photograph
by Greg Heins.

five-thirty tavern. Much of what the people do and believe and share is evident then. The City Cafe in Gainesboro had three calendars that I could see from the walk. Inside were no interstate refugees, no wild-eyed children just released from the glassy cell of a stationwagon backseat, no longhaul truckers talking in CB numbers. There were only townspeople wearing overalls, or catalog-order suits with five-and-dime ties, or uniforms. That is, here were farmers and mill hands, bank clerks, the dry goods merchant, a policeman, and chiropractor's re-

ceptionist. Because it was Saturday, there were also mothers and children.

I ordered my standard on-the-road breakfast: two eggs up, hashbrowns, tomato juice. The waitress, whose pale, almost translucent skin shifted hue in the gray light like a thin slice of mother of pearl, brought the food. Next to the eggs was a biscuit with a Smiley button stuck in it. She said, "You from the North?"

"I guess I am." A Missourian gets used to Southerners thinking him a Yankee, a Northerner considering him a cracker, a

Westerner sneering at his effete Eastern-ness, and the Easterner taking him for a cowhand.

"So whata you doin' in the mountains?"

"Talking to people. Taking some pictures. Looking mostly."

"Lookin' for what?"

"A three-calendar cafe that serves Smiley buttons on the biscuits."

"You needed a smile. Tell me really."

"I don't know. Actually, I'm looking for some jam to put on this biscuit now that you've brought one."

She came back with grape jelly. In a land of quince jelly, apple butter, apricot jam, blueberry preserves, pear conserves, and lemon marmalade, you always get grape jelly.

"Whata you lookin' for?"

Like anyone else, I'm embarrassed to eat in front of a watcher, particularly if I'm getting interviewed. "Why don't you have a cup of coffee?"

"Cain't right now. You gonna tell me?"

"I don't know how to describe it to you. Call it harmony."

She waited for something more. "Is that it?" Someone called her to the kitchen. I had managed almost to finish by the time she came back. She sat on the edge of the booth. "I started out in life not likin' anything, but then it grew on me. Maybe that'll happen to you." She watched me spread the jelly. "Saw your van." She watched me eat the biscuit. "You sleep in there?" I told her I did. "I'd love to do that, but I'd be scared spitless."

"I don't mind being scared spitless. Sometimes."

"I'd love to take off cross country. I like to look at different license plates. But I'd take a dog. You carry a dog?"

"No dogs, no cats, no budgie birds. It's a one-man campaign to show Americans a person can travel alone without a pet."

"Cain't travel without a dog!"

"I like to do things the hard way."

"Shoot! I'd take me a dog to talk to. And for protection."

"It isn't traveling to cross the country and talk to your pug instead of people. Besides, being alone on the road makes you ready to meet someone when you stop. You get sociable traveling alone."

She looked out toward the van again. "Time I get the nerve to take a trip, gas'll cost five dollars a gallon."

"Could be. My rig might go the way of the steamboat." I remembered why I'd come to Gainesboro. "You know the way to Nameless?"

"Nameless? I've heard of Nameless. Better ask the amlance driver in the corner booth." She pinned the Smiley on my jacket. "Maybe I'll see you on the road. His name's Bob, by the way."

"The ambulance driver?"

"The Smiley. I always name my Smileys—otherwise they all look alike. I'd talk to him before you go."

"The Smiley?"

"The amlance driver."

And so I went looking for Nameless, with a Smiley button named Bob.

Developing Comprehension Skills

1. How does William Least Heat Moon judge restaurants? How do restaurants with several calendars differ from those with none?

2. "Best of all, Nameless," the author writes. "The logic!" Why do you think he was attracted to a town called Nameless? What did he mean by "the logic"?

3. What does Least Heat Moon say he is looking for as he travels back road America? Why might this be important to him?

4. How do you know that both he and the waitress are interested in people?

5. How are Least Heat Moon's ideas of the best way to travel similar to those of the waitress? How are they different? Whose ideas do you think are the best? Why?

6. Why do you think Least Heat Moon recalls and writes about this incident in Gainesboro, Tennessee? What did he gain from the experience?

Reading Literature: Nonfiction

1. **Understanding Journals.** What characteristics of a journal does this selection have? How does it differ from John Steinbeck's journal?

2. **Recognizing Dialect.** Language may be used in different ways by different people. **Dialect** includes the vocabulary, grammar, and pronunciation that are common to speakers in a certain group or region. Find one example of the dialect of the people of Gainesboro. Why is the use of dialect fitting in this journal about travel on back roads?

3. **Examining Characterization.** Least Heat Moon shows the character of the waitress through her actions and her words. Tell what each of the following comments reveals about the waitress:

   a. I'd love to take off cross country.
   b. You need a smile.
   c. You sleep in there? . . . I'd love to do that, but I'd be scared spitless.
   d. I always name my Smileys. . . .

4. **Recognizing Paradox.** A **paradox** is a statement that seems at first to contradict itself. On closer examination, though, it is found to be true. For example, Least Heat Moon says, "You get sociable traveling alone." Why does this comment seem to be a contradiction? Why could it actually be true?

5. **Understanding Titles.** The complete title of Least Heat Moon's book is *Blue Highways: A Journey into America.* You already know that "Blue Highways" refers to the small roads marked by blue on a road map. The word *into* in the title is also important. What does it reveal about the purpose of Least Heat Moon's travels?

Developing Vocabulary Skills

Using Synonyms and Antonyms To Find Word Meaning. As you recall from Chapter 2, synonyms and antonyms can be used as context clues. Each sentence or sentence group below contains an underlined word and a synonym or antonym for that word. Write the meaning of each underlined word and then write its synonym or antonym.

1. Eleanor Roosevelt gave ten dollars and a job offer to a disheveled young man. He later appeared at the White House, well-groomed and ready to work.

2. One of the Roosevelt boys came home late in a ramshackle car. The broken-down auto made the White House guards suspicious.

3. For young Sam Levenson, the Sabbath was sacred, but it had a secular value as well.

4. During Passover, dramatic chronicles were read, such as the story of Moses.

5. Charley's owner thought that he was a unique dog, different from all others.

6. Charley had great tolerance for most living things, but this broad-mindedness did not include bears.

Developing Writing Skills

1. **Writing an Explanation.** The poet Robert Louis Stevenson wrote, "To travel hopefully is a better thing than to arrive." What do you think he meant by this comment? In one paragraph, explain how Stevenson's quotation applies to William Least Heat Moon.

   Pre-Writing. Discuss Stevenson's quotation with your family or friends. Then make notes on how the statement applies to "Blue Highways." Decide on the way to organize your ideas into a paragraph. You might, for example, begin with an explanation of the quotation. You could then give reasons telling why it applies to Least Heat Moon.

   Writing. Combine your ideas into paragraph form. Remember to give examples to prove your point.

   Revising. Team up with a partner to edit each other's paragraphs. If your partner spots unclear sentences, rewrite them using specific language. If your paragraph needs more development, use more examples to support your topic sentences.

2. **Writing a Dialogue.** John Steinbeck and William Least Heat Moon both enjoyed traveling through America. Imagine that the two of them meet. Create a dialogue between the two that shows how their attitudes about travel are alike and how they differ.

3. **Understanding a Quotation.** Least Heat Moon claims that a café "shows the tone, the voice of a small town." Think of some of the businesses, buildings, and recreation spots where you live. Which one best represents your city or town? Write a short composition that describes this place.

Developing Skills in Critical Thinking

Analyzing Connotations. Connotations are the feelings and ideas that people think of when they hear a word. Least Heat Moon enjoys reading the names of small towns in his road atlas. What feelings and ideas do you associate with these town names: Bear Wallow, Mud Lick, Peavine, Milky Way, Weakly, Only, Clouds, Subtle, and Nameless? What kind of town would you expect each to be? Why would such towns appeal to Least Heat Moon?

Developing Skills in Speaking and Listening

Holding a Panel Discussion. A panel discussion is an opportunity to exchange ideas with others. This discussion is carried on by a small number of speakers before an audience.

With several of your classmates, present an informal panel discussion on this topic: Which is the best place to live in America—a city, a small town, or the country? Each panelist should be prepared to explain and defend his or her viewpoint with logical reasons.

From

North to the Orient

ANNE MORROW LINDBERGH

Piloting a small plane over Alaska, the Lindberghs suddenly realize that they must land. How will they land at night in unknown territory?

"What time does it get dark at Nome?" My husband pushed a penciled message back to me. Dark? I had completely forgotten that it ever was dark. We had been flying in the land of the midnight sun, though actually its period was over in August. The sun set, but the sky did not darken on either of the flights, from Baker Lake to Aklavik, or from Aklavik to Barrow. But tonight—for it was about eight-thirty in the evening—the light was fading rather fast. Streaks of the remaining sunset ran gold in the inlets and lagoons of the coast. We had turned the corner of Alaska after leaving Point Barrow and were flying south to the little mining town, Nome, on the Bering coast. An unknown route, an unknown harbor; we must have light to land safely.

"WXB - - - WXB - - - WXB," I called back to our friend at the Barrow radio station. I had tried in vain to reach Nome. "Nil - - - hrd (nothing heard) - - - from - - - WXY (Nome) - - - or - - - WXW (Kotzebue) - - - what - - - time - - - does - - - it - - - get - - - dark - - - at - - - Nome?" His faint signals

traced dim incomprehensible marks on my brain, then faded away. It was no use; I could not make them out. I would have to let go of that thread and pick up another.

"Can't - - - copy - - - ur (your) - - - sigs (signals) - - - will - - - contact - - - NRUL (the *Northland*)." I signed off. There was no time to lose. Again I tried, "NRUL - - - de - - - KHCAL - - - nil - - - hrd - - - from - - - WXY - - - what - - - time - - - does - - - it - - - get - - - dark - - - at Nome?" No answer. The sparks from the exhaust flashed behind us in the growing dusk.

Was it really going to get dark? It had not been dark since Baker Lake, since that evening when we set out recklessly at seven to fly all night. It had seemed, I remembered, a kind of madness to start at that hour. It would soon be dark, or so I thought, and to fly at night, in a strange country, through uncertain weather to an unknown destination—what were we thinking of! Spendthrifts with daylight, we who usually counted every coin; who always rose early to fly, at three or four in the morning, not to waste a second of the precious light; we were down at the field, the engine warmed up and ready to start with the first streaks of dawn, in order "to get there by dark." Dark—that curfew hour in a flier's mind, when the gates are closed, the portcullis dropped down, and there is no way to go around or to squeeze under the bars if one is late.

But that night at Baker Lake, we were going north, into the midnight sun.

"And it will be light all the way?" we had asked incredulously. (Though of course we knew it to be so.)

"Sure—it won't get dark at all—going north like that." The game warden had nodded his head. "Light all the way!"

Going into that strange world of unending day was like stepping very quietly across the invisible border of the land of Faery that the Irish poets write of, that timeless world of Fionn and Saeve, or the world of Thomas the Rhymer. It was evening when we left Baker Lake, but an evening that would never flower into night, never grow any older. And so we had set out, released from fear, intoxicated with a new sense of freedom—out into that clear unbounded sea of day. We could go on and on and never reach the shores of night. The sun would

Left: Charles and Anne Morrow Lindbergh before the test flight for the 1930 Pacific survey flight. Lindbergh Picture Collection, Yale University Archives, New Haven, Connecticut.

Below: A page of Anne Morrow Lindbergh's diary. From *Locked Rooms and Open Doors* by Anne Morrow Lindbergh. Harcourt Brace Jovanovich, Inc., Orlando, Florida.

set, darkness would gather in the bare coves, creep over the waste lands behind us, but never overtake us. The wave of night would draw itself together, would rise behind us and never break.

But now—going south—my husband switched on the instrument lights. We were running short of fuel. Our gasoline barrels were on the icebound *Northland* and we had not refueled since Aklavik. There was no chance of turning back. We must land before dark.

"NRUL - - - NRUL - - - what - - - time - - - does - - - it - - - get - - - dark - - - at - - - Nome?"

At Barrow, I remembered, we had even wanted the dark. When I went to bed the first night, I had pulled down the shades, trying to create the feeling of a deep black night. For sleep, one needs endless depths of blackness to sink into; daylight is too shallow, it will not cover one. At Aklavik, too, I had missed night's punctuality. It was light when we went to bed and light when we rose. The same light shed over breakfast and lunch and supper and continued on through bedtime, so that I hardly knew when to feel tired or when to feel hungry.

But now, seeing signs of approaching night—the coves and lagoons took up the light the sky was losing—I was afraid. I felt the terror of a savage seeing a first eclipse, or even as if I had never known night. What was it? Explorer from another planet, I watched with fear, with amazement, and with curiosity, as Emily Dickinson watched for day:

Will there really be a morning?
Is there such a thing as day?
Could I see it from the mountains
If I were as tall as they?

Has it feet like water-lilies?
Has it feathers like a bird?
Is it brought from famous countries
Of which I have never heard?

"Feathers like a bird," perhaps answered my own questioning. The shadow of a wing covered all the sky. We would be covered, inclosed, crushed. Wisps of evening fog below grew luminous in the approaching dark. I remembered now what night was. It was being blind and lost. It was looking and not seeing—that was night.

"WXY - - - WXY - - - WXY - - - what - - - time - - - does - - - it - - - get - - - dark - - - at - - - Nome?"

Suddenly an answer: "WXN - - - WXN - - - Candle - - - Candle—" One of the relay stations on the coast had heard us. "Will - - - stand - - - by - - - in - - - case - - - you - - - don't - - - get - - - WXY," came their message. At last someone to answer.

"What - - - time - - - does - - - it - - - get - - - dark - - - at - - - Nome?"

There was a silence while he relayed the message to Nome. I looked out and caught my breath. The sea and sky had merged. The dark had leaped up several steps behind me when my back was turned. I would have to keep my eye on him or he would sneak up like the child's game of steps. But the radio was buzzing. My head went down again.

"The - - - men - - - are - - - going - - - to - - - put - - - flares - - - on - - - Nome - - - River," came back the answer. "It's - - - overcast - - - and - - - getting - - - dark." Then continuing, "When - - - u (you) - - - expect - - - arrive - - - so - - - they - - - no (know) - - - when - - - lite - - - flares?"

I passed my scribbled message forward. The lights blinked on in the front cockpit. I read by my own light the reply, "Arrive in about 1½ hours—don't lite flares until plane circles and blinks lites."

An hour and a half more! It would be night when we landed! Turned inland, we were over the mountains now and there were peaks ahead. It was darker over the land than over the water. Valleys hoard darkness as coves hoard light. Reservoirs of darkness, all through the long day they guard what is left them from the night before; but now their cups were filling up, trembling at the brim, ready to spill over. The wave of night climbed up behind us; gathering strength from every crevice, it towered over us.

Suddenly my husband pulled the plane up into a stall, throttled the engine, and, in the stillness that followed, shouted back to me, "Tell him there's fog on the mountains ahead. We'll land for the night and come into Nome in the morning."

"All right, where are we?"

"Don't know exactly—northwest coast of Seward Peninsula."

Without switching on the light I started tapping rapidly, "WXN - - - WXN - - - WXN - - - fog - - - on - - - mountains - - - ahead - - - will - - - land - - - for - - - night - - - and - - - come - - - into - - - Nome - - - morning - - - position - - - northwest - - - coast - - - Seward - - - Peninsula," I repeated twice.

"Hurry up! Going to land," came a shout from the front cockpit. We were banking steeply.

No time to try again. No time to listen for reply. I did not know if they had received it, but we could not wait to circle again. We must land before that last thread of light had gone.

Down, down, down, the cold air whistling through the cowlings as we dived toward the lagoon. I must wind in the antenna before we hit the water. The muscles in my arms stiffened to soreness turning the wheel at top speed, as though I were reeling in a gigantic fish from the bottom of the sea. One more turn—jiggle, snap, the ballweight clicked into place—all wound up, safe. Now—brace yourself for the landing. How can he see anything! Spank, spank, spank. There we go—I guess we're all right! But the ship shot on through the water—on and on. Must have landed "down wind." Now it eased up a little. There, I sighed with relief. We were taxiing toward that dark indistinct line ahead—a shore. About half a mile off, my husband pulled back the throttle, idled the engine for a few seconds, then cut the switch. In the complete stillness that followed, he climbed out onto the pontoon.

"Think we'd better anchor here." He uncoiled the rope and threw out our anchor. Splash! There it stayed under about three feet of water with the rope floating on top. Heavens! Pretty shallow—thought we had more room than that. Well, we were anchored anyway. We were down—we were safe. Somewhere out on the wild coast of Seward Peninsula.

At Nome it was dark now. The bonfire that was to have welcomed us lit up an empty shore as the crowd straggled home. It was dark where we were on the coast of Seward Peninsula. A little light surprised us from the blackness miles away—a single Eskimo camp perhaps. We made a bed in the baggage compartment out of our parachutes, our flying suits, and sleeping bag, and stretched out. The wave of night broke over us and we slept.

We slept—but not for long. I had only time to turn over twice—fly around the world, run from savages, drop pebbles in the Black Sea, paint the corners of the Mediterranean a deeper blue with a very long paint brush—when—putt, putt, putt— something broke into the Mediterranean and my sleep. Putt, putt, putt—I wasn't in the Mediterranean. I was nowhere. I was in Alaska, on a lagoon, far off from civilization, where perhaps no white man had been before, Putt, putt, putt. Were those voices?

"Hul-lo!"

"Charles! What's that!"

We both woke with a terrible start. My husband crawled aft, pushed back the sliding hatch and looked out. (The savages! I thought—they've come back again!)

"Hello," said my husband tentatively. Two small boats, both roofed with skins, were alongside our pontoons. In the cave-like mouth of one, a lantern lit up a circle of dark faces.

"Hul-lo!" I heard the same guttural voice hesitating with the words, "We—hunt— duck."

"Oh," said my husband, a little bewildered. "That's nice." (We were not in the wilds of Alaska after all.)

"You—land—here?" came the voice from the cave.

"Yes," answered my husband, "we came for the night." (Smiling.) "Do you see many of these around here?"

"Yes—yes—" said the man vaguely, not understanding at all.

"Get many ducks?" (What was one to make conversation about at three-thirty in the morning on the northwest coast of Seward Peninsula!)

"Well, guess I'll go back to bed." My husband closed the hatch and the boats disappeared.

To sleep again, but I could not get back to the Mediterranean.

Developing Comprehension Skills

1. As Anne Morrow Lindbergh and her husband set out for Nome, why did they feel a sense of excitement and freedom?

2. In the Arctic Circle, there is no darkness during the summer months. How does Anne Morrow Lindbergh feel about days with no darkness?

3. Why did the Lindberghs have to land? What emergency arrangements did the crew at Nome make? How did the coming of night make the Lindberghs' problems more serious?

4. Why did Lindbergh quote Emily Dickinson's poem? How were Dickinson's feelings similar to her own?

5. What clues do you find about the kind of plane the Lindberghs flew? How would the Lindberghs' flight be different today?

6. Lindbergh commented on her reactions to light and dark. How do you think light and dark usually affect people? Why do you think this is so?

Reading Literature: Nonfiction

1. **Recognizing Journal Writing.** How is Anne Morrow Lindbergh's writing typical of journal writing? How is it different? Does her journal remind you more of Steinbeck's or the journal of Least Heat Moon? Compare and contrast the three journals in terms of purpose and style. Which did you enjoy reading the most? Why?

2. **Understanding Sequence.** As Lindbergh's story begins she and her husband are trying to get landing information. Then she switches to a flashback. A **flashback**, as you recall, is an incident that occurred earlier in time. For example, Lindbergh writes, "It had seemed, I remembered, a kind of madness to start at that hour. . . ." Find the spot in the journal where the flashback ends. What did you learn about Lindbergh from this flashback? Now list the main events of the selection in the order in which they really occurred.

3. **Analyzing Suspense.** As Lindbergh describes flight problems, the reader feels growing tension about the outcome of the flight. What problems and obstacles help to build this suspense? At what point in the story do you feel the tension is greatest? Why? How does the constant repetition of "What time does it get dark at Nome?" add to the suspense?

4. **Appreciating Metaphors.** A **metaphor** is a figure of speech comparing two unlike things. The comparison is direct and does not use the words *like* or *as*. Lindbergh's poetic style is marked by graceful metaphors. Explain the comparison suggested by each of the following metaphors:

   a. an evening that would never flower into night
   b. the shores of night
   c. spendthrifts with daylight, we who usually counted every coin
   d. that last thread of light

   What feelings about night and day are created by Lindbergh's metaphors?

5. **Identifying Onomatopoeia.** The technique of **onomatopoeia** is the use of words that imitate sounds. Writers use onomatopoeia to help the reader "hear" the sounds in a selection. *Bang* and *whirr* are examples of ono-

matopoeia. Locate at least two uses of onomatopoeia in the selection. What sound is each word intended to imitate?

6. **Analyzing Style.** As Anne Morrow Lindbergh writes about her dangerous flight, she uses both past and present tense. Here is an example:

> We dived toward the lagoon. I must wind in the antenna. The muscles in my arm stiffened. . . . There we go—I guess we're all right! But the ship shot on through the water—on and on.

Which verbs are past tense and which are present tense? What does the use of present tense verbs add to this passage? Do the present tense verbs help you to feel what Lindbergh was feeling better than past tense verbs? Explain your answer.

Developing Vocabulary Skills

Determining Meaning with Context Clues. You have studied the following context clues in Chapter 2:

definition/restatement comparison/contrast
synonym/antonym example
inference cause and effect

The sentences below are taken from selections you have read. Choose the best meaning for each underlined word from the three given. Write the letter of your answer. Then write what type of context clue helped you determine the meaning of the word.

1. We gingerly tested each toehold and fingerhold for loose rock before putting our weight on it.
   a. quickly   b. carefully   c. noisily

2. "They're not active at this season," he said quietly. "A snake takes on the temperature of its surroundings. They can't stand too much heat for that reason, and when the weather is cool, as now, they're sluggish."
   a. slow-moving   b. hibernating
   c. energetic

3. Sitting bolt upright, I listened intently.
   a. carelessly   b. carefully   c. straight

4. My return over the river was accomplished with such verve that I paddled the canoe almost her full length up on the beach on the other side.
   a. vigor and energy   b. acute pain
   c. disinterest

5. His faint signals traced dim incomprehensible marks on my brain, then faded away. I could not make them out.
   a. psychological   b. distinct
   c. not understandable

6. Dark—that curfew hour in a flier's mind, when the gates are closed, the portcullis dropped down, and there is no way to go around or to squeeze under the bars if one is late.
   a. curtain   b. iron grating
   c. darkness

Developing Writing Skills

1. **Defending a Choice.** Imagine that you must choose to live either in the dark or in the light for a period of several years. In one paragraph, tell why you would choose one situation rather than the other.

2. **Writing from a Different Point of View.** Imagine that you are an Eskimo duck hunter who watched the Lindberghs' landing. Write

two or three paragraphs in your journal describing your thoughts and feelings as you watched the plane land.

Pre-Writing. Reread the section of Lindbergh's journal about their landing. In the library, find a picture that shows what the Lindberghs' plane looked like. Finally, make notes about what you, as one of the Eskimo hunters, would see and feel as the plane lands nearby. Would you be surprised, fearful, amazed, or simply curious? Now organize your notes into groups. One set of notes could describe the setting. Another could describe the plane itself. The third could tell about your meeting with the Lindberghs.

Writing. Following your writing plan, connect the details into clear descriptive sentences. Try to use sensory details in your descriptions.

Revising. Does your writing paint a clear word picture of how the landing looked? Does your writing include descriptions with sensory details? Do these details tell a reader your reaction to the landing? If not, add more specific descriptions. Ask an editing partner to check the spelling and punctuation in your sentences.

Developing Skills in Study and Research

1. **Using a Map.** In an atlas, locate Alaska's "land of the midnight sun." Trace the Lindberghs' journey from Baker Lake to Aklavik to Point Barrow and then toward Nome. Find the northwest coast of Seward peninsula, where the Lindberghs landed. Using the map's legend and scale of miles, determine how far the Lindberghs flew each day.

2. **Using Biographical Reference Books.** In your library, find the *Dictionary of American Biography* and *Current Biography*. These reference works can help you locate information about famous Americans. The one volume *Dictionary of American Biography* briefly identifies famous persons. *Current Biography* has many volumes. You can use the index to locate the volume with the entry you are seeking.

   Look up Charles Lindbergh and Anne Morrow Lindbergh in these reference works. Take notes on the Lindberghs' major achievements. For what accomplishments is each of them best known?

Humorous and Personal Essays

Essays are a special kind of nonfiction. They express a writer's personal feelings. Essays can be humorous or serious. They can entertain, inform, or persuade.

The essays in this section deal with many subjects. Some may make you laugh. Others might make you think about everyday events in a new way. As you read, try to determine the purpose of each writer.

Not To Be Reproduced, 1937,
RENÉ MAGRITTE. Museum
Boymans-van Beuningen, Rotterdam.
Copyright © Georgette Magritte.

Fresh Air Will Kill You

ART BUCHWALD

Take a trip with a humorist to a place with a strange new atmosphere—fresh air. As you read this essay, try to figure out how Art Buchwald keeps you laughing.

Smog, which was once the big attraction of Los Angeles, can now be found all over the country from Butte, Montana, to New York City, and people are getting so used to polluted air that it's very difficult for them to breathe anything else.

I was lecturing recently, and one of my stops was Flagstaff, Arizona, which is about seven thousand miles above sea level.

As soon as I got out of the plane, I smelled something peculiar.

"What's that smell?" I asked the man who met me at the plane.

"I don't smell anything," he replied.

"There's a definite odor that I'm not familiar with," I said.

"Oh, you must be talking about the fresh air. A lot of people come out here who have never smelled fresh air before."

"What's it supposed to do?" I asked suspiciously.

"Nothing. You just breathe it like any other kind of air. It's supposed to be good for your lungs."

"I've heard that story before," I said.

"How come if it's air, my eyes aren't itching and watering?"

"Your eyes don't water with fresh air. That's the advantage of it. Saves you a lot in paper tissues."

I looked around and everything appeared crystal clear. It was a strange sensation and made me feel very uncomfortable.

My host, sensing this, tried to be reassuring. "Please don't worry about it. Tests have proved that you can breathe fresh air day and night without its doing any harm to the body."

"You're just saying that because you don't want me to leave," I said. "Nobody who has lived in a major city can stand fresh air for a very long time. He has no tolerance for it."

"Well, if the fresh air bothers you, why don't you put a handkerchief over your nose and breathe through your mouth?"

"Okay, I'll try it. If I'd known I was coming to a place that had nothing but fresh air, I would have brought a surgical mask to protect myself."

We drove in silence. About fifteen minutes later he asked, "How do you feel now?"

"Okay, I guess, but I miss sneezing."

"We don't sneeze too much here," the man admitted. "Do they sneeze a lot where you come from?"

"All the time. There are some days when that's all you do."

"Do you enjoy it?"

"Not necessarily, but if you don't sneeze, you'll die. Let me ask you something. How come there's no air pollution around here?"

"Flagstaff can't seem to attract industry. I guess we're really behind the times. The only smoke we get is when the Indians start signaling each other. But the wind seems to blow it away."

The fresh air was making me feel dizzy. "Isn't there a diesel bus around here that I could breathe into for a couple of hours?"

"Not at this time of day. I might be able to find a truck for you."

We found a truck driver, and slipped him a five-dollar bill, and he let me put my head near his exhaust pipe for a half hour. I was immediately revived and able to give my speech.

Nobody was as happy to leave Flagstaff as I was. My next stop was Los Angeles, and when I got off the plane, I took one big deep breath of the smog-filled air, my eyes started to water, I began to sneeze, and I felt like a new man again.

A coal-fired electrical power plant on the Mississippi River. H. Armstrong Roberts, Inc., Chicago. Photograph by H. Abernathy.

Developing Comprehension Skills

1. The odor in Flagstaff, Arizona, seemed strange to Buchwald. Why?

2. How did Buchwald finally ease his dizziness and discomfort?

3. When the narrator arrived in Los Angeles, how did he react to the smog? Why would this air seem natural to him?

4. What is Art Buchwald making fun of in this essay?

5. Which part of Buchwald's essay do you find funniest? Why?

Reading Literature: Nonfiction

1. **Understanding Essays.** An **essay** is a short, personal piece of nonfiction that expresses one person's ideas or opinions about a topic. Essays that have a serious tone and a formal structure are called **formal** essays. Essays that are lighter and more casual are **informal** essays. Which type of essay is Buchwald's? What details led you to your conclusion?

2. **Identifying Satire.** Writing that criticizes a subject by the use of humor or wit is called **satire**. The aim of satire is to make people aware of a situation or problem. In your opinion, is satire an effective method of pointing out a problem? Why or why not?

3. **Understanding Irony.** Irony, as you know, is the contrast between what is expected and what actually happens. In "Fresh Air Will Kill You," for example, it is ironic that the narrator nearly chokes on fresh air. Explain the irony of these humorous statements:

   a. Smog, which was once the big attraction of Los Angeles . . .

   b. If I'd known I was coming to a place that had nothing but fresh air, I would have brought a surgical mask. . . .

   c. I took one deep breath of the smog-filled air, my eyes started to water, I began to sneeze, and I felt like a new man again.

   Find three other sentences in which the humor is ironic.

4. **Appreciating Dialogue.** Dialogue is written conversation between two or more characters. Most of "Fresh Air Will Kill You" is written as a dialogue between the writer and his host in Flagstaff, Arizona. How do you react differently to a dialogue than you would to a simple explanation of the problem? Do you think that a dialogue is an effective way to present the topic?

5. **Identifying Theme.** Even though Buchwald's essay is humorous, it takes a serious stand on an important issue. In your opinion, what is the theme of Buchwald's essay? Find the sentence that you think best sums up the main idea of the essay.

Developing Vocabulary Skills

Finding Meaning from Word Parts and Context Clues. Decide on the meaning of each underlined word below. Use your knowledge of word parts and context clues. Write the meaning of the word. Then tell whether you used context clues, word parts, or both to figure out the meaning.

1. Smog . . . can now be found all over the country . . . and people are getting so used to polluted air that it's very difficult for them to breathe anything else.

2. My host, sensing this, tried to be <u>reassuring</u>. "Please don't worry about it."

3. No calendar: Same as an <u>interstate</u> pit-stop.

4. One calendar: <u>Preprocessed</u> food assembled in New Jersey.

5. To the rider of back roads, nothing shows the <u>tone</u>, the voice of a small town, more quickly than the breakfast grill or the five-thirty tavern.

6. In a land of quince jelly, apple butter, apricot jam, blueberry preserves, pear <u>conserves</u>, and lemon marmalade, you always get grape jelly.

Developing Writing Skills

1. **Analyzing the Classification of a Selection.** In "Fresh Air Will Kill You," Art Buchwald seems to mix fact with fiction. Look over the essay and decide what is true and what is made up by Buchwald. Consider the purpose of this essay. Then write a paragraph explaining why the selection is classified as nonfiction.

2. **Writing an Informal Essay.** An environmental problem is anything affecting the air, land, or water in a negative way. It may deal with human or animal life, pollution, or the loss of natural resources. Write an essay expressing your viewpoint on an environmental problem.

   Pre-Writing. Choose an environmental issue that concerns you. You might consider endangered species, water pollution, or chemical dumping. Use the *Readers' Guide* to find three articles on the topic. Read these articles carefully and take notes on important facts. Then organize your notes. You might use the following method:

   a. In one paragraph, explain the environmental problem.

   b. In a second paragraph, explain the causes of the problem.

   c. In a third paragraph, explain how the problem might be solved.

   Writing. Keep your audience in mind as you write. Use information and language that is appropriate for them. Use facts to support each main idea.

   Revising. Consider these questions as you revise your essay:

   a. Have I explained the problem and the effects clearly?

   b. Have I discussed the causes of the problem?

   c. Have I stated my feelings strongly?

   d. Have I presented a workable solution to the problem?

   If necessary, clarify your stand and your main points.

3. **Writing a Dialogue.** Art Buchwald uses humorous dialogue in "Fresh Air Will Kill You." Write your own dialogue to highlight an important issue. Your dialogue, for instance, may be between two characters in one of the following situations:

   a child who watches a lot of TV and a friend who doesn't

   a police officer and a rookie on their first day together walking their beat

   a pair of elderly Americans in a nursing home

   You may make your dialogue humorous if you wish.

Reading Graphs. In his essay, Art Buchwald mentions that Flagstaff has an altitude of "about seven thousand miles above sea level." The graph below shows the actual altitude of Flagstaff, as well as six other cities in the United States. Follow these guidelines when reading a graph for information:

1. Read the title to know what the graph is about.

2. Look for a key to abbreviations.

3. Read the headings on the top, bottom, and sides of the graph.

4. Find the information you need by locating the point where the vertical and horizontal columns meet.

Altitude of United States Cities

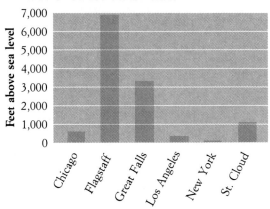

What is the actual altitude of Flagstaff? Which of the seven cities has the highest altitude? the second highest? the lowest? Does the graph give you enough information to tell which city in the U.S. has the highest altitude? How could you find this?

At the Funeral

MARK TWAIN

Mark Twain presents his own special set of rules for how to act at a funeral. As you read, try to decide why he would put together such a strange list.

Do not criticize the person in whose honor the entertainment is given.

Make no remarks about his equipment. If the handles are plated, it is best to seem to not observe it.

If the odor of the flowers is too oppressive for your comfort, remember that they were not brought there for you and that the person for whom they were brought suffers no inconvenience from their presence.

Listen, with as intense an expression of attention as you can command, to the official statement of the character and history of the person in whose honor the entertainment is given. If these statistics should seem to fail to tally with the facts, in places, do not nudge your neighbor or press your foot upon his toes, or manifest, by any other sign, your awareness that taffy is being distributed.

If the official hopes expressed concerning the person in whose honor the entertainment is given are known by you to be oversized, let it pass politely—do not interrupt.

Cosmos, 1957, BEN SHAHN. Copyright © 1985 Estate of Ben Shahn/V.A.G.A., New York.

At the moving passages, be moved—but only according to the degree of your intimacy with the parties giving the entertainment, or with the party in whose honor the entertainment is given. Where a blood relation sobs, an intimate friend should choke up, a distant acquaintance should sigh, a stranger should merely fumble sympathetically with his handkerchief. Where the occasion is military, the emotions should be graded according to military rank, the highest officer present taking precedence in emotional violence, and the rest modifying their feelings according to their position in the service.

Do not bring your dog.

Developing Comprehension Skills

1. According to Mark Twain, how can a person decide how much emotion to show at a funeral?

2. Twain also gives advice about how to listen to the speeches made about the deceased person. He advises, "do not . . . manifest, by any other sign, your awareness that taffy is being distributed." What did he mean?

3. "If the official hopes . . . are known by you to be oversized," Twain says, "let it pass. . ." What are these "official hopes"?

4. What do you think is the most worthwhile advice Twain gives?

5. Do you think that Twain means for any of his rules to be taken seriously? Explain.

Reading Literature: Nonfiction

1. **Understanding Humorous Essays.** In "At the Funeral," Mark Twain makes readers laugh about funerals. The laughter is aimed at showing readers the foolishness of funeral customs.

   What does Twain find ridiculous about the funeral service itself? about the casket and flowers? about the mourners' behavior? Do you think this essay could be classified as satire? Why or why not?

2. **Identifying Tone.** Tone, as you know, is a writer's attitude toward the subject. As Mark Twain begins to set forth his rules, his tone appears to be serious. Quickly, however, it becomes clear that his tone is not what it seemed to be. What lets you know that Twain's tone is not really serious?

3. **Recognizing Understatement.** The opposite of exaggeration is **understatement**. It is a figure of speech in which the writer says less than he or she actually means. For example, to refer to icy waters as "a little chilly" would be understatement. When there is a great contrast between what is said and what is meant, the result can be humorous.

   Explain this understatement from "At the Funeral": "If the odor of the flowers is too oppressive for your comfort, remember that . . . the person for whom they were brought suffers no inconvenience from their presence." Explain how this is an example of understatement.

4. **Appreciating Style.** Style refers to a writer's special way of expressing himself or herself. Mark Twain's style is marked by a great deal of wit and humor. To create humor, Twain uses language in fresh, unexpected ways. For example, Twain refers to the funeral as "the entertainment." Find two more examples of Twain's unexpected use of language. How do these phrases add to the humor of the essay?

Developing Vocabulary Skills

Learning About Greek Roots. On page 309 you studied Greek root words. Here are some other commonly used Greek roots:

Root	Meaning	Example
ortho	right, straight	orthodontist
pathos	suffering, disease	pathetic
therme	heat	thermal
metron	measure	meter
logos	thought	logical

Find the Greek root or roots in the following words. Give the meaning of the root and the meaning of the word.

biologist	orthopedic
pathology	thermometer
logic	autobiography
biographer	unorthodox

Developing Writing Skills

1. **Understanding the Author.** It is sometimes possible to tell a great deal about a writer from the way he or she writes. The subject matter of the writing can also tell you something about the person. What conclusions might you draw about Twain after reading "At the Funeral"? Write a paragraph in which you state your ideas about the man. Support your conclusions with evidence from this or other Twain stories.

2. **Writing a Humorous Essay.** Develop your own set of humorous rules for one of the following:
   a. how to win a game gracefully
   b. how to avoid chores
   c. how to impress your friends.

   Pre-Writing. Think of some of the more foolish ways people behave in each of the situations listed above. List them. Also list a few examples of each type of behavior.

   Writing. When writing your rules, try to keep a "serious" tone. Then add humor by using unexpected language or by combining different styles of language.

   Revising. Check to see that the tone of your essay is the same throughout. Have another person read your rules to see if the humor you intended comes through.

Developing Skills in Study and Research

Using Audio-Visual Resources. Some libraries have collections of films, videocassettes, and recordings. These may be listed in a file or catalog of their own. Ask your librarian about the audio-visual resources at your library. See if the library has a recording of selected examples of Mark Twain's nonfiction. You might, for example, find a copy of Hal Holbrook's famous recording *Mark Twain Tonight*. Listen to a selection from the recording you find. What was your reaction to the reading? Do you think the actor did a good job of re-creating Twain's humor, personality, and style?

The Fraudulent Ant

MARK TWAIN

In this humorous essay, Mark Twain makes fun of the humble ant. As you read, try to figure out why Twain would choose the tiny ant as his target.

It seems to me that in the matter of intellect the ant is strangely overrated. During many summers, now, I have watched him, when I ought to have been in better business, and I have not yet come across a living ant that seemed to have any more sense than a dead one. I refer to the ordinary ant, of course; I have had no experience of those wonderful African ones which vote, keep drilled armies, hold slaves, and dispute about religion. Those ants may be all that the naturalist paints them, but I am persuaded that the average ant is a sham. I admit his industry, of course; he is the hardest working creature in the world—when anybody is looking—but his leather-headedness is the point I make against him.

He goes out foraging, he makes a capture, and then what does he do? Go home? No. He doesn't know where home is. His home may be only three feet away—no matter, he can't find it. His capture is generally something which can be of no use to himself or anybody else; it is usually seven times bigger than it ought to be. He hunts out the awkwardest place to take hold of it; he lifts it bodily in the air, and starts; not toward home, but in the opposite direction; not calmly and wisely, but with a frantic haste. He fetches up against a pebble, and instead of going around it, he climbs over it backwards dragging his booty after him, tumbles down on the other side, jumps up in a passion, kicks the dust off his clothes, moistens his hands, grabs his property viciously, yanks it this way, then that, shoves it ahead of him a moment, turns tail and lugs it after him another moment, gets madder and madder, then presently hoists it into the air and goes tearing away in an entirely new direction.

At the end of half an hour, he fetches up within six inches of the place he started from and lays his burden down. Now he wipes the sweat from his brow and then marches aimlessly off, in as violent a hurry as ever. He traverses a good deal of zigzag country and by and by stumbles on his same booty again. He does not remember ever seeing it before; he looks around to see which is not the way home, grabs his bundle and starts; he goes through the same

Leaf cutter ant. Robert and Linda Mitchell, Lubbock, Texas.

adventures he had before and finally stops to rest.

A friend comes along. Evidently the friend remarks that a last year's grasshopper leg is a very noble acquisition and contracts to help him freight it home. They take hold of opposite ends of that grasshopper leg and begin to tug with all their might in opposite directions. presently they take a rest and confer together. They decide that something is wrong; they can't make out what. Each accuses the other of being an obstructionist. They warm up, and the dispute ends in a fight. They lock themselves together and chew each other's jaws for a while; then they roll and tumble on the ground till one loses a horn or a leg and has to haul off for repairs. They make up and go to work again in the same old insane way, but the crippled ant is at a disadvantage. Tug as he may, the other one drags off the booty and him at the end of it.

By and by, when that grasshopper leg has been dragged all over the same old ground once more, it is finally dumped at about the spot where it originally lay. The two perspiring ants inspect it thoughtfully and decide that dried grasshopper legs are a poor sort of property after all; and then each starts off in a different direction to see if he can't find an old nail or something else that is heavy enough to afford entertainment and at the same time is valueless enough to make an ant want to own it.

The Fraudulent Ant 443

I once saw an ant go through such a performance as this with a dead spider of fully ten times his own weight, which he finally left in the middle of the road to be confiscated by any other fool of an ant that wanted him. I measured the ground which this fool had traversed, and arrived at the conclusion that what he had accomplished inside of twenty minutes would constitute some such job as this—relatively speaking—for a man; to wit, to strap two eight-hundred-pound horses together, carry them eighteen hundred feet, mainly over (not around) boulders averaging six feet high, and in the course of the journey climb up and jump from the top of one precipice like Niagara, and three high steeples; and then put the horses down, in an exposed place, without anybody to watch them, and go off and indulge in some other fool task.

Science has discovered that the ant does not lay up anything for winter use. He does not work, except when people are looking, and only then when an observer has a green, naturalistic look and seems to be taking notes. He cannot stroll around a stump and find his way home again. This amounts to idiocy. His much admired industry is but a vanity, since he never goes home with anything he starts with. This disposes of the last remnant of his reputation and wholly destroys his main usefulness as a moral agent.

It is strange, beyond comprehension, that so obvious a humbug as the ant has been able to fool so many nations for so many ages without being found out.

Developing Comprehension Skills

1. What reputation does the ant have? Where did this reputation come from?

2. Why does Mark Twain consider ants "fraudulent"? What does he think dishonest about them?

3. What traits of the ant does Twain make fun of? Do you think his criticisms are justified?

4. Do you think Twain is really as critical of the ant as he appears to be? If not, what do you think his purpose was in writing the essay?

Reading Literature: Nonfiction

1. **Identifying Satire.** Satire, as you know, combines criticism with humor. As he makes fun of the ant, Twain also satirizes human society. Reread the essay. Which descriptions of the ant might apply to humans as well?

2. **Appreciating Description.** Description is writing that helps a reader to picture scenes, events, or characters. Twain uses detailed descriptions in "The Fraudulent Ant." For example, in paragraphs two through five,

Twain describes a typical ant's bumbling pursuit of his "booty." Reread these paragraphs, and notice the specific details that Twain includes. How does Twain help the reader to visualize the ant's adventures? What purpose does Twain accomplish by carefully describing the ant's mission in such great detail?

3. **Recognizing Personification.** When Mark Twain describes the ant dusting off his clothes and moistening his hands, he is using personification. **Personification** is a technique that gives human traits to a non-human subject. Find three other examples of personification in this essay. How does personification add to the humor?

4. **Appreciating Allusion.** You recall that an **allusion** is a reference to a well-known person, place, event or work of literature. "Science has discovered that the ant does not lay up anything for winter use," Twain says. His statement may be an allusion to a fable, "The Ant and the Grasshopper." This fable tells of an admirable ant who works hard all summer to store up food for winter while the grasshopper plays. How might this fable have given Twain the idea for his essay?

5. **Recognizing Analogy.** An **analogy** is a point-by-point comparison of two somewhat similar things. Analogies sometimes make a point by comparing something new with something familiar. Reread Twain's analogy on page 444 that compares ants hauling a spider to a man carrying horses. What is the point of this analogy? Do you think such a comparison helps you understand the true nature of the ant's feat? How does it add to the humor of the essay?

6. **Recognizing Rhetorical Questions.** A rhetorical question is a question that does not require an answer. It is asked to make people think about a situation. It can also be used to point out a shocking or ridiculous situation. For example, look at the second paragraph of "The Fraudulent Ant." Twain writes, "He goes out foraging, and then what does he do? Go home?" What trait of the ant does the rhetorical question point out? Do you think this rhetorical question helps Twain make his point? Explain your answer.

Developing Vocabulary Skills

Understanding Latin Roots. You have studied some Latin roots on page 309. Here are some others:

Root	Meaning	Example
lumen	light	illuminate
revelare	to disclose	reveal
trudere	to thrust, push	intrude
vigil	awake, watch	vigilant

Read the following sentences from selections in this chapter. Use your knowledge of Latin roots and word parts to determine the meaning of the underlined words. Write each word and its meaning.

1. The truth is that my first sight of the wolf's paw-prints was a <u>revelation</u>.

2. In fact, I was on the point of abandoning my interest in the <u>spectacle</u> until some expert in psychic research happened along. . . .

3. The female was still invisible, and the male had so far relaxed his attitude of <u>vigilance</u>. . . .

4. It would have been a tragedy if my accidental <u>intrusion</u> had unduly disturbed these wolves.

5. They . . . I slowly and <u>incredulously</u> began to realize, were . . . playing a game of tag.

6. Although her eyes were lovely and her hair beautiful, she had <u>protruding</u> teeth.

7. "You'll never see the money or the young man again," a friend <u>predicted</u> gloomily.

8. Wisps of evening fog below grew <u>luminous</u> in the approaching dark.

Developing Writing Skills

1. **Drawing Conclusions.** How does Mark Twain poke fun at human customs in both "At the Funeral" and "The Fraudulent Ant"? Write one paragraph discussing Twain's message.

   Pre-Writing. Review both essays. List the criticisms Twain makes about people. Decide on the main points you will mention in your paragraph. Jot these down, together with specific examples to illustrate them. Determine the most logical order for presenting your ideas.

   Writing. Write a topic sentence that states your idea about the point Twain is making in his essays. Then follow your writing plan as you write your ideas. When needed, add specific examples from real life to back up Twain's ideas.

   Revising. Study the draft of your paragraph carefully. Does it contain a strong topic sentence? Is the organization clear? Did you include examples to support your ideas? When you are satisfied with the content, proofread your paragraph.

2. **Developing an Argument.** In "The Fraudulent Ant," Mark Twain takes a commonly accepted idea and tries to show that it is false. Think of other commonly held beliefs about people or nature that may be false. Choose one for your subject. You may choose, for example, any common saying such as, "The early bird catches the worm." In three or four paragraphs, try to persuade your audience that the idea is not true. Use personal experiences as evidence. You may also refer to the experiences of others in real life, books, or films to support your argument.

3. **Writing a Letter.** Write a humorous reply to Mark Twain on behalf of the ant population. Defend the honor of the ant by proving Twain's arguments to be false. You may use information from an encyclopedia and books about ants to support your opinion. You may also add humor by making up ridiculous explanations for all ants' behavior that Twain criticizes.

Developing Skills in Speaking and Listening

Using Oral Interpretation. The second and third paragraphs of "The Fraudulent Ant" are uproarious examples of the best of humorous essays. Twain's description emphasizes the ridiculousness of each of the ant's actions. Read these paragraphs aloud, using your voice to convey the tone and humor of Twain's writing. As you read, try to appear relaxed, and maintain eye contact with your audience.

A Loud Sneer for Our Feathered Friends

RUTH McKENNEY

Two sisters are "sentenced" to a horrible summer camp. Read to see how Ruth McKenney and her sister stir up trouble—and laughs.

From childhood, my sister and I have had a well-grounded dislike for our friends the birds. We came to hate them when she was ten and I was eleven. We had been exiled by what we considered an unfeeling family to one of those horrible girls' camps where Indian lore is abundant and the management puts up neatly lettered signs reminding the clients to be Good Sports. From the moment Eileen and I arrived at dismal old Camp Hi-Wah, we were Bad Sports, and we liked it.

We refused to get out of bed when the bugle blew in the morning. We fought against scrubbing our teeth in public to music and sneered when the flag was ceremoniously lowered at sunset. We avoided doing a good deed a day, and complained loudly about the food, which was terrible. We bought some chalk once and wrote all over the Recreation Cabin, "We hate Camp Hi-Wah." It made a wonderful scandal, although unfortunately we were immediately accused of the crime. All the other little campers loved dear old Camp Hi-Wah, which shows you just what kind of people they were.

The first two weeks Eileen and I were at Camp Hi-Wah, we sat in our cabin grinding our teeth at our counselor and writing letters to distant relatives. These letters were, if I say so myself, real masterpieces of double dealing and heartless trickery. In our childish, and we hoped, appealing scrawl, we explained to Great-Aunt Mary Farrel and Second Cousin Joe Murphy that we were having such fun at dear Camp Hi-Wah making Indian pocketbooks.

"We would simply L-O-V-E to make you a pocketbook, dear Aunt Mary," we wrote, "only the leather costs $1 for a small pocketbook or $1.67 for a large size pocketbook, which is much nicer because you can carry more things in it. The rawhide you sew it up with, just exactly the way the Indians did, costs 40 cents more. We burn pictures on the leather but that doesn't cost anything. If we O-N-L-Y had $1 or $1.67 and 40 cents for the rawhide, we could make you the S-W-E-L-L-E-S-T pocketbook."

As soon as we had enough orders for Indian pocketbooks with pictures burned on them, we planned to abscond with the funds sent by our trusting relatives and run away to New York City, where, as we used to explain dramatically to our cabin-mates, we intended to live it up. After a few days, our exciting plans for our immediate future were talked about all over the camp, and admirers came from as far away as Cabin Minnehaha, which was way down at the end of Hiawatha Alley, just to hear us tell about New York and good times.

Fame had its price, however. One of the sweet little girls who lived in our cabin turned out to be such a Good Citizen ("Camp Hi-Wah Girls Learn to Be Good Citizens") that she told our dreadful secret to our counselor. Our mail was impounded for weeks, and worst of all, we actually had to make several Indian pocketbooks with pictures burned on them. My pictures were all supposed to be snakes, although they were pretty blurred. Eileen specialized in what she believed to be the likeness of a werewolf, but Cousin Joe, who had generously ordered three pocketbooks, wrote a nice letter thanking Eileen for his pretty pocketbooks with the pretty pictures of Abraham Lincoln on them. We were terribly disgusted by the whole thing.

It was in this mood that we turned to birds. The handicraft hour at Camp Hi-Wah, heralded by the ten-thirty A.M. bugle, competed for popularity with the bird walks at the same hour. You could, as Eileen said, "name your own poison." After three weeks of burning pictures on leather, we were ready for anything, even birds.

So one hot morning in July, the two McKenney sisters, big and bad and fierce for their age, answered the bird-walk bugle call, leaving the Indian-pocketbook teacher to mourn her two most backward pupils. We were dressed, somewhat reluctantly, to be sure, in the required heavy stockings for poison ivy and brambles, and carried, each of us, in our dirty hands a copy of a guide to bird lore called *Bird Life for Children*.

Bird Life for Children was a volume that all the Good Citizens in Camp Hi-Wah pretended to find fascinating. Eileen and I thought it was stupefyingly dull.

Bird Life for Children was full of horrid pictures in full color of robins and pigeons and redbirds. Under each picture was a ridiculous paragraph describing how the bird in question spent his spare time, what he ate, and why children should love him. Eileen and I hated the book so, we were quite prepared to despise birds when we started off that morning on our first bird walk. We had no idea of what we were going to suffer that whole awful summer, because of our feathered friends.

In the first place, since we had started off making leather pocketbooks, we were three weeks behind the rest of the Hi-Wah bird-lovers. They had been tramping through blackberry bushes for days and days and had already got the hang of the more ordinary bird life around camp.

On that first bird walk, Eileen and I trotted anxiously along behind the little band

Untitled (Woodpecker Habitat), 1946,
JOSEPH CORNELL. Mr. and Mrs. E. A. Bergman
Collection, Chicago.

of serious-minded bird-lovers, trying desperately to see, or at least hear, even one bird, even one robin. But alas, while other bird-walkers saw, or pretended to see—for Eileen and I never believed them for a moment—all kinds of hummingbirds and hawks and owls, we never saw or heard a single, solitary feathered friend, not one.

By the time we staggered into camp for lunch, with stubbed toes, scratched faces, and tangled hair, Eileen and I were soured for life on birds. Our bird logs, which we carried strapped to our belts along with the Guide, were still blank, while all the other little bird-lovers had lengthy entries, such as "Saw redbird at 10:37 A.M. Molting."

Still, for the next three days we stayed honest and suffered. For three terrible mornings we endured being dolts among bird-walkers, the laughingstock of Camp

Hi-Wah. After six incredibly tiresome hours, our bird logs were still blank. Then we cracked under the strain. The fourth morning we got up feeling grim but determined. We sharpened our pencils before we started off on the now familiar trail through the forest.

When we got well into the woods and Mary Mahoney, the premier bird-walker of Camp Hi-Wah, had already spotted and logged her first redbird of the morning, Eileen suddenly stopped dead in her tracks. "Hark!" she cried. She had read that somewhere in a book. "Quiet!" I echoed instantly.

The bird-walkers drew to a halt respectfully and stood in silence. They stood very still. It was not good form even to whisper while fellow bird-walkers were logging a victim. After quite a long time the Leader, whose feet were flat and often hurt her, whispered impatiently, "Haven't you got him logged yet?"

"You drove him away," Eileen replied sternly. "It was a yellow-billed cuckoo."

"A yellow-billed cuckoo?" cried the Leader incredulously.

"Well," Eileen said modestly, "at least *I* think it was." Then, with many a pretty hesitation and thoughtful pause, she recited the features of the yellow-billed cuckoo, as recorded in *Bird Life for Children*.

The leader was terribly impressed. Later on that morning I logged a kingfisher, a red-headed woodpecker, and a yellow-bellied sapsucker, which was all I could remember at the moment. Each time, I kept

the bird-walkers standing around for the longest time, gaping into blank space and listening desperately to the rustle of the wind in the trees and the creak of their shoes as they went from one foot to another.

In a few days Eileen and I were the apple of our Leader's eye, the modest heroes of the Camp Hi-Wah bird walks. Naturally, there were nasty children around camp, former leading bird-walkers, who spread foul rumors up and down Hiawatha Alley that Eileen and I were frauds. We soon stopped this ugly talk, however. Eileen was the pitcher, and a very good one, too, of the Red Bird ball team and I was the first base. When Elouise Pritchard, the worst gossip in Cabin Sitting Bull, came up to bat, she got a pitched ball right in the stomach. Of course it was only a soft ball, but Eileen could throw it pretty hard. To vary this routine, I tagged Mary Mahoney, former head bird-walker out at first base, and Mary had a bruise on her thigh for weeks. The rumors stopped abruptly.

We had begun to get pretty bored with logging rare birds when the game took on a new angle. Mary Mahoney and several other bird-walkers began to see the same birds we did on our morning jaunts into the forest. This made us pretty mad, but there wasn't much we could do about it. Next, Mary Mahoney began to see birds we weren't logging. The third week after we joined the Camp Hi-Wah Bird Study Circle, everybody except the poor, dumb Leader and a few backward but honest bird-lovers was logging the rarest birds seen around Camp Hi-Wah in twenty years. Bird walks developed into a race to see who could shout "Hark!" first and keep the rest of the little party in fidgety silence for the next five minutes.

The poor bird-walk Leader was in agony. Her reputation as a bird-lover was in shreds. Her talented pupils were seeing rare birds right and left, while the best she could log for herself would be a few crummy old redbirds and a robin or so. At last our Leader's morale collapsed. It was the day when nearly everybody in the group swore that she saw and heard a bona-fide nightingale.

"Where?" cried our Leader desperately, after the fourth nightingale had been triumphantly logged in the short space of five minutes. Heartless fingers pointed to a vague bush. The Leader strained her honest eyes. No notion of our fraud crossed her innocent, unworldly mind.

"I can't see any nightingale," our Leader cried and burst into tears. Then, full of shame, she sped back to camp, leaving the Camp Hi-Wah bird-lovers to their nightingales and guilty thoughts.

Eileen and I ate a hearty lunch that noon because we thought we would need it. Then we strolled down Hiawatha Alley and hunted up Mary Mahoney.

"We will put the Iron Cross on you if you tell," Eileen started off, as soon as we found Mary.

"What's the Iron Cross?" Mary squeaked, startled out of her usual poise.

"Never mind," I growled. "You'll find out if you tell."

We walked past Cabin Sitting Bull, past the flagpole, into the tall grass beyond the ball field.

"She'll tell," Eileen said finally.

"What'll we do?" I replied mournfully. "They'll try us at campfire tonight."

They did, too. It was terrible. We denied everything, but the Head of Camp sentenced us to no desserts and eight-o'clock bedtime for two weeks. We thought over what to do to Mary Mahoney for four whole days. Nothing seemed sufficiently frightful, but in the end we put the wart curse on her. The wart curse was simple but horrible. We dropped around to Cabin Sitting Bull one evening and in the presence of Mary and her allies we drew ourselves up to our full height and said solemnly in unison, "We put the wart curse on you, Mary Mahoney." Then we stalked away.

We didn't believe for a moment in the wart curse, but we hoped Mary would. At first she was openly contemptuous, but to our delight, on the fourth evening she developed a horrible sty in her eye. We told everybody a sty was a kind of a wart and that we had Mary in our power. The next day Mary broke down and came around to our cabin and apologized in choked accents. She gave Eileen her best hair ribbon and me a little barrel that had a picture of Niagara Falls inside it, if you looked hard enough. We were satisfied.

Developing Comprehension Skills

1. What scheme did Ruth and Eileen develop to escape from Camp Hi-Wah?

2. Why did Ruth and Eileen take up bird walking? When they saw no birds, how did they make the walks more interesting?

3. What did Ruth and Eileen do to stop Mary and other campers from spreading rumors?

4. What did the counselors and other campers learn about Ruth and Eileen?

5. Were the girls harmless pranksters, or do you think they were cruel to the other girls and their leader? Explain your answer.

Reading Literature: Nonfiction

1. **Understanding Essays.** Personal essays take many forms. Ruth McKenney's essay is similar to a short story, except that it is true. How are its plot, setting, and characters similar to those in a short story?

2. **Recognizing Exaggeration.** Humorists can often get their audience to laugh by exaggerating ordinary situations. The McKenney sisters' antics at camp are certainly funny. What incidents do you think may have been exaggerated to make them more humorous?

3. **Appreciating Language.** Another way McKenney creates humor is by using fresh, unexpected language. For example, she often uses words in unusual combinations. Explain what is unexpected about this language from McKenney's essays:

   > wonderful scandal
   > masterpieces of double dealing and heartless trickery
   > a fine vulture

How do each of these examples add to the humor of this personal essay? What do they tell you about the writer who used them?

4. **Analyzing Point of View.** Even a true story can be told in many different ways, depending on the point of view. "A Loud Sneer for Our Feathered Friends" is told in first person from Ruth's point of view. How do you think the story might be told differently by Eileen? by Mary Mahoney? by a third-person narrator? Which incidents would seem most different when told by Eileen or Mary?

5. **Identifying Tone.** Tone, as you know, is a writer's attitude toward the subject. Ruth McKenney's negative language might suggest that she is heartless and nasty. Is this language misleading? Is the actual tone different? What details can you find that reveal Ruth's real personality?

Developing Vocabulary Skills

Adding to Your Knowledge of Root Words. Here are some additional Greek and Latin roots that may help you determine the meaning of unfamiliar words:

Greek Root	Meaning	Example
peri	surrounding	periscope
psyche	soul, mind	psychology
techne	art, science, skill	technical
toxi	poison	toxic

Latin Root	Meaning	Example
fluere	to flow	fluid
ruptus	broken	rupture
solus	alone	solo
verus	true	verify
voluntas	free will	volunteer

The words in the left column are from the selections you have read in this chapter. On your own paper, match them with the definitions on the right by putting the correct letter next to the number of the word.

1. involuntary   a. to break into the middle of something
2. fluently   b. outside the normal boundaries
3. interrupt   c. actual; in fact
4. veritable   d. moving smoothly and easily
5. peripheral   e. having lost control through liquor, drugs, or emotion
6. technique   f. not done by choice
7. intoxicated   g. suddenly or sharply
8. abruptly   h. having to do with the mental process
9. solitary   i. the way in which artistic, scientific, or mechanical work is done
10. psychic   j. lonely; without others

Developing Writing Skills

1. **Writing a Character Sketch.** Imagine what the camp counselors at Camp Hi-Wah would have thought of Ruth McKenney. Write a counselor's report describing Ruth.

   Pre-Writing. Put yourself in the place of Ruth's counselor. Imagine how she might feel about Ruth. Decide whether your character sketch will be objective or subjective. List character traits you have observed in Ruth. Then list the incidents that demonstrate each trait. Group together descriptions that concern the same general trait. Plan your character sketch around these general traits.

   Writing. Begin with a topic sentence that states your general impression of Ruth. Describe each character trait in a paragraph. Use first-person point of view, taking the role of Ruth's counselor. If you are writing objectively, develop each paragraph with facts. Avoid judgment words. If you are writing subjectively, allow feelings to come through by using judgment words and opinions.

   Revising. Ask another person to read your character sketch. Ask the person to see if your writing remains objective or subjective throughout. Ask also if you have used enough examples to support your characterization of Ruth.

2. **Writing a Humorous Essay.** Have you ever been involved in a funny prank? As a child, did you get into mischief? In two or three paragraphs, write about one such funny experience. In the introduction, try to get your readers' attention. Try using fresh language to add to the humor of your writing.

Developing Skills in Critical Thinking

Recognizing the Use of Loaded Language. Ruth McKenney's story of her summer at Camp Hi-Wah is told in a highly subjective manner. Ruth quite purposefully presents every person and situation in the worst possible light. To do this, she uses highly emotional, or loaded, language. What examples of loaded language can you find in the selection? How do they add to the humor of the essay?

Primal Screen

ELLEN GOODMAN

Today the average American family spends about thirty hours a week watching television. What does columnist Ellen Goodman think these viewing habits are doing to American families?

Someday, I would like to see a television series about a family that sits around the set watching a series about a family that sits around the set.

It might not make the Nielsen top ten, but it isn't such a strange idea. Especially when you think about what's going on now.

Night after night, inside the tube, warm and wiggly families spend their prime time "communicating" like crazy and "solving problems" together like mad. Meanwhile, outside the tube, real families sit and wait for a commercial break just to talk to each other.

About the only subject that never comes up before our glazed eyes is what the medium does to our family life. But, I suppose we already know that.

According to a recent Gallup Poll, television comes out as a major heavy in our family lives. On the scale of problems, TV didn't rate as bad as inflation, but it ran neck-and-neck with unemployment.

According to a recent Roper Poll, it even causes fights. When people were asked what husbands and wives argued about, money was the champion. But television was a strong contender. Considering how much time we spend in front of the tube, that may not be such a shock.

To a certain extent, we blame the programs. In the Gallup Poll, for example, people worried most about the overemphasis on sex and violence. Surely half of those fights between husbands and wives must be about the more fundamental issue of turning it off.

Deep down below our poll-taking consciousness, we know that the worst aspect of our addiction isn't what's on TV, but how long the TV is on. We can't help but be aware of what happens when we spend more time facing the screen than facing each other.

In that same Gallup Poll, a large number of us said that the way to improve family life is by sharing—sharing family needs, recreational activities and chores. But when you are watching, you aren't doing. The only experience you share is a vicarious one.

Still Life #31, 1963, TOM WESSELMANN. Collection of Mrs. Melvin Hirsch, Los Angeles. Courtesy of Sidney Janis Gallery, New York.

I am absolutely convinced that the average wife feels tuned out by the twelfth consecutive weekend sports event because she is being tuned out. The average kid develops that distant, slack-jawed, hypnotic stare because he or she is hooked.

In the same way, the people who spend night after night in front of the tube should not worry about it. They've become an audience and not a family. Television simply presents us with one model of family life. Watching it makes us fit another model.

But the striking thing in all of this research about how we feel and behave is the role of choice. On the one hand, we have real anxiety about what TV is doing to us. On the other hand, we let it happen.

We choose to turn it on and each other off. We choose peace and quiet when we let the kids watch TV instead of running around the living room. We choose to "relax" in the semi-comatose slump.

The average viewing time of the American child between six and sixteen years of age is twenty to twenty-four hours a week. A large percentage of parents place no restrictions on either the number of hours watched or the type of program viewed.

At the very least, we behave as if we were powerless to wrench each other away.

I grant you that there are a lot of things that touch on our families that are totally out of our individual control. We can't regulate foreign affairs. We can't set the price for oil. We have about as great a chance of controlling inflation as we do of capping Mount St. Helens.

But a television set has a dial and a plug. And we have hands. It is absurd to let our feelings of helplessness in the world start creeping into our private lives.

Just once, we ought to create a private show about a real-life family that kicked the habit.

Developing Comprehension Skills

1. What effect does television watching have on the family, according to Goodman?

2. What does research show about Americans' attitudes toward television programming? about their viewing habits? How do these attitudes contradict each other?

3. Goodman ends with a plea for action. What does she urge Americans to do?

4. Do you think that Goodman's criticisms are fair? Do you agree with her that television has a negative effect on families? Why?

Reading Literature: Nonfiction

1. **Evaluating Support for Opinions.** Writers often use the essay form to present and explain an opinion. An essay is successful if the reader decides that the opinion expressed is a sound one. A sound opinion is one that is well supported by facts.

   What is Goodman's opinion about television and the American family? Find facts in the essay that support this opinion. Does Goodman convince you that her opinion is a sound one? List several facts that she uses to support her opinions.

2. **Analyzing the Introduction.** Goodman captures her readers' interest with a humorous introduction. Later in the essay, she becomes more serious. Do you think that humor is a good way to introduce this subject? Why or why not?

3. **Recognizing Contrast.** Contrast is the technique of emphasizing one thing by comparing it to something very different. Many times, Ellen Goodman makes her point by using contrast. For example, she contrasts television watching with more constructive activities a family could be sharing. Explain the contrasts in these sentences:

   a. They've become an audience and not a family.
   b. We choose to turn it on and each other off.
   c. When you are watching, you aren't doing.

What point is Goodman trying to make with each of these contrasts?

4. **Appreciating Repetition.** Ellen Goodman often uses repetition to help make her writing striking and memorable. She repeats the same word or phrase at the beginning of different sentences. Locate the use of repetition in this paragraph:

> We choose to turn it on and each other off. We choose peace and quiet when we let the kids watch TV instead of running around the living room. We choose to 'relax.'

What effect does the repetition have? Find another example of repetition in the essay.

Developing Vocabulary Skills

Recognizing Word Families. Many words in English are related to each other. They are parts of word families that are built on the same root word. Each sentence below has an underlined word with a Greek or Latin root. Write the word on your paper, underline the root, and give the meaning of the root. Then create a word family for the word by writing as many related words as you can.

Example:
Mark Twain implies that bringing your dog to a funeral might be disruptive.
disruptive—to break

rupture   interruption
interrupt   corrupt
corruption   abrupt

1. Although he has never found one, William Least Heat Moon predicts that a seven-calendar cafe would serve superb food.

2. Art Buchwald cannot envision a world without smog.

3. In "The Fraudulent Ant," Twain tries to discredit the idea that ants are intelligent.

4. The McKenny sisters claimed they had seen many rare and spectacular birds.

Developing Writing Skills

1. **Analyzing Tone.** What tone does Ellen Goodman use in her article? Does it stay the same throughout, or does it change? Write a paragraph that analyzes the tone of the essay. Use examples from the essay itself to support your answer.

2. **Supporting an Opinion.** What effect does television have on people today? Write a few paragraphs supporting your opinion.

    Pre-Writing. To help clarify your opinion, discuss one or more of these issues with your friends or family:

    Does television provide inexpensive and enjoyable entertainment?
    Does television help to educate people?
    Does television make people violent?
    Do television commercials make people feel dissatisfied with themselves?

State your opinion about one of these questions. List the reasons that led you to that opinion. Then write down specific facts and examples for each point you are trying to make. You may find that you need to do research to provide solid facts.

   Writing. Write an attention-getting introduction. You may wish to use an anecdote or startling statistic. Devote one paragraph to each main reason. Give examples and facts to support each reason. End with a conclusion that includes a suggestion to improve the situation.

Revising. Ask a friend to act as your editor. See if this person thinks your introduction is attention-getting and your arguments convincing.

Developing Skills in Study and Research

1. **Reading Tables.** Tables are listings of facts. These facts are often listed as numbers. Usually a table has several columns with headings at the top and sides. These headings tell you what kind of information you can find.

   To read a table, notice the title and the headings. To locate specific information in a table, find the headings at the top and at the side that reflect the information you need. The spot where these two columns meet should provide you with the facts you need. Here is a table from the *1985 Information Please Almanac* that shows the television viewing habits of various age groups:

Weekly TV Viewing by Age (in hours and minutes)	Time per week 1982	1983
Women 18–34 years old	26 h 56 min	30 h 19 min
Women 35–54	33 h 23 min	33 h 23 min
Women 55 and over	37 h 14 min	41 h 13 min
Men 18–34	24 h 39 min	28 h 30 min
Men 35–54	26 h 56 min	27 h 50 min
Men 55 and over	32 h 59 min	35 h 53 min
Female Teens	21 h 20 min	24 h 16 min
Male Teens	23 h 40 min	25 h 17 min
Children 6–11	24 h 00 min	24 h 50 min
Children 2–5	25 h 29 min	27 h 09 min
Total Persons	**28 h 22 min**	**30 h 47 min**

   Source: A. C. Nielsen Company

Who watches more TV, male teens or female teens? Which age group watches the least TV, according to the table? Which age group watches the most? How many hours do children five years and under watch each week? Which age group has the smallest increase in viewing time for the two years given? Go to the library and find the most current TV viewing statistics. Compare them to the table. What conclusions can you draw?

2. **Using the SQ3R Study Method.** The SQ3R study method is a good way to understand and remember new written material. SQ3R involves these steps:

   Survey. Scan the selection to get a general idea of what it's about. Read the introduction and the conclusion. Notice the title and subheadings. Read the introduction and summary.

   Question. Prepare questions. Cover what you think you should be able to answer when you finish your reading. Use study questions presented at the end of the selection. You may also make up questions by turning the subheads into questions.

   Read. Look for answers to the questions. Find main ideas and supporting details in each section. Examine topic sentences.

   Recite. Say your answers out loud, and make notes on them. Write down other important points.

   Review. Quickly skim your notes and main points in the selection. Look up answers to questions you are unsure of.

   Apply the SQ3R method to the next selection, "Your Chances for the Presidency."

Articles

Articles are probably the most familiar kind of nonfiction. Articles are fairly brief reports that often appear in newspapers and magazines. They can deal with almost any subject in either a humorous or serious way. Articles entertain as well as inform. The articles in this section cover a wide variety of subjects. Each contains a wealth of information, some humorous, some serious. As you read, see if the main purpose of each article is to inform or entertain.

The Mt. Kilauea Volcano, Hawaii, April 1983. Copyright © 1984 Eric Meola.

Your Chances for the Presidency

RICHARD ARMOUR

If you're tall, you may be one step closer to the Presidency, says Richard Armour. What other "important" traits does it take to become President of the United States?

People sometimes (though not very often, I'll admit) ask me why I did not become President of the United States. I have a ready answer for them.

I point out that, while I have the legal qualifications to be President (I was born in the United States and am over thirty-five), I could not possibly attain that office. The Constitution is *for* me, but tradition is *against* me. You see, I am an only child, and no person who was an only child has ever been elected President. The closest anyone came to it was Franklin Roosevelt, who had a half-brother. Thus he barely made it.

So if you aspire to become President, I hope you are not an only child, as I am. In fact, history indicates that it helps to come from a very large family. Twenty-five of our Presidents came from families of five or more children, seven came from families of ten or more children, and the record is a tie between Madison and Benjamin Harrison, both of whom came from families of twelve children. Apparently it does something for you to have the companionship and the competition of a large number of brothers and sisters.

You had also better plan to get married. Only two Presidents went into the White House as bachelors, Cleveland and Buchanan, and only Buchanan remained a bachelor.

Height Helps

It is a great help to be tall. At a time when the average height for males was several inches shorter than today, our first President, George Washington, was six feet two. Our third President, Thomas Jefferson, was a slight bit taller—six feet two and a half. Our tallest President, as you know, was Lincoln, who stood six feet four and in his tall stovepipe hat must have seemed even taller. In addition, thirteen other Presidents have been six feet or more, and with few exceptions the taller of the two major candidates has been the winner.

Don't give up, though, if you are really short. James Madison made it, and he was only five feet four. Van Buren and Benjamin

Presidential campaign memorabilia. H. Armstrong Roberts, Inc., Chicago.

Harrison were five feet six, and both Adamses were five feet seven. Nonetheless, height seems to help, perhaps by making the candidate impressive, able to be singled out in a crowd, and to be looked up to in more ways than one.

As for weight, there has been great variety, all the way from Madison, who weighed a mere 100 pounds, to Taft, who weighed nearly 350—and once got stuck in the bathtub in the White House and had to be pried out. So I guess you can weigh just about whatever you wish—or whatever you can't help weighing, whether you wish it or not.

Choose the Right Career

You may not be able to do much about the number of your brothers and sisters or your height, but you can pick the career that, according to history, has given us far more Presidents than any other. That career is law. Out of thirty-eight Presidents in thirty-nine Presidencies (Grover Cleveland throws off the count by having been elected twice, with Benjamin Harrison in between), twenty-six were lawyers.

Political experience is of course good preparation for the Presidency. Eight Presidents served in the House of Representatives, six served in the Senate, and eleven served in both the House and Senate. Of the thirty-nine Presidents, only fifteen had no service whatsoever in the Congress. Aside from national office, many Presidents got their political experience as governors, mayors, and in various municipal or state offices. It would seem the natural road to the White House to be in some sort of public service.

How about sports? Taft, Wilson, Harding, Coolidge, Eisenhower, and Ford were among those who went in for (or out for) golf. Teddy Roosevelt, who built himself up with dumbbells from a puny boyhood, took up boxing. Many Presidents went fishing, and a large number favored horseback riding. You know that Kennedy liked touch football, but you may not know that Teddy Roosevelt went in for jujitsu, Hoover for the medicine ball, and Benjamin Harrison and Teddy Roosevelt for hunting. Gerald Ford, once a star football lineman for the University of Michigan, is an avid swimmer and skier.

Music Strikes a Sour Note

Oddly, very few of the Presidents could play a musical instrument. Jefferson and Tyler played the violin, Truman and Nixon the piano, Coolidge the harmonica, and Harding the alto horn and the cornet. From this it will be seen that there were just two two-President instruments, the violin and the piano, and one two-instrument President, Harding.

But times change, styles change. History goes in cycles. The "in" becomes "out" and the "out" becomes "in." What I have been describing has to do with the past, and maybe a little of the present. If you model yourself on past Presidents (a tall, married lawyer from a large family who likes sports but can't play a musical instrument), you may not be what the American public will want by the time you are ready to run for the highest office in the land. Someone may come along who catches the national imagination because she is five feet two—an only child who hates sports and plays in an orchestra.

Developing Comprehension Skills

1. What family size has been common to many Presidents? What physical size?

2. What career did most Presidents choose before they were in office?

3. What was the most popular hobby of American Presidents?

4. What does Richard Armour suggest about future Presidents? Will they follow the pattern set in the past?

5. Do you think Armour really believes that matching certain statistics helps a person become President? Do you think that there could be some sound reasons why so many Presidents shared certain characteristics?

Reading Literature: Nonfiction

1. **Understanding Articles.** An **article** is a brief essay that informs or persuades. An article is usually found in a book, magazine, or newspaper. An article is often more objective than a personal or humorous essay. It presents factual information rather than opinions.

   In what way is "Your Chances for the Presidency" more objective than the other essays you have read? Are there any personal touches, where the writer's personality or feelings are visible? What effect does this personal writing have on the article?

2. **Analyzing Structure.** Armour's article contains an easily identified introduction, body, and conclusion. The introduction presents the topic of becoming President. How does Armour capture the reader's attention in the introduction? The body, or main part of the essay, explains certain traits that Presidents have had in common. Which trait does each body paragraph discuss? The conclusion of the article is the last paragraph. Armour not only summarizes the main point, but also presents a thought-provoking idea. With what idea does Armour leave his readers?

3. **Recognizing Satire.** Satire, as you know, is writing that criticizes something in a humorous way. There is an element of satire in Richard Armour's article. He shows how people can misuse statistics to "prove" things that aren't necessarily true. What does Armour "prove" about Presidents that isn't necessarily true? What qualifications for becoming President does Armour *not* mention? Do you think these are more important than those Armour does mention?

Developing Vocabulary Skills

Forming Words by Joining Word Parts. Look at the example for the vocabulary exercise on page 457. Notice that the family of words related to *disruptive* was made by adding prefixes and/or suffixes to a Latin root. The following lists provide you with root words, prefixes, and suffixes. Combine parts from both columns to make new words. You may wish to add both a prefix and a suffix to a root. Remember that the spelling of a part may change when it is combined with another part. Give the meaning of each new word.

Example: dict + pre = predict

Root Words	Prefixes/Suffixes
dict	-able/-ible
spect	-im-/-in-
mis	pre-
cred	dis-
vis	-or
	-ation

Developing Writing Skills

1. **Comparing and Contrasting Personal Traits.** What are your chances for the Presidency? In an essay, explain your chances based on the qualifications that Armour mentions. Conclude by telling whether or not you would like to be President. You might organize your essay by writing one paragraph of comparison and one paragraph of contrast.

2. **Writing a Campaign Commercial.** Campaign commercials try to persuade viewers that a candidate is qualified for a certain position. Imagine you are running for some school or public office. Write the script for your own sixty-second radio commercial.

    Pre-Writing. Discuss the qualifications for the office you are running for with family members, teachers, or friends. Another source of ideas may be newspapers, news magazines, and television interview programs. List six or eight of the most important qualifications you can think of. Write personal experiences and accomplishments that prove you have these qualifications.

    Writing. Try to persuade the audience that you are the best candidate. Present facts, but feel free to use loaded, or emotional, language as well.

    Revising. Read your commercial to a classmate. Ask if it is convincing.

Developing Skills in Study and Research

Taking Notes in Outline Form. You have used outlines to organize your ideas before you write. You can also use outlines to help you understand someone else's writing.

Look at this partial outline of "Your Chances for the Presidency." Complete the outline by filling in the remaining ideas.

    I. No only child has ever been President.
    II. Most Presidents are from big families.
    III.
    IV. Most Presidents have been tall.
    V. Presidents have varied in weight.
    VI.
    VII.
    VIII.
    IX. Presidents have played various sports.
    X.

Develop this outline in more detail by adding subpoints under each main heading. Use capital letters to show subpoints. You must include at least two subpoints for each main heading. Here are the subpoints for one main heading:

    II. Most Presidents are from big families.
        A. Twenty-five came from families with five or more children.
        B. Seven came from families with ten or more children.
        C. Two came from families with twelve children.

Developing Skills in Critical Thinking

Recognizing False-Cause Reasoning. When one event happens after another, people may assume that the first event caused the second event. This error in reasoning is called **false-cause reasoning**. Richard Armour intentionally uses false-cause reasoning in this selection. What traits does Armour suggest cause people to vote for a candidate? Think about elections you have witnessed. Is there any evidence that the traits and the election really are related?

The First Basketball Game

RAYMOND P. KAIGHN
As told to Bob Brooks

Basketball did not exist before 1891. Today, it is one of the most popular sports in the world. Read to discover the surprising facts about the origin of the game.

On a cold December day in 1891, our class trotted into the gym at the YMCA Training School in Springfield, Massachusetts, resigned to our daily workout in Swedish gymnastics. We wished these exercises had never slipped by United States Customs. After a season of football, they were mighty boring.

That day we were all set for another dull dose—but we hadn't reckoned on Jim Naismith, the assistant coach, a man as determined as he was imaginative.

Jim had been working for days, trying to figure out a game with the excitement of football but without its danger of injury. Football is dangerous for indoor play because you tackle the man when he's running with the ball. But why, thought Jim, couldn't you tackle the ball instead of tackling the man?

When we came to class that day, Jim pointed out a peach basket at each end of the gym. The baskets were fastened at the base of the balcony running track. Some of us groaned. We were going to play guinea pig, we feared, for another instructor's crazy ideas on winter indoor athletics.

When Jim got through telling us the rules, though, we perked up. He showed us the soccer ball we'd use, and then chose eighteen men to play—nine for each side. I was one of them.

He threw the ball into play from the center, and we all scrambled for it. Equipment, dumbbells, and Indian clubs, stowed around the sides of the gym, tumbled everywhere as we chased the ball. The racket sounded like league night at a bowling alley.

At first every fellow tried madly to throw the ball into the peach baskets, regardless of where he was on the floor. I'm afraid that Jim's hopes of close teamwork didn't pan out in those first minutes of play. "Pass it! Pass it!" he would yell, blowing his whistle to stop the rough play.

As we kept playing the game each day, more teamwork crept into the scrimmages. No doubt it was mostly because of Jim's constant emphasis on passing the ball. "Pass it" became the slogan of the class.

With the game growing more and more popular, we wanted to give it a name. Since the baskets were there, we just got in the habit of calling it basketball—and the name stuck.

The selection of baskets as the goals for this new game was an accident. Jim had wondered what to have the players do with the ball, and finally he decided the ball should be put some place where it would stay. The best idea, he reasoned, was to throw it into a raised box.

So he asked the janitor of the gym to fasten up a couple of old boxes. The janitor couldn't find any and put up two half-bushel peach baskets instead. Jim settled for them, and, without realizing it, chose the principle of his game.

Jim developed thirteen basic rules for that first scrimmage—compared with two hundred fifty rules in present-day basketball. One of these original regulations was that, when the ball went out of bounds, it went to the side that first got hold of it.

This always produced an uproar, with all eighteen men diving after the ball and scattering all the apparatus stacked under the running track. When the ball went into the balcony, we'd stampede up the narrow stairway or climb up over the railing by jumping on each other's shoulders to get at the ball.

Even with these complications, the out-of-bounds regulation wasn't changed until the year 1913.

Most basketball players worry about getting the ball in the basket. Our biggest problem was getting it out of the basket. Since we used a basket with the bottom still in it, the ball—naturally—just sat inside until somebody lifted it out. At first we'd set a ladder against the balcony and have someone climb up each time we made a goal, or else we'd hoist a teammate up on our shoulders to lift it out.

This slowed up the game so much that we began getting the school kids, who jammed the balcony to watch us play, to reach over the railing and throw the ball back to us.

Two years later, a man from a sporting goods company saw the game and devised a heavy cord net basket fastened around an iron hoop. He put a drawcord through a pulley and fastened it to the net. Then the referee just pulled the cord and bounced the ball back through the top of the basket.

Several years afterward, some nameless genius reasoned that it might be more practical for the ball to drop directly through the basket. So an opening was made in the bottom of the net.

Those school kids gave players another headache. They'd often help their favorite team by leaning over the gallery rail to knock a ball in or out of the basket. We kept bawling them out for it, but they didn't stop. So one day Jim put a large square of wooden planking behind the basket. This was the start of our present-day backboard.

At Christmas vacation a few days after that first scrimmage, we all took the basketball idea home with us. Later on, the YMCA began spreading it and has since helped carry the game all over the world. The Springfield gym floor was well below street level, and we'd always have a large crowd of spectators—teachers, sports enthusiasts, and just plain curious people—who'd look through the windows or come in to see us play.

We soon found out just how popular this new game was when girls began playing it. Shortly after that first scrimmage, some teachers from a grade school had watched us from the balcony. They took the game back with them to their school and introduced it to girls.

The number of players in those early days was an up-and-down regulation. In 1894, when basketball was played on all shapes of courts, the number varied with the size of the court. This got confusing when a team played on one court at home, then had to add or subtract from its squad when it played on another court. In 1897, the number was permanently set at five.

At first, the game had two officials—a referee to control the ball and an umpire to control the men.

Sometimes the crowd gave an official more trouble after a game than the players did during the game. One umpire once told Jim Naismith that, whenever he worked a

Dr. James Naismith (2nd row, wearing suit) and the first basketball team, 1891. The Bettmann Archive, New York.

game, he was careful to see that a window in the room where he dressed was left unlatched. Then immediately after the game he could, if necessary, grab his clothes and leave unnoticed.

The fouls were simple. You couldn't shoulder, hold, push, trip, or strike an opponent; you couldn't bat the ball with your fist though you could with your hands; and you couldn't run with the ball. That was it.

The second foul against a man put him out of the game until the next goal was made—or, if the umpire thought he was trying to injure an opposing player, the man could be put out for the whole game, with no substitute allowed.

By the second year, the pivot was allowed so that a man could turn in his position to pass or shoot the ball, provided he didn't advance.

Then came dribbling, which was first a defensive measure. When a player had the ball and was so closely guarded he couldn't pass it, he had to lose it deliberately, then recover it again. So he'd roll or bounce it. And that was the start of present-day dribbling.

Another big development was speeding the game up to satisfy the public's desire for fast action. Probably the most noticeable part of this change was the way the ball was put into play after a goal. At first, the referee brought it back to the middle and tossed it up. That was soon cut to the current practice of having the opposing team put it into play as soon as the goal is made.

The game invented by Jim Naismith is classed today as one of the world's most popular sports. It is played in more than seventy countries. Its original eighteen men have been joined by some forty million who play the game each year and many millions more who watch.

It is America's favorite spectator and participant sport.

Developing Comprehension Skills

1. Why did coach Jim Naismith invent the sport of basketball? How did the game get its name?

2. What made the first basketball game so rough? Was this what Naismith had in mind?

3. How did the net and the backboard become part of the game?

4. How does today's out-of-bounds rule differ from the rule in the early game? Give three other examples of changes in the game over the years.

5. Do you think the addition of rules added to the enjoyment of the game or lessened it?

Reading Literature: Nonfiction

1. **Evaluating Point of View.** "The First Basketball Game" is told from the first-person

point of view, using the pronouns *we* and *our*. The article was written by one of the world's first basketball players. How does a firsthand account make the article seem more interesting and informative?

2. **Recognizing Explanatory Writing.** Explanatory writing explains something. One kind of explanatory writing tells how to do something. It may also explain how something happens, works, or develops. A second kind tells why something is the way it is or why it should be different. A third kind defines a term or idea. Which type is used in "The First Basketball Game"?

3. **Identifying Development.** In explanatory writing, the main ideas may be developed in several ways. Incidents, examples, reasons, or statistics may be used to provide more detailed information about the topic. For the most part, how are the main ideas in this article developed?

4. **Recognizing Sequence.** The sequence of events in a selection is the order in which the writer presents them. "The First Basketball Game" is written mainly in chronological order, or time sequence. The writer starts at the beginning and tells the major events in the order in which they occurred. Make a list of those events. Why do you suppose the writer chose chronological order for his article about the beginnings of basketball? Does the writer ever depart from strict chronological order? What purpose may he have had for doing so?

Developing Vocabulary Skills

Creating Words. When new discoveries or ideas are developed, it is often necessary to cre-

ate new words to describe them. Imagine that you are an inventor with five new inventions or ideas to name. Use the prefixes, suffixes, and root words you have studied to create names for your discoveries. Write each name and then write a description of the invention. Your new words may be humorous if you wish.

Examples:
triphone—a telephone that allows three people to speak or listen at the same time.
ruptology—the study of broken things.

Developing Writing Skills

1. **Analyzing Explanatory Writing.** Write two or three paragraphs comparing and contrasting "The First Basketball Game" with an encyclopedia article on basketball. You might find similarities and differences in the kind of information each article includes. You might also discuss the purposes for each kind of article.

2. **Writing an Explanatory Article.** Have you ever been curious about how a certain sport, art, or process developed? Choose a subject you are interested in. Then write an explanatory article that tells how your subject came to be.

   Pre-Writing. Read a general encyclopedia article on your subject. Then consult a book or an expert in the field, if that is possible. Take notes from all of your sources on the development of your subject. Organize your notes in chronological order.

   Writing. Use your notes to write your explanation in paragraph form. Write simply and clearly. Be sure not to leave out any steps. Use transitional words such as *first*, *next*, and *then* to make your order clear.

Revising. Ask a classmate to read your paragraph. Is it clear? Have any steps been left out? Is it interesting? Revise as necessary. Then proofread your draft and make a clean, final copy.

Developing Skills in Study and Research

Consulting an Almanac. "The First Basketball Game" is an interesting look at the beginnings of basketball. But if you want current facts about modern basketball, you must refer to a more current reference source.

One useful reference tool for up-to-date facts about sports is an almanac. Published yearly, almanacs contain facts and statistics on current events, government, economics, population, sports, and other fields. The alphabetical index in an almanac will direct you to information about basketball. Use an almanac in your library to find the following information:

1. last year's National Basketball Association champion, individual scoring leader, and all-star team
2. last year's NBA rookie of the year
3. last year's college championship team
4. location of the Basketball Hall of Fame
5. winner of the NBA championship in 1968

What other information about basketball can the almanac provide you with?

Developing Skills in Critical Thinking

Understanding the Problem-Solving Process. One important critical thinking skill is that of finding solutions to problems. In successful problem-solving, the problem is first identified. Then different solutions are considered. The solution that seems most likely to succeed is then tried.

Early basketball players faced many problems. They tried to solve these problems in different ways. Explain why each of the following was a problem. Tell what the possible solutions were. Then tell how the problem was solved.

1. Football was dangerous for indoor play.
2. Someone had to lift the basketball out of the peach basket.
3. School kids in the balcony knocked the basketball into or out of the basket.

Developing Skills in Speaking and Listening

Preparing To Give a Formal Speech. A formal speech covers a specific subject in depth. It is usually longer than an informal talk. It requires careful planning and preparation. In the next few lessons, you will learn step by step how to prepare and give a formal speech.

1. The first step in preparing to give a speech is to decide on a topic. The best topic is one that is unusual or that deals with a familiar topic in a fresh way. A good topic will interest both you and your audience. Limit the subject to fit the available time.
2. Next, determine the purpose of your speech. The purpose may be to inform, to persuade, or to entertain.
3. Finally, identify your audience. You should know your audience's age, background, and knowledge of your topic. Then you can decide how to present your material.

Prepare to give a formal speech to your class. After you complete the first three steps, save your notes in a folder. You will use these notes in the next selection.

Clever Hans

EVON Z. VOGT *and* RAY HYMAN

Can animals think? In 1904, a horse nicknamed Clever Hans seemed to prove that they can. Read to see how clever Hans really was.

Wilhelm von Osten, Clever Hans and Oskar Pfungst,
Courtesy of the General Research Division, the New York Public Library,
Astor, Lenox and Tilden Foundations.

The following true account shows how a famous mystery of the past was solved because one man used the "scientific method" and refused to believe everything he saw.

In the year 1904, there appeared in Berlin a Russian trotting horse known as Clever Hans. Here was a horse, so it seemed, that could have settled the age-old question of animal consciousness. For Hans was renowned for his ability to solve arithmetical problems, to spell and define words, to identify musical notes and intervals, and to behave in other ways that indicated he had powers of abstract reasoning.

The public sang his praises in songs, articles, and books. His picture appeared on post cards and liquor labels. Children's toys were made in his image. Men of renown investigated him and found him to be truly endowed with human intelligence. He was intensively studied by a committee consisting of a circus manager, several educators, a zoologist, a veterinarian, a physiologist, and the famous psychologist Carl Stumpf. The committee reported that no trickery or known cues were involved. Hans had achieved the developmental stage of a fourteen-year-old child.

The horse's trainer, Von Osten, a man of about seventy years of age, stood proudly at the horse's right. A former arithmetic teacher, he had spent three years teaching Hans the three R's. His approach was not that of the circus performer but that of the patient schoolmaster. Instead of the whip, he used occasional rewards of carrots, which he kept stuffed into his pockets. He declined to profit commercially from Hans' fame. Even the group that gathered in the courtyard to watch Hans go through his paces came free of charge.

Hans could answer almost any question put to him in German. He could count up to one hundred, and he could do all the basic arithmetical operations, including those involving compound fractions and decimals. He could spell words, identify persons and objects by name, designate the pitch of musical notes, and even express a like or dislike for certain kinds of music. Hans, of course, could not talk in a vocal sense. He responded to questions by tapping with his hoof, shaking his head, or walking over and pointing to letters on a board or objects on a rack.

Other animals, to be sure, had been advertised as capable of such feats. But these other animals had been trained to respond to cues and signs from their masters.

Furthermore, it developed that Hans could often perform even when his master was not present. In September, 1904, after examining Hans thoroughly, a commission of thirteen outstanding scientists and animal experts could only report:

> In spite of the most attentive observation, nothing in the way of movements or other forms of expression which might have served as a sign could be discovered. . . . This is a case which appears to differ from any hitherto discovered . . . and therefore it is worthy of a serious and incisive investigation.

It remained for the psychologist Oskar Pfungst to carry out this "serious and incisive investigation." The results of Pfungst's systematic inquiry are recorded in his book *Clever Hans*. This amazing document not only presents us with an illustration of scientific investigation at its best but unfolds its findings in the manner of the best detective thrillers.

Mr. Pfungst first took pains to make friends with Hans. Then, when Mr. Von Osten was not present, he put questions to Hans. To the scientist's amazement, the horse answered correctly each problem put to him. Mr. Pfungst knew that he was not coaching or signaling the horse. Yet, with no one else present, the horse was going through his paces with perfect precision.

Some other eminent men had gone through the same experience with Hans. Faced with this unexplainable situation, they honestly admitted their bewilderment and publicly endorsed the claim that Hans was capable of abstract reasoning. Mr. Pfungst was also honest enough to admit his bafflement. It is at this point that his scientific training distinguished him from the other eminent onlookers. Instead of jumping from his inability to explain the horse's behavior to the conclusion that Hans was part-human, Pfungst investigated further.

He designed a series of experiments in which the horse was questioned in the usual fashion. Half of the questions were ones to which the questioner knew the answer and half were ones to which the questioner did not know the answer. The results were clear-cut: Hans could answer questions only when his questioner knew the answer. When his questioner was ignorant, so was Hans. Obviously, then, Hans was getting his cues from the questioner. But what were these cues, and how was Hans receiving them? After eliminating auditory and tactual cues, Pfungst used blinders to block the horse's view of the questioner. Here Hans balked. He insisted on turning his head and orienting himself so that he could see his interrogator. As long as Hans could not see his questioner, he could not answer his question.

So far two facts had been established. Hans could answer questions only when the questioner knew the answer, and he had to see the questioner to give him the answer. Here the investigation met a snag. It appeared that the horse was responding to visual cues, and Pfungst, to whom the horse responded perfectly, was unable to detect any behavior or postures in himself that could serve as a sign.

Again, Pfungst revealed the ideal of scientific spirit. He did not give up. He kept looking and finally discovered the answer where all others had failed. The horse was responding to a postural cue from the questioner, a cue so small and subtle that it was almost impossible to detect.

When the questioner asked his question, he focused attention upon the horse's hoof, which began tapping the answer. In many questioners, this close attention produced a tenseness that was translated into an almost imperceptible slouching of the head—just a trace of the more overt gesture of bending over and watching the hoof. This was a sufficient cue for Hans to begin tapping. When Hans had tapped a sufficient number of times in response to the question, the questioner, confident that the horse was not going to tap any more, would almost imperceptibly raise his head and straighten up. This was Hans' cue to stop tapping.

Pfungst had been unable to discover this cue by studying himself. It was only after long observation of other questioners that he discovered it. Pfungst did not stop his investigations at this point. Instead, he carried his investigations into the laboratory. He wanted to know if naive questioners would unintentionally give the same cues that the successful questioners had given to Hans.

For these experiments, Pfungst played the part of Hans. His right hand became the right foreleg of Hans. A questioner would stand before Pfungst. He would merely think of a question that could be answered in terms of a number of taps of the hand. Pfungst would look for the cue, the almost imperceptible slouch, to begin tapping. He would tap, all the while observing the questioner; when he thought he observed a slight relaxation in the questioner, he would cease tapping.

In all, Pfungst went through these paces with twenty-five different persons who ranged in age from five upward. None of these subjects were aware of the purpose of the experiment. The results were startling. All but two of the subjects gave the same involuntary head movements that Pfungst had discovered in the questioners of Hans. Pfungst was able to use these involuntary movements to successfully "read" the minds of his questioners. He was able to devise other kinds of experiments to correspond with Hans' complete repertoire. In each case, the subjects gave involuntary cues; and in each case, when being told, they denied any knowledge of these involuntary movements.

Still Pfungst wasn't satisfied. He carried on with further experiments. He found that he could train a subject to give him cues of various kinds, even while the subject did not know he was being trained to give such cues. He then built special apparatus to record such movements objectively.

The results of all these experiments were undeniably clear. When subjects asked a question and then concentrated on the movements of the experimenter, they invariably made involuntary movements that cued the experimenter when to start and stop. And the experimenter had little trouble in utilizing these cues to read the minds of the questioners in a manner similar to that of Hans.

One question remained to be answered. How did Hans learn to respond to these cues? Did his owner, Mr. Von Osten, deliberately train him to react to these cues? Or did he accidentally pick them up by the simple process of noting that he was rewarded with a carrot if he stopped at certain signs? All the facts lead to the conclusion that Mr. Von Osten was as much the dupe of his involuntary actions as were all the later investigators.

Von Osten spent three years patiently training his horse. Others who came after him, knowing the real secret of Hans' success, succeeded in teaching other horses Hans's complete repertoire in a matter of weeks.

Developing Comprehension Skills

1. What unusual ability did Hans seem to have?

2. How was Pfungst's procedure different from that of other scientists?

3. Which things indicated that Hans's amazing ability was not a trick?

4. How did Pfungst prove that Hans received clues from a questioner? Do you think Hans was intentionally taught to respond to these clues?

5. How did Clever Hans's actual abilities differ from the abilities people thought he had?

6. In your opinion, does the truth about Hans make him any less clever?

Reading Literature: Nonfiction

1. **Recognizing Explanatory Writing.** "Clever Hans" is basically an explanation of how one scientist made a discovery. It is an example of **explanatory writing**. Explanatory writing must be clear, detailed, and accurate. Find the passages that explain the following:

   a. how Hans was trained

   b. how Oskar Pfungst discovered that Hans got signals from a questioner

   c. how Pfungst discovered that Hans's cues were visual

   d. how Pfungst discovered that the cue was a slouching of the head

   e. how Pfungst proved that his theory was correct

   In each of these cases, the writer explains a process. Is each process explained clearly? Are any important steps or details left out? Was each process easy to understand? Why or why not?

2. **Determining Motivation.** "Clever Hans" focuses on *what* happens rather than *why* something happens. However, it does give some clues about the characters' motivation. In other words, it provides hints as to why people act the way they do.

   Reread the paragraph about Von Osten's training methods. Then infer why Von Osten trained Hans. Do you think his goal was money, fame, or amusement? Similarly, why do you think Osker Pfungst kept trying to discover the truth about Hans?

3. **Identifying Tone.** You know that **tone** is a writer's attitude toward his or her subject matter. Nonfiction writers use an **objective** tone if they want to present information without including their own opinions. Most newspaper news stories, for example, are written objectively to present facts fairly. Nonfiction writers can also use a more **subjective** tone. Subjective writing shows either approval or disapproval of the subject matter.

   Is the tone of "Clever Hans" objective or subjective? What do you think the author's opinion of Oskar Pfungst was? Which words and phrases help you reach that conclusion?

4. **Inferring Character Traits.** In "Clever Hans," the actions of Pfungst are told in detail. These actions reveal a great deal about the man. Which of the following words would you use to describe Pfungst: *resourceful, persistent, careless, casual, emotional, thorough,* or *determined*? Can you think of two other traits that Pfungst's actions reveal about him? Find specific examples that suggest these traits to you.

Developing Vocabulary Skills

Determining Word Meaning. Sometimes no clues are given for the meaning of an unfamiliar word. In this case, you will need to use the dictionary. Read the following sentences. Use your knowledge of word parts and context clues to decide on the meaning of the underlined words. If no clues are given, use the dictionary. Write each underlined word and its meaning on your paper. Then explain how you determined the meaning.

1. . . . and in the course of the journey climb up and jump from the top of one precipice like Niagara. . . .

2. We choose to "relax" in the semicomatose slump.

3. Teddy Roosevelt went in for jujitsu. . . .

4. . . . we'd always have a large crowd of spectators—teachers, sports enthusiasts, and just plain curious people—who'd look through the windows or come in to see us play.

5. The results of Pfungst's systematic inquiry are recorded in his book *Clever Hans*.

6. . . . this close attention produced a tenseness that was translated into an almost imperceptible slouching of the head—just a trace of the more overt gesture.

7. He insisted on turning his head and orienting himself so that he could see his interrogator. As long as Hans could not see his questioner, he could not answer his question.

Developing Writing Skills

1. **Analyzing Style.** Like fiction writers, nonfiction writers can keep readers interested and involved by using various writing techniques. For example, a writer may create suspense. The writer may also entertain the readers with humor, or puzzle the reader with strange circumstances. How do the writers of "Clever Hans" hold the reader's interest? In one paragraph, analyze how readers are kept interested in "Clever Hans" throughout the article. Find specific sentences that build interest.

2. **Supporting an Opinion.** In addition to wondering whether animals can think, people have also wondered if animals feel emotion. What do you think? State your opinion in one paragraph. Try to prove your opinion with incidents, facts, and examples from personal experience and reference sources.

3. **Writing Description and Explanation.** As he studied Hans the horse, Oskar Pfungst found that appearances can be misleading. Tell about something or someone that proved to you that things are not always what they seem to be.

   Pre-Writing. Here are some ideas for possible topics:

   A Job That Looked Easy
   A Lucky Day That Wasn't
   An Elderly Person Who Is Young
      (or, A Young Person Who Is Old)

   You can also think of another topic that interests you. Jot down details about your subject's appearance. Then make notes about how the appearance differed from the actual facts. Organize your notes to emphasize the contrast.

   Writing. In one paragraph, describe the appearance that gave you a first impression.

In another paragraph, explain how the person or thing actually differed from its appearance. Use specific details. You may then write a paragraph that describes the conclusion you drew from the situation.

Revising. Exchange papers with an editing partner. Find out what your editor would like to know more about. Be sure that your descriptions and explanations are clear. Add any details that are missing.

Developing Skills in Critical Thinking

Drawing Conclusions Based on Facts. Scientist Oskar Pfungst used a careful reasoning process to determine the truth about Hans. First he observed Hans carefully and noticed many facts about Hans. Then he drew conclusions based on those facts. Finally, he tested each conclusion, or theory.

In one instance, Pfungst decided that Hans was getting visual cues or signals. He tested that conclusion by putting blinders on Hans. When Hans became disturbed by the blinders, Pfungst was led to believe that his assumption was correct. He then conducted other experiments to check his idea further.

Oskar Pfungst tested many other conclusions about Hans. What theory was he testing when he did each of the following:

1. questioned Hans without knowing the answers half the time
2. took the part of Hans and tapped his foot to answer

Developing Skills In Speaking and Listening

Preparing To Give a Speech. In the exercises for "The First Basketball Game," you completed the first steps in giving a speech. The next step is to gather information for your speech.

To gather information for an informative speech, you can draw on personal experiences. You can also interview people. Most of your information, though, will probably come from sources in the library. Use the card catalog, the *Readers' Guide*, encyclopedias, and other reference books to gather information.

When you find helpful information, take notes on note cards. See pages 362 and 464 for guidelines on note-taking. Save your work in your speech folder.

Body Talk

KATHLYN GAY

Do people speak only with words? Read to find out how you can "listen" to people by watching their body language.

Sitting, standing, running, walking, skipping, leaning—people perform many actions with the body. Whatever one does with his or her body positions can telegraph a message to someone else. This is especially true in sports such as basketball, football, or baseball. Coaches instruct players to look for ways opponents might telegraph what they are going to do.

Anyone who has played or watched these sports knows that members of a team do not want to give away a play that might win points. Thus, players make certain movements to fake a play. A basketball player leans forward as if to dribble the ball, but whirls and shoots instead. A football player pretends to pass, but this "fake" provides an opening to run. A runner on base leads off as if to steal home but only wants to shake up the pitcher.

In sports or everyday living there are many different messages sent with positions of the body. But how do you figure out what a person says with posture?

Posture can tell you a great deal about a person's attitude. Usually people tense their bodies when they are listening or watching with interest. That doesn't mean being uptight or rigid. Rather, people hold a position of forwardness, or openness. They seem to be taking in what is going on around them. Just the opposite is true in a situation like this one: A salesperson is talking to a group. Some people slouch down in their chairs. Others lean their heads on their hands with elbows propped on the table. A few have their arms crossed. Most are so overrelaxed they look like wet noodles draped over furniture. The message? No sale!

Here's another scene: An older sister is working a crossword puzzle. Her posture should tell you whether or not she wants to be disturbed. She might be hunched over at a table, staring at the squares and lists of words. The tip of her pencil is in her mouth or else her tongue might protrude slightly between her teeth. Such body positions often signal concentration. A person in such a posture is usually in deep thought and does not want to be bothered.

When looking for clues as to what body posture has to tell you, there's no better place to observe than at a busy airport or train station. People may exhibit impatience by the way they pace back and forth. A person who is not too uptight about waiting may sit casually on a seat or lean easily against a post, watching the parade of people go by. Then there are "expectant" postures. People press against railings and lean forward, watching for relatives or friends who are arriving. There are slumped postures that indicate disappointment or sadness. Postures can also say a person is eager to visit a new place or is confused or tired of traveling.

Boredom, excitement, happiness, sorrow, and many other human conditions are shown with posture. One posture that demonstrates confidence is sitting with hands clasped behind the head. Other postures also say "I'm in charge." A store manager or floor walker might pace with shoulders "squared," head tilted back, eyes watchful. This lets people know that he or she has authority.

A policeman's stance is another familiar pose. He "anchors" himself with feet spread slightly apart. His thumbs may be caught in his belt; chest and chin are thrust forward. He says with his posture, "I am here to enforce the law." In contrast, a policeman in another country might not use such posture. The Italian policeman, for example, would be more likely to lean for-

Seated Youth, 1917, WILHELM LEHMBRUCK.
The National Gallery of Art. Andrew W. Mellon Fund, Washington, D.C.

Body Talk 479

ward when talking to a person. He would be demonstrating that he is a "servant of the people."

In noting postures, there's this to remember: The body can assume nearly a thousand different positions, but people usually use only a few common ones. While growing up, each person learns patterns for posing and holding his or her body, just as we all learn gestures, facial expressions, and the language of touch. These patterns add to the vocabulary, or coded symbols, of body talk.

Developing Comprehension Skills

1. What is "body talk"?

2. How can body talk be useful in sports?

3. How reliable does Kathlyn Gay think body language is for revealing a person's attitude?

4. How reliable do you think body language is for revealing a person's attitude? Can you think of two examples from your own experience?

5. Do you think you would be able to understand the body talk in another country or culture? Why or why not?

Reading Literature: Nonfiction

1. **Understanding the Author's Purpose.** What is the purpose of Kathlyn Gay's article? Do you think that she accomplishes this purpose?

2. **Understanding Explanatory Writing.** You remember that one type of explanatory writing explains a process or tells how to do something. Another type defines a term or idea. A third type gives reasons for an opinion. What type of explanatory writing is "Body Talk"?

3. **Understanding Organization.** As Kathlyn Gay explains different types of body talk, she arranges her information in the order of its familiarity. In other words, she begins with subjects that are familiar to the reader and moves to less familiar ones. She begins with the topic of body talk in sports, a subject that is familiar to most readers. She then goes on to less familiar situations. Why is this type of organization a good one to use when explaining an unfamiliar subject?

4. **Understanding Development.** The main ideas in an article may be developed with examples, reasons, or facts and figures. What type of development does Kathlyn Gay use throughout most of her article? Find one main idea in this article that is supported with this type of development. Then list the items of information that are used to develop this idea.

5. **Recognizing Simile.** The figure of speech that uses *like* or *as* to compare two unlike things is a **simile**. Kathlyn Gay refers to peo-

ple who "look like wet noodles draped over furniture." Explain her simile. How does it help to describe these people?

6. **Appreciating Parallelism.** When a writer uses parallelism, he or she repeats the same sentence structure or phrasing with different words. Writers use parallelism to get readers to notice an important point, or to help create interest.

The first sentence of "Body Talk" uses a series of words that all end with *-ing*. What effect does this use of parallelism have on you as you begin reading this article?

Can you find parallel sentences in the second paragraph of "Body Talk"? Explain the effect this device has on the reader.

Developing Vocabulary Skills

Learning Prefixes That Refer to Amount. There is a special group of commonly-used Greek and Latin prefixes that mean a number or amount. Study the following list. You may already know some of these prefixes.

Prefix	Meaning	Example
mono-, uni-	one	monologue
di-, bi-, duo-	two	dialogue
tri-	three	triangle
quad-	four	quadrangle
pent-	five	pentagon
deca-, deci-	ten	decagon
poly-, multi-	many	polyester
semi-	half	semicolon
pan-, omni-	all	Pan-American

Use this chart to help you define the underlined words in the statements below. Then, based on your understanding of the word, answer the question that is in parentheses.

1. Babe Didrikson won the female <u>decathlon</u> in the 1932 Olympics. (Is this statement true or false? Remember, Babe won two events.)

2. Dick Gregory's mother was an <u>omnipresent</u> influence during his childhood. (Name another author for whom this was true.)

3. Russell Baker would have been happier if the magazines he sold were issued <u>biannually</u>. (Do you agree? Why?)

4. Athletes such as Willie Mays have well-developed <u>bicep</u> and <u>tricep</u> muscles. (Try to guess why these muscles have been given these names. Then consult a dictionary to check your answer.)

5. A <u>multiplicity</u> of calendars on a cafe's walls indicates good food. (Would a one-calendar restaurant be a good place to dine?)

Developing Writing Skills

1. **Writing an Explanation.** Author Kathlyn Gay writes, "Whatever one does with his or her body postures can telegraph a message to someone else." Review the article, "Clever Hans." In two or three paragraphs, explain how Clever Hans responded to body language that "telegraphed a message."

Pre-Writing. Review "Clever Hans." Make notes on signals people unknowingly gave Hans and on his response to them. Decide on an order for presenting your information. In your first paragraph, you might summarize what body language is. In a second paragraph, you could discuss Hans's unusual abilities. In a third paragraph, you could then show how these abilities could be explained in body language.

Writing. Use your pre-writing notes to write a rough draft of your paragraphs. Begin each paragraph with a strong topic sentence. Use several examples to support each point. Write clearly and simply.

Revising. Check to see if you have applied the ideas from "Body Language" to "Clever Hans." Have you stated the main idea of each paragraph in your topic sentence? Have you developed each idea with specific examples? Are your sentences clear and complete?

2. **Combining Description and Explanatory Writing.** Kathlyn Gay describes various body postures and what they might signal — *disappointment, concentration, impatience, confidence.* Find a magazine or newspaper photograph that shows a person communicating a certain attitude through his or her posture. In two paragraphs, describe the body posture, and then tell what it "says" about the person.

3. **Writing an Article.** What can hands communicate? What can eyes signal? What can the facial expressions of others tell you? These are three other types of nonverbal communication, or body talk. Using Kathlyn Gay's article as a model, write your own article explaining one or more of these types of body talk. To illustrate your ideas about body talk, use specific examples from your own experiences with people. The entries in your journal may provide you with details.

Developing Skills in Speaking and Listening

1. **Using Body Language.** Whenever you speak, your posture, expressions, and gestures can say as much as your words. Look at the following sentence:

I couldn't believe what I was seeing.

Say this sentence several times. Each time, try to communicate one of the feelings listed below. Show your feelings through gestures, posture, and the expression on your face.

surprise	anger
disgust	happiness
wonder	excitement

2. **Preparing a Speech.** You have learned how to gather information for your informative speech. The next step is to organize the information. This process is the same as that of organizing a composition. Begin by reading through your notes several times. Then identify the main ideas in your notes. Divide your note cards into separate groups, one group for each main idea. Finally, arrange the groups, along with the ideas within each group, in a logical order. You will have an opportunity to test your speechwriting skills in the writing activity for the following selection, "Pompeii."

Write a draft, or outline, of your speech. Plan to begin your speech with an attention-getting introduction. Effective openers include an *anecdote,* a *question,* a *thought-provoking question,* an *analogy,* or *startling facts.* End with a good conclusion. Your conclusion should summarize the main idea of your speech in a forceful and interesting way. A strong summary statement, a quotation, or a challenge is sometimes used.

You now have the skeleton for your speech. Save your materials in your speech folder.

Pompeii

ROBERT SILVERBERG

The city of Pompeii died in a volcanic eruption nineteen hundred years ago. How does this article bring it back to life?

Not very far from Naples a strange city sleeps under the hot Italian sun. It is the city of Pompeii, and there is no other city quite like it in all the world. No one lives in Pompeii but crickets and beetles and lizards, yet every year thousands of people travel from distant countries to visit it.

Pompeii is a dead city. No one has lived there for nearly 2,000 years—not since the summer of the year A.D. 79, to be exact.

Until that year Pompeii was a prosperous city of 25,000 people. Nearby was the Bay of Naples, an arm of the blue Mediterranean. Rich men came down from wealthy Rome, 125 miles to the north, to build luxurious seaside villas. Fertile farmlands occupied the fields surrounding Pompeii. Rising sharply behind the city was the 4,000-foot bulk of Mount Vesuvius, a grass-covered slope where the shepherds of Pompeii took their goats to graze. Pompeii was a busy city and a happy one.

It died suddenly, in a terrible rain of fire and ashes.

The tragedy struck on the 24th of August, A.D. 79. Mount Vesuvius, which had slumbered quietly for centuries, exploded with savage violence. Death struck on a hot summer afternoon. Tons of hot ashes fell on Pompeii, smothering it, hiding it from sight. For three days the sun did not break through the cloud of volcanic ash that filled the sky. And when the eruption ended, Pompeii was buried deep. A thriving city had perished in a single day.

Centuries passed. Pompeii was forgotten. Then, 1,500 years later, it was discovered again. Beneath the protecting shroud of ashes, the city lay intact. Everything was as it had been the day Vesuvius erupted. There were still loaves of bread in the ovens of the bakeries. In the wine shops, the wine jars were in place, and on one counter could be seen a stain where a customer had thrown down his glass and fled.

Modern archaeology began with the discovery of buried Pompeii. Before then, the digging of treasures from the ground had been a haphazard and unscholarly affair. However, the excavation of Pompeii was done in a systematic, scientific manner, and so the science of serious archaeology can be said to have begun there. Since the year 1748, generations of skilled Italian workmen have been carefully removing the ashes that buried Pompeii, until today almost four-fifths of the city has been uncovered.

Other Roman cities died more slowly. Wind and rain and fire wore them away. Later peoples tore down the ancient monuments, using the stone to build houses and churches. Over the centuries, the cities of the Caesars vanished, and all that is left of them today are scattered fragments.

Not so with Pompeii. It was engulfed in an instant, and its people's tragedy was our great gain. The buildings of Pompeii still stand as they stood 2,000 years ago, and within the houses we can still see the pots and pans, the household tools, the hammers and nails. On the walls of the buildings are election slogans and the scrawlings of unruly boys. Pompeii is like a photograph in three dimensions. It shows us exactly what

Ruins, Pompeii, Italy. Photo Researchers, New York. Copyright © 1977 Susan McCartney.

Election slogan from a wall in Pompeii. "All the fruitsellers with Helvius Vestalis support the election of M. Holconius Priscus as duumvir." Line art from the Museum of Fine Arts, Boston.

a city of the Roman Empire was like, down to the smallest detail of everyday life.

To go to Pompeii today is to take a trip backward in a time machine. The old city comes to vivid life all around you. You can almost hear the clatter of horses' hoofs on the narrow streets, the cries of children, the loud hearty laughter of the shopkeepers. You can almost smell meat sizzling over a charcoal fire. The sky is cloudlessly blue, with the summer sun almost directly overhead. The grassy slopes of great Vesuvius pierce the heavens behind the city, and sunlight shimmers on the water of the bay a thousand yards from the city walls. Ships from every nation are in port, and the babble of strange languages can be heard in the streets.

Such was Pompeii on its last day. And so it is today, now that the volcanic ash has been cleared away. A good imagination is all that is necessary to restore it to bustling vitality.

The Last Day

As its last day of life dawned, in A.D. 79, Pompeii found itself in the midst of a long, sleepy Mediterranean summer. It was a city several hundred years old. Its founders were an Italian people called the Oscans, who had built the city long before Rome had carved out its worldwide empire.

Greeks from Naples had settled in Pompeii, too, and the walls that surrounded the city were built in the Greek style.

For more than 150 years, Pompeii had been part of the Roman Empire. The Roman dictator Sulla had besieged and captured the town in 89 B.C., giving it to his soldiers and making it a Roman colony. By A.D. 79, it had become a fashionable seaside resort, an Atlantic City or a Miami Beach of its day. Important Romans had settled there. The great orator Cicero had been proud of his summer home in Pompeii. It was a city of merchants and bankers, too.

Pompeii had not had unbroken peace. Twenty years earlier, in the year 59, a contest of gladiators had been held in the big outdoor stadium of Pompeii. A team of gladiators from the neighboring town of Nocera had come to fight against Pompeii's best gladiators. Tempers grew hot as local favorites were pitted against each other in combat to the death. Men from Pompeii began to hurl insults at Nocerans. Words led to blows. Then daggers flashed. A massacre resulted, in which dozens of Nocerans perished and only a few escaped.

Nocera appealed to Rome, and the Roman Senate issued a stern decree: the amphitheater of Pompeii would be closed for ten years. No more gladiatorial games! It was like having our Congress declare that neither the Yankees nor the Dodgers could play baseball for a decade.

The ruling was considered a great tragedy in sports-loving Pompeii. But an even greater one was in store four years later, in A.D. 63, for an earthquake rocked the town. Nearly every building in Pompeii toppled. Hundreds of people died.

One who survived the earthquake of 63 was the banker, Caecilius Jucundus. He was a plump, well-fed man with a harsh smile and beady eyes and a big wart on his left cheek. At the moment the earth shook, Caecilius was in the Forum, the main square of Pompeii. Much business was transacted in the Forum, which was lined with imposing stone columns arranged in a double row, one above the other.

As statues of the gods and slabs of marble tumbled to the ground, fat Caecilius sank to his knees in terror. "If my life is spared," he cried to the heavens, "I'll sacrifice a bull to the gods!"

We know that Caecilius escaped—and that he kept his vow. For when he rebuilt his house after the earthquake, he added a little strip of marble above his family's altar, and on it was a scene showing the earthquake and depicting the bull he had sacrificed. Next to the altar the fat moneylender kept his treasure chest, crammed full with gold coins—and, facing it, a portrait of himself, wart and all.

Sixteen years passed after the dreadful earthquake of 63. Sixteen years later, signs of the catastrophe could still be seen every-

Amphitheater with Mt. Vesuvius in background, Pompeii, Italy. Photo Researchers, New York. Photograph by John Verde.

where, for the Pompeiians were slow to rebuild. The private homes were back in order, of course, but the big public places still showed the effects of the quake. The columns of the Forum remained fallen. The Basilica, or law court, still looked devastated. The Temple of Apollo was not yet restored to its former glory. Such repairs took time and cost a great deal of money. The Pompeiians were in no hurry. Time passes slowly along the Mediterranean coast. The columns could be rebuilt next year, or the year after next, or the year after that. In time, everything would be attended to. Commerce and daily life were more important.

But time was running short.

At dawn, on the 24th of August, in the year 79, Pompeii's 25,000 people awakened to another hot day in that hot summer. There was going to be a performance in the arena that night, and the whole town was looking forward to the bloody contests of the gladiators, for the Senate's ban had long since ended. The rumble of heavy wooden wheels was heard as carts loaded with grain entered the city from the farms outside the walls. Over the centuries the steady stream of carts traveling in and out of the city had worn ruts deep into the pavement of Pompeii's narrow streets.

Wooden shutters were drawn back noisily. The grocers and sellers of fruit opened their shops, displaying their wares on trays set out on the sidewalk. In the wine shops, the girls who sold wine to the thirsty sailors got ready for another busy day.

Outside, children headed toward school, carrying slates and followed by their dogs. Nearly everyone in Pompeii had a dog, and barking could be heard everywhere as the Pompeiian pets greeted one another. A small boy who had just learned the Greek alphabet stopped in front of a blank wall and took a piece of charcoal from his tunic. Hastily he scribbled the Greek letters: *alpha, beta, gamma.*

In the Forum, the town's important men had gathered after breakfast to read the political signs that were posted during the night. Elsewhere in the Forum, the wool merchants talked business and the men who owned the vineyards were smiling to each other about the high quality of this year's wine, which would fetch a good price in other countries.

The quiet morning moved slowly along. There was nothing very unusual about Pompeii. But tragedy was on its way. Beneath Vesuvius' vinecovered slopes, a mighty force was about to break loose.

No one in Pompeii knew the dangerous power imprisoned in Vesuvius. For 1,500 years the mountain had slept quietly; but far beneath the crest a boiling fury of molten lava had gradually been gathering strength. The solid rock of Vesuvius held the hidden forces in check. The earthquake 16 years before had been the first sign that the trapped fury beneath the mountain was struggling to break free. Pressure was building up. In the city at the base of the mountain, life went on in complete ignorance of the looming catastrophe.

Vesuvius Explodes

At 1 o'clock in the afternoon on the 24th of August, in the year 79, the critical point was reached. The walls of rock could hold no longer.

The mountain exploded, raining death on thousands.

Like many tragedies, this one was misunderstood at first. Down in Pompeii, four miles from Vesuvius, a tremendous explosion was heard, echoing ringingly off the mountains on the far side of the city.

"What was that?" people cried from one end of town to another. They stared at each other, puzzled, troubled. Were the gods fighting in heaven? It that what the loud explosion was?

"Look!" somebody shouted. "Look at Vesuvius!"

Thousands of eyes swiveled upward. Thousands of arms pointed. A black cloud was rising from the shattered crest of the mountain. Higher and higher it rose. An eyewitness, the Roman philosopher Pliny, described the cloud as he saw it from Misenum, 22 miles from Pompeii on the opposite side of the Bay:

"Better than any other tree, the pine can give an idea of the shape and appearance of this cloud," Pliny wrote in his notebook later that day. "In fact it was projected into the air like an enormous trunk and then spread into many branches, now white, now black, now spotted, according to whether earth or ashes were thrown up."

Minutes passed. The sound of the great explosion died away, but it still tingled in everyone's ears. The cloud over Vesuvius still rose, black as night, higher and higher.

"The cloud is blotting out the sun!" someone cried in terror.

Still no one in Pompeii had perished. The fragments of rock thrown up when the mountain exploded all fell back on the volcano's slopes. Within the crater, sizzling masses of molten rock were rushing upward, and upwelling gas drove small blobs of liquefied stone thousands of feet into the air. They cooled, high above the gaping mouth of the volcano, and plummeted earthward.

A strange rain began to fall on Pompeii—a rain of stone.

The stones were light. They were pumice stones, consisting mostly of air bubbles. They poured down as though there had been a sudden cloudburst. The pumice stones, or lapilli, did little damage. They clattered against the wooden roofs of the Pompeiian houses. They fell by the hundreds in the streets. The people who had rushed out of houses and shops to see what had caused the explosion now scrambled to take cover as the weird rain of lapilli continued.

"What is happening?" Pompeiians asked one another. They rushed to the temples—the Temple of Jupiter, the Temple of Apollo, the Temple of Isis. Bewildered priests tried to calm bewildered citizens. Darkness had come at midday, and a rain of small stones fell from the sky, and who could explain it?

Some did not wait for explanation. In a tavern near the edge of the city, half a dozen gladiators who were scheduled to compete in that night's games decided to flee quickly. They had trumpets with them that were used to sound a fanfare at the amphitheater. But they tossed the trumpets aside, leaving them to be found centuries later. Covering their heads with tiles and pieces of wood, the gladiators rushed out into the hail of lapilli and sprinted toward the open country beyond the walls, where they hoped they would be safe.

Vesuvius was rumbling ominously, now. The sky was dark. Lapilli continued to pour down, until the streets began to clog with them.

"The eruption will be over soon!" a hopeful voice exclaimed.

But it did not end. An hour went by and darkness still shrouded everything, and still the lapilli fell. All was confusion now. Children struggled home from school, panicky in the midday darkness.

The people of Pompeii knew that doom was at hand now. Their fears were doubled when an enormous rain of hot ashes began to fall on them, along with more lapilli. Pelted with stones, half smothered by the ashes, the Pompeiians cried out to the gods for mercy. The wooden roofs of some of the houses began to catch fire as the heat of the ashes reached them. Other buildings were collapsing under the weight of the pumice stones that had fallen on them.

In those first few hours, only the quick-witted managed to escape. Vesonius Pri-mus, the wealthy wool merchant, called his family together and piled jewelry and money into a sack. Lighting a torch, Vesonius led his little band out into the nightmare of the streets. Overlooked in the confusion was Vesonius' black watchdog, chained in the courtyard. The terrified dog barked wildly as lapilli struck and drifting white ash settled around him. The animal struggled with his chain, battling fiercely to get free, but the chain held, and no one heard the dog's cries. The humans were too busy saving themselves.

Many hundreds of Pompeiians fled in those first few dark hours. Stumbling in the darkness, they made their way to the city gates, then out, down to the harbor. They boarded boats and got away, living to tell the tale of their city's destruction. Others preferred to remain within the city, huddling inside the temples, or in the public baths, or in the cellars of their homes. They still hoped that the nightmare would end— that the tranquillity of a few hours ago would return.

It was evening now. New woe was in store for Pompeii. The earth trembled and quaked! Roofs that had somehow withstood the rain of lapilli went crashing in ruin, burying hundreds who had hoped to survive the eruption. In the Forum, tall columns toppled as they had in 63. Those who remembered that great earthquake screamed in new terror as the entire city seemed to shake in the grip of a giant fist.

Three feet of lapilli now covered the ground. Ash floated in the air. Gusts of poi-

Above right: the Mt. Kilauea Volcano, April 1983. Copyright © 1984, Eric Meola.

Left: Pompeiians caught by the lava flow as they ran toward Porta Nocera, August 24, 79 A.D.
Photo Researchers, New York. Photograph by Leonard von Matt.

sonous gas came drifting from the belching crater, though people could still breathe. Roofs were collapsing everywhere. The cries of the dying filled the air. Rushing throngs, blinded by the darkness and the smoke, hurtled madly up one street and down the next, trampling the fallen in a crazy, fruitless dash toward safety. Dozens of people plunged into dead-end streets and found themselves trapped by crashing buildings. They waited there, too frightened to run farther, expecting the end.

The rich man Diomedes was another of those who decided not to flee at the first sign of alarm. Rather than risk being crushed by the screaming mobs, Diomedes calmly led the members of his household into the solidly built basement of his villa. There were sixteen people altogether, as well as his daughter's dog and her beloved little goat. They took enough food and water to last for several days.

But for all his shrewdness and foresight, Diomedes was undone anyway. Poison gas was creeping slowly into the underground shelter! He watched his daughter begin to cough and struggle for breath. Vesuvius was giving off vast quantities of deadly carbon monoxide, that was now settling like a blanket over the dying city.

The poison gas thickened as the terrible night continued. It was possible to hide from the lapilli, but not from the gas, and Pompeiians died by the hundreds. Carbon monoxide gas keeps the body from absorbing oxygen. Victims of carbon monoxide poisoning get sleepier and sleepier, until they lose consciousness, never to regain it. All over Pompeii, people lay down in the beds of lapilli, overwhelmed by the gas, and death came quietly to them.

Two prisoners, left behind in the jail when their keepers fled, pounded on the sturdy wooden doors. "Let us out!" they called, but no one heard, and the gas entered. They died, not knowing that the jailers outside were dying as well.

In a lane near the Forum, a hundred people were trapped by a blind-alley wall. Others hid in the stoutly built public bathhouses, protected against collapsing roofs but not against the deadly gas. Near the house of Diomedes, a beggar and his little goat sought shelter. The man fell dead a few feet from Diomedes' door; the faithful goat remained by his side, its silver bell tinkling, until its turn came.

All through the endless night, Pompeiians wandered about the streets or crouched in their ruined homes or clustered in the temples to pray. By morning, few remained alive. Not once had Vesuvius stopped hurling lapilli and ash into the air, and the streets of Pompeii were filling quickly. At midday on August 25th, exactly twenty-four hours after the beginning of the holocaust, a second eruption racked the volcano. A second cloud of ashes rose above Vesuvius' summit. The wind blew ash as far as Rome and Egypt. But most of the new ashes descended on Pompeii.

The deadly shower of stone and ashes went unslackening into its second day. But it no longer mattered to Pompeii whether the eruption continued another day or another year. For by midday on August 25th, Pompeii was a city of the dead.

Pompeii Today

Arriving at Pompeii today, you leave your car outside and enter through an age-old gate. Just within the entrance is a museum that has been built in recent years to house many of the smaller antiquities found in the ruins. Here are statuettes and toys, saucepans and loaves of bread. The account books of the banker Caecilius Jucundus are there, noting all the money he had lent at steep interest rates. Glass cups, coins, charred beans and peas and turnips, baskets of grapes and plums and figs, a box of chestnuts—the little things of Pompeii have all been miraculously preserved for your startled eyes.

Then you enter the city proper. The streets are narrow and deeply rutted with the tracks of chariot wheels. Only special narrow Pompeiian chariots could travel inside the town. Travelers from outside were obliged to change vehicles when they reached the walls of the city. This provided a profitable monopoly for the Pompeiian equivalent of cab drivers, more than twenty centuries ago!

At each intersection, blocks of stone several feet high are mounted in the roadway, so designed that chariot wheels could pass on either side of them.

"Those are steppingstones for the people of Pompeii," your guide tells you. "Pompeii had no sewers, and during heavy rainfalls the streets were flooded with many inches of water. The Pompeiians could keep their feet dry by walking on those stones."

The houses and shops are of stone. The upper stories, which were wooden, were burned away in the holocaust or simply crumbled with the centuries. The biggest of the shops are along the Street of Abundance, which must have been the Fifth Avenue of its day. Silversmiths, shoemakers, manufacturers of cloth—all had their shops here. And every few doors, there is another thermopolium, or wine shop. In many of these, the big jars of wine are still intact, standing in holes in marble counters just the way bins of ice cream are stored in a soda fountain today.

The center of the city's life was the Forum, a large square which you enter not far from the main gate of the city. Before the earthquake of 63, Pompeii's Forum must have been a truly imposing place, enclosed on three sides by a series of gates supported by huge columns. At the north end, on the fourth side, stood the temple of Jupiter, Juno, and Minerva, raised on a podium ten feet high. But the earthquake toppled the temple and most of the columns, and not much rebuilding had been done at the time of the eruption. Pompeii's slowness to rebuild was our eternal loss, for little remains of the Forum except the stumps of massive columns.

Other public buildings were also on the main square: the headquarters of the wool industry, and several other temples, including one dedicated to Vespasian (father of Titus), a Roman emperor who was worshiped as a deity. Near the Forum was a macellum, or market, where food-stuffs were sold and where beggars wandered.

Pompeii had many beggars. One of them was found in April, 1957, at the gate of the road leading to the town of Nocera. A cast taken of him shows him to have been less than five feet tall, and deformed by the bone disease known as rickets. On the last day of Pompeii's life, this beggar had gone about asking for alms, and some generous citizen had given him a bone with a piece of meat still on it. When the eruption came, the beggar tried to flee, jealously guarding his sack containing the cutlet—and he was found with it, 2,000 years later.

Pompeii was a city of many fine temples, both around the Forum and in the outlying streets. One of the most interesting is one dating from the sixth century B.C., the oldest building in the city. Only the foundation and a few fragmented columns remain, but this temple was evidently regarded with great reverence, since it was located in the center of a fairly large triangular space adjoining the main theater. Nearby is the Temple of Isis, which was rebuilt after the earthquake and so is in fairly good preservation. Isis, an Egyptian goddess, was one of the many foreign gods and goddesses who had come to be worshiped in the Roman Empire by the time of the destruction of Pompeii. Her gaudily decorated temple at Pompeii is the only European temple of Isis that has come down to us from the ancient world.

But many temples, bathhouses, amphitheaters, and government buildings have survived in other places. What makes Pompeii uniquely significant is the wealth of knowledge it gives us about the private lives of its people. Nowhere else do we have such complete information about the homes of the ancients, about their customs and living habits, about their humble pots and pans.

The houses in Pompeii show the evolution of styles over a period of several centuries. Many of the houses are built to the same simple plan: a central court, known as the atrium, around which a living room, bedrooms, and a garden are arrayed. This was the classic Roman style of home. Some of the later and more impressive houses show the influence of Greek styles, with paintings and mosaic decorations as well as baths, reception rooms, huge gardens, and sometimes a second atrium.

The houses of Pompeii are known by name, and a good deal is known of their occupants. One of the most famous is the House of the Vetti Brothers, which is lavishly decorated with paintings, mosaics, and sculptures. The inscriptions on these houses are often amusing today. One businessman had written on the walls of his villa, WELCOME PROFITS! Another greeted his visitors with the inscribed words, PROFITS MEAN JOY!

Mosaic from a house in Pompeii with the inscription, "Cave Canem." First century, A.D. Scala/Art Resource, New York.

At the so-called House of the Tragic Poet, a mosaic shows a barking dog, with the inscription *cave canem*—"Beware of the dog." On the building known as the House of the Lovers, which received its name because the newly married Claudius Elogus lived there, someone had written a line of verse dedicated to the newlyweds on the porch: *Amantes, ut apes, vitam mellitem exigunt.* ("Lovers, like bees, desire a life full of honey.")

One interesting house uncovered since World War II is the Villa of Giulia Felix ("Happy Julia") which was of exceptional size. Apparently Giulia found the expense of this elegant house too much for her budget, because she had opened her baths to the public and advertised the fact with a sign on the gate. For a fee, Pompeiians who scorned the crowds at the public baths could bathe at Giulia's in privacy and comfort. Even this income did not seem to have been enough, for another sign uncovered in 1953 announced that the magnificent villa was for rent.

One of the truly fascinating aspects of Pompeii is the multitude of scribbled street signs. Notices were painted directly on the stone, and have come down to us. At the big amphitheater, an inscription tells us, "The troupe of gladiators owned by Suettius Centus will give a performance at Pompeii on May 31st. There will be an animal show. The awnings will be used." And at the theater, a message to a popular actor reads, "Actius, beloved of the people, come back soon; fare thee well!"

There are inscriptions at the taverns, too. "Romula loves Staphyclus" is on one wall. Elsewhere there is a poem that sounds like one of today's hit tunes: "Anyone could as well stop the winds blowing, / And the waters from flowing, / As stop lovers from loving."

Developing Comprehension Skills

1. Robert Silverberg writes of Pompeii, "There is no other city quite like it in all the world." What did he mean?

2. Why does the author say that modern archaeology began with Pompeii?

3. How are the remains of Pompeii different from the remains of other ancient cities?

4. On the day of the eruption of Mount Vesuvius in A.D. 79, what warning did the Pompeiians have? How did their reactions vary?

5. Do you think modern people would react to a natural disaster differently than the citizens of Pompeii did? Explain your answer.

Reading Literature: Nonfiction

1. **Identifying Description and Narration.** For the most part, "Pompeii" is an explanatory article. In it, the author explains what Pom-

peii was like and how it died. However, the author uses both description and narration to present information. In the following paragraph, for example, the first sentence is explanatory, the second is description, and the third is narration:

> One who survived the earthquake of 63 was the banker, Caecilius Jucundus. He was a plump, well-fed man with a harsh smile and beady eyes and a big wart on his left cheek. At the moment the earth shook, Caecilius was in the Forum, the main square of Pompeii. . . .

Find other passages that combine narration, explanation, and description. Explain what each kind of writing adds to the selection.

2. **Appreciating Imagery.** To capture the sights, sounds, and smells of bustling Pompeii, the author of this article used a great deal of imagery. Imagery, as you know, is description that appeals to one or more of the senses—sight, sound, touch, taste, and smell. An example of sound imagery is "the rumble of heavy wooden wheels." An example of sight imagery is "drifting white ash." Find three more examples of imagery in the article. How does each help you to experience Pompeii and feel the terror of the doomed citizens?

3. **Recognizing Sources of Information.** A writer of nonfiction must get information from several reliable, or truthful, sources. Where do you think the author of "Pompeii" found most of his information? What additional sources of information might he have used?

4. **Combining Fact and Fiction.** In order to give readers a good understanding of life in a past age, a writer often combines fact and fiction. The writer first studies all the real evidence that is available. He or she then creates characters or situations to fit those facts. Find two examples in "Pompeii" of a fictional incident that seems to have been based on facts.

5. **Identifying Figures of Speech.** Figures of speech are used to describe things in fresh, imaginative ways. Silverberg uses a great many figures of speech in his writing. For example, throughout the article, Silverberg personifies the city of Pompeii. This means that he gives it human characteristics. At other times, Silverberg uses metaphors in his descriptions. A metaphor compares unlike things. It does not use *like* or *as* to make the comparison. Find several examples of each type of figure of speech. Explain the comparison in each one.

6. **Understanding Analogies.** An analogy is a comparison of two basically different things that are alike in some ways. This analogy makes the point that Pompeii was a popular vacation spot: "By A.D. 79, it had become a fashionable seaside resort, an Atlantic City or a Miami Beach of its day." Explain the comparison.

The following analogies are also from "Pompeii." Explain the analogy in each, and the point the author is making.

a. No more gladiatorial games! It was like having our Congress declare that neither the Yankees nor the Dodgers could play baseball for a decade.

b. The biggest of the shops are along the Street of Abundance, which must have been the Fifth Avenue of its day.

c. Pompeii is like a photograph in three

dimensions. It shows us exactly what a city of the Roman Empire was like.

Developing Vocabulary Skills

Analyzing Your Vocabulary Skills. Use the skills you have learned to define the underlined words in the following sentences from "Pompeii." Write each underlined word and its definition. Then explain how you determined the meaning. Did you use a context clue? If so, which one? Were word parts helpful? If so, write the meaning of the word part that you recognized. Were there any words you needed to look up in the dictionary? Why?

1. Before then, the digging of treasures from the ground had been a haphazard and unscholarly affair. However, the <u>excavation</u> of Pompeii was done in a systematic, scientific manner. . . .

2. Not so with Pompeii. It was <u>engulfed</u> in an instant.

3. . . . on it was a scene showing the earthquake and <u>depicting</u> the bull he had sacrificed.

4. Many of the houses are built to the same simple plan: a central court, known as the <u>atrium</u>, around which a living room, bedrooms, and a garden are arrayed.

5. Her <u>gaudily</u> decorated temple at Pompeii is the only European temple of Isis that has come down to us. . . .

6. The pumice stones, or <u>lapilli</u>, did little damage.

7. But for all his shrewdness and <u>foresight</u>, Diomedes was undone anyway.

8. Just within the entrance is a museum that has been built in recent years to house many of the smaller <u>antiquities</u> found in the ruins.

9. A cast taken of him shows him to have been less than five feet tall, and deformed by the bone disease known as <u>rickets</u>.

10. And every few doors, there is another <u>thermopolium</u>, or wine shop.

Developing Writing Skills

1. **Comparing Fiction and Nonfiction.** In Chapter 1, you read the short story "The Dog of Pompeii." It, like the nonfiction article "Pompeii," is about the ancient city of Pompeii and its destruction. What do the short story and the article have in common? What similar information do they present? In what ways are the two pieces about Pompeii different? In a short composition, compare and contrast the views of Pompeii presented in the short story and in the nonfiction article.

2. **Describing a Place.** Review the third paragraph of "Pompeii." In it, the author describes ancient Pompeii. In a composition, describe a city you know well. Use precise words to describe its size, location, appearance, and mood.

   Pre-Writing. If possible, observe the city you have chosen. Take notes, using descriptive words and phrases. Use sensory images to describe sights, sounds, and smells. Describe details that reveal the city's mood. Organize your list of sensory descriptions. You might use the following groupings: size, appearance, location, and mood.

   Writing. Use your organized notes to develop your paragraph. Focus on one aspect of the city in each paragraph. Use specific adjectives and strong, active verbs. Include an interesting introduction and conclusion.

Revising. Ask someone to imagine the city as you read your composition aloud. Ask if you have provided enough sensory details. Check to see if each paragraph develops description of a different aspect of the city. Look for confusing or vague words, and replace them with more specific ones.

3. **Writing a Speech.** Refer to the materials you have been gathering in your speech folder. Use your organized note cards to write the first draft of your speech. Develop each main idea with the specific facts you have gathered. Make your introduction and conclusion strong and interesting.

When your first draft is completed, revise it. Improve the organization and strengthen the development, if necessary. Read the speech aloud. Have someone listen and comment on it.

Developing Skills in Critical Thinking

Using Inferences. An inference, as you have learned, is a conclusion based on factual evidence. For example, archaeologists found a stain on a counter of a wine shop in Pompeii. When the author says that "a customer had thrown down his glass and fled," he is basing the statement on an inference. How did he reach his conclusion?

Read the following statements. Explain the evidence on which each is probably based.

1. Over the centuries the steady stream of carts had worn ruts deep into the pavement of Pompeii's narrow streets.

2. A small boy who had just learned the Greek alphabet stopped in front of a blank wall and took a piece of charcoal from his tunic. Hastily he scribbled the Greek letters. . . .

3. Near the house of Diomedes, a beggar and his little goat sought shelter. The man fell dead a few feet from Diomedes' door; the faithful goat remained by his side, its silver bell tinkling until its turn came.

Developing Skills in Speaking and Listening

Developing a Speech. After you have organized and written your speech, you must rehearse your speech many times. You may choose to memorize your entire speech. You may also refer to an outline or notes. Find the method that works best for you.

Consider these guidelines when giving your speech:

Dress appropriately.

Maintain eye contact with your audience.

Glance at your notes. Do not read directly from your cards.

Speak loudly enough to be heard. Pronounce words clearly and distinctly.

Use natural gestures and facial expressions to emphasize key points.

Be comfortable. Stand tall, but try to appear relaxed and confident.

When you have practiced your speech enough to feel comfortable, you will have the confidence you need to deliver it well.

CHAPTER 5 Review

Using Your Skills in Reading Nonfiction

The following paragraphs are nonfiction. They come from *Black Boy*, by Richard Wright. Read them, and answer the questions that follow.

> In Memphis we lived in a one-story brick tenement. The stone buildings and the concrete pavements looked bleak and hostile to me. The absence of green, growing things made the city seem dead. Living space for the four of us—my mother, my brother, my father, and me—was a kitchen and a bedroom. In the front and rear were paved areas in which my brother and I could play, but for days I was afraid to go into the strange city streets alone.
>
> It was in this tenement that the personality of my father first came fully into the orbit of my concern. He worked as a night porter in a Beale Street drugstore and he became important and forbidding to me only when I learned that I could not make noise when he was asleep in the daytime. He was the lawgiver in our family and I never laughed in his presence. I used to lurk timidly in the kitchen doorway and watch his huge body sitting slumped at the table.

1. Is this a passage from an autobiography, a biography, an article, a personal essay, or a true adventure? What clues led you to your conclusion?

2. What is Richard Wright's tone?

3. What is the setting for this passage?

4. What can you tell about the narrator of this selection?

Using Your Comprehension Skills

1. The following passages are from a long short story that you will read in Chapter 6. Explain whether the narrator's purpose in each of these passages is to describe, define, explain, or persuade.

    a. As you see, my experiments are completed. I have included in my report all of my formulae, as well as mathematical analysis in the appendix.

    b. I want to be left to myself. I am touchy and irritable. I feel the darkness closing in. I don't blame anyone. I knew what might happen.

2. The following sentences are from the same story. Decide which of these statements are facts and which are opinions. Explain your answers.

 a. I've quit my job with Donnegan's Plastic Box Company.
 b. There's something mighty strange about you, Charlie.
 c. He snapped at my hand.
 d. He was unusually disturbed and vicious.

Using Your Vocabulary Skills

Read these sentences from Chapter 6. In the underlined words, find prefixes, suffixes, and Greek and Latin roots. What do these word parts tell about the meaning of each word?

1. Dr. Nemur said Dr. Strauss was nothing but an opportunist.
2. I had the feeling that she was an unreachable genius.
3. Nemur was unacquainted with Hindustani and Chinese.
4. The disproving of a theory was as important to the advancement of learning as a success would be.
5. I should look up all the words in the dictionary.
6. My television set is broken.

Using Your Writing Skills

Choose one of the writing assignments below.

1. Identify two authors in this chapter who are similar in some way. They may have similar careers, similar ideas, or similar backgrounds, for example. Write a report comparing these two authors. Your report should point out both similarities and differences between the two authors.
2. Choose two famous people who interest you. You might choose two former Presidents, for example, or two sports figures. Write an imaginary dialogue between these two people. Have them discuss important issues or ideas. Remember to make your dialogue flow logically as one person reacts to and responds to the other.

Using Your Skills in Study and Research

You have learned about a number of individuals and events in this chapter. Choose a person or subject that interested you. Use the *Readers' Guide*, card catalog, and vertical file to find more information on that person. Collect facts, photos, and graphic aids. Present your findings to the class.

CHAPTER 6

The Long Short Story

Blue Caterpillar, 1961, HELEN FRANKENTHALER.
Collection of the Artist. Courtesy of Skira, S.A.
Geneva, Switzerland.

Reading Literature: The Long Short Story

What Is a Long Short Story?

Sometimes a story is too long to be read at one sitting. Yet it still concentrates on only a few major characters. Its plot is simple, not complicated. Every detail counts. Such a story is a **long short story**.

The History of the Long Short Story

It is clear that the long short story is very much like any other short story. However, the long short story is also similar to another form of literature, called the **novel**. The first novels appeared in the seventeenth and eighteenth centuries. They differed from earlier literature, such as epics, in that they told about the lives of ordinary people. Novels covered long periods of time and dealt with dozens of different incidents, settings and characters. Because of the length of the novel, all of these elements could be covered in great depth.

Occasionally, a writer would develop a story that was not clearly either a novel or a short story. Such stories were not as complex as novels. However, they were not short enough to be called short stories. They also covered a longer period of time and more incidents than a short story. New terms developed for these selections: **the short novel** or **long short story**. No matter what they are called, however, they make wonderful reading.

The Elements of the Long Short Story

You learned about the elements of a short story in Chapter 2. A long short story uses these same elements.

Conflict. One of the most important elements of a long short story is the conflict. Conflict, as you know, is a struggle between forces.

You need to know what the conflict of any story is in order to understand why the characters feel and act as they do. Conflict can be either external or internal. External conflict is a struggle between characters or between a character and an outside force. Internal conflict is a mental struggle within a character.

Point of View. Point of view refers to the eyes and mind through which something is written. A story may be told from first-person point of view. This means that the narrator, or person telling the story, is part of the action. A story may also be told from the third-person point of view. Then, the narrator is outside the story. The long short story you will read in this chapter is told from the first-person point of view. The character telling the story is also the main character. As you read, be aware of how the first-person point of view affects the information you receive.

Static and Dynamic Characters. The characters in a story can be either static or dynamic. A **static character** stays the same throughout the story. A **dynamic character** changes in response to the events that occur in the story.

The main character in the story you are about to read is a dynamic character. As this story unfolds, you will see many changes take place within him. Try to notice how the writer gives you clues about these changes.

How To Read a Long Short Story

1. Allow yourself enough time to read the long short story comfortably. Remember, you will probably not be able to read the whole story at one sitting.
2. Notice how the conflict in the story creates a feeling of tension and suspense.
3. Be aware of how the main character develops. First look at his or her changing reactions to other people. Then try to see how others react to the character.
4. Appreciate how the writer brings this story to a close. Then ask yourself if there are any questions the story does not answer. Even though there is a definite conclusion, is there more you would like to know?

Comprehension Skills: Grammar and Mechanics

Sentences and Sentence Fragments

Authors usually write in complete sentences. You remember that a sentence expresses a complete thought. It tells you what is happening, and who or what is involved in the action.

The dishes | crashed to the floor.

what   what happened

Sometimes, however, writers use sentence fragments. A sentence fragment is only part of a sentence. Here is an example of a sentence fragment. The fragment is underlined.

I've been given a lab of my own and permission to go ahead with the research. I'm onto something. <u>Working day and night.</u>

Writers sometimes use fragments to imitate the way people really speak and think. Fragments often tell something about the mood of the character. The character may be in a hurry or upset.

Using Grammar and Spelling Clues

You learn about characters by the way they speak or write in a story. Charlie, the character in the long short story you are about to read, uses incorrect grammar when the story begins. Read the following passage. What does Charlie's writing tell you about him?

I told him I saw a inkblot. He said yes and it made me feel good. I thot that was all but when I got up to go he said Charlie we are not thru yet.

The following lines occur later in the story. Charlie's writing has changed. What does this change tell you about Charlie?

The day was good for me. Seeing the past more clearly, I've decided to use my knowledge and skills to work in the field of increasing human intelligence levels.

Using Punctuation Clues

End Marks. End marks tell the reader how a sentence should be spoken. They can also tell you how the character is feeling.

The period (.) tells you that the sentence is a statement or a command: *I had a test today. Let me try again.*

The question mark (?) signals a question: *What is on this card?*

A sentence that ends with an exclamation point (!) is said with excitement or strong emotion: *What a dope I am!*

Quotations. Quotations tell what a character says. There are two types of quotations, direct and indirect.

A direct quotation tells the exact words of the person who is speaking. A direct quotation is enclosed in quotation marks (" ").

"All right, Charlie," Miss Kinnian said, "it's time to begin learning foreign languages."

An indirect quotation tells what the person said. However, it does not repeat his or her exact words. No quotation marks are needed for an indirect quotation.

Miss Kinnian said I should start to learn foreign languages.

Exercises: Understanding Grammar and Mechanics

A. Read each word group below. Tell whether it is a sentence or a fragment.

1. Took a test.
2. I imagined all sort of things.
3. The one with the inkblots on the pieces of cardboard.

B. Tell whether each of these quotations is a direct or an indirect quotation. Then use punctuation clues to determine how a sentence should be read.

1. She says I'm a fine person.
2. "He's a scream," one of the girls said.
3. Dr. Strauss says I should keep writing things down in my journal.
4. I jumped up and shouted, "Leave him alone! It's not his fault!"

Vocabulary Skills: How New Words Are Created

Creating New Words

Language is a living thing that grows and develops with the changing time. New words are added to our vocabulary to keep pace with the ideas and inventions that are constantly being developed. Old words may be changed to meet current needs. In this chapter, you will learn about the different ways new words are formed.

Compound Words. Sometimes new words are formed by joining words that are already in use. These are called **compound words**. For example, when the typewriter was invented, the words *type* and *writer* were combined to name the new machine.

There are three different ways of writing compound words. They may be one word (touchdown), they may be two words (nose dive), or they may be hyphenated (single-handed).

Blends and Clipped Words. The **blend** is similar to a compound word. Words are combined, but in this case, some letters are dropped. *Motocross*, for example, is a blend of *motor* and *cross country*.

Clipped words are merely shortened forms of longer words. *Memo* and *champ*, for example, are the clipped forms of *memorandum* and *champion*. A few clipped words such as *bus* (from the word *omnibus*) are acceptable in any situation. However, most clipped words should not appear in formal writing and speaking. They should be used only in more casual circumstances.

Acronyms. Some words are made from the first letters of a group of words. These words are called acronyms. The word *sonar*, for example, was formed from **so**und **n**avigation **a**nd **r**anging. Many acronyms come from the names of organizations and government agencies. The shortened form is easier to remember. Most people have heard of NASA. Few, however, may know the agency's actual name, National Aeronautics and Space Administration.

Words from Names and Places. Proper names of people and places have also become part of our vocabulary. *August* was named for Roman emperor Augustus Caesar. The word *dunce* comes from the medieval teacher Johannes Duns Scotus. His students were called "Dunsmen." A country club near Tuxedo Lake, New York, gave its name to a style of formal suit, the *tuxedo*.

Words from Specialized Fields. Most technical and professional fields have a vocabulary of special terms called **jargon**. Members of these fields use jargon to communicate efficiently with each other. Some of this specialized vocabulary gradually becomes part of our regular vocabulary. For example, computer terms such as *word processor*, *software*, *byte*, and *BASIC* are now familiar to much of the general public.

Exercises: Finding the Origin of Words

A. Tell whether the words listed below are acronyms, blends, clipped words, compounds, or words made from a name. Use a dictionary to help you decide.

1. turtleneck	6. twirl	11. blastoff	16. teddy bear
2. gasohol	7. bedlam	12. grumble	17. kneepad
3. typo	8. quicksand	13. SALT	18. limo
4. vet	9. bunsen burner	14. paisley	19. babel
5. WHO	10. mezzo	15. NOW	20. sweatshirt

B. Try writing at least two of your own blends and acronyms. Think of some new products you would like to see on the market or a special-interest group you would like to form. For example, a combination crayon and pencil might be called a *crencil*. Or, you might use the acronym SNAP for a Student News Assembly Period.

C. Sometimes familiar words have a different meaning when they are used as part of a specialized jargon. Use a dictionary to answer the following questions.

1. What does *interest* mean to a banker?

2. What does *pan* mean to a TV director?

3. How is the word *down* used by a football player?

4. What would a geologist mean by the word *fault*?

Flowers for Algernon
Part One

DANIEL KEYES

Charlie is a mentally retarded man who wishes he were more like everyone else. What risks will he take to make his dream come true?

progris riport 1—march 5, 1965

Dr. Strauss says I shud rite down what I think and evrey thing that happins to me from now on. I dont know why but he says its importint so they will see if they will use me. I hope they use me. Miss Kinnian says maybe they can make me smart. I want to be smart. My name is Charlie Gordon. I am 37 years old. I have nuthing more to rite now so I will close for today.

progris riport 2—martch 6

I had a test today. I think I faled it. And I think maybe now they wont use me. What happind is a nice young man was in the room and he had some white cards and ink spillled all over them. He sed Charlie what do yo see on this card. I was very skared even tho I had my rabits foot in my pockit because when I was a kid I always faled tests in school and I spillled ink to.

I told him I saw a inkblot. He said yes and it made me feel good. I thot that was all but when I got up to go he said Charlie we are not thru yet. Then I don't remember so

good but he wantid me to say what was in the ink. I dint see nuthing in the ink but he said there was picturs there other pepul saw some picturs. I couldnt see any picturs. I reely tryed. I held the card close up and then far away. Then I said if I had my glases I coud see better I usally only ware my glases in the movies or TV but I said they are in the closit in the hall. I got them. Then I said let me see that card agen. I bet Ill find it now.

I tryed hard but I only saw the ink. I told him maybe I need new glases. He rote something down on a paper and I got skared of faling the test. I told him it was a very nice inkblot with littel points all around the edges. He looked very sad so that wasnt it. I said please let me try agen. Ill get it in a few minits because Im not so fast sometimes. Im a slow reeder too in Miss Kinnians class for slow adults but I'm trying very hard.

He gave me a chance with another card that had 2 kinds of ink spilled on it red and blue.

Women Dreaming of Escape, 1945, JOAN MIRÓ. Mr. and Mrs. Morton Neumann Collection, Chicago. Copyright © 1985. A.D.A.G.P., Paris/V.A.G.A., New York.

He was very nice and talked slow like Miss Kinnian does and he explained it to me that it was a *raw shok*.[1] He said pepul see things in the ink. I said show me where. He said think. I told him I think a inkblot but that wasn't rite eather. He said what does it remind you—pretend something. I closed my eyes for a long time to pretend. I told him I pretend a fowntan pen with ink leeking all over a table cloth.

I don't think I passed the *raw shok* test.

progris riport 3—martch 7

Dr Strauss and Dr Nemur say it dont matter about the inkblots. They said that maybe they will still use me. I said Miss Kinnian never gave me tests like that one only spelling and reading. They said Miss Kinnian told that I was her bestist pupil in the adult nite school because I tryed the hardist

---

1. **Rorschach.** The Rorschach Ink-Blot Test is used to diagnose mental illness. The patient is asked to tell the psychologist what he or she sees in a series of standardized ink blots. The patient's replies indicate his or her inner feelings.

and I reely wantid to lern. They said how come you went to the adult nite scool all by yourself Charlie. How did you find it. I said I asked pepul and sumbody told me where I shud go to lern to read and spell good. They said why did you want to. I told them becaus all my life I wantid to be smart and not dumb. But its very hard to be smart. They said you know it will probly be tempirery. I said yes. Miss Kinnian told me. I dont care if it herts.

Later I had more crazy tests today. The nice lady who gave it to me told me the name and I asked her how do you spellit so I can rite it my progris report: THEMATIC APPERCEPTION TEST.[2] I dont know the frist 2 words but I know what *test* means. You got to pass it or you get bad marks. This test lookd easy becaus I could see the picturs. Only this time she dint want me to tell her the picturs. She said make up storys about the pepul in the picturs.

I told her how can you tell storys about pepul you never met. I said why shud I make up lies. I never tell lies any more becaus I always get caut.

She told me this test and the other one the raw-shok was for getting personality. I laffed so hard. I said how can you get that thing from inkblots and fotos. She got sore and put her picturs away. I don't care. It was sily. I gess I faled that test too.

---

2. **Thematic Apperception Test (TAT)**. This is a psychological test where the subject is shown a series of pictures and asked to make up a story about them. This test is used to identify personality traits.

Later some men in white coats took me to a difernt part of the hospitil and gave me a game to play. It was like a race with a white mouse. They called the mouse Algernon. Algernon was in a box with a lot of twists and turns like all kinds of walls and they gave me a pencil and a paper with lines and lots of boxes. On one side it said START and on the other end it said FINISH. They said it was *amazed* and that Algernon and me had the same amazed to do. I dint see how we could have the same amazed if Algernon had a box and I had a paper but I dint say nothing. Anyway there wasnt time because the race started.

One of the men had a watch he was trying to hide so I wouldnt see it so I tryed not to look and that made me nervus.

Anyway that test made me feel worse than all the others because they did it over 10 times with different amazeds and Algernon won every time. I dint know that mice were so smart. Maybe thats because Algernon is a white mouse. Maybe white mice are smarter than other mice.

progris riport 4—Mar 8

Their going to use me! Im so exited I can hardly write. Dr Nemur and Dr Strauss had an argament about it first. Dr Nemur was in the office when Dr Strauss brot me in. Dr Nemur was worryed about using me but Dr Strauss told him Miss Kinnian rekemmended me the best from all the people who she was teaching. I like Miss Kinnian becaus shes a very smart teacher. And she said Charlie your going to have a second chance. If you volenteer for this experiment you mite get smart. They dont know if it will be perminint but theirs a chance. Thats why I said ok even when I was scared because she said it was an operashun. She said dont be scared Charlie you done so much with so little I think you deserv it most of all.

So I got scaird when Dr. Nemur and Dr. Strauss argud about it. Dr. Strauss said I had something that was very good. He said I had a good *motorvation*. I never even knew I had that. I felt proud when he said that not every body with an eye-q of 68 had that thing. I dont know what it is or where I got it but he said Algernon had it too. Algernons motor-vation is the cheese they put in his box. But it cant be that because I didn't eat any cheese this week.

Then he told Dr. Nemur something I dint understand so while they were talking I wrote down some of the words.

He said Dr. Nemur I know Charlie is not what you had in mind as the first of your new brede of intelek * * (coudnt get the word) superman. But most people of his low ment * * are host * * and uncoop * * they are usually dull apath * * and hard to reach. He has a good natcher hes intristed and eager to please.

Dr Nemur said remember he will be the first human beeng ever to have his intelijence tripled by surgicle meens.

Dr. Strauss said exakly. Look at how well hes lerned to read and write for his low mentel age its as grate an acheve * * as you and I lerning einstines therey of * * vity without help. That shows the inteness motor-vation. Its comparat * * a tremen * * achev * * I say we use Charlie.

I dint get all the words but it sounded like Dr Strauss was on my side and like the other one wasnt.

Then Dr Nemur nodded he said all right maybe your right. We will use Charlie. When he said that I got so exited I jumped up and shook his hand for being so good to me. I told him thank you doc you wont be sorry for giving me a second chance. And I mean it like I told him. After the operashun Im gonna try to be smart. Im gonna try awful hard.

Developing Comprehension Skills

1. What kind of experiment did the doctors want to perform on Charlie?

2. Why did the doctors ask Charlie to keep a diary?

3. What did Charlie's reaction to the two psychological tests tell you about his mental abilities?

4. Why did Charlie go to adult evening school? Why did this surprise the doctors?

5. What was special about Algernon? Why was Charlie's race against Algernon important?

6. Dr. Strauss had to persuade Dr. Nemur that Charlie was the right subject for the experiment. What impressed Dr. Strauss about Charlie? Do you agree with his reasoning? Why or why not?

Reading Literature: The Long Short Story

1. **Recognizing the Long Short Story.** Sometimes a short story is too long to be read in one sitting. In this case, it is called a **long short story**. Usually, such a story covers a longer period of time than a typical short story. It also has more characters, settings, and incidents.

   How does the length of "Flowers for Algernon" compare with the short stories you read in Chapter 2? In Part One of "Flowers for Algernon," how many characters are introduced? Based on what you have read, what incidents might you still expect to happen in the story?

2. **Understanding Form.** "Flowers for Algernon" is written as though it were a diary, or journal. In a diary the writer records thoughts, feelings, and experiences. Do you think the diary form is a good way to tell this story? How will it help the reader to see changes in Charlie? What things will the diary *not* show?

3. **Analyzing Language.** Charlie writes in simple language and uses very short, simple sentences. He often shows that he does not understand the meaning of certain words. For example, Charlie writes, "Its very hard to be smart. They said you know it will probly be tempirery. I said yes. Miss Kinnian told me. I dont care if it herts." What does this passage say about the risks of Charlie's operation? Do you think Charlie understands these risks? Do you think he even understands the word *temporary*? In general, what does Charlie's writing tell you about him? What does it imply about the way he might view the world around him?

4. **Recognizing Motivation.** Charlie is eager to have the experimental operation. Examine his journal closely for clues to his motivation, or reasons for wanting it. Why does Charlie want desperately for the doctors to "use" him? Is this motive the same as his motive for going to night school?

5. **Suspending Disbelief.** In fiction and drama, authors sometimes ask readers to accept something that may not really be possible. For example, a writer may ask the readers to accept that a character has supernatural powers of some kind.

   Charlie reports a long conversation between Dr. Strauss and Dr. Nemur. He also records dozens of other details about the selection process. Is it likely that Charlie would be able to remember so much?

6. **Recognizing Foreshadowing.** Foreshadowing, you remember, is an author's clues to an event that will happen later in a story. Look again at the passage given in question 3. Explain how this passage might be a clue to the success or failure of the experiment. Are there any other hints in Part One about what will happen in the rest of the story?

Developing Vocabulary Skills

1. **Creating Words from Names and Places.** Some words in English were once the names of people or places. In Part One of this selection, you read about a *Rorschach Test*. This widely-used personality test was named for its creator, Swiss psychiatrist Hermann Rorschach. Research the words in the list below. Write the origin of each word. Then write its definition.

   a. melba toast
   b. diesel
   c. pasteurization
   d. Frisbee
   e. boycott
   f. tuxedo
   g. Richter scale
   h. alexandrite
   i. January
   j. watt
   k. Alençon lace
   l. sideburns
   m. sandwich
   n. mason jar
   o. ampere
   p. graham cracker

2. **Understanding Acronyms.** As you know, acronyms are words formed from the first letters of a group of words. Look at the list that follows. If an acronym is given, write the group of words for which it stands. If a group of words is given, write the acronym. Use a dictionary if you need help.

   a. UNICEF
   b. Wide Area Telecommunications Service
   c. Beginners All-purpose Symbolic Instruction Code
   d. OSHA
   e. HUD
   f. CARE
   g. Women Appointed for Voluntary Emergency Service
   h. lasar
   i. North Atlantic Treaty Organization
   j. Organization of Petroleum Exporting Countries

Developing Writing Skills

1. **Analyzing Character.** In Part One of "Flowers for Algernon," readers learn more about Charlie Gordon than his intelligence level. Readers also learn about his interests, his hopes, and his special personal qualities. In a brief composition, analyze Charlie Gordon's personality. Be sure to support your opinions with specific examples and quotations from Part One.

2. **Using Point of View.** In many ways, Charlie's view of the world is childlike. A child's understanding is limited. He or she may see events differently from the way they really happen. Take the viewpoint of a child. Write two or three paragraphs describing an incident in the grownup world. The incident may be real or imaginary. Try to write your description with a child's innocence, trust, and lack of experience.

   Pre-Writing. Think of an incident to report. You might choose something in the news, such as an election or a natural disaster. You might also report a process, such as the construction of a building, the making of a television program, or the making of a meal. Make notes on the actual event. Then consider how a child would view the event.

For example, a child might see things in terms of a world of toys and make-believe. Adjust your notes to this point of view. Then arrange your notes in logical order. For example, chronological, or time, order would be best for describing a process.

Writing. As you write, remember to use simple sentences made up of words a child might use. Remember that a child's view of things may be either very inaccurate or very much on target.

Revising. Exchange papers with an editing partner. Ask the person if the child's point of view comes through. Also ask your partner if your paragraphs need further details and explanation.

3. **Writing a Definition.** In the story, scientists try to judge Charlie's intelligence. What *is* intelligence? What does being smart mean to you? In two paragraphs, write your own definition of *intelligence*. You may want to tell what it is and what it is not. Give examples to support your ideas.

Developing Skills in Study and Research

Using Several Sources. In Part One, Charlie takes two tests that tell the doctors something about him. All of us take tests that measure what we know or can do. Locate information about the tests you or your classmates may be taking sometime. These could include the *Pre-liminary Scholastic Aptitude Test* (PSAT), the *Scholastic Aptitude Test* (SAT), and the *American College Test.* (ACT). Check with your school counselor for general information about the tests. Ask your librarian if your library has test preparation manuals. Ask older students to tell you what they know about the various examinations. Take notes on the information you receive from all of these sources. Share what you find with your classmates.

Developing Skills in Critical Thinking

Making Inferences. Charlie is baffled by the tests he is given because he cannot think beyond a certain level. When he is asked to imagine pictures in inkblots, he can see only inkblots. When he is asked to make up a story about a picture, he refuses to "make up lies." He cannot use his imagination. He also cannot interpret what he sees.

As Charlie describes the events of his life, the reader must look beyond Charlie's simple, matter-of-fact reporting. The reader must make inferences about what is really happening. For example, what conclusions can you draw from the following?

1. the doctors' possible reasons for wanting to perform surgery on Charlie

2. the purpose of the race between Charlie and Algernon

3. Charlie's relationship with Miss Kinnian

Flowers for Algernon
Part Two

The operation has been performed, and Charlie eagerly awaits the result. Will he finally be "smart" like other people?

progris riport 5—*Mar 10*

Im skared. Lots of the nurses and the people who gave me the tests came to bring me candy and wish me luck. I hope I have luck. I got my rabits foot and my lucky penny. Only a black cat crossed me when I was comming to the hospitil. Dr Strauss says dont be supersitis Charlie this is science. Anyway Im keeping my rabits foot with me.

I asked Dr Strauss if Ill beat Algernon in the race after the operashun and he said maybe. If the operashun works Ill show that mouse I can be as smart as he is. Maybe smarter. Then Ill be abel to read better and spell the words good and know lots of things and be like other people. I want to be smart like other people. If it works perminint they will make everybody smart all over the wurld.

They dint give me anything to eat this morning. I dont know what that eating has to do with getting smart. Im very hungry and Dr. Nemur took away my box of candy. That Dr Nemur is a grouch. Dr Strauss says

I can have it back after the operashun. You cant eat befor a operashun. . . .

progress report 6—*Mar 15*

The operashun dint hurt. He did it while I was sleeping. They took off the bandijis from my head today so I can make a PROGRESS REPORT. Dr. Nemur who looked at some of my other ones says I spell PROGRESS wrong and told me how to spell it and REPORT too. I got to try and remember that next time.

I have a very bad memary for spelling. Dr Strauss says its ok to tell about all the things that happin to me but he says I should tell more about what I feel and what I think. When I told him I dont know how to think he said try. All the time when the bandijis were on my eyes I tryed to think. Nothing happened. I don't know what to think about. Maybe if I ask him he will tell me how I can think now that Im suppose to get smart. What do smart people think about. Fancy things I suppose. I wish I knew some fancy things already.

progress report 7—*Mar 19*

Nothing is happining. I had lots of tests and different kinds of races with Algernon. I hate that mouse. He always beats me. Dr. Strauss said I got to play those games. And he said some time I got to take those tests over again. Those inkblots are stupid. And those pictures are stupid too. I like to draw a picture of a man and a woman but I wont make up lies about people.

I got a headache from trying to think so much. I thot Dr Strauss was my friend but he don't help me. He dont tell me what to think or when Ill get smart. Miss Kinnian dint come to see me. I think writing these progress reports are stupid too.

progress report 8—*Mar 23*

Im going back to work at the factory. They said it was better I shud go back to work but I cant tell anyone what the oper-ashun was for and I have to come to the hospital for an hour evry night after work. They are gonna pay me mony every month for learning to be smart.

Im glad Im going back to work because I miss my job and all my frends and all the fun we have there.

Dr Strauss says I shud keep writing things down but I dont have to do it every day just when I think of something or some-thing speshul happins. He says dont get dis-coridged because it takes time and it hap-pins slow. He says it took a long time with Algernon before he got 3 times smarter than he was before. Thats why Algernon beats me all the time because he had that

operashun too. That makes me feel better. I coud probly do that amazed faster than a reglar mouse. Maybe some day Ill beat him. That would be something. So far Algernon looks smart perminent.

Mar 25. (I dont have to write PROGRESS REPORT on top any more just when I hand it in once a week for Dr Nemur. I just have to put the date on. That saves time)

We had a lot of fun at the factery today. Joe Carp said hey look where Charlie had his operashun what did they do Charlie put some brains in. I was going to tell him but I remembered Dr Strauss said no. Then Frank Reilly said what did you do Charlie forget your key and open your door the hard way. That made me laff. Their really my friends and they like me.

Sometimes somebody will say hey look at Joe or Frank or George he really pulled a Charlie Gordon. I dont know why they say that but they always laff. This morning Amos Borg who is the 4 man at Donnegans used my name when he shouted at Ernie the office boy. Ernie lost a packige. He said Ernie for godsake what are you trying to be a Charlie Gordon. I dont understand why he said that.

Mar 28. Dr Strauss came to my room tonight to see why I dint come in like I was suppose to. I told him I dont like to race with Algernon any more. He said I dont have to for a while but I shud come in. He had a present for me. I thot it was a little television but it wasnt. He said I got to turn it on when I go to sleep. I said your kidding why shud I turn it on when Im going to sleep. Who ever herd of a thing like that. But he said if I want to get smart I got to do what he says. I told him I dint think I was going to get smart and he puts his hand on my sholder and said Charlie you dont know it yet but your getting smarter all the time. You wont notice for a while. I think he was just being nice to make me feel good because I dont look any smarter.

Oh yes I almost forgot. I asked him when I can go back to the class at Miss Kinnians school. He said I wont go their. He said that soon Miss Kinnian will come to the hospittil to start and teach me speshul.

Mar 29. Tha crazy TV kept up all night. How can I sleep with something yelling crazy things all night in my ears. And the nutty pictures. Wow. I don't know what it says when Im up so how am I going to know when Im sleeping.

Dr Strauss says its ok. He says my brains are lerning when I sleep and that will help me when Miss Kinnian starts my lessons in the hospitl (only I found out it isn't a hospitl its a labatory.) I think its all crazy. If you can get smart when your sleeping why do people go to school. That thing I don't think will work. I use to watch the late show on TV all the time and it never made me smart. Maybe you have to sleep while you watch it.

progress report 9—*April 3*

Dr Strauss showed me how to keep the TV turned low so now I can sleep. I don't hear a thing. And I still don't understand what it says. A few times I play it over in the morning to find out what I lerned when I was sleeping and I don't think so. Miss Kinnian says Maybe its another langwidge. But most times it sounds american. It talks faster than even Miss Gold who was my teacher in 6 grade.

I told Dr Strauss what good is it to get smart in my sleep. I want to be smart when Im awake. He says its the same thing and I have two minds. Theres the *subconscious* and the *conscious* (thats how you spell it). And one dont tell the other what its doing. They dont even talk to each other. Thats why I dream. And boy have I been having crazy dreams. Wow. Ever since that night TV. The late late late show.

I forgot to ask him if it was only me or if everybody had those two minds.

(I just looked up the word in the dictionary Dr Strauss gave me. The word is *subconscious. adj. Of the nature of mental operations yet not present in consciousness; as, subconscious conflict of desires.*) There's more but I still dont know what it means. This isnt a very good dictionary for dumb people like me.

Anyway the headache is from the party. My friends from the factery Joe Carp and Frank Reilly invited me to go to Muggsys Saloon for some drinks. I don't like to drink but they said we will have lots of fun. I had a good time.

Joe Carp said I shoud show the girls how I mop out the toilet in the factory and he got me a mop. I showed them and everyone laffed when I told that Mr. Donnegan said I was the best janiter he ever had because I like my job and do it good and never miss a day except for my operashun.

I said Miss Kinnian always said Charlie be proud of your job because you do it very good.

Everybody laffed and we had a good time and they gave me lots of drinks and Joe said Charlie is a card when hes potted. I dont know what that means but everybody likes me and we have fun. I cant wait to be smart like my best friends from work Joe Carp and Frank Reilly.

Flower Head, about 1940, WILLIAM BAZIOTES. University of Oklahoma Museum of Art, Norman, Oklahoma.

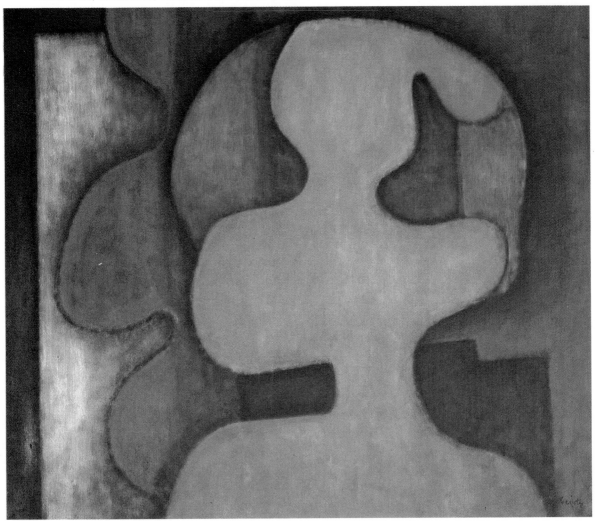

I dont remember how the party was over but I think I went out to buy a newspaper and coffe for Joe and Frank and when I came back there was no one their. I looked for them all over till late. Then I dont remember so good but I think I got sleepy or sick. A nice cop brot me back home Thats what my landlady Mrs Flynn says.

But I got a headache and a big lump on my head. I think maybe I fell but Joe Carp says it was the cop they beat up drunks some times. I don't think so. Miss Kinnian says cops are to help people. Anyway I got a bad headache and Im sick and hurt all over. I dont think Ill drink anymore.

April 6. I beat Algernon! I dint even know I beat him until Burt the tester told me. Then the second time I lost because I got so exited I fell off the chair before I finished. But after that I beat him 8 more times. I must be getting smart to beat a smart mouse like Algernon. But I don't feel any smarter.

I wanted to race Algernon some more but Burt said thats enough for one day. They let me hold him for a minit. Hes not so bad. Hes soft like a ball of cotton. He blinks and when he opens his eyes their black and pink on the eges.

I said can I feed him because I felt bad to beat him and I wanted to be nice and make friends. Burt said no Algernon is a very specshul mouse with an operashun like mine, and he was the first of all the animals to stay smart so long. He told me Algernon is so smart that every day he has to solve a

test to get his food. Its a thing like a lock on a door that changes every time Algernon goes in to eat so he has to lern something new to get his food. That made me sad because if he couldn't lern the test he woud be hungry.

I don't think its right to make you pass a test to eat. How would Dr. Nemur like it to have to pass a test every time he wants to eat. I think Ill be friends with Algernon.

April 9. Tonight after work Miss Kinnian was at the laboratory. She looked like she was glad to see me but scared. I told her dont worry Miss Kinnian Im not smart yet and she laffed. She said I have confidence in you Charlie the way you struggled so hard to read and rite better than all the others. At werst you will have it for a little wile and your doing somthing for science.

We are reading a very hard book. Its called *Robinson Crusoe* about a man who gets merooned on a desert Iland. Hes smart and figers out all kinds of things so he can have a house and food and hes a good swimmer. Only I feel sorry because hes all alone and has no frends. But I think their must be somebody else on the iland because theres a picture with his funny umbrella looking at footprints. I hope he gets a frend and not be lonly.

April 10. Miss Kinnian teaches me to spell better. She says look at a word and close your eyes and say it over and over until you remember. I have lots of truble with through that you say threw and enough and tough that you dont say enew and tew. You get to say enuff and tuff. Thats how I use to write it before I started to get smart. Im confused but Miss Kinnian says theres no reason in spelling.

Apr 14. Finished *Robinson Crusoe.* I want to find out more about what happens to him but Miss Kinnian says thats all there is. Why.

Apr 15. Miss Kinnian says Im lerning fast. She read some of the Progress Reports and she looked at me kind of funny. She says Im a fine person and ill show them all. I asked her why. She said never mind but I shouldnt feel bad if I find out everybody isnt nice like I think. She said for a person who god gave so little to you done more then a lot of people with brains they never even used. I said all my friends are smart people but there good. They like me and they never did anything that wasnt nice. Then she got something in her eye and she had to run out to the ladys room.

Apr 16. Today, I lerned, the comma, this is a comma (,), a period, with a tail, Miss Kinnian, says its importent, because, it makes writing, better, she said, somebody, coud lose, a lot of money, if a comma, isnt, in the, right place, I dont have, any money, and I dont see, how a comma, keeps you, from losing it,

Apr 17. I used the comma wrong. Its punctuation. Miss Kinnian told me to look up long words in the dictionary to lern to spell them. I said whats the difference if you can read it anyway. She said its part of your education so now on Ill look up all the words Im not sure how to spell. It takes a long time to write that way but I only have to look up once and after that I get it right.

You got to mix them up, she showed? me" how. to mix! them (and now, I can! mix up all kinds" of punctuation, in! my writing? There, are lots! of rules? to lern; but Im gettin'g them in my head.

One thing I like about, Dear Miss Kinnian: (thats the way it goes in a business letter if I ever go into business) is she, always gives me' a reason" when—I ask. She's a gen'ius! I wish I cou'd be smart" like, her;

(Punctuation, is: fun!)

April 18. What a dope I am! I didn't even understand what she was talking about. I read the grammar book last night and it explanes the whole thing. Then I saw it was the same way as Miss Kinnian was trying to tell me, but I didn't get it.

Miss Kinnian said that the TV working in my sleep helped out. She and I reached a plateau. Thats a flat hill.

After I figured out how punctuation worked, I read over all my old Progress Reports from the beginning. Boy, did I have crazy spelling and punctuation! I told Miss Kinnian I ought to go over the pages and fix all the mistakes but she said, "No, Charlie, Dr. Nemur wants them just as they are. That's why he let you keep them after they were photostated, to see your own progress. You're coming along fast, Charlie."

That made me feel good. After the lesson I went down and played with Algernon. We don't race any more.

April 20. I feel sick inside. Not sick like for a doctor, but inside my chest it feels empty like getting punched and a heartburn at the same time. I wasn't going to write about it, but I guess I got to, because its important. Today was the first time I ever stayed home from work.

Last night Joe Carp and Frank Reilly invited me to a party. There were lots of girls and some men from the factory. I remembered how sick I got last time I drank too much, so I told Joe I didn't want anything to drink. He gave me a plain coke instead.

We had a lot of fun for a while. Joe said I should dance with Ellen, and she would teach me the steps. I fell a few times and I couldn't understand why because no one else was dancing besides Ellen and me. And all the time I was tripping because somebody's foot was always sticking out.

Then when I got up I saw the look on Joe's face and it gave me a funny feeling in my stomach. "He's a scream," one of the girls said. Everybody was laughing.

"Look at him. He's blushing. Charlie is blushing."

"Hey, Ellen, what'd you do to Charlie? I never saw him act like that before."

I didn't know what to do or where to turn. Everyone was looking at me and laughing and I felt naked. I wanted to hide. I ran outside and I threw up. Then I walked home. It's a funny thing I never knew that Joe and Frank and the others liked to have me around all the time to make fun of me.

Now I know what it means when they say "to pull a Charlie Gordon."

I'm ashamed.

progress report 11

April 21. Still didn't go into the factory. I told Mrs. Flynn my landlady to call and tell Mr. Donnegan I was sick. Mrs. Flynn looks at me funny lately like she's scared.

I think it's a good thing about finding out how everybody laughs at me. I thought about it a lot. It's because I'm so dumb and I don't even know when I'm doing something dumb. People think it's funny when a dumb person can't do things the same way they can.

Anyway, now I know I'm getting smarter every day. I know punctuation and I can spell good. I like to look up all the hard words in the dictionary and I remember them. I'm reading a lot now, and Miss Kinnian says I read very fast. Sometimes I even understand what I'm reading about, and it stays in my mind. There are times when I can close my eyes and think of a page and it all comes back like a picture.

Besides history, geography and arithmetic, Miss Kinnian said I should start to learn foreign languages. Dr. Strauss gave me some more tapes to play while I sleep. I still don't understand how that conscious and unconscious mind works, but Dr.

Strauss says not to worry yet. He asked me to promise that when I start learning college subjects next week I wouldn't read any books on psychology—that is, until he gives me permission.

I feel a lot better today, but I guess I'm still a little angry that all the time people were laughing and making fun of me because I wasn't so smart. When I become intelligent like Dr. Strauss says, with three times my I.Q. of 68, then maybe I'll be like everyone else and people will like me.

I'm not sure what an I.Q. is. Dr. Nemur said it was something that measured how intelligent you were—like a scale in the drugstore weighs pounds. But Dr. Strauss had a big argument with him and said an I.Q. didn't weigh intelligence at all. He said an I.Q. showed how much intelligence you could get, like the numbers on a measuring cup. You still had to fill the cup up.

Then when I asked Burt, who gives me my intelligence tests and works with Algernon, he said that both of them were wrong (only I had to promise not to tell them he said so). Burt says that the I.Q. measures a lot of different things including some of the things you learned already, and it really isn't any good at all.

So I still don't know what I.Q. is except that mine is going to be over 200 soon. I didn't want to say anything, but I don't see how if they don't know what it is, or where it is—I don't see how they know how much of it you've got.

Dr. Nemur says I have to take a Rorshach Test tomorrow. I wonder what that is.

April 22. I found out what a Rorshach is. It's the test I took before the operation— the one with the inkblots on the pieces of cardboard.

I was scared to death of those inkblots. I knew the man was going to ask me to find the pictures and I knew I couldn't. I was thinking to myself, if only there was some way of knowing what kind of pictures were hidden there. Maybe there weren't any pictures at all. Maybe it was just a trick to see if I was dumb enough to look for something that wasn't there. Just thinking about that made me sore at him.

"All right, Charlie," he said, "you've seen these cards before, remember?"

"Of course I remember."

The way I said it, he knew I was angry, and he looked surprised. "Yes, of course. Now I want you to look at this. What might this be? What do you see on this card? People see all sorts of things in these inkblots. Tell me what it might be for you—what it makes you think of."

I was shocked. That wasn't what I had expected him to say. "You mean there are no pictures hidden in those inkblots?"

He frowned and took off his glasses. "What?"

"Pictures. Hidden in the inkblots. Last time you told me everyone could see them and you wanted me to find them too."

He explained to me that the last time he had used almost the exact same words he was using now. I didn't believe it, and I still have the suspicion that he misled me at the time just for the fun of it. Unless—I don't know any more—could I have been that feeble-minded?

We went through the cards slowly. One looked like a pair of bats tugging at something. Another one looked like two men fencing with swords. I imagined all sorts of things. I guess I got carried away. But I didn't trust him any more, and I kept turning them around, even looking on the back to see if there was anything there I was supposed to catch. While he was making his notes, I peeked out of the corner of my eye to read it. But it was all in code that looked like this:

WF+A DdF−Ad orig. WF—A SF+obj

The test still doesn't make sense to me. It seems to me that anyone could make up lies about things that they didn't really imagine? Maybe I'll understand it when Dr. Strauss gives me permission to read up on psychology.

April 25. I figured out a new way to line up the machines in the factory, and Mr. Donnegan says it will save him ten thousand dollars a year in labor and increased production. He gave me a $25 bonus.

I wanted to take Joe Carp and Frank Reilly out to lunch to celebrate, but Joe said he had to buy some things for his wife, and Frank said he was meeting his cousin for lunch. I guess it'll take a little time for them to get used to the changes in me. Everybody seems to be frightened of me. When I went over to Amos Borg and tapped him, he jumped up in the air.

People don't talk to me much any more or kid around the way they used to. It makes the job kind of lonely.

April 27. I got up the nerve today to ask Miss Kinnian to have dinner with me tomorrow night to celebrate my bonus.

At first she wasn't sure it was right, but I asked Dr. Strauss and he said it was okay. Dr. Strauss and Dr. Nemur don't seem to be getting along so well. They're arguing all the time. This evening I heard them shouting. Dr. Nemur was saying that it was his experiment and his research, and Dr. Strauss shouted back that he contributed just as much, because he found me through Miss Kinnian and he performed the operation. Dr. Strauss said that someday thousands of neuro-surgeons might be using his technique all over the world.

Dr. Nemur wanted to publish the results of the experiment at the end of this month. Dr. Strauss wanted to wait a while to be sure. Dr. Strauss said Dr. Nemur was more interested in the Chair[3] of Psychology at Princeton than he was in the experiment. Dr. Nemur said Dr. Strauss was an opportunist trying to ride to glory on his coattails.

When I left afterwards, I found myself trembling. I don't know why for sure, but it was as if I'd seen both men clearly for the first time. I remember hearing Burt say Dr. Nemur had a shrew of a wife who was pushing him all the time to get things published

---

3. **Chair**, position as head of the department of a school or college.

so he could become famous. Burt said that the dream of her life was to have a big shot husband.

April 28. I don't understand why I never noticed how beautiful Miss Kinnian really is. She has brown eyes and feathery brown hair that comes to the top of her neck. She's only thirty-four! I think from the beginning I had the feeling that she was an unreachable genius—and very, very old. Now, every time I see her she grows younger and more lovely.

We had dinner and a long talk. When she said I was coming along so fast I'd be leaving her behind, I laughed.

"It's true, Charlie. You're already a better reader then I am. You can read a whole page at a glance while I can take in only a few lines at a time. And you remember every single thing you read. I'm lucky if I can recall the main thoughts and the general meaning."

"I don't feel intelligent. There are so many things I don't understand."

"You've got to be a little patient. You're accomplishing in days and weeks what it takes normal people to do in a lifetime. That's what makes it so amazing. You're like a giant sponge now, soaking things in. Facts, figures, general knowledge. And soon you'll begin to connect them, too. You'll see how different branches of learning are related. There are many levels, Charlie, like steps on a giant ladder that take you up higher and higher to see more and more of the world around you.

"I can see only a little bit of that, Charlie, and I won't go much higher than I am now, but you'll keep climbing up and up, and see more and more, and each step will open new worlds that you never even knew existed." She frowned. "I hope . . . I just hope to God—"

"What?"

"Never mind, Charles. I just hope I wasn't wrong to advise you to go into this in the first place."

I laughed. "How could that be? It worked, didn't it? Even Algernon is still smart."

We sat there silently for a while, and I knew what she was thinking about as she watched me toying with the chain of my rabbit's foot and my keys. I didn't want to think of that possibility any more than elderly people want to think of death. I knew that this was only the beginning. I knew what she meant about levels because I'd seen some of them already. The thought of leaving her behind made me sad.

I'm in love with Miss Kinnian.

Developing Comprehension Skills

1. How did Charlie feel immediately after the operation? Give two examples that show his feelings.

2. When did you first notice a change in Charlie? Do you think he was aware of the change at the time?

3. Was it true, as Charlie said, that all his co-workers liked him? Explain.

4. After the operation, why do you think Charlie's co-workers began to fear him? Do you think people would really react this way?

5. How did Charlie's feelings for Algernon begin to change? Why?

6. Do you think the doctors had a right to experiment on Charlie, even with his permission? Explain your opinion.

Reading Literature: The Long Short Story

1. **Appreciating Character Development.** At the beginning of the story, Charlie is innocent and trusting. As Charlie's intelligence grows, his awareness also increases. He begins to see the people in his life more clearly. After the second party, what does he realize about his co-workers? What does he realize in Part Two about his doctors? How does this new awareness make him feel? Why?

2. **Recognizing Irony.** Irony is a situation in which the truth is the opposite of what at first seems to be true. On page 516, Charlie recalls the comments made by Joe Carp and Frank Reilly after the operation. Charlie's comment is "That made me laff. Their really my friends and they like me." What is ironic about Charlie's comment?

Explain the irony in this statement: "I just cant wait to be smart like my best friends Joe Carp and Frank Reilly."

3. **Inferring Actions.** At the beginning of Part Two, Charlie still does not understand everything that happens to him. For that reason, readers must infer what actually happened from details in Charlie's report. For example, Charlie talks of going with friends to a party. He ends up alone and confused, with a lump on his head. Read Charlie's description on page 519. What can you conclude about what happened at the party and afterward? Find two other examples of actions that the reader must infer from Charlie's remarks.

4. **Making Inferences About Character Traits.** Daniel Keyes characterizes Charlie entirely through Charlie's own words. From Charlie's comments, readers can infer Charlie's character traits. What does each of these statements show about Charlie?

   a. I got my rabits foot and my lucky penny.
   b. I said can I feed him [Algernon] because I felt bad to beat him and I wanted to be nice and make friends.
   c. I feel sorry because hes [Robinson Crusoe] all alone and has no friends.

Developing Vocabulary Skills

Learning About Compound Words. You recall that a compound word is made by joining two separate words. Compounds may be written as one word (keyhole); they may be hyphenated (absent-minded); or they may be two words (jet lag). Skim Part Two of "Flowers for Algernon," looking for compound words. Try to find at least fifteen.

Developing Writing Skills

1. **Analyzing Character Development.** As Charlie's mental abilities grow, he goes through many changes. How are these changes similar to the stages that a child goes through while growing up? Write a composition explaining your ideas.

   Pre-Writing. Think about how children change as they grow up. Begin by listing traits of children, such as innocence and playfulness. Then list ways that children develop. You might mention such things as how the older child relates to others and feels emotionally. Now review "Flowers for Algernon." Look for ways that Charlie's actions and thoughts reflect these changes. Organize your notes by grouping main ideas and supporting examples together. Put the main ideas in chronological, or time, order or order of importance.

   Writing. In your introduction, state your main idea. Then write a topic sentence that states the main idea of each paragraph. Make sure that you include specific examples and quotations to support each topic sentence. Conclude the composition with a summary of your main points.

   Revising. Ask someone else to read your essay. See if the person thinks you have explained your ideas thoroughly. Are there more details the person wants to know? Are any passages confusing?

2. **Writing an Imaginary Diary.** "Flowers for Algernon" is fiction written in the form of a diary. Write your own imaginary diary or journal concerning a new achievement in sci-ence. This achievement may be real or imaginary. You may wish to skim newspapers or magazines for ideas.

   Write the diary entry from the point of view of someone who is directly involved. For example, you might write the diary entry for an astronaut on a new space mission. Imagine the feelings and attitudes the person would have. Try to express them clearly.

Developing Skills in Critical Thinking

1. **Recognizing False Analogies.** An analogy compares two things that are basically different, but that are similar in some ways. An analogy is often a good way to explain an unfamiliar idea. If an analogy is carried too far, however, it is considered weak, or false.

   Find the two analogies for IQ, or intelligent quotient, on page 522. One analogy compares IQ to a scale. The other compares IQ to the numbers on a measuring cup. What is helpful about each of these analogies? What are the weaknesses of each analogy?

2. **Understanding Levels of Thinking.** Charlie's early progress reports demonstrate a very simple level of thinking. Charlie understands and reports only the actual, literal facts. The progress reports in Part Two show Charlie advancing to higher levels of thinking. When does he first draw a conclusion based on the facts that he observes? How does Charlie apply problem-solving skills to a problem in the factory?

Flowers for Algernon
Part Three

Charlie has become a man of superior intelligence. He no longer has to feel lonely or "different." . . . or does he? Read to discover the new problems Charlie faces.

progress report 12

April 30. I've quit my job with Donnegan's Plastic Box Company. Mr. Donnegan insisted it would be better for all concerned if I left. What did I do to make them hate me so much?

The first I knew of it was when Mr. Donnegan showed me the petition. Eight hundred names, everyone in the factory, except Fanny Girden. Scanning the list quickly, I saw at once that hers was the only missing name. All the rest demanded that I be fired.

Joe Carp and Frank Reilly wouldn't talk to me about it. No one else would either, except Fanny. She was one of the few people I'd known who set her mind to something and believed it no matter what the rest of the world proved, said or did—and Fanny did not believe that I should have been fired. She had been against the petition on principle and despite the pressure and threats she'd held out.

"Which don't mean to say," she remarked, "that I don't think there's something mighty strange about you, Charlie. Them changes. I don't know. You used to be a good, dependable, ordinary man—not too bright maybe, but honest. Who knows what you done to yourself to get so smart all of a sudden. Like everybody around here's been saying, Charlie, it's not right."

"But how can you say that, Fanny? What's wrong with a man becoming intelligent and wanting to acquire knowledge and understanding of the world around him?"

She stared down at her work and I turned to leave. Without looking at me, she said: "It was evil when Eve listened to the snake and ate from the tree of knowledge. It was evil when she saw that she was naked. If not for that, none of us would ever have to grow old and sick and die."

Once again, now, I have the feeling of shame burning inside me. This intelligence has driven a wedge between me and all the people I once knew and loved. Before, they laughed at me and despised me for my ignorance and dullness; now, they hate me for my knowledge and understanding. What in God's name do they want of me?

They've driven me out of the factory. I don't have a job. Now I'm more alone than ever before. . . .

May 15. Dr. Strauss is very angry at me for not having written any progress reports in two weeks. He's justified because the lab is now paying me a regular salary. I told him I was too busy thinking and reading. When I pointed out that writing was such a slow process that it made me impatient with my poor handwriting, he suggested I learn to type. It's much easier to write now because I can type seventy-five words a minute. Dr. Strauss continually reminds me of the need to speak and write simply so people will be able to understand me.

I'll try to review all the things that happened to me during the last two weeks. Algernon and I were presented to the American Psychological Association sitting in convention with the World Psychological Association. We created quite a sensation at the convention. Dr. Nemur and Dr. Strauss were proud of us.

I suspect that Dr. Nemur, who is sixty— ten years older than Dr. Strauss—finds it necessary to see tangible results of his work. Undoubtedly the result of pressure by Mrs. Nemur.

Contrary to my earlier impression of him, I realize that Dr. Nemur is not at all a genius. He has a very good mind, but it struggles under the spectre of self-doubt. He wants people to take him for a genius. Therefore it is important for him to feel that his work is accepted by the world. I believe that Dr. Nemur was afraid of further delay because he worried that someone else might make a discovery along these lines and take the credit from him.

Dr. Strauss on the other hand might be called a genius, although I feel his areas of knowledge are too limited. He was educated in the tradition of narrow specialization; the broader aspects of background were neglected far more than necessary— even for a neurosurgeon.

I was shocked to learn the only ancient languages he could read were Latin, Greek, and Hebrew, and that he knows almost nothing of mathematics beyond the elementary levels of the calculus of variations. When he admitted this to me, I found myself almost annoyed. It was as if he'd hidden this part of himself in order to deceive me, pretending—as do many people, I've discovered—to be what he is not. No one I've ever known is what he appears to be on the surface.

Dr. Nemur appears to be uncomfortable around me. Sometimes when I try to talk to him, he just looks at me strangely and turns away. I was angry at first when Dr. Strauss told me I was giving Dr. Nemur an inferiority complex. I thought he was mocking me and I'm oversensitive about people making fun of me.

How was I to know that a highly respected psycho-experimentalist like Nemur was unacquainted with Hindustani and Chinese? It's absurd when you consider the work that is being done in India and China today in the very field of his study.

I asked Dr. Strauss how Nemur could refute Rahajamati's attack on his method if Nemur couldn't even read them in the first place. That strange look on Strauss' face

Relativity, 1953, M. C. ESCHER. National Gallery of Art. Gift of Mr. C. V. S. Roosevelt, Washington, D.C.

can mean only one of two things. Either he doesn't want to tell Nemur what they're saying in India, or else—and this worries me—Dr. Strauss doesn't know either. I must be careful to speak and write clearly and simply so people won't laugh.

May 18. I am very disturbed. I saw Miss Kinnian last night for the first time in over a week. I tried to avoid all discussions of intellectual concepts and to keep the conversation on a simple, everyday level, but she just stared at me blankly and asked me what I meant about the intricate mathematical variance equivalent in Dorbermann's *Fifth Concerto.*

When I tried to explain she stopped me and laughed. I guess I got angry, but I suspect I'm approaching her on the wrong level. No matter what I try to discuss with her, I am unable to communicate. I must review Vrostadt's equations on *Levels of Semantic Progression.* I find I don't communicate with people much any more. Thank God for books and music and things I can think about. I am alone at Mrs. Flynn's boarding house most of the time and seldom speak to anyone.

May 20. I would not have noticed the new dishwasher, a boy of about sixteen, at the diner where I take my evening meals if not for the incident of the broken dishes.

They crashed to the floor, sending bits of white china under the tables. The boy stood there, dazed and frightened, holding the empty tray in his hand. The catcalls from the customers (the cries of "hey, there go the profits!" . . . "Mazeltov!" . . . and "well, he didn't work here very long . . ." which invariably seem to follow the breaking of glass or dishware in a public restaurant) all seemed to confuse him.

When the owner came to see what the excitement was about, the boy cowered as if he expected to be struck. "All right! All right, you dope," shouted the owner, "don't just stand there! Get the broom and sweep that mess up. A broom . . . a broom, you idiot! It's in the kitchen!"

The boy saw he was not going to be punished. His frightened expression disappeared and he smiled as he came back with the broom to sweep the floor. A few of the rowdier customers kept up the remarks, amusing themselves at his expense.

"Here, sonny, over here there's a nice piece behind you. . . ."

"He's not so dumb. It's easier to break 'em than wash 'em!"

As his vacant eyes moved across the crowd, he slowly mirrored their smiles and finally broke into an uncertain grin at the joke he obviously did not understand.

I felt sick inside as I looked at his dull, vacuous smile, the wide, bright eyes of a child, uncertain but eager to please. They were laughing at him because he was mentally retarded.

And I had been laughing at him too.

Suddenly I was furious at myself and all those who were smirking at him. I jumped up and shouted, "Shut up! Leave him alone! It's not his fault he can't understand! He can't help what he is! But he's still a human being!"

The room grew silent. I cursed myself for losing control. I tried not to look at the boy as I walked out without touching my food. I felt ashamed for both of us.

How strange that people of honest feelings and sensibility, who would not take advantage of a man born without arms or eyes—how such people think nothing of abusing a man born with low intelligence. It infuriated me to think that not too long ago I had foolishly played the clown.

And I had almost forgotten.

I'd hidden the picture of the old Charlie Gordon from myself because, now that I was intelligent, it was something that had to be pushed out of my mind. But today in looking at that boy, for the first time I saw what I had been. I was just like him!

Only a short time ago, I learned that people laughed at me. Now I can see that unknowingly I joined with them in laughing at myself. That hurts most of all.

I have often reread my progress reports and seen the illiteracy, the childish naiveté, the mind of low intelligence peering from a dark room, through the keyhole at the dazzling light outside. I see that even in my dullness I knew I was inferior, and that other people had something I lacked—something denied me. In my mental blindness, I thought it was somehow connected with the ability to read and write, and I was sure that if I could get those skills I would automatically have intelligence too.

Even a feeble-minded man wants to be like other men.

A child may not know how to feed itself, or what to eat, yet it knows of hunger.

This then is what I was like. I never knew. Even with my gift of intellectual awareness, I never really knew.

This day was good for me. Seeing the past more clearly, I've decided to use my knowledge and skills to work in the field of increasing human intelligence levels. Who is better equipped? Who else has lived in both worlds? These are my people. Let me use my gift to do something for them.

Tomorrow, I will discuss with Dr. Strauss how I can work in this area. I may be able to help him work out the problems of widespread use of the technique that was used on me. I have several good ideas.

There is so much that might be done with this technique. If I could be made into a genius, what about thousands of others like myself? What fantastic levels might be achieved by using this technique on normal people? on geniuses?

There are so many doors to open. I am impatient to begin.

Developing Comprehension Skills

1. Why was Charlie fired from the factory?

2. What conclusion does Charlie reach about Dr. Nemur and Dr. Strauss? Do you think his view of them is correct? Could his tremendous intelligence have affected the way he saw these men?

3. "I must be careful to speak and write clearly and simply so people won't laugh," Charlie writes. In addition to this difficulty, what other similar problems did Charlie face before and after the operation?

4. What did Charlie realize after he saw the boy in the restaurant? Why does he say he felt ashamed for both of them?

5. Why did Charlie decide to "work in the field of increasing human intelligence levels"?

6. Charlie writes, "How strange that people of honest feelings and sensitivity . . . think nothing of abusing a man born with low intelligence." Do you agree that people are cruel to those with mental handicaps? Can you think of reasons why this might be so?

Reading Literature: The Long Short Story

1. **Recognizing Theme.** When an idea is considered many times throughout a work of fiction, it is probably a theme of the work. A long short story such as "Flowers for Algernon" may have several themes. The idea of loneliness occurs often in "Flowers for Algernon." Does Charlie feel more alone before or after his operation? What might be an explanation for this? What do you think "Flowers for Algernon" says about the causes and effects of loneliness?

2. **Analyzing Style.** In Part Three, Charlie uses correct grammar, punctuation, and spelling. He also uses longer or more complex sentences. How does this affect the reader's view of Charlie? What does it say about the importance of language in creating a good impression?

3. **Appreciating Imagery.** Another way Charlie shows increased intelligence is through the use of imagery in his writing. Read the following statement from his diary:

> I have often reread my progress reports and seen . . . the mind of low intelligence peering from a dark room, through the keyhold at the dazzling light outside.

What picture does this statement create? What is "the dazzling light outside"?

4. **Explaining Analogies.** You remember that an analogy is a comparison between two similar things. Charlie makes this analogy: "Even a feeble-minded man wants to be like other men. A child may not know how to feed itself, or what to eat, yet it knows of hunger." What point does Charlie wish to make with this analogy?

5. **Recognizing Allusions.** Charlie asks Fanny Girden, "What's wrong with a man becoming intelligent?" She replies by saying, "It was evil when Eve listened to the snake and ate from the tree of knowledge. It was evil when she saw that she was naked. If not for that, none of us would ever have to grow old and sick and die."

What point does Fanny intend to make by comparing Charlie's experience with Eve's experience? Is her comparison fair? Explain.

Developing Vocabulary Skills

Identifying Blends and Clipped Words. You remember that blends are made by taking parts of two separate words and blending them together into one word. *Motel*, for example, is a blend of *motor* and *hotel*.

Clipped words are shortened forms of longer words. Examples of clipped words in this selection are *photo*, from *photography*, and *lab*, from *laboratory*.

Tell whether the words below are clipped words or blends. Then tell the word or words from which each one was made.

1. flu
2. deli
3. flabbergast
4. skyjack
5. chortle
6. cab
7. telethon
8. gym
9. moped
10. brunch
11. ad
12. sub
13. splurge
14. heliport
15. phone

Developing Writing Skills

1. **Analyzing Theme.** Charlie writes "Before, they laughed at me and despised me for my ignorance and dullness; now, they hate me for my knowledge and understanding." Do you think that being "different" makes a person unpopular with others? In two or three paragraphs, explain what "Flowers for Algernon" says about being different. Be sure to use quotations and examples from the story to support your ideas.

2. **Writing a Dialogue.** Imagine the following situations, which might have occurred in "Flowers for Algernon":
   a. the meeting with Mr. Donnegan where Charlie is fired
   b. Charlie's date with Miss Kinnian
   c. Charlie giving advice to the dishwasher

Choose one of these situations. Write your own imaginary dialogue to show what might have happened.

Pre-Writing. Think about each character's role in the conversation you have selected. Then make notes for what you think each character would say. How would each character respond to the other? Keep in mind Charlie's level of understanding and use of language at that point in the story.

Writing. Use your notes as you write the dialogue. Try to show how these people would really talk. Also remember that sometimes characters may interrupt each other or use incomplete sentences. Keep your dialogue smooth. Allow one idea to lead logically to the next.

Revising. Read your dialogue aloud or ask two people to read it aloud to you. Listen for awkward parts. Check to see that the conversation makes sense and sounds natural. Make any changes that are needed to improve your dialogue.

Developing Skills in Critical Thinking

Evaluating Humor. Laughter usually occurs in situations that are pleasant or amusing. Laughter, however, can also be cruel. Cruel humor often comes from a person's prejudices or feelings of being better than others.

In Part Two, what makes Joe's and Frank's jokes about Charlie cruel rather than humorous? In Part Three, why do the diners in the restaurant laugh at the dishwasher? Do you think their laughter is cruel? Why or why not? Think of examples of jokes that arise from prejudice. Can you think of reasons why people laugh at such jokes? Explain your answer.

Flowers for Algernon
Part Four

The experiment draws to a close. What does Charlie discover about his future? Was the experiment worth the price he must pay?

progress report 13

May 23. It happened today. Algernon bit me. I visited the lab to see him as I do occasionally, and, when I took him out of his cage, he snapped at my hand. I put him back and watched him for a while. He was unusually disturbed and vicious.

May 24. Burt, who is in charge of the experimental animals, tells me that Algernon is changing. He is less cooperative; he refuses to run the maze any more; general motivation has decreased. And he hasn't been eating. Everyone is upset about what this may mean.

May 25. They've been feeding Algernon, who now refuses to work the shifting-lock problem. Everyone identifies me with Algernon. In a way we're both the first of our kind. They're all pretending that Algernon's behavior is not necessarily significant for me. But it's hard to hide the fact that some of the other animals who were used in this experiment are showing strange behavior.

Dr. Strauss and Dr. Nemur have asked me not to come to the lab any more. I know what they're thinking but I can't accept it. I am going ahead with my plans to carry their research forward. With all due respect to both these fine scientists, I am well aware of their limitations. If there is an answer, I'll have to find it out for myself. Suddenly, time has become very important to me.

May 29. I have been given a lab of my own and permission to go ahead with the research. I'm onto something. Working day and night. I've had a cot moved into the lab. Most of my writing time is spent on the notes which I keep in a separate folder, but from time to time I feel it necessary to put down my thoughts from sheer habit.

I find the calculus of intelligence to be a fascinating study. Here is the place for the application of all the knowledge I have acquired.

May 31. Dr. Strauss thinks I'm working too hard. Dr. Nemur says I'm trying to cram a lifetime of research and thought into a few weeks. I know I should rest, but I'm driven on by something inside that won't let me stop. I've got to find the reason for the sharp regression in Algernon. I've got to know if and when it will happen to me.

June 4
Letter to Dr. Strauss (copy)

Dear Dr. Strauss:

Under separate cover I am sending you a copy of my report entitled, "The Algernon-Gordon Effect: A Study of Structure and Function of Increased Intelligence," which I would like to have published.

As you see, my experiments are completed. I have included in my report all of my formulae, as well as mathematical analysis in the appendix. Of course, these should be verified.

Because of its importance to both you and Dr. Nemur (and need I say to myself, too?), I have checked and rechecked my results a dozen times in the hope of finding an error. I am sorry to say the results must stand. Yet for the sake of science, I am grateful for the little bit that I here add to the knowledge of the function of the human mind and of the laws governing the artificial increase of human intelligence.

I recall your once saying to me that an experimental failure or the disproving of a theory was as important to the advancement of learning as a success would be. I know now that this is true. I am sorry, however, that my own contribution to the field must rest upon the ashes of the work of two men I regard so highly.

Yours truly,
Charles Gordon

June 5. I must not become emotional. The facts and the results of my experiments are clear, and the more sensational aspects of my own rapid climb cannot obscure the fact that the tripling of intelligence by the surgical technique developed by Drs. Strauss and Nemur must be viewed as having little or no practical applicability (at the present time) to the increase of human intelligence.

As I review the records and data on Algernon, I see that, although he is still in his physical infancy, he has regressed mentally. Motor activity is impaired; there is a reduction of glandular activity; there is an accelerated loss of coordination.

There are also strong indications of progressive amnesia.

As will be seen by my report, these and other physical and mental deterioration syndromes can be predicted with significant results by the careful application of my formula.

The surgical stimulus to which we were both subjected has resulted in an intensification and acceleration of all mental processes. The unforeseen development, which I have taken the liberty of calling the Algernon-Gordon Effect, is the logical extension of the entire intelligence speed-up. The hypothesis here proven may be described simply in the following terms: Artificially increased intelligence deteriorates at a rate of time directly proportional to the quantity of the increase.

I feel that this, in itself, is an important discovery.

As long as I am able to write, I will continue to record my thoughts in these progress reports. It is one of my few pleasures. However, by all indications, my own mental deterioration will be very rapid.

I have already begun to notice signs of emotional instability and forgetfulness, the first symptoms of the burnout.

June 10. Deterioration progressing. I have become absent-minded. Algernon died two days ago. Dissection shows my predictions were right. His brain had decreased in weight and there was a general smoothing out of cerebral convolutions, as well as a deepening and broadening of brain fissures.

I guess the same thing is or will soon be happening to me. Now that it's definite, I don't want it to happen.

I put Algernon's body in a cheese box and buried him in the back yard. I cried.

June 15. Dr. Strauss came to see me again. I wouldn't open the door and I told him to go away. I want to be left to myself. I am touchy and irritable. I feel the darkness closing in. It's hard to throw off thoughts of suicide. I keep telling myself how important this journal will be.

It's a strange sensation to pick up a book you enjoyed just a few months ago and discover you don't remember it. I remembered how great I thought John Milton was, but when I picked up *Paradise Lost* I couldn't understand it at all. I got so angry I threw the book across the room.

I've got to try to hold on to some of it. Some of the things I've learned. Oh, God, please don't take it all away.

June 19. Sometimes, at night, I go out for a walk. Last night, I couldn't remember where I lived. A policeman took me home. I have the strange feeling that this has all happened to me before—a long time ago. I keep telling myself I'm the only person in the world who can describe what's happening to me.

June 21. Why can't I remember? I've got to fight. I lie in bed for days and I don't know who or where I am. Then it all comes back to me in a flash. Fugues of amnesia. Symptoms of senility—second childhood. I can watch them coming on. It's so cruelly logical. I learned so much and so fast. Now my mind is deteriorating rapidly. I won't let it happen. I'll fight it. I can't help thinking of the boy in the restaurant, the blank expression on his face, the silly smile, the people laughing at him. No—please—not that again. . . .

June 22. I'm forgetting things that I learned recently. It seems to be following the classic pattern—the last things learned are the first things forgotten. Or is that the pattern? I'd better look it up again to make certain. . . .

I reread my paper on the Algernon-Gordon-Effect and I get the strange feeling that it was written by someone else. There are parts I don't even understand.

Motor activity impaired. I keep tripping over things, and it becomes increasingly difficult to type.

June 23. I've given up using the typewriter. My coordination is bad. I feel I'm moving slower and slower. Had a terrible shock today. I picked up a copy of an article I used in my research, Krueger's "Uber psychische Ganzheit," to see if it would help me understand what I had done. First I thought there was something wrong with my eyes. Then I realized I could no longer read German. I tested myself in other languages. All gone.

June 30. A week since I dared to write again. It's slipping away like sand through my fingers. Most of the books I have are too hard for me now. I get angry with them because I know that I read and understood them just a few weeks ago.

I keep telling myself I must keep writing these reports so that somebody will know what is happening to me. But it gets harder to form the words and remember spelling. I have to look up even simple words in the dictionary now and it makes me impatient with myself.

Dr. Strauss comes around almost every day, but I told him I wouldn't see or speak

Synchromy in Green and Orange, 1916, STANTON MACDONALD-WRIGHT. Walker Art Center. Gift of the T. B. Walker Foundation, Minneapolis.

to anybody. He feels guilty. They all do. But I don't blame anyone. I knew what might happen. But how it hurts.

July 7. I don't know where the week went. Todays Sunday I know because I can see through my window people going to church. I think I stayed in bed all week but I remember Mrs. Flynn bringing food to me a few times. I keep saying over and over I've got to do something but then I forget or maybe its just easier not to do what I say I'm going to do.

I think of my mother and father a lot these days. I found a picture of them with me taken at a beach. My father has a big ball under his arm and my mother is holding me by the hand. I dont remember them the way they are in the picture. All I remember is my father drunk most of the time and arguing with mom about money.

He never shaved much and he used to scratch my face when he hugged me. My Mother said he died but Cousin Miltie said he heard his dad say that my father ran away with another woman. When I asked my mother she slapped me and said my father was dead. I dont think I ever found out the truth but I dont care much. (He said he was going to take me to see cows on a farm once but he never did. He never kept his promises to anyone. . . .)

July 10. My landlady Mrs. Flynn is very worried about me. She says the way I lay around all day and dont do anything I remind her of her son before she threw him out of the house. She said she doesn't like loafers. If Im sick its one thing, but if Im a loafer thats another thing and she won't have it. I told her I think Im sick.

I try to read a little bit every day, mostly stories, but sometimes I have to read the same thing over and over again because I don't know what it means. And its hard to write. I know I should look up all the words in the dictionary but its so hard and Im so tired all the time.

Then I got the idea that I would only use the easy words instead of the long hard ones. That saves time. I put flowers on Algernons grave about once a week. Mrs. Flynn thinks Im crazy to put flowers on a mouses grave but I told her that Algernon was special.

July 14. Its sunday again. I dont have anything to do to keep me busy now because my television set is broke and I dont have a job and any money to get it fixed. (I think I lost this months check from the lab. I dont remember)

I get awful headaches and asperin doesnt help me much. Mrs. Flynn knows Im really sick and she feels very sorry for me. Mrs. Flynns a wonderful woman whenever someone is sick.

July 22. Mrs. Flynn called a strange doctor to see me. She was afraid I was going to die. I told the doctor I wasnt too sick and I only forget sometimes. He asked me did I have any friends or relatives and I said no I dont have any. I told him I had a friend called Algernon once but he was a mouse and we used to run races together. He looked at me kind of funny like he thought I was crazy. He smiled when I told him I used to be a genius. He talked to me like I was a baby and he winked at Mrs. Flynn. I got mad and chased him out because he was making fun of me the way they all used to do before.

July 24. I have no more money and Mrs Flynn says I got to go to work somewhere and pay the rent because I havent paid for two months. I dont know any work but the job I used to have at Donnegans Box Company. I dont want to go back because they all knew me when I was smart and maybe they'll laugh at me. But I dont know what else to do to get money.

July 25. I was looking at some of my old progress reports and its very funny but I cant read what I wrote. I can make out some of the words but they dont make sense to me.

Miss Kinnian came to the door but I said go away I don't want to see you. She cried and I cried too but I wouldnt let her in because I didn't want her to laugh at me. I told her I didnt like her any more. I told her I didnt want to be smart any more. Thats not true. I still love her and I still want to be smart but I had to say that so shed go away. She gave Mrs. Flynn money to pay the rent. I dont want that. I got to get a job.

Please . . . please let me not forget how to read and write. . . .

July 27. Mr. Donnegan was very nice when I came back and asked him for my old job of janitor. First he was very suspicious but I told him what happened to me then he looked very sad and put his hand on my shoulder and said Charlie Gordon you sure got guts.

Everybody looked at me when I came downstairs and started working in the toilet sweeping it out like I used to. I told myself Charlie if they make fun of you dont get sore because you remember their not so smart as you once thot they were. And besides they were once your friends and if they laughted at you that doesnt mean anything because they liked you too.

One of the new men who came to work there after I went away made a nasty crack he said hey Charlie I hear your a very smart fella a real quiz kid. Say something intelligent. I felt bad but Joe Carp came over and grabbed him by the shirt and said leave him alone you lousy cracker or I'll break your neck. I dint expect Joe to take my part so I guess hes really my friend.

Later Frank Reilly came over and said Charlie if anybody bothers you or trys to take advantage you call me or Joe and we will set em straight. I said thanks Frank and I got choked up so I had to turn around and go into the supply room so he wouldnt see me cry. Its good to have friends.

July 28. I did a dumb thing today I forgot I wasn't in Miss Kinnians class at the adult center any more like I used to be. I went in and sat down in my old seat in the ·

Man Sitting at Table, 1961,
GEORGE SEGAL. Stadtisches Museum,
Abteiberg Monchengaladbach, Germany.

back of the room and she looked at me funny and she said Charles. I dint remember
she ever called me that before only Charlie
so I said hello Miss Kinnian Im redy for my
lesin today only I lost my reader that we was
using. She startid to cry and run out of the
room and everybody looked at me and I
saw they wasnt the same pepul who used to
be in my class.

Then all of a suddin I remembered some
things about the operashun and me getting

smart and I said holy smoke I reely pulled a
Charlie Gordon that time. I went away before she come back to the room.

Thats why Im going away from New
York for good. I dont want to do nothing
like that agen. I dont want Miss Kinnian to
feel sorry for me. Evry body feels sorry at
the factery and I dont want that eather so
Im going someplace where nobody knows
that Charlie Gordon was once a genus and
now he cant even reed a book or rite.

Im taking a cuple of books along and even if I cant reed them Ill practise hard and maybe I wont forget every thing I lerned. If I try reel hard maybe Ill be a little bit smarter than I was before the opera- shun. I got .my rabits foot and my lucky penny and maybe they will help me.

If you ever reed this Miss Kinnian dont be sorry for me Im glad I got a second chanse to be smart becaus I lerned a lot of things that I never even new were in this world and Im grateful that I saw it all for a littel bit. I dont know why Im dumb agen or what I did wrong maybe its because I dint try hard enuff. But if I try and practis very hard maybe Ill get a littl smarter and know what all the words are. I remember a littel bit how nice I had a feeling with the blue book that has the torn cover when I red it. Thats why Im gonna keep trying to get

smart so I can have that feeling agen. Its a good feeling to know things and be smart. I wish I had it rite now if I did I would sit down and reed all the time. Anyway I bet Im the first dumb person in the world who ever found out somthing importent for sience. I remember I did somthing but I dont remember what. So I gess its like I did it for all the dumb pepul like me.

Goodby Miss Kinnian and Dr. Strauss and evreybody. And P.S. please tell Dr Nemur not to be such a grouch when pepul laff at him and he woud have more frends. Its easy to make frends if you let pepul laff at you. Im going to have lots of frends where I go.

P.P.S. Please if you get a chanse pleese put some flowers on Algernons grave in the bak yard. . . .

Developing Comprehension Skills

1. What did Charlie's research reveal about his own future?

2. How did Charlie react as his condition began to worsen?

3. As Charlie's intelligence declined, his memory of the boy in the restaurant haunted him. Why?

4. How did Joe and Frank change their attitude toward Charlie? What do you think made them change?

5. At the end of the story, why did Charlie decide to leave town? Where do you think he

was going? What do you think will happen to him?

6. What price did Charlie pay for his temporary intelligence? What did he gain? Taking all of this into account, do you think the experiment was worth the pain?

Reading Literature: The Long Short Story

1. **Recognizing Foreshadowing.** Both Charlie and the reader receive several clues as to the outcome of the experiment. What is fore- shadowed by the change in Algernon?

2. **Analyzing Style.** As Charlie's abilities decrease, his style of writing gradually changes back to its earlier, simple level. When do you first notice Charlie's return to shorter sentences and simpler vocabulary? When does the punctuation become inaccurate? When does he lose capitalization skills and the ability to spell correctly? How does Charlie's writing at the end of the journal compare with the beginning of the journal?

3. **Appreciating Character Development.** In Part Four nearly every progress report shows evidence that Charlie is losing his memory. He is also losing the ability to do certain things. For every entry, identify those things Charlie can no longer do well. Is Charlie aware that he is losing his abilities? How does he react?

4. **Understanding the Significance of a Title.** "Everyone identifies me with Algernon," Charlie writes. Why do people make such a comparison? How does Charlie feel about the comparison? Charlie asks that flowers be put on Algernon's grave. Why is this important to Charlie? What do the flowers for Algernon represent?

5. **Analyzing Tone.** Review Charlie's letter to Dr. Strauss. What is the tone of this letter? Considering the message, does the tone surprise you? Why or why not?

6. **Inferring Character Traits.** In Part Three, Charlie showed impatience with the doctors. Have Charlie's feelings about the doctors changed in Part Four? Explain. What other evidence do you find that Charlie has learned to understand and accept his co-workers? What do you think is responsible for this change?

7. **Recognizing the Climax.** The climax of a story is its turning point, or point of highest interest. At that point, the main character takes an action or becomes aware of something that leads to the end of the conflict. What do you think is the climax of "Flowers for Algernon"? What questions or problems are left unanswered at the end of the story? Would you have enjoyed the story more if all of these questions were answered? Explain your answer.

Developing Vocabulary Skills

1. **Recognizing Specialized Language.** In the introduction to this chapter, you learned about jargon, the specialized vocabulary of a particular profession.

   Parts Three and Four of "Flowers for Algernon" contain much specialized language. Skim them to find answers to the questions below. Then use a dictionary to find the meaning of each word.

   a. Find a term that is used in the field of mathematics.
   b. Find three terms used in psychology.
   c. Find three terms that are used in the field of medicine.

   Now give two examples of jargon from three of the fields listed below. You may have to consult reference works.

space	business	law
sports	carpentry	dance
religion	auto mechanics	

2. **Reviewing How Words Are Created.** Tell whether the words listed on the next page are acronyms, blends, clipped words, compounds, or words made from the name of a person or place. Write what each acronym

stands for. Tell what word or words are used for clips and blends. Explain the origin of words based on people or place names. You may need to use a dictionary.

a. marathon
b. folklore
c. glop
d. wig
e. cardigan
f. VISTA
g. printout
h. leotard
i. dorm
j. telecast
k. smog
l. cologne
m. AWOL
n. hideout
o. scuba
p. cattail
q. derrick
r. splatter
s. pest
t. martial

Developing Writing Skills

1. **Analyzing a Story.** You may feel that Charlie's operation was not worth all the pain it caused him and others. On the other hand, you may see benefits that made the pain and disappointment worthwhile. In a brief composition, state your opinion of the value of the operation. Support your opinion with evidence from the story.

   Pre-Writing. Think about the advantages and disadvantages of the experiment. Think about its effects on Charlie, as well as on the other characters in the story. Write your opinion of the experiment in sentence form. Then list examples, incidents, and quotations that help to support it. Decide how to organize the reasons. One way is in their order of importance. Save the most convincing argument for last.

   Writing. Include your opinion in the introduction. Make each of your supporting reasons the main idea of one paragraph. Use examples and quotations for support. Close your composition with a strong concluding paragraph.

   Revising. Reread your rough draft. Be sure that each topic statement is supported with at least three examples, incidents, or quotations. Ask someone to read your composition. Have the reader tell you which arguments are most convincing and which are least convincing. Strengthen or remove the weakest ones.

2. **Writing a Script.** "Flowers for Algernon" was made into a motion picture, called *Charly*. In the movie, incidents in the diary were acted by the performers.

   Choose one day's diary entry. Write the movie script that would cover the same events. Describe the setting carefully. Re-create the dialogue. Be certain that each character speaks in a realistic manner.

Developing Skills in Speaking and Listening

Holding a Panel Discussion. Hold a panel discussion with several of your classmates. Your discussion should be on the subject of medical experiments. Consider one of the topics below, or one of your own choosing. Prepare for your discussion by reading several current newspaper or magazine articles on the topic.

1. Do doctors have the right to experiment on human beings? on animals?
2. Should scientists attempt to increase human intelligence?

CHAPTER 6 **Review**

Using Your Skills in Reading Long Short Stories

This passage comes from Nikolai Gogol's long short story "The Diary of a Madman." The main character realizes that he can hear something no one else can. Read this entry from his diary. Then answer the questions that follow.

Her lap dog was too slow to get into the store while the door was open and had to stay in the street. I knew that little dog. She's called Madgie. Then, a minute or so later, I heard a thin little voice: "Hello, Madgie." Well, I'll be. Who's that talking? I turned around and saw two ladies walking under their umbrellas: one old, the other young and pretty. But they had already passed when I heard again, just next to me: "You ought to be ashamed, Madgie!" What on earth was going on? I saw Madgie and a dog that had been following the two ladies sniffing at one another. "Maybe I'm drunk," I said to myself, "but it's not likely. It doesn't happen to me very often." "No, Fidele, you're wrong." With my own eyes I saw Madgie forming the words, "I was, bow-wow, I was bow-wow, very sick." Talk about a lap dog! I must say I was quite surprised to hear her talking.

1. How is the form of Gogol's short story like "Flowers for Algernon"?

2. From the main character's diary, what can you tell about him and about his mental state? What specific clues helped you reach this conclusion?

3. What kind of conflict would you expect to find in this story?

Using Your Comprehension Skills

The following dialogue is from a play that you will read in Chapter 7. Find the sentence fragments in this portion of dialogue. What do they tell you about how the speaker is feeling and acting?

> **Adams.** Listen. Please. For just one minute. Maybe you think I am half cracked. But this man. . . .

Now read the following lines, also from a play in Chapter 7. How do the punctuation marks help the actor know how to read his lines? Find the grammatical error in this speech. What does it suggest about the character?

Charlie. There's something that ain't legitimate. Maybe under normal circumstances we could let it go by, but these aren't normal circumstances. Why, look at this street! Nothin' but candles. Why, it's like goin' back into the Dark Ages or somethin'!

Using Your Vocabulary Skills

In one of the plays in Chapter 7, the family is British, and the son is an electrician. In the following sentences and phrases, identify words that come from the dialect of the British or from the specialized vocabulary of electricity. Infer the meaning of these words from context clues.

1. On the inside of the street door, a wire letter-box.
2. Just now my dynamos don't leave me any time for falling in love.
3. And, power! You say—and the trams go whizzing. . . .
4. I wish for two hundred pounds.
5. He was telling his mates a story.

Using Your Writing Skills

Choose one of the following writing assignments.

1. In "Flowers for Algernon," Charlie Gordon changes greatly over a period of less than five months. Explain, in two or three paragraphs, how Charlie changes both intellectually and emotionally. Make sure that you support your statements with specific evidence from Charlie's diary.

2. Did you notice any of the changes in characters in the nonfiction selections of Chapter 5? Choose one of these characters from Chapter 5 and write three diary entries from that person's point of view. Show through the diary how the person's attitudes or feelings are changing. For example, you might show how Marjorie Kinnan Rawling's attitude toward snakes changes. You might also show how Eleanor Roosevelt's attitude toward public life changes.

Using Your Skills in Critical Thinking

Charlie's thinking skills progress from a very basic, surface understanding of events to an understanding that includes the ability to make inferences and draw conclusions. Give examples of Charlie's thinking at each of these levels.

CHAPTER 7

Drama

Man Walking, 1958, NATHAN OLIVEIRA.
Hirshhorn Museum and Sculpture Garden,
Smithsonian Institution, Washington, D.C.

Reading Literature: Drama

What Is Drama?

Drama is a form of literature that is meant to be performed before an audience. Drama, or plays, tell a story through the words and actions of the characters.

The History of Drama

Drama, like poetry, is a very old form of literature. The ancient Greeks were the first to record their plays in written form. Drama festivals were held, and they attracted large audiences. To encourage writers, prizes were given for the best plays.

Another great time for drama and playwrights was during the sixteenth century in England. William Shakespeare is thought by many to be the finest playwright of all time. His plays explored a wide range of human emotions. Those that ended in disaster were called **tragedies**. The lighter plays were called **comedies**. A third type, the **historical drama**, retold the stories of famous historical figures.

Today, plays are performed on television, on the radio, and in the movies. Of course, plays are still performed live before an audience. This remains the best "stage" for a drama.

The Elements of Drama

Seeing a play being performed is very different from reading one. As part of an audience, you can watch the actors. You can see their appearance, their facial expressions, and how they speak and move. You can also see how lighting, scenery, and music affect the play.

The reader of a play must imagine all of these parts of a play. A good understanding of the elements of drama can help.

Dialogue. Dialogue is the conversation among characters. Much of the story of the play is told through the words of the characters.

Stage Directions. These directions give the actors, actresses, and director instructions for performing the play. For example, they might tell the actors and actresses where to move or how to speak. Stage directions may also describe the setting, sound effects, and props.

Narrator. A narrator is a character who introduces and comments on the action. In this chapter, both "The Hitchhiker" and "The Monsters Are Due on Maple Street" make use of this device.

Sound Effects. These are the sounds that are to be made part of the play. They are especially important in radio plays, where they help the listener picture the action.

Types of Plays

You will read three different types of plays in this chapter: a radio play, a play for television, and a stage play. Each type is different.

Radio Play. All the action in a radio play must be presented through sound effects, narration, and dialogue. Music is also important in a radio play. It sets the mood for the scene that is taking place.

Television Play. A television play is written to take advantage of the capabilities of television. Scenes can change quickly and dramatically. The camera can focus the viewer's attention on a specific action.

Stage Play. A stage play usually has only a few simple settings. Success depends on what the audience sees and hears. The stage directions for a stage play, then, are specific about scenery, lighting, and costumes. The actors must create and maintain the mood of the play.

How To Read a Play

1. Picture the play in your mind as though it were being performed. Use the stage directions to "see" the setting, to place the characters on stage, and to tell you how lines should be read.
2. Read the dialogue carefully. Remember that most of the story is told through these conversations.

Comprehension Skills: Evaluation

Evaluating What You Read

It is important to evaluate, or judge, the material you read. This is true whether you read a book, a story, a play, or a newspaper article. Learn to recognize the qualities that make certain pieces of literature better than others.

To evaluate a piece of literature, you must look at it objectively. You must consider each element that makes up that piece of writing. You must then judge whether the material meets your standards.

To evaluate a selection, first look at the ideas the author presents. In your opinion, are they important enough to think about and write about?

Second, look at how the writer presented his or her ideas. Consider the elements of literature that you have studied so far. In a play, for example, are the characters and dialogue realistic? Does the play have a definite mood? Is the theme clear? Is the conflict believable? Look for specific evidence in the piece to support your opinions.

As the last step in your evaluation, try to decide whether the author accomplished his or her purpose. Perhaps the purpose of a certain play is to create a mood of mystery. To decide whether the author was successful, examine your own reaction. Did you feel the suspense building throughout the play? Were you anxious to unlock the mystery? If not, the author's purpose was probably not accomplished.

Understanding Evaluations

Many writers evaluate other writers' work. These evaluations, called reviews, appear in newspapers and magazines every day. The evaluations usually focus on the writer's personal reaction to the selection. They also tell which elements the reviewer felt were done well or poorly.

Not every reviewer feels the same about every book or play. Often, you can read many different points of view about the same play, book, or story. To decide which of these reviews you should believe, ask yourself questions like these:

Did the reviewer explain exactly how the subject meets or fails to meet certain standards?

Do the reviewers standards seem similar to your own?

Did the reviewer give evidence from the piece to support his or her opinion?

What qualifies this reviewer to judge other people's work?

Is the reviewer known for slanted opinions? For example, does he or she have a history of always giving good reviews to comedies and bad reviews to mysteries?

Become an active reader. Think about what you read and learn to make your own decisions about the material. Begin to develop your own standards by which you can recognize excellent work.

Exercises: Understanding Evaluations

A. Read the following statements. Decide whether each one could be used in a good evaluation.

1. Anyone who doesn't laugh at the jokes in this play has no sense of humor.

2. The play takes place in a darkened room that looks like a basement. That setting helps to create the depressing mood of the play.

3. The dialogue is not realistic enough. Few people in such a frightening situation would act so unconcerned.

4. The play was long and boring. I didn't think it was ever going to end.

5. The play had a happy ending. Unfortunately, the ending didn't fit together with the rest of the play. I felt puzzled instead of satisfied.

B. Imagine you are writing an evaluation of the following selections. Think of three elements that you could examine for each one.

"The Most Dangerous Game"   (short story)
"Barter"   (poem)
"Babe"   (biography)
"The Monkey's Paw"   (drama)

Vocabulary Skills: Levels of Language

Recognizing Levels of Language

When you dress to go out, you choose clothes that fit the place where you are going. Similarly, when you write or speak, you must choose the type of language that suits your purpose.

There are two types, or levels, of English. **Standard English** follows all the rules of good grammar and usage. It is understood and accepted everywhere English is spoken. **Nonstandard English** does not follow all of the rules of the language. It is not acceptable in most situations.

Writers sometimes use different levels of language to fit a specific character or narrator. A careful reader recognizes the different types of language and why they are being used.

Standard English

There are two types of Standard English: formal standard English and informal standard English.

Formal standard English is correct, serious, and dignified. It often uses long, complex sentences and an advanced vocabulary. Formal English is used in speeches, essays, reports, and official documents. Look at the following example of this level of English.

> No one in Pompeii knew the dangerous power imprisoned in Vesuvius. For 1,500 years the mountain had slept quietly; but far beneath the crest a boiling fury of molten lava had gradually been gathering strength.
> —Robert Silverberg, "Pompeii"

Informal standard English is the language of everyday speech. It is correct, yet at the same time relaxed, casual, and friendly. Here is an example of informal standard English.

> I feel a lot better today, but I guess I'm still a little angry that all the time people were laughing and making fun of me because I wasn't so smart.　　　　—Daniel Keyes, "Flowers for Algernon"

Nonstandard English

Nonstandard English often contains errors in grammar, usage, punctuation, and spelling. Here is an example.

> **Charlie.** That don't prove a thing. Any guy who'd spend his time lookin' up at the sky early in the morning—well, there's something wrong with that kind of person. There's something that ain't legitimate.
> —Rod Serling, "The Monsters Are Due On Maple Street"

Slang. Popular words and phrases that are new to the language are called **slang**. Slang changes quickly. When you have trouble understanding an outdated slang word or phrase, such as "it gave me the willies," try to guess its meaning using context clues.

Dialect

People speak and write differently, depending on where they live. The types of language used in different areas are called **regional dialects**. Regional dialects may differ in three ways: in vocabulary, in pronunciation, and in grammar. As you read, be aware that some strangeness in the dialogue may be due to the dialect of the characters.

The following line is from "The Monkey's Paw," one of the plays in this chapter. What tells you that you are reading a type of dialect?

> **Sergeant.** How are you, ma'am? (*to Herbert*) How's yourself, laddie?

Exercise: Understanding the Levels of Language

Decide whether the following sentences are standard or nonstandard English. Then tell whether the standard passages are formal or informal.

1. A society girl who found social life boring, born to wealth but with a deep concern for the poor, Eleanor Roosevelt has become a defender of human rights, friend of the forgotten, citizen of the world.

2. I didn't see—anybody. There wasn't nothing but a bunch of steers—and the barbed wire fence.

3. It's just a ham radio set. A lot of people have them.

4. That don't seem likely. Sky's just as blue as anything. Not a cloud.

The Hitchhiker
A Play for Radio

LUCILLE FLETCHER

On a cross country drive, Ronald Adams sees the same hitchhiker again and again. Who is this hitchhiker? What does he want of Adams?

CHARACTERS

Orson Welles, *narrator*	Henry	Long Distance Operator
Ronald Adams	Woman	Albuquerque Operator
Mother	Girl	New York Operator
Voice	Gallup Operator	Mrs. Whitney
Mechanic		

Welles (*narrating*). Good evening, this is Orson Welles. . . .

Music. *In.*

Welles. Personally I've never met anybody who didn't like a good ghost story, but I know a lot of people who think there are a lot of people who don't like a good ghost story. For the benefit of these, at least, I go on record at the outset of this evening's entertainment with the sober assurance that, although blood may be curdled on the program, none will be spilt. There's no shooting, knifing, throttling, axing, or poisoning here. No clanking chains, no cobwebs, no bony and/or hairy hands appearing from secret panels or, better yet, bedroom curtains. If it's any part of that dear old phosphorescent foolishness that people who don't like ghost stories don't like, then again, I promise you we haven't got it. What we do have is a thriller. If it's half as good as we think it is, you can call it a shocker, and we present it proudly and without apologies. After all, a story doesn't have to appeal to the heart—it can also appeal to the spine. Sometimes you want your heart to be warmed—sometimes you want your spine to tingle. The tingling, it's to be hoped, will be quite audible as you listen tonight to *The Hitchhiker*— That's the name of our story, *The Hitchhiker*—

Sound. *Automobile wheels humming over concrete road.*

Music. *Something weird and shuddery.*

Adams (*narrating*). I am in an auto camp on Route Sixty-Six just west of Gallup, New Mexico. If I tell it, perhaps it will help me. It will keep me from going mad. But I must tell this quickly. I am not mad now. I feel perfectly well, except that I am running a slight temperature. My name is Ronald Adams. I am thirty-six years of age, unmarried, tall, dark, with a black mustache. I drive a 1940 Ford V-8, license number 6V-7989. I was born in Brooklyn. All this I know. I know that I am, at this moment, perfectly sane. That it is not I, who has gone mad—but something else—something utterly beyond my control. But I must speak quickly . . . very quickly. At any moment the link with life may break. This may be the last thing I ever tell on earth . . . the last night I ever see the stars. . . .

Music. *In.*

Adams (*narrating*). Six days ago I left Brooklyn to drive to California. . . .

Mother. Goodbye, son. Good luck to you, my boy. . . .

Adams. Goodbye, mother. Here—give me a kiss, and then I'll go . . . .

Mother. I'll come out with you to the car.

Adams. No. It's raining. Stay here at the door. Hey—what is this? Tears? I thought you promised me you wouldn't cry.

Mother. I know dear. I'm sorry. But I—do hate to see you go.

Adams. I'll be back. I'll only be on the coast three months.

Mother. Oh—it isn't that. It's just—the trip. Ronald—I really wish you weren't driving.

Adams. Oh—mother. There you go again. People do it every day.

Mother. I know. But you'll be careful, won't you. Promise me you'll be extra careful. Don't fall asleep—or drive fast—or pick up any strangers on the road . . . .

Adams. Lord, no. You'd think I was still seventeen to hear you talk—

Mother. And wire me as soon as you get to Hollywood, won't you, son?

Adams. Of course I will. Now don't you worry. There isn't anything going to happen. It's just eight days of perfectly simple driving on smooth, decent, civilized roads, with a hotdog or a hamburger stand every ten miles. . . . (*Fade*)

Sound. *Auto hum.*

Music. *In.*

Adams (*narrating*). I was in excellent spirits. The drive ahead of me, even the loneliness, seemed like a lark. But I reckoned without *him*.

Music. *Changes to something weird and empty.*

Adams (*narrating*). Crossing Brooklyn Bridge that morning in the rain, I saw a

Brooklyn Bridge, 1919,
JOSEPH STELLA. Yale University
Art Gallery, Société Anonyme
Collection, New Haven Connecticut.

man leaning against the cables. He seemed to be waiting for a lift. There were spots of fresh rain on his shoulders. He was carrying a cheap overnight bag in one hand. He was thin, nondescript, with a cap pulled down over his eyes. He stepped off the walk right in front of me and, if I hadn't swerved hard, I'd have hit him.

Sound. *Terrific skidding.*

Music. *In.*

Adams *(narrating).* I would have forgotten him completely, except that just an hour later, while crossing the Pulaski Skyway over the Jersey flats, I saw him again. At least, he looked like the same person. He was standing now, with one thumb pointing west. I couldn't figure out how he'd got there, but I thought probably one of those fast trucks had picked him up, beaten me to the Skyway, and let him off. I didn't stop for him. Then—late that night, I saw him again.

Music. Changing.

Adams (*narrating*). It was on the New Pennsylvania Turnpike between Harrisburg and Pittsburgh. It's two hundred and sixty-five miles long, with a very high speed limit. I was just slowing down for one of the tunnels—when I saw him—standing under an arc light by the side of the road. I could see him quite distinctly. The bag, the cap, even the spots of fresh rain spattered over his shoulders. He hailed me this time. . . .

Voice (*very spooky and faint*). Hall-ooo. . . . (*It echoes as though coming through the tunnel.*) Hall-ooo. . . !

Adams (*narrating*). I stepped on the gas like a shot. That's lonely country through the Alleghenies, and I had no intention of stopping. Besides, the coincidence, or whatever it was, gave me the willies. I stopped at the next gas station.

Sound. Auto tires screeching to stop . . . horn honk.

Mechanic. Yes, sir.

Adams. Fill her up.

Mechanic. Certainly, sir. Check your oil, sir?

Adams. No, thanks.

Sound. Gas being put into car.

Mechanic. Nice night, isn't it?

Adams. Yes. It—hasn't been raining here recently, has it?

Mechanic. Not a drop of rain all week.

Adams. I suppose that hasn't done your business any harm.

Mechanic. Oh—people drive through here all kinds of weather. Mostly business, you know. There aren't many pleasure cars out on the Turnpike this season of the year.

Adams. I suppose not. (*casually*) What about hitchhikers?

Mechanic (*laughing*). Hitchhikers *here*?

Adams. What's the matter? Don't you ever see any?

Mechanic. Not much. If we did, it'd be a sight for sore eyes.

Adams. Why?

Mechanic. A guy'd be a fool who started out to hitch rides on this road. Look at it. It's two hundred and sixty-five miles long, there's practically no speed limit, and it's a straightaway. Now what car is going to stop to pick up a guy under those conditions? Would you stop?

Adams. No. (*He answers slowly, with puzzled emphasis.*) Then you've never seen anybody?

Mechanic. Nope. Mebbe they get the lift before the Turnpike starts—I mean, you know—just before the toll house—but then it'd be a mighty long ride. Most cars wouldn't want to pick up a guy for that long a ride. And you know—this is pretty lonesome country here—mountains, and woods . . . You ain't seen anybody like that, have you?

Adams. No. (*quickly*) Oh no, not at all. It was—just a—technical question.

Mechanic. I see. Well—that'll be just a dollar forty-nine—with the tax. . . . (*Fade*)

Sound. *Auto hum up.*

Music. *Changing.*

Adams (*narrating*). The thing gradually passed from my mind, as sheer coincidence. I had a good night's sleep in Pittsburgh. I did not think about the man all next day—until just outside of Zanesville, Ohio, I saw him again.

Music. *Dark, ominous note.*

Adams (*narrating*). It was a bright sunshiny afternoon. The peaceful Ohio fields, brown with the autumn stubble, lay dreaming in the golden light. I was driving slowly, drinking it in, when the road suddenly ended in a detour. In front of the barrier, he was standing.

Music. *In.*

Adams (*narrating*). Let me explain about his appearance before I go on. I repeat. There was nothing sinister about him. He was as drab as a mud fence. Nor was his attitude menacing. He merely stood there, waiting, almost drooping a little, the cheap overnight bag in his hand. He looked as though he had been waiting there for hours. Then he looked up. He hailed me. He started to walk forward.

Voice (*far off*). Hall-ooo . . . Hall-oo. . . .

Adams (*narrating*). I had stopped the car, of course, for the detour. And for a few moments, I couldn't seem to find the new road. I knew he must be thinking that I had stopped for him.

Voice (*sounding closer now*). Hall-ooo . . . Hallll . . . ooo. . . .

Sound. *Gears jamming . . . sound of motor turning over hard . . . nervous accelerator.*

Voice (*closer*). Hall . . . oooo. . . .

Adams (*with panic in his voice*). No. Not just now. Sorry. . . .

Voice (*closer*). Going to California?

Sound. *Starter starting . . . gears jamming.*

Adams (*as though sweating blood*). No. Not today. The other way. Going to New York. Sorry . . . sorry . . . .

Sound. *Car starts with squeal of wheels on dirt . . . into auto hum.*

Music. *In.*

Adams (*narrating*). After I got the car back onto the road again, I felt like a fool. Yet the thought of picking him up, of having him sit beside me was somehow unbearable. Yet, at the same time, I felt, more than ever, unspeakably alone.

Sound. *Auto hum up.*

Adams (*narrating*). Hour after hour went by. The fields, the towns ticked off, one by one. The lights changed. I knew now that I was going to see him again. And though I dreaded the sight, I caught myself searching the side of the road, waiting for him to appear.

Scund. *Auto hum up . . . car screeches to a halt . . . impatient honk two or three times . . . door being unbolted.*

Sleepy Man's Voice. Yep? What is it? What do you want?

Adams (*breathless*). You sell sandwiches and pop here, don't you?

Voice (*cranky*). Yep. We do. In the daytime. But we're closed up now for the night.

Adams. I know. But—I was wondering if you could possibly let me have a cup of coffee—black coffee.

Voice. Not at this time of night, mister. My wife's the cook and she's in bed. Mebbe further down the road—at the Honeysuckle Rest . . . .

Sound. *Door squeaking on hinges as though being closed.*

Adams. No—no. Don't shut the door. (*shakily*) Listen—just a minute ago, there was a man standing here—right beside this stand—a suspicious looking man . . . .

Woman's Voice (*from distance*). Hen-ry? Who is it, Henry?

Henry. It's nobuddy, mother. Just a feller thinks he wants a cup of coffee. Go back into bed.

Adams. I don't mean to disturb you. But you see, I was driving along—when I just happened to look—and there he was . . . .

Henry. What was he doing?

Adams. Nothing. He ran off—when I stopped the car.

Henry. Then what of it? That's nothing to wake a man in the middle of his sleep about. (*sternly*) Young man, I've got a good mind to turn you over to the local sheriff.

Adams. But—I—

Henry. You've been taking a nip, that's what you've been doing. And you haven't got anything better to do than to wake decent folk out of their hard-earned sleep. Get going. Go on.

Adams. But—he looked as though he were going to rob you.

Henry. I ain't got nothin' in this stand to lose. Now—on your way before I call out Sheriff Oakes. (*Fade*)

Sound. *Auto hum up.*

Adams (*narrating*). I got into the car again, and drove on slowly. I was beginning to hate the car. If I could have found a place to stop . . . to rest a little. But I was in the Ozark Mountains of Missouri now. The few resort places there were closed. Only an occasional log cabin, seemingly deserted, broke the monotony of the wild wooded landscape. I had seen him at that roadside stand; I knew I would see him again—perhaps at the next turn of the road. I knew that when I saw him next, I would run him down . . . .

Sound. *Auto hum up.*

Adams. But I did not see him again until late next afternoon . . . .

Sound. *Warning system at train crossing.*

Adams (*narrating*). I had stopped the car at a sleepy little junction just across the border into Oklahoma—to let a train pass by—when he appeared, across the tracks, leaning against a telephone pole.

Sound. *Distant sound of train chugging . . . bell ringing steadily.*

Adams (*narrating, very tensely*). It was a perfectly airless, dry day. The red clay of Oklahoma was baking under the southwestern sun. Yet there were spots of fresh rain on his shoulders. I couldn't stand that. Without thinking, blindly, I started the car across the tracks.

Sound. *Train chugging closer.*

Adams (*narrating*). He didn't even look up at me. He was staring at the ground. I stepped on the gas hard, veering the wheel sharply toward him. I could hear the train in the distance now, but I didn't care. Then something went wrong with the car. It stalled right on the tracks.

Sound. *Train chugging closer. Above this, sound of car stalling.*

Adams (*narrating*). The train was coming closer. I could hear its bell ringing, and the cry of its whistle. Still he stood there. And now—I knew that he was beckoning—beckoning me to my death.

Sound. *Train chugging close. Whistle blows wildly. Then train rushes up and by with pistons going.*

Adams (*narrating*). Well—I frustrated him that time. The starter had worked at last. I managed to back up. But when the train passed, he was gone. I was all alone in the hot dry afternoon.

Sound. *Train retreating. Crickets begin to sing in background.*

Music. *In.*

Adams (*narrating*). After that, I knew I had to do something. I didn't know who this man was or what he wanted of me. I only knew that from now on, I must not let myself be alone on the road for one single moment.

Sound. *Auto hum up. Slow down. Stop. Door opening.*

Adams. Hello, there. Like a ride?

Girl. Well what do you think? How far you going?

Adams. Amarillo . . . I'll take you all the way to Amarillo.

Girl. Amarillo, Texas?

Adams. I'll drive you there.

Girl. Gee!

Sound. *Door close—car starts.*

Music. *In.*

Girl. Mind if I take off my shoes? My dogs are killing me.

Adams. Go right ahead.

Girl. Gee, what a break this is. A swell car, a decent guy, and driving all the way to Amarillo. All I been getting so far is trucks.

Adams. Hitchhike much?

Girl. Sure. Only it's tough sometimes, in these great open spaces, to get the breaks.

Adams. I should think it would be. Though I'll bet if you get a good pick-up in a fast car, you can get to places faster than— say, another person, in another car?

Girl. I don't get you.

Adams. Well, take me, for instance. Suppose I'm driving across the country, say, at a nice steady clip of about forty-five miles an hour. Couldn't a girl like you, just standing beside the road, waiting for lifts, beat me to town after town—provided she got picked up every time in a car doing from sixty-five to seventy miles an hour?

Girl. I dunno. Maybe and maybe not. What difference does it make?

Adams. Oh—no difference. It's just a— crazy idea I had sitting here in the car.

Girl (*laughing*). Imagine spending your time in a swell car thinking of things like that!

Adams. What would you do instead?

Girl (*admiringly*). What would I do? If I was a good-looking fellow like yourself? Why—I'd just enjoy myself—every minute of the time. I'd sit back, and relax, and if I saw a good-looking girl along the side of the road . . . (*sharply*) Hey! Look out!

Adams (*breathlessly*). Did you see him too?

Girl. See who?

Adams. That man. Standing beside the barbed wire fence.

Girl. I didn't see—anybody. There wasn't nothing but a bunch of steers—and the barbed wire fence. What did you think you was doing? Trying to run into the barbed wire fence?

Adams. There was a man there, I tell you . . . a thin gray man, with an overnight bag in his hand. And I was trying to— run him down.

Girl. Run him down? You mean—kill him?

Adams. He's a sort of—phantom. I'm trying to get rid of him—or else prove that he's real. But (*desperately*) you say you didn't see him back there? You're sure?

Girl (*queerly*). I didn't see a soul. And as far as that's concerned, mister . . .

Adams. Watch for him the next time, then. Keep watching. Keep your eyes peeled on the road. He'll turn up again—maybe any minute now. (*excitedly*) There. Look there—

Sound. *Auto sharply veering and skidding. Girl screams.*

Sound. *Crash of car going into barbed wire fence. Frightened lowing of steer.*

Girl. How does this door work? I—I'm gettin' outta here.

Adams. Did you see him that time?

Girl (*sharply*). No. I didn't see him that time. And personally, mister, I don't expect never to see him. All I want to do is to go on living—and I don't see how I will very long driving with you—

Adams. I'm sorry. I—I don't know what came over me. (*frightened*) Please—don't go . . . .

Girl. So if you'll excuse me, mister—

Adams. You can't go. Listen, how would you like to go to California? I'll drive you to California.

Girl. Seeing pink elephants all the way? No thanks.

Adams (*desperately*). I could get you a job there. You wouldn't have to be a waitress. I have friends there—my name is Ronald Adams—You can check up.

Sound. *Door opens.*

Girl. Uhn-hunh. Thanks just the same.

Adams. Listen. Please. For just one minute. Maybe you think I am half cracked. But this man. You see, I've been seeing this man all the way across the country. He's been following me. And if you could only help me—stay with me—until I reach the coast—

Girl. You know what I think you need, big boy? Not a girl friend. Just a good dose of sleep . . . There, I got it now.

Sound. *Door opens . . . slams.*

Adams. No. You can't go.

Girl (*screams*). Leave your hands offa me, do you hear! Leave your—

Adams. Come back here, please, come back.

Sound. *Struggle . . . slap . . . footsteps running away on gravel . . . lowing of steer.*

Adams (*narrating*). She ran from me, as though I were a monster. A few minutes later, I saw a passing truck pick her up. I knew then that I was utterly alone.

Sound. *Lowing of steer up.*

Adams (*narrating*). I was in the heart of the great Texas prairies. There wasn't a car on the road after the truck went by. I tried to figure out what to do, how to get hold of myself. If I could find a place to rest. Or even, if I could sleep right here in the car for a few hours, along the side of the road . . . I was getting my winter overcoat out of the back seat to use as a blanket, (Hall-ooo) when I saw him coming toward me, (Hall-ooo), emerging from the herd of moving steer . . .

Voice. Hall-ooo . . . Hall-oooo . . .

Sound. *Auto starting violently . . . up to steady hum.*

Music. *In.*

Adams (*narrating*). I didn't wait for him to come any closer. Perhaps I should have spoken to him then, fought it out then and there. For now he began to be everywhere. Whenever I stopped, even for a moment—for gas, for oil, for a drink of pop, a cup of coffee, a sandwich—he was there.

Music. *Faster.*

Adams (*narrating*). I saw him standing outside the auto camp in Amarillo that night, when I dared to slow down. He was sitting near the drinking fountain in a little camping spot just inside the border of New Mexico.

Music. *Faster.*

Adams (*narrating*). He was waiting for me outside the Navajo Reservation, where I stopped to check my tires. I saw him in Albuquerque where I bought twelve gallons of gas . . . I was afraid now, afraid to stop. I began to drive faster and faster. I was in lunar landscape now—the great

arid mesa country of New Mexico. I drove through it with the indifference of a fly crawling over the face of the moon.

Music. *Faster.*

Adams (*narrating*). But now he didn't even wait for me to stop. Unless I drove at eighty-five miles an hour over those endless roads—he waited for me at every other mile. I would see his figure, shadowless, flitting before me, still in its same attitude, over the cold and lifeless ground, flitting over dried-up rivers, over broken stones cast up by old glacial upheavals, flitting in the pure and cloudless air . . .

Music. *Strikes sinister note of finality.*

Adams (*narrating*). I was beside myself when I finally reached Gallup, New Mexico, this morning. There is an auto camp here—cold, almost deserted at this time of year. I went inside, and asked if there was a telephone. I had the feeling that if only I could speak to someone familiar, someone I loved, I could pull myself together.

Sound. *Nickel put in slot.*

Operator. Number, please?

Adams. Long distance.

Sound. *Return of nickel: buzz.*

Long Distance. This is long distance.

Adams. I'd like to put in a call to my home in Brooklyn, New York. My name is Ronald Adams. The number there is Beechwood 2-0828.

Long Distance. Thank you. What is your number?

Adams. 312.

Albuquerque Opr. Albuquerque.

Long Distance. New York for Gallup. (*Pause*)

New York Opr. New York.

Long Distance. Gallup, New Mexico, calling Beechwood 2-0828. (*Fade*)

Adams. I had read somewhere that love could banish demons. It was the middle of the morning. I knew Mother would be home. I pictured her, tall, white-haired, in her crisp house dress, going about her tasks. It would be enough, I thought, merely to hear the even calmness of her voice . . . .

Long Distance. Will you please deposit three dollars and eighty-five cents for the first three minutes. When you have deposited a dollar and a half, will you please wait until I have collected the money?

Sound. *Clunk of six coins.*

Long Distance. All right, deposit another dollar and a half.

Sound. *Clunk of six coins.*

Long Distance. Will you please deposit the remaining eighty-five cents.

Sound. *Clunk of four coins.*

Long Distance. Ready with Brooklyn—go ahead, please.

Adams. Hello.

Mrs. Whitney. Mrs. Adams' residence.

Adams. Hello. Hello—Mother?

Mrs. Whitney (*very flat and rather proper . . . dumb, too, in a flighty sort of way*). This is Mrs. Adams' residence. Who is it you wished to speak to, please?

Adams. Why—who's this?

Mrs. Whitney. This is Mrs. Whitney.

Adams. Whitney? I don't know any Mrs. Whitney. Is this Beechwood 2-0828?

Mrs. Whitney. Yes.

Adams. Where's my mother? Where's Mrs. Adams?

Mrs. Whitney. Mrs. Adams is not at home. She is still in the hospital.

Adams. The hospital!

Mrs. Whitney. Yes. Who is this calling please? Is it a member of the family?

Adams. What's she in the hospital for?

Mrs. Whitney. She's been prostrated for five days. Nervous breakdown. But who is this calling?

Adams. Nervous breakdown? But—my mother was never nervous . . . .

Mrs. Whitney. It's all taken place since the death of her oldest son, Ronald.

Adams. The death of her oldest son, Ronald . . . ? Hey—what is this? What number is this?

Mrs. Whitney. This is Beechwood 2-0828. It's all been very sudden. He was killed just six days ago in an automobile accident on the Brooklyn Bridge.

Operator *(breaking in).* Your three minutes are up, sir. *(Silence)*

Operator. Your three minutes are up, sir. *(pause)* Your three minutes are up, sir. *(fade)* Sir, your three minutes are up. Your three minutes are up, sir.

Adams *(narrating in a strange voice).* And so, I am sitting here in this deserted auto camp in Gallup, New Mexico. I am trying to think. I am trying to get hold of myself. Otherwise, I shall go mad . . . . Outside it is night—the vast, soulless night of New Mexico. A million stars are in the sky. Ahead of me stretch a thousand miles of empty mesa, mountains, prairies—desert. Somewhere among them, he is waiting for me. Somewhere I shall know who he is, and who . . . I . . . am . . . .

Music. *Up.*

The Grey Hills, 1942, GEORGIA O'KEEFFE. Indianapolis Museum of Art. Gift of Mr. and Mrs. James W. Fesler.

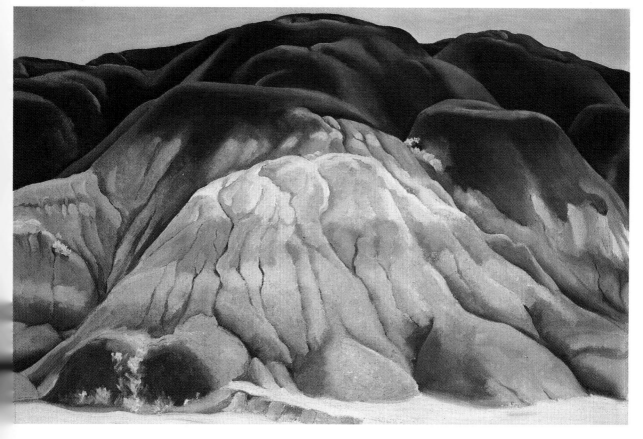

Developing Comprehension Skills

1. Ronald Adams says of the hitchhiker, "There was nothing sinister about him." If that were true, why was Adams so disturbed by him? What clues told Adams that there was something odd about the hitchhiker?

2. Where was the hitchhiker when Adams first spotted him? From what you learn at the end of the play, why was that location particularly important?

3. What finally convinced Adams that the hitchhiker was a threat?

4. Who or what was the hitchhiker? How did Adams finally learn who he was? How does the hitchhiker's identity explain why Adams could not escape him and why others could not see him?

5. Did you like the ending of this play, or were you disappointed when you found out the truth about Adams and the hitchhiker? Explain your reasons for deciding whether or not the ending is a strong one.

Reading Literature: Drama

1. **Understanding the One-Act Play.** A **one-act play** is a short play that builds quickly to a climax. It usually contains only a few characters. Why is the story of "The Hitchhiker" especially suited for presentation as a one-act play?

2. **Recognizing the Radio Play.** A **radio play** is a short drama relying on dialogue, music, and sound effects to tell a story. The listener does not actually see any of the action. Instead, the sound and dialogue help the listener picture the action in his or her imagination.

Look again at the play you have just read. Examine the stage directions. These are the instructions to the director, actors, and actresses. How do these show that this play is intended for radio? Look carefully at the **dialogue tags**, or tag lines, which indicate how the actors are to say their lines. Why would these be especially important in a radio play?

3. **Identifying the Prologue.** "The Hitchhiker" begins with a prologue. A **prologue** is a short message delivered before a play begins. In radio drama, a prologue helps to set the mood of the play. It can also provide clues to later events in the play.

In this prologue, the listener is warned that "The Hitchhiker" will shock and tingle the spine. Does the play have this effect on you? Find specific passages that shock, or surprise you. In what other ways is the listener prepared for the play?

4. **Understanding Plot.** A play, like a short story and a true adventure story, has a plot. The elements of plot are shown in the diagram below:

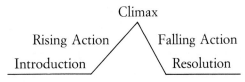

Tell which incidents in "The Hitchhiker" belong at each point in the plot diagram.

5. **Understanding Setting.** At the beginning of Adams's story, the setting is bustling New York City. As the play continues, the landscape becomes more and more lonely and barren. Describe the changes in setting, using details from the play. How do these changes reflect what is happening to Adams?

6. **Inferring Character and Action from Dialogue.** In a radio play, characters and actions are revealed through dialogue. For example, in the scene between Adams and the Girl, what do the following lines tell you about the characters and the action?

 a. "Mind if I take off my shoes? My dogs are killing me."

 b. "Listen. Please. For just one minute . . . This man . . . He's been following me. Stay with me—until I reach the coast—"

 c. **Adams.** No, you can't go.
  Girl (*screams*). Leave your hands offa me, do you hear! Leave your—
  Adams. Come back here, please, come back.

7. **Building Suspense.** Suspense, as you know, is the tense feeling the reader or listener gets while waiting for something to happen. As this drama unfolds, the hitchhiker appears more and more frequently. By the end, "He didn't even wait for me to stop," Adams says. How does the quickened pace of events add to the suspense?

Developing Vocabulary Skills

1. **Recognizing Standard and Nonstandard English.** A careful reader or writer should be aware that there are different levels, or classifications, of English. **Standard English** follows traditional rules of grammar and usage. It is acceptable in all situations. **Nonstandard English** does not follow all the rules of good grammar and usage. It should be avoided in most situations, especially in discussions, speeches, and in most writing.

 Writers sometimes use nonstandard English to make the dialogue in a story or play sound more realistic. Look at the following example:

> Mebbe they get the lift before the Turnpike starts—I mean, you know—just before the toll house.

How do the nonstandard elements make this sentence sound realistic?

 Now read the following passages of dialogue from the play. On your paper, *Standard* or *Nonstandard* to indicate what type of language each is. Then, rewrite each nonstandard passage in standard English.

 a. The peaceful Ohio fields, brown with the autumn stubble, lay dreaming in the golden light.

 b. There aren't many pleasure cars out on the Turnpike this season of the year.

 c. I ain't got nothin' in this stand to lose.

 d. You see, I've been seeing this man all the way across the country.

 e. And personally, mister, I don't expect never to see him.

 f. There wasn't nothing but a bunch of steers—and the barbed wire fence. What did you think you was doing?

2. **Identifying Slang.** One type of nonstandard English is slang. **Slang** is made up of popular words and phrases that quickly pass out of common use.

 Look at the following sentences from "The Hitchhiker." What does each underlined slang term mean? What standard word or phrase could be substituted for each?

 a. Besides, the coincidence, or whatever it was, gave me the willies.

 b. Suppose I'm driving across country at a nice steady clip of about forty-five miles an hour.

c. Only it's tough sometimes, in these great open spaces, to get the breaks.
d. Keep your eyes peeled on the road.
e. My dogs are killing me.

Developing Writing Skills

1. **Analyzing a Play.** In the prologue, the narrator states that while "The Hitchhiker" presents no blood, shooting, or creaking doors, it is nonetheless a thriller. How would you define a "thriller"? Do you agree that this play is a thriller? In a composition of at least four or five paragraphs, explain and support your answer. Use evidence from the play to support your opinion.

   Pre-Writing. Discuss the term *thriller* with your teacher and classmates. Then develop a definition of *thriller.* List several reasons why "The Hitchhiker" does or does not qualify as a thriller.

   Choose two or three of the most convincing reasons. For each, list supporting examples and quotations from the play. Organize this list in logical order.

   Writing. Begin your composition with an introductory paragraph that presents your definition of *thriller.* In the body of your composition, use each reason from your pre-writing list as a topic sentence for one paragraph. Support each topic sentence with the examples and quotations that you also listed in pre-writing. Summarize your major ideas in a concluding paragraph.

   Revising. Check the organization of each paragraph. Does each have a topic sentence? Is each well supported with evidence from the play? When you are satisfied with the content, proofread your work.

2. **Translating a Story into a Radio Play.** Write one scene from a short story as though it were a scene in a radio play. You might choose a scene from "Feathered Friend" or "The Foghorn" from Chapter 2. Develop the action and the characters through dialogue. Include instructions for music and sound. Also include tag lines directing actors and actresses how to say their lines.

Developing Skills in Speaking and Listening

1. **Creating Sound Effects.** Think of ways to create specific sound effects, such as the sound of thunder or the roar of a crowd. You might crackle paper, for instance, to imitate the sound of walking in dried leaves. Present five of your own sound effects in class. Have your classmates shut their eyes and try to guess what sound you are trying to create.

   As a more advanced experience, work with a partner to devise sound effects for a short story. As one person reads the story aloud, the other creates the sound effects.

2. **Retelling an Urban Myth.** "The Hitchhiker" is based on an urban myth. **Urban myths** are modern folk tales told across the country. Each story may appear in many versions. However, the teller always insists that the story happened in that town or to someone he or she knows. These stories often contain elements of horror. Well known urban myths include baby sitter stories and tales of animals in the sewers of a city.

   Think of an urban myth you might have heard. Retell this story for your classmates. Try to create an appropriate mood through your choice of words and the tone of your voice.

The Monsters Are Due on Maple Street

ROD SERLING

Fear and suspicion have replaced peace and harmony on Maple Street. What has turned neighbor against neighbor? As you read this television drama, try to determine just who the "monsters" are.

CHARACTERS

Narrator	Voice Five	Ice cream vendor
Tommy	Pete Van Horn	Second Boy buying ice cream
Steve Brand	Charlie	Charlie's wife
Don Martin	Sally, *Tommy's mother*	Other Residents of Maple Street
Myra Brand, *Steve's wife*	Man One	
Woman	Les Goodman	
Voice One	Ethel Goodman, *Les's wife*	
Voice Two	Man Two	
Voice Three	Figure One	
Voice Four	Figure Two	

ACT ONE

(*Fade in on a shot of the night sky. The various heavenly bodies stand out in sharp, sparkling relief. The camera moves slowly across the heavens until it passes the horizon and stops on a sign that reads "Maple Street." It is daytime. Then we see the street below. It is a quiet, tree-lined, small-town American street. The houses have front porches on which people sit and swing on gliders, talking across from house to house.* Steve Brand *is polishing his car, which is parked in front of his house. His neighbor,* Don Martin, *leans against the fender watching him. An ice cream vendor riding a bicycle is just in the process of stopping to sell some ice cream to a couple of kids. Two women gossip on the front lawn. Another man is watering his lawn with a garden hose.*

As we see these various activities, we hear the Narrator's *voice.*)

Narrator. Maple Street, U.S.A., late summer. A tree-lined little world of front porch gliders, hop scotch, the laughter of children, and the bell of an ice cream vendor.

(There is a pause and the camera moves over to a shot of the ice cream vendor and two small boys who are standing alongside just buying ice cream.)

Narrator. At the sound of the roar and the flash of the light, it will be precisely six-forty-three P.M. on Maple Street.

(At this moment Tommy, *one of the two boys buying ice cream from the vendor, looks up to listen to a tremendous screeching roar from overhead. A flash of light plays on the faces of both boys and then moves down the street and disappears.*

Various people leave their porches or stop what they are doing to stare up at the sky.

Steve Brand, *the man who has been polishing his car, stands there transfixed, staring upwards. He looks at* Don Martin, *his neighbor from across the street.)*

Steve. What was that? A meteor?

Don. That's what it looked like. I didn't hear any crash though, did you?

Steve. Nope. I didn't hear anything except a roar.

Myra *(from her porch).* What was that?

Steve *(raising his voice and looking toward the porch).* Guess it was a meteor, honey. Came awful close, didn't it?

Myra. Too close for my money! Much too close.

(The camera moves slowly across the various porches to people who stand there watching and talking in low conversing tones.)

Narrator. Maple Street. Six-forty-four P.M. on a late September evening. *(He pauses.)* Maple Street in the last calm and reflective moment *(pause)* before the monsters came!

(The camera takes us across the porches again. A man is replacing a light bulb on a front porch. He gets off his stool to flick the switch and finds that nothing happens.

Another man is working on an electric power mower. He plugs in the plug, flicks the switch of the mower off and on, but nothing happens.

Through a window we see a woman pushing her finger up and down on the dial hook of a telephone. Her voice sounds far away.)

Woman. Operator, operator, something's wrong on the phone, operator! *(Myra Brand comes out on the porch and calls to Steve.)*

Myra *(calling).* Steve, the power's off. I had the soup on the stove, and the stove just stopped working.

Woman. Same thing over here. I can't get anybody on the phone either. The phone seems to be dead.

(We look down again on the street. Small, mildly disturbed voices are heard coming from below.)

Voice One. Electricity's off.

Voice Two. Phone won't work.

Voice Three. Can't get a thing on the radio.

Voice Four. My power mower won't move, won't work at all.

Voice Five. Radio's gone dead!

(Pete Van Horn *a tall, thin man, is seen standing in front of his house.*)

Pete. I'll cut through the back yard to see if the power's still on, on Floral Street. I'll be right back!

(*He walks past the side of his house and disappears into the back yard.*

The camera pans down slowly until we are looking at ten or eleven people standing around the street and overflowing to the curb and sidewalk. In the background is Steve Brand's *car.*)

Steve. Doesn't make sense. Why should the power go off all of a sudden and the phone line?

Don. Maybe some kind of an electrical storm or something.

Charlie. That don't seem likely. Sky's just as blue as anything. Not a cloud. No lightning. No thunder. No nothing. How could it be a storm?

Woman. I can't get a thing on the radio. Not even the portable.

(*The people again begin to murmur softly in wonderment.*)

Charlie. Well, why don't you go downtown and check with the police, though they'll probably think we're crazy or something. A little power failure and right away we get all flustered and everything—

Steve. It isn't just the power failure, Charlie. If it was, we'd still be able to get a broadcast on the portable.

(*There is a murmur of reaction to this.* Steve *looks from face to face and then at his car.*)

Steve. I'll run downtown. We'll get this all straightened out.

(*He gets in the car and turns the key.*

Looking through the open car door, we see the crowd watching Steve *from the other side. He starts the engine. It turns over sluggishly and then stops dead. He tries it again, and this time he can't get it to turn over. Then very slowly he turns the key back to "off" and gets out of the car.*

The people stare at Steve. *He stands for a moment by the car and then walks toward them.*)

Steve. I don't understand it. It was working fine before—

Don. Out of gas?

Steve (*shakes his head*). I just had it filled.

Woman. What's it mean?

Charlie. It's just as if (*pause*) as if everything had stopped. (*Then he turns toward* Steve.) We'd better walk downtown.

(*Another murmur of assent to this.*)

Steve. The two of us can go, Charlie. *(He turns to look back at the car.)* It couldn't be the meteor. A meteor couldn't do this.

(He and Charlie exchange a look. Then they start to walk away from the group.

Tommy *comes into view. He is a serious-faced young boy in spectacles. He stands half-way between the group and the two men who start to walk down the sidewalk.)*

Tommy. Mr. Brand—you'd better not!

Steve. Why not?

Tommy. They don't want you to.

(Steve and Charlie exchange a grin and Steve looks back toward the boy.)

Steve. *Who* doesn't want us to?

Tommy *(jerks his head in the general direction of the distant horizon).* Them!

Steve. Them?

Charlie. Who are them?

Tommy *(intently).* Whoever was in that thing that came by overhead.

(Steve knits his brows for a moment, cocking his head questioningly. His voice is intense.)

Steve. What?

Tommy. Whoever was in that thing that came over. I don't think they want us to leave here.

(Steve leaves Charlie, walks over to the boy, and puts his hand on the boy's shoulder. He forces his voice to remain gentle.)

Steve. What do you mean? What are you talking about?

Tommy. They don't want us to leave. That's why they shut everything off.

Steve. What makes you say that? Whatever gave you that idea?

Woman *(from the crowd).* Now isn't that the craziest thing you ever heard?

Tommy *(persistent but a little frightened).* It's always that way, in every story I ever read about a ship landing from outer space.

Woman *(to the boy's mother,* Sally, *who stands on the fringe of the crowd).* From outer space yet! Sally, you better get that boy of yours up to bed. He's been reading too many comic books or seeing too many movies or something!

Sally. Tommy, come over here and stop that kind of talk.

Steve. Go ahead, Tommy. We'll be right back. And you'll see. That wasn't any ship or anything like it. That was just a . . . a meteor or something. Likely as not—*(He turns to the group, now trying very hard to sound more optimistic than he feels.)* No doubt it did have something to do with all this power failure and the rest of it. Meteors can do some crazy things. Like sunspots.

Don *(picking up the cue).* Sure. That's the kind of thing—like sunspots. They raise Cain with radio reception all over the world. And this thing being so close—why, there's no telling the sort of stuff it can do. (*He wets his lips and smiles nervously.*) Go ahead, Charlie. You and Steve go into town and see if that isn't what's causing it all.

(Steve *and* Charlie *walk away from the group down the sidewalk as the people watch silently.*

Tommy *stares at them, biting his lips, and finally calls out again.*)

Tommy. Mr. Brand!

(*The two men stop.* Tommy *takes a step toward them.*)

Tommy. Mr. Brand . . . please don't leave here.

(Steve *and* Charlie *stop once again and turn toward the boy. In the crowd there is a murmur of irritation and concern, as if the boy's words—even though they didn't make sense—were bringing up fears that shouldn't be brought up.*

Tommy *is both frightened and defiant.*)

Tommy. You might not even be able to get to town. It was that way in the story. Nobody could leave. Nobody except—

Steve. Except who?

Tommy. Except the people they sent down ahead of them. They looked just like humans. And it wasn't until the ship landed that—(*The boy suddenly stops, conscious of the people staring at him and his mother and of the sudden hush of the crowd.*)

Sally (*In a whisper, sensing the antagonism of the crowd*). Tommy, please son . . . honey, don't talk that way—

Man One. That kid shouldn't talk that way . . . and we shouldn't stand here listening to him. Why this is the craziest thing I ever heard of. The kid tells us a comic book plot, and here we stand listening—

(Steve *walks toward the camera and stops beside the boy.*)

Steve. Go ahead, Tommy. What kind of story was this? What about the people they sent out ahead?

Tommy. That was the way they prepared things for the landing. They sent four people. A mother and a father and two kids who looked just like humans . . . but they weren't.

(*There is another silence as* Steve *looks toward the crowd and then toward* Tommy. *He wears a tight grin.*)

Steve. Well, I guess what we'd better do then is to run a check on the neighborhood and see which ones of us are really human.

(*There is laughter at this, but it's a laughter that comes from a desperate attempt to lighten the atmosphere. The people look at one another in the middle of their laughter.*)

Charlie (*rubs his jaw nervously*). I wonder if Floral Street's got the same deal we got. (*He looks past the houses.*) Where is Pete Van Horn anyway? Isn't he back yet?

(*Suddenly there is the sound of a car's engine starting to turn over.*

We look across the street toward the drive- way of Les Goodman's *house. He is at the wheel trying to start the car.*)

Sally. Can you get started, Les?

(Les Goodman *gets out of the car, shaking his head.*)

Les. No dice.

(*He walks toward the group. He stops sud- denly as, behind him, the car engine starts up all by itself.* Les *whirls around to stare at the car.*

The car idles roughly, smoke coming from the exhaust, the frame shaking gently.

Les's *eyes go wide, and he runs over to his car.*

The people stare at the car.)

Man One. He got the car started somehow. He got *his* car started!

(*The people continue to stare, caught up by this revelation and wildly frightened.*)

Woman. How come his car just up and started like that?

Sally. All by itself. He wasn't anywheres near it. It started all by itself.

(Don Martin *approaches the group and stops a few feet away to look toward* Les's *car.*)

Don. And he never did come out to look at that thing that flew overhead. He wasn't even interested. (*He turns to the group, his face taut and serious.*) Why? Why

didn't he come out with the rest of us to look?

Charlie. He always was an oddball. Him and his whole family. Real oddball.

Don. What do you say we ask him?

(*The group starts toward the house. In this brief fraction of a moment, it takes the first step toward changing from a group into a mob. The group members begin to head pur- posefully across the street toward the house.* Steve *stands in front of them. For a moment their fear almost turns their walk into a wild stampede, but* Steve's *voice, loud, incisive, and commanding, makes them stop.*)

Steve. Wait a minute . . . wait a minute! Let's not be a mob!

(*The people stop, pause for a moment, and then, much more quietly and slowly, start to walk across the street.*

Les *stands alone facing the people.*)

Les. I just don't understand it. I tried to start it, and it wouldn't start. You saw me. All of you saw me.

(*And now, just as suddenly as the engine started, it stops, and there is a long silence that is gradually intruded upon by the fright- ened murmuring of the people.*)

Les. I don't understand. I swear . . . I don't understand. What's happening?

Don. Maybe you better tell us. Nothing's working on this street. Nothing. No lights, no power, no radio, (*then mean- ingfully*) nothing except one car—yours!

(The people's murmuring becomes a loud chant filling the air with accusations and demands for action. Two of the men pass Don *and head toward* Les, *who backs away from them against his car. He is cornered.)*

Les. Wait a minute now. You keep your distance—all of you. So I've got a car that starts by itself—well, that's a freak thing—I admit it. But does that make me a criminal or something? I don't know why the car works—it just does!

(This stops the crowd momentarily, and Les, *still backing away, goes toward his front porch. He goes up the steps and then stops, facing the mob.)*

Les. What's it all about, Steve?

Steve *(quietly).* We're all on a monster kick, Les. Seems that the general impression holds that maybe one family isn't what we think they are. Monsters from outer space or something. Different from us. Aliens from the vast beyond. *(He chuckles.)* You know anybody that might fit that description around here on Maple Street?

Les. What is this, a gag? *(He looks around the group again.)* This a practical joke or something?

(Suddenly the car engine starts all by itself, runs for a moment, and stops. One woman begins to cry. The eyes of the crowd are cold and accusing.)

Les. Now that's supposed to incriminate me, huh? The car engine goes on and off

and that really does it, doesn't it? *(He looks around at the faces of the people.)* I just don't understand it . . . any more than any of you do! *(He wets his lips, looking from face to face.)* Look, you all know me. We've lived here five years. Right in this house. We're no different from any of the rest of you! We're no different at all. . . . Really . . . this whole thing is just . . . just weird—

Woman. Well, if that's the case, Les Goodman, explain why—*(She stops suddenly, clamping her mouth shut.)*

Les *(softly).* Explain what?

Steve *(interjecting).* Look, let's forget this—

Charlie *(overlapping him).* Go ahead, let her talk. What about it? Explain what?

Woman *(a little reluctantly).* Well . . . sometimes I go to bed late at night. A couple of times . . . a couple of times I'd come out here on the porch, and I'd see Mr. Goodman here in the wee hours of the morning standing out in front of his house . . . looking up at the sky. *(She looks around the circle of faces.)* That's right, looking up at the sky as if . . . as if he were waiting for something, *(pauses)* as if he were looking for something.

(There's a murmur of reaction from the crowd again as Les *backs away.)*

Les. She's crazy. Look, I can explain that. Please . . . I can really explain that . . . .

She's making it up anyway. *(Then he shouts.)* I tell you she's making it up!

(He takes a step toward the crowd and they back away from him. He walks down the steps after them, and they continue to back away. Suddenly he is left completely alone, and he looks like a man caught in the middle of a menacing circle as the scene slowly fades to black.)

American Street, 1983,
ROGER BROWN. Courtesy of Phyllis
Kind Gallery, Chicago and New York.
Photograph by William Bengtson.

ACT TWO

SCENE 1. (*Fade in on Maple Street at night. On the sidewalk, little knots of people stand around talking in low voices. At the end of each conversation they look toward* Les Goodman's *house. From the various houses, we can see candlelight but no electricity. The quiet that blankets the whole area is disturbed only by the almost whispered voices of the people standing around. In one group* Charlie *stands staring across at the* Goodmans' *house. Two men stand across the street from it in almost sentry-like poses.*)

Sally (*in a small, hesitant voice*). It just doesn't seem right, though, keeping watch on them. Why . . . he was right when he said he was one of our neighbors. Why, I've known Ethel Goodman ever since they moved in. We've been good friends—

Charlie. That don't prove a thing. Any guy who'd spend his time lookin' up at the sky early in the morning—well, there's something wrong with that kind of person. There's something that ain't legitimate. Maybe under normal circumstances we could let it go by, but these aren't normal circumstances. Why, look at this street! Nothin' but candles. Why, it's like goin' back into the Dark Ages or somethin'!

(Steve *walks down the steps of his porch, down the street to the* Goodmans' *house, and then stops at the foot of the steps.* Les *is standing there;* Ethel Goodman *behind him is very frightened.*)

Les. Just stay right where you are, Steve. We don't want any trouble, but this time if anybody sets foot on my porch—that's what they're going to get—trouble!

Steve. Look, Les—

Les. I've already explained to you people. I don't sleep very well at night sometimes. I get up and I take a walk and I look up at the sky. I look at the stars!

Ethel. That's exactly what he does. Why, this whole thing, it's . . . it's some kind of madness or something.

Steve (*nods grimly*). That's exactly what it is—some kind of madness.

Charlie's Voice (*shrill, from across the street*). You best watch who you're seen with, Steve! Until we get this all straightened out, you ain't exactly above suspicion yourself.

Steve (*whirling around toward him*). Or you, Charlie. Or any of us, it seems. From age eight on up!

Woman. What I'd like to know is—what are we gonna do? Just stand around here all night?

Charlie. There's nothin' else we *can* do! (*He turns back, looking toward* Steve *and*

Less *again*.) One of 'em'll tip their hand. They got to.

Steve (*raising his voice*). There's something you can do, Charlie. You can go home and keep your mouth shut. You can quit strutting around like a self-appointed judge and climb into bed and forget it.

Charlie. You sound real anxious to have that happen, Steve. I think we better keep our eye on you, too!

Don (*as if he were taking the bit in his teeth, takes a hesitant step to the front*). I think everything might as well come out now. (*He turns toward* Steve.) Your wife's done plenty of talking, Steve, about how odd you are!

Charlie (*picking this up, his eyes widening*). Go ahead, tell us what's she's said.

(Steve *walks toward them from across the street*.)

Steve. Go ahead, what's my wife said? Let's get it all out. Let's pick out every idiosyncrasy of every single man, woman, and child on the street. And then we might as well set up some kind of citizens' court. How about a firing squad at dawn, Charlie, so we can get rid of all the suspects. Narrow them down. Make it easier for you.

Don. There's no need gettin' so upset. Steve. It's just that . . . well . . . Myra's talked about how there's been plenty of nights you spent hours down in your basement workin' on some kind of radio or something. Well, none of us have ever seen that radio—

(*By this time* Steve *has reached the group. He stands there* defiantly.)

Charlie. Go ahead, Steve. What kind of "radio set" you workin' on? I never seen it. Neither has anyone else. Who do you talk to on that radio set? And who talks to you?

Steve. I'm surprised at you, Charlie. How come you're so dense all of a sudden? (*He pauses*.) Who do I talk to? I talk to monsters from outer space. I talk to three-headed green men who fly over here in what look like meteors.

(Myra Brand *steps down from the porch, bites her lip, calls out*.)

Myra. Steve! Steve, please. (*Then looking around, frightened, she walks toward the group*.) It's just a ham radio set, that's all. I bought him a book on it myself. It's just a ham radio set. A lot of people have them. I can show it to you. It's right down in the basement.

Steve (*whirls around toward her*). Show them nothing! If they want to look inside our house—let them go and get a search warrant.

Charlie. Look, buddy, you can't afford to—

Steve (*interrupting him*). Charlie, don't start telling me who's dangerous and who isn't and who's safe and who's a menace.

(*He turns to the group and shouts.*) And you're with him, too—all of you! You're

standing here all set to crucify—all set to find a scapegoat—all desperate to point some kind of a finger at a neighbor! Well now, look, friends, the only thing that's gonna happen is that we'll eat each other up alive—

(*He stops abruptly as* Charlie *suddenly grabs his arm.*)

Charlie (*in a hushed voice*). That's not the only thing that can happen to us.

(*Down the street, a figure has suddenly materialized in the gloom. In the silence we hear the clickety-clack of slow, measured footsteps on concrete as the figure walks slowly toward them. One of the women lets out a stifled cry. Sally grabs her boy, as do a couple of other mothers.*)

Tommy (*shouting, frightened*). It's the monster! It's the monster!

(*Another woman lets out a wail and the people fall back in a group staring toward the darkness and the approaching figure.*
The people stand in the shadows watching. Don Martin joins them, carrying a shotgun. He holds it up.)

Don. We may need this.

Steve. A shotgun? (*He pulls it out of* Don's *hand.*) No! Will anybody think a thought around here! Will you people wise up. What good would a shotgun do against—

(*The dark figure continues to walk toward them as the people stand there, fearful, mothers clutching children, men standing in front of their wives.*)

Charlie (*pulling the gun from* Steve's *hands*). No more talk, Steve. You're going to talk us into a grave! You'd let whatever's out there walk right over us, wouldn't yuh? Well, some of us won't!

(*Charlie swings around, raises the gun, and suddenly pulls the trigger. The sound of the shot explodes in the stillness.*
The figure suddenly lets out a small cry, stumbles forward onto his knees, and then falls forward on his face. Don, Charlie, and Steve race forward to him. Steve is there first and turns the man over. The crowd gathers around them.)

Steve (*slowly looks up*). It's Pete Van Horn.

Don (*in a hushed voice*). Pete Van Horn! He was just gonna go over to the next block to see if the power was on—

Woman. You killed him, Charlie. You shot him dead!

Charlie (*looks around at the circle of faces, his eyes frightened, his face contorted*). But . . . but I didn't know who he was. I certainly didn't know who he was. He comes walkin' out of the darkness—how am I supposed to know who he was? (*He grabs* Steve.) Steve—you know why I shot! How was I supposed to know he wasn't a monster or something? (*He grabs* Don.) We're all scared of the same thing. I was just tryin' to . . . tryin' to protect my home, that's all! Look, all of you, that's all I was tryin' to do. (*He looks down wildly at the body.*) I didn't know it was somebody we knew! I didn't know—

(*There's a sudden hush and then an intake of breath in the group. Across the street all the lights go on in one of the houses.*)

Woman (*in a hushed voice*). Charlie . . . Charlie . . . the lights just went on in your house. Why did the lights just go on?

Don. What about it, Charlie? How come you're the only one with lights now?

Les. That's what I'd like to know.

(*Pausing, they all stare toward* Charlie.)

Les. You were so quick to kill, Charlie, and you were so quick to tell us who we had to be careful of. Well, maybe you had to kill. Maybe Pete there was trying to tell us something. Maybe he'd found out something and came back to tell us who there was amongst us we should watch out for—

(Charlie *backs away from the group, his eyes wide with fright.*)

Charlie. No . . . no . . . it's nothing of the sort! I don't know why the lights are on. I swear I don't. Somebody's pulling a gag or something.

(*He bumps against* Steve, *who grabs him and whirls him around.*)

Steve. A gag? A gag? Charlie, there's a dead man on the sidewalk, and you killed

him! Does this thing look like a gag to you?

(Charlie *breaks away and screams as he runs toward his house.*)

Charlie. No! No! Please!

(*A man breaks away from the crowd to chase* Charlie.

As the man tackles him and lands on top of him, the other people start to run toward them. Charlie *gets up, breaks away from the other man's grasp, and lands a couple of desperate punches that push the man aside. Then he forces his way, fighting, through the crowd and jumps up on his front porch.*

Charlie *is on his porch as a rock thrown from the group smashes a window beside him, the broken glass flying past him. A couple of pieces cut him. He stands there perspiring, rumpled, blood running down from a cut on the cheek. His wife breaks away from the group to throw herself into his arms. He buries his face against her. We can see the crowd converging on the porch.*)

Voice One. It must have been him.

Voice Two. He's the one.

Voice Three. We got to get Charlie.

(*Another rock lands on the porch.* Charlie *pushes his wife behind him, facing the group.*)

Charlie. Look, look I swear to you . . . it isn't me . . . but I do know who it is . . . I swear to you, I do know who it is. I know who the monster is here. I know who it is that doesn't belong. I swear to you I know.

Don (*pushing his way to the front of the crowd*). All right, Charlie, let's hear it!

(Charlie's *eyes dart around wildly.*)

Charlie. It's . . . it's . . .

Man Two (*screaming*). Go ahead, Charlie.

Charlie. It's . . . it's the kid. It's Tommy. He's the one!

(*There's a gasp from the crowd as we see* Sally *holding the boy.* Tommy *at first doesn't understand and then, realizing the eyes are all on him, buries his face against his mother.*)

Sally (*backs away*). That's crazy! He's only a boy.

Woman. But he knew! He was the only one! He told us all about it. Well, how did he know? How could he have known?

(*Various people take this up and repeat the question.*)

Voice One. How could he know?

Voice Two. Who told him?

Voice Three. Make the kid answer.

(*The crowd starts to converge around the mother, who grabs* Tommy *and starts to run with him. The crowd starts to follow, at first walking fast, and then running after him. Suddenly* Charlie's *lights go off and the lights in other houses go on, then off.*)

Man One (*shouting*). It isn't the kid . . . it's Bob Weaver's house.

Woman. It isn't Bob Weaver's house, it's Don Martin's place.

Charlie. I tell you it's the kid.

Don. It's Charlie. He's the one.

(*People shout, accuse, and scream as the lights go on and off. Then, slowly, in the middle of this nightmarish confusion of sight and sound the camera starts to pull away until, once again, we have reached the opening shot looking at the Maple Street sign from high above.*)

SCENE 2. (*The camera continues to move away while gradually bringing into focus a field. We see the metal side of a spacecraft that sits shrouded in darkness. An open door throws out a beam of light from the illuminated interior. Two figures appear, silhouetted against the bright lights. We get only a vague feeling of form.*)

Figure One. Understand the procedure now? Just stop a few of their machines and radios and telephones and lawn mowers. . . . Throw them into darkness for a few hours, and then just sit back and watch the pattern.

Figure Two. And this pattern is always the same?

Figure One. With few variations. They pick the most dangerous enemy they can find

. . . and it's themselves. And all we need do is sit back . . . and watch.

Figure Two. Then I take it this place . . . this Maple Street . . . is not unique.

Figure One *(shaking his head)*. By no means. Their world is full of Maple Streets. And we'll go from one to the other and let them destroy themselves. One to the other . . . one to the other . . . one to the other—

SCENE 3. *(The camera slowly moves up for a shot of the starry sky, and over this we hear the* Narrator's *voice.)*

Narrator. The tools of conquest do not necessarily come with bombs and explosions and fallout. There are weapons that are simply thoughts, attitudes, prejudices—to be found only in the minds of men. For the record, prejudices can kill and suspicion can destroy. A thoughtless, frightened search for a scapegoat has a fallout all its own for the children . . . and the children yet unborn, *(a pause)* and the pity of it is . . . that these things cannot be confined to . . . The Twilight Zone!

(Fade to black.)

The Milky Way. United States Naval Observatory, Washington, D.C.

Developing Comprehension Skills

1. What incident at the beginning of the play upset the peacefulness of Maple Street?

2. How did Tommy help to create the hysteria on Maple Street?

3. Why did the people of Maple Street become suspicious of Les Goodman? Do you think the neighbors wanted to believe that Les was an enemy? Why?

4. Which character was the most reasonable person in the play? Which character was the least reasonable? Find specific incidents from the play to support your choices.

5. Act Two, Scene 2 describes a conversation between two aliens. From this conversation, could you determine their mission on Earth? What was their plan to complete this mission? Did this plan succeed on Maple Street? Explain your answer.

6. In a similar situation, do you think that real people would act as the characters in this play acted? Give reasons for your answer.

Reading Literature: Drama

1. **Recognizing a Television Play.** In a television play, camera directions are used to describe visual effects and camera movements. For example, the opening camera directions are to "fade in on shot of night sky." The direction "fade in" means that a picture of the sky gradually appears on the TV screen. Find five other camera directions used in "The Monsters Are Due on Maple Street." Explain how these camera directions help to focus the viewer's attention on the action.

2. **Understanding the Importance of the Setting.** The setting of "The Monsters Are Due on Maple Street" is Maple Street, U.S.A. What details in the setting tell you that Maple Street is an ordinary street in an ordinary small town? Why is an ordinary setting important to this play?

3. **Recognizing Conflict.** In an external conflict, a character struggles with another character, the forces of nature, or problems of society. What kinds of external conflict are present in "The Monsters Are Due on Maple Street"?

4. **Identifying Contrasts in Mood.** At the beginning of the play, the mood is cheerful and peaceful. Find specific incidents and dialogue that help convey this pleasant mood. How has the mood changed by the end of the play? Find evidence from the play to support your statement.

5. **Recognizing the Narrator's Function.** Reread the narrator's lines in the first scene of "The Monsters Are Due on Maple Street." Besides setting the scene, this prologue serves another purpose. The prologue foreshadows, or gives clues to, the conflict of the play. What specific comment by the narrator sets the stage for the conflict that follows?

   The narrator also delivers an epilogue, or concluding remarks at the close of the play. What is the narrator's message? Are these remarks intended as a warning to the audience? Explain your answer.

6. **Understanding Irony.** In spoken irony, a speaker says the opposite of what is meant. The speaker does this to make a point, or achieve a desired effect. In a mocking way, for example, Steve says, "How about a firing squad at dawn, Charlie, so we can get rid of all the suspects?" What point is Steve actu-

ally trying to make? Does this comment have the effect Steve was hoping for? How do you know? Find two other examples of Steve's use of irony. What is Steve's purpose in each? Does he achieve his purpose in each instance?

Developing Vocabulary Skills

Identifying Formal and Informal English. There are two types of standard English. **Formal English** is language that is used in more serious or formal situations. It uses long, complex sentences and a sophisticated vocabulary. **Informal English** is the comfortable, correct language used in every day situations. It is the language of most conversations, newspapers, and magazines. It uses shorter sentences and a simpler vocabulary.

Look at the following passages drawn from "The Hitchhiker" and "The Monsters Are Due on Maple Street." Decide whether the passage is an example of *Formal Standard English* or *Informal Standard English*.

1. I would see his figure, shadowless, flitting before me, still in its same attitude, over the cold and lifeless ground, flitting over dried-up rivers, over broken stones cast up by old glacial upheavals, flitting in the pure and cloudless sky.

2. I saw a man leaning against the cables. He seemed to be waiting for a lift.

3. A scapegoat has a fallout all its own for the children . . . and the children yet unborn.

4. I don't know why the lights are on. I swear I don't.

5. There are weapons that are simply thoughts, attitudes, prejudices—to be found only in

the minds of men. For the record, prejudices can kill and suspicion can destroy.

Developing Writing Skills

1. **Using Contrast.** Review what you learned about a radio play in "The Hitchhiker." Now, consider the television play, "The Monsters Are Due on Maple Street." How does a TV play differ from a radio play? Write two or three paragraphs explaining the differences between these two types of drama. Consider such elements as sound effects, stage directions, and dialogue, as well as the plays' effect on the audience. What are the strengths of each form? What are the weaknesses? Which elements are most important in each type of play?

2. **Assuming a Different Point of View.** Imagine that you are one of the aliens portrayed in Act Two, Scene 2. Write a report for your commander on the progress of your mission on Earth. Make sure your report is objective. Objective writing is factual. It is unemotional and shows none of the writer's own feelings.

   Pre-Writing. Think about how the alien would view the events on Maple Street. You might begin by explaining the procedure the aliens used. Then tell the results. Organize these results in a logical order. What facts would be most important to the commander?

   Writing. Be objective as you write your report. Include enough details to make your report a complete record of the plan and events that took place on Maple Street. Then, imagine what the aliens will do next. Conclude your report with a statement of the next step in the aliens' plan.

Revising. Ask a classmate to read your report and comment on how well you maintained the alien's point of view. Then check to be sure that you included all the necessary information. Revise as necessary. Finally, proofread for errors in grammar, usage, and mechanics. Then make a clean, final copy.

3. **Describing Setting.** Imagine that you are writing a TV play of Richard Connell's "The Most Dangerous Game" or Farley Mowat's "Never Cry Wolf." Choose a scene that you found particularly exciting or interesting. Then write the opening camera directions to set the scene for the viewer. Describe the setting in detail. Which details of the setting do you consider most important? Direct the camera to focus on these details.

Developing Skills in Study and Research

Researching a Historical Event. The events in "The Monsters Are Due on Maple Street" may be compared with the Salem witch trials in eighteenth-century New England. Use the encyclopedia and the card catalog to find information on the Salem witch trials. Take notes on similarities to the events in this play.

Developing Skills in Critical Thinking

1. **Recognizing Weak Opinions.** Sound opinions are based on truth or logical reasoning. They are supported by a great deal of evidence, or facts. Weak opinions have too few facts to support them.

   Charlie says that Les Goodman is a "real odd ball." He bases that opinion partially on the fact that Les doesn't go outside to look at the flying object. On what other information does Charlie base his conclusion about Les? Is Charlie's opinion sound or unsound?

2. **Recognizing the Either/Or Problem.** The **either/or problem** is another kind of faulty logic. Someone claims that there are only two choices when there are actually more. The residents of Maple Street fall into this trap. They claim that *either* someone acts like everybody else *or* else he or she is a "monster." How do the residents use this kind of faulty reasoning to accuse Les, Steve, and Tommy?

3. **Recognizing Scapegoats.** A **scapegoat** is a person or group who is blamed for the problems of others. This blame is placed without any real evidence. People sometimes create scapegoats out of fear or to shift attention away from the real problem.

   Who are the scapegoats in this story? Why do you think the other residents on Maple Street are so quick to turn on them?

Developing Skills in Speaking and Listening

Discussing an Issue. The author raises a number of thought-provoking issues in the play. One interesting issue centers on the following questions:

1. When faced with a threat, do people usually turn on each other?

2. What happens to people who do not conform with others in a group? At what point are they often treated as outcasts?

Discuss one of these issues with your classmates. Support your opinions with personal and historical examples. Listen courteously to other people's ideas. If you disagree with something that is said, do so in a polite manner.

The Monkey's Paw

W. W. JACOBS
Dramatized by Louis N. Parker

Most people would like to have control over their future. . . or would they? Read to see if the magic charm in this play brings people the happiness they seek.

CHARACTERS

Mr. John White
Mrs. Jenny White, *his wife*
Herbert White, *their son*
Sergeant-Major Morris
Mr. Sampson

SCENE. *The living-room of an old-fashioned cottage on the outskirts of Fulham near London, England. Set corner-wise in the left angle at the back is a deep window; further front, three or four steps lead up to a door. Further forward is a dresser, with plates, glasses, and cups. At back is an alcove, with the street door fully visible. On the inside of the street door is a wire letter-box. On the right is a cupboard and a fireplace. In the center is a round table. Against the wall is an old-fashioned piano. On each side of the fireplace is a comfortable armchair. Other chairs are placed about the room. On the mantelpiece are a clock, old china figures, and other small objects. An air of comfort pervades the room.*

ACT ONE

At the rise of the curtain, Mrs. White, *a pleasant-looking old woman, is seated in the armchair below the fire, attending to a kettle and keeping a laughing eye on* Mr. White *and* Herbert. *These two are seated at the right angle of the table nearest the fire with a chess-board between them.* Mr. White *is evidently losing.* Herbert, *a fine young fellow, is looking with satisfaction at the move he has just made.* Mr. White *makes several attempts to move, but thinks better of them. There is a shaded lamp on the table. The door is tightly shut. The curtains of the window are drawn; but every now and then the wind is heard whistling outside.*

Mr. White (*moving at last, and triumphant*). There, Herbert, my boy! Got you, I think.

Herbert. Oh, you're a smart one, Dad, aren't you?

Mrs. White. Mean to say he's beaten you at last?

Herbert. No! Why, he's overlooked—

Mr. White (*very excited*). I see it! Let me have that back!

Herbert. I can't. Rules of the game!

Mr. White (*disgusted*). I don't hold with those rules. You turn what ought to be an innocent relaxation—

Mrs. White. Don't talk so much, Father. You put him off—

Herbert (*laughing*). Not him!

Mr. White (*trying to distract his attention*). Hark at the wind.

Herbert (*drily*). Ah! I'm listening. Check.

Mr. White (*still trying to distract him*). I should hardly think Sergeant-Major Morris would come tonight.

Herbert. Mate. (*He rises.*)

Mr. White (*with an outbreak of disgust and sweeping the chessmen off the board*). That's the worst of living so far out. Your friends can't come for a quiet chat, and you addle your brains over a confounded—

Herbert. Now, Father! Morris will turn up all right.

Mr. White (*still in a temper*). Lover's Lane, Fulham! Of all the beastly, slushy, out-o-the-way places to live in—! Pathway's a bog, and the road's a torrent. (*He speaks to* Mrs. White, *who has risen and is at his side.*) What's the County Council thinking of, that's what I want to know? Just because this is the only house on the road, it doesn't matter if nobody can get near it, I suppose.

Mrs. White. Never mind, dear. Perhaps you'll win tomorrow. (*She moves to back of table.*)

Mr. White. Perhaps I'll—perhaps I'll—! What do you mean? (*He bursts out laughing.*) There! You always know what's going on inside of me, don't you, Mother?

Mrs. White. Ought to, after thirty years, John. (*She goes to the dresser and busies herself wiping the tumblers on a tray there.*)

(Mr. White *rises and goes to the fireplace.*)

Herbert. And it's not such a bad place, Dad. After all, it's one of the few old-fashioned houses left near London. None of your stucco villas. Comfortable, I call it. And so do you, or you wouldn't have bought it.

Mr. White (*growling*). Nice job I made of that, too! With two hundred pounds still to pay on it.

Herbert (*leaning on the back of his father's chair*). Why, I shall work that off in no time, Dad. Matter of three years, with the raise promised me.

Mr. White. If you don't get married.

Herbert. Not me. I'm not that sort.

Mrs. White. I wish you would, Herbert. A good, steady, lad—(*She brings the tray with a bottle of whisky, glasses, a lemon, spoons, small cakes, and a knife to the table.*)

Herbert. Lots of time, Mother. Sufficient for the day—as the saying goes. Just now my dynamos don't leave me any time for falling in love. Jealous they are, I tell you!

Mr. White (*chuckling*). I lay awake at night often, and think: If Herbert took a nap, and let his what-d'you-call-ums—dynamos, run down, all Fulham would be in darkness. Lord! What a joke!

Herbert. Joke! And me getting fired! Pretty idea of a joke you've got.

(*There is a knock at the outer door.*)

Mrs. White. Hark!

(*The knock is repeated, louder.*)

Mr. White (*going toward the door*). There he is. That's the Sergeant-Major. (*He unlocks the outer door.*)

Herbert (*removes the chess board*). Wonder what yarn he's got for us tonight. (*He places the chessboard on the piano.*)

Mrs. White (*busies herself putting the other armchair nearer the fire*). Don't let the door slam, John!

(Mr. White *opens the door a little, struggling with the wind.* Sergeant-Major Morris, *a veteran with a distinct military appearance, missing his left arm, is seen to enter.* Mr. White *helps him off with his coat, which he hangs up in the outer hall.*)

Mr. White (*at the door*). Slip in quick! It's as much as I can do to hold it against the wind.

Sergeant. Awful! Awful! (*He is busy taking off his jacket.*) And a mile up the road—by the cemetery—it's worse. Enough to blow the hair off your head.

Mr. White. Give me your stick.

Mrs. White. So cold you must be! Come to the fire.

Sergeant. How are you, ma'm? (*He speaks to* Herbert) How's yourself, laddie? Not on duty yet, eh? Day shift, eh?

Herbert. No sir. Night shift. But there's half an hour yet.

(*The* Sergeant *sits in the armchair above the fire, toward which* Mrs. White *is motioning him.* Mr. White *mixes grog for Morris.*)

Sergeant. Thank you kindly, ma'm. That's good—hah! That's a sight better than the trenches. That's better than sitting in a puddle with the rain pouring down in buckets, and the natives taking pot-shots at you.

Mrs. White. Didn't you have an umbrella with you?

Sergeant. Umbrell—? Ho! ho! That's good! Eh, White? That's good. Did you hear what she said? Umbrellas!— And galoshes! And hot-water bottles!—Ho, yes! No offense, ma'm, but it's easy to see you were never a soldier.

Herbert (*rather hurt*). Mother spoke out of kindness, sir.

Sergeant. And well I know it; and no offense intended. No, ma'm, hardship, hardship is the soldier's lot. Starvation, fever, and get yourself shot. That's a bit of my own wisdom.

Mrs. White. You don't look to have taken much harm—except—(*She indicates his empty sleeve. She takes the kettle to the table, then returns to the fire.*)

Sergeant (*showing a medal hidden under his coat*). And that I got this for. No, ma'm. Tough. Thomas Morris is tough. (*Mr. White is holding a glass of grog under the Sergeant's nose.*) And sober. What's this now?

Mr. White. Put your nose in it; you'll see.

Sergeant. Whisky? And hot? And sugar? And a slice o' lemon? No. I said I'd never—but seeing the sort o' night. Well! (*He waves the glass at them.*) Here's another thousand a year!

Mr. White (*also with a glass*). Same to you, and many more.

Sergeant (*to* Herbert, *who has no glass*). What? Not you?

Herbert (*laughing and sitting across the chair*). Oh! It isn't for want of being sociable. But my work doesn't go with it. Not even a little. I've got to keep a cool head, a steady eye, and a still hand. The flywheel might gobble me up.

Mrs. White. Don't, Herbert. (*She sits in an armchair below fire.*)

Herbert (*laughing*). No fear, Mother.

Sergeant. Ah! You electricians!—Sort of magicians, you are. Light! you say—and light it is. And, power! you say—and the trams go whizzing. And, knowledge! you say—and words go humming to the ends of the world. It beats me—and I've seen a bit in my time, too.

Herbert (*nudges his father*). Your Indian magic? All a fake, Governor. The fakir's fake.

Sergeant. Fake, you call it? I tell you, I've seen it.

Herbert (*nudging his father with his foot*). Oh, come, now! Such as what?

Sergeant. I've seen a man with no more clothes on than a baby, (*He speaks to* Mrs. White) if you know what I mean— take an empty basket—empty, mind!— as empty as—as this glass—

Mr. White. Hand it over, Morris. (*Morris hands it to* Herbert, *who goes quickly behind table and fills it.*)

Sergeant. Which was not my intention, but used for illustration.

Herbert (*while mixing*). Oh, *I've* seen the basket trick; and I've read how it was done. Why, I could do it myself, with a bit of practice. Ladle out something stronger. (Herbert *brings him the glass.*)

Sergeant. Stronger?—What do you say to an old fakir chucking a rope up in the air—in the *air*, mind you!—and swarming up it, same as if it was hooked on—and vanishing clean out of sight?—I've seen *that.*

(Herbert *goes to the table, plunges a knife into a cake and offers it to the* Sergeant *with exaggerated politeness.*)

Sergeant (*eyeing it with disgust*). Cake—? What for?

Herbert. That yarn takes it.

(Mr. *and* Mrs. White *are delighted.*)

Sergeant. You doubt my word?

Mrs. White. No, no! He's only teasing you. You shouldn't, Herbert.

Mr. White. Herbert always was one for a bit of fun!

(Herbert *puts the cake back on the table. Then he comes around in front and, moving the chair out of the way, sits cross-legged on the floor at his father's side.*)

Sergeant. But it's true. Why, if I chose, I could tell you things—But there! You won't get more yarns out of *me.*

Mr. White. Nonsense, old friend. (*He puts down his glass.*) You're not going to get angry about a bit of fun. (*He moves his chair nearer* Morris's.) What was that you started telling me the other day about a monkey's paw, or something? (*He nudges* Herbert *and winks at* Mrs. White.)

Sergeant (*gravely*). Nothing. Leastways, nothing worth hearing.

Mrs. White (*with astonished curiosity*). Monkey's *paw*—?

Mr. White. Ah—you were telling me—

Sergeant. Nothing. Don't go on about it. (*He puts his empty glass to his lips—then stares at it.*) What? Empty again? There! When I begin thinking of the paw, it makes me that absent-minded—

Mr. White (*rises and fills glass*). You said you always carried it on you.

Sergeant. So I do, for fear of what might happen. (*He is suddenly sunk in deep thought.*) Ay!—ay!

Mr. White (*handing him his glass refilled*). There. (*He sits again in the same chair.*)

Mrs. White. What's it for?

Sergeant. You wouldn't believe me, if I were to tell you.

Herbert. *I* will, every word.

Sergeant. Magic, then? Don't you laugh!

Herbert. I'm not. Got it on you now?

Sergeant. Of course.

No Place Like Home, 1877, THOMAS HICKS. Private collection.

Herbert. Let's see it.

(Seeing that the Sergeant *doesn't know where to put his glass,* Mrs. White *rises from her chair and takes the glass from him. She places it on the mantelpiece and remains standing, a look of curiosity on her face.)*

Sergeant. Oh, it's nothing to look at. *(He hunts in his pocket.)* Just an ordinary— little paw—dried to a mummy. *(He produces it and holds it toward Mrs. White.)* Here.

Mrs. White *(leaning forward eagerly, then starting back with a cry of disgust).* Oh!

Herbert. Give us a look. (Morris *passes the paw to Mr. White,* from whom Herbert *takes it.)* Why, it's all dried up!

Sergeant. I said so.

(The wind blows.)

Mrs. White *(with a slight shudder).* Hark at the wind! *(She sits again in her old place.)*

Mr. White (*taking the paw from* Herbert). And what's special about it?

Sergeant (*impressively*). That paw has had a spell put upon it!

Mr. White. No? (*In great alarm he thrusts the paw back into* Morris's *hand.*)

Sergeant (*pensively*). Ah! By an old fakir. He was a very holy man. He'd sat all doubled up in one spot, going on for fifteen years thinking of things. And he wanted to show that fate ruled people. That everything was cut and dried from the beginning, as you might say. That there wasn't any getting away from it. And that, if you tried to, you would suffer. (*He pauses solemnly.*) So he put a spell on this bit of a paw. It might have been anything else, but he took the first thing that came handy. Ah! He put a spell on it, and made it so that three people (*looking at them with deep meaning.*) could each have three wishes.

(*All but* Mrs. White *laugh rather nervously.*)

Mrs. White. Ssh! Don't!

Sergeant (*more gravely*). But, mark you, though the wishes would be granted, those three people would have cause to wish they hadn't been.

Mr. White. But how could the wishes be granted?

Sergeant. He didn't say. It would all happen so naturally, you might think it a coincidence.

Herbert. Why haven't you tried it, sir?

Sergeant (*gravely, after a pause*). I have.

Herbert (*eagerly*). You've had your three wishes?

Sergeant (*gravely*). Yes.

Mrs. White. Were they granted?

Sergeant (*staring at the fire*). They were.

Mr. White. Has anybody else wished?

Sergeant. Yes. The first owner had his three wish—(*He is lost in recollection.*) Yes, oh, yes, he had his three wishes all right. I don't know what his first two were, (*very impressively*) but the third was for death. (*All shudder.*) That's how I got the paw.

(*Pause.*)

Herbert (*cheerfully*). Well! Seems to me you've only got to wish for things that can't bring any bad luck. (*He rises.*)

Sergeant (*shaking his head*). Ah!

Mr. White (*tentatively*). Morris—if you've had your three wishes—it's no good to you, now—what do you keep it for?

Sergeant (*still holding the paw; looking at it*). Fancy, I suppose. I did have some idea of selling it, but I don't think I will. It's done mischief enough already. Besides, people won't buy. Some of them think it's a fairy tale. And some want to try it first, and pay after.

(*There is a nervous laugh from the others.*)

Mrs. White. If you could have another three wishes, would you?

Sergeant (*slowly—weighing the paw in his hand and looking at it*). I don't know—I don't know—(*Suddenly, with violence, he flings it in the fire.*) No! I'm damned if I would!

(*There is movement from all.*)

Mr. White (*rises and quickly snatches it out of the fire*). What are you doing? (*White goes to the fireplace.*)

Sergeant (*rising and following him*). Let it burn! Let the infernal thing burn!

Mrs. White (*rises*). Let it burn, Father!

Mr. White (*wiping it on his coatsleeve*). No. If you don't want it, give it to me.

Sergeant (*violently*). I won't! I won't! My hands are clear of it. I threw it on the fire. If you keep it, don't blame me, whatever happens. Here! Pitch it back again.

Mr. White (*stubbornly*). I'm going to keep it. What do you say, Herbert?

Herbert (*laughing*). I say, keep it if you want to. Stuff and nonsense, anyhow.

Mr. White (*looking at the paw thoughtfully*). Stuff and nonsense. Yes. I wonder—(*casually.*) I wish—(*He was going to say some ordinary thing, like "I wish I were certain."*)

Sergeant (*misunderstanding him; violently*). Stop! Mind what you're doing. That's not the way.

Mr. White. What is the way?

Mrs. White (*moving away to the back of the table, and beginning to put the tumblers straight and the chairs in their places*). Oh, don't have anything to do with it, John. (*She takes glasses to the dresser. She rinses them in a bowl of water on the dresser, and wipes them with a cloth.*)

Sergeant. That's what I say, m'am. But if I didn't tell him, he might go wishing something he didn't mean to. You hold it in your right hand and wish aloud. But I warn you! I warn you!

Mrs. White. Sounds like the Arabian Nights. Don't you think you might wish me four pair of hands?

Mr. White (*laughing*). Right you are, Mother!—I wish—

Sergeant (*pulling his arm down*). Stop it! If you must wish, wish for something sensible. Look here! I can't stand this. Gets on my nerves. Where's my coat? (*He goes into the alcove.*)

(*Mr. White crosses to the fireplace and carefully puts the paw on the mantelpiece.*)

Herbert. I'm coming your way, to the plant, in a minute. Won't you wait? (*He helps Morris with his jacket.*)

Sergeant (*picking up his coat*). No. I'm all shook up. I want fresh air. I don't want to be here when you wish. And wish you will as soon as my back's turned. I know. I know. But I've warned you.

Mr. White (*helping him into his coat*). All right, Morris. Don't you fret about us. (*He gives him money.*) Here.

Sergeant (*refusing it*). No, I won't—

Mr. White (*forcing it into his hand*). Yes, you will. (*He opens door.*)

Sergeant (*turning to the room*). Well, good night all. (*He speaks to* Mr. White.) Put it in the fire.

All. Good night. (*The* Sergeant *exits.* Mr. White *closes the door, comes toward the fireplace, absorbed in the paw.*)

Herbert. If there's no more in this than there is in his other stories, we shouldn't make much out of it.

Mrs. White (*to* Mr. White). Did you give him anything for it, Father?

Mr. White. A trifle. He didn't want it, but I made him take it.

Mrs. White. There, now! You shouldn't. Throwing your money about.

Mr. White (*looking at the paw, which he has picked up again*). I wonder—

Herbert. What?

Mr. White. I wonder, whether we hadn't better chuck it on the fire?

Herbert (*laughing*). Why, we're all going to be rich and famous and happy.

Mrs. White. Throw it on the fire, indeed, when you've given money for it! So like you, Father.

Herbert. Wish to be an Emperor, Father to begin with. Then you can't be hen-pecked!

Mrs. White (*going for him in front of the table with a dust cloth*). You young—! (*He follows him to the back of the table.*)

Herbert (*running away from her, hiding behind table*). Steady with that dust cloth, Mother!

Mr. White. Be quiet there! (Herbert *catches* Mrs. White *in his arms and kisses her.*) I wonder—(*He has the paw in his hand.*) I don't know what to wish for, and that's a fact. (*He looks about him with a happy smile.*) I seem to've got all I want.

Herbert (*with his hands on the old man's shoulders*). Old Dad! If you'd only cleared the debt on the house, you'd be quite happy, wouldn't you? (*He laughs.*) Well—go ahead! wish, for the two hundred pounds—that'll just do it.

Mr. White (*half laughing*). Shall I?

Herbert. Go on! Here!—I'll play slow music. (*He goes to the piano.*)

Mrs. White. Don't, John. Don't have anything to do with it!

Herbert. Now, Dad! (*He plays.*)

Mr. White. I will! (*He holds up the paw, as if half ashamed*) I wish for two hundred pounds. (*There is a crash on the piano. At the same instant* Mr. White *utters a cry and lets the paw drop.*)

Mrs. White *and* **Herbert.** What happened?

Mr. White (*gazing with horror at the paw*). It moved! As I wished, it twisted in my hand like a snake.

Herbert (*picks the paw up*). Nonsense, Dad. Why, it's as stiff as a bone (*He lays it on the mantelpiece.*)

Mrs. White. Must have been your fancy, Father.

Herbert (*laughing*). Well—? (*He looks around the room.*) I don't see the money, and I bet I never shall.

Mr. White (*relieved*). Thank God, there's no harm done! But it gave me a shock.

Herbert. Half-past eleven. I must get along, I'm on at midnight. (*He fetches his coat.*) We've had quite a merry evening.

Mrs. White. I'm off to bed. Don't be late for breakfast, Herbert.

Herbert. I shall walk home as usual. Does me good. I shall be with you about nine. Don't wait, though.

Mrs. White. You know your father never waits.

Herbert. Good night, Mother. (*He kisses her. She lights a candle on the dresser, goes up the steps and exits.*)

Herbert (*coming to his father, who is sunk in thought*). Good night, Dad. You'll find the cash tied up in the middle of the bed.

Mr. White (*staring, seizes* Herbert's *hand*). It moved, Herbert.

Herbert. Ah! And a monkey is hanging by his tail from the bed-post watching you count the golden sovereigns.

Mr. White (*accompanying him to the door*). I wish you wouldn't joke, my boy.

Herbert. All right, Dad. (*He opens the door.*) Lord! What weather! Good night. (*He exits.*)

(*The old man shakes his head, closes the door, locks it, puts the chain up, and slips the lower bolt. He has some difficulty with the upper bolt.*)

Mr. White. This bolt's stiff again! I must get Herbert to look to it in the morning. (*He comes into the room, puts out the lamp, crosses toward the steps; but he is irresistibly attracted toward the fireplace. He sits down and stares into the fire. His expression changes: he sees something horrible in the flames.*)

Mr. White (*with an involuntary cry*). Mother! Mother!

Mrs. White (*appearing at the door at the top of the steps with a candle*). What's the matter?

Mr. White (*mastering himself; rises*). Nothing—I—haha!—I saw faces in the fire.

Mrs. White. Come along. (*She takes his arm and draws him toward the steps. He looks back frightened toward the fireplace as they reach the first step.*)

CURTAIN

ACT TWO

There is bright sunshine. The table, which has been moved nearer the window, is laid for breakfast. Mrs. White *is busy about the table.* Mr. White *is standing in the window looking off. The inner door is open, showing the outer door.*

Mr. White. What a morning Herbert's got for walking home!

Mrs. White. What's the time? (*She looks at the clock on the mantelpiece.*) Quarter to nine, I declare. He's off at eight. (*She crosses to the fire.*)

Mr. White. Takes him half an hour to change and wash. He's just by the cemetery now.

Mrs. White. He'll be here in ten minutes.

Mr. White (*coming to the table*). What's for breakfast?

Mrs. White. Sausages. (*She stands at the mantelpiece.*) Why, if here isn't that dirty monkey's paw! (*She picks it up, looks at it with disgust, puts it back. She takes sausages in the dish from before the fire and places them on the table.*) Silly thing! The idea of us listening to such nonsense!

Mr. White (*goes up to the window again*). Ay—the Sergeant-Major and his yarns! I suppose all old soldiers are alike—

Mrs. White. Come on, Father. Herbert hates us to wait. (*They both sit and begin breakfast.*)

Mrs. White. How could wishes be granted, nowadays?

Mr. White. Ah! Been thinking about it all night, have you?

Mrs. White. You kept me awake, with your tossing and tumbling—

Mr. White. Ay, I had a bad night.

Mrs. White. It was the storm, I expect. How it blew!

Mr. White. I didn't hear it. I was asleep and not asleep, if you know what I mean.

Mrs. White. And all that rubbish about its making you unhappy if your wish was granted! How could two hundred pounds hurt you, eh, Father?

Mr. White. Might drop on my head in a lump. Don't see any other way. And I'd try to bear that. Though, mind you, Morris said it would all happen so naturally that you might take it for a coincidence.

Mrs. White. Well—it hasn't happened. That's all I know. And it isn't going to. (*A letter is seen to drop in the letter-box.*) And how you can sit there and talk about it—(*There is a sharp knock at the door. She jumps to her feet.*) What's that?

Mr. White. Postman, of course.

Mrs. White (*seeing the letter from a distance; in an awed whisper*). He's brought a letter, John!

Mr. White (*laughing*). What did you think he'd bring? Ton of coals?

Mrs. White. John—! John—! Suppose—?

Mr. White. Suppose what?

Mrs. White. Suppose it was two hundred pounds!

Mr. White (*suppressing his excitement*). Eh!—Here! Don't talk nonsense. Why don't you fetch it?

Mrs. White (*crosses and takes the letter out of the box*). It's thick, John—(*feels it*)—and—and it's got something crisp inside it. (*Takes the letter to* Mr. White.)

Mr. White. Who—who's it for?

Mrs. White. You.

Mr. White. Hand it over, then. (*He examines it with ill-concealed excitement.*) The idea! What a superstitious old woman you are! Where are my specs?

Mrs. White. Let me open it.

Mr. White. Don't you touch it. Where are my specs?

Mrs. White. Don't let sudden wealth sour your temper, John.

Mr. White. Will you find my specs?

Mrs. White (*taking them off the mantelpiece*). Here, John, here. (*He opens the letter.*) Take care! Don't tear it!

Mr. White. Tear what?

Mrs. White. If it was banknotes, John!

Mr. White (*taking a thick, formal document and a crisp-looking slip out of the envelope*). You've gone dotty.—You've made me nervous. (*He reads*) "Sir,—Enclosed please find receipt for your payment of interest on the mortgage on your house, duly received."

(*They look at each other.* Mr. White *sits down to finish his breakfast silently.* Mrs. White *goes to the window.*)

Mrs. White. That comes of listening to tipsy old soldiers.

Mr. White (*pettish*). What does?

Mrs. White. You thought there were banknotes in it.

Mr. White. I didn't! I said all along—

Mrs. White. How Herbert will laugh, when I tell him!

Mr. White (*with gruff good-humor*). You're not going to tell him. You're going to keep your mouth shut. That's what you're going to do. Why, I should never hear the last of it.

Mrs. White. Serve you right. I shall tell him. You know you like his fun. See how he joked you last night when you said the paw moved. (*She is looking through the window.*)

Mr. White. So it did. It did move. That I'll swear to.

Mrs. White (*abstractedly; she is watching something outside*). You thought it did.

Mr. White. I say it did. There was no thinking about it. You saw how it upset me, didn't you? (*She doesn't answer.*) Didn't you?—Why don't you listen? (*He turns around.*) What is it?

Mrs. White. Nothing.

Mr. White (*turns back to his breakfast*). Do you see Herbert coming?

Mrs. White. No.

Mr. White. He's about due. What is it?

Mrs. White. Nothing. Only a man. Looks like a gentleman. Leastways, he's in black, and he's got a top-hat on.

Mr. White. What about him? (*He is not interested; goes on eating.*)

Mrs. White. He stood at the garden-gate as if he wanted to come in. But he couldn't seem to make up his mind.

Mr. White. Oh, you're full of fancies.

Mrs. White. He's going—no; he's coming back.

Mr. White. Don't let him see you peeping.

Mrs. White (*with increasing excitement*). He's looking at the house. He's got his hand on the latch. No. He turns away again. (*eagerly*) John! He looks like a sort of lawyer.

Mr. White. What of it?

Mrs. White. Oh, you'll only laugh again. But suppose—suppose he's coming about the two hundred—

Mr. White. You're not to mention it again! You're a foolish old woman. Come and eat your breakfast. (*eagerly*) Where is he now?

Mrs. White. Gone down the road. He has turned back. He seems to have made up his mind. Here he comes! Oh, John, and me all untidy! (*Crosses to the fire. There is a knock.*)

Mr. White (*to* Mrs. White *who is hastily smoothing her hair*). What does it matter? He's made a mistake. Come to the wrong house. (*Goes to the fireplace.* Mrs. White *opens the door.* Mr. Sampson, *dressed from head to foot in solemn black, with a top-hat, stands in the doorway.*)

Sampson (*outside*). Is this Mr. White's house?

Mrs. White. Come in, sir. Please step in. (*She shows him into the room. He is awkward and nervous.*) You must overlook our being so untidy; and the room all messy; and John in his garden-coat. (*To* Mr. White *she says reproachfully.*) Oh, John.

Sampson (*to* Mr. White). Morning. My name is Sampson.

Mrs. White (*offering a chair*). Won't you be seated? (Sampson *stands quite still.*)

Sampson. Ah—thank you—no, I think not—I think not. (*He pauses.*)

Mr. White (*awkwardly, trying to help him*). Fine weather for the time o' year.

Sampson. Ah—yes—yes—(*He pauses; he makes a renewed effort.*) My name is Sampson—I've come—

Mrs. White. Perhaps you was wishful to see Herbert; he'll be home in a minute. (*She points.*) Here's his breakfast waiting—

Sampson (*interrupting her hastily*). No, no! (*He pauses.*) I've come from the electrical plant—

Mrs. White. Why, you might have come with him.

(*Mr. White sees something is wrong and tenderly puts his hand on her arm.*)

Sampson. No—no—I've come—alone.

Mrs. White (*with a little anxiety*). Is anything the matter?

Sampson. I was asked to call—

Mrs. White (*abruptly*). Herbert! Has anything happened? Is he hurt? Is he hurt?

Mr. White (*soothing her*). There, there, Mother. Don't you jump to conclusions. Let the gentleman speak. You've not brought bad news, I'm sure, sir.

Sampson. I'm—sorry—

Mrs. White. Is he hurt? (Sampson *bows.*) Badly?

Sampson. Very badly. (*He turns away.*)

Mrs. White (*with a cry*). John—! (*She instinctively moves toward* Mr. White.)

Mr. White. Is he in pain?

Sampson. He is not in pain.

Mrs. White. Oh, thank God! Thank God for that! Thank—(*She looks in a startled fashion at* Mr. White—*realizes what* Sampson *means, catches his arm, and tries to turn him toward her.*) Do you mean—?

(*Sampson avoids her look. Mrs. White gropes for her husband. He takes her two hands in his and gently lets her sink into the armchair above the fireplace. Then he stands on her right, between her and* Sampson.)

Mr. White (*hoarsely*). Go on, sir.

Sampson. He was telling his mates a story. Something that had happened here last night. He was laughing and wasn't noticing and—and—(*hushed*) the machinery caught him—

(*A little cry comes from* Mrs. White; *her face shows her horror and agony.*)

Mr. White (*vague, holding* Mrs. White's *hand*). The machinery caught him—yes—and him the only child—it's hard, sir—very hard—

Sampson (*subdued*). The Company wished me to convey their sincere sympathy with you in your great loss—

Mr. White (*staring blankly*). Our—great—loss—!

Sampson. I was to say further—(*He speaks as if apologizing.*) I am only their servant—I am only obeying orders—

Office Board for Smith Bros. Coal Company (detail), 1879, JOHN F. PETO. Addison Gallery of American Art, Phillips Academy, Andover, Massachusetts.

Mr. White. Our—great—loss—

Sampson *(laying an envelope on the table and edging toward the door).* I was to say, the Company disclaims all responsibility, but, in consideration of your son's services, they wish to present you with a certain sum as compensation. *(He gets to the door.)*

Mr. White. Our—great—loss—*(suddenly, with horror).* How—how much?

Sampson *(in the doorway).* Two hundred pounds. *(He exits.)*

(Mrs. White gives a cry. The old man takes no heed of her, smiles faintly, puts out his hands like a sightless man, and drops, a senseless heap, to the floor. Mrs. White stares at him blankly and her hands go out helplessly toward him.)

CURTAIN

ACT THREE

Night. On the table a candle is flickering at its last gasp. The room looks neglected. Mr. White *is dozing fitfully in the armchair.* Mrs. White *is in the window peering through the blind.* Mr. White *starts, wakes, looks around.*

Mr. White (*fretfully*). Jenny—Jenny.

Mrs. White (*in the window*). Yes.

Mr. White. Where are you?

Mrs. White. At the window.

Mr. White. What are you doing?

Mrs. White. Looking up the road.

Mr. White (*falling back*). What's the use, Jenny? What's the use?

Mrs. White. That's where the cemetery is; that's where we've laid him.

Mr. White. Ay—ay—a week ago today—what time is it?

Mrs. White. I don't know.

Mr. White. We don't take much account of time now, Jenny, do we?

Mrs. White. Why should we? He doesn't come home. He'll never come home again. There's nothing to think about—

Mr. White. Or to talk about. (*He pauses.*) Come away from the window; you'll get cold.

Mrs. White. It's colder where he is.

Mr. White. Ay—gone for ever—

Mrs. White. And taken all our hopes with him—

Mr. White. And all our wishes—

Mrs. White. Ay, and all our—(*with a sudden cry*) John! (*She comes quickly to him; he rises.*)

Mr. White. Jenny! For God's sake! What's the matter?

Mrs. White (*with dreadful eagerness*). The paw! The monkey's paw!

Mr. White (*bewildered*). Where? Where is it? What's wrong with it?

Mrs. White. I want it! You haven't done away with it?

Mr. White. I haven't seen it—since—why?

Mrs. White. I want it! Find it! Find it!

Mr. White (*groping on the mantelpiece*). Here! Here it is! What do you want of it? (*He leaves it there.*)

Mrs. White. Why didn't I think of it? Why didn't you think of it?

Mr. White. Think of what?

Mrs. White. The other two wishes!

Mr. White (*with horror*). What?

Mrs. White. We've only had one.

Mr. White (*tragically*). Wasn't that enough?

Mrs. White. No! We'll have one more. (Mr. White *crosses the room.* Mrs. White *takes the paw and follows him.*) Take it. Take it quickly. And wish—

Mr. White (*avoiding the paw*). Wish what?

Mrs. White. Oh, John! John! Wish our boy alive again!

Mr. White. Good God! Are you mad?

Mrs. White. Take it. Take it and wish. (*She is overcome with grief.*) Oh, my boy! My boy!

Mr. White. Get to bed. Get to sleep. You don't know what you're saying.

Mrs. White. We had the first wish granted—why not the second?

Mr. White (*hushed*). He's been dead ten days, and—Jenny! Jenny! I only knew him by his clothing—if you weren't allowed to see him then—how could you bear to see him now?

Mrs. White. I don't care. Bring him back.

Mr. White (*shrinking from the paw*). I dare not touch it!

Mrs. White (*thrusting it into his hand*). Here! Here! Wish!

Mr. White (*trembling*). Jenny!

Mrs. White (*fiercely*). Wish. (*She goes on frantically whispering "Wish."*)

Mr. White (*shuddering, but overcome by her insistence*). I—I—wish—my—son—alive again. (*He drops it with a cry. The*

candle goes out. There is utter darkness. He sinks into a chair. Mrs. White hurries to the window and draws the blind back. She stands in the moonlight. Pause.)

Mrs. White (*drearily*). Nothing.

Mr. White. Thank God! Thank God!

Mrs. White. Nothing at all. Along the whole length of the road not a living thing. (*She closes the blind.*) And nothing, nothing, nothing left in our lives, John.

Mr. White. Except each other, Jenny—and memories.

Mrs. White (*coming back slowly to the fireplace*). We're too old. We were only alive in him. We can't begin again. We can't feel anything now, John, but emptiness and darkness. (*She sinks into the armchair.*)

Mr. White. Not for long, Jenny. There's that to look forward to.

Mrs. White. Every minute's long, now.

Mr. White (*rising*). I can't bear the darkness!

Mrs. White. It's dreary—dreary.

Mr. White (*goes to the dresser*). Where's the candle? (*He finds it and brings it to the table.*) And the matches? Where are the matches? We mustn't sit in the dark. (*Lights a match and then the candle.*) There. (*He turns with the lighted match toward Mrs. White, who is rocking and moaning.*) Don't take on so, Mother.

Mrs. White. I'm a mother no longer

Mr. White (*lights candle*). There now; there now. Go on up to bed. Go on, now—I'm coming.

Mrs. White. Whether I'm here or in bed, or wherever I am, I'm with my boy, I'm with—

(*There is a low, single knock at the street door.*)

Mrs. White (*starting*). What's that!

Mr. White (*mastering his horror*). A rat. The house is full of 'em. (*There is a louder, single knock; Mrs. White starts up. He catches her by the arm.*) Stop! What are you going to do?

Mrs. White (*wildly*). It's my boy! It's Herbert! I forgot it was a mile away! Don't hold me! I must open the door!

(*The knocking continues in single knocks at irregular intervals, constantly growing louder and more insistant.*)

Mr. White (*still holding her*). For God's sake!

Mrs. White (*struggling*). Let me go!

Mr. White. Don't open the door! (*He drags her away.*)

Mrs. White. Let me go!

Mr. White. Think what you might see!

Mrs. White (*struggling fiercely*). Do you think I fear the child I bore! Let me go!

(*She wrenches herself loose and rushes to the door, which she tears open.*) I'm coming, Herbert! I'm coming!

Mr. White (*cowering in the extreme corner, left front*). Don't do it! Don't do it!

(*Mrs. White works on the outer door, where the knocking continues. She slips the chain and lower bolt, and unlocks the door.*)

Mr. White (*suddenly*). The paw! Where's the monkey's paw? (*He gets on his knees and feels along the floor for it.*)

Mrs. White (*tugging at the top bolt*). John! The top bolt's stuck. I can't move it. Come and help. Quick!

Mr. White (*wildly groping*). The paw! There's a wish left.

(*The knocking grows louder.*)

Mrs. White. Do you hear him? John! Your child's knocking!

Mr. White. Where is it? Where did it fall?

Mrs. White (*tugging desperately at the bolt*). Help! Help! Will you keep your child from his home?

Mr. White. Where did it fall? I can't find it—I can't find—

(*The knocking is now tempestuous, and there are blows upon the door as of a body beating against it.*)

Mrs. White. Herbert! Herbert! My boy! Wait! Your mother's opening to you! Ah! It's moving! It's moving!

Mr. White. God forbid! *(He finds the paw.)* Ah!

Mrs. White *(slipping the bolt).* Herbert!

Mr. White *(raising himself to his knees; holding the paw high).* I wish him dead. *(The knocking stops abruptly.)* I wish him dead and at peace!

Mrs. White *(flinging the door open simultaneously).* Herb—

(There is only a flood of moonlight and emptiness. The old man sways in prayer on his knees. The old woman lies half swooning, wailing against the doorpost.)

CURTAIN

Bust of a Man, 1964, LESTER JOHNSON. Miami University Art Museum. Gift of Ruth Mayer Durchslag, Oxford, Ohio.

Developing Comprehension Skills

1. At the beginning of the play Mr. White says, "I seem to've got all I want." To the Whites, what are the most important things in life?

2. Sergeant-Major Morris tells the Whites that the first owner's third wish was for death. What does this imply about the first two wishes?

3. What price did the Whites pay for the granting of their first wish?

4. If Mr. White had not used the third wish, what would his wife have seen at the door?

5. Do the characters in this play act as you would expect real people to act? Find several examples to support your answer.

6. The fakir who put a spell on the monkey's paw did so to prove that people had no control over their lives. Based on the Whites' experiences, do you think the fakir proved his point? Explain your reasoning.

Reading Literature: Drama

1. **Understanding Stage Plays.** "The Monkey's Paw" was originally written as a short story. This version is intended to be acted out on stage. How do you think the short story was changed to make it into a stage play? For example, did dialogue become more important in the dramatic version? If so, why? What other things may have had to change?

   What advantages would a stage play have over a television version of this story? over a radio play? In what ways might the other two versions have been better?

2. **Understanding Foreshadowing.** Foreshadowing, as you know, is a writer's use of clues to hint at events that will occur later. In "The

Monkey's Paw," the Sergeant-Major states that the first owner of the monkey's paw wished for death as his third wish. How does this comment foreshadow the Whites' tragedy? Find and explain one other example of foreshadowing in the play.

3. **Recognizing Structure.** When a play is divided into three acts or three scenes, the action usually follows a set pattern. Most often, the first part prepares the audience for an important occurrence. That important event usually occurs in the second part. Then, the third part shows the consequences of that event. Does "The Monkey's Paw" follow this three-part structure? Explain your answer.

4. **Identifying Suspense.** The playwright does a number of things to create suspense throughout "The Monkey's Paw." One especially suspenseful scene, for example, occurs as the Whites wait for their two hundred pounds. In this instance, tension grows while a number of incidents and conversations postpone the arrival of the money. Finally, the outcome becomes clear and the suspense is replaced by the horror of the son's death. Find two other suspenseful moments in the play. Explain how the suspense is created in each case.

5. **Identifying Mood.** In a play, dialogue and details of setting help to establish mood. The mood, or atmosphere, changes several times during "The Monkey's Paw." The play begins with a warm, cozy mood as Mr. White and Herbert play chess. What details in the setting of this scene contribute to this mood? How does the family's dialogue help create this mood?

Once the monkey's paw is revealed, the mood becomes eerie. How does the weather contribute to the mood? In Act Two, what is the mood before Sampson arrives? What details add to this mood? Explain how the mood changes again in Act Three.

6. **Noticing Elements of Folklore.** "The Monkey's Paw" contains a number of elements that are common in folklore. One is the use of a magic charm, in this case the monkey's paw. Another is the number "three." The number three has been thought by many people and cultures to have magic or supernatural qualities. Some of these qualities were thought to be lucky. The old saying "the third time's a charm" reflects this belief. What things in "The Monkey's Paw" occur in threes? Are any of these things "lucky"? Explain your answer.

Developing Vocabulary Skills

Understanding Dialect. The English language spoken in the United States differs from the English language spoken in England. Even within a country, the way English is used changes slightly from region to region, and sometimes from person to person. These minor differences in vocabulary, pronunciation, and grammar make up the **dialect** of a country or region.

Carefully read the following passages from "The Monkey's Paw." Each underlined word is an expression used by a speaker of English dialect. Using context clues or the dictionary, determine the meaning of the underlined word. Then write a word that an American speaker of English might use.

1. Pathway's a <u>bog</u>, and the road's a torrent.

2. You've gone <u>dotty</u>—you've made me nervous.

3. And, power! you say—and the <u>trams</u> go whizzing by.

4. It must have been your <u>fancy</u>, Father.

5. He was telling his <u>mates</u> a story.

6. <u>Hark</u> at the wind.

Developing Writing Skills

1. **Analyzing the Function of Characters.** Minor characters are not as fully developed as the main characters in a play. Still, minor characters often serve an important purpose. In one paragraph, explain who the minor characters in "The Monkey's Paw" are and what function they serve in the play.

   Pre-Writing. Review the play, and notice who the minor characters are. Decide why each minor character is important in this play. Make notes on the purposes of each minor character, along with specific actions that each one performs.

   Writing. Write a topic sentence that makes a general statement about the importance of minor characters in the play. Support that topic sentence with the specific examples from your pre-writing notes. Try to show clearly how each character affects what happens in the rest of the play.

   Revising. Check for a clear topic sentence. Have you explained all functions of the minor characters? Add necessary ideas, and omit unrelated ones.

2. **Using Comparison and Contrast.** Both "The Hitchhiker" and "The Monkey's Paw" contain supernatural elements. Supernatural ele-

ments, you will remember, are events beyond the realm of normal human experience. Write two paragraphs comparing and contrasting the supernatural elements in these two plays. Be sure to include a discussion of the reactions of the characters to these elements.

3. **Writing Stage Directions.** Write stage directions for Acts Two and Three of "The Monkey's Paw." Imagine what lighting, music, costumes, and sound effects would be most effective in staging this play. Try to picture these elements in detail. Think about how they could reflect the characterization and mood of the play.

Developing Skills in Study and Research

Using Specialized Reference Works. Did you wonder why the writer chose a monkey's paw as the magic object in this play? The monkey's paw has its roots in early superstitions. Specialized reference works can help you to find out about the origins, or beginnings, of superstitions and folklore.

Check to see if *Funk and Wagnall's Standard Dictionary of Folklore, Mythology and Legend* is in your library. If it is, look up *monkey.* Can you find information about the monkey's paw? How did this animal's paw come to have superstitious meaning? Also check to see if your library has the *Dictionary of Superstition and Mythology.* If so, what can you learn about Indian folklore? Take notes on the significance of the monkey's paw and Indian beliefs about magic. Ask your teacher or librarian to direct you to other reference materials that could provide information about superstitions.

Developing Skills in Speaking and Listening

1. **Imitating a Dialect.** As you have learned, dialect is a way of speaking that is characteristic of the people in a certain region. Dialect includes the grammar, expressions, and pronunciations of the people. Dialect can be used to add realism and color to the dialogue in a story or play. The characters in "The Monkey's Paw," for example, speak a dialect common in England.

In your library, locate books and recordings featuring different British dialects. Ask your librarian for help. Practice imitating one of these dialects. Work with a partner to improve your dialect. What does this experience teach you about language?

2. **Listening to a Play.** Listen to a recording of a play. Let your imagination assist you in visualizing the setting, characters, and action. After you have listened to the play, write a brief description of how you have imagined the setting and the characters. Try to determine what costuming, set, makeup, lighting, and music would best convey the mood and the characters. If any of your classmates have listened to the same play, compare your conclusions with theirs. Decide what it was in the recording that helped you to visualize the play.

Using Your Skills in Reading Drama

1. In this chapter you read a radio play, a television play, and a stage play. Each kind of play has its own special characteristics. How does "The Hitchhiker" take advantage of the special qualities of radio? How does "The Monsters Are Due on Maple Street" take advantage of television? Why is "The Monkey's Paw" especially well suited for stage presentation? What did the writers of these plays have to take into consideration?

2. The plays in this chapter all contain supernatural elements. As you know, supernatural elements are those beyond ordinary human experience. Identify the supernatural elements in each play. Then find two short stories in Chapter 2 that have supernatural elements. Compare these short stories to the three plays in this chapter. How are the moods similar? How are the settings, characters, and themes alike? How are they different? How would each short story have to be changed if it were presented as a drama?

Using Your Skills in Comprehension

The authors of all three plays in this chapter intend to create an eerie, suspenseful mood. Does each author achieve that purpose?

Another purpose of "The Monsters Are Due on Maple Street" and "The Monkey's Paw" is to suggest a theme, or idea, to the audience. What are the themes of these two plays? Do you think the authors succeeded in making the audiences understand these themes?

Using Your Skills in Vocabulary

The following lines are from the plays in Chapter 7. Decide whether standard or nonstandard English is used in each passage. If the language is standard, tell whether it is formal or informal.

1. **Henry.** It's nobuddy, mother. Just a feller thinks he wants a cup of coffee. Go back into bed.

2. **Welles.** I go on record at the outset of this evening's entertainment with the sober assurance that although blood may be curdled on this program none will be spilt.

3. **Adams.** Let me explain about his appearance before I go on. I repeat. There was nothing sinister about him.

4. **Sampson.** The Company disclaims all responsibility, but, in consideration of your son's services, they wish to present you with a certain sum as compensation.

5. **Charlie.** Go ahead, Steve. What kind of "radio set" you workin' on? I never seen it.

Using Your Writing Skills

Choose one of the following writing assignments.

1. How do the authors of "The Hitchhiker," and "The Monsters Are Due on Maple Street," and "The Monkey's Paw" create suspense? In a brief composition, explain how each playwright builds suspense. Point out similarities in the techniques the playwrights use. Give examples of specific incidents in each play that are especially suspenseful.

2. Assume that you are rewriting one of the short stories in Chapter 2 as a stage play. Choose the story that you would like to adapt, and write the opening scene for a play. Begin by determining the setting and writing the opening stage directions to set the scene. Imagine how the action and characters of the short story would be presented in a drama. Write dialogue for the opening scene. Include in your dialogue directions to the actors. These directions should tell the actor how to act while delivering the dialogue.

Using Your Skills in Speaking and Listening

Complete this activity in a group with two or three other people. Choose a news story or other event that everyone in your class is familiar with. Take turns retelling this event to the class. One person should relate the story using formal, standard English. One should tell it using informal, or conversational English. The third person should use nonstandard English. If possible, a fourth person should use a dialect. With the class, discuss the effect the different types of language had on the report.

Handbook for Reading and Writing

Literary Terms

Adage. An adage is a traditional saying that is assumed to express a basic truth. "Seeing is believing" is an example of an adage.

For more about adages, see page 84.

Alliteration. The repetition of initial consonant sounds is called alliteration. Alliteration is used in prose and poetry, as well as in everyday speech. It adds a musical quality and rhythm to writing. It also helps to create mood and emphasis.

Life has loveliness to sell,
    All beautiful and splendid things.
Blue waves whitened on a cliff,
    Soaring fire that sways and sings
("Barter," page 274)

For more about alliteration, see pages 179–180.

Allusion. A writer's reference to a well known work of literature, a famous person, or a historical event is called an allusion. This technique is often used to emphasize an idea, event, or character. The allusion to *Dr. Jekyll and Mr. Hyde* in "Travels with Charley" on page 414, refers to a book by Robert Louis Stevenson. In this novel, a doctor takes a drug that changes him from a kind and caring person into an ugly and evil monster.

For more about allusion, see page 144.

Analogy. An analogy makes a point by point comparison of two things. These things are basically different, but have some similarities. Mark Twain makes an analogy between ants and men in "The Fraudulent Ant," page 442.

For more about analogies, see page 445.

Article. An article is a brief essay that informs or persuades. Articles are generally found in magazines or newspapers. They are usually objective and present facts rather than opinions. "The First Basketball Game" on page 465 is an example.

For more about articles, see page 305.

Assonance. The repetition of vowel sounds within words is called assonance. Assonance can create a certain mood and give a musical quality to prose and poetry. Note how the repetition of the long *o* sound in this example creates the feeling of cold.

It is a cold and snowy night. The main street
    is deserted.
The only things moving are swirls of snow.
As I lift the mailbox door, I feel its cold
    iron.
("Driving to Town Late To Mail a Letter,"
page 264)

For more about assonance, see pages 181 and 182.

Autobiography. A story about a person's life written by that person is an autobiography. It is written from the first-person point of view and generally focuses on significant events in the person's life. An example of an autobiography is the selection by Willie Mays on page 404.

For more about autobiography, see page 305.

Biography. A factual account of someone's life is called a biography. Biographies often include important events as well as less important yet interesting facts about a person's life. While biographies focus on the subject's personality, they may also provide details about the times when the person lived. "Eleanor Roosevelt: Citizen of the World" on page 363, is an example of a biography.

For more on biography, see page 304.

Character. Every person (or animal) who participates in the action of a story, poem, or play is a character. The most important character or characters are called the major characters. Everyone else in the selection is called a minor character. In "The Beau Catcher" (page 79), Genevieve is a major character, while Bert is a minor character.

A dynamic character is one that changes during the course of a story. A static character is one who remains the same throughout the course of the story.

For more about characters, see pages 13 and 161. See also *Character Trait* and *Characterization*.

Characterization. The method a writer uses to make the characters come alive is called characterization. A writer can describe characters either directly or indirectly.

In direct description, the writer makes specific statements about the character.

> With a name like that, you will picture Sven at once as a six-foot-six Nordic giant, built like a bull and with a voice to match. ("Feathered Friend," page 19)

In indirect description, the writer does not state directly how a character looks or acts. Instead, the writer provides indirect clues to characterization. The reader must gain an understanding of the character by examining that character's actions, what he or she says or thinks, and by what others in the story say about the character.

For more about characterization, see pages 49 and 50. See also *Character, Character Trait,* and *Description*.

Character Trait. A quality exhibited by a character through his or her actions, statements, or thoughts is a character trait. In "Zlateh the Goat" (page 25), for example, Aaron exhibits the character trait of perseverance.

For more about character traits, see page 24. See also *Character* and *Characterization*.

Chronological Order. See *Time Order*.

Climax. The climax of a story usually involves an important event, decision, or discovery. It is the turning point of the story and affects the final outcome. In "Beauty Is Truth" (page 110), for example, the climax occurs when Jeanie's piece of writing is read aloud in class.

For more about climax, see page 13. See also *Plot*.

Comparison. A comparison is used in prose or poetry to show how two different things may actually have something in common. Writers use comparisons to make things clearer for the reader. In this example, William compares his frightening situation to a nightmare.

> I cried out to Doug, but the words caught in my dry throat. I was like one in a nightmare who struggles to shout—who is then seized with a fear that promises to destroy him.
> ("Of Men and Mountains," page 311)

For more about comparison, see page 77. See also *Contrast, Metaphor, Simile*.

Concrete Poem. A poem that is placed on the page so that it forms a shape is called a concrete poem. The picture or design made by the words of the poem adds additional meaning to the words themselves. "The Universe" (page 238) is an example of a concrete poem.

For more about concrete poems, see page 225. See also *Poetry*.

Conflict. The struggle a character faces in a story creates the conflict. Conflict is nec-essary in any story or play. It is the basic framework for the plot. There are two types of conflict, external and internal.

A struggle between two characters, or between a character and a force such as nature, is called external conflict. In "The Most Dangerous Game" (page 85), the external conflict is the life-or-death struggle between Rainsford and Zaroff.

The struggle within a character is called internal conflict. This struggle often involves a decision the character must make, sometimes relating to different desires or courses of action. In "The Fan Club" (page 44), Laura must decide whether or not to join in the ridiculing of Rachel.

For more about conflict, see page 31. See also *Plot*.

Contrast. Contrast is often used by writers to show how two things are different. In "Rattlesnake Hunt" (page 326), contrast is used to show the different types of snake hunting devices.

> He does not use the forked stick of conventional snake hunting, but a steel prong, shaped like an *L*, at the end of a long stout stick.

For more about contrast, see page 77. See also *Comparison*.

Description. In a description, details are given to help the reader get a precise picture of a character, setting, or action. There are two types of description, direct and indirect.

In direct description, the writer makes specific statements that tell about a character, setting, or event.

> The jungle weeds were crushed down and the moss was lacerated. One patch of weeds was stained crimson. A small, glittering object not far away caught Rainsford's eye. ("The Most Dangerous Game," page 85)

In indirect description, the reader learns about characters, setting, and events by inferring information from what other characters say and do.

For more about description, see page 144. See also *Characterization* and *Imagery*.

Dialect. The types of language used in different geographical areas are called regional dialects. They may vary in vocabulary, pronunciation, and grammar. William Least Heat Moon uses dialect to indicate the different speech patterns in "Blue Highways," page 420.

For more about dialect, see page 606.

Dialogue. Conversation between characters in a story or play is called dialogue. In stories, the exact words are set off by quotation marks.

> "I'll try discus," said one girl.
> "Hurdles for me," said a second.
> "I'm a javelin thrower," said a third.
> "What are you going to try out for, Babe?" asked the coach.
> ("Babe Didrickson Zaharias," page 346)

In a play, no quotation marks are used but dialogue tags or taglines are often used to indicate how the actors are to say their lines.

For more about dialogue, see pages 548 and 549.

Dialogue Tags. See *Dialogue*.

Direct Description. See *Characterization* and *Description*.

Drama. Literature that is meant to be performed on stage before an audience is a drama, or play. A drama is told through dialogue and the actions of the characters. Like other forms of fiction, drama uses characters, setting, plot, dialogue, and sometimes a narrator. Written drama may also include suggestions for the set, costumes, sound, and lighting, as well as instructions for the actors. Most plays are divided into parts called acts. Each act may be divided into smaller parts called scenes.

A radio play, such as "The Hitchhiker" (page 554), relies on dialogue, music, and sound effects to tell a story. A television play, such as "The Monsters Are Due on Maple Street" (page 569), includes camera directions. A stage play is similar to a television play. However, it usually has only a few simple settings. "The Monkey's Paw" (page 586) is an example of a stage play.

For more about drama, see pages 548 and 549. See also *Stage Directions*.

Dynamic Character. See *Character*.

Essay. A short, personal piece of nonfiction in which the writer expresses an opinion on a given topic or gives information, is called an essay. An informal essay is often humorous. It reflects the writer's feelings in a light and casual way, such as in "Fresh Air Will Kill You" (page 434). A formal essay examines a topic in a logical, thorough way. It usually has a serious tone and a formal structure. "Primal Screen" (page 454) is an example of a formal essay.

For more about the essay, see page 305. See also *Nonfiction*.

External Conflict. See *Conflict*.

Falling Action. Falling action is that part of the plot following the climax, in which the story draws to a conclusion. For example, in "The Force of Luck," on page 118, the climax occurs when the men find the nest containing the first two hundred dollars. The falling action occurs when the men find the second two hundred dollars in the clay jar.

For more on falling action, see pages 13 and 82. See also *Climax* and *Plot*.

Fiction. A work of fiction is imaginative writing, although it may be inspired by actual events or real people. Some types of fiction are short stories, legends, and drama.

See also *Science Fiction*.

Figurative Language. Speaking or writing about familiar things in a fresh, new way is called figurative language. This type of writing gives new meaning to ordinary words.

Figurative language is used in all types of writing. It includes several specific ways of putting words together. These are known as figures of speech. The most common figures of speech are: simile, metaphor, personification, and hyperbole.

For more about figurative language, see page 223. See also *Hyperbole*, *Metaphor*, *Personification*, and *Simile*.

Flashback. Flashback occurs when a writer interrupts the normal order of a story to tell about something that happened earlier in time. You will find an example of flashback in "North to the Orient" (page 425).

For more about flashback, see page 430.

Folk Tale. A story that is passed on orally from generation to generation is called a folk tale. The original author, or storyteller, is generally unknown. A folk tale often involves an unexpected or miraculous event and usually presents a lesson to be learned. "The Force of Luck" (page 118) is an example of a folk tale.

For more about folk tales, see pages 125 and 126.

Foot. See *Rhythm*.

Foreshadowing. A clue or hint of a future event to take place in a story is called foreshadowing. The writer uses this technique to prepare the reader for an important event or to create suspense. In "The Dog of

Pompeii" (page 33), the author gives several hints that another earthquake could take place. When discussing earthquakes never striking twice, a stranger interjects, "Don't they? How about the two towns in Sicily that have been ruined three times within fifteen years by the eruptions of Mt. Etna?" This foreshadows the event to come.

For more about foreshadowing, see pages 40 and 41.

Free Verse. When there is no set pattern of accented and unaccented syllables in a poem, it is called free verse. Although there is no regular rhyme or meter in free verse, the poem may still have a rhythmic flow. Much of the poetry written in the twentieth century is free verse. "Youth to Age" (page 244) and "Kidnap Poem" (page 246) are examples.

For more about free verse, see page 201. See also *Poetry* and *Rhythm*.

Humor. Writing that amuses the reader has the quality of humor. A certain setting, character, action, or use of words can suggest humor. Sometimes the author uses humor to create a situation that is the opposite of what the reader expects, as in "The Ransom of Red Chief" (page 135).

For more about humor, see page 433. See also *Hyperbole, Irony, Understatement,* and *Parody.*

Hyperbole. A figure of speech in which obvious exaggeration is used is called hyperbole. It often gives the reader a humorous image of what the writer is describing. The exaggeration may also be used for emphasis in making a point.

> His pulse is so slow we think him dead.
> ("The Bat," page 216)

For more about hyperbole, see pages 195 and 196. See also *Figurative Language.*

Imagery. Any kind of description that makes an object or experience so realistic that it re-creates a vivid sensory experience for the reader is called imagery. Sensory details are used to help us see, feel, smell, hear, or taste the things described.

> The sun was dropping low in the west. Masses of white clouds hung above the flat marshy plain and seemed to be tangled in the tops of distant palms and cypresses. The sky turned orange, then saffron.
> ("Rattlesnake Hunt," page 326)

For more about imagery, see page 222. See also *Figurative Language.*

Indirect Description. See *Characterization* and *Description.*

Internal Conflict. See *Conflict.*

Introduction. The first part of the plot is the introduction. In it, the reader is introduced to the main characters and the setting.

> Tito and his dog Bimbo lived under the city wall where it joined the inner gate. They

really didn't live there. They just slept there. They lived anywhere.
("The Dog of Pompeii," page 33)

For more about the introduction, see pages 13 and 107. See also *Plot*.

Irony. The contrast between what is expected or what appears to be true, and what actually happens is called irony. For example, in "Richard Cory" (page 294) it is ironic that a man who appeared to have everything and was admired by everyone was, in fact, so unhappy that he took his own life.

For more about irony, see page 23.

Journal. A daily record of events and personal feelings is called a journal. A journal may be written in a formal or an informal manner. It may record the writer's thoughts or observations in a natural, unstructured way or it may involve careful planning and more formal language. An example is "Travels with Charley" on page 414.

For more about journals, see page 413.

Long Short Story. A story that is too long to be read in one sitting is called a long short story. It can also be referred to as a short novel. Like a short story, it concentrates on only a few major characters; however, it may cover a greater length of time and deal with more than one event. "Flowers for Algernon" (page 508) is an example of a long short story.

For more about a long short story, see page 502.

Metaphor. A metaphor is a figure of speech that makes a comparison of two unlike things that have something in common. Unlike the simile, the comparison is made without the use of the words *like* or *as*. In the following example, the moon is compared to a balloon.

who knows if the moon's
a balloon, coming out of a keen city
in the sky-filled with pretty people?
("who knows if the moon's," page 234)

For more about metaphor, see pages 191 to 193 and 223. See also *Comparison, Figurative Language*, and *Simile*.

Mood. The feeling or atmosphere the writer creates for the reader is called the mood. There are several ways mood can be established in a piece of writing. The description of the setting, what characters say, the use of imagery and figurative language—all can be used to develop mood.

For more about mood, see page 71.

Motive. A dynamic character's reason for wanting to change is a motive. In "The Beau Catcher," on page 79, Genevieve's motive to change is to attract a "beau."

For more about motives, see page 161. See also *Character*.

Narrator. A narrator is the person from whose point of view a story is told. There are different types of narrators. The first-person narrator is usually a character in the story, such as the archaeologist in "Humans

Are Different" (page 106). The third-person narrator tells the story from outside the action. There are two types of third-person narrator. A narrator who knows how all the characters feel is *omniscient* as in "The Dog of Pompeii" (page 33). The third-person narrator may be *limited*, telling only what one character thinks and feels, as in "The Test" (page 72).

For more about narrator, see pages 23 and 549. See also *Point of View*.

Nonfiction. Writing that presents factual information is called nonfiction. It may contain narration, description, or exposition. Autobiographies and biographies are examples of nonfiction. Other types are articles, journals, and essays. All of the selections in Chapter 5 are nonfiction.

For more about nonfiction, see pages 304 and 305. See also *Autobiography, Biography, Essay, Journal,* and *True Adventure Story*.

Onomatopoeia. The use of words that imitate the sounds they describe is called onomatopoeia.

"Maaaa," was the goat's reply.
("Zlateh the Goat," page 25)

For more about onomatopoeia, see page 187.

Oral Tradition. Stories and songs that are retold to new generations over the years are part of an oral tradition. They are the product of many storytellers and have changed as details were added or left out.

For more about oral tradition, see page 12.

Paradox. A statement that at first seems to contradict itself, but on closer examination is found to be true is called a paradox. In "Blue Highways," on page 420, the main character says, "You get sociable traveling alone." At first, the statement seems to be contradictory, but a closer look reveals its truth.

For more about paradox, see page 423.

Parody. Parody is used when a writer pokes fun at another kind of literature by imitating it in an exaggerated or humorous way. Parody points out the humor in something that is ordinarily taken seriously. In "The Storyteller" (page 61), the author makes fun of, or parodies, a fairy tale.

For more about parody, see page 66.

Personification. A figure of speech in which human qualities are given to animals, objects, or ideas is personification. In his poem "Bicycles" (page 266), Andrei Voznesensky talks about them as if they were human.

Huge and surprised
They stare at the sky.

. . . they lie Forgotten,
Asleep. Asleep.

For more about personification, see pages 193, 194, and 223. See also *Figurative Language*.

Play. See *Drama*.

Plot. The sequence of actions and events in a story is called the plot. One event logically follows the next. Usually, each thing that happens is caused by what precedes it. The elements, or parts of the plot include the introduction, the rising action, the climax, the falling action, and the resolution.

For more about plot, see page 13. See also *Climax, Falling Action, Introduction, Resolution,* and *Rising Action.*

Poetry. Poetry is language arranged in lines. It condenses ideas and feelings into a few exact words. The sounds of the words and their arrangement are often as important as the meaning of the words themselves.

In the past, poets followed definite rules for form, rhythm, and rhyme. Lines of verse were regular and divided into groups called stanzas. Modern poets sometimes ignore these rigid rules, but their work still falls under the broad definition of poetry.

For more about poetry, see pages 200 and 201. See also *Concrete Poem, Free Verse, Rhyme, Rhyme Scheme, Rhythm,* and *Stanza.*

Point of View. The narrative method used in writing is called the point of view. It may be a first-person point of view, as in "Feathered Friend" (page 19), or it may be a third-person point of view, as in "The Richer, the Poorer" (page 157).

For more about point of view, see page 70. See also *Narrator.*

Prologue. A short message given before a play begins is called the prologue. For an example of a prologue, see "The Hitchhiker" (page 554).

For more about prologue, see page 566.

Purpose. The purpose is the writer's reason for writing. It may be to amuse, to inform, to persuade, or to express feelings about a certain subject. The writer must decide on his or her purpose before beginning the process of writing.

For more about purpose, see page 3. See also *Theme.*

Repetition. A literary technique in which a word or group of words is repeated in a selection is called repetition. Poets often repeat a word or phrase to give special emphasis to a thought or action.

Rain that fosters growing plants
Takes the creases out of pants.

Rain that settles summer dust
Causes mildew, causes rust.

Rain that, with its cleansing fall
Washes autos, makes them stall.

Rain that fills the dried up creek
Causes people's roofs to leak.
("Rain," page 210)

For more about repetition, see page 219.

Resolution. The fifth, or last part of the plot is the resolution. The loose ends of a story are tied up in the resolution. Any remaining questions that the reader might have are answered.

So now if you visit any space station, don't be surprised if you hear an inexplicable snatch of bird song. There's no need to be alarmed. On the contrary, in fact it will mean that you're being doubly safeguarded, at practically no extra expense.
("Feathered Friend," page 19)

For more about resolution, see page 13. See also *Plot*.

Rhyme. The repetition of sounds at the ends of words is called rhyme. Rhyming words usually come at the ends of lines in poetry. The rhyming words in this example are *drily/highly* and *air/there*.

"A planet doesn't explode of itself," said
    drily
The Martian astronomer, gazing off into the
    air—
"That they were able to do it is proof that
    highly
Intelligent beings must have been living
    there."
("Earth," page 296)

For more about rhyme, see page 183. See also *Rhyme Scheme*.

Rhyme Scheme. Rhyme schemes are different patterns in which end rhyme can be used in poetry. When a rhyme scheme is written, a different letter of the alphabet is used to stand for each different rhyming sound.

The rain to the wind said,	*a*
"You push and I'll pelt."	*b*
They so smote the garden bed	*a*
That the flowers actually knelt	*b*
And lay lodged—though not dead.	*a*
I know how the flowers felt.	*b*

("Lodged," page 286)

For more about rhyme scheme, see pages 183 and 184. See also *Rhyme*.

Rhythm. The pattern of accented and unaccented syllables in poetry is called rhythm. The accented or stressed syllables are marked with /, while the unaccented or light syllables are marked with ⌣. The pattern these syllables make in a line of poetry may be divided into units. Each unit is called a foot. Rhythm may emphasize ideas, create a mood, or stress the musical quality of a poem.

  ⌣ / ⌣ / ⌣ / ⌣ /
The Penguin sits upon the shore,
  ⌣ / ⌣ / ⌣ / ⌣ /
And loves the lit-tle fish to bore;
  ⌣ / ⌣ / ⌣ / ⌣ /
He has one en-er-vat-ing joke,
  ⌣ / ⌣ / ⌣ / ⌣ /
That would a very saint provoke.
("A Penguin," page 280)

For more about rhythm, see pages 185 and 186.

Rising Action. The second part of the plot is the rising action. In this part, it becomes apparent that the characters face a problem, or conflict. One event logically follows the other. The events in the rising action build to the climax, the third part of the plot. In "The Most Dangerous Game" (page 85), the rising action occurs as Rainsford tries desperately to avoid being found by the General.

For more about rising action, see pages 13, 102, and 103. See also *Plot*.

Satire. Writing that criticizes a subject by combining the use of humor or wit with criticism is called satire. In "Fresh Air Will Kill You" (page 434), the writer criticizes the effects of pollution in a satirical way.

For more about satire, see page 296.

Science Fiction. Science fiction is a special kind of fiction that uses a base of scientific knowledge to create fantasy. It frequently presents an imaginary view into the future. "Feathered Friend" (page 19) and "Humans Are Different" (page 106) are examples of science fiction.

For more about science fiction, see pages 22 and 23. See also *Fiction*.

Sensory Image. See *Imagery*.

Sequence. A series of events or ideas put in a particular order is called sequence. The writer often tells a story in chronological sequence or time order. Sometimes a selection has ideas arranged in a logical sequence, with an opinion followed by reasons to back it up.

For more on sequence, see page 361. See also *Time Order*.

Setting. The time and place in which the events or actions of a story occur are called the setting. All stories have a setting, but some are described in greater detail than others depending on the importance of the setting to the story.

For example, little time is spent describing the setting for "The First Basketball Game" (page 465). Where the game originated is much less important than the development of the game itself.

On the other hand, the setting for "Of Men and Mountains" (page 311) is described in great detail. It is an essential factor in the development of the story.

For more about setting, see page 13.

Short Story. A short story is a work of fiction that can be read at one sitting. It usually tells about one major character and one major conflict. The four main elements of a short story are: setting, character, plot, and theme. All the selections in Chapter 2 are short stories.

For more about the short story, see page 12. See also *Character*, *Plot*, *Setting*, and *Theme*.

Simile. A simile is a figure of speech that states a comparison between two things that are unlike, but have something in common. Similes use the words *like* or *as*.

She stands
In the quiet darkness,
This troubled woman
Bowed by
Weariness and pain
Like an
Autumn flower
In the frozen rain.
("Troubled Woman," page 262)

For more about simile, see pages 189, 190, and 223. See also *Comparison*, *Figurative Language*, and *Metaphor*.

Speaker. The speaker of a poem is the voice through which the ideas in the poem are presented. The speaker and the poet are not necessarily the same. The speaker of a poem may be compared to the narrator in prose writing.

For more about the speaker, see page 222.

Stage Directions. In drama, stage directions are guidelines for the actors in the performance of the play. These directions may tell the actors how to read certain words, or how to move, or what background sounds or actions are needed. In "The Monkey's Paw" (page 586), the following stage directions may be found:

very excited, trying to distract his attention, leaning back on his chair, rather hurt.

For more about stage directions, see page 549.

Stanza. A group of lines that form a unit in poetry is called a stanza. It is comparable to a paragraph in prose. There is usually a space between stanzas of a poem. Stanzas may be divided by the ideas presented in the poem or by the pattern of rhyme used. An example of a poem with several stanzas is "The Optileast and the Pessimost," on page 207.

For more about stanzas, see page 245.

Static Character. See *Character*.

Style. The special way a writer expresses his or her ideas is called the writer's style of writing. Style refers to how something is said, not to what is said. The length and order of sentences, choice of words, and use of figurative language all contribute to a writer's style.

For more about style, see page 41.

Suspense. The feeling created when the reader becomes unsure of the outcome of events is called suspense. In "The Old Man" (page 146), the writer builds suspense throughout the story, so that the reader is anxious about what might happen.

For more about suspense, see page 103.

Symbol. A symbol is a person, place, object, or idea that stands for or represents something else. A dove, for example, is the symbol for peace. A character such as Superman is a symbol for goodness and justice.

In "The Foghorn" (page 164), the fog horn represents loneliness.

For more about symbols, see page 171.

Theme. The theme of a piece of writing is a thought or idea that the author wishes to share with the reader. A writer rarely states the theme directly. Instead, the idea must be inferred by the reader after a careful examination of the selection. The theme of "The Beau Catcher" (page 79), for example, might be that the true key to popularity is self confidence.

A universal theme is one that is concerned with feelings and ideas shared by all people in all walks of life.

For more about theme, see pages 50, 71, and 285.

Time Order. The progression of events in the order in which they occurred in time is called time, or chronological, order. Time order is a common method of organizing the details of a piece of writing. "Clever Hans" (page 471), is written in time order, as are the journals in Chapter 5.

For more about time order, see page 14.

Tone. The author's attitude toward a subject is the tone of the selection. It tells how the writer feels about the material he or she is writing about. Tone should not be confused with mood. Mood refers to the feelings created in the reader. In "Fresh Air Will Kill You" (page 434), for example, the tone is sarcastic with an underlying seriousness. The mood, however, is light and humorous.

For more about tone, see pages 161, 162, and 223.

True Adventure Story. A type of nonfiction that has characters, external conflict, and focuses on one memorable event is called a true adventure story. "Of Men and Mountains," page 311, tells of one exciting adventure experienced by the writer.

For more about true adventure stories, see page 310.

Understatement. The opposite of exaggeration is understatement. The writer makes a calm, simple statement when the situation really calls for something more forceful. Farley Mowat uses understatement in "Never Cry Wolf" (page 333), when he suddenly finds himself nose to nose with a wolf. Instead of describing the heart-stopping terror he felt, Mowat noted only that "my head was full of the most disturbing thoughts."

For more about understatement, see page 342.

Universal Theme. See *Theme*.

Urban Myth. A modern folk tale told all across the country is called an urban myth. Each story may appear in many versions, but usually contains elements of horror, such as in "The Hitchhiker" (page 554). The storyteller almost always insists that the event happened locally and to people known to the storyteller.

For more about urban myth, see page 568. See also *Oral Tradition*.

Summary of Comprehension Skills

Cause and Effect. Events are sometimes related by cause and effect. One event is the cause of another event. The second event is the effect of the first event.

There are certain key words that tell a reader to look for a cause and effect relationship. These key words include: *because, so that, since, in order that,* and *if—then.*

Sometimes, when one event happens after another, a reader or writer assumes that the first caused the second, when, in fact, the two events have no relationship to each other. This is called *false cause and effect reasoning.*

For more about cause and effect, see page 14. See also *False Cause and Effect Reasoning* in the Summary of Critical Thinking Terms, pages 648 and 649.

Chronological Order. See *Paragraph Organization.*

Circular Reasoning. See the Summary of Critical Thinking Terms, page 647.

Comparison and Contrast. When a reader finds similarities between two works of literature, it is called making comparisons. Finding the differences between selections is called making contrasts. Some of the elements that can be compared and contrasted are character, setting, plot, and theme.

For more about comparison and contrast, see pages 268 and 361.

Errors in Reasoning. See the Summary of Critical Thinking Terms, page 648.

Evaluations. After finishing a selection, a reader should be able to make a judgment, or evaluation, about it. A fair evaluation is an objective one. It is based on established standards of good writing. When evaluating a piece of writing, you should consider each element individually. Elements to examine include character development, setting, plot, mood, theme, and the writer's style.

For more about evaluations, see page 533. See also, the Summary of Critical Thinking Terms, page 648.

Fact and Opinion. Facts are statements that can be proved. Opinions express only the writer's beliefs. They cannot be proved. Facts and opinions are often combined in writing. To read effectively, a reader should be able to distinguish between facts and opinions. In the example that follows, the writer begins with an opinion. The opinion is underlined. Then the writer presents two statements of fact to back up his or her opinion.

Woody Guthrie was the most influential musician of our time. Folk singer, guitarist, and composer, he wrote over 1,000 songs, mainly on social and political themes. His work has influenced many younger performers.

For more about separating fact and opinion, see page 306. See also, the Summary of Critical Thinking Terms, page 648.

Figurative Language. Figurative language is a way of speaking or writing that describes familiar things in fresh, new ways. Figurative language means more than it says on the surface.

For example, if someone is "up to their eyeballs in homework," it does not mean that the person is surrounded by stacks of books and papers that reach eye level. The writer is using figurative language to say that the student has an exceptional amount of homework to do.

The opposite of figurative language is literal language. Literal language means exactly what it says.

For more about figurative language, see page 223.

Inferences. A logical guess based on given evidence is called an inference. Often a reader is expected to make inferences. One must infer what the writer has not stated directly by examining clues or hints. For example, you might read a sentence such as the following:

Allan entered, panting and shaking the water from his umbrella and briefcase.

From the information given, you can infer that it is raining outside and that Allan has probably been running to get out of the bad weather. Because he is carrying a briefcase, you can infer that he is an adult and not a child.

Literal Language. See *Figurative Language*.

Long Sentences. See *Punctuation Clues*.

Main Idea. See *Paragraph Organization*.

Outcomes. When a reader makes a reasonable guess about what will happen next in a story, he or she is predicting an outcome. Some outcomes are easy to predict, while others are more difficult.

When you predict outcomes, use the clues that the writer has given you. Consider information about the characters, the plot, and the setting. Use your personal knowledge and experience to judge what people do in similar situations.

For more about predicting outcomes, see pages 14 and 15.

Overgeneralization. See the Summary of Critical Thinking Terms, page 649.

Paragraph Organization. There are four basic kinds of paragraphs. To understand a paragraph, it is necessary to recognize the sequence, or the order in which the information is presented. A *narrative paragraph* tells about a series of events. The sentences are usually arranged in the order in which the events happen. Therefore, the sequence they follow is in time order or chronological order. Here is an example from "The Dog of Pompeii."

> It was then the crashing began. First a sharp crackling, like a monstrous snapping of twigs. Then an explosion that tore earth and sky. . . . A house fell. Then another. (page 37)

For more about recognizing time order, see page 14.

A *descriptive paragraph* describes a person, an object, or a scene. Details are usually arranged in the order or sequence in which you would notice them. This is called spatial order. In "The Storyteller," the writer describes the scene in spatial order.

> The occupants of the carriage were a small girl, and a smaller girl, and a small boy. An aunt belonging to the children occupied one corner seat, and the further corner seat on the opposite side was occupied by a bachelor. . . . (page 61)

A *persuasive paragraph* tries to persuade the reader. Sentences are arranged in a logical sequence. The writer's argument must make sense to the reader. Usually a persuasive paragraph is logically arranged with reasons presented in the order of importance to the writer. The reasons explain why the reader should think or behave in a certain way.

Ellen Goodman's essay "Primal Screen," page 454, is an example of persuasive writing.

An *explanatory paragraph* explains something. After the topic sentence, the other sentences give details, usually in chronological order or order of importance.

> "They're not active at this season," he said quietly. "A snake takes on the temperature of its surroundings. They can't stand too much heat for that reason, and when the weather is cool, as now, they're sluggish." ("Rattlesnake Hunt," page 326)

Punctuation Clues. Punctuation tells a reader where to pause, when to break a thought, and how to interpret a sentence. Punctuation is especially important in poetry. In this form of writing, words are arranged in lines. The reader might logically assume that each line is a complete thought. This is rarely the case, however, and the careful reader will look for periods, question marks, and exclamation marks to signal the actual end of a thought.

Sometimes, a poem will be only one or two *long sentences*. When this is the case, the reader will have to divide the long sentence into meaningful phrases or shorter sentences.

For more about punctuation clues, see page 203.

Purpose. Before beginning to write, a person must decide what he or she wants to accomplish with the writing. This is called the writer's purpose. The purpose of a piece of writing can be to inform, to entertain, to persuade, or to express feelings or thoughts. The writer often chooses his or her topic or organization after considering the purpose of the writing. Treatments of elements such as plot, character, and setting also depend on the author's purpose.

For more about an author's purpose, see page 306.

Sentence Fragments. An incomplete sentence, one that is missing either a subject or a verb, is called a sentence fragment. Professional writers sometimes use sentence fragments so that their writing sounds like everyday conversation. In your writing, however, you should use complete sentences.

For more about sentence fragments, see page 504.

Sequence. See *Paragraph Organization.*

Slanted Writing. See the Summary of Critical Thinking Terms, pages 649–650.

Spatial Order. See *Paragraph Organization.*

Time Order. See *Paragraph Organization.*

Transitional Words. Words or phrases that suggest the relationship of ideas within or between paragraphs are called transitional words. Examples of transitional words are: *tomorrow*, *then*, *for a long time*, *seldom*, and *meanwhile.*

For more about transitional words, see page 14.

Word Choice. A writer's choice of words depends on many factors. A writer considers all of the following when he or she chooses a word: the mood of the selection, the tone, his or her personal style, the setting, and the audience to whom the writing is aimed.

For more about word choice, see page 271.

Word Order. For emphasis, a writer will occasionally arrange the words in a sentence in an order that is different than normal. Usually, a sentence will contain a subject followed by a verb. Sometimes, however, the sentence will be reversed. The verb will come before the subject. Poets, especially, like to use this reverse word order. To understand such a poem, it may be necessary to put the sentences back in the usual order by finding out who or what the sentence is about (the subject) and then asking what the subject does or what happens to the subject (the verb).

For more about word order, see page 202.

Summary of Vocabulary Skills

1. Word Parts

Some words are made by combining word parts. When you know the meanings of the word parts, you can often discover the meaning of the whole word. Three kinds of word parts are base words, prefixes, and suffixes.

Base Word. A word to which other word parts are added is called a base word. For example, the base word in *reapply* is *apply*. The base word in *careful* is *care*.

Prefix. A prefix is a word part added to the beginning of a base word. When you add a prefix to a base word, you change the meaning of the word.

> **Prefix + Base Word = New Word**
> un- + happy = unhappy

For a list of frequently used prefixes, see page 308.

Suffix. A suffix is a word part added to the end of a base word. The new word that is created has a different meaning from the base word alone.

> **Base Word + Suffix = New Word**
> hope + -less = hopeless

For a list of frequently used suffixes, see page 309.

You must make spelling changes before you can add suffixes to some words.

1. When a suffix beginning with a vowel is added to a word ending in silent *e*, the *e* is usually dropped.

   > come + -ing = coming

   The *e* is not dropped when a suffix beginning with a consonant is added.

   > rare + -ly = rarely

2. When a suffix is added to a word ending in *y* preceded by a consonant, the *y* is usually changed to an *i*.

   > pretty + -est = prettiest

   When *y* is preceded by a vowel, the base word does not change.

   > play + -ful = playful

3. Double the final consonant when adding *-ing*, *-ed*, or *-er* to a one-syllable word that ends in one consonant preceded by one vowel.

   > hop + ed = hopped

   When two vowels precede the final consonant in a one-syllable word, the final consonant is not doubled.

   > hear + -ing = hearing

2. Context Clues

Clues to the meaning of a new word can often be found in context. Context refers to the sentences and paragraphs that surround the word. Look for the following context clues as you read:

Antonyms. An antonym, or opposite, may be used as a clue to the meaning of a word. The antonym may be in the same sentence or in a nearby sentence. It often appears in the same position in the sentence as the new word.

> Frank is <u>taciturn</u>, but the other members of his family are all very talkative.

Taciturn is the opposite of "very talkative." Therefore, you can infer that *taciturn* means "quiet or silent."

For more about antonyms, see page 59.

Comparison and Contrast Clues. Writers often compare one idea with another. Sometimes an unfamiliar word may be used in one part of the comparison. Then the other part of the comparison may give you a clue to the meaning of the word. Key words such as *also, as, similar to, both, than,* and *in addition* indicate a comparison.

> The mayor requested a few more days to <u>deliberate</u> on the issue. His committee members also wanted more time to think about the matter.

The comparison tells you that *deliberate* means "think."

Writers also show how certain things are opposites by using contrast. A contrast clue tells what the new word is not. Some key words in contrast clues are *although, however, yet, on the other hand,* and *different from*.

> Fred and Meghan had <u>disparate</u> opinions on the new regulation. Usually, however, their viewpoints are similar.

From this example, *disparate* must mean the opposite of "similar."

For more about comparison and contrast clues, see pages 16 and 17.

Definition or Restatement. The most direct clues to the meaning of a word are definition and restatement.

When definition is used, the meaning of a word is stated directly.

> A <u>philatelist</u> is a person who collects stamps.

When restatement is used, the unfamiliar word is restated in a different way.

> Sharon is a <u>philatelist</u>. That is, she collects stamps.

The following key words and punctuation tell you to look for a definition or restatement: *is, who is, which is, that is, in other words, or,* dashes, commas, and parentheses.

For more about definition and restatement clues, see page 16.

Example Clues. In an example clue, a new word is related to a group of familiar words. The new word may be an example of a familiar term. Sometimes, familiar terms are examples of the new word.

The following key words signal an example clue: *for example, an example, one kind, some types, for instance,* and *such as.*

> The students learned about freshwater animals, such as the <u>hydra</u>, in biology class.

For more about example clues, see pages 83 and 84.

Inference Clues. Writers sometimes leave clues about the meaning of unfamiliar words in different parts of the sentence. For example, clues to a new word in the subject can often be found in the predicate.

> The restored <u>galleon</u> sailed into the harbor.

From this sentence, you can guess that a *galleon* is a type of sailing ship.

Sometimes the sentence in which a new word appears has no clues to its meaning. However, it may be possible to find clues to the meaning somewhere else in the same paragraph.

> Luke had never played <u>lacrosse</u> before. His nine teammates showed him how to catch and throw the small rubber ball with the basket of the long-handled racket. Then they explained the strategy for getting the ball down the field and into the other team's goal.

Context clues tell you that *lacrosse* must be a game played on a field by two ten-person teams. The players use long-handled rackets with baskets on the end to move a ball down the field and into the opponent's goal.

Sometimes the main idea of a paragraph will give you a clue about the meaning of a new word. In this example there are several clues that help you guess the meaning of the underlined word.

> The year had produced a <u>copious</u> harvest. The barn was filled to the rafters with hay. Countless jars of preserved fruits, vegetables, and jellies lined the pantry shelves, and the cellar overflowed with bushel baskets of apples, turnips, potatoes, and yams.

The main idea of the paragraph tells you that *copious* means "plentiful" or "abundant."

For more about inferring meanings from context, see page 17.

Synonyms. A word that means the same or nearly the same as another word is called a synonym. Sometimes a word is used in the same sentence or paragraph as its synonym. The writer counts on you to understand either the word or its synonym. In the following example you can infer that *aversion* means "dislike."

> Lela has an <u>aversion</u> to trying anything new. Because of this dislike, she misses many interesting opportunities.

For more on synonyms, see page 31.

3. Word Origins

Words in the English language come from many different sources. One ancient source is thought to be a prehistoric language called Indo-European. The first settlers of the island now called Great Britain spoke a form of Indo-European. However, in the centuries since that time, the English language has changed. Words have become part of the language in the following ways:

Acronyms. Words that are made from the first letters of other words are called acronyms. For example, the organization WHO takes its name from its longer title, <u>W</u>orld <u>H</u>ealth <u>O</u>rganization.

Blended Words. Blended words are similar to compound words. Two words are joined together to make a new word. In this case, however, some letters from one or both of the words are dropped. *Brunch* is a blended word made from *breakfast* and *lunch*.

Borrowed Words. Throughout its history, the English language has taken words from other languages. Many words came from the French, Spanish, Italian, Latin, and Greek languages, as well as others.

Clipped Words. New words are often made by shortening existing words. For example, *photo* was clipped from *photograph*. *Referee* was shortened to make the word *ref*.

Compound Words. Two words may be combined to form one new word. An example is *cheerleader*.

Root Words. Many Greek and Latin word parts are used as prefixes and suffixes in English words. If you know the meaning of the Greek and Latin word parts, you can figure out the meaning of the whole word. For example, the Greek prefix *bio-* means "life." The word part *logy* means "the study of." Together, these word parts make the word *biology*, which is another word for the study of life.

Words from Names and Places. Some words are based on the name of a person or a place. For example, pasteurization is a method of destroying harmful bacteria in milk. The process was developed by Louis Pasteur, a French chemist.

Words from Sounds. Some words imitate sounds. These words are called echoic words. Some examples are *hush* and *tweet*.

Words from Specialized Areas. Sometimes members of a professional or technical field have a special vocabulary of words pertaining to their work. Such words are called *jargon*. Occasionally, jargon words become part of our everyday vocabulary.

For more about word origins, see pages 506 and 507.

4. Reference Books: The Dictionary, Glossary, and Thesaurus

A **dictionary** is an alphabetical listing of words and their meanings. If context clues and word parts do not give enough information to allow you to understand an unfamiliar word, you can use a dictionary.

A **glossary** can be found in the back of some nonfiction books. Like the dictionary, it is an alphabetical listing of words and their meanings. However, the words a glossary defines are limited to the new or unfamiliar words in the book. The definition of a word in the glossary is often limited to the way it is used in a particular selection.

A **thesaurus** lists words with other words of similar meanings, and sometimes with opposites. The thesaurus usually gives some explanation of the differences. You use a thesaurus when you need to find the exact word for your meaning.

For more about reference books, see Guidelines for Study and Research.

5. Levels of Language

Standard English is English that is accepted and understood everywhere English is spoken. Standard English may be formal or informal. Formal standard English is used in serious or formal situations, such as in business letters, classroom assignments, and speeches. Informal standard English is used in everyday conversation. It follows all the rules of grammar, just as formal English does, but it sounds more natural. It also uses some words or meanings called colloquialisms, words not used in formal English.

Nonstandard English includes language that does not follow the traditional rules of grammar. Words such as *ain't* and local dialects are considered nonstandard.

Slang is a type of nonstandard English. It includes new words or words with new meanings. Some slang words are used for only a short time.

For more about recognizing the levels of language, see pages 552 and 553.

Guidelines for the Process of Writing

You will do many different types of writing, both in and out of school. You may write short stories, business reports, or speeches. No matter what you write, however, you should follow the same steps. These steps are the process of writing.

The process of writing has three stages: **pre-writing**, **writing**, and **revising**.

Stage 1: Pre-Writing

The pre-writing stage is also called the planning stage. During this stage you think about ideas, do your research, and organize. The five pre-writing steps are below.

1. Choose and limit a topic. If you are not assigned a specific topic, you have the opportunity to choose one of your own. Make a list of interesting ideas or topics. Choose the one that is most interesting to you. Then list the things you might say about that topic. Limit your list to ideas that will match the length of the piece you plan to write.

For example, a student was asked to write a paragraph on one of the elements in the short story "The Fan Club." He listed the elements of a short story and did some thinking about which ones were most important to "The Fan Club." He also

thought about which elements had affected him the most. Finally he circled the one he thought he would like to write about.

characterization   setting   point of view
theme   plot   (mood)

2. Decide on your purpose. Decide how you want to handle the topic. Do you plan to explain it, describe it, or criticize it? Do you intend to teach, persuade, or simply amuse your readers? Your purpose will determine how you write about your subject.

The student writing about elements of short stories thought that he could write about either how mood is important to the story or how mood was created. He decided to explain how a writer creates mood.

3. Decide on your audience. Identify who will read your writing. You will then be more able to choose the level of language you will use and the details you will include.

4. Gather supporting information. List all you know about the topic. Then decide whether or not you need more information. If you do, you may need to refer to reference sources such as encyclopedias.

The student writing about elements in short stories skimmed his literature textbook looking for sections that discussed mood. After reviewing them, he reread "The Fan Club," taking notes on anything he felt helped create mood.

Mood

Feeling reader gets
How created?
— setting
— word choice
— descriptive words, adjectives
— specific details
— character description

"The Fan Club"

Mood is gloomy, unhappy
Laura has a splattered book, stringy hair
Setting is school on Monday A.M.
   rain, damp, cold
   building "loomed," "massive," "dark"
   students "cold," "unkind," "hostile"
   pushing and shoving in halls
Tailor shop small, greasy, tattered awning

5. Organize your ideas. Review the list of details that you made. Cross out anything that does not fit your main idea or purpose.

Choose a logical order for your details. A descriptive paragraph might use spatial order. A story might be written in time order. If you are explaining something, you may choose to organize your points in order of importance. Make an outline showing the order in which you will present your ideas.

Here is the student's outline for his paragraph. He has written out his main idea and underlined it. This will help him keep to his subject.

Mood in "The Fan Club"

Main Idea: <u>The gloomy, unhappy mood in the story comes from the writer's use of setting and her word choice.</u>

Important details:
  I. Mood is feeling reader gets
 II. Mood of "The Fan Club"
    A. Gloomy, unhappy
    B. Tense, uncomfortable
III. Mood in "The Fan Club" created by:
    A. Setting
      1. School on rainy Monday morning
      2. Weather—damp, cold
    B. Word choice
      1. School is "looming," "massive," "dark"
      2. Students are "cold," "unkind," "hostile"
      3. Crowds shove, throng, stream, cluster

Stage 2: Writing a First Draft

You are now ready to put your ideas down on paper. Follow your outline as you write, keeping your purpose and audience in mind. Do not be concerned with such things as spelling and punctuation at this point. These can be corrected later during the revision stage. The important thing now is just to get your ideas down in written form. If better ideas come to you as you write, do not hesitate to include them in your draft.

This is how the student in the example wrote the first draft of his paragraph.

First Draft

```
The mood of a story is the feelings people get by reading. The
Fan club mood is tension and uncomfortable. The Writer makes this
mood with her choice of setting and using lots of descriptive
words. The setting is a rainey Monday morning at school. It is
damp and cold outside the building is "masive and dark." The
students inside are "cold," "unkind" and "hostile." The halls
were crowded with poeple pushing and shoving other kids. These
things give an atmosfere of unhappyness, and confusion.
```

Stage 3: Revising

The revision stage gives you a chance to polish your work. Read what you have written and then ask yourself these questions.

1. Is my writing interesting? Will others want to read it?
2. Did I stick to my topic? Are there any unnecessary details? Should any other details be added?
3. Is my organization easy to follow? Do my ideas flow together smoothly?
4. Is every group of words a sentence? Is every word the best word?

Mark any corrections on your first draft.

Proofreading. After you have revised the content of your writing, you will need to give it a careful proofreading. Check for any errors in capitalization, punctuation, grammar, and spelling. Correct your errors. Use the symbols at the right.

Notice how the sample draft has been revised. The writer has improved the piece by deleting unnecessary words, changing words, and shifting ideas around. He has also corrected several errors in capitalization, punctuation, grammar, and spelling. Study this draft and compare it to the final draft at the bottom of page 637.

Proofreading Symbols

Symbol	Meaning	Example
∧	insert	masíve
≡	capitalize	club
/	lower case	Writer
∿	transpose	poeple
ℯ	take out	lots of
¶	paragraph	¶The
⊙	add a period	cold⊙
∧	add a comma	Inside∧

Revised Draft

The mood of a story is the feelings ^that the reader gets while ~~people get by~~ reading. ^In "The
~~Fan club~~ "the ~~mood is~~ tense ~~and~~ gloomy ~~uncomfortable~~ The Writer ~~makes~~ (it) creates this
mood with her choice of setting and ~~using lots~~ use of descriptive
words. The setting is a rainy Monday morning at school. ^It is
damp and cold (outside) the building ~~is~~ looms "massive and dark." ^The
students (inside) are "cold," "unkind" and "hostile." The halls
~~were~~ are crowded with people pushing and shoving ~~other kids~~. These
~~things~~ factors give an atmosphere of unhappiness, and confusion.

Writing the Final Copy. When you are completely satisfied with your work, make a clean, neat final copy. Proofread your paper once more, looking for any errors.

Notice that in making his final copy, the student found and corrected an error in punctuation. He also improved the wording of one phrase.

Final Copy

The mood of a story is the feeling that the reader gets while reading it. In "The Fan Club," the mood is tense and gloomy. The writer creates this mood with her choice of setting and use of descriptive words. The setting is a rainy Monday morning at school. Outside, it is damp and cold. The building looms "massive and dark." Inside, the students are "cold," "unkind," and "hostile." The halls are crowded with people pushing and shoving. These factors all work together to build an atmosphere of unhappiness and confusion.

Checklist for the Process of Writing

Pre-Writing

1. Choose and limit a topic.
2. Decide on your purpose.
3. Decide on your audience.
4. Gather supporting information.
5. Organize your ideas.

Writing Your First Draft

1. Begin writing. Keep your topic, purpose, and audience in mind at all times.
2. As you write, you may add new details.
3. Concentrate on ideas. Do not be concerned with grammar and mechanics at this time.

Revising

1. Read your first draft. Ask yourself these questions:
   a. Do you like what you have written? Is it interesting? Will others want to read it?
   b. Did you accomplish what you set out to do?
   c. Is your writing organized well? Do the ideas flow smoothly from one paragraph to the next? Are the ideas arranged logically?
   d. Does each paragraph have a topic sentence? Does every sentence stick to the topic? Should any sentence be moved?
   e. Should any details be left out? Should any be added?
   f. Does every sentence express a complete thought? Are your sentences easy to understand?
   g. Is every word the best possible word?
2. Mark any changes on your paper.

Proofreading

Ask yourself these questions as you check your writing for errors in grammar and usage, capitalization, punctuation, and spelling.

Grammar and Usage

a. Is every word group a complete sentence?
b. Does every verb agree with its subject?
c. Have you used the correct form of each pronoun?
d. Is the form of each adjective correct?
e. Is the form of each adverb correct?

Capitalization

a. Is the first word in every sentence capitalized?
b. Are all proper nouns and adjectives capitalized?
c. Are titles capitalized correctly?

Punctuation

a. Does each sentence have the correct end mark?
b. Have you used punctuation marks such as commas, apostrophes, hyphens, colons, semicolons, question marks, quotation marks, and underlining correctly?

Spelling

a. Did you check unfamiliar words in a dictionary?
b. Did you spell plural and possessive forms correctly?

Preparing the Final Copy

1. Make a clean copy of your writing. Make all changes and correct all errors. Then ask yourself these questions:

   a. Is your handwriting neat and easy to read?
   b. Are your margins wide enough?
   c. Is every paragraph indented?

2. Proofread your writing again. Read it aloud. Correct any mistakes neatly.

Guidelines for Study and Research

1. Using Reference Materials

The Dictionary

The dictionary is an alphabetical listing of words and their meanings. The **glossary** in a nonfiction book is like a dictionary. However, it limits its entry words to words from that book.

How To Find a Word. Guide words help you find the word you are looking up. Guide words are printed in heavy black type at the top of each page. They show the first and last words on the page. If the word you are looking for falls alphabetically between the two guide words, then you know your word is on that page.

What the Entry Word Tells You. The entry word is printed in bold type and divided into syllables. This division shows you where to break a word at the end of a line of writing.

How To Find the Pronunciation. The respelling that appears in parentheses after each entry word, tells how that word should be pronounced. Special symbols are used to indicate pronunciation. A key to these symbols can be found at the bottom of the dictionary page or the page opposite it. (For the meaning of symbols in the respelling below, refer to the pronunciation key in the Glossary.)

> **ap·pa·ri·tion** (ap′ ə rish′ ən) *n*. Something that appears unexpectedly.

Accent marks show which syllable or syllables to stress when you pronounce the word. Words with more than one syllable may have more than one accent. The heavy accent, the primary accent, is printed in bold type. The secondary accent is a lighter stress. It is printed in lighter type.

How To Find the Part of Speech and Definitions. An abbreviation following the respelling tells the part of speech of the word. The definition, or meaning, of the word follows. Some words have many definitions listed. In addition, many words can be used as more than one part of speech. Definitions for each part of speech are together.

After some entries, subentries are listed. Subentries are familiar phrases in which the entry word appears.

For more about using a dictionary, see pages 204 and 205.

The Thesaurus

A thesaurus is a listing of words and related words such as synonyms. It is an invaluable aid when you are looking for just the right word to express your meaning. The thesaurus also lists antonyms, words that have the opposite meaning from the entry word.

Suppose you needed a word to use instead of the word *sad.* You would find the listing for *sad* in the thesaurus. There would be listed such related words as *melancholy* and *unhappy.* You might also find antonyms for the word, such as *glad.*

Each thesaurus is organized a little differently. To use a thesaurus, you need to read the directions in that book.

The Encyclopedia

The encyclopedia contains articles about a wide variety of topics. The articles are listed in alphabetical order, according to their titles. Many encyclopedias are several volumes long. An index telling what topics are discussed appears in the final volume. The index will list the volume and page where you can find each article.

Readers' Guide to Periodical Literature

Magazines are a good source of information for anyone writing a report. They give current information on many interesting topics. To find magazine articles, use the *Readers' Guide to Periodical Literature.*

The *Readers' Guide* is an alphabetical listing of topics that have been discussed in magazine articles during a specific period of time. Under the topic, the guide lists the titles of articles on that subject and the magazines in which they were printed.

For more on using the *Readers' Guide,* see pages 343–344.

Specialized Reference Works

Almanacs and yearbooks are useful sources of up-to-date facts and statistics. They are published annually and provide information on current events, government, sports, population, and other fields. The *Guinness Book of World Records* and the *Information Please Almanac* are examples.

Atlases such as the *National Geographic Atlas of the World,* contain maps as well as information on subjects related to specific geographic areas.

Literary reference books are helpful in locating quotations and finding specific poems and stories. *Bartlett's Familiar Quotations* and *Granger's Index to Poetry* are examples.

Biographical references can help you locate information on specific people. *Twentieth Century Authors* and *Who's Who* are two examples.

For more on specialized reference works, see page 607.

2. Finding the Right Resource Material

The Classification of Books

The library contains many different sources of information. Among them are magazines, records, filmstrips, movies, and microfilm, as well as books.

The books in a library are divided into two groups: fiction and nonfiction.

Fiction books are arranged alphabetically according to the author's last name. The name appears on the spine of the book.

Nonfiction books are usually arranged according to the Dewey Decimal System. Each book is assigned a number in one of ten categories. That number is a call number and is printed on the spine of the book. The categories of the Dewey Decimal System are shown below. The books are arranged on the shelves in numerical order. Biographies are usually in a separate section of the library.

THE DEWEY DECIMAL SYSTEM

000–099	General Works	encyclopedias, almanacs, handbooks
100–199	Philosophy	conduct, ethics, psychology
200–299	Religion	the Bible, mythology, theology
300–399	Social Science	economics, law, education, commerce, government, folklore
400–499	Language	languages, grammar, dictionaries
500–599	Science	mathematics, chemistry, physics
600–699	Useful Arts	farming, cooking, sewing, radio, nursing, engineering, television, business, gardening, cars
700–799	Fine Arts	music, painting, drawing, acting, photography, sports
800–899	Literature	poetry, plays, essays
900–999	History	biography, travel, geography

The Card Catalog

The card catalog lists all the books in the library. The cards are arranged in alphabetical order according to the words at the top.

Each book has three cards. The author card lists the author's name on the first line. The title card lists the title of the book on the first line. The subject card lists the subject or topic of the book on the first line. On the top left corner of each card you will find the call number.

Your library may also have a catalog for audio-visual materials such as records, films, or video cassettes.

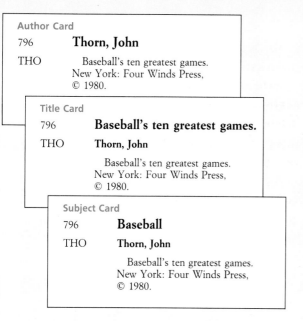

Author Card
796
THO   **Thorn, John**
           Baseball's ten greatest games.
           New York: Four Winds Press,
           © 1980.

Title Card
796
THO   **Baseball's ten greatest games.**

           Thorn, John

           Baseball's ten greatest games.
           New York: Four Winds Press,
           © 1980.

Subject Card
796
THO   **Baseball**

           Thorn, John

           Baseball's ten greatest games.
           New York: Four Winds Press,
           © 1980.

contain the information you need. Knowing about the parts of a book will help you decide.

The title page gives the complete title of the book, the names of the authors or editors, the name of the publisher, and the place of publication.

The copyright page gives the copyright dates, the copyright holder, and the dates of editions or printings. If your topic requires up-to-date information, it is important to know when the book was written.

The table of contents is an outline of the contents of the book, arranged in order of appearance. Skimming the chapter and part heads can tell you whether the book might be useful in your research.

The bibliography is a list of sources that have been used in preparing the book. These sources can provide further information on a subject.

The index is an alphabetical list of subjects covered in the book and their page numbers.

For more on the parts of a book, see page 213.

The Vertical File

The vertical file is a cabinet containing brochures, pamphlets, catalogs, and other current information on a variety of subjects. The material is arranged alphabetically.

The Parts of a Nonfiction Book

After you locate the books for your research, you must determine whether they

3. Preparing to Study

Preparations in Class

The first step to studying is listening carefully to assignment directions.

1. Concentrate on only the directions about to be given.

2. Note how many steps there are.
3. Relate a key word to each step, such as *Read, Answer,* or *Write.*
4. If you do not understand a step, ask questions.
5. Write the directions down.

An assignment notebook will help you organize your studying. For each assignment, write the following:

1. The subject
2. The assignment and any details
3. The date the assignment is given
4. The date the assignment is due

Your Schedule for Study Time

Some assignments can be completed in a small amount of time. These are short-term goals. Set aside time each day to work on these assignments.

Assignments that cannot be completed overnight are called long-term goals. They become more manageable when you break them down into smaller tasks and do each part separately.

A study plan will help you complete your work. On your plan, show what you will accomplish each day and the times you will work on your project.

4. Study and Research

Three Types of Reading

There are three types of reading that you will find useful in your studying. Each is used for a particular purpose.

Scanning is a kind of fast reading. It lets you find a specific piece of information quickly. Scanning means moving your eyes rapidly over the page. Look for key words that point out the information you need.

Skimming is another type of fast reading. It gives you an overview of the material you are about to read. Skimming means moving your eyes quickly over the material looking for titles, subtitles, and illustrations that will give you clues about the content of the material.

The third kind of reading is **in-depth reading.** The SQ3R study method is an effective way to plan in-depth reading.

The SQ3R Study Method

SQ3R stands for five steps: Survey, Question, Read, Recite, and Review.

Survey. Get a general idea of what the material is about. Look at graphic aids, such as pictures, maps, graphs, or tables. Read the titles and subtitles. Read the introduction and the summary.

Question. Read any study questions provided. If there are none, make your own by turning titles and headings into questions.

Read. Read the material. Keep the study questions and main ideas in mind.

Recite. After reading, recite the answers to the study questions. Write a few notes to help you remember any important ideas.

Review. Look back at the study questions and try to answer them without using your notes. Finally, study your notes.

Note-Taking

Taking notes when you study has two uses: 1) it helps you concentrate on the material and 2) it gives you something to study for a review.

Notes should be written clearly so you will be able to understand them later. They do not have to be written in sentences. You may want to write a **summary**, or a short version, of the original material. Or you may want to **paraphrase** the information. When you paraphrase what someone has written, you put the main ideas of the selection in your own words.

When you are researching a subject for a writing project, use note cards. Be sure to write down where your information came from. You may need to refer to that source again. Include the following source information in your notes.

Books. Give the title, the author, the copyright date, and the page number.

Magazine or Newspaper Articles. Give the name and date of the periodical, the title of the article, the name of the author, and the page numbers of the article.

Encyclopedias. Give the name of the set, the title of the entry, the volume number where the entry appears, and the page numbers of the entry.

Direct Interviews. Write the name of the person you interviewed and the date.

Outlining

An **outline** is a way of organizing ideas and facts. It helps you see which ideas are main ideas and which ones are supporting details. When you make an outline, you begin to see the connections between ideas.

To make an outline follow the form below.

Sample Note Card

Title of book   Copyright date
Baseball's Ten Greatest Games, 1980

Author   Page number
John Thorn   page 78

Leo Durocher was let go by the Dodgers in 1948 and then hired as manager of the Giants.

I. Main Idea
  A. Subtopic
    1. Detail
    2. Detail
  B. Subtopic

II. Main Idea
  A. Subtopic
  B. Subtopic
    1. Detail
    2. Detail

Preparing a Bibliography

A bibliography lists the sources you used in gathering information for a report. The bibliography comes at the end of your paper and should be arranged alphabetically according to the author's last name. If no author is indicated, use the title of the source. Sample bibliography entries follow:

Bibliography

Encyclopedia "Football." The World Book Encyclopedia. 1984 ed.

Magazine Kaplan, J. "These Dodger Kids Are on the Ball." Sports Illustrated, 30 July 1984, pp. 20–22.

Newspaper Rapoport, Ron. "Suwanee Fosters Bears' Hopes," Chicago Sun Times, 27 Dec. 1984, p. 112.

Book Thorn, John. Baseball's Ten Greatest Games. New York: Four Winds Press, 1980.

Summary of Critical Thinking Terms

Analysis. When you analyze, you break something down into small parts and study each part carefully. It is often difficult to understand a piece of writing fully when you look at it all at once. That is why analysis is such a useful skill. When you analyze, you focus on each part individually.

For example, when you analyze a story, you may want to look at its characters, its setting, its dialogue, or any other element.

As you study each part separately, you understand the whole selection better. Also, analysis helps you see the similarities and differences between selections.

Bandwagon. The bandwagon approach urges one to take a certain action just because others are doing so. One type of bandwagon is **snob appeal**. In this case, someone does something because the "popular" people are doing it.

Categorizing and Classifying. Categorizing and classifying mean grouping according to common elements. For example, imagine that you wanted to talk about an element of short stories, such as mood. You would review short stories you have read. Then you might group together stories with a light, humorous mood. Other short stories with a mood of sadness could be grouped together, as could those with a mood of terror.

Pieces of writing that are categorized or classified together have some element in common. That element could be similar characters, setting, or theme. It could be similar plots or point of view. When you classify literature, first decide on the element that the pieces have in common.

For more about classifying, see page 272.

Cause and Effect. See *Summary of Comprehension Skills*, page 625.

Circular Reasoning. This occurs when a writer tries to prove a statement by merely rephrasing the same idea in different words. The following is an example of circular reasoning.

This project is necessary for the development of our town because it is needed if we expect the town to grow.

Connotation. Connotation refers to the emotional meaning a word carries with it. This meaning can go far beyond the **denotation**, or straight dictionary meaning of the word. The denotation of *mother*, for example, is simply "a female parent." The connotation, however, carries strong feelings that may include tenderness, love, warmth, or security.

Either/Or Thinking. If someone insists that there are only two possibilities, or alternatives, in a situation when there may be other choices, either/or thinking is being used. If, for example, someone says, "You either want this job or you don't," he or she is guilty of either/or thinking. The speaker is not allowing for the possibility that you may see advantages and disadvantages to both choices.

Errors in Reasoning. Errors in reasoning can confuse readers and listeners. These errors can also lead to false conclusions.

See *Bandwagon, Circular Reasoning, Either/Or Thinking, Exaggeration, False Cause and Effect Reasoning, False Analogy, Overgeneralization, Scapegoat, Stacking,* and *Stereotype.*

Evaluation. When you evaluate a piece of writing, you study it carefully and decide on its value.

Writing can be evaluated in several ways. First, you can judge the skills of the writer. Has the writer achieved his or her purpose? Are the important elements in this type of writing developed well? Has the writer used effective methods of presenting ideas? Is the writing organized logically?

The second type of evaluation involves judging what the writer says, not only how he or she says it. Is the writing truthful and accurate? Has he or she left out important facts?

Finally, is the writer qualified to write about this subject? Do you suspect that the writer is biased in any way?

When you evaluate what writers write, watch for evidences of loaded language and errors in reasoning such as those discussed in this Summary.

Exaggeration. A writer may exaggerate or overstate the facts in a piece of writing. This may sometimes be used to make an incident more humorous.

Fact and Opinion. Facts are statements that can be proved to be true. Opinions, on the other hand, are statements of a person's beliefs. They may or may not be supported by facts.

> Fact: This rose is yellow.
> Opinion: This yellow rose is beautiful.

Opinions, although they cannot always be proved, should be based on evidence. You are often asked to give your opinion about an issue or question. You should be able to point to the reasons why you hold that opinion.

For more about separating fact and opinion, see pages 324, 325, and 344.

False Analogy. An analogy compares two things that are basically different, yet similar in some ways. A false analogy carries the comparison too far.

False Cause and Effect Reasoning. When one event happens shortly after another, someone may incorrectly assume that the first event caused the second. Many superstitions are based on this error in reasoning. If a black cat crosses your path and you then have bad luck, you might incorrectly decide that the two events are related.

Generalizations. A generalization is a statement about a group that is supposedly true of all members of the group. Although any generalization should be accurate and based on facts, readers should be aware that many generalizations are faulty and not based on facts.

A fair generalization might be the following statement:

To be healthy, all people need exercise.

The following is an example of a faulty generalization:

All people need daily exercise to be healthy.

If even one person does not need daily exercise to be healthy, the generalization is faulty.

For more about generalizations, see pages 78 and 284.

Inferences. See the *Summary of Comprehension Skills*, page 626.

Judgment Words. These are words used to express a particular feeling about a subject. When a writer says that something is *good*, *bad*, *evil*, or other such words, he or she is making a judgment. To be effective, a judgment must be supported by facts.

Loaded Language. Language that carries very powerful emotional connotations is called loaded language. It is sometimes used to sway an audience by appealing to their emotions rather than their logic. A careful reader will always check to see that such language is supported by facts.

See also *Connotation* and *Judgment Words*.

Objective / Subjective Language. Objective language conveys information in a fair and impartial way without giving a personal opinion. Subjective language uses words that have an appeal.

Overgeneralization. Conclusions that are made about entire groups or classes of things are generalizations. When one makes a generalization that is too broad and not backed by fact, he or she is making the error of overgeneralization.

See also *Generalization*.

Scapegoat. A scapegoat is a person or group that is blamed for the problems of others without any real evidence.

Slanted Writing. When a writer uses loaded language or errors in reasoning to lead the reader to a certain point of view, he or she is using slanted writing.

Slanted writing is a powerful tool. It can easily sway a careless reader. Be alert to this kind of writing when you read and avoid it in your own writing.

Stacking. When a writer presents only one side of a question in order to make a point, he or she is using stacking.

Stereotype. A broad and unfair generalization about a particular ethnic, racial, political, social, or religious group is called a stereotype.

Glossary

The **glossary** is an alphabetical listing of words from the selections, with meanings. The glossary gives the following information:

1. **The entry word broken into syllables.**

2. **The pronunciation of each word.** The **respelling** is shown in parentheses. The most common way to pronounce a word is listed first. The Pronunciation Key below shows the symbols for the sounds of letters and key words that contain those sounds.

    A **primary accent ′** is placed after the syllable that is stressed the most when the word is spoken. A **secondary accent ′** is placed after a syllable that has a lighter stress.

3. **The part of speech of the word.** These abbreviations are used:
    n. noun   *v.* verb   *adj.* adjective   *adv.* adverb

4. **The meaning of the word.** The definitions listed in the glossary apply to selected ways a word is used in these selections.

5. **Related forms.** Words with suffixes such as *-ing, -ed, -ness,* and *-ly* are listed under the base word.

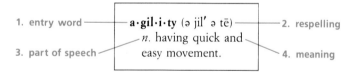

1. entry word ——— **a·gil·i·ty** (ə jil′ ə tē) ——— 2. respelling
3. part of speech ——— *n.* having quick and easy movement. ——— 4. meaning

Pronunciation Key

a	fat	i	hit	o͞o	look		a *in* ago	ch	chin
ā	ape	ī	bite, fire	o͞o	tool		e *in* agent	sh	she
ä	car	ō	go	ou	out	ə	i *in* sanity	th	thin
e	ten	ô	law, horn	u	up		o *in* comply	th	then
ē	even	oi	oil	ur	fur		u *in* focus	zh	leisure
				′l	able	ər	perhaps	ng	ring

A

ab·scond (əb skänd′ *or* ab skand′) *v.* to run away quickly and hide.

ab·stract (ab strakt′) *v.* to steal or take dishonestly.

ab·stract·ed (ab strak′ tid) *adj.* preoccupied.

a·byss (ə bis′) *n.* a deep crack in the earth.

ad·dle (ad′ ′l) *v.* to make confused.

af·fa·ble (af′ ə b′l) *adj.* pleasant and easy to talk to.

aft (aft *or* äft) *adv.* the rear of an airplane.

a·gil·i·ty (ə jil′ ə tē) *n.* having quick and easy movement.

alms (ämz) *n.* money or things given to poor people.

am·ble (am′ b′l) *v.* to walk leisurely.

a·men·i·ty (ə men′ ə tē *or* ə mē′ nə tē) *n.* anything that adds to one's comforts.

am·ne·sia (am nē′ zhə *or* am nē′ zhē ə) *n.* loss of memory.

an·guished (an′ gwisht) *adj.* showing great pain or grief.

a·nom·a·lous (ə näm′ ə ləs) *adj.* not in the usual way.

an·thol·o·gy (an thäl′ ə jē) *n.* a collection of written works.

an·tiq·ui·ty (an tik′ wə tē) *n.* ancient or old.

ap·pa·ra·tus (ap′ ə rat′ əs *or* ap′ə rāt′ əs) *n.* instruments or equipment for a specific use.

ap·pa·ri·tion (ap′ ə rish′ ən) *n.* something that appears unexpectedly.

ap·pli·ca·bil·i·ty (ap′ li kə bil′ ə tē) *n.* appropriateness.

ap·point·ment (ə point′ mənt) *n.* equipment.

ap·pre·hen·sive (ap rə hen′ siv) *adj.* anxious and fearful.

ar·chae·ol·o·gist (är kē äl′ ə jist) *n.* one who scientifically studies the life and culture of ancient peoples.

ar·chae·ol·o·gy (är kē äl′ ə jē) *n.* the study of ancient cultures.

ar·dent (är′ d′nt) *adj.* very enthusiastic.

ar·id (ar′ id *or* er′ id) *adj.* very dry or barren.

ar·ray (ə rā′) *v.* to place in a certain order.

ar·ro·gant (ar′ ə gənt) *adj.* too full of pride and feelings of self-importance.

as·cend (ə send′) *v.* to go from lower to higher.

as·sail (ə sāl′) *v.* to attack with questions or arguments.

a·tone·ment (ə tōn′ mənt) *n.* something done to make up for wrong doings.

at·trib·ute (a′ trə byoot′) *n.* a characteristic or quality of a person or thing.

au·di·to·ry (ô′ də tôr′ ē) *adj.* having to do with the sense of hearing.

B

bar·ba·rous (bär′ bər əs) *adj.* cruel or brutal.

bar·ter (bär′ tər) *n.* to trade by exchanging goods without the use of money.

base (bās) **1.** *n.* the part on which something rests. **2.** *adj.* showing little honor or decency.

bas·re·lief (bä′ rə lēf′ *or* bas′ rə lēf′) *adj.* figures that are carved in a flat surface so that they project only a little from the background.

ba·zaar (bə zär′) *n.* a shop or market that sells various kinds of goods.

beau (bō) *n.* sweetheart.

Bed·lam (bed′ ləm) *n.* a hospital for the mentally ill.

be·hoove (bi hoov′) *v.* to become necessary for.

be·lat·ed (bi lāt′ id) *adj.* late.

ben·e·dic·tion (ben′ə dik′ shən) *n.* a blessing, especially at the end of a religious service.

ben·e·fac·tor (ben′ ə fak′ tər) *n.* a person who has given financial help.

berth (burth) *n.* a built-in bed.

be·siege (bi sēj′) *v.* surround by armed forces, usually for attack.

bid·ing (bīd′ iŋ) *v.* waiting patiently for an opportunity.

bi·zarre (bi zär′) *adj.* odd or eccentric.

bland·ly (bland′ lē) *adv.* smoothly or agreeably.

bo·a (bō′ ə) *n.* a long scarf usually made of fur or feathers.

bog (bäg *or* bôg) *n.* a swamp.

boo·ty (boot′ ē) *n.* a prize or gain often associated with a robbery.

borsch (bôrsh) *n.* a Russian soup made of beets.

bris·tle (bris′ ′l) *v.* to become tense with anger, fear, or irritation.

buoy·ant (boi′ ənt *or* boi′ yənt) *adj.* cheerful.

C

cal·is·then·ics (kal′ əs then′ iks) *n.* exercises.

cal·li·o·pe (kə lī′ ə pē′ *or* kal′ ē ōp) *n.* in Greek mythology, the Muse of epic poetry.

cam·o·mile (kam′ ə mīl′ *or* kam′ ə mēl) *n.* a plant whose dried flower heads are sometimes used in medicinal tea.

can·vass (kan′ vəs) *v.* to go among people to try to get orders.

car·i·bou (kar′ ə boo′) *n.* a large North American deer with branching antlers.

cat·a·pult (kat′ ə pult′ *or* kat′ ə poolt) *v.* to move quickly.

Cau·ca·sus (kô′ kə səs) *n.* a region in the U.S.S.R. near the Black Sea.

caul·dron (kôl′ drən) *n.* a large kettle.

cau·ter·ize (kôt′ ər īz′) *v.* to burn with a hot needle or iron or caustic substance to destroy dead tissue.

cha·teau (sha tō′) *n.* a large country house especially found in France.

col·lab·o·rate (kə lab′ ə rāt′) *v.* work together.

co·ma·tose (kō′ mə tōs′ *or* käm′ ə tōs′) *adj.* as if in a stupor or coma.

com·mer·cial (kə mur′ shəl) *adj.* designed to have popular appeal.

com·mun·ion (kə myoon′ yən) *n.* the act of sharing one's thoughts and emotions with another.

con·cus·sion (kən kush′ ən) *n.* a hurt suffered by the brain resulting from a blow on the head.

con·demn (kən dem′) *v.* to declare guilty of a wrong doing.

con·done (kən dōn′) *v.* forgive or pardon.

con·sole (kən sōl′) *v.* to comfort.

con·tig·u·ous (kən tig′ yoo wəs) *adj.* touching along most of or all of one side.

con·va·lesce (kän′ və les′) *v.* to regain strength gradually after an illness.

con·verge (kən vurj′) *v.* to come together at the same point.

cor·rupt (kə rupt′) *v.* to change someone or something from good to bad.

cos·mop·o·lite (käz mäp′ ə līt′) *n.* citizen of the world.

Cos·sack (käs′ ak *or* käs′ ək *or* kô′ sak) *n.* a person of southern Russia, famous as a cavalryman and a horseman.

coun·ter·prop·o·si·tion (koun′ tər präp ə zish′ ən) *n.* a proposal in response to one that is unsatisfactory.

court·plas·ter (kôrt′ plas′ tər) *n.* cloth covered with an adhesive material used for protecting minor bruises.

cow·er (kou′ ər) *v.* to tremble or crouch from someone's blows.

crepes·su·zette (krāp′ soo zet′) *n.* thin, filled pancake served in a sauce.

cre·vasse (kri vas′) *n.* a deep crack or break.

cru·ci·fy (kroo′ sə fī′) *v.* to put to death by nailing to a cross and leaving to die.

cu·bit (kyoo′ bit) *n.* an ancient measure, from the elbow to the end of the middle finger.

cul·ti·vat·ed (kul′ tə vāt′ id) *adj.* refined or cultured.

---

at, āte, fär; pen, ēqual; sit, mīne; sō, côrn, join, took, fool, our; us, turn; chill, shop, thick, they, sing; **zh** *in* measure; ′l *in* idle; ə *in* alive, cover, family, robot, circus.

cun·ning (kun′ iŋ) *adj.* clever or sly.

cyn·i·cal (sin′ i k'l) *adj.* doubting the sincerity of people's actions or motives.

Czar (zär) *n.* the title of any former emperor of Russia. (also Tsar)

D

daft (daft) *adj.* foolish; crazy.

das·tard·ly (das′ tərd lē) *adj.* cowardly.

de·bil·i·tat·ing (di bil′ ə tāt′ iŋ) *adj.* weakening.

de·cry (di krī′) *v.* to strongly speak out against.

de·plor·a·bly (di plôr′ ə b'lē) *adv.* very bad; regrettable.

der·e·lict (der′ ə likt′) *n.* a very poor person without a home or job.

de·ri·sive (di rī′ siv) *adj.* ridiculing.

der·vish (dur′ vish) *n.* a member of a Moslem order who often practices whirling and howling as a religious act.

de·scend·ing (di send′ iŋ) *adj.* moving from higher to lower.

des·ig·nate (dez′ ig nāt) *v.* to indicate by name.

de·te·ri·o·ra·tion (di tir′ ē ə rā′ shən) *n.* becoming worse.

dev·as·tate (dev′ ə stāt′) *v.* to destroy or to make waste.

de·vour (di vour′) *v.* to eat or destroy with great force.

di·a·tribe (dī′ ə trīb′) *n.* very abusive criticism.

din·ghy (din′ gē *or* diŋ′ ē) *n.* a small boat used to take one to a larger boat.

dis·crim·i·na·tion (dis krim′ ə nā′ shən) *n.* showing favoritism in treatment.

dis·dain (dis dān′) *n.* the act of treating as unworthy.

dis·gorge (dis gôrj′) *v.* to force something out of the throat.

di·shev·eled (di shev′ 'ld) *adj.* having untidy hair or clothes.

dis·mal (diz′ m'l) *adj.* gloomy; depressing.

dis·patch (dis pach′) *v.* **1.** send off quickly. **2.** kill.

di·ver·sion (də vur′ zhən) *n.* anything that distracts the attention.

dog·ged·ly (dôg′ id lē *or* däg′ id lē) *adv.* persistently or stubbornly.

dolt (dōlt) *n.* a stupid person.

dove·tail (duv′ tāl′) *v.* to join together to make a logically connected whole.

dow·dy (dou′ dē) *adj.* not stylish or neat in appearance.

droll (drōl) *adj.* amusing in an odd way.

dun (dun) *adj.* grayish brown.

dy·na·mo (dī′ nə mō′) *n.* a dynamic or forceful person.

E

earth·en·ware (ur′ thən wer′) *adj.* made of baked clay.

ec·cen·tric (ik sen′ trik) *adj.* not usual or normal in behavior; odd.

ed·dy (ed′ ē) *n.* a current of air moving with a circular motion against the main current.

ef·fete (e fēt′ *or* i fēt′) *adj.* worn out; not forceful.

e·go·tism (ē′ gə tiz'm) *n.* too high an opinion of oneself.

e·merge (i murj′) *v.* to become visible.

em·phat·ic (im fat′ ik) *adj.* very definite. — **emphatically** *adv.*

en·sue (in soo′ *or* in syoo′) *v.* to follow immediately. —**ensuing** *adj.*

e·rup·tion (i rup′ shən) *n.* a bursting forth of lava.

es·ker (es′ kər) *n.* a winding sandy ridge.

es·tu·ar·y (es′ choo wer′ ē) *n.* an arm or inlet of the sea.

e·vade (i vād′) *v.* to avoid by cleverness.

ex·ca·va·tor (eks′ kə vāt′ ər) *n.* a person or thing that uncovers by digging.

ex·cel (ik sel′) *v.* to be better or superior to others.

ex·clu·sive (iks klōō′ siv) *adj.* shutting out certain people; snobbish.

ex·ile (eg′ zīl *or* ek′ sīl) *v.* force to leave.

F

fa·kir (fə kir′) *n.* a Hindu or Moslem beggar often claiming to perform miracles.

fat·back (fat′ bak′) *n.* the fat from the back of a hog, often dried and salted in strips.

fa·tigue (fə tēg′) *n.* a tired feeling; mental or physical exhaustion.

fat·u·ous·ly (fach′ ōō wəs lē) *adv.* silly or foolishly.

fe·do·ra (fə dôr′ ə) *n.* a hat made of felt with a lengthwise crease in the crown and a slightly curved brim.

fee·ble·mind·ed (fē′ b'l mīn did) *adj.* mentally retarded.

fe·roc·i·ty (fə räs′ ə tē) *n.* force or cruelty.

fifth·col·um·nist (fifth käl′ əm nist *or* fifth käl′ ə mist) *n.* a person who spies or is involved in other revolutionary activities within the borders of a nation.

floun·der (floun′ dər) *v.* to struggle awkwardly to move.

foil (foil) *n.* a person or thing that sets off another by contrast.

for·age (fôr′ ij *or* fär′ ij) **1.** *n.* food for animals. **2.** *v.* to seek food.

fo·rum (fôr′ əm) *n.* a public marketplace of an ancient Roman city.

fos·ter (fôs′ tər *or* fäs′ ter) *v.* to help grow.

fran·ti·cal·ly (fran′ ti kəl lē) *adv.* acting with wild emotion.

fraud·u·lent (frô′ jə lənt) *adj.* acting with the intent of cheating or tricking.

fren·zied (fren′ zēd) *adj.* with a wild outburst of feeling or action.

friv·o·lous (friv′ ə ləs) *adj.* unimportant or silly.

fru·gal·ly (frōō′ g'l lē) *adv.* not in a wasteful manner.

fugue (fyōōg) *n.* a loss of memory during which time one appears to behave normally, yet when returning to consciousness the person cannot remember that period of time.

fu·tile (fyōōt′ 'l) *adj.* hopeless, useless.

G

gape (gāp) *v.* to open wide.

gar·goyle (gär′ goil) *n.* an ornament that looks like a carved animal or creature.

gaud·i·ly (gôd′ i lē) *adv.* showy but lacking good taste.

gid·dy (gid′ ē) *adj.* not serious; light-headed.

gin·ger·ly (jin′ jər lē) *adv.* in a very cautious manner.

glad·i·a·tor (glad′ ē āt′ ər) *n.* a man who fought other men or animals with a sword or other weapon in an arena for the entertainment of others in ancient Rome.

gon·do·lier (gän′ də lir′) *n.* the person who rows a gondola, or boat, used in Venice, Italy.

grave (grāv) *adj.* important; serious.

grave·ly (grāv′ lē) *adv.* of a dangerous or threatening nature.

grit (grit) *n.* courage or perseverance.

gro·tesque (grō tesk′) *adj.* distorted or strange.

gul·den (gōōl′ dən) *n.* a former coin used in Germany and Austria.

gump·tion (gump′ shən) *n.* courage and boldness.

gut·ta·per·cha (gut′ ə pur′ chə) *adj.* made from a rubberlike gum produced from Southeast Asian trees.

gut·tur·al (gut′ ər əl) *adj.* a rasping sound produced in the throat.

---

at, āte, fär; pen, ēqual; sit, mīne; sō, côrn, join, took, fōōl, our; us, turn; chill, shop, thick, *th*ey, si**ng**; **zh** *in* measure; ′l *in* idle; ə *in* alive, cover, family, robot, circus.

H

Ha·nuk·kah (khä′ noo kä′ *or* hä′ noo kə) *n.* a Jewish holiday celebrated by the lighting of candles for eight days.

hav·er·sack (hav′ ər sak′) *n.* a canvas bag worn over one shoulder, usually for carrying food and supplies.

her·ald (her′ əld) *v.* to announce.

her·ni·a (hur′ nē ə) *n.* the bulging of an organ of the body through a tear in the wall of a surrounding structure.

her·pe·tol·o·gist (hur′ pə täl′ ə jist) *n.* one who studies reptiles and amphibians.

hoard (hôrd) *v.* to accumulate and store away.

hol·o·caust (häl′ ə kôst *or* hō′ lə kôst′) *n.* a total destruction of life.

hone (hōn) *v.* to sharpen.

hos·tile (häs t′l) *adj.* unfriendly.

hum·mock (hum′ ək) *n.* very low hill.

I

id·i·o·syn·cra·sy (id′ ē ə sing′ krə sē *or* id′ ē ə sin′ krə sē) *n.* any personal peculiarity.

im·pel (im pel′) *v.* to force or compel.

im·per·a·tive (im per′ ə tiv) *adj.* absolutely necessary.

im·per·cep·ti·ble (im′ pər sep′ tə b′l) *adj.* extremely slight so as not to be easily seen. —**imperceptibly** *adv.*

im·plic·it (im plis′ it) *adj.* suggested, but not plainly expressed.

im·pos·ing (im pō′ zing) *adj.* impressive because of size.

in·au·gu·rate (in ô′ gyə rāt′) *v.* to make a formal beginning.

in·cen·di·ar·y (in sen′ dē er′ ē) *n.* bomb.

in·cense (in′ sens) *n.* a substance producing a pleasant odor when burned.

in·con·ti·nent·ly (in känt″ n ənt lē) *adv.* not held back.

in·cred·u·lous (in krej′ oo ləs) *adj.* showing doubt. —**incredulously** *adv.*

in·do·lent (in′ də lənt) *adj.* lazy. —**indolently** *adv.*

in·dulge (in dulj′) *v.* to satisfy.

in·dus·tri·ous (in dus′ trē əs) *adj.* hard working or steady effort.

in·ef·fa·ble (in ef′ ə b′l) *adj.* too overwhelming to be expressed in words.

in·ev·i·ta·ble (in ev′ ə tə b′l) *adj.* that is certain to happen.

in·ex·pli·ca·ble (in eks′ pli kə b′l *or* in′ iks plik′ ə b′l) *adj.* that cannot be explained.

in·fal·li·ble (in fal′ ə b′l) *adj.* not capable of error.

in·fin·i·tes·i·mal (in′ fin ə tes′ ə m′l *or* in fin′ ə tes′ ə m′l) *adj.* too small to be measured accurately.

in·i·ti·a·tive (i nish′ ē ə tiv *or* i nish′ ə tiv) *n.* the act of making the first move.

in·teg·ri·ty (in teg′ rə tē) *n.* having sound moral principles; honesty.

in·tern·ment (in turn′ mənt) *n.* to hold within a definite area.

in·ter·vene (in′ tər vēn′) *v.* to come between.

in·tol·er·a·ble (in täl′ ər ə b′l) *adj.* painful or unbearable.

in·tox·i·cate (in täk′ sə kāt) *v.* to make wild with excitement.

in·var·i·a·ble (in ver′ ē ə b′l) *adj.* unchanging. —**invariably** *adv.*

ir·ra·tion·al (i rash′ ə n′l) *adj.* senseless or unreasonable.

J

jav·e·lin (jav′ lin *or* jav′ ə lin) *n.* the throwing of a spear in a field event.

ju·jit·su (joo jit′ soo) *n.* a system of wrestling in Japan.

K

Kan·ga·roo court (kan gə roo′ kôrt) *n.* a court set up with no legal authority that holds trials and punishes people in an illegal way.

kin·dling (kin′ dling) *n.* bits of dry wood for starting a fire.

knout·er (nout′ ər) *n.* a person that whips criminals, especially in Russia.

L

lab·y·rinth (lab′ ə rinth′) *n.* a structure containing a complicated network of winding passages that are difficult to follow; a maze.

lac·er·ate (las′ ə rāt′) *v.* to tear unevenly.

lack·a·dai·si·cal (lak′ ə dā′ zi k′l) *adj.* showing a lack of interest or energy.

la·ment (lə ment′) *n.* a sad cry.

la·pil·li (lə pil′ ī) *n.* a small piece of rock ejected from a volcano.

lax·ness (laks′ nəs) *n.* a carelessness.

lin·go (lin′ gō) *n.* a vocabulary that one is not familiar with.

list·less (list′ lis) *adj.* having or showing no interest in what is going on. —**listlessly** *adv.*

loom (lōōm) *v.* to threaten. —**looming** *adj.*

lor·ry (lôr′ ē *or* lär′ ē) *n.* a low, flat wagon.

lout (lout) *n.* a clumsy, stupid person.

lu·mi·nous (lōō′ mə nəs) *adj.* glowing in the darkness.

M

mack·i·naw (mak′ə nô′) *n.* a short, woolen coat, usually plaid.

mag·nan·i·mous (mag nan′ ə məs) *adj.* generous in overlooking insults or injuries.

mag·ni·tude (mag′ nə tōōd *or* mag′ nə tyōōd) *n.* greatness or importance.

maim (mām) *v.* to injure, causing the loss or crippling of a part of the body.

ma·lar·i·a (mə ler′ ē ə) *n.* a disease transmitted by the bite of an infected mosquito.

mal·ice (mal′ is) *n.* a desire to harm or do mischief.

ma·li·cious (mə lish′ əs) *adj.* spiteful.

man·gle (man′ g′l) *v.* to damage by repeated rough cutting; spoil. —**mangled** *adj.*

ma·ni·a (mā nē ə *or* mān′ yə) *n.* a violent or wild form of mental disorder. —**maniac** *n.*

mar·tyr (mär′ tər) *n.* a person who chooses to die rather than give up his principles.

max·im (mak′ sim) *n.* a statement of a general truth stated in a few words.

me·di·e·val (mē′ dē ē′ v′l) *adj.* characteristic of the Middle Ages.

met·a·mor·pho·sis (met′ ə môr fə sis *or* met′ ə môr fō′ sis) *n.* a complete change.

mo·rale (mə ral′ *or* mô ral′) *n.* a condition of the mind involving courage, discipline, and confidence.

mo·sa·ic (mō zā′ ik) *n.* a picture or design made by inlaying small bits of colored stone, tile, or glass in mortar.

mun·dane (mun dān′ *or* mun′ dān) *adj.* ordinary.

murk (mʉrk) *n.* dark or gloom.

N

na·ive (nä ēv′) *adj.* unsophisticated.

na·ive·te (nä ēv tā′ *or* nä ēv′ tā) *n.* the quality of being simple or childlike.

neu·ro·sur·geon (noor′ ō sʉr′ jən *or* nyoor′ ō sʉr′ jən) *n.* a doctor specializing in surgery involving some part of the nervous system.

niche (nich) *n.* a hollow spot.

Nor·dic (nôr′ dik) *adj.* of a physical type with characteristics like the tall, blond people of Scandinavia.

O

ob·scure (əb skyoor′ *or* äb skyoor′) *v.* conceal or hide.

o·gre (ō′ gər) *n.* cruel or coarse man.

---

at, āte, fär; pen, ēqual; sit, mīne; sō, côrn, join, took, fōol, our; us, tʉrn; chill, shop, thick, they, sing; zh *in* measure; ′l *in* idle; ə *in* alive, cover, family, robot, circus.

om·i·nous (äm′ ə nəs) *adj.* threatening. —
ominously *adv.*

op·pres·sive (ə pres′ iv) *adj.* difficult to put up
with.

or·nate (ôr nāt′) *adj.* having a great deal of or
too much decoration.

o·vert (ōvʉrt′ *or* ō′vʉrt) *adj.* open; not hidden
in any way.

P

pal·at·a·ble (pal′ it ə b′l) *adj.* suitable for eating or drinking.

pa·la·tial (pə lā′ shəl) *adj.* large and splendid,
like a palace.

pan·de·mo·ni·um (pan′ də mō′ nē əm) *n.* a
place of noise and confusion.

peck (pek) *n.* large amount; eight quarts.

per·ceive (pər sēv′) *v.* to take note of.

per·emp·to·ry (pə remp′ tə rē) *adj.* that cannot
be changed.

pet·ri·fied (pet′ rə fīd) *adj.* inflexible or rigid.

pet·u·lant (pech′ ᴏᴏ lənt) *adj.* irritable or impatient.

phil·o·pro·gen·i·tive·ness (fil′ ə prō jen′ ə tiv
nes) *n.* having the ability to produce many
offspring.

phos·pho·res·cent (fäs′ fə res′ ənt) *adj.* giving
off a continuing light without heat.

pil·lar (pil′ ər) *n.* **1.** a tall, slender structure
used to support a large structure or to stand
alone as a monument. **2.** a person who is the
primary support of an organization or institution.

plain·tive (plān′ tiv) *adj.* sorrowful.

pla·teau (pla tō′) *n.* a period during which
there is very little change.

plum·met (plum′ it) *v.* to plunge straight
downward.

poign·an·cy (pᴏin′ yən sē) *n.* a touching or
moving emotion.

pon·der (pän′ dər) *v.* to think about and consider carefully.

port·cul·lis (pôrt kul′ is) *n.* an iron grating sus-
pended by chains, lowered to bar the en-
trance to a castle.

pre·car·i·ous (pri ker′ ē əs) *adj.* insecure; de-
pendent on another. —**precariously** *adv.*

prec·i·pice (pres′ ə pis) *n.* a very steep.

pre·dom·i·nance (pri däm′ ə nəns) *n.* authority
over others.

prej·u·dice (prej′ ə dis) *n.* an opinion formed
before the facts are known.

pri·me·val (prī mē′ v′l) *adj.* from the earliest
times.

pros·trate (präs′ trāt) *adj.* lying flat, usually
with the face down.

pro·trude (prō trᴏᴏd) *v.* to jut out or project.
—**protruding** *adj.*

pro·vi·sion (prə vizh′ ən) *n.* food and other
supplies assembled for one's future needs.

pun·gent (pun′ jənt) *adj.* strong smelling.

Q

quar·ry (kwôr′ ē *or* kwär′ ē) *n.* an animal that
is being hunted or pursued.

R

ram·shack·le (ram′ shak′ ′l) *adj.* shaky; likely
to fall apart.

rank (raŋk) **1.** *n.* position. **2.** *v.* to assign a
certain position. **3.** *adj.* producing an excess
of luxurious crop.

rav·el (rav′ ′l) *v.* to make clear or to untangle.
—**ravelling** *adj.*

re·cip·ro·cate (ri sip′ rə kāt′) *v.* to give in
return.

re·coil (ri kᴏil′) *n.* the act of flying back when
let go.

rec·on·noi·tre (rē′ kə nᴏit′ ər *or* rek′ ə nᴏit′ ər)
v. to make a survey to gather information.

re·gres·sion (ri gresh′ ən) *n.* a move backward.

ren·e·gade (ren′ ə gād′) *n.* a person who aban-
dons one's religion, party, or principles and
goes over to the other side.

re·past (ri past′ *or* ri päst′) *n.* meal.

rep·er·toire (rep′ ər twär *or* rep′ ə twär) *n.* all of the special skills of an individual.

re·pose (ri pōz′) *n.* to lie quietly and calmly.

re·pug·nance (ri pug′ nəns) *n.* a dislike.

re·qui·em (rek′ wē əm *or* räk′ wē əm *or* rēk′ wē əm) *n.* a church service to pray for the soul of a dead person.

res·in (rez′ ′n) *n.* a sticky substance that comes from various trees or plants.

res·o·lute (rez′ ə lo͞ot′) *adj.* determined. — **resolution** *n.*

re·spec·tive (ri spek′ tiv) *adj.* relating separately to each of two or more persons or things.

re·ver·ber·a·tion (ri vur′ bə rā′ shən) *n.* reechoing sound.

re·vive (ri vīv′) *v.* to bring back to consciousness.

right·eous (rī′ chəs) *adj.* doing what is moral.

Ri·o (rē′ ō) *n.* Rio de Janeiro; a seaport in southeast Brazil.

row·el (rou′ əl) *n.* a small revolving wheel with sharp points.

ru·ble (ro͞o′ b′l) *n.* a unit of money used in the Soviet Union.

S

saf·fron (saf′ rən) *adj.* orange yellow.

san·i·tar·i·um (san′ ə ter′ ē əm) *n.* **1.** an institution for the care of ill people. **2.** a quiet resort where people go to rest or recuperate.

sar·cas·tic (sär kas′ tik) *adj.* with the intent to hurt by mocking or ridiculing.

sa·vor (sā′ vər) *v.* to enjoy with appreciation.

scape·goat (skāp′ gōt′) *n.* a person who is blamed for the mistakes or crimes of others.

scav·enge (skav′ inj) *v.* to look for food.

scrim·mage (skrim′ ij) *n.* fight.

scru·ple (skro͞o′ p′l) *n.* a feeling of doubt coming from difficulty in deciding what is right.

scut·tle (skut′ ′l) *v.* to move quickly away from danger.

scythe (sīth) *n.* a tool for cutting long grass.

sham (sham) *n.* a fraud; not real.

sheep·ish (shēp′ ish) *adj.* embarrassed.

shun (shun) *v.* to avoid.

sin·gu·lar (sing′ yə lər) *adj.* remarkable or unique. —**singularly** *adv.*

sin·is·ter (sin′ is tər) *adj.* evil or wicked, usually in a dark, mysterious way.

slake (slāk) *n.* an amount that satisfies.

sleuth (slo͞oth) *n.* a detective.

slew (slo͞o) *v.* to turn on a fixed point.

sloth (slôth *or* slōth *or* släth) *n.* a slow-moving mammal of Central or South America that hangs, back down, from branches.

slug·gish (slug′ ish) *adj.* lacking energy.

smote (smōt) *v.* to attack with a powerful and disastrous effect.

so·lic·i·tous (sə lis′ ə təs) *adj.* showing concern or care. —**solicitously** *adv.*

sov·er·eign (säv′ ren *or* säv′ ər in) *n.* a British gold coin, no longer minted.

spec·tre (spek′ tər) *n.* an object of fear.

squan·der (skwän′ dər *or* skwôn′ dər) *v.* to spend in a wasteful manner.

stance (stans) *n.* the way one stands.

stealth·y (stel′ thē) *adj.* slyly or secretively.

stock·ade (stä kād′) *n.* enclosure for military prisoners.

strife (strīf) *n.* fighting or quarreling.

sub·merge (səb murj′) *v.* hide.

sub·ter·fuge (sub′ tər fyo͞oj′) *n.* a plan or action to avoid a difficult situation.

sub·ter·ra·ne·an (sub′ tə rā′ nē ən) *n.* beneath the surface of the earth.

suf·fused (sə fyo͞oz ′d′) *adj.* spread over with glow or color.

---

at, āte, fär; pen, ēqual; sit, mīne; sō, côrn, join, to͝ok, fo͞ol, our; us, turn; chill, shop, thick, they, sing; zh *in* measure; ′l *in* idle; ə *in* alive, cover, family, robot, circus.

sul·try (sul′ trē) *adj.* very hot and moist.

sup·ple (sup′ ′l) *adj.* easily bent or moved.

sup·press (sə pres′) *v.* to hold or keep back.

surge (surj) *n.* violent movement or motion.

sur·pass (sər pas′ *or* sər päs′) *v.* to be superior to or greater than. —**surpassingly** *adv.*

syl·van (sil′ vən) *adj.* of the woods.

syn·drome (sin′ drōm) *n.* a set of characteristics identifying a certain condition.

T

tac·it (tas′ it) *adj.* not expressed openly; implied, yet unspoken.

tac·tu·al (tak′ choo wəl) *adj.* pertaining to the sense of touch.

taint (tānt) *v.* to affect with something unpleasant.

tal·ly (tal′ ē) *v.* to add up.

tan·gi·ble (tan′ jə b'l) *adj.* that can be touched or felt by touching.

tap·es·try (tap′ is trē) *n.* a heavy, woven cloth with designs, often used as a wall hanging.

tem·pest (tem′ pist) *n.* outburst.

ten·ta·tive (ten′ tə tiv) *adj.* not final or certain. —**tentatively** *adv.*

terse (turs) *adj.* concise; using no more words than necessary.

teth·er (te*th*′ ər) *v.* to fasten with a rope.

the·o·rem (thē′ ə rəm *or* thir′ əm) *n.* a statement that may not appear true, but can be proved by other accepted statements and is, therefore an established principle or law.

this·tle·down (this′ 'l doun′) *n.* down attached to the flowerhead of the thistle.

throng·ing (thrông′ ing) *adj.* gathered together; crowded.

trans·fig·ure (trans fig′ yər) *v.* to change the outward appearance.

trav·erse (tra vurs′ *or* trə vurs′) *v.* to travel back and forth over.

treach·er·ous·ly (trech′ ər əs lē) *adv.* giving a false appearance of safety or security.

trep·i·da·tion (trep′ ə dā′ shən) *n.* a feeling of anxiety or uncertainty.

tri·fle (trī f'l) *n.* a very small amount.

tulle (tool) *n.* a very thin netting material, often used in veils.

U

un·can·ny (un kan′ ē) *adj.* mysterious in a way that can make uneasy or frighten.

un·daunt·ed (un dôn′ tid *or* un dän′ tid) *adj.* without hesitation due to fear.

un·slack·en·ing (un slak′ 'n ing) *adv.* without stopping or letting up.

V

vac·u·ous (vak′ yoo wəs) *adj.* showing a lack of intelligence.

vague (vāg) *adj.* not sharp or certain in thought or feeling.

ven·ti·late (ven′ t' lāt) *v.* to furnish with an opening for the escape of air or gas.

ver·i·fy (ver′ ə fī′) *v.* to confirm the truth of.

verve (vurv) *n.* energy; enthusiasm.

vil·la (vil′ ə) *n.* a large country house.

vul·ner·a·ble (vul′ nər ə b'l) *adj.* that can be hurt or injured.

W

wel·ter·weight (wel′ tər wāt′) *adj.* between a lightweight and a middleweight, often used in a description of a boxer.

whim (whim *or* wim) *n.* a sudden.

wist·ful (wist′ fəl) *adj.* showing longings or yearnings. —**wistfully** *adv.*

with·er (wi*th*′ ur) *v.* to dry up or decay. —**withered** *adj.*

Y

yeo·man·ry (yō′ mən rē) *n.* assistants to the sheriff.

Biographies of Authors

Russell Baker

Robert Bly

Ray Bradbury

Richard Armour (*born 1906*) has written thousands of light, humorous poems and essays. In addition to his humorous writing, he is also the author of many serious books and articles. Armour, who received his education at Harvard University, has taught English at a number of colleges. *Nights with Armour* and *Armour's Almanac* are two well known collections of his humorous observations.

Russell Baker (*born 1925*) planned on being a novelist, but found himself with a newspaper career instead. He wrote political satire for the *New York Times* for many years. Later, his topics included subjects such as tax reform and current trends. He received the 1979 Pulitzer Prize for distinguished commentary. In 1982, he won another Pulitzer Prize for his book of memoirs called *Growing Up.* Baker states that he wrote *Growing Up* because he wanted young people to understand how they are connected to their parents and their past.

Robert Bly (*born 1926*) is the founder of his own poetry magazine, designed to introduce Americans to works by poets of other nations. Bly collects and translates many of the poems himself. His dedication to this effort comes from his belief that English and American poets are too tied down to form and tradition. Bly is also known for his dramatic poetry readings, in which he uses masks and costumes.

Ray Bradbury (*born 1920*) believes that science fiction and fantasy offer original approaches to solving modern problems. He began writing as a child, while growing up in Waukegan, Illinois, and claims to have lived in a fantasy world for most of his life. Since then Bradbury has written over a thousand stories in addition to novels, plays, and movie and television scripts. *The Martian Chronicles* and *Fahrenheit 451* are two of his popular works. Although he often portrays a future world filled with sophisticated technology, Bradbury claims that he has never flown in an airplane or learned to drive a car.

Art Buchwald

Art Buchwald (*born 1925*) left high school without a diploma to join the marines. Later he left college without a degree to live in Paris. It was there he got his first job as a newspaper correspondent. Today he is one of the most successful humorists in the country with a column syndicated in nearly four hundred newspapers. His writing often pokes fun at politicians and current events.

Diana Chang (*born 1934*) is the daughter of Eurasian/Chinese parents. Although she was born in New York, she spent her childhood in China. Chang is the author of *The Frontiers of Love* and *Eye to Eye,* two recently published novels. She also writes poetry, which has appeared in many magazines and anthologies.

Anton Chekhov (*1860–1904*), a Russian author, began writing stories while studying medicine. He was able to continue both careers throughout his life. His writing generally deals with the problems of ordinary people. It is realistic, sometimes sad, but never without a touch of humor. Chekhov's short stories and plays have had a great influence on other writers. They are still being read and produced.

Anton Chekhov

Arthur C. Clarke (*born 1917*) is a British novelist whose writing ranges from serious scientific work to wildly imaginative science fiction. Clarke specializes in the area of space travel. Additionally, he was the first person to create plans for the use of satellite relays for radio and television. Clarke also writes about his hobby, skin-diving.

Elizabeth Coatsworth (*born 1893*) inherited a love of travel from her parents, who took her to many countries as a child. After graduating from college, she spent a year in the Orient. That experience and her love of the New England countryside have served as a basis for much of her writing. In addition to novels, poetry, and essays for adults, she has published more than ninety books for young people. *The Cat Who Went to Heaven* won the Newbery Medal in 1931.

Richard Connell (*1893–1949*) began his writing career at the age of ten, covering local baseball games for the newspaper his father edited. As a student at Harvard University, Connell served as the editor of *Lampoon,* the school's humor magazine. In World War I he edited the army camp's weekly newspaper. About three hundred of Connell's stories have appeared in English and American magazines.

Arthur C. Clarke

Photograph © 1985 Jill Krementz

Emily Dickinson

William O. Douglas

Daphne du Maurier

Paul Laurence Dunbar

e. e. cummings (*1894–1962*) revised the rules of punctuation, capitalization, and verse form in order to create his unique poetry. He was born and raised in Massachusetts and earned two degrees from Harvard. During World War I Cummings went to France as a volunteer ambulance driver. He spent several years there after the war, writing and painting. Although Cummings showed exceptional talent as a painter, it was his controversial poetry that made him famous. As an extension of his unusual use of grammar, he chose to eliminate capital letters in his name and signed his work 'e. e. cummings.'

Emily Dickinson (*1830–1886*) began her life just as any other upper-class girl might during the 1800's. However, during her twenties, something occurred in Dickinson's life that caused her to shut herself off from society. She stayed in her Amherst, Massachusetts home where she secretly wrote hundreds of poems. Dickinson's poems were full of her observations about the mysteries of life. Only seven of her poems were published during her lifetime but over a thousand poems were found after her death.

William O. Douglas (*1898–1980*) spent thirty-six years as a Justice of the Supreme Court of the United States. He favored a strict enforcement of the free speech amendment and was concerned about both civil liberties and civil rights. Along with his legal activities, Douglas displayed a love for the rugged outdoor life. This is reflected in his book *Of Men and Mountains.*

Daphne du Maurier (*born 1907*) grew up in England, part of a family of actors, writers, and artists. Her life had a fairy-tale quality, yet she often longed for quiet and solitude. To satisfy this need, she began to write. Du Maurier has penned novels, plays, biographies, and short stories. Many of them are based on romance and intrigue. One of her most famous books, *Rebecca,* received a National Book Award.

Paul Laurence Dunbar (*1872–1906*) was the son of former slaves. Because he was unable to afford college, Dunbar gave up hopes of a career as a lawyer or minister. Instead, he became an elevator operator and wrote poetry in his spare time. Dunbar's first collection of poems, *Oak and Ivory,* was published in 1893. He followed that with the writing of novels, short stories, and more than five hundred poems.

James A. Emanuel

James A. Emanuel (*born 1921*) did not begin writing poetry until the age of forty. Born in Nebraska, he spent several years in the army and working at odd jobs. He later earned both a master's degree and a doctoral degree. Included in Emanuel's published collections are *The Panther Man* and *The Treehouse and Other Poems.*

Lucille Fletcher (*born 1912*) has written novels, short stories, and movie and television scripts. She is best known, however, for her radio dramas that were listened to by millions during the golden age of radio. *Sorry, Wrong Number,* one of Fletcher's most famous stories, was first a novel and then adapted for stage, screen, and television.

Alyesa Forsee began her career as a high school teacher in Minnesota. She later became a college instructor and adult-education teacher. In 1956 she turned from teaching to writing. Her work has concentrated on biographies, such as *Eleanor Roosevelt,* and books for children. Besides writing, Forsee also enjoys playing the violin.

Robert Francis

Robert Francis (*born 1901*) has devoted his life to writing and teaching English. Although his award-winning work includes fiction, essays, autobiography, and nonfiction, Francis is best known for his poetry. Among the eight volumes of poems he has published is *The Orb Weaver.* Francis also enjoys teaching and playing the violin.

Robert Frost (*1874–1963*) was the only American poet to be awarded four Pulitzer Prizes and a congressional medal. He also had the honor of presenting one of his poems at the inauguration of President John Kennedy. Frost's poems are often set in rural New England. They focus on the individual's search for courage and integrity. His work is known for its easy-going conversational style. This simplicity, however, is deceiving. Under the surface of his poetry, a reader can find many serious thoughts and themes.

Robert Frost

Kathlyn Gay (*born 1930*) has always been concerned with the way people get along with each other. Much of her writing has focused on the varied people and cultures that exist in our country. Gay has helped write many textbooks and teaching materials, as well as fiction, essays, and plays. Her interest in drama and theater has led to articles on using drama skills in teaching and the way our bodies send silent messages. *Body Talk* and *Look Mom! No Words* are examples.

Nikki Giovanni

Ellen Goodman

Dick Gregory

O. Henry

Nikki Giovanni (*born 1943*) founded her own publishing company at the age of twenty-seven. Prior to that, she had graduated from Fisk University, attended the University of Pennsylvania and Columbia University. She has taught at the college level and enjoys lecturing and reading her poetry to audiences. Giovanni's poetry such as *Black Feeling, Black Talk* reflects her childhood in Tennessee and her attitudes about the Black experience.

Ellen Goodman (*born 1941*) was raised in Massachusetts, the daughter of a lawyer and a politician. A columnist, Goodman won the Pulitzer Prize for distinguished commentary in 1980. She writes seriously about what have been called "soft subjects" such as fads, divorce, and feminism.

Dick Gregory (*born 1932*) has achieved recognition as an entertainer as well as a writer. Born in St. Louis, Missouri, Gregory attended college in Illinois, then served in the U.S. Army. His first book, *From the Back of the Bus,* was published in 1962. It was followed by an autobiography, a cookbook, and political essays.

O. Henry (*1862–1910*) was the pen name of William Sydney Porter. Before gaining fame as a writer, O. Henry worked as a ranch hand, store clerk, and a bank teller. He began writing while serving a jail sentence for embezzlement. Whether he was actually guilty of the crime is still in doubt. Some of O. Henry's popular short story collections are *Of Cabbages and Kings* and *The Four Hundred.* These stories often tell about simple people who become caught up in uncontrollable situations. Surprise endings are a trademark of O. Henry's work.

Oliver Herford (*1863–1935*) was born in England but his family moved to the United States when he was a child. He studied at Antioch College in Ohio, then continued his studies in Paris and London. Herford's writings, which he often illustrated, were widely read in the early 1900's. They frequently appeared in popular magazines, such as *Life* and *Harper's Weekly.*

Calvin C. Hernton (*born 1932*) is both a writer and a college instructor. Most of his work focuses on race relations. Although Hernton concentrates on poetry, he is also the author of several plays and a novel, *Scarecrow.*

John Hersey

Langston Hughes

Layle Silbert

David Ignatow

Hannah Kahn

John Hersey (*born 1914*) was born in China, the son of American citizens. After college, he became the private secretary, driver, and handyman for noted author Sinclair Lewis. A short time later he began a writing career of his own. His many awards include the 1945 Pulitzer Prize for *A Bell for Adano.* As the writer of contemporary history novels, he believes, "Truth is said to be stranger than fiction; fiction can be stronger than truth."

Langston Hughes (*1902–1967*) was born in Mississippi. He attended school in Cleveland, worked in Mexico, and continued with his schooling at Columbia University in New York. Most famous for his poetry, Hughes also wrote novels, plays, radio and movie scripts, children's stories, and nonfiction. In works such as *Montage of a Dream Deferred*, Hughes demonstrated his ability to re-create the structures and rhythm of blues and jazz. His writing is said to have captured the soul of urban Black life.

David Ignatow (*born 1914*) has been an editor of poetry journals as well as a critic, teacher, and writer. His poems often portray life in the city. Ignatow's poetry collections include *The Gentle Weight Lifter* and *Figures of the Human.* He is a native of Brooklyn, New York.

W. W. Jacobs (*1863–1943*) was born in London, where he worked as a postal clerk for many years. He began his literary career by writing short stories for "pocket money." After the publishing of his first novel, however, Jacobs decided on writing as a career. Though a shy and mild-mannered man, his work leaned toward sea adventures, humorous fiction, and horror stories. "The Monkey's Paw" has been popular for over half a century as a story and as a play.

Hannah Kahn (*born 1911*) worked as an interior designer and wrote poetry in her spare time. At the age of fifty, she began attending college classes at night. She received her degree twelve years later. Kahn published her first poetry collection in 1963. Since then her work has appeared in magazines, newspapers, and poetry collections.

Daniel Keyes (*born 1927*) began his teaching career in New York. From there he went on to serve as the director of the creative writing center at Ohio University. Keyes has also devoted time to the study of

Naoshi Koriyama

Sam Levenson

Anne Morrow
Lindbergh

Willie Mays

abnormal psychology. Some of his writing is based on the observations he made while studying unusual cases. The award-winning *Flowers for Algernon* was first written as a short story. It was later expanded into a novel and a movie called "Charly."

Naoshi Koriyama (*born 1926*) was born in Kikai Island, Japan. His native tongue is Japanese but he set himself the challenge of composing his poetry in English. He attended college in Japan and also earned a degree from New York State College for Teachers in Albany. Along with writing poetry, Koriyama teaches English literature in Japan.

William Least Heat Moon (*born 1940*), is also known as William Trogden. After some personal and professional disappointments, Least Heat Moon decided to take a long trip, in hopes of finding a new life. He chose the back roads of the United States, represented by blue lines on highway maps. This resulted in his first book, *Blue Highways*, a journal of his 14,000 mile journey. The insights he gained from traveling and writing caused Trogden to adopt his Sioux name, Least Heat Moon.

Sam Levenson (*1911–1980*) was an author, entertainer, and humorist who appeared on popular radio and television programs for over thirty years. His books, such as *In One Era and Out the Other* and *Everything But Money*, are filled with practical advice and stories on family life. In his work, he frequently suggests that old-fashioned methods and traditions are best.

Anne Morrow Lindbergh (*born 1906*) is the wife of the famous aviator, Charles Lindbergh. She has written essays, an autobiography, memoirs, and poetry. The long essay, *Gift from the Sea*, is one of her most popular books. Lindbergh and her husband shared a strong sense of adventure. She, too, learned how to fly and navigate an airplane. The trips they made provided material for much of her writing.

Alonzo Lopez was born in Arizona and attended Yale University, Wesleyan University, and the Institute of American Indian Arts. Lopez writes poetry in his native Navajo language, as well as in English. His poems focus on the Navajo culture.

Willie Mays (*born 1931*) is best known for his achievements in professional baseball. Born in Alabama, the son of a semi-professional

Eve Merriam

Farley Mowat

Pauli Murray

Gloria Oden

baseball player, Mays began his major league career with the New York Giants in 1951. Over the years he earned the National League batting title and was twice named Most Valuable Player. Mays has written several books about baseball, including his autobiography.

Ruth McKenney (*1911–1972*) wrote *My Sister Eileen*, an account of the youthful adventures she shared with her sister. That book was made into a movie of the same name and a Broadway play entitled *Wonderful Town*. McKenney wrote several other humorous books. Most of them are based on personal experiences.

Eve Merriam (*born 1916*) has written everything from advertising copy and song lyrics to television scripts and plays. Her poetry collections include *Family Circle* and *It Doesn't Always Have to Rhyme*. Her poetry often expresses the problems she sees in society. Merriam addressed the issue of women's rights in her book, *Growing Up Female in America*.

Farley Mowat (*born 1921*) is a Canadian naturalist who prefers a simple life and people who live such lives. He spent two years living with the Ihalmuit Eskimos. Mowat's concern over the destruction of the natural environment is expressed in *People of the Deer* and *A Whale for the Killing*. His writing also takes a humorous approach, as shown in *Owls in the Family*.

Pauli Murray (*born 1910*) is a lawyer who has used her skills to gain rights for women and minorities. She was a "freedom rider" in the 1940's, protesting segregation on buses. Murray's poetry has frequently appeared in periodicals. She also wrote a family history, *Proud Shoes*.

Gloria Oden (*born 1923*) published her first book of poetry in 1952. Before she became a college professor and a poet, Oden was an editor of math, science, and language textbooks. Her award-winning poetry has appeared in numerous anthologies.

Marjorie Kinnan Rawlings (*1896–1953*) has been a newspaperwoman, poet, and novelist. In 1928, needing solitude, she purchased an orange grove and devoted herself to farming and writing. Rawlings used the Florida back country as the setting for many of her novels and short stories. She won a Pulitzer Prize for *The Yearling*.

Edwin A. Robinson

Saki

Carl Sandburg

Rod Serling

Richard Rive (*born 1931*) lives in South Africa and has devoted much time to the study of contemporary African literature. He has received a Fulbright Scholarship and has done graduate work at Columbia University. *African Songs*, a collection of short stories, and *Emergency*, a novel, are examples of his work. Rive enjoys spending his free time mountain climbing and spear fishing.

Edwin A. Robinson (*1869–1935*) used his New England background as a setting and model for his poetry. President Theodore Roosevelt admired Robinson's work and aided his career by giving him employment. In his poetry, Robinson mixes realism with irony and humor. His first successful publication was *The Town Down the River*.

Theodore Roethke (*1908–1963*) based many of his poems on the experiences he had growing up around his father's greenhouse in Saginaw, Michigan. He was educated at the University of Michigan and at Harvard, then went on to teach at several colleges. Roethke published several collections of poetry, including *Open House* and *Words for the Wind*. In 1954 he won the Pulitzer Prize for *The Waking*.

Saki (*1870–1916*) was the pen name of Hector Hugo Munro. He was born in India to Scottish parents, then was sent to England as a child. Saki traveled widely and began a writing career as a journalist. He also wrote novels and short stories, which were famous for their unique blend of horror and humor. Saki was killed during World War I.

Carl Sandburg (*1878–1967*) was the son of Swedish immigrants who settled in Illinois. Sandburg held a variety of jobs, in addition to serving in the army and traveling around the country collecting folk music. His experiences are reflected in his poetry, fiction, and nonfiction. Sandburg intended his work to be both for and about the common man. Thus, his style is rough and bold, using free verse and street talk.

Rod Serling (*1924–1975*) is best known for his television series "The Twilight Zone" and "Night Gallery." His first television drama, "Patterns," brought him overnight success in the television industry. However, he soon switched from drama to fantasy writing to avoid censorship problems. Serling's writing consists of screenplays, books, and television dramas. His many honors include Emmy Awards for "Patterns," "Twilight Zone," and "Requiem for a Heavyweight."

Isaac Bashevis Singer

John Steinbeck

May Swenson

Sara Teasdale

Robert Silverberg (*born 1935*) was born in New York. He began writing as soon as he graduated from Columbia University, producing an amazing number of books. Silverberg's science fiction works include *Needle in a Timestack* and *Lost Race of Mars*. His nonfiction topics include space exploration, archaeology, and ancient history.

Isaac Bashevis Singer (*born 1904*) grew up in Poland the son and grandson of rabbis. Although he studied at a rabbinical seminary, he eventually turned to writing as a career. Singer has lived in the United States since 1935, but he still writes in Yiddish, the language of his youth. Much of Singer's writing is set in nineteenth century Polish villages. He often blends superstition and the supernatural with the normal routines of everyday life. He received the Nobel Prize in literature in 1978 for his work which includes stories, novels, memoirs, and tales for children.

John Steinbeck (*1902–1968*) developed a sympathy for the common working man while working at a variety of jobs. He was a painter, caretaker, brick hauler, and fruit picker after attending Stanford University. In *The Grapes of Wrath*, which won a Pulitzer Prize, Steinbeck told the story of migrant workers living during the Depression. He also earned fame for *Tortilla Flat, Of Mice and Men,* and *The Red Pony.* He received the Nobel Prize for Literature in 1962.

May Swenson (*born 1919*), a native of Utah, is an award-winning poet. Her work has been called experimental because she often shapes her verse into typed pictures. She believes that this visual approach gives added meaning to her words.

Sara Teasdale (*1884–1933*), was born and educated in St. Louis, Missouri. She was a shy, sensitive woman who withdrew from normal life after an unhappy marriage. Her poems often revealed her feelings about love. One of her poetry volumes, *Love Songs*, won an award that later came to be called the Pulitzer Prize.

Theodore L. Thomas (*born 1920*) is a practicing patent attorney who writes stories as a hobby. Besides his science fiction stories and novels like *The Clone*, Thomas has written a newspaper column on scientific topics and a series on patent lawyers. Before turning to law and writing, Thomas was a chemical engineer.

Mark Twain

Louis Untermeyer

Alice Walker

Dorothy West

Mark Twain (*1835–1910*) was the pen name of Samuel Clemens. Twain grew up in Hannibal, Missouri and used his many adventures on the Mississippi River in writing *The Adventures of Tom Sawyer* and *The Adventures of Huckleberry Finn.* He was fun-loving and lived the life he wrote about. Twain, who is considered one of the greatest American humorists, is also known for his newspaper articles and lectures.

Louis Untermeyer (*1895–1977*) did not become a writer until the age of thirty-eight. Before that he worked in his family's jewelry business for twenty years. Despite his late start, Untermeyer had a long and distinguished career as a writer, editor, and teacher. His works include poetry, short stories, biographies, essays, a novel, and a play.

Andrei Voznesenski (*born 1933*) is a Russian poet who was originally schooled in architecture. He gained popularity in the 1960's, when Russian audiences were eager to hear the bold work of young poets, in contrast to the restricted poetry of the Stalin era. Voznesenski says that he was strongly influenced by the poet, Boris Pasternak.

Alice Walker (*born 1944*) grew up on a small farm in Georgia. One of eight children, she worked her way through college to become an award-winning writer. Walker, who has taught at several colleges, has also written poetry and a biography of Langston Hughes. Her writing reflects the social injustice experienced by some blacks. She was awarded the Pulitzer Prize in 1983 for *The Color Purple,* her most recent novel.

Dorothy West (*born 1910*) grew up in Boston and was educated at Boston University and Columbia University School of Journalism. After serving as editor of *Challenge* and *New Challenge,* she worked as a relief investigator in Harlem during the depression. She then began to write short stories based on her experiences. These were syndicated in newspapers across the country. In addition to short stories, she has also written a novel, *The Living Is Easy.*

John Hall Wheelock (*born 1886*) worked as an editor for forty-six years. He has published more than a dozen collections of his own poetry. Born in Long Island, New York, Wheelock attended Harvard University, and studied in Germany. *Dear Men and Women* and *The Gardener and Other Poems* are two of Wheelock's books of verse.

Index of Titles and Authors

Index of Fine Art

Index of Skills

Skills in Comprehending Literature

Vocabulary Skills

Homographs 239
Idioms 283
Inference 162
Inflected Forms 259
Jargon 507, 542–543, 633
Levels of Language 552–553, 567, 584, 633
Prefixes 308, 324, 331, 342, 481, 629
Punctuation Clues 504, 627
Sentences and Sentence Fragments 504, 628
Slang 553, 567
Standard and Nonstandard English
   See *Levels of Language.*
Suffixes 309, 356, 361, 383–384, 629
Synonyms See *Context Clues.*
Synonymies 250
Thesaurus 633
Using Synonyms and Antonyms To Find
   Word Meanings 423–424
Word Families 457
Word Parts 115–116, 308–309, 375, 394,
   411, 463, 469, 476, 496, 629
   Adding Affixes to Base Words, 308, 318,
   402, 457, 629
   Greek and Latin Word Parts, 309, 441,
   445–446, 452–453, 463, 632
   Inferring Meaning from Familiar Word
   Parts, 115
Words from Names and Places 507, 513,
   542–543, 632
Words from Specialized Areas See *Jargon.*

Writing Skills

Adage 84, 612
Analysis 318, 384, 437, 543, 568
Article 482, 612
Argument 78, 446
   See also *Opinion.*

Autobiography 613
   Writing about Yourself, 402–403, 412
Campaign Commercials 464
Character 613
   Analyzing Characters, 32, 324, 356–357,
   513, 606
   Character Development, 526, 613
   Character Traits, 26, 613
   Writing a Character Sketch, 453
Children's Stories 67
Classification 437
Climax 132–133, 613
Comparison and Contrast 41–42, 357, 464,
   584, 606–607, 614
   Of Characters, 104, 331, 357, 375, 411–
   412
   Of Poems, 220, 293
   Of Purpose, 342–343
   Of Selections, 96, 116, 172, 584
Defending a Choice 431
Defining a Term 78, 126, 231, 514
Description 60, 251, 476–477, 482, 614
   Indirect Description, 162–163
Dialogue 298, 362, 424, 437, 533, 615
Diary 526
Essay 437, 441, 453, 615–616
Explanations 126–127, 384, 412, 424, 476–
   477
Explanatory Writing 469–470, 481–482
First Draft 384, 635–636, 638
Humor 145, 384, 617
Hyperbole 104, 617
Imagery 240, 271–272, 617
Imagining the Background for a Story 108
Interviews 104
Irony 162, 618
Journals 419, 618
Letters 319, 446
Mood 67, 145, 172, 231, 618
Motivation 318–319

Study and Research Skills

Acknowledgments

(continued from copyright page)

from *Lost Cities and Vanished Civilizations*; copyright © 1962 by Robert Silverberg. Patricia Ayres and Eve Merriam: For "The Optileast and the Pessimost" by Eve Merriam, from *There Is No Rhyme for Silver*; published by Atheneum Publishers; copyright © 1962 by Eve Merriam, all rights reserved. Robert Bly: For "Driving to Town Late To Mail a Letter" by Robert Bly, from *Silence in the Snowy Fields*; Wesleyan University Press, 1962, copyright © 1960 by Robert Bly. Branden Press: For "Rain" by Richard Armour, from *Armoury of Light Verse*, 1962, Branden Press, 21 Station Street, Brookline, MA 02147. Brandt & Brandt Literary Agents, Inc.: For "The Most Dangerous Game" by Richard Connell; copyright 1924 by Richard Connell, copyright renewed 1952 by Louise Fox Connell. Diana Chang Hermann: For "Saying Yes" by Diana Chang, from *Asian-American Heritage: An Anthology of Prose and Poetry*, edited by David Hsin-Fu Wand. Don Congdon Associates, Inc.: For "The Fog Horn" by Ray Bradbury; copyright © 1953 by Ray Bradbury, renewed in 1981 by Ray Bradbury. Kirby Congdon: For "Television-Movie" by Kirby Congdon. Dodd, Mead & Company, Inc.: For "Life" by Paul Laurence Dunbar, from *The Complete Poems of Paul Laurence Dunbar*. Doubleday & Company, Inc.: For "The Old Man," from *Echoes From the Macabre* by Daphne du Maurier; copyright © 1952, 1959, 1970, 1971, 1976 by Daphne du Maurier. For "The Bat" and "The Sloth" by Theodore Roethke, from *The Collected Poems of Theodore Roethke*; copyright 1938 and 1950 by Theodore Roethke. For "The Ransom of Red Chief," from *Whirligigs* by O. Henry; copyright 1907 by Doubleday & Company, Inc. Dover Publications: For "Friendship" (Oglala Sioux), from *The Indians Book*, recorded and edited by Natalie Curtis; copyright © 1950. E. P. Dutton, Inc.: For "Not Poor, Just Broke," From *Nigger, An Autobiography* by Dick Gregory with Robert Lipsyte; copyright © 1964 by Dick Gregory Enterprises, Inc. For an edited excerpt from *Willie Mays: My Life In and Out of Baseball*, as told to Charles Einstein; copyright © 1966 by Willie Mays. James A. Emanuel: For "Get Up, Blues" by James A. Emanuel. Aylesa Forsee: For "Eleanor Roosevelt" by Aylesa Forsee, from *American Women Who Scored Firsts*. Samuel French, Inc.: For *The Monkey's Paw* by W. W. Jacobs, dramatized by Louis N. Parker (entire play); copyright 1910 by Samuel French Ltd., copyright 1937 (in renewal) by Louis N. Parker. *Caution:* Professionals and amateurs are hereby warned that *The Monkey's Paw*, being fully protected under the copyright laws of the United States of America, the British Commonwealth countries, including Canada, and the other countries of the Copyright Union, is subject to a royalty. All rights, including professional, stock, amateur, motion picture, recitation, public reading, radio, television and cablevision broadcasting, and the rights of translation into foreign languages, are strictly reserved. Amateurs may produce this play upon payment of a royalty of ten dollars ($10.00) for each performance, payable one week before the play is to be given, to Samuel French, Inc. at 45 West 25th Street, New York, N.Y. 10010, or at 7623 Sunset Blvd., Hollywood, Calif. 90046, or if in Canada, to Samuel French (Canada) Ltd., 80 Richmond Street East, Toronto M5C 1P1. Copies of this play, in individual paper covered acting editions, are available from Samuel French, Inc. at the above addresses. Grove Press, Inc.: For "Bicycles" by Andrei Voznesensky, translated by Anselm Hollo, from *Selected Poems of Andrei Voznesensky*; copyright © 1964. Harcourt Brace Jovanovich, Inc.: For "Arithmetic" by Carl Sandburg, from *The Complete Poems of Carl Sandburg*; copyright 1950 by Carl Sandburg, renewed 1978 by Margaret Sandburg, Helga Sandburg Crile and Janet Sandburg. For "Dark" (pages 111–121), from *North to the Orient* by Anne Morrow Lindbergh; copyright 1935, 1963 by Anne Morrow Lindbergh. For "Feathered Friend," from "The Other Side of the Sky" by Arthur C. Clarke; copyright © 1957 by Royal Publications, Inc., from *The Other Side of the Sky* by Arthur C. Clarke. For "A Loud Sneer for Our Feathered Friends," from *My Sister Eileen* by Ruth McKenney; copyright 1938, 1966 by Ruth McKenney. For "The Dog of Pompeii," from *The Donkey of God* by Louis Untermeyer; copyright 1932 by Harcourt Brace Jovanovich, Inc.; renewed 1960 by Louis Untermeyer. For "Medicine," from *Once* by Alice Walker; copyright © 1968 by Alice Walker. Harper & Row, Publishers, Inc.: For "Zlateh the Goat" (text only), from *Zlateh the Goat and Other Stories* by Isaac Bashevis Singer; text copyright © 1966 by Isaac Bashevis Singer. For an abridged and adapted version of "Mildred Didrikson Zaharias (1912–1956)" (text only, pages 145–163), from *Women Who Made America Great* by Harry Gersh (J. B. Lippincott Company); copyright © 1962 by Harry Gersh. For abridged and adapted pages 314–325 of *Of Men and Mountains* by William O. Douglas; copyright 1950 by William O. Douglas. Harvard University Press: For "I'm Nobody!" by Emily Dickinson, reprinted by permission of the publishers and the Trustees of Amherst College, from *The Poems of Emily Dickinson*, edited by Thomas H. Johnson, Cambridge, Mass.: The Belknap Press of Harvard University Press, copyright 1951, © 1955, 1979, 1983 by the President and Fellows of Harvard College. Calvin Hernton: For "The Distant Drum," from *Soulscript*; copyright © 1970 by Calvin Hernton. Alfred A. Knopf, Inc.: For "Not To Go With the Others" by John Hersey, from *Here to Stay*; copyright © 1962 by John Hersey. Holt, Rinehart and Winston, Publishers: For "Lodged," from *The Poetry of Robert Frost*, edited by Edward Connery Lathem; copyright 1928, © 1969 by Holt, Rinehart and Winston, copyright © 1956 by Robert Frost. Indiana University Press: For "Where the Rainbow Ends" by Richard Rive, from *Poems From Black Africa*, edited by Langston Hughes. International Creative Management: For *The Monsters Are Due on Maple Street* by Rod Serling; copyright © 1960 by Rod Serling. Ted Joans: For "Voice in the Crowd" by Ted Joans. Daniel Keyes: For "Flowers For Algernon" by Daniel Keyes; copyright © 1959 by Mercury Press, Inc. Reprinted by permission of the author. Naoshi Koriyama: For "Time and Space" by Naoshi Koriyama, first appeared in *The Mainichi Daily News* in 1979; copyright © 1979 by Naoshi Koriyama. Frederick Laing: For "The Beau Catcher" by Frederick Laing. Little, Brown and Company: For "The Universe" by May Swenson, from *To Mix With Time*; copyright © 1961 by May Swenson. For an edited excerpt "Nameless Tennessee" by William Least Heat

Moon, from *Blue Highways: A Journey Into America*; copyright © 1982 by William Least Heat Moon. For an adapted excerpt from *Never Cry Wolf* by Farley Mowat; copyright © 1963 by Farley Mowat. Liveright Publishing Corp.: For "who knows if the moon's" by E. E. Cummings, from *Tulips & Chimneys*; copyright 1923, 1925, renewed 1951, 1953 by E. E. Cummings; copyright © 1973, 1976 by the Trustees for the E. E. Cummings Trust, copyright © 1973, 1976 by George James Firmage. Macmillan Publishing Co., Inc.: For "Barter" by Sara Teasdale, from *Collected Poems*; copyright 1917 by Macmillan Publishing Co., Inc., renewed 1945 by Mamie T. Wheless. Rona Maynard: For "The Fan Club" by Rona Maynard. William Morris Agency, Inc. and Lucille Fletcher: For *The Hitch Hiker* by Lucille Fletcher; copyright © 1947 by Lucille Fletcher. William Morrow & Company, Inc.: For "Kidnap Poems," from *The Women and the Men* by Nikki Giovanni; copyright © 1970, 1974, 1975 by Nikki Giovanni. Museum of New Mexico Press: For "The Force of Luck," from *Cuentos, Tales From the Hispanic Southwest*, adapted by Rudolfo A. Anaya; copyright © 1980. New American Library: For "The Confession" by Anton Chekhov, from *Selected Stories*, translated by Ann Dunnigan; copyright © 1960 by Ann Dunnigan. Gloria Oden: For "The Way It Is," from *Poetry Is Alive and Well and Living in America* by G. C. Oden and May Swenson; copyright © 1969 by Media Plus, Inc. The Putnam Publishing Group: For "Fresh Air Will Kill You," from *Have I Ever Lied To You?* by Art Buchwald; copyright © 1966, 1967, 1968 by Art Buchwald. Random House, Inc.: For "Poem," from *The Dream Keeper and Other Poems* by Langston Hughes; copyright 1932 by Alfred A. Knopf, Inc., renewed 1960 by Langston Hughes. For "Troubled Woman," from *Selected Poems of Langston Hughes*; copyright 1926 by Alfred A. Knopf, Inc., renewed 1954 by Langston Hughes. St. Martin's Press, Inc.: For an edited version of Chapter Two from *Growing Up* by Russell Baker; copyright © 1982 by Russell Baker. Saturday Review: For "Concrete Trap," from *Poems* by Elizabeth Coatsworth; copyright 1957, The Macmillan Co., New York. For "Ride a Wild Horse" by Hannah Kahn, from *Saturday Review*, from *Into the Sun*, March, 1953 issue. Charles Scribner's Sons: For "A Mother in Mannville," from *When the Whippoorwill* by Marjorie Rawlings; copyright 1940 by Marjorie Kinnan Rawlings, copyright renewed 1968 by Norton Baskin. For an excerpt from *Body Talk* by Kathlyn Gay; copyright © 1974 by Kathlyn Gay. For an adaptation of "Rattlesnake Hunt," from *Cross Creek* by Marjorie Kinnan Rawlings; copyright 1942 by Marjorie Kinnan Rawlings, copyright renewed 1970 by Norton Baskin. For "Earth," from *The Gardener and Other Poems* by John Hall Wheelock; copyright © 1961 by John Hall Wheelock. Silvermine Publishers: For "Words" and "Youth to Age" by Pauli Murray, from *The Dark Testament and Other Poems* by Pauli Murray; copyright © 1970. Simon & Schuster, Inc.: For "A Penguin" by Oliver Herford, from *Pith and Vinegar*, edited by William Cole; copyright © 1969 by William Cole. For "Friday Night Dinner," from *Everything But Money* by Sam Levenson; copyright © 1949, 1951, 1952, 1953, 1955, 1958, 1959, 1961, 1966 by Sam Levenson. For "Primal Screen," from *At Large* by Ellen Goodman; copyright © 1981 by the Washington Post Company, reprinted by permission of Summit Books, a division of Simon & Schuster, Inc. Theodore L. Thomas: For "The Test" by Theodore L. Thomas, first appeared in *The Magazine of Fantasy and Science Fiction*; copyright © 1962 by Mercury Press, Inc. The University of Chicago Press: For "Clever Hans," from *Water Witching U.S.A.* by Evon Z. Vogt and Ray Hyman. The University of Massachusetts Press: For "Seagulls" by Robert Francis, from *Robert Francis: Collected Poems, 1936–1976*; copyright © 1942, 1970 by Robert Francis, University of Massachusetts Press, 1976. Viking Penguin, Inc.: For an excerpt from *Travels With Charley* by John Steinbeck; copyright © 1961, 1962 by The Curtis Publishing Co., Inc., copyright © 1962 by John Steinbeck. For "The Story Teller," from *The Short Stories of Saki* (H. H. Munro); copyright 1930, renewed copyright © 1958 by The Viking Press, Inc. Wesleyan University Press: For "Two Friends" by David Ignatow, from *Figures of the Human*; copyright © 1963 by David Ignatow. Dorothy West; by permission of The Bertha Klausner International Literary Agency, Inc. For "The Richer, the Poorer" by Dorothy West. The authors and editors have made every effort to trace the ownership of all copyrighted selections found in this book and to make full acknowledgment for their use.